❧ MARIPOSA ROAD ❦

MARIPOSA ROAD

The First Butterfly Big Year

ROBERT MICHAEL PYLE

Houghton Mifflin Harcourt

Boston New York

2010

For information about permission to reproduce selections from this book,
write to Permissions, Houghton Mifflin Harcourt Publishing Company,
215 Park Avenue South, New York, New York 10003.

www.hmhbooks.com

CREDITS
Page 24: Selection from "Garland Ranch Song" by Donald Marsh, reprinted
by permission of the author; page 82: Poem from the Crooked Garden, reprinted by
permission of James Price, Crooked Garden curator; page 226: E-mail from
Christopher Benshoof, reprinted by permission of the author; page 336: Passage from
"Oahe" Alma Mater, reprinted by permission of Ron Hopkins, principal, Kahlotus
High School, Washington; page 344: Excerpt from "Old Friends' Reunion at
Yellowstone," reprinted by permission of John Lane.

ENDPAPER CREDITS
The following have kindly granted permission to reprint their photographs.
(*front*) Palaeno sulphur: Kenelm W. Philip, Alaska Lepidoptera Survey. Bartram's scrub-
hairstreak: Alana Edwards. Swamp metalmark: Susan S. Borkin. Isabella's longwing:
Jan Dauphin. Astarte fritillary: D. Nunnallee. Loammi skipper: Linda F. Cooper.
Two-barred flasher: Benton Basham. Thorne's hairstreak: Kojiro Shiraiwa. Gillett's
checkerspot: Scott Hoffman Black, Xerces. Florida purplewing: Alana Edwards. Hessel's
hairstreak: Pat Sutton. Hawaiian blue: Jim Snyder. (*back*) Miami blue: ©Paula Cannon.
Huachuca giant-skipper: Hank & Priscilla Brodkin. Martial scrub-hairstreak: Alana
Edwards. Orange-barred sulphur: ©Paula Cannon. Hermes copper: Kojiro Shiraiwa.
Giant swallowtail: ©Paula Cannon. Arogos skipper: Linda F. Cooper.
Avalon hairstreak: Jim P. Brock. Regal fritillary: Jim Wiker. Malachite: ©Paula Cannon.
Red-bordered satyr: Jim P. Brock. Atala hairstreak: Alana Edwards.

Library of Congress Cataloging-in-Publication Data
Pyle, Robert Michael.
Mariposa road : the first butterfly big year / Robert Michael Pyle.
p. cm.
ISBN 978-0-618-94539-9
1. Butterflies—North America. 2. Pyle, Robert Michael—Travel—North America.
3. North America—Description and travel. I. Title
QL548.P944 2010
595.78'9097—dc22 2010005763

Book design by Lisa Diercks
Linocut on title page by Thea Linnaea Pyle
This book is typeset in Hightower and Whitman.

Printed in the United States of America
DOC 10 9 8 7 6 5 4 3 2 1

To my Thea

to the memory of these ones, all gone too soon,
who would have enjoyed the journey:

Harry Foster, Charles Lee Remington, Karölis Bagdonas,
MaVynee Betsch, Lee G. Miller, George Austin, Charles Slater,
William H. Howe, Barry Sullivan, Larry Everson,
George Schiel, and Mike Uhtoff

Finally we learned to know why we did these things. The animals were very beautiful. Here was life from which we borrowed life and excitement. In other words, we did these things because it was pleasant to do them.

—John Steinbeck, *The Log from the Sea of Cortez*
(with E. F. Ricketts)

CONTENTS

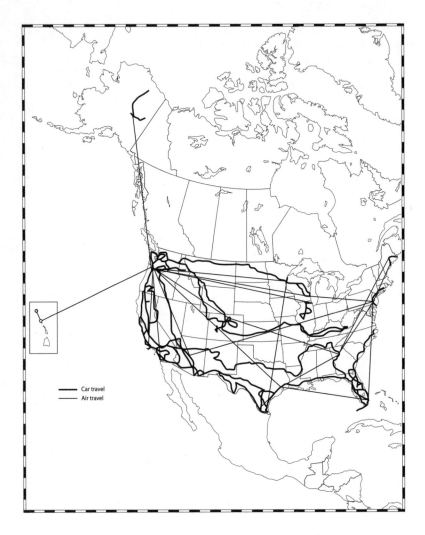

Route map for Mariposa Road

(after S. Jepsen and S. Tenney, Xerces Society)

WHY A BUTTERFLY BIG YEAR?

Late one afternoon in North Florida, I came to a place called Butterfly Knoll. Its faded, split-log archway was painted with a zebra, a monarch, a red-spotted purple, a dogface, and a sulphur. There was no house there now, and just weeds where the garden once grew. What fond fools, I wondered, with what dreams, had come and gone here?

I too was a fool with a butterfly dream: to travel the continent and see as many North American butterflies, north of Mexico, as I possibly could in one calendar year. And why would a person spend a perfectly good year this way? Plastered to the Oregon coast by high wind and rain; driving thousands of miles through desiccated desert boneyards that haven't seen a raindrop or a flower for months; slogging through chiggers in an Illinois canebrake in matched heat and humidity in the nineties; crawling prone through icy Minnesota bogs in the snows of November—all in search of *butterflies*?

Otherwise sensible people have attempted birding Big Years for more than half a century. The first great narrative of a Big Year, though the listing itself was so secondary as to be almost a whim, was Roger Tory Peterson and James Fisher's wonderful 1955 classic, *Wild America*. The next was Kenn Kaufman's magical *Kingbird Highway*. These two books directly inspired the present one. Both fine butterfliers, Peterson and Kaufman attended to some extent to scaled as well as feathered fliers. But neither they nor anyone else, by my reckoning, had ever attempted a butterfly Big Year.

The diversity of American birds and butterflies is roughly the same, but there are profound differences between a Big Year for birds and one for butterflies. Consider the weather: birds fly in the rain and snow, butterflies mostly don't. Or take migration and life span: most butterflies live for a week or two and have strictly limited, frustratingly variable flight periods: if you miss them, you can't pick them up somewhere else, later in the migration, as you can with many birds. But there are similarities too, so a butterfly Big Year ought appeal to birders as well as butterfliers—that is, if anybody ever did one.

My previous book, *Sky Time in Gray's River,* was very much a *home* book. When I finished it, I found myself hankering after another road romp like the one in *Chasing Monarchs,* which recounted my 1996 trip to follow the western monarch migration all autumn long. When I suggested the Big Year idea to my literary agent, Laura Blake Peterson, it caught her fancy. We proposed it to Lisa White at Houghton Mifflin Harcourt, publisher of *Wild America* and *Kingbird Highway* as well as *Chasing Monarchs.* And when Lisa went for it, there was no turning back.

I saw the project as being somewhat like *Chasing Monarchs,* only instead of tracking one species in more or less one direction for one season, this would be eight hundred species in every direction for one whole year. Such a broad remit requires a structure, of course, to avoid absolute chaos. So here's the basic setup: my objectives were to find, experience, and definitively identify as many species of butterflies as I could in one full year. The count area would be North America north of Mexico; but unlike the birders, I included Hawaii (they get the offshore waters, useless to me). I would include immature stages (eggs, larvae, and pupae) if identified with certainty, since the adult butterfly is but one-quarter of the animal; birders, after all, count nestlings, and I had no songs to count.

Although I wrote and photographed the first field guide in this country that used photographs of wild butterflies instead of specimens or drawings (*Watching Washington Butterflies,* 1974), I decided to take no photographs at all. Butterfly photography has evolved, is time-consuming, and would make for a very different experience. I would watch the butterflies and use nets for careful examination in hand when my binoculars were insufficient for the purpose. Usually, this would involve harmless catch-and-release, at which I am adept.

However, for difficult species neither at risk nor protected, I would take modest numbers of voucher specimens for expert confirmation and museum deposition. In the event, this practice proved essential for a number of taxa that cannot reliably be identified otherwise. A panel of distinguished lepidopterists would certify my final total.

My methods and tools offered the advantage of simplicity. Unlike many male biologists of my acquaintance, I am neither a gearhead nor a natural mechanic, and I lean seriously toward low-tech. My primary items of equipment were a pair of 6X24 Leitz Trinovid binoculars that I have carried for thirty-five years; an even older companion, a Colorado cottonwood branch-and-hoop butterfly net named Marsha, who has had a hard life (her story is told in *Walking the High Ridge: Life as Field Trip*); a fine aluminum Japanese net, with extendable handle and collapsable rim, named Akito for the admired lepidopterist who gave it to me; a pocket net named Mini-Marsha; and a basic BioQuip quick-leap-out-of-the-car net; as well as forceps, field notebooks, and mechanical pencils. No laptop, no GPS unit—just a stack of maps and a traveling library of field guides.

My friend Benton Basham, the first Big Year birder to exceed seven hundred species, likes to say that, in a Big Year, strategy is everything. My primary strategies, then, were these: first, I figured that if I went after certain butterflies I considered to be "grails"—that is, species I'd always wanted to see or see better—then the more common butterflies would likely fall into the net along the way, as it were. Second, I posited a number of sorties out and back, to and from my home in southwest Washington State. I pictured these outings like the ray petals of a daisy, with Gray's River as the flower's disk.

As for tactics, my chief means of travel would be Powdermilk, my 1982 Honda Civic hatchback, which has been a character in several of my previous books, augmented from time to time by rental cars and other vehicles. As for flying, several birding Big Years in recent times have taken great advantage of air travel. I had neither the money nor the desire for that. I would make several flights, particularly to Alaska and Hawaii; but for these, I would exclusively use frequent flier miles or tickets donated by kind supporters. Train travel for several legs would likewise be done with Amtrak miles I had saved. On the whole, I would go solo; but my wife and field pal, Thea, would join me for some of the best bits.

Out of necessity and inclination, my travels would be done on half a shoestring. Not, perhaps, as short as Kenn Kaufman's knotted shoestring for *Kingbird Highway*: I never ate kibbles. But I did eat wild food, road finds, and an awful lot of peanuts. With no budget for lodging, I converted Powdermilk into the smallest camper on the road.

Certain principles molded my approach. I could have relied on knowledgeable lepidopterists, many of whom I know, to guide me to all the special species, and in some cases I did just that. But after a lifetime of butterfly studies, I wanted to test my own knowledge and experience, to rely on research in my library and others, and on intuition. I harbored a deep desire to follow hunch and happenstance as much as guides, to romance chance more than sure things or, as the birders call them, "stakeouts." Nor did I rely on tools such as listserves, e-mail chains, and rare species alerts to any great extent. In fact, I was virtually offline for the year, one of its greatest attractions for me.

Of course I researched my routes and target species to some extent, but not as thoroughly as some would do. I knew that, with butterflies, flexibility and spontaneity would trump the hard and fast plan in every case, especially given the vagaries of the weather and flight periods. This M.O. meant that I could afford few set dates, and except for a handful of lectures to pay some bills back home, I made few commitments. It also meant—along with the sheer distances I had to cover in a very short summer—that I had to turn down many kind and attractive invitations, especially in Ohio, Vermont, and a few other places that I deeply regretted missing out on.

I was determined not to succumb to contempt for the familiar. As Kenn Kaufman described this regrettable but common condition in *Flights Against the Sunset*, "The search for rare finds is the big thing (or even the only thing) for many, and common birds become part of the background, an annoyance to be ignored while one searches for the next rarity." The equivalent for butterfliers would be relegation of painted ladies or snouts, when superabundant during mass movements, to the category of "junk bugs," which I have heard all too often. I wanted to see the beauty in every butterfly.

Some find the very activity of listing to be demeaning of the organisms tallied, and it certainly can be. But it can also be just plain fun, as many naturalists have experienced with day lists, yard lists, and annual counts. I have always enjoyed the sheer *play* involved in listing, though I don't even maintain a serious life list for birds or butterflies. My intent here was to let the game drive the days enough to keep me moving but not so much as to call all the shots. My promise to the butterflies, my readers, and myself was never to let mere listing, ticking, or twitching the species supersede or get in the way of solid, meaningful encounter with the animal and its habitat. And while I concentrated on butterflies, I attended to all of the flora and fauna, including people.

All the above means that I surely saw fewer species of butterflies than I would have had I single-mindedly employed every tool, guide, and lead available to me. But I probably had more fun my way. And that was my most important principle: to have a good time and a heck of a field trip. As will come clear, the book is as much about what I missed as about what I found.

It might fairly be asked (and it has been) whether I could have found a more trivial pursuit, or a more indulgent caper, to pursue in these parlous times. Maybe not. Yet, prithee consider that it was also relatively harmless. And that, after forty years of close involvement with butterfly conservation, I saw this as a grand habitat transect: an opportunity to gain a broad sense of how our butterflies are faring versus development, climate change, exotic biota, and our own land management choices, such as burning and big agribiz. Another socially redeeming element of the gambol was the Xerces Society's Butterfly-A-Thon (www.xerces.org), whereby people pledged pennies, dimes, or dollars to Xerces for every species I saw, with all receipts destined directly for butterfly habitat conservation work.

Finally, a word about names. I usually use those suggested by my friends on the North American Butterfly Association (NABA)'s common names committee, but not always. Sometimes, they are just unsuitable names; other times, they usurp perfectly good traditional names. So sometimes I opt for the vernaculars offered by the older Xerces Society/Smithsonian Institution book *Common Names of North American Butterflies*, edited by Jacqueline Miller. I also use certain scientific names, for both their beauty and interest. In that department, my be all and end all is Jonathan Pelham's *Catalogue of the Butterflies of the United States and Canada*, whose publication in 2008 was an enormous boon to the whole project. This magisterial work absolved me of any and all taxonomic decisions and formed the ultimate authority for my list, as well as my running orders on the ground. I thanked the gods (and Jon) for it every day. By whatever name, the identity of the butterfly I am referring to will always be clear in context.

And so I set out. My only responsibilities: cover the miles, see the butterflies, and come home safe to Thea. What a year it was—and what an extraordinary privilege! The playwright Gennadi Bashknev, writing of his Buryat minority in Russia, said that they deserve "a low bow and an unhurried narrator." That expresses exactly what I hoped to be for these butterflies and their necessary places: an unhurried narrator, bowing low.

MARIPOSA ROAD

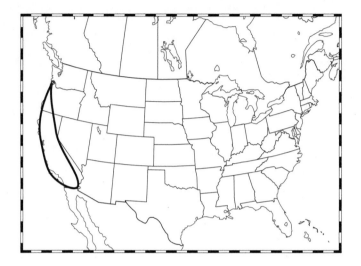

Cabbages and Kings

The days are lengthening. The sun is returning. The whole year is beginning. All nature, with bud and seed and egg, looks forward with optimism.

—Edwin Way Teale, *Wandering Through Winter*

1. SOMETHING NICE IN THE WOODSHED

Moments past midnight, January 1, 2008, I am sitting on an anvil block in the former smithy of our homestead in southwest Washington. Outside, a crust of frozen hail whitens the ground. The sun shone today, but it was *cold*—this is the frozen North, after all. Even so, I am looking up at a butterfly: first of the year—first individual, first species.

I expected to begin among the orange of monarchs, hanging in their winter roosts in California. I'll get to those soon enough. But the oranges I am actually looking at are those of rotted, rat-gnawed life jackets, the handle of a peavey, my Stihl chain saw, bar guard, and earmuffs; and that of a Sunkist oranges box, slug-eaten and full of kindling. The mellow, sun-dried oak in my woodpile is almost orange, though a little closer really to the Baltic amber of the Sierra Nevada Celebration Ale in my wineglass, lifted to the new year, the journey ahead, and this butterfly, which is also orange.

I spotted it a few days ago when I came out here to the former smithy, now woodshed, for Christmas firewood: that unmistakable silhouette of a winter nymph, outlined against an algal-dimmed windowpane. Thrilled, I hoped it would still be here—not shifted, stirred by the day's sun and hunkered down behind the woodpile, or eaten by a mouse—by New Year's. I checked on it each day, resisting the temptation to tape or Velcro it down. Yet here it is: a live butterfly, ringing in the new year, north of the 46th parallel.

A hibernating California tortoiseshell, it is perched in the upper left corner of the upper right pane of a six-eyed window on the north side of this outbuilding in the lower left corner of the upper left state in the Lower 48. Its spiny feet, or tarsi, grip the wooden window frame; its cloaked, closed wings almost graze the glazing. It

3

has moved in the days since I first saw it, but only a slight reorientation. Sloppy cobwebs hang all over and around the window, but it has avoided them, and the big English hunting spiders are frozen or hibernating too. Handsaws and an old hand scythe hang on nails beside the window, old license plates stand up below. Canoe paddles, lawn rakes, a chipper, and a weedwhacker guard the sleeping creature.

The tortoiseshell's orange and black, which give it its name, barely show. Mostly I can see the dark bark brown of the underside, with straw patches and sea blue chevrons. The crenelated edges of the wings suggest a leaf, making the nymph cryptic in the forest, but not here, where it stands right out against the hail-reflected pallor outside the window. Maybe to a mouse it is a leaf in a cobweb. But to me, it is much more. How lucky to begin this Big Year right *here*, at *home*, rather than in some distant grove of gum trees. Thea told me she saw a tortoiseshell in here around Halloween—was it the same one? It's got a couple of months to go. Good luck, little butterfly; and to me too. You are my beginning, and I hope to see you here when I return.

2. A BIG BLOW

After the holiday festivities and heavy preparations, I was still unready to take off on New Year's Day. But on the second day of the
year, I got away before 9 A.M. with 354,490.35 miles on Powdermilk's
odometer. Thea crossed the long bridge over the Columbia River to
Astoria, Oregon, with me for a goodbye breakfast date at the Pig &
Pancake. Parting was hard—but it wasn't going to be the only time
this year, nor the longest separation.

I headed out across Youngs Bay and into the Lewis and Clark
Valley, sodden, brown and green below, gray and white above.
Downed trees, fresh stumps, and battered houses spoke to a recent,
powerful storm. Driving through the dull, leaden landscape, I felt
the first twinge of the solitude that would mark much of my time
over the months to come. And then I felt an overwhelming drowsi-
ness and had to take a nap already. A marginal narcoleptic since
high school, I can never tell when I am going to have to pull over
and take a snooze. With as far as I had to go, and no one to share the
driving, that could be a problem.

For now, I pulled into Fort Clatsop, part of the new Lewis and
Clark National Historical Park. The weather was foul—much like
that endured by Lewis and Clark themselves when they wintered
here two hundred years ago. I napped beside a huge pile of fresh
rounds from wind-thrown hemlocks, drugged by the overpowering
scent of terpenes. When I came to half an hour later, I braved the
rain to search under the eaves of picnic shelters and interpretive
kiosks for more diapausing nymphalid butterflies—there were five
or six more species that could conceivably be found this way—but
saw only banana slugs. When I moved on, mist was settling into
the early dark. Down the coast, the great lump of Haystack Rock

5

loomed out of sea spray at Cannon Beach, and an October day I remembered, when the town was alive with butterflies on autumn flowers, seemed geologic ages away.

Around ten, I settled into a rest area on the Trask River, south of Tillamook, on a dark and stormy coastal night. I'd made a bed from the back seat laid lengthwise, where the passenger seat used to be, propped on my book boxes and topped with a body pillow. I drank the miniature bottle of Tullamore Dew Irish whiskey that my stepdaughter, Dory, gave me in my Christmas stocking to toast the start, and that providential tortoiseshell. Cozy in my chrysalis, about as tight as a midwinter butterfly still months from emergence, I slept eight hours solid, safely out of the heavy rain that beat on Powdermilk's protective roof. I awoke to Steller's jay calls after the first night of many on my traveling pallet. The only other two vehicles in the rest area belonged to people living in their cars but, unlike me, not by choice.

On many passes down the Oregon coast, Thea and I have stopped at Bear Creek Artichokes near Beaver, for both local produce and butterflies. The summer nectar was long gone or far in the future now, but I hoped to find a cabbage white caterpillar on the winter broccoli and kale fields. This tough introduced pierid is one of the only species one can sometimes see this far north active in the winter as a nonhibernating immature. We'd found a larva on our own kale back at Thanksgiving. But this time the fields at Bear Creek lay fallow. I stopped anyway for Longbottom coffee and a French Topaz apple, which I had on the Salmon River estuary in the sun, Sitka spruces and vine maples overhead, a rainbow to the east.

The night was balmy on the buttoned-up waterfront of Bandon. The deserted pier was illuminated by an octopus, a seal, a shark, and other sea beasts all formed by Christmas lights. I thought of sleeping there, but a wandering constable dissuaded me. It was midnight when I went to ground at Ophir Wayside State Park north of Gold Beach, just about at the bottom of Oregon. Soon any semblance of mildness went out with the tide, as this wild night on the coast got under way.

I bedded down in winds of true gale force, and I was grateful for my strong, warm holt. A tent would not have cut it. The blast rose to over eighty miles an hour, rocking Powdermilk like a cradle. Then still fiercer, less cradle than punching bag. I was afraid that Powdermilk might actually blow over, or a lamp standard come crashing down on us, or driftwood be cast up in my lap, for I was only yards from the shore. I realized that I should have parked end-on to the coast-wise wind, instead of broadside. I would have re-oriented if I could have done so without opening the door, which easily could have blown right off. In any case, I slept very little.

After a brief surcease the next day, the wind regained its edge and pinned me down. In the damp, hammering air, a heavy, bearded man in a Storey County Jeep Posse windbreaker and ball cap got out of a big, shiny red F-150 to walk a dachshund for a pee. The dog had on a little yellow rain slicker, but the wind blew it over his head, so the man gave up and took it off. Breasting the blow to pee my-self, I saw there was plenty of cakile here. This succulent mustard, also known as beach radish, comes in two species along the West Coast, one introduced and the other possibly indigenous. Cakile and cabbage whites have coadapted to the Pacific beaches, so that in summer you can find the whites tossing like bits of sea foam right down to the tide line. These wide-ranging species are beach buddies around many a northern shoreline. I'd planned to comb the cakile at Coquille, but it was dusk when I got there, so I checked the radishes here. I combed a stretch of wind-battered beach bashed by high gray seas, poked under driftwood, on marah straw in the dunes, and under the bathroom eaves: no cabbage white chrysalides.

Three brown pelicans came coasting into the wind, shooting the tubes, making slow, careless headway south. Would I make any more speed against this wind than they? I wondered. After resist-ing it for years, I'd finally agreed to carry a cell phone for the trip, mostly for the family's peace of mind, and so Thea could reach me if she needed to. Now I used the unfamiliar implement to beg a bed for the night in Eureka. There would be a warm welcome and a fine dinner, eve, and overnight to come with Redwood Coast naturalists Tom and Sue Leskiw, and excellent Indica India Pale Ale at the Lost Coast Brewery's Eureka Alehouse. But first, many more miles to cover. Blow, winds, blow!

Highway 101 curled past Otter Point and on across the Rogue River into Gold Beach. This should be one of the great town approaches anywhere. But in a stroke of world-class philistinism, a big plastic Motel 6 sign stood out on the forested hillside, directly framed by the Art Deco pillars of the historic bridge. North of Brookings, yellow-flowered hillsides kicked in—but it was European gorse, not the native spring goldfields. Equally exotic pyracantha and pampas grass violated the verges southward, but there were protected acres too, and botanical waysides, and Oregon Dunes National Recreation Area, all among the wind-driven gray and occasional sun splashes on the waves. Then, for the first of many entries I would make this year, came California. "Entering Smith River, Easter Lily Capital of the World," read the sign, followed by one of the best street names ever: Wonder Stump Road.

3. TALK TO ME OF MENDOCINO

It was a wild drive down the Eel River and the Avenue of the Giants, rain and fog bringing daytime darkness among the looming great trees. With early nightfall came a power outage throughout the area. I deemed it necessary to drive Powdermilk through one of the drive-through trees, which I had denigrated as a boy ranger in Sequoia National Park in 1969. Stepping outside, looking at Powdermilk *completely inside* a redwood—then looking up to see a cavern open to the sky, black foliage against the slate night—that was worth the schmaltz, the insult, and the two bucks. In the drive-through village, the red neon word "cocktails" glowed in the black night. I ducked into the saloon, dark except for that sign, a cozy heater, and the 49ers game, all on generator, to ask for a drive-through tree brochure. I felt nibbles on my finger. It was a black feral kitty called Friday, taking shelter from the storm on a barstool, playing with my half-gloved hand.

From there, U.S. Highway 1 to the coast was signposted "closed"—but I checked at a candlelit Willits store, and the clerk said she thought it might be open after all. So, up and over the road littered with redwood wind-throw and rocks. I saw only three other cars on the pass, maybe half a dozen all the way to Fort Bragg. Finally I dropped down to the coast, got out to see breakers, smell the ocean air, and stretch, and saw two glows in the sky—an actual *star* to the north, maybe Polaris, the first in several nights; and Fort Bragg to the south. I checked some pink rocketlike mustard and fennel in the headlights for whites and anise swallowtails, but no larvae presented themselves.

Once in old Fort Bragg, I had no choice but to visit the North Coast Brewing Company, a warm and cozy pub with sofas and a

fire that served fine Red Seal Ale, made right there and cask-condi-
tioned. I settled back with my notes and listened to the quiet talk of
the few people who'd braved the weather to come out. A fellow on
a long walk for MoveOn.org, asked about his schedule, said, "I've
got from now on." I couldn't think of a better philosophy, and as
it was only early January, it still seemed to apply to me. That's if I
didn't spend the whole year in alehouses. I spent the night in the
pub parking lot.

In the morning, I made a mistake, buying a restaurant breakfast
in town. Driving back north on Highway 1 to investigate cypress av-
enues I'd seen in the night coming in, I came to a big white Grange
hall. Fort Bragg Grange #603 was hopping. Being a Granger myself
(a member of the venerable Patrons of Husbandry), I stopped in
to see what was up. That's when I discovered my error. My Grange
brothers and sisters had a great five-dollar breakfast going, held
every first Sunday, serving from three hundred to seven hundred
people. Aggrieved that I was too full for pancakes and local eggs, I
had coffee, donated two bucks to the scholarship fund, and headed
into likely looking habitat out back.

The path through the old Inglenook Cemetery took me into a
eucalyptus grove and on into dunes. The rim of a dune crested
with wild buckwheat led to another euc forest; I slid down its steep
face to get into it. These were big, amazing eucs—they reminded
me of the old-growth jarrah and karri forest I had visited on a recent Australian trip. I was looking for monarchs, as most of the
California colonies now overwinter in eucalyptus trees. Those who
would eliminate these highly intrusive exotics refer to their taken-
over territory as "biological deserts." This grove certainly wasn't
that—I flushed great horned owls—but the abundant life inside
was not all native, with periwinkle for a ground cover, for example.
Wind-battered and salt-scorched, the habitat yet seemed good for
adaptable monarchs. I looked and looked but saw none.

At little Cleone the grocery was busy with people whose power
was still out. I asked the proprietor about monarchs in the vicinity.
She said she knew of none, but a patron told me she saw *big* hatches
of them last year—"the road was black with them"—near Ukiah,
and up 10 Mile River Road, too, near here. Those, certainly, will
have been California tortoiseshells. Bursting out like that in the

western mountains, they are mistaken for monarchs more than any other butterfly but painted ladies. But at least she'd noticed them.

Beyond the blue nursery named in cerise letters "Fuchsiarama," I came to the Mendocino Coast Botanical Gardens. Stanley the Cat lay sacked out before the wood stove in the shop. Huge, and one of the prettiest cats I've ever seen, he was white and tawny with brown stripes. He loved my petting, and missing my own cat, Firkin, I loved petting him. I'd hoped to butterfly on the early flowers here, but it was too windy, cold, and expensive to bother with the garden. So I luxuriated with Stanley before the fire, considering my next moves. They turned out to be sodden explorations of old sheds, water tower, shacks, and barns at funky Caspar, California, above a deep declivity full of willow, looking in vain for wintering tortoiseshells and anglewings; and all around nearby umbels and crucifers, finger-freezing inspections for *Papilio zelicaon* and *Pieris rapae* chrysalides. As desperate as these efforts may seem looking back, they were not unreasonable. Or productive.

It just kept raining and blowing. There were more birds than butterflies, like some versus none. Out the road to Pomo Bluffs, western meadowlarks were seeding and bugging with starlings, and a great blue heron stood so tall I thought it was a caricature of a statue, so broad in flight it might have been an albatross gone to ground in the storm. Beautiful kestrels lined the wires. But as for butterflies, I might as well have been looking for Bigfoot—I'd have seen just about as many.

Some ten years before, I had camped on the Mendocino Headlands. Now I found the headlands off-limits to camping, so I ferreted out a place to sleep on a quiet side street of Mendocino. The pub no longer had baskets of peanuts, but they still had Red Seal Ale. Eric Schramm recognized me from a story in the local paper. A dealer in wild mushrooms of many species, he was in town for a major mushroom festival. In the morning I picked up a copy of the *Mendocino Pilot* to see if the rumor was true. It was. There was the headline, "Butterfly Traveler Flies This Way." Shortly before I'd taken off from home, Al Wagar, a long-ago forestry professor of mine, now president of the Washington Butterfly Association, drove down to Gray's River with the young lepidopterist David Droppers to buy my first tank of gasoline and present me with a very welcome

Federal Lands Pass. Then Al sent out a press release with the photo of the ceremonial fill-up and a note about the Butterfly-A-Thon. That's why I was in the Mendocino paper. Then at Moody's Organic Coffee Bar, Susan Maresco, mushroom publisher, recognized me from a recent lecture I'd given in Port Townsend. I began to wonder whether maintaining anonymity might prove challenging. I had avoided most publicity for my trip so as not to squander precious time on interviews. As things turned out, my concern about recognition was well placed—only, usually it would be a case of mistaken identity. Eric and Susan, the mushroom folks, may have been the sole strangers to get my field marks right all year long.

There was one more thing I had to do before leaving town. Prevented from camping there again, I wanted to visit the unforgettable headland. I had dug out my old tape of the McGarrigle Sisters singing what must be one of the most haunting songs ever: Kate McGarrigle's "Talk to me of Mendocino." I listened to it several times on the stunning bluffs, as all the black birds—turkey vultures, crows, ravens, pelagic and double-crested cormorants—basked with pleasure on the rocks. The day was actually sunny! But when I was ready to head to Gualala, my first real field target, it was raining again.

Yet when I reached the mouth of the Navarro River, the sun came on strong. I walked the roadside and took a good look at nettles, cow parsnip, German ivy, and mustards, but nothing flew except common goldeneyes landing in the river. Common mergansers stood all along a log with a double-crested cormorant in the middle and a mother and pup harbor seal basking at each end. Sharp fins of rock cut the surf and defined scooped beaches and coves of stilling beauty. Two turkey vultures stood spread-winged as if crucified atop wooden power poles—a third would have made it just too Golgotha to be real. North of Punta Arenas, a whole kettle of TVs worked its way north. Surely there could be a bit of butterfly flight as well? I explored a perfect place for mourning cloaks beside a riverside rug of yellow willow leaves, but no cloaks deigned to appear.

Just as the McGarrigle girls sang "Talk to Me of Mendocino" for about the fortieth time, following John Lane's directions I arrived at Fish Rock Road with sea lions oinking from the rocks below. My old friend John Lane is the preeminent historian of California monarchs. I had long been fascinated with reports of monarchs in Mendocino—well north of any other known wintering site for the famous annual migrant. Particularly in view of climate change, I wondered whether monarchs might be pushing the northern edge of the envelope for winter survival, perhaps someday even reaching the mild southwest Oregon coast (not that it had been so mild for me). I'd asked John for the details of his sightings in the 1970s, when he was conducting monarch surveys up and down the coast. No one had confirmed winter monarchs in Mendocino since then.

For hours I negotiated a mugho pine slope to a west-facing ravine under tan oak, holly oak, and California myrtle, then up into evergreen blackberry, manzanita, Douglas-fir, and grand fir; next madroña, sword fern, bracken, a little salal, and dewberry; and finally to eucalypts on top. The bright red berries of toyon were good to see after all the exotic pyracantha. A ridge fronted what really felt like Mexican monarch forest. I perched in the sun beneath a mossy-footed Doug-fir that was three feet through, commanding the slope with its broad limbs and canopy globe; then again in a fairy ring of some thirty redwood stems. As the sun sank into a western haze, the air cooled, the sea lions complained, and a western gray squirrel levitated in the tall pines. Among many mushrooms— russulas, corals—shone a golden clump of chanterelles. I didn't take them and later thought, What was I *thinking*? It wasn't raining, and I could have cooked.

Lying back on a pine-needle cushion, I scanned the canopy in a good open stand of *Pinus muricata*, overtopped by a feeding flock of warblers doing their treetop pinball, draped in terpy fragrance, serenaded by sea lions. Not a glint of orange. But after weeks of rain, this was heavenly, monarchs or no. Talk to me of Mendocino.

From there it was a wild drive, in every sense, of fog, wind, and rain down Highway 1 and over the hills to Tomales Bay, where my friend Barbara Deutsch had invited me to stay in the marsh house she and her husband, Barry, have so lovingly converted to a *pied-à-eau*. Barbara gave me hot tea, a deep bath, and a book-filled room with an actual bed. If the mythical monarchs of Mendocino had failed to show, I thought as I drifted off, at least Marin ought to come through.

"Look," said Barbara, "there it is." Through the mist I saw the violet bars, a little green with algae. I'd been intrigued by a spot known as the "Purple Gate site," which had proved a reliable monarch refuge for some seasons past. A poetic plantswoman committed to justice and conservation, Barbara Deutsch knows a great deal about what butterflies want and what they need. The rain stopped long enough for us to have a good look among the tall eucalypts, but we failed to find any monarchs. Between the resumed downpour and poor recent reports, we passed on a couple of other Marin locations, retreated to a good lunch at the Parkdale in Stinson Beach, and parted till later. At least I'd finally seen the Purple Gate.

Back on Highway 1, I was almost blown off the Muir Beach overlook by the high, wild wind. Dropping down into the sheltered folds between the hills and headlands, I made it to Muir Woods. There I found Mía Monroe, manager, chief ranger, naturalist, and genius loci of Muir Woods National Monument, in her office. So devoted to her work and to this park is Mía that she was featured in *Sunset* magazine as one of ten "druids" of the National Park Service. Mía is also the Xerces Society's Monarch Project leader for California. This afternoon Mía was heavily occupied by preparations for the Muir Woods Centennial, which would culminate the next day, with many events and visitations in honor of John Muir, the park, and redwood conservation.

I don't know how, but Mía found time to escape from her centennial duties and walk with me to the Cathedral Grove, where she has hosted everyone from the Dalai Lama to the secretary-general of the United Nations. This was the first time I'd observed her in her home habitat, impressive in her sequoia green uniform and brown Stetson Smokey hat in its own plastic shower cap. Today was a designated day of silence in the park, perfect for walking among the ruddy giants swaddled in fern, moss, and soft, sempervirens rain. We would meet up later, with Barbara, in better monarch weather.

I exited the traffic hell of I-580/880 at San Leandro and found the resort called Monarch Bay, where clusters had been reported in golf course eucalypts. I toured the entire links in the dark, the nearest trees illuminated by the driving range lights. Bright spots turned out to be golf balls perched high in the eucalyptus branches. There were no stars out, but Mars shone through as a bright saffron hole in the hooded night. It is amazing how much the pendent bundles of both red and blue gum leaves can resemble a cluster of monarchs in the dull sodium glow of the Bay Area sky.

From there, I continued around the bay to sanctuary in Campbell, an erstwhile village now surrounded by San Jose. My big sister, Susan Kafer, a librarian, and her husband, Ted, a retired sixth-grade teacher who restores Model A's, dwell in a pleasant house in Campbell and make it mine when needed. The next day, ten days into the butterfly Big Year with just one butterfly under my belt, I decided it was time to quit screwing around and go find a bloody monarch. While most of the winter colonies haunt the coast, a few have been known inland. One of these was Ardenwood Historic Farm in nearby Fremont. I was met by two turkey vultures on an expired Canada goose at the gate, and by Ranger Ira Beltz. He showed me how eucalyptus longhorn borers had ravaged the blue eucs (*E. globulus compacta*), leading to the introduction of two species of Australian wasps for biocontrol. Then the lerp psyllid, an aphidlike plant louse, hit the typical blue gums, but not subspecies *compacta*. And now eucalyptus tortoise beetles are attacking them, especially red gums, their leaves scalloped as if by pinking shears.

I was fascinated by the biology but hot to see monarchs, if they indeed were there. And they were—my first butterflies since the tortoiseshell in the woodshed. Ira led me to the tree, I scanned the branches, and there they were: a compact cluster of some dozens, sixty feet up in a tall red gum, one of a long, deep colonnade along the railroad tracks. A couple of the hunkered butterflies had orange showing, and a few actually took wing and fluttered about in the overcast damp at about 55°F.

A group of school kids arrived and became excited: "I see one!" "There goes one!" "Whoooa!" A spotting scope was set up on the monarchs at kid height. Teachers applied the "five-second rule" at the scope, which would have killed me right off. Some were sadly rushed to get a good look at the cluster, but they loved it just the same. Park naturalist Caterina Meyers said there were about eighty. She had found them here, the first ones seen since the big storm, before which several hundred had been present in several clusters. Doubtless there were some other clusterettes we hadn't yet spotted. Another naturalist, Christina Garcia, wondered if I was the well-known Hawaiian ornithologist Robert L. Pyle but figured I was too young. She was right, and in fact *that* Bob Pyle had recently passed on. She told me that some folks wonder if she is Jerry Garcia's sister, and I said some folks wonder if I *am* Jerry—or least they used to, before *he* passed.

After the kids moved on, I remained to watch my first monarchs well beyond the five-second rule. Now there were several in the air at once—just flying about at fifty feet or so, flirting with various branches. The year's first mosquitoes appeared as well, and something told me they wouldn't be the last. It was so fine to see that embered orange blazing away at the accumulated days of gray! The cluster was about the size of a medicine ball; eighty looked about right, or maybe a hundred. More seemed to come from across the tracks as the day brightened. Half a dozen spun in the air over the path, and a hummingbird zipped between two of them.

But there were more monarchs to come. On Saturday morning, I drove 17 across the hills to Santa Cruz and met Mía, Barbara, and Park Ranger Martha Nitzberg at Natural Bridges State Beach in full, warm sun. Natural Bridges has traditionally been one of the best of the central coast monarch groves, but this year there were few monarchs in residence. On the boardwalk down to the main eucalyptus grove, only a couple flew over. We ran into the monarch expert John Dayton, who has performed much research in the area. Then a nice, big *Vanessa atalanta* appeared, open-winged on the blue-green and tan trunk of a slender red gum. Most people know this butterfly as the red admiral, a latter-day contraction of its older English name, red admirable. Since it is not closely related to the true admirals (genus *Limenitis*) but is instead a lady (genus *Vanessa*), I prefer to call it by its original, descriptive name. This one was an overwinterer, its bands more orangy than the crimson a new one would display. A pair of them rose, chased about, and basked on brambles. Then on the other side of the ravine, in the sunny open, a colorful circus took place involving monarchs, red admirables, Anna's hummingbirds, and chestnut-backed chickadees.

After a Thai lunch, John, Barbara, Mía, and I walked through the Australian plant and eucalyptus collection of 150 species in the UCSC Arboretum. Most monarch overwintering in California now takes place in eucalypts, and we discussed the kind of density that they seem to need. People who want to rid California of eucalypts, a laudable goal on the surface, ask why monarchs cannot merely move over to native trees. But the native forests have been radically reduced and fragmented; and as John Lane has written, no one knows exactly what sorts of groves monarchs used in Old California, since historical accounts are few and vague. Some experimental plantings of redwoods, cypresses, live oaks, and pines are taking place and should be expanded. But trees grow only so fast: you could spend fifty years reconstructing a forest that the monarchs then rejected. Until the proper native structure can be restored, the monarchs will depend on exotic gum trees, no matter how galling to native plant activists. If the day *Eucalyptus* met these shores was bad luck for the California flora, it was just good luck for monarchs that eucs furnished the right thermal qualities, shelter traits, and leaf shape for them. Without their remarkable adaptive shift, the phenomenon of the westernmost monarchs wintering along the California coast might well have become extinct long ago.

Barbara, Mía, and I overnighted at Ranger Martha and her husband, Mark's West Cliff home. As it happened, the popular band known as the 5M's—the Mostly Mediocre Monarch Mariposa Musicians—were holding their regular rehearsal there that night. Speaking of good luck, the harmonica player was absent, and I had my blues harp with me, so I got to sit in. Band member Julie nursed her little twins, Zephyr and Ryder, as her clear soprano joined the fine concordance.

Sunday morning, after Martha's fresh persimmon bread, found us finally among a bunch of monarchs worth the name. Lighthouse Field held about five thousand, according to John Dayton, including many on the wing, basking, and nectaring on red gum and ice plant flowers. A large cluster clothed two ascending Monterey cypress boughs that met at the top, creating a gothic arch of ecclesiastical gold. This was the grand monarch spectacle I'd been imagining from the first.

The monarchs of Lighthouse Field were far from the last I would see this year. In fact, I would run into *Danaus plexippus* on more days in 2008 than any other species. And over the next few days, I visited several more of the classic winter locales along the California coast. First, just around Monterey Bay, came Pacific Grove—so-called Butterfly Town, U.S.A.—in the popular mind to monarchs as San Juan Capistrano is to swallows. But it was something of a downer. Ro Vaccaro, the almost indomitable Butterfly Lady of Pacific Grove, had died just a few days before. In George Washington Park, the Monterey pines were hurting from the storms and pine canker. And in the usual cluster area, I saw nothing but a monarch-colored sunset streaming through the trees.

Next I called on a quintessentially Californian, New Age mecca that is also a de facto monarch preserve. Esalen Institute once sponsored a monarch conference in exchange for the assembled experts' management advice for their own colony. As we all soaked in the famous baths, sea otters over our left shoulders, monarchs over our right, it was wonderful to see how people's egos and agendas dropped away with their clothes.

This time, some two to three thousand monarchs hung pendent in a single coast redwood, like some pagan Yule tree ornaments. Later, the westering moon illuminated them coolly: when I focused my binoculars on their dim forms, one monarch's outline stood out sharply, engraved in silver filigree against the full moon.

In Morro Bay State Park, where I had camped beneath clusters on my *Chasing Monarchs* trip in 1996 and the following year with Thea, I now found the eucalyptus grove thinned out dramatically and both the monarchs and native western gray squirrels gone. The ranger told me that the visitors preferred the more open grove. But then a turkey vulture roost moved in, so they have buzzard breath and droppings instead of butterflies. He said the turkey vultures probably got all the squirrels—did he really believe they were raptors?—and as for the monarchs, "There are lots of 'em at Pismo," as if that excused their loss here. Normally there are, but this year, the worst for winter monarchs in California since 1994, when they virtually disappeared, I found them confined to several boughs of a single red gum at Pismo State Beach. A young woman excited to have found them and eager to share said, "There are at least a million!" but sadly it wasn't so—not in the whole state. There were perhaps five thousand. Here, at least, experiments were under way to regenerate native forests that might someday prove capable of holding monarchs through the winter without the benefit of eucalypts.

Finally, I would visit the largest Californian monarch colony, the Ellwood Main Monarch Grove and the Coronado Butterfly Preserve near Santa Barbara. Long threatened with development, it recently gained protection thanks to the fervent efforts of local conservationists and monarch lovers. This year, as late copper sun shimmered through the cluster, Ellwood displayed maybe ten thousand butterflies, magnificent to be sure—but a fraction of the number in a good year. The dry conditions foreshadowed dreadful fires to come.

So if our morning's spectacle at Lighthouse Field wasn't the biggest bunch of monarchs I would see, it was the most beautifully set, and memorable. Nearby, a *Vanessa* flew up from a dead pine and lichen clump garlanded with mallow. As Barbara and I watched and waited for it to alight for a good look, a black phoebe launched from a downed cypress post and scarfed up what was my first West Coast lady, or would have been, anyway. We three made our goodbyes, knowing we'd hook up later in the year for further adventures.

I could taste the salt from the nearby surf as I rounded the packed Santa Cruz shore walk. Down on a little pocket beach, a pair of wandering tattlers bracketed a trio of sanderlings on the taupe sand until the oystery surf came in and they all dissipated like the morning's mist. It was hard to pull away from the sunny, lively scene, but I reminded myself there were more butterflies than monarchs to see. Forty-five thousand surfers were staged just north of Santa Cruz for a contest, so I made sure to head south.

5. BIXBY CREEK AND BEYOND

At five, I pulled into Moss Landing State Beach for the masses of shore birds—red knots, avocets, black-bellied plovers—and for the winkled sunset at the lip of the beach. Then, in a bay between the sea to the west, U.S. 101 on the east, and the many stories of lights and two tall rubied towers of the Moss Landing Power Plant on the south, I made out a pod of some fifty sea otters only ten or twenty yards offshore. I camped there, among sea otters and surfers. In the morning, the otters were still there; I hadn't imagined them after all.

Otters lolled and floated and preened. One lay there with its hands up as if about to clap or giving benediction. Next to it, another rolled and rolled, while two more wrestled through the pod, bumping into the sleepers. Some somersaulted, some nibbled and preened and played with their flippers. A harbor seal's shiny knob kept popping up among the otters, and one gray gull remained with them for hours, like their familiar. About as many harbor seals lay hauled out on the sand as there were otters in the water, and on the beach of the little embayment below me lay one sea otter. I was afraid it was dead, but it looked up, turned over, and scrubbed its hoary face. After a few minutes, Shore Otter entered the water and paddled out, turning over, scrubbing its whole body as it went, much more mobile in the water than on land. Benedictine Otter stayed just that way, tail afloat, hands akimbo. As the surfer dudes grew thick, the butterfly dude split. And when I looked back from a boat launch off 101, Shore Otter was out among the others.

Circling the bay south, past oceans of artichokes that would have painted ladies if they were not so sprayed, I entered old Monterey, then weathered the mercantile mess of Cannery Row to buy monarch, sea otter, and hammerhead shark postcards, the last for my shark-freak grandson David. I reckoned John Steinbeck would deplore what the place had become. Later, I read in *The Log from the Sea of Cortez* that he harbored reservations already in the late forties: "As the book began to be read, tourists began coming . . . first a few, then in droves." What would he think of Steinbeck Plaza today? I felt actually hot in Monterey for the first time, but there were no butterflies at the flowers. A nectar-rich garden that should have furnished ladies or something had a black phoebe in residence instead. I was beginning to think that these flycatchers might present me with some serious competition.

I spent the day on the Monterey Peninsula, and when I found a place to sleep, it was in the parking lot of Our Lady of Mt. Carmel Catholic Church, in Carmel Valley. I awakened on the middle day of January to the puling of a western gray squirrel. This most gorgeously plumed of American tree squirrels is endangered in Washington but fortunately still common in California. Slow, though; it is too often seen in one dimension on the blacktop. Far better to watch it from bed in the first sun to hit the top of a tall pine. Tall too, between a yellow-green *Liquidambar* and an incense cedar, stood the six-foot cross, painted brown with California poppies trailing up the lower third. The church custodian, truly Christian, left his guest to his morning ablutions.

I thought I might wear out my welcome by cooking breakfast there, so I dropped down to the village for coffee. At the bakery, I saw a flight of blue butterflies arrestingly arrayed up the legs of a business-suited woman in sheer stockings and a slit skirt. At the risk of arrest, I inquired for the sake of science if they were on her stockings or her skin. No worries: this was California, and the young lady was happy to talk about her legs.

"My skin," she said. "It took me a long time to bring them out."

"Now with the sun," I said, "they might fly away."

"Not yet!" she said. "But they do fade in the sun. That's why I did the inside first."

Sun! Clear, still, warming. I hurried to Garland Ranch Regional Park, where I'd come with John Lane, Thea, and a National Wildlife Federation butterfly class from a Conservation Summit at Asilomar years ago. It was now popular with women walkers in pairs, arriving in their pairs of SUVs, and folks with pairs of dogs, or all six combined. As I arrived, I faced a problem that I knew would arise sometime: after last night's big fish meal, I had a mighty motion in the offing, and no loo, in a public place. Stream on my right, highway on my left. But across it, a big pile of road gravel, shielded by cottonwoods. Not exactly sanctioned by that excellent field text *How to Shit in the Woods,* but it served admirably. Black-capped chickadees and yellow-rumped warblers, a.k.a. butterbutts, worked the willows along the stream all the while.

I paused on the bridge over the Carmel River to look for mourning cloaks in the nice willow and cottonwood riparian edge. There was a stream flow gauge with a recording chart that told the whole story of the terrible drought afflicting California: the most likely cause for the monarch dearth. The water flow for the year 2007 measured 200 acre-feet through December 7, the lowest ever; the figure for 1998 was 250,000 acre-feet. A "No Fishing" sign looked like a Darwin fish with a red slash through it. Nearby, the welcome sign gave warnings about rattlesnakes and mountain lions. Then I saw a sign for a restroom—*now* they told me.

I set out on the extensive trails. Everywhere it looked like there might be butterflies, there was a black phoebe stationed. A man in a fur cap warned me of a dead skunk up the trail—that could be good for my purposes, as all the nymphs love to come to carrion. I began to smell the skunk, and my first spring tincture of cottonwood-balsam—a heady mix. I carried sticky yellow and green on my fingers from a violated bud.

As I came down the upper side of the Lupine Loop through dappled oak woods, scrub jays calling, I saw a movement intersecting my path from the left. We saw each other a moment later, and it stopped—bobcat! Just nineteen yards away (I stepped it off), the bobcat paused, and we looked at each other (I with my binos) for three or four minutes. I saw its stocky, spotty legs, its white-tipped little tail flicking, and when it tilted its ear, the white spot on the back of it; mustard-colored eyes, big kitty grin. The puss looked slightly over its shoulder a couple of times, then turned and trotted into the brush, and I saw its ruff, or shaggy sideburns, wagging as it went. I breathed again. My best bobcat sighting ever, by far. I felt its fresh pugmark where it turned to go, in damp earth between the moss and short spring grass and bracken—put my left index finger in a fresh bobcat's print. And there was a musk.

A way down the trail I found another print—it must use this trail frequently. And then I came to the Rancho Loop/Live Oak trail junction, and atop a low slab bench a poem, in gold letters, was baked onto a black plaque—"Garland Ranch Song," by Donald Marsh:

> I'll be with you
> In fairy lantern
>
> Bobcat time.
> Bobcat saw me
>
> And danced
> In fiddleneck field.

The poem went on about bobcat for several more lines, leaving me almost as amazed as by the animal itself.

Back down on Monterey Bay, I sought out the Pacific Grove Museum of Natural History to see what Edwin Way Teale in *Wandering Through Winter* called "one of the finest mounted sea otters in the country . . . in the superb little museum at Pacific Grove." *He* (with prominent penis and testicles and a broad, tawny head) was still here, gnawing on a red abalone; he'd been found perished off the mouth of Bixby Creek, down the coast. Beside him reclined a criminally cute baby sea otter, toylike, with little rabbit's foot–size brown, furry feet and tail. I also visited the bobcats, much smaller than the one I'd danced with. One of these was batting at a buckeye butterfly, which certainly could have been there for me too, in my personal opinion.

Heading down the Cabrillo Highway, I picked up a locally made tamale at Carmel General Store, converted from an old canopy gas station outside town. It was so good I wished I'd bought several. Late, I reached Bixby Canyon and camped at the north end of the soaring bridge to the Big Sur coast, behind three granite boulders, by the sign that reads "WARNING / STEEP SLOPE / STAY BACK."

One truck pulled in for a while, and a patrolman stopped to see if he was okay but didn't bother me.

The historic Bixby Creek Bridge, built in 1932, must be one of the most spectacular in the West. The downstream pedestrian bay frames the very debouchure of little Bixby Creek far below. The white hems of the waves come in to it, past it, and take it into their lacy embrace, then pull its silty plume back out into the bay. A murre, a gull, and a pelican all fished along the plume's border with dark water. After a long search of the extensive kelp canopy, I spotted the telltale staple with one bifurcated end that meant a sea otter, playing with its toes off the mouth of Bixby Creek—maybe a direct descendent of the one found here that resides still in the "superb little museum" in Pacific Grove.

Lawrence Ferlinghetti, owner of City Lights Bookshop in San Francisco, urged Jack Kerouac to use his cabin up in the canyon to unwind from his unwanted "King of the Beatniks" notoriety. He did so and was charmed with the setting, the jays, a donkey, and the stream. His demons came with him, though, and later his buddies arrived with a great deal of wine, and the idyll ended badly. A stark but luminous novel, *Big Sur*, came out of this visit. It includes a long poem composed of Jack's dictation taken from the waves themselves, when he would wander down the creek to its mouth and listen for what the ocean had to say.

Two young men from Tübingen asked me about the place and its literary connections. They knew Kerouac, having read *On the Road* by its title *auf Deutsch, Unter Weg.* "*Ich bin unter Weg auch,*" I told them, "*aber, mit Schmetterlingen.*"

Then a New Zealand couple—Anglo man, Maori woman—came by to chat. The man wanted to see the coast redwood groves to the south, having seen the giants in the Sierra. She said I looked like Kenny Rogers and asked if I would be photographed with her—she in her little knit top and shorts, I in jeans, chambray, khaki vest, and broad hat. The man said that their daughters refused to leave the car just to see some bridge: "They say, 'It's too gay!' " But when their mum went back and showed them her snapshot with Kenny Rogers, they shyly tripped over to me and asked if I was indeed the singer.

"They tell me so," I drawled. Their mom said I was driving this little car so as to be anonymous on my holiday. "That's right," I said, "this old Honda's my disguise. The Hummer's back at the ranch." Then I asked them not to tell anyone I was out here. They promised and, squeaking with excitement, asked for a picture of their own. One held up her little pink cell-phone camera and got the three of us, me framed between Shana and Aria, with their pink braces, pink lip gloss, sparkly jeans, and pink flip-flops.

"I have 'The Gambler' on my telephone," Shana said as they giddily skittered back to their car, never even looking at the canyon or the bridge. I called out, "Now, remember, girls—you gotta know when to fold 'em."

In the late, warm morning I headed up Bixby Canyon. I'd been here once before. A few years ago, a friend of Barbara's borrowed the key to Lawrence Ferlinghetti's gate and cabin from a friend of the poet-bookseller. Mía, Barbara, other friends, and I came down from a monarch meeting at Asilomar and spent the day around the cabin and the canyon. This was not the same cabin that Kerouac had memorialized in *Big Sur,* but there was an enchanting Buddhist grotto at the head of a derelict pool, with a plaque that read "Temple of the Zen Fool" and a small Buddha said to have been presented to Ferlinghetti by Allen Ginsberg. And there had been West Coast ladies a-wing. So while I didn't have the entrée this time, a look about in the vicinity seemed a good thing to do.

And right away, at last, there was a butterfly! On the hills and roadsides by the first bridge, a pink convolvulus was blooming. Palisades of *Delairea odorata,* an introduced South African liana for some reason called German ivy, hung from trees, shrubs, and power-line guy wires, so there was plenty of good nectar, and the air was over 70°F. At first I saw only bees on the flowers, but then a white appeared on a dappled bank below the road. It flew to a *Senecio* leaf, basked, and flew up over the road and upslope; then another. They were fresh *Pieris marginalis venosa,* the most dramatically dark-veined race of a West Coast species called the margined white. As well as crisp blackish vein-scaling below, the male I saw well had a black spot on each dorsal forewing and charcoal vein-ends, crenelated on the edges. Very different from the lineny *P. m.*

marginalis that would be flying at home in March, it was my first nonhibernating, spring-emergent species for the year.

Farther up Bixby Creek, in Los Padres National Forest, I rounded a bend and came to a sunny glade beneath redwoods and thought, Good spot for *Polygonia,* when a *Polygonia* popped up! Polygon = angled, so *Polygonia* = anglewings, also known as commas for the silvery marks they bear on their ventral hindwings. It circled high, back and forth in the sun patch, dallied with another in a slow courtship flutter, then they parted. One lit briefly on Marsha's rim, then on foliage, where I got just one shot, missed, and it left the territory. I saw that it was a satyr anglewing, a common nettle feeder and overwinterer. It had weathered well, burned-out redwoods furnishing fine hibernacula. I headed down-canyon and down-coast, elated by butterflies at last.

Beyond Big Sur, above the big elephant seal beach at Point Piedra Blancas, I saw a life mammal by moonlight. The massive animals were just visible down below but hugely audible. They gave a remarkable convocation of growls, grunts, hoots, clicks, and kronks, with sea lions barking behind like a backup chorus. The lights of Hearst Castle, like a twin-towered mission, glowed on a hill to the south. And in the morning, the three towers of the nuclear power plant and the long wild spit of Los Osos del Oro loomed beyond Morro Bay. I walked the Elfin Forest, a fascinating chaparral of California sagebrush, Morro manzanita, gnarly and lichen-hung coast live oak, and many other species. A botanical wonderland, it was nearly nectarless at this season except for fuchsia-flowered currants that the hummingbirds loved. We were months away from the flight of the locally endemic Morro blue. But the satyrs of Big Sur and the bright new whites of Bixby Creek were on the books.

As I pushed on south, I couldn't keep from smiling. In fact, I would catch myself smiling over and over, all year long. Often when I did, I would think back to Bixby Creek and something Kerouac had said in *Big Sur.* "The sea drove me away," he wrote, "and yelled 'Go to your desire.' As I hurried up the valley it added one last yell: —'And laugh!'"

6. VENTURA HIGHWAY

"Today would be Charles's eighty-sixth birthday!" said Debra at break-fast. "January nineteenth—what an appropriate way to spend it."

And it was. Charles Lee Remington was founder of the Lepidop-terists' Society and one of the foremost students of butterfly biology over the twentieth century. He was a major mentor of mine since I was twelve and eventually served as my major professor at Yale University. John Piot is Remington's nephew. His wife, Debra, was preparing a Ph.D. dissertation on Remington and his conservation legacy. We were at table in their sunny condominium at Shadow Hills above Santa Barbara, where the Piots were wintering from their home in Maine. We'd met at a Remington memorial seminar in New Haven the previous fall, and they'd offered me their hospi-tality during the Big Year, having no idea how much I would exploit that rash invitation.

In bright sun, Painted Rock Canyon, where manzanita bloomed prolifically, held nothing for us but two pallid and flimsy geome-ters. These inchworm moths (geo = earth, meter = measure, hence earth-measurers), many of them diurnal, often cause false alarms. We visited Painted Rock and the Chumash Indian cave and had a fine spring walk down the canyon, but there was nothing out yet. That's just the way it is with butterflies: you can lay the party, but it doesn't mean anyone will show up. What did show up was a road-runner—we got a good, close, long look, with its iridescent tail and crest raised when it did what it was supposed to do. Then down at Arroyo Burro estuary and beach, looking for pygmy-blues, what we found was another stunning bird. The exotic mandarin drake must be the most spectacular duck going, with its upswept primaries of saffron-buff and stripy green head like that of a wood duck in drag.

On the strength of that, we retreated to the Beach Cafe for mahi-mahi and macadamias with Island Pale Ale from nearby Carpinteria and celebrated the good Uncle Professor Remington's birthday with a worthy midcoast Syrah.

"Ventura Highway, in the su-un-shine," is that how the seventies band America put it? That was me on Sunday morning. On the salt marsh and native plants nature trail at Sandyland Cove I saw a golden-crown's crown against golden pussy willows as the Amtrak Pacific Surfliner tooted past and a solo monarch sailed toward the south. As I entered Ventura, I rued the lack of a DeLorme atlas and gazetteer for Southern California, since I had insensibly passed that particular Rubicon and needed its detailed maps. None of the bookstores I checked had it. So I went on gut and bad maps to find my objective, for I had a particular one that day, "the free wind blowin' through my hair."

When an organism is first named in the scientific literature, the provenance of the original specimen described is designated as that species' type locality (TL). Descriptions from eighteenth- and nineteenth-century authorities often gave vague locality data, such as "Oregon Territory," "Rocky Mountains," or if you were lucky, "*Californie Sud.*" But my target insect, though long known to science, wasn't given its current name until 1971, so its TL was precisely defined, in the manner of more modern authors. The reason for its recent naming makes an interesting story in itself. The specific epithet long applied to the common butterfly we call the West Coast lady was *Vanessa carye*. When William Field, a curator at the Smithsonian Institution, revised the painted ladies of the genus *Vanessa*, he discovered that *V. carye* actually applied to a South American species, leaving our lady nameless. Bill gallantly remedied her identity crisis by naming the species for his young daughter, Annabella. While he was at it, he separated the true ladies from the admirables, resurrecting the 1807 genus *Cynthia* for them. This was later sunk as a subgenus, but it still leaves the West Coast lady with the charming and utterly feminine appellation of *Vanessa (Cynthia) annabella*. It was this lovely creature—the one likely snatched from before my eyes by the phoebe of Lighthouse Field—that I was seeking today at its TL.

Revisiting type localities is worthwhile, to see if the animals or plants described from them (topotypes) still occupy the sites. One too often finds that they have been eradicated, or the very location scarified, paved, or otherwise altered beyond recognition.

Sometimes type localities are just hard to find or access. By one in the afternoon, I located the general area of *Vanessa annabella's* TL in Ventura: the "first valley 1/8 mile north of Arroyo Verde Park." My mission required ranging over "No Trespassing" ranch land, but the sign threatening me with death and dismemberment was pretty rusty. The first fence above the road was easy. The second, admitting into spring green chaparral and grassy hills, was double and difficult, a real belly crawler. Secreted under a spreading palo verde, I perched on a low limb to see if anyone was on my tail and to lunch on a hard-boiled egg and water. Only raven and redtail witnessed, and they forgave my trespasses. Crossing a ridge, I descended into what must be "the" valley, full of beat range and dense scrub, and on the far (ocean-facing) slope, tall prickly pear cactus. The overall aspect brought to mind Tajikistan in November, about as dry and grazed. But here there were cattle, not goats, and towhees instead of hawfinches. At least the cows had cleared the exotic pampas grass.

I cast about for ladies, but the arroyo was thick with coyote brush, California sagebrush, and prickly pear. It was all but impassable, even if I'd worn my jeans instead of, dumbly, my shorts (hey, it's Ventura!). The bottom of the caved-in cattle trail felt miles from Ventura Highway. Marah vine tendriled and bloomed beneath palo verde in moist shade, around a handsome clump of mushrooms with veils, vulvas, and brown caps split from the centers into white stars. A tiny buzz alerted me to a blue-gray gnatcatcher, distant barks to dogs—I didn't like to hear them, recalling as they did a Mexican pooch attack, complete with bites, a year before. Now that I was past the yearlong incubation period for rabies, I could go this entire year without a dog bite and not be at all disappointed.

An old track led over to the next drainage, dropped to a *very* serious fence above a new home site, then turned back uphill. Horse prints gave me hope of exit, then an old, rusty pony shoe, small and round. Up the next ridge, I saw that I'd made it to the park, which I had rejected as an access point because of cost and crowds. I over-looked an Ultimate Frisbee game and a trail, mostly deserted as the day waned and the clouds closed in.

I continued to the top to watch for hilltopping, an activity in which ladies often partake late in the afternoon. From my high vantage, the only orange fliers I saw were a flicker and a ladybird beetle. From the very head of Annabella Valley, I could see Powder-milk way, way below. A merlin alighted for about half a second on the path before me, then flew up into low brush. I didn't make out what it caught. I don't suppose it really was my hilltopping Anna-bella's butterfly, but you never know. Kestrels catch grasshoppers, after all.

From the ridge high behind the valley, I found my way down openings and cow trails to the exact point where I'd come in. Back to base at 4:30 from my three-hour tour, ladyless, I headed home for Debra's pizza. John had looked up the weather. Another northern front was on the way, and the forecast was bad for days to come, all over. Bad, anyway, for butterflies, and for fools who would seek them in midwinter. They wanted me to stay. So I did, but at early light, I got out to make hay before the storm.

Malibu-bound, I took Highway 1 out of Oxnard into the Santa Monica Mountains National Recreation Area. The lepidopter-ist Sandy Russell had told me of a certain canyon where she had found Sonoran blues. Marah, yellow bladderpod, and lots of mal-low—West Coast lady food—lined the road. In Deer Canyon—off road, down creek, up ravine—I got into a confiding pack of wren-tits, a life bird that took me about three seconds to place and an-other second to fall in love with. They foraged seeds overhead, like bigger, slower chickadees, and whirred when they flew. A spotted towhee screed and California towhees scraped socially on the dirt road. Abundant lemonade berry bushes should have sucked some-thing into their overflowing nectar stand but didn't. I found a sylvan oak glade defaced by junk and bullets. I'll never understand some recreators' contempt for the beautiful places they visit: the worst litter is often in the prettiest spots. Sycamore State Park in the next valley would have been free of such blight, but it charged admis-sion, banned nets, and had lots of people. I often took the mess of secondhand spots over the tidier but also expensive, regulated, and crowded beauty spots.

But the free places weren't always vandalized. Mulholland Highway, a name out of the Tom Petty songbook this time, took me to a little fishers' path down to a lovely green stream lined with big tasseled sedges under willows and California sycamores. Reminiscent of papyrus, three feet tall with some twenty leaves in a starburst and flowers in the center, they were probably a kind of *Cyperus* escaped from someone's water garden. At the entry booth to Leo Carillo State Beach at the bottom, the ranger had never heard of the trail I was seeking, nor did he know the flowering shrubs. Bushtits were working the bare limbs of a little tree when a wrentit hopped up and landed among them. When I later described the scene to a friend as having "two tits in the bush," I think I was misapprehended, especially as I'd just been describing the nude baths at Esalen.

My friend may have taken me for a loon as well as a lech when I told her that the next birds I saw were *parrots*. But it's true: hearing a raucous clatter, I looked up and—ye gods! Parrots! Five black-hooded parakeets—blue-black face, chartreuse breast, green back, red leggings—sat in the California sycamores. "I've got a flock of frigging *parrots* here," I noted, "and I can't find one bloody butterfly!"

But it wasn't long before I did—find a butterfly, that is. Returning north from Malibu town, I noticed a bright yellow mustard field against the blue chaparral on the uphill slope. The edge of the field was actually a trail. A couple with daypacks came down it, and we exchanged greetings of the day. Then at the top of the field, where habitats met, before the trail switchbacked up into the chaparral that would become a tinderbox the following summer, a white butterfly apparated out of thin air. It showed no sign of settling, so I thought I'd better net it, and Marsha caught it on our second attempt.

A fresh little male, it struck me at first as a spring white, not a terribly common butterfly. But on close examination it turned out to be the small, dark spring "vernalis" form of the checkered white, a much more widespread species. That made more sense, since *Pontia sisymbrii* is a specialist on native crucifers for the most part, while *P. protodice* happily occupies weedy sites such as this, laying its eggs on almost any available mustard. Either way, it was a butterfly, and it was about time.

Without the atlas, I'd failed to find Sandy's canyon. But back in Santa Barbara, Debra presented me with the Southern California edition DeLorme, which she'd kindly tracked down. So I tried again the next day, and this time, with better maps and directions, I had no trouble finding the North Malibu Canyon trailhead. The coastal chaparral was lush after all the rain. A footbridge over a runnel was blocked by two slats, but the sign was gone. Especially in a case like this, when it's not even there, I adhere to my friend Karölis Bagdonas's dictum: "Signs like that mean nothing to us." The trail led to a bench above the stream, where old rusted pots and a clearing suggested a former "grow"—a marijuana garden, perhaps why the path had been closed. Foot-tall shooting stars bloomed beneath oaks, their cerise, black-beaked flowers nodding, the central velvety bits between anthers and petals banded deep grape and lemon.

Then I came to a National Park Service sign hanging from an oak: "Research Area/Please Do Not Disturb." Signs like that *do* mean something to us, so I pressed on undisturbingly. But the next sign was even more meaningful: "*DANGER—MOUNTAIN LION CAPTURE AREA. Captured Mountain Lions Are Extremely Dangerous. PLEASE STAY AWAY FROM THIS AREA AND KEEP PETS AWAY.*" I spotted a fresh scrape; then three more around the signs. As Richard Nelson wrote about warm bear crap in *Heart and Blood,* "Information like this should never be taken lightly." I retreated, watching my back, lifting Marsha to look big. Alert for pugmarks, I saw two old ones and a bit of scat. Much as I'd've liked to have seen a cougar to match the bobcat, this sign really did mean something to me. The many hollowed caves in red rocks above were perfect for pumas.

Down by the "grow," a few little yellow lotuses were in bloom. I checked for green hairstreaks, and by the gods, there was a butterfly! Not a greenie but a brownie: a beautiful fresh brown elfin, thumbnail-size, rich loam brown with eye-opening violet and russet scaling over the sawing hindwings. Back at the bridge, a western fence lizard skittered, just as at home, except with *Dudleya* instead of *Sedum* on the mossy balds it claimed. That *Dudleya* didn't have the Sonoran blues around it that I'd hoped for, but the brown elfin was nothing to sneer at.

Not far up-canyon a sign read "Malibu Ponderosa.com—135.68 acres—(Raw Land)—$1,300,000." Human invasion of mountain lion habitat should be considered illegal occupation, rather than grounds for removing the original occupants. But such is the Californian way. Just across the Santa Monicas, Sheetrock palaces clotted the hills in unstable sites prone to wildfires, landslides, and earthquakes. The pumas will be back.

7. PROTECTING OUR BORDERS

"Is this *right*," fulminated the right-wing talk show host, "for illegal immigrants to identify with this song?" After his cordial reception of some Mexican singers, he had induced them to sing a Spanish version of "This Land Is Your Land" and was now using them to incite hysterical call-ins. The presidential primaries were under way, and the Republican candidates were outdoing themselves to sound tough on undocumented immigrants. As I drove Highway 126 east from Ventura to Santa Paula, the orange and lemon groves and crop fields were full of chemicals and Mexicans. "Mitt Romney," I asked the radio, "just who would *you* have doing this work?"

I'd spent a couple more days in Santa Barbara, waiting on the weather. Debra, hearing a rumor of a sun spot out by UCSB, dragged me out for a look. What we saw were Heermann's gulls tussling with the wind and the pelicans bouncing on the wild surf, ditto for a completely crazy windsurfer. In Goleta we spent over an hour in heavy rain turning over leaves checking for chrysalides of cloudless sulphurs and searching senna stalks for *Phoebis sennae* pupae, but they might as well have been fool's gold—invisible fool's gold. The next day saw even heavier rain, house-shaking thunder, and fresh snow over the Santa Barbara hills. I had no choice but to flee to the deserts.

The hills were green as only California January hills can be. I-5 was closed by snow at Castaic, just north of my route, the section known as the Grapevine impassable. Sycamore Road, coming in from the north side, split for a massive old California sycamore hulk, ten feet high, four feet through, hollow and burned out but alive. Its interpretive plaque had been stolen by scrap-metal thieves. I checked on the lush mallow at its base for electric lady larvae, salvaged some fallen lemons from the adjacent grove, and carried on. Then, speaking of scrap metal, somewhere before Fillmore, an old gold crown fell out of my jaw. I couldn't imagine hanging around looking for a dentist, let alone the expense. I called my friend and dentist David Branch, and on his advice, bought some fix-it at a Rite Aid and plunked the crown back in as best I could. The Sespe Condor Sanctuary lay just above on the north. I hated to give the Sespe Wild a miss, but black clouds, rain, and thick fog looked back from up there, and the roads to the edge were steep and muddy. I watched out for California condors anyway and saw exactly as many as I did butterflies.

Santa Clarita, near the highway, presented a faux-Spanish mess of malls and condos at the very edge of the L.A. octopus. Over Escondido Summit, 3,258 feet, some blue sky showed through snowy mountains with lots of ravens. Then onto the Pearblossom Highway, which would take me to the deserts. At a blatant tourist trap, "Charlie Brown's—Antelope Valley's Largest Gift Shop," I stopped for pistachios and honey. Outside, the workers were laughing over the rare pleasure of throwing snowballs. Inside, a local girl was opening a pack of chocolate-covered insects. She said she'd eat a "worm" if I'd eat a cricket. So she popped the caterpillar, I crunched the cricket, and we did a high-five. "Pretty unusual to have snowballs around here, eh?" I asked.

"Yeah, but not as unusual as *this*," she said, pointing at the chocolate bugs. On my way out, I handed a buck to a shivering hobo. It was *cold*, more like Wyoming than SoCal.

Joshua trees appeared just twenty-six miles south of Edwards Air Force Base, where Powdermilk had turned over 250,000 miles in 1996 on the monarch chase. Rapture Road was a dusty track with old trailers among the creosote bush. Mariposa Road was a big fib, running south into a black cloud wall. Looking down toward Apple Valley, beyond the waste of Victorville (closed Route 66 museum, tiny 1970s Amshak, homeless guys in the chilly sunshine of a weedy park), it was all ravens, rocks, and rainbows. The highway ran a straight line east under the snowy San Bernardinos. When the sun downed into them and their clouds, it left gold and purple stripes across the rocks and playas to the north.

Some years, spring strikes early in the California deserts, and several species of butterflies emerge before January runs out. This was not one of those years. I decided there wasn't much point in spending a day in Joshua Tree National Park. As much as I love that tumbled-boulder landscape, southward seemed a better bet. The day grew warm, but Big Morongo Canyon had a hibernal aspect to it, with snow just above. A loop on foot up a side canyon with burro, deer, and coyote sign revealed just one or two flying insects and a couple of ants. As I came down out of Morongo from the north, giant ranks of windmills surrounded the Palm Springs blob on the valley floor; heading out the south side, ranks of date palms took over. Traveling toward Mecca takes you from mansions to the barrio inside a mile. At the north end of the Salton Sea, everything was doubled in the calm purple water, like the two-sterned coot on the surface and the two-necked stilt bending constantly to kiss its own reflection on impossibly long pink legs. Gold willows framed a sky that grew deeper and deeper rose. When it reached the color of raw tuna, I knew I had to turn back north to make a rare date in La Quinta.

I had long planned to meet up with George Exum and Carol Carver, good friends from Puget Island in our home county. Their daughter Maya, whom I'd known since birth, was living in Palm Springs with a friend from home, working in the hospitality trade. As a concierge at the Hyatt, Maya received certificates good for meals at fine restaurants in the area, so the four of us dined at a fancy Italian place in Palm Desert. Several waiters hovered throughout, showing surprising deference and bearing course after bottle after course. My lamb chops were rare and worthy of Puget Island. With our wine, the tariff bumped four hundred dollars. We were unsure just how much the coupon would cover. When the entire bill was comped, George made discreet inquiries. He learned that a rumor had begun in the kitchen that Kenny Rogers was out there with a party. Celebrities often came in, after all, and apparently my vest and hat hadn't hurt. Not about to disabuse the proud staff, George just winked at the headwaiter and put his wallet away.

George and Carol had seen a monarch at Sonny Bono National Wildlife Refuge on the Salton Sea the day before. As I passed down the west side of that great but shrinking salty lake the next morning, clouds of white fog and snow geese drifted over the blinding soft white powder of the former lakebed. Godetia Ditch, Verbena Ditch, and Aster Wash gave no sign of the advertised nectar. Grand Ditch was more like its name. The Anza-Salton Seaway cut through impressive creosote badlands grading into flats of ocotillo, whose first scarlet buds were breaking.

Anza-Borrego Desert State Park is famous for its butterflies, and I hoped to prove up on that reputation. The village of Borrego Springs lies in the middle of the park. At noon I pulled into the Roadrunner Club at Borrego Springs Resort to look over the flowers and right away saw the first butterfly in days—a male monarch in good condition, nectaring on purple verbena, basking, and flying all around the entry gate. Then another, out over the road. I wondered if there was a roost nearby. Only one winter roost had ever been reported in the interior of Southern California; what were monarchs doing in Anza-Borrego and Sonny Bono in January?

I parked at the Tamarisk Grove Campground to take the trail to Yaqui Wells. From fine desert of saltbush and barrel cactus, I descended into San Felipe Wash. Beside it, someone had built a five-stone circle with a cairn in the middle, topped by a Corona bottle cap: Yaqui or Honkee? A phainopepla flashed from a mesquite covered in mistletoe with red-berry poop spattered all over its limbs. Saltbush was putting forth galaxies of crumb-size seeds that small black ants were harvesting, carrying them ten or twelve feet back home and down into holes. Other ants were coming out of the same holes bearing husks—the *empties*—and depositing them in a neat rubbish heap about a foot from the holes: putting out the recycling.

The "well" was a room-size cove surrounded by fragrant *Distichlis* grass with a tiny pool in the bottom the size and shape of a large T-bone steak (well, it did used to water cattle). The spring face it collected from was damp but not flowing, barely earning its description as "year-round" but perhaps a lot for this dried-out year. A raven and three phainopeplas remarked my entry to the premises. If the well was a modest thing, two other features impressed me greatly. First, a trio of big dead ironwood trees, rusty, tan, and gray, with great knots, hollows, and witchy, curvy limbs. Second, two of the best outhouses I have ever seen: squat, square, solid granite-masonry-built boxes, open to the sky. Unvandalized, as were the old trees, the gents' bore an old wooden "MEN" sign, the women's had the female symbol with flared skirt. Obedient small mammals had left their pellets in neat piles by the toilets. My good impression of the park did not prevent an underoccupied ranger from berating me for parking in the empty campground. I tried to plead reciprocity with my Federal Lands Pass, but it just didn't fly.

Nor did the vaunted butterflies. I had planned to walk up Plum Canyon, well known for several early species, including the coveted Sonoran blues that would be flying by now in an average year, but now it was just plum cold. A few miles on, I walked a stretch of the Pacific Crest Trail, looping back through a wash on the Sentenac Birding Trail. Just inside the crossing, behind a creosote, there were two nice little chairs, a shelter with numerous water jugs, and a sign that invited walkers to "Relax / Enjoy / Trail Ratz Dave, Dave, & John / Class of 2003."

South of Anza, the smell of damp burned fields on the air toward El Centro could only mean rain. When I reached a rest area on Interstate 8, it was raining so hard that I had to sleep in the tipped-back driver's seat rather than arrange my bunk and get soaked in the process.

These constant weather systems from the west were keeping me largely innocent of butterfly encounters. If only I could get some sun tomorrow, I felt I could do some good with the southernmost, border species. But it was supposed to rain some more. So I sat there ensconced in my chrysalis listening to Beethoven, eating pistachios, and reading Fred Heath's book about the SoCal species I *could* be seeing. It was dispiriting but not surprising when I opened my eyes to cold, gray rain. It was a long way to drive from Gray's River just to get rained on like this. I, who generally like rain, said rude words. Great-tailed grackles and house sparrows hunkering beneath sodden palms seemed to agree.

In the loveliness that is Calexico, I parked between a duty-free store and the double-fenced railroad track to have breakfast and watch Customs and Immigration agents take apart cars and trucks.

One sedan had its whole bumper assemblage down on the ground. I was glad I had no plans to go into Mexico and back—they'd take one look at Powdermilk and I'd be there a week. Four agents stood about drinking coffee as a dozen cars waited in the queue. One kicked desultorily at a bumper and pored over a magazine he'd found in one of the cars. The border was a gaily painted sheet metal wall up against Mexicans' backyards. A two-towered white church poked up beyond, and the saltcedar stream coming across, the New River, was snowy with detergent suds. Gazing into Mexicali, I listened to the Grateful Dead singing "Mexicali Blues." "Is there anything a man don't stand to lose / when the devil wants to take it all away?" Like sunshine?

As I was going west, a big Border Patrol roadblock tried to wave me through, but not to be cheated out of a chance to use my new interpretive Xerces Society business cards, I stopped anyway. An agent read the story on the back and said, "Oh, yeah? I've seen *lots* of butterflies out here." He paused. "But not in the rain." A little farther on, a Say's phoebe awaited sun and my butterflies by the road. There must've been something to eat around there, as I saw sixteen kestrels over those big black burned fields that I'd smelled last night, mostly in pairs. Three more Border Patrol agents checked me out separately and, seeing I was birding, drove on.

As I headed west into creosote, the verges turned purple, yellow, and white with blossom. The Yula Desert was in bloom—acres of mauve sand verbenas, sprinkled with lots of a tall desert sunflower, apricot mallow, big white, floppy evening primroses, and several I didn't know at all. Then, *un milagro!* The sun came out. I hiked the broad wash, along a silt cliff, and up the sandy slopes. I sweated in too many layers and loved it. But in such a nectar trove, in warm sun, I saw *no* butterflies. It seemed almost unbelievable, and certainly unacceptable. I scanned a slow 360° with my binos, seeing only one Say's phoebe and one black phoebe. "Ah! That's it!" I said. "The damn phoebes got 'em all!" Then my crown fell out again.

Two BP agents and a sheriff's deputy stopped to make sure I was okay. Abandoned water containers increased as the bush thickened near the border. It's not the immigrants you worry about but the drug and people smugglers, who can get violent when discovered. But I saw no more travelers than butterflies.

My new gazetteer showed something intriguingly called "Crucifixion Thorn Natural Area." The name referred to a tree, *Castela emory,* with truly fearsome thorns that looked like no fun at all. A related Middle Eastern species is identified with the Christian crown of thorns. The flower buds resembled those of redbud. I'd have loved to have seen it in bloom—or anything at all: when I found it, the Nine-inch Nails preserve had bare soil and no blossom. The agent who stopped to see if he could help me was powerless to do so.

At In-Ko-Pah rock park, I was nearly blown off the top of a tall stone tower by a frigid wind as I scanned back toward that warm, flowered desert that might have been a mirage. West of Jacumba, east of Campo, the clock tower of an old feldspar mill was ringed by a spooky neon circle that shone like a blue beacon in the night. An agent followed me for twenty miles until I was waved through a checkpoint. A helicopter was circling and spraying the fields with light. A car was stopped, and I saw a Mexican woman escorted into a people cage on the back of a Border Patrol truck. Zombied out by the time I reached Ocean Beach, I found that the cheap surfer motels I'd been told about had gone out with the tide. But I checked into the Dolphin for fifty bucks. The stars were actually out, but after a hard sleep, I woke up to rain over San Diego.

At Cabrillo National Monument, sun shimmered on the ocean between pelicans and Coronado Island. Peterson and Fisher, as told in *Wild America,* went out there for petrels and auks. On their own winter wander, Edwin and Nellie Teale visited the twenty-mile crescent beach known as the Silver Strand, way down below me—which is where I went next, all the way down to the Tijuana Estuary.

The Silver Strand is a spectacular crescent guarding San Diego, and a nice beach if it didn't have a freeway alongside it. Beyond it lies Imperial Beach, then, across the Tijuana River, flooded rural country of horse farms, community gardens, and open space. Monument Road led to Border Field State Park, at the extreme southwest corner of the United States. Helicopters thwapped overhead continuously, and cordial BP agents were on me in minutes. "We can't keep you out," said one. "It's a state park, after all. But you'd best be out before twilight. It's a whole different world out here after dark."

The only way to get to the corner of the country was by the beach. I waded past brush into the glasswort marsh and polluted mud flats behind the beach, made it to a bridge over a little slough, and to the edge of the snowy plover–least tern preserve. From there it was south along the strand. Just a few miles from downtown San Diego, this was essentially a wilderness beach, except for the slight tincture of sewage.

I came to the border, defined by steel palings four to six inches apart, running out into the ocean. I stood on the extreme southwest square inch of the United States, insofar as the current state of the tide allowed. The BP surveyed my progress with a gimlet eye from a rise above as a bunch of Mexican guys watched my approach and waved from their hangout in front of the Tijuana bullring. When I placed one foot in Mexico, cheers arose from the young Mexicans; the agents just stared and wondered what the hell I was up to.

On their side, colorful buildings ran down to the shore. A couple with their arms around each other walked down the beach with their son; another strolled holding hands, and a man was surfcasting. Still another couple, and an Indian woman in a blue serape, stood on a circular deck before the tall white lighthouse, taking the sun, waiting for it to set. On our side, there was no one at all but the BP and me. I thought, These really are two different cultures. A gull perched on the outermost paling of the wall, and I wondered about its nationality. Number 2284 was the last solid sheet of iron seaward, or the first of the gathering rank of them stretching farther and farther by the day toward the Rio Grande.

I left the beach just after sunset, figuring I had enough light to get back before the action began. I'd reached the closed park headquarters when I heard a rustling in the brush beside the road and a grunt. I thought it was a wild pig, but then I glimpsed a figure in black running through the bush. Moments later, agents appeared and dove in. Then I heard "Take him! Take him!"

Back at the car, because of the fetid drainage, I washed my Croc-clad feet and prepared to don clean socks and pants. As I was sitting in my hatch, rinsing my feet with my pants off, an agent came running past from right to left. Then another. An SUV arrived, then a Humvee driven by the first woman I'd seen. The agents left their vehicles, doors open, and ran toward the action. This all happened about thirty feet in front of me, and they paid me no more mind than an armadillo. I got my pants and shoes on before they all came back, with a parade of five or six people lined up against one of the vehicles.

Driving out, I paused to thanked them for their hospitality. "I'll get out of your hair now," I said. They smiled and waved, told me to have a good night and find lots of butterflies. There was no gunplay, and they didn't seem rough on their catch. But I found it astonishing that this stylized, nightly struggle and dance went on right there around me, as if I were just one of the cottontails I caught in my headlights on the way out. Driving north, I turned on the news. As if scripted, George Bush came on and said, "We've effectively ended the policy of catch-and-release at our borders."

8. THE CROWS OF CAPISTRANO

Up above the old adobes, latter-day bishops' palaces of extraordinary ostentation overtopped the green hills at San Juan Capistrano. The ruined mission where the (barn) swallows nest after their "miraculous return" each year squatted under palms across from Starbucks. My coffee was free with a gift card I had, but mission admission was nine dollars, so I walked around it, not in. The swallow story was handed out for free, but at this season, only crows (*Corvus brachyrhynchos*) flew around the mission walls. Perhaps this was as it should be. St. John Capistrano, born Giovanni Chiori in 1386, whipped the Turks at Belgrade, coming to the assistance of "Hungary's greatest strategist," John Corvinus, a.k.a. János Corvinus, whose name means literally "John of the Crows," hence, the famous crows of Capistrano.

By noon I reached Silverado Canyon, in further search of the Sonoran blue and its *Dudleya*. This tip-off came from Larry Orsak's *Butterflies of Orange County*. Larry, an early president of the Xerces Society and colleague of mine in early butterfly conservation plots, wrote that valuable book while still a kid. Much of the landscape he wrote about I found burned over and badly eroding. Long, narrow Silverado Canyon had escaped so far, but above the national forest boundary, all entry was blocked as a fire closure from November '07 to November '09—great for the pumas we were to beware of but bad for butterfly hunters. Retreating downstream, I found some of the desired *Dudleya*, with its fleshy, blue-green leaves, as Larry said, growing among licorice ferns behind the fire station. But *Philotes sonorensis* didn't make the scene.

Even when clement, those January days were just too darned short. I "rushed" (as much as any rushing can be done in Orange

44

County) to Huntington Beach State Beach, per Fred Heath's book. An equestrian area offered masses of mustard, mallows, and nettle—all manna for early fliers—but it was just too early in the year, too late in the day, too cold. My third green flash of the trip gleamed over Huntington Beach at sunset. Then I skirted the endless refineries around Long Beach and the entire mess and mass of Los Angeles on the water side, about which the less said the better.

On an ocean overlook past Point Dume, I bedded down. Until, that is, a state patrolman stopped and kicked me out. He was nice but told me scary stories of lone sleepers such as I in such places. "I just can't let you sleep here," he said. "I found a man beaten here just last month." When I asked him where I should go, the state park being closed, he suggested the Wal-Mart in Oxnard—forty miles north! So be it. It was my first.

The next night, during a long, fast-for-me drive north on 101, dodging crazy lane changers and appalling headlights, Powdermilk's oil light came on. As she hadn't burned oil since an engine rebuild a few years ago, this was a real scare, especially because the reservoir was more than two quarts down. I found some expensive oil, negotiated the San Jose freeway maze, and hauled into safe harbor in Campbell after a four-hundred-mile day, just in time to watch the weather with Susan and Ted. It was set to deteriorate again already. And it did; chilly walks and drives in potential Bay Area habitats were pleasant, but pointless as far as the quarry was concerned.

Yet somehow, the first of February came in on a raft of *sun*—the only day of it for a week to come. I got the heck out of doors. First stop, a huge mustard meadow opposite the *San Jose Mercury News* near Milpitas. But when I saw both a black phoebe *and* a Say's phoebe swinging slo-mo arcs around the field from pillar to post, I knew I was doomed by the competition. The first butterfly out of the grass would be snapped up by one or the other of the flycatchers faster than you can say *fee-bee*.

Next I drove to the big salt marsh at funky Alviso, and trails into San Francisco Bay National Wildlife Refuge, to seek pygmy-blues. But as I read later in Arthur Shapiro's *Butterflies of the San Francisco Bay Area*, the pygmies don't turn up in the *Salicornia* until later broods spread in, since they cannot withstand the winter flooding.

They overwinter instead on upland chenopods. Art, consummate butterfly ecologist at UC Davis, also advised that the host plant for the Sonoran blue in this area is *Dudleya cymosa* var. *setchellii*. It was in search of that I next went, first up Calaveras, then down Sierra, far above the East Bay, across the grazed green hills reminiscent of Cumbria, then down, a little south, and back up into Alum Rock Park. I found a little *Dudleya*, but Alum Rock was the main hope.

One long-ago visit here, Super Bowl Sunday dawned sunny and warm. Having never seen that stunning little California endemic the Sonoran blue, and knowing it was an early emerger, I wondered if it could possibly be out at that date. I telephoned a guru of the blues, Bob Langston, for his advice. He thought it possible, and the place to try was Alum Rock Park, up against the hills east of San Jose. Barbara Deutsch took me there. We learned from the ranger that the road to the habitat, shared with inholders above, was off-limits to visitors. One of us spotted my Audubon field guide on their shelf and brazenly pointed it out. Through this shameless ploy we were given permission to go up. We managed to find both male and female *Philotes sonorensis* and get good looks at them on the wing and perched. I will never forget my first sight of this ethereally blue creature painted with fire-engine red spots on the forewings above, the only American butterfly so adorned.

So here I was back at Alum Rock, a handsome and highly popular canyon spa of former days, the old stonework now mere artifacts but its popularity intact. The day waning, I decided that my long-ago permission had been granted for life and headed up the blocked and posted road on foot toward the extensive *Dudleya* habitat. As the sun climbed higher and higher on the walls, I chased its receding beams, but like a rainbow, it wouldn't let me quite get to them. I concluded the blues just weren't out yet. On the way down, I searched tons of *Dudleya* duff for overwintering pupae. Mountain lion warnings below were echoed by large puma poop in the road up there. When I got down, the poor ranger was awaiting me so he could go home, but he did not challenge my permit for life.

Recalling that earlier Super Bowl Sunday at Alum Rock, among the mythic Sonoran blues, I surely would have stayed to reprise it this year had the forecast not been so bleak for game day. Over sister Susan's beef stew and an ale with Ted, I watched the storms roll in one after another on their TV's Doppler. For fifty years I'd known how very much the field lepidopterist is at the mercy of the elements, but never had that reality been driven home more forcefully than this first month and a day of 2008.

Groundhog Day impressed the point with a nine-pound hammer, and if not for some good people, it would have been a dead loss. For many years, UC Berkeley Professor Jerry Powell had held an annual open house for lepidopterists at the Essig Museum of Entomology. This year's was to be the last such soiree before the collections were moved. I was eager to attend, but by the time I got repacked and made my getaway from Campbell, time was tight. In rain like pitchforks, murderous traffic, and rotten signage, I made a wrong exit from 580 onto the Bay Bridge and an unscheduled visit to Treasure Island. When I finally got to the Berkeley campus, I was way late. Then the parking permit machine at the gate was jammed, and the only thing I could do was park right behind Wellman Hall and dash in.

"Here's Pyle, better late than never," announced the ever-plain-spoken Powell.

I was just in time to report my progress and my grand total of seven species so far to my underwhelmed brethren of the net. It was fine to see Jerry and many other good friends, several of whom I'd known for most of my life. They were all rooting for my Big Year, and at least they, if anyone, understood about the raw deal I'd had from the weather. As for the fifty-dollar parking ticket I got from the campus police, after I'd resolved it months later, Jerry told me it may have been the first parking fine ever forgiven by the UC Berkeley traffic department.

Two nights later, arriving in Crescent City late and tired, I found the Wal-Mart and settled into the lot. I was no sooner snoozing than a cop tapped at my window, checked my ID, and said, "I'm afraid you can't sleep here."

"But, Officer," I whined, "it's a *Wal-Mart!*"

"Yeah," said the polite young policeman. "Well, I'm sorry to say, this is probably the only Wal-Mart in the country where you can't camp." Seems there's a Del Norte County ordinance against "sleeping out." I must have looked fairly dejected at that news, because he let me stay. "But just for tonight," he said and promised to keep an eye on me from time to time during the short remainder of the night.

The fourth of February came with bright sun, blue skies, and frost. At the pier, heavy fog along the bay shore, reflected in the snowcap of the Coast Range hills behind, made a white comforter disturbed by a foghorn embedded in it somewhere. Black oyster-catchers and surf scoters conspired in the brilliance of red and black. An oystercatcher got up and began to approach the rock's shore but thought better of it, tucked its bill under its wing, and showing one pink eye, napped right next to a napping turnstone below a napping gull on the top of the rock. I yawned.

And then, at eleven, it happened. I passed a pea patch and ducked in to check it out: the Crescent Elk Middle School Commu-nity Garden and Composting Project. There were several patches of winter crucifers. I looked carefully over arugula, broccoli, kale, then checked the nearby project hut and potting shed—and there on the sunny side, about eight feet up, nestled right in the groove of the green-painted plywood known as T111, was a buffy brown cabbage white chrysalis! I climbed up on a potting bench to pal-pate it and make sure it was full, soft, pliable—in a word, loaded. It was—cocked and ready to go, as soon as the temperature and day length conspired to bring it out.

Pieris rapae is the single most abundant and widespread butterfly in the United States. Introduced from Europe, perhaps as pupae on a cabbage crate, the small white (as it is known in England) first turned up in Quebec in 1861. Since then it has spread to al-most every corner of the continent, except the Far North and the Deep South. A remarkably adaptive and resilient animal, it occurs in places that most butterflies find inhospitable. A competitor for cruciferous crops such as Brussels sprouts, it was fought relent-lessly with DDT in England. But *P. rapae* became resistant even as its predatory beetles were being knocked out, leading to a net increase of larvae on the poisoned sprouts. While it is considered a pest in cabbage fields and broccoli patches in the United States, and often called the "cabbage moth," its eggs and larvae are easy to remove by hand in the kitchen garden. I actually appreciate it for its simple beauty and because—as today—it is often the only butterfly around.

A week later I would spot another *Pieris rapae* chrysalis on the chain-link fence at David Branch's Magnolia Pea-Patch in Seattle. It was green, against a background of dark green plastic slats between the steel diamonds; the same color as the T111 of the garden hut with the brown cabbage chrysalis in Crescent City. This pair of pupae displayed the dimorphism expressed by the chrysalides of many whites and swallowtails. Folklore (including that of many lepidopterists) says that these color phases reflect the colors of pupation sites. Instead of such a "chameleon model," Charles Remington preferred the hypothesis of "balanced polymorphism" to account for such color phases. By this model, populations adapt a ratio of green to brown expression that optimizes the chances of finding the "right" substrate color in a given environment—more green ones in a wet setting, more brown in the desert, but some of each in either. My Crescent City chrysalis and its Seattle opposite seem to support that explanation, but they constituted a small sample. Of course, both mechanisms might apply but to different species in different places.

I left the chrysalis in its perfect cubby; there was no need to remove and hatch it out, since it could be nothing else. This one small white's pupa was butterfly number 8: I had reached 1 percent of the fauna in five weeks. And when I made it home, just as Thea was rising, there were 358,613.0 miles on the odometer. That made the first outing 4,122.65 miles, or 515 miles per species. At that rate, satisfying my goal of 500 species would require only a little bit over a quarter of a million miles and about six years. At any rate, I now had my cabbage, to go with all the kings I'd seen overwintering along the California coast.

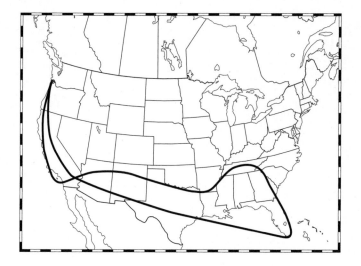

East to Atala

Stuck in the ruts to the who knows where.

—Jack Gladstone, "The Roman Road"

1. STUCK IN LODI AGAIN

This was not good. My butt was petrified from the miles, Powder-milk's oil was low again, and the rain came down in strata more than sheets. Hunkered in the El Rancho Motel, I was suffering a crisis of confidence, stuck in Lodi again. And it really was "again." The first time I was stuck in Lodi was in 1969. On our way to Sequoia National Park for summer jobs, my former wife, JoAnne, and I got lost passing through the torn-up streets. Too tired to travel on, we took a room in a flophouse in the old downtown. Our bed cost us $2.50, and we felt proud and adventurous. Until we discovered the bedbugs.

The El Rancho cost rather more, and it had no bedbugs. But I was depressed all the same. Back home, I'd seen to seemingly endless details, observed Valentine's Day suitably with Thea, celebrated Darwin's birthday with naturalist friends, and visited with the tortoiseshell in the woodshed every day. It was hard to leave, but I was missing species down south; or would have been, if the season hadn't remained adverse. At last, on February 17, a sunny, mild day with crocuses bursting, the tortoiseshell spread its wings. I took it outside. It flew from my hand to an oak, basked in the sun, and took off to the south. I did the same.

The sun stayed with me to the southern Oregon town of Myrtle Creek, where there really was a lot of "myrtle," or California laurel. I hiked over a mossy knoll with lomatium, saxifrage, and stonecrop in bloom among Garry oak and poison oak beneath madroña. Honeybees and bumblebees worked the bloom, and I thought I saw a butterfly's shadow, but the hoped-for Moss's elfins were truant. The day was not without a butterfly. Along the Cow Creek National Back Country Byway, I walked the old railroad bed under pillowed and caved basalt with the same flowers on its sunny south face. Beautiful waterfalls turned into cascades along Cow Creek. A California tortoiseshell appeared, alighted up a ferny cleft, and when a western fence lizard made a lunge at it, flew down behind an incense cedar. If it was my avatar, it made good time here from Gray's River.

But then the day grew cold, and I got on to the Shakespeare Festival town of Ashland for one of my few planned social visits. Mike and Kathy Uhtoff, dear old friends and great naturalists and conservationists of long standing, settled here years before to run the Northwest Nature Shop. I'd often visited for book signings, to lead butterfly outings and classes, and once, when Mike was head of the chamber of commerce, to serve as the town Santa Claus at his request. But this visit was different. Mike had Alzheimer's, and I wanted to see him while he could still recall some of our adventures together. Their daughter Marie sat me down to meat loaf, mac and cheese, brownies, and red wine to await Mike and Kathy's return from a conservation meeting. Then we talked, and we were still talking over waffles in the morning. A natural teacher, Mike had a witty, subtle sensibility and always a story or a scheme at hand. Now it was like when you start to tell something but forget your point. We all know that feeling, but for Mike, it happened every time. Yet he chuckled about it.

As I was leaving, Mike handed me a fine book, *Oregon's Dry Side*, by Alan St. John. He said I should get together with the author, whom I knew as a good butterfly photographer. Mike began to tell something Alan had shown him for the first time. "A book?" "No." "A natural history experience?" "Yeah, a plant—hazardous plant." "Oh, poison oak?" "Yes! Poison oak. It erupted all over!" We both laughed, and hugged, and I took off. That was the last time I would see Mike, laughing there under the madroñas. He died just about a year later.

As always when in Ashland, I stopped into Puck's donut shop, kitty-cornered from the Northwest Nature Shop, but this time I took little pleasure in the sin. I pointed south into California, and rain again. I opened the window for cool air, and the rain came in, but my glasses were already wet.

And now Lodi, in pummeling rain, after hours on I-5, with the oil light screaming on the dashboard. I'd taken Powdermilk in to Dave, her longtime keeper at Stirling Honda in Longview, to check on the earlier oil loss. He'd found evidence of a small leak that must have originated with a new timing belt or some other measure during prophylactic work I'd had done to prepare for the trip. Dave doubted the leak would amount to much. For a while it hadn't, but here we were, down again. That can wreck a good engine quick-time. Plus, engine oil is costly, and I was already operating in the unanticipated condition of the highest gas prices in American history. My seat was nearly worn out, and I was already stiff and sore from sitting. Then I made the mistake of looking carefully at my highway atlas . . . I'm driving *where*? To freaking *Florida*?

For the first time, it hit me, what so many others had asked me over the past few months but what I had never once questioned myself: *Can I really do this thing?*

And it scared me. I thought of a sign I had seen back in November, another scary time, when I was two hundred feet up in a giant karri tree in South West Australia. At the point where the precarious spiral ladder grew even steeper and narrower to reach the fire-watch platform atop the tree, the sign said: *"Reassess Your Situation Now: Turn Back if You Are Not Comfortable."* Then, as now, that seemed like damn good advice.

So there in the El Rancho, I reassessed my situation. I almost decided I'd have to make some radical changes in my plan. It wouldn't be the first time I'd ever fallen back on a Plan B, making concessions from the original concept of a big trip. Now, in my funk, I nearly concluded that I was going to have to change to Plan F, relying on public conveyances and rental cars to reach Thea in Florida and then to get back to Texas and the West, leaving Powdermilk in Tucson. It was a body blow of a reversal, and I didn't like it a bit.

But then, somewhere in the night, the word "wend" came to me. I realized that relief might be a part of my revisionary musings, because of my lithified ass, the scary map, and the acknowledgment of how very far away Florida really was. But I didn't *want* that kind of relief—or the hassles and expense of alternative plans, the loss of freedom to explore where I wanted, and least of all, to be without Powdermilk. So, I thought: *wend*. Don't even try to make it one long, stultifying haul. I had a suspicion that it was freeway speeds that raised the oil pressure and caused the leak. So go slow. Check the oil. You've got time. Just wend. After all, I had reassessed my situation up in the karri tree, carried on, and stood atop the old-growth canopy, where I finally stopped shaking.

I awoke happier, sun through the shades, ready to blow Lodi. First, a good breakfast at the Hollywood Cafe, which dated from the period of that '69 flophouse. Then I wended my way south through the unlovely and ruined San Joaquin Valley. And even though the general state of the valley is one of lost horizons, chemicals, and subdivisions supplanting fields that supplanted one of the richest grasslands in the world, I soon found three butterflies, two of them new. First, in a big mustard patch by a Baptist church, two nice fresh cabbage whites were flying about—my first adults on the wing. Next, after a walkabout all over a major vacant lot in Manteca, full of weedy nectar flowers such as fiddleneck and filaree, and thinking how impossible was this nothingness, an orange flutter resolved into a West Coast lady. A very fresh little male, it was the first since that likely candidate the phoebe snatched at Lighthouse Field. Netted and released, he returned to nectaring on yellow and white rocket and *Lamium*.

Finally, I called in at Caswell Memorial State Park. An interpretive sign told the pioneer Minnie Elizabeth Hope's recollection of sportsmen coming from San Francisco to Stockton by boat, then by livery to her dad's ranch to hunt coon, wildcats, and ducks. Now the surroundings are all so devastated, for as far as you can think or see, that this little remnant of the valley oak woodland is inordinately important. It was stuffed with birds. As there were many nettles and hollow trees, I searched for the trio of hibernating, nettle-feeding nymphs that includes Milbert's tortoiseshell. What I found was a different *Nymphalis* that feeds on willows instead of nettles. About to leave, I spotted something dark on the brick wall of the john, a good basking site, right beside a big hollow oak. *Yes!* A mourning cloak, big and brown, yellow borders winter-faded. I watched it bask, then fly up, do a slow circle toward me and away across the picnic lawn, then off, up, over trees toward the Stanislaus

River. It took me back to my very first cloak, which performed a similar getaway over the crown of a giant Colorado cottonwood, fifty years ago. That long-ago *Nymphalis antiopa* might be why I was here at all.

I hopped back over to I-5 to get to Bakersfield. This was the San Joaquin Valley; the northern part of the Central Valley is the Sacramento. The winds split, up-valley and down-valley, through the Carquinez Strait, which is the windy bridge I crossed after Berkeley heading home last time. That night, cheese and crackers and carrot and celery sticks made a modest dinner, augmented later by a good bowl of local pea soup from Andresen's in Santa Nella. The woman at the counter said the farmers around here consider themselves an endangered species. It hadn't looked that way to me in the valley. But later, looking down at the lights all along the valley floor from a rest area up against soft green hills on the west side of the valley, I could see that plenty of conversion was going on.

Above, what was going on was a total eclipse of the moon, halfway there already. I rode with it, exiting at Crows Landing for the perfect dark vantage, above the sparkled valley floor and away from the freeway lights, to watch totality. Luna was a plummy yo-yo strung in a cat's cradle between Regulus and Saturn, Procyon and Spica. Her facial features stood out on her soft, rouged or bruised complexion. A barn owl called before the last crescent of light left, and when it was less than a little skim of silver sheen on the right side, a coyote sang. At full dark, a long meteor tailed off to my right in the direction of the owl. Later, from farther south, the one-third moon was like a bright acorn in its cap. As the last bit was given back, inside a rosy ring and under a mackerel cloud, the texture was borrowed from the breast feathers of a garganey teal.

After I'd set up camp at Buttonwillow, beneath a tall palm tree among cotton fields and dust storms, the map didn't look so scary. Wending or not, I was making the miles, and the oil stayed up. Death Valley tomorrow, then Nevada, Arizona . . . and on to freaking Florida.

2. LIFE VALLEY

Jawbone. Indian Wells. Owens Lake, stretched out in color fields of beige, black, white, and all dun tones between. Then Powdermilk turned 360,000 miles on the way to Olancha. On Washington's Birthday, hopeful ravens stalked the dusty creosote farm of a campground. I rubbed my eyes against the mesmerizing play of light across the Panamint Range to the west.

Desert gold (*Geraea canescens*), pungent with orange disks, erupted from the Scotty's Castle turnoff in Death Valley. The sun grew very hot, very fast. At two hundred feet below sea level, the desert gold became thick across the desert, which went on forever. But it was cloudy now, with rain squalls across the valley. West of Furnace Creek, I took an hour's hike up and down shallow washes north of the road. The sun and rain played tag, and the alluvial flats brimmed with G. *canescens* for miles, uncountable millions of them. Brown-eyed evening primrose was also abundant, its eye actually henna red; and on the floors of the washes grew the odd, softly reptilian turtleback plant. There was the grapey purple notch-leaf *phacelia*, with its ferny leaves and sagey-minty fragrance; the two-foot, big-flowered golden camissonia; and the lovely and tender pink desert five-spot, as well as a little white ground-hugging aster. After a while I wondered if this situation might exceed even my Washington record for being in a place with the most flowers, in partial sun, with the fewest butterflies, and that's saying a lot.

Coming back from my hike, I concentrated on the chenopods. The shrubs were mostly creosote, but there were a few desert holly, so I was hoping for western pygmy-blues, which feed as larvae on members of the chenopod family. I tapped one; about to do a second, I discerned a dark spot on a leaf stem—a male *Brephidium exilis,* just emerged, still drying its wings. This tiniest of North American butterflies is way under a dime's worth of bronzy wings, with deep blue highlights and a scintillant spot row on the ventral hindwings. A few yards away, a fresh one was spreading its wings to the sun—shiny-brown copper, tarnished in the middle: the smallest butterfly of all in the midst of the biggest landscape I'd ever seen. Then a rain squall reached me, and the desert *did* smell like rain, as Gary Nabhan's bewitching book by that name insists. Afterward, the sun came out fierce as the flowers. Though I scanned the entire panorama with my binoculars, there was nary another flicker of wings.

I came to the lowest point on the California state highway system—242 feet below mean sea level. To the south lay the silvery salt flats and damps of Cottonball Basin and Marsh; silvery clouds and snows of the sunstruck Panamint Range and Tuki Mountain beyond, and desert gold below. All the earth tones of last night had gone to the sheens of precious metals. The substance that made fortunes here was not a metal but unromantic borax. Chinese workmen gathered the borax ore—called "cotton ball"—at Old Harmony Borax Works. From there it was transported by twenty mule-team wagons, one of which was currently on display here in the park. The matchup of the old television show *Death Valley Days* with its sponsor, 20 Mule Team borax soap, was inspired; its host, a young Hollywood actor named Ronald Reagan, was also well cast, some say for the last time.

Beyond Zabriskie Point and comatose Death Valley Junction, I hit the Nevada state line at Amargosa Valley and gassed up at Terrible's in Pahrump. Terrible seemed to own half the casinos and gas stations in the region. Great name, Pahrump, but terrible in the flesh, like a bunch of board games emptied out across the raw desert basin. There is certainly no sign ordinance, nor any garish scruple. The spare desertscape is unforgiving.

But Pahrump is not the bottom of the deck. It's just a patch of purgatory, a speed bump on the way to hell—because then comes Lost Vegas. There was a lot of traffic coming toward me on the 160, the canyon road jammed with glaring, speeding pellets at escape velocity. And there was snow! Fairly heavy snow, in fact, magnifying the blinding lights as I crested the basin rim and dropped past Red Rock Canyon, down toward the light box of the city. If it could snow in Santa Barbara, I guessed it might as well snow in Las Vegas. It just seemed par for my course.

The blaze of Vegas looked like Christmas lights from up there, especially through the falling flakes. But once into the electrical wen, I just wanted out. Thanks to misleading signage, I missed the 215 bypass and had to fiddle around Frank Sinatra Drive to get back. I could have returned on the Strip, but having seen that exemplar of excess, I had no desire to experience it again. Give me the strips of *Phacelia* any day. But what a trial, navigating the fast flood of shiny, roaring motors parting around my deliberate little rig.

After attending to my notes over a High Scaler IPA at Boulder City Brewery, I found a five-dollar federal campsite at Boulder Beach on Lake Mead. When I called Thea on the rarely handled mobile, I heard my grandchildren in the background. They were visiting for the weekend, and they'd just had chocolate pudding by the fire. Lonely as could be for them all, especially after the ordeal of the past hour, I signed off before the doubt storm of Lodi could roll back in. The morning looked better after a good sleep.

The "lake," hugely drawn down, may cease providing water after 2012. Crossing Boulder Dam, I ogled the handsome Art Deco details, such as the copper, winged and muscled gynanders guarding the flag, and clock towers announcing Nevada time on one side, Arizona on the other in that beautiful thirties script. At the vista point, I clicked the couples' cameras for them. Dion and Angela of Baton Rouge were en route to the Grand Canyon. Dion said, "You give me a call when you get to Baton Rouge, I'll show you some *goood* places to eat!"

I was in the last class of drive-overs: a giant, high freeway bridge was being built alongside to take traffic off dam. The dam opened (or, more accurately, closed) in July 1935, "a vision of lonely lands made fruitful," as the plaque put it. The diminished river ran below into its canyon, but no one looked downstream. My grandfather Robert Campbell Pyle drove through here in the Depression when construction was under way. What he remembered vividly, and told a thousand times, was coming across a group of construction workers cooling off in the river on a torrid afternoon. There were both men and women present, and as GrandPop put it, still amazed and scandalized after all those years, "They were *stark nekked*—didn't have a stitch on, not a *stitch.*" According to the southern humorist Lewis Grizzard, " 'Naked' means you have no clothes on; '*nekked*' means you have no clothes on, and you are up to something."

Off U.S. 93 toward Kingman, a side road led down to Willow Beach past an Easterish array of golden camissonia and purple *Phacelia crenulata.* A turquoise-and-carnelian-speckled lizard skittered into a draw beneath a slope of delicate yellow poppies, and a black-throated sparrow sang in a creosote. A shadow crossing over the road perched and became a butterfly: the first painted lady of the year. Three or four more *Vanessa cardui*, very fresh and very small, hugged a two- to ten-inch lens of moist earth at the base of the south-facing road cut. Resident in Mexico, painted ladies filter north in great numbers during springs with ample nectar and suitable travel conditions. In 1992 and 2002, incoming painted ladies were so thick as to cause stretches of I-5 to close for hours at a time. A painted lady flight was coming on now, and its vanguard made my dozenth butterfly: emergent offspring of the border crossers, almost neon pink in their orange.

Down at Willow Beach on "Lake Mohave," where palms and elms grew together above Davis Dam, I swam in the enslugged Colorado . . . for about three minutes, it was so cold. As I dried off, wondrously refreshed and merely naked, I recalled Robin Mallow, the BLM station host back in Jawbone. Pink face framed in a white bob, demeanor pleasant as her name, she whispered a warning: "If you go to Saline Valley, you'll have to be careful. It's clothing optional." And I thought of GrandPop some seventy-five years ago, coming upon those clothing-optional folks from the boomtown dam: "They were *stark nekked*—didn't have a stitch on, not a *stitch.*"

3. OIL CAPS AND CRAWDADS

I skirted Phoenix but dove into Tucson in hopes of early butterflies. The frontage road past Pacheco State Park was a paintbox
of lupines, California poppies, and fiddlenecks, minus butterflies.
But some sort of sulphur flew along River Road on the outskirts of
Tucson, buoying hope. The botanical gardens were dry, but I came
away with gulf fritillaries, cloudless sulphurs, and probable southern dogfaces.

New Mexico arrived with a windy little hamlet called Road Forks,
one fork to Rodeo, the other to Douglas, Arizona. Both lay months
down the line for me. Instead I headed east, then south toward
Playas and the border. Aside from a cloud of horned larks following
a plow across an irrigated field, it was all creosote bush, white cows,
and puffy bunch grass on black gravel. The Continental Divide
came without warning on undulating tableland at 4,486 feet. Now
I was on the Atlantic slope, between the Pyramid Mountains and
the Brockman Hills, running on down to Thea in a week, if I could
make it.

On NM 9, guarded by a raven, I met the first two Border Patrol
agents, with two trailers, comparing notes. I stopped, and we chatted amiably. One asked if I was a U.S. citizen, and did I have any
bodies under all my stuff? I said I could just about fit myself in.
"Never mind that, have you got anything else?" the other one asked,
still smiling. "No, sir—even back in the sixties, Nature was always
my drug of choice."

"Can't beat fresh air, can you?"

"That's right—live longer, feel better. But I have a glass of wine
now and then, and I'll have a Mexican beer in El Paso."

"Nothing wrong with that. Have a good trip."

The Border Patrol had makeshift stations, plus lots of water jugs, Porta Pottis, and an observation crane. Pink and purple and blue strata and swirls wrapped all the way around, with no clear distinction between the land and the sky.

After dark, it was a grim night on the road for a lot of animals. I hate this part of any road trip. First, I passed and returned to a jackrabbit, hit and disabled but alive and alert. I pulled it off to the verge by the rear feet and stood poised with a rock but hadn't the stomach for it—I wasn't sure it was fatally injured, though it seemed likely. A couple stopped because of my blinkers to see if I needed help, and they offered to take care of it. "It'll die sometime," the man said. "It's just the cycle of nature." He said he'd toss it in the back and take it to his dad's chickens, who needed protein. I thanked them but said I'd handle it.

"Just hit it on the head," said the young farm wife, not unkindly. Instead, I carried it by the scruff and placed it beside a low shrub with some green, where it sat on its haunches and didn't object to a little petting of neck and ears. Both times I picked it up, it made a pitiful high, short, soft squeal. There I left it.

Next came a recently dead doe in the road. A couple of Border Patrollers stopped and leaped out when I pulled over to haul it into the brush, then wished me a good night. Many jackrabbits appeared in the headlights, but it was the cottontails that dashed out on the side—two had near escapes, and finally one came right to me and I hit it, killing it outright. I moved it so the harrier or raven who came for it wouldn't be hit too. Many cottontails lay dead-on-road, and both spotted and striped skunks. A coyote's eyes fired beside a creosote bush, but it stayed put. Imperceptibly I crossed the Rio Grande.

Diesel-sour, roadkilled out, and hungry, I had all of Texas to cross at its widest girth. Of course some could do that in a day or two, cruising through on the interstate. The speed limit was eighty miles per hour, but I was doing fifty-five, a perfectly good speed, as it was back in 1982, when I bought Powdermilk, after Jimmy Carter made it national. And I had more in mind than simply covering miles. I hit the Central Time Zone, and there went an hour. I would need it, coming back.

Out in the middle of nowhere stood the tiny white adobe, tin-roofed "CALERA CHAPEL (MISSION MARY) EST. 1902—OPEN TO THE PUBLIC." I pulled the rope that hung down from the belfry. The little bell had a high, clear timbre that lingered on the desert air, wavering into silence. On the plain pine altar, the Bible was open to the Gospel According to St. John 3, "Nicodemus": "The wind bloweth where it listeth, and thou hearest the sound thereof, but canst not tell whence it cometh, and whither it goeth." So it was outside, and the scripture might have gone on about the white flicker of litter on the wind that "doth become a butterfly and settleth beside me" before it bleweth off into the ferocious thorns and the rest of Texas. A fresh male western white, I'd have said, but that didn't occur here. Kaufman and Brock, in their *Kaufman Field Guide to Butterflies of North America,* reminded me that heavily marked spring checkered whites can look just about the same, and I wasn't going to be fooled again for a spring white, as I had at Malibu. So it was a checkered white, not new but a butterfly—the only one in West Texas, as far as I could see.

After all the aridity, Balmorhea State Park's cienaga and seductive, spring-fed pools were restorative. I saw the endangered Pecos gambusia and Comanche pupfish, but in the small butterfly garden, there was all of one dandelion blooming. The dusty drive out to Balmorhea Lake revealed only a weedy, wintry shoreline redeemed by a covey of scaled quail with their puffy, translucent buff crests like hoodies. If you are a butterflier, it's best to be a birder too, since that way you can almost always occupy yourself.

I needed a room. All the motels in Ozona were expensive, unappealing, and full. So I did not hesitate when, in Sonora, I saw the sign for Zola's Motel: "American owned, Si Habla Espanol Un Poco—single $27.00 + tax." The owner, a slim Texan with the handle Pat Jungler, was in no hurry as he checked me in. I asked about the music stand and guitars sitting about his living room. Pat, a picker, was practicing for a funeral on the morrow. And the name? It really came from Emile Zola. And the price: "I just can't see charging any more than that for a night's sleep," Pat said. My very basic room had no phone but forty-one channels, including the Hillary-Barack debate dubbed in Spanish.

In the morning, coming out of the Sonora library, I spotted a fresh dark skipper gliding about the lawn with a bright gulf fritillary. Deep black velvet with a bright white fringe, it was a mournful duskywing, *Erynnis tristis*. Then, across the street, I noticed the Buckeye Trailhead into Eaton Hill Wildlife Sanctuary. I hiked several of the trails in warm sun. Rounding a hillside among juniper scrub, I whacked a few of the "cedars" for possible juniper hairstreaks. A little brown rocket launched off of a branch. I caught it, and it was no cedar hairstreak but a female Henry's elfin—a life butterfly! Things, I thought, are getting better.

And then they got worse. The oil had finally dropped enough to put in a quart. But when I next raised the hood to check the level, I found that I had failed to replace the oil cap. The viscid Quaker State had been hurled all over the inside of the hood and was dripping everywhere. I'd done that once years before, and Dave at the Honda shop never let me live it down. Now I was miles from anywhere, with no way to keep oil in the engine. I stuffed a rag into the hole, but by the time I got to the first gas station, it was soaked. The woman behind the counter told me she thought the AutoZone in Kerrville was open late. I hadn't intended to go through Kerrville, but now I detoured there and found the shop buttoned up tight. The only other option seemed to be Wal-Mart, so for about my second time ever, I entered and passed the greeters. There were no oil caps. I thought, Why not use a cork? No big corks, either. How about a rubber sink plug, then? Those, they had. I bought a tapered plug that I thought should fit, and a gallon jug of oil, and hastened to a well-lit service station to top it up and plug the spout. But the stopper was a little large, and as I tried to fit it in, I pushed too hard and shoved it right down inside the valve cover. There were moving parts in there. "Shit," I said for the forty-third time that night and went into the station to ask for a metal clothes hanger, which they actually had.

So there I was, fishing under my hood, when a snappy white Jeep drove up and a trim, capable-looking fellow popped out. "What's the problem here?" he asked, and before I knew it, Granger Ellington was doing the fishing. Eventually he got the plug out, shoved a rag back in, and said, "Now we need to go to the Watering Hole for a beer." Who was I to argue with my Samaritan? So Granger led me out of town to his local, which really was called The Old Watering Hole. There I passed the next several hours with Granger, his buddies, and lots and lots of Bud Light. Or in my case, a distinctly lesser amount of Shiner Bock. Granger was a linchpin of this whole little society, and a society of regulars it was, *Cheers* with a drawl. I was introduced around, and no one seemed to think that butterflies were the least strange. Dale the Poet read me his epic poem as Nadine in Green swayed to country music pouring out of the juke.

I had to step outside for air. This was no Mendocino brewpub; except for the beer and the smoke, it was better. If you could take it. These guys did it every night. Finally, Granger was ready to leave. He took me home to his cabin beneath bald cypresses along the Guadalupe River. His girlfriend, Leslie, a barmaid in a different saloon, was already asleep. Her little daughter Grace and Aragon the cat gave up their bed for me. In the morning, I was away early into the fresh Hill Country air.

I had no choice but to join the 10 again, into the fiery furnace of San Antonio traffic, to seek the oil cap grail. The big Honda dealer's service reception department had green, gold, blue, and red "teams" to manage the patrons—a far cry from good ol' Dave in Longview. Curtis Monday in Parts found my cap to be back-ordered, but he directed me to a nearby AutoZone, where Isaac Aguilar went up a high ladder and, not finding it, located one at another AutoZone and sent me there. Replete with fine Texas courtesy and a new oil cap, I was back on the road before noon.

Across a different Colorado River, near the Attwater Prairie-Chicken Refuge, white lilies starred the sunny verge among scarlet phlox. Figuring they ought to have something on them, I jumped out and caught a female pearl crescent nectaring on both. Not far away, on a back-beach berm bright with blue-eyed grass, my first phaon crescent pumped its wings in thin sun. I shirked Houston altogether by passing through Bonus, indeed a bonus. Then Peachland, with peaches coming into bloom, and Flora, Fig Ridge, Winnie, Lissie, and Sweeny, with baseball coming into play. A springy, chewy smell to the air, with ocean notes, presaged the Gulf of Mexico. Sleep came easily at Jamaica Beach, north of Galveston.

A grandfatherly policeman checked me out, but he just wanted me to move Powdermilk a little away from the ramp. I hope he came through all right when that beach and everything around it were devastated a few months later. Laughing gulls awakened me to Leap Day. In Galveston proper, I noticed the massive edifices of the National Weather Service and the Bishop's Palace. They, at least, will have survived the hurricane, though neither sphere of influence did much to protect this unlucky city when the time came.

After the ferry at Bolivar, I found the Louis Smith–Boy Scout Woods Bird Sanctuary on High Island. From a small birding grandstand, I watched half a dozen monarchs tilting above a glade and nectaring on lantana as a pair of pearl crescents mobbed them. Lemony cloudless sulphurs visited red hibiscus. Like a mini version, a little yellow (*Pyrisitia lisa*) flitted and nectared on a yellow ground rose with strawberry fruits. Mexican workers were bucking and shredding chinaberry trees felled by the hurricane, their fresh-cut wood the color of salmon fillets. The chain saws and shredders made it a rummy day for birders. In this case, the butterflier had it better.

I'd noticed pint-size earthen mounds sticking out of the fields, and I asked a bulky fellow at a "Live Mullet" stand what they were. "Them are *crawfish*," he said. I might have guessed it from their form, but—in the fields! I guess those "fields" were right at the water table. No wonder they eat a lot of crayfish down there—they were everywhere. The man's barefoot boy confronted me. With a cross, curious, and accusational expression and not a trace of shyness, he asked in a thick accent, "What's on your car?" "Rack." "What for?" "My boat." "Is it a big, big boat?" "Yep." "What's your name?" "Bob, what's yours?" "Canyon." "That's a great name." His ma, or grandma, I couldn't tell which, said, "*I* thought so." "Yew get pretty good mileage in that little car?" asked Pappy. "Yep," I told him, but I didn't want to say just *how* good.

That good mileage sometimes led me to neglect gassing up when I should have. Now I was very low, and failing to find anyone pumping. One station's smashed pumps stood at forty-five degrees to the ground, the premises mere girders. I detoured through Port Arthur to find some fuel before hitting a long lonely stretch. Positively hammered by some hurricane or other, Port Arthur was a ruin of refineries and wrecked buildings. In spite of all the gasworks, I had to look far and wide over for a working filling station, or anything open at all. At last, a quick-mart. A friendly customer asked me to send her a souvenir from Washington. "Have a safe trip, baby," she said, "but I'd get out of *here* pretty soon, if I was you."

After the refinery swarm, I crossed a high bridge over the Intra-coastal Waterway. In Sabine Lake, two brown pelicans flew over two white pelicans. This put me on "Louisiana's Outback—the Creole Nature Trail." Right at sunset, another little ferry took me across the mouth of Calcasieu Lake to Cameron. East would have been into the battered bayous, and dark. I veered north through Lake Charles and Baton Rouge.

I remembered Dion's invitation from Boulder Dam for "some good places to eat" around here, but it was too late to take him up on the offer. Still, I had to try crayfish after all those mounds. At Cajun Tales Seafood in Welsh I asked the proprietor, Jim Louvier, how I should have my crawdads. He said they were all good, so I ordered the crawfish platter: crawfish gumbo, fried crawfish tails, crawfish pie, crawfish cocktail, and crawfish étouffée. Everything was rich and excellent. None of it stuck in my craw, but I did have to box some of it up: crawfish to go.

Now I was on the Gulf. All I had to do was round it—all the way to Sanibel.

March arrived in the parking lot of the St. Tammany Parish visitor center. Along the marsh boardwalk out behind, a turtle basked by its hibernaculum, and a green anole in the gazebo displayed its painted-lady-colored gular pouch. Nothing yet was on the wing. But later on the Tammany Trace, a Rails-to-Trails footpath outside town full of cyclists and joggers, three cloudless sulphurs circled high in a dervish triad. Worn red admirables and fresh Horace's duskywings danced around the gravel edges. Along the horse path, little bees were pollinating small white violets with fine purple nectar guides.

It was early in the day for a beer, but I had to stop in and check out Abita Springs brewpub, one of the few in the vast good-beer desert of the South. I didn't think too much of their amber lager at Cajun Tales the night before, but the draft Jockamo IPA, well hopped (for the South), was much better. Under an umbrella in the sweet southern breeze, I pored over my *Tulane Studies in Zoology Butterflies of Louisiana* by Edward Nelson Lambremont (1954), bought, read, and reread as a kid. Parishes, as opposed to counties, seemed so exotic back then; now here I was, actually in one, beneath Spanish moss. I'd have loved to sneak the rest of last night's crayfish with my IPA, but since I seldom bothered to keep ice, I feared it might have spoiled already in the morning heat. So I put it out for the many cats around the periphery of the pub, and soon a pretty calico was at my étouffée as purple martins from their apartment house by the bandstand opposite took care of any stray mosquitoes.

East from Abita Springs on the Hickory Highway, loads of pink rhodies and early cherries bloomed, and sulphurs, duskywings, and dark swallowtails zipped along piney tracksides. Walking one of these sandy roads, I missed a tiny member of the group actually called roadside-skippers by flicking my net from the side instead of striking from above as it flew up. I walked back and forth looking for that roadside-skipper but kept being faked out by bees that resembled it on the wing. The skipper itself did not reappear.

The flapping of mourning doves caused me to turn my head. There in a tall huckleberry, nectaring on the pale bells, sat a Hunter's butterfly, a very old name for the American painted lady. The pink flush at the base of the ventral forewing on *Vanessa virginiensis* rivals the brightest pinks I know in the animal kingdom, more intense than any flamingo or mandrill's butt. Together with the blueberry flowers, rosy too, it made a stunning tableau in pinks. Now I had seen 80 percent of the American *Vanessa* species. I wouldn't have a crack at the fifth species for nearly another ten months.

At the end of Louisiana, beside a trashy and rutted fishermen's parking lot, the Chevron Boardwalk was occupied by a great blue heron, cerise samaras of swamp maples, bald cypresses pretty kicked about by hurricanes, and cadres of beer cans in the marsh. One frog clicked, one chirped. I crossed the Pearl River into Mississippi: my fiftieth state to set foot in, and my ninth for the year. There were no in-out signs for either state, but a wonderful "Welcome to Pearlington" sign featured a green frame of fancy scrollwork from old wooden furniture, dragons, iron pokers, cherubs, fools, ladies, an alligator, and a big leaf, all glued in, and two bill-to-bill coots on top. Someone really cared, to do that.

To and through Biloxi the road was slow, with much devastation. The whole first row of buildings—mansions, marinas, lighthouse, roads—was all wrecked. They were being replaced by garish and supposedly impregnable casinos. Much new building and repair was going on, including big new bridges. Big old houses farther back looked all right, but much of the way along the beach was still one-lane, crowded, and chaotic. The low sun lit up a new gambling fortress that would soon light up the night by itself.

Crossing Alabama, I avoided getting stuck inside of Mobile with the Gray's River Blues again. After slipping into Florida, I camped at a spot most of the way to Tallahassee at four in the morning.

It's a good thing Thea's coming, I thought at breakfast beneath a bowered lane of live oaks, as I ate the very last helping of her superlative granola. A short mile down a forest road in Apalachicola National Forest, I netted a bird-struck sleepy orange, a male with its tails gone: the first of thousands of *Abaeis nicippe* I guessed I would see. The underside had taupy, rosy reticulation; the upper side was pure Florida orange juice. By a live oak festooned with Spanish moss, a smaller but equally fetching sulphur appeared. The barred yellow shows dramatic seasonal dimorphism, the summer form milky white below, and this winter expression rusty red, much like the sleepy. A redbird called from the wood as a broad-tailed hawk cried overhead. The cardinal told me I was back east, while the presence of palmettos testified that I had made it to Florida after all. Take that, Lodi!

I came to Wakulla Spring, said to be the largest and deepest spring in the world. Near the entrance, five big Florida cooters basked, one with its feet splayed like ginkgo leaves. James Fisher in *Wild America* (1955) wrote of watching "one of the rarer birds in America, the curious anomalous rail-crane, the limpkin, teaching its young to eat giant snails in the shallows," right here at Wakulla. Edwin Way Teale, describing Wakulla as "the River of Limpkins" in *North with the Spring* (1951), wrote of their "caterwauling crescendo" as "the voice of the dark, the swamp, the vast wilderness of ancient times [that] links us—as it will link men and women of an even more urbanized, regimented, crowded tomorrow—with days of a lost wildness." That tomorrow had come. As much as I wanted to see and hear if the limpkins were still there, I gave Wakulla Springs State Park, its stiff fee, and its hordes of people a reluctant pass.

Highway 267 is the Big Bend Scenic Byway. There was a "Tupelo Honey" sign, and one for "Mayhaw Jelly"—is mayhaw the British "may" crossed with the American hawthorn, both names for *Crataegus*? Actually the Brits also use (and originated) "hawthorn," even calling the tree's scarlet pomes "haws." But in the English spring, when its white clouds of flowers bloom, the plant takes on the seasonal appellation "may." I'd never seen this hybrid word form, possibly a usage from colonial times, before.

St. Marks National Wildlife Refuge had a handsome brick lighthouse, its whitewash stained green with algae, and lots of herons, ibises, and alligators, but no butterflies along its breezy dikes. At 4:30 P.M., tired from three pretty rangy nights, I almost quit for the day. But I decided to try one last look along a sunny, sandy road.

In Aucilla Wildlife Management Area, between Newport and Perry, I walked and tapped junipers. That strategy produced only a geometrid moth, but then a dark butterfly on a redbud bough put up a second. They both alighted and began to nectar on the red-bud's flowers. The first was a duskywing with bright, glassy spots at the tips, probably a Horace's; the other, a juniper hairstreak of the uncommon southern subspecies known as Sweadner's. Its olive green and warm brown wings, white stripes, and wavy tails, backlit, showed well against the redbud tips. A barred owl called deep in Aucilla, "Who cooks for you," echoing my thoughts exactly, and a rich rusty brown thrasher crossed the road.

Then came a hard night's drive down the west coast of Florida, a solid fifty miracle miles like Aurora Avenue in Seattle, or Colfax Avenue in Denver, or Speedway in Tucson, but lacking the shabby charm of their fifties remains. Just a sodium vapor–lit strip of mer-cantile dross, a once wondrous coast now sacrificed to the appe-tites of mammon, all fast food, car lots, and "gentlemen's clubs." Heavy fogs making their way through North Florida, swirling in streetlights the color of frozen citrus concentrate, gave a dishonest impression of relief to the flat landscape.

At six in the morning on Monday, March 3, two weeks and 4,378.8 miles from home, I arrived at Coquina House on Sanibel Island. A pleasant, well-appointed, single-level home with a pool and palm trees, a beach ten minutes away by foot, and a lake with gators right behind, it had belonged to the parents of my friend David Campbell. A professor of biology at Grinnell College and a distinguished writer, David had offered us the use of this house for years. We were finally taking him up on it. I settled into Sanibel, and after some sleep, a swim, and getting the water going, I pre-pared for Thea's arrival. I'd made it across the country, if only just in time, and picked up a few butterflies along the way.

5. THE BLUE FROG

Thea's flight was delayed by a storm in Houston. When she called, it was snowing in Memphis. In David's Toyota, Constanza, I collected her at Fort Myers airport. She wore a big smile, and so did I. The fact that we'd pulled off this rendezvous, and had a South Florida adventure to look forward to together, seemed remarkable. First, that I'd actually made it here. Second, that our frequent flier miles had accommodated the dates and destination. And third, but really most on our minds, that Thea's health was holding. Four and a half years earlier, she had suffered and withstood ovarian cancer. Fit, strong, and positive, Thea had since regained her health. So far, so good.

After our reunion, we took David's tip and visited Manatee Park by the power plant canal from the Caloosahatchee River. The vaunted *Sirenia* were in absentia, but there were many fishers— little blue, tricolored, great, snowy, and green herons, as well as ospreys, anhingas, and kingfishers. Naturalist Wendy told us the anhingas were not normal here but present because of increasing salinity bringing their prey, as well as stingrays, into the channel. She showed us larvae of monarchs and gulf fritillaries she was rearing on milkweed and passion vine. A Cassius blue basked on a star-shaped grass, and three female orange-barred sulphurs, as big as the abundant palm warblers, flew around a red maple. As the wind rose, one took shelter in a cluster of leaves of its own yellows, oranges, and green: one of the most elegant blendings I've ever seen, right down to bogus disease spots on the "leaves" of its wings.

Sanibel Island, across a causeway from Fort Myers, has long drawn shellers to its beaches. Butterfliers too have taken to this subtropical retreat, among them Jo Brewer and Dave Winter. Jo, author of *Wings in the Meadow*, was virtually a cofounder of the Xerces Society, and Dave was a great student of moths and author of a classic text of field and lab techniques for lepidopterists. Both New Englanders, first friends and later mates, they loved coming to Sanibel and adjacent Captiva to warm up and swing their nets. When Thea and I visited the Sanibel Nature Center, Dee Serage-Century showed me Jo and Dave's collection and photocopied their helpful *Butterflies of Sanibel* booklet for me.

Dee explained that Hurricane Charley, in 2004, pruned the black mangroves well and gave lots of new growth, leading to a population explosion of mangrove buckeyes. But the storm had the opposite effect on red mangroves, which were flattened, and the mangrove skippers dependent upon that species crashed. An intimate meeting with the spectacular mangrove skipper was one of the chief hopes we harbored for our trip.

On the nature center's trails, we glimpsed those mangrove buckeyes, gulf fritillaries, and a white peacock nectaring on beggar's ticks. Exotic Cuban brown anoles skipped and jumped all over the boardwalks, very cute but hard on the native green anoles. Their tails twitched so fast that they kept giving false alarms for butterfly movement.

Early the next morning we bicycled to the beach, that remarkable, shifting, and shining sediment of shells for which Sanibel is so famous. The fauna varies from beach to beach and season to season. There were few of the tiny, rainbow-shelled coquinas this time compared to my visit a few years before, but fighting conchs, left-handed whelks, calico scallops, cockles, pens, olives, murexes, and others abounded. One stretch of beach was all urchins. Thea, who grew up with agate vacations on subtler Pacific Northwest beaches, went crazy over them all. I gathered iridescent shards of pen shells, for what, I don't know. As a natural passion, seashells came even before butterflies for me; a visit to Sanibel at age nine would have done me in from overstimulus. This plenitude of seashells mocked their absence when they most mattered to me, as it mocked the paucity of butterflies so far this year. I couldn't alter the dearth of seashells in my landlocked Colorado boyhood, but the present parsimony of butterflies was about to be redressed.

I thought I'd put my tooth troubles behind me, but now that Thea and I were ready to play, a nasty pain arose in a crowned tooth opposite the crown that had fallen out before. Only one dentist would help me on an emergency basis. At his upscale practice in Naples, Dr. Alan Rembos saw me right away and did the job with care and expedition. As he, Sue, and Marcy worked, he told me about a patient who'd just put in a $400,000 waterfall at his home. Naples was clearly one of the most affluent, boob-jobbed, and Botoxed towns I'd ever seen, and I was concerned about the effect of the bill on my budget. But when I explained my project, Dr. Rembos said, "We think it's great what you're doing. This one's on us." And then, as if that kindness weren't enough, he told me that I must visit Pelican Preserve, a gated community in Fort Myers where his father-in-law lived, and see its excellent butterfly garden.

On the seventh of March, sunny and hot after rain and wind, Thea and I set off in Constanza for the Everglades. As we left the island, the verges lit up white and yellow with great southern whites and dainty sulphurs. A pause at Estero Bay River Scrub, a state buffer preserve, produced the first fiery skipper and half a dozen gopher tortoises. Coy but confiding, some up to fifteen inches long, they basked beside the cavelike holes they'd dug in the limy soil. On our way out of town, we bought green tamales to munch along the Tamiami Trail.

As southwest Florida has depreciated under the weight and wants of way too many people, the Audubon Society's Corkscrew Swamp Sanctuary has maintained a measure of the state's subtropical richness. Even Corkscrew was at risk from the lack of water afflicting much of South Florida. Still, queens, crescents, and zebra longwings appeared, and then an eye-popping ruddy daggerwing dallied over the boardwalk. Two enormous palamedes swallowtails coursed low over wapato in the dry cypress swamp as an eastern tiger swallowtail sailed overhead. A trio of especially sharp skippers drew our eyes as they flew out at the swallowtails or one another: a black-and-white two-spotted skipper; a smaller, rich roan and russet southern broken-dash; and sipping from a pickerelweed just beyond an alligator, a striking, big silver-spotted skipper.

There was just a little water at Cabbage Ponds. The overseeing eight-foot alligator in the damps, wearing a cute shriveled hat of swamp cabbage, was not even submerged. A little blue heron and an immature white ibis fished in parallel past the gator, on either side, just far enough from its jaws to be safe. Purple gallinules paddled among baby alligators. After the noisy knot of people glued to the gators moved on, Thea pointed out something odd, clinging to umbels on the other side of the muddy pond. "It's *blue*," she said, "almost turquoise."

I saw it too. "What do you think it could be?" I asked. Thea figured it was a frog, and I had to agree. But what a strange color! It looked almost artificial.

Back at the visitor center, we spoke with Brad Kolhoff and Gerald Griggs, naturalists at Corkscrew. Brad did his senior project at Florida Gulf Coast University on butterflies and asked me to sign his field guide. As we were talking, Thea spotted the blue frog again: on the front page of the Corkscrew newsletter! They have been seen here before, but seldom. According to Ed Carlson, sanctuary director, it was "a rare color form" of the green tree frog (*Hyla cinerea*), "lacking the yellow pigment needed to mix with blue to make green." When we told Brad and Gerald what we had observed, they were first incredulous, then skeptical; and when it became clear that we really had seen it, just plain envious. I described where it was, in hopes that they might be able to find it there still. But that's Thea all over: she always spots the best stuff.

Having reached the eastern shore and settled into a room in Florida City, we marked our great day with tuna, tilapia, and wine at the Mutineers. There were giant koi carp, turtles, and wood ducks in the moat, but no frogs of any hue.

From the boardwalk of the Anhinga Trail at Royal Palm in Everglades National Park, you look right into anhinga nests, the birds' silver-pinioned wings spread like awnings over their snaky-necked babies. Their more familiar relatives, often seen from our bed at home, double-crested cormorants, sat upright all along the railing as we passed. But as spectacular as the birds might be, we were attending to the little-noticed butterflies. Ocola panoquins, with purplish sheen and improbably long forewings, clung to Spanish needles. Big foxy viceroys, mimicking red-brown queens here instead of monarchs, flap-glided over the black sloughs. Barred yellows here expressed the white summer form, so different from the winter reds I'd seen just days before in Texas. The most brilliant of the giant sulphurs, the large orange, also made an appearance.

The pine rockland scrub at Long Pine Hammock furnished just the butterfly we were looking for, the Florida duskywing. Drab at first glance, *Ephyriades brunnea* rewards a close look with deep patterns of rich brown and fugitive tones of violet. Then Thea said, "There goes an atala! No—but it's got atala's colors!" And it did: as the amazing insect fluttered slowly out of the palmettos, we clearly saw its blue-black wings, white polka dots, and fiery red tip. This was a wasp moth whose picture I'd long known from the cover of *Florida Arthropods*, but had never seen—the faithful beauty. Its scientific name is almost as beautiful as the moth itself: *Composia fidelissima*. An atala hairstreak here would be remarkable, though its host plant, coontie, was present. But the moth really did resemble it, as Thea's instant reaction demonstrated. It made me wonder whether these two organisms are involved in a Muellerian mimetic ring that might also include the great purple hairstreak. Like many brightly colored diurnal moths, *Composia* is likely unpalatable to birds, as atala (red-tipped too) certainly is. Later we saw *C. fidelissima*'s screaming red, blue-backed larvae on the toxic devil's potato.

Our drive out to Flamingo, the park's hurricane-battered, distal point in Florida Bay, was mainly remarkable for swallow-tailed kites that knifed right overhead, and for the rare American crocodile we inspected just at sunset, lying on the canal bank, waiting for dusk. Under the thinnest of crescent moons, we watched for the Florida panther on our way back. We didn't see it, but Mario's Station, a Cuban cantina in Homestead, made a good consolation find, with thin, tasty steaks, thick, pasty yucca, and sweet plantains.

Sunday brought daylight-savings time, which is really noticed at the end of those short, subtropical days. We spent it under clouds at a series of small reserves. Florida Audubon's Mary Krome Bird Refuge in Homestead, just a corner between suburb and avocado grove, gave us a suitably tiny butterfly, the easily overlooked three-spotted skipper. The big deal at Camp Owaissa Bauer, a pine-and-hammock preserve, was a female dina yellow. She displayed an orange blush at her rims and heliotrope spotting beneath like an imperial moth, capped off by purple frosting on the forewing's rusty tip.

Last, the consummate Florida naturalist Roger Hammer showed us his impressive garden-habitat-jungle with its many palms, orchids, and other subtropical plants. A rich orange Julia longwing floated over his remarkable limestone pool full of bright blue cichlids, big pacas, tilapia, and other fish. Our first giant swallowtail shadowed over, as twenty-one young Polydamas swallowtail larvae quietly browsed on Dutchman's pipe. By cutting the petiole and feeding right off the stem, they mainline both nutrients and strong protective toxins. An *Electrostrymon angelia*, as brilliant as its scientific name, the only fulvous hairstreak I would see all year long, alighted above our heads, like the halo that among us only Thea deserved.

Eumaeus atala isn't like other hairstreaks, most of which are small, brown or gray, with thin tails tipping their hindwings. Two inches across, its rounded, tailless wings are velvety black with iridescent rows of pale blue spots and rays of emerald or sapphire. The abdomen, and a spot next to it, are bright, toxic orange. So rare was the tropical atala considered in the United States, even unto extinction after Hurricane Donna in 1960, that the Xerces Society took its name for its conservation journal. Then, surprise! It came back on its own in the 1980s, exploiting ornamental coontie and other cycads in Miami parks and gardens. Roger Hammer introduced atala to Fairchild Tropical Botanic Garden, where it was now reported to thrive.

Thea and I had seen live ones in a butterfly house, and two related cycadians in Mexico, but neither of us had ever seen atala in the wild. Now we had ventured to Fairchild, in Coral Gables, in search of this foremost Florida grail. But when we found the admission to be twenty dollars each, we passed. At a workers' entrance, I asked the guard if I could see a staff member. Everett Skinner, in charge of that area, overheard. He instructed Phillip to admit us for twenty minutes, just to the Cycad Garden. "But you might not see them," he said as he drove off. In Cycad Circle and Cycad Vista, a gardenia bower was being erected for a fancy wedding. Otherwise there were few flowers around, and it was late and cool. The coontie showed feeding damage, however, and Thea soon spotted an atala chrysalis.

Eventually we found three of the reddish pellets. That was fine for free, and we were glad we'd saved the forty bucks.

On our way out, Thea spied a canna-feeding Brazilian skipper on a white cucurbit vine. Then she cried, "And there's a mangrove skipper!" Two or three of the *Phocides pigmalion* flew all over a purple-flowering bush, their wings matte black in dull light, flashing blue and purple in late sun, with sky-bright slashes, a Harry Potter zigzag, blue dots at the spiracles, blue eyebrows, and white palpi—as fancy as an atala any day.

From Matheson Hammock, Miami and Miami Beach sprawled before us across Biscayne Bay—as close as we needed to get to the action. Our vice of choice lay in the red mangroves along the trails. There we found the cut flaps of mangrove skippers' larval nests, occupied by the flocculent boxcars of caterpillars with their red heads and yellow headlights protruding. One chrysalis, puffed up and frosted white, was ready to pop.

On our last day in Homestead, we fended off the heat with Key lime milk shakes from Robert Is Here, a fruit stand dating from 1960. Just down the road at Navy Wells Pineland Preserve, among poison ivy and poisonwood, grew croton: foodplant of Bartram's hairstreak and Florida leafwing, rare butterflies we tried but failed to find. We did see rattlebox moths, whose scientific name, *Utetheisa bella,* speaks to their gorgeous pinks and oranges. The sandy paths were alive with harlequin meadowhawks, as distracting as the many buckeyes, and diminutive baracoa skippers. At Castellow Hammock Preserve, Roger's base as manager of the county's nature reserves, he showed us a few of the hundred-plus known forms of *Liguus fasciatus.* These beautiful banded snails clung to sunburned trunks of the gumbo-limbos in pastel colors. But the unfairly named dingy purplewing we sought, also a gumbo-limbo feeder, did not come out to play.

It is one thing to seek out uncommon endemic species and regional specialties on their native host plants in remnant habitats, and a satisfying thing it is, if too often elegiac. But sometimes the spectacles one remembers best involve weeds. Driving north from Castellow, we saw many whites over roadside lantanas. Great southern and checkered whites, raised on weedy crucifers and fueled by abundant lantana and *Bidens,* swirled around us in a virtual snowstorm. A male *protodice* hung from its chrysalis, just out, and mating pairs of *monuste* lumbered by in flight. Thea found a mallow scrub-hairstreak larva on a yellow mallow in the verge along with its attending ant, as I scanned the rows of an avocado plantation. Through binoculars, the flurry become an outright blizzard. But abundance is not the only measure. These thousands took nothing away from those single checkered whites in Malibu and West Texas, back when butterflies were rare.

We'd left far too little time for the Big Cypress National Preserve. Handsome cinder-block and thatch dwellings of Miccosukee Indians lined the berms on the way there. On canals west of Shark Valley, thistles dripped with tawny skippers, palatkas enormous next to tiny, black-rimmed least skippers. We shared the memorable sights and sounds of Sweetwater Strand with another couple, also stopped for the gathering sunset: bald cypresses occupied by ibises and an-hingas, swallow-tailed kites swirling overhead between green nee-dles and pearly sky, egrets pacing among cypress butts and knees in the black snake water, gators honking and roaring, and ibises, flying in, yawping.

The next day, back on Sanibel, the Ding Darling National Wildlife Refuge's Indigo Trail took us along the eastern shore. A reef of rose-ate spoonbills shimmered off to the east. Under the round umbrel-las of sea grape leaves bloomed samphire, glasswort, and sea purs-lane's small pink flowers, but few butterflies stirred in the heat.

In the late afternoon we walked white sand to the lighthouse; then, at sunset, to our own beach. It was strewn with living straw-berry scallops, rims a-shimmer with their iridescent azure eyes. Microscopic *Noctiluca* never did light up the sea for us, as I so vividly recalled from my first visit to the island. But between the mangrove skippers and the Paul Newman scallops, their bioluminescence was hardly missed.

Our last night was a short one. At four in the morning I took Thea back across the causeway to the airport, and she was away, all too soon. Now, when Thea turns on her laptop, the blue eyes of a calico scallop flash back from the screen saver, and the memory of a blue frog is never far from her mind.

6. THE CROOKED WAY TO KISSIMMEE

On Sanibel and its daughter isle, Captiva, landscapers seem to have studiously avoided the provision of any useful plants. The chief floral element, a yellow composite, is at least native but never attracted a butterfly in our experience. Sanibel gardeners eschew the butterflies' favorite, lantana, with apparent disgust. Yet our best resource was a patch of golden mound lantana, not far from Campbell's house by bicycle, that somehow escaped the pogrom. So I was excited to visit a large garden planted expressly for Florida butterflies, the one Dr. Rembos had recommended.

At Pelican Preserve in Fort Myers, the Crooked Garden had more nectar than I'd seen on Sanibel for weeks—purple trailing lantana, golden mound lantana, penta, flame vine, ageratum, and much more. Beginning with a monarch on a bright red penta, I saw a dozen species in no time—among them queens, buckeyes, gulfs, peacocks, zebras, and an überfly of a black swallowtail on ageratum—wow! Spectacular she was, and new for the year. Jim Price, resident curator of the Crooked Garden, joined me and pointed out their live pupae, including a green one on a parsley leaf. Then a rosy orange-barred sulphur dropped a big teardrop pearl of an egg on a fresh leaf of *Cassia*.

Jim is an advanced martial artist and a retired pharmaceutical rep. After building a small butterfly garden for his wife, he came here and saw the beginnings of one that could be "like a racetrack for wheelchairs"—that is, big! He went away with the title of curator. The garden that resulted is big, all right—twelve thousand square feet big. At first, the butterfly garden was a joke, here in the Kingdom of Golf. But since then, many residents and others—Dr. Rembos's dad among them—have come to admire, enjoy, and contribute to it. Now the source of much proprietary pride, the Crooked Garden is often called "the treasure of Pelican Preserve." I told Jim honestly that it was one of the best I'd seen, by several measures—so much nectar, many caterpillar host plants, and highly varied overall.

Intense, driving, and emotional, Jim is the perfect complement to Robert Cramer, the soft-spoken and laid-back landscape supervisor. Robert is a great plantsman, Jim a great doer. They make an effective team. Jim's poem for the place is mounted on a stucco wall behind a bench on the whimsical scenic overlook in the northwest corner of the garden:

> There is a crooked garden with
> crooked little paths
> And crooked little caterpillars
> crawling through the grass.
> There are crooked little butterflies
> Enjoying garden treats,
> And all these wonders here to view
> From this crooked garden seat.

After sorting, packing, swimming three times in the pool, shutting up Coquina House, and making the visit I'd promised myself to the famous shell museum, I made my getaway just in time—Sanibel was filling up like crazy for the weekend. I paid the six-dollar bridge toll for the last time and struck north for Kissimmee. East of Alva I passed into orange groves, and all of a sudden it hit me—*orange blossom!* The late golden afternoon was awash in the heavenly scent, which some find almost unbearably cloying. The trees bore both fruit and flower at the same time. As I northed toward Sebring, the citrus sun strobed through the rows of orange trees, spilling an orange splash behind the orange-dotted groves, everything in sight bathed in the sweet perfume.

At Annie's 98 Restaurant on Highway 98, I could hear the races at Sebring Speedway tearing open the night. (Later, everyone leaving the races thought he was at the speedway; two cars were in the ditch, and several more belonged there.) I guess I could have been a little speedier myself getting here—I was two hours later than planned—but my friends waited for me. Alana Edwards and Buck and Linda Cooper are some of the best butterfliers in Florida. They'd offered to show me some fine habitat and hospitality; I was only sorry that Alana's mom, Lana, was ill and couldn't join us. Buck treated us to catfish and beer as we made plans for the dawning. There was karaoke, including a truly bad "I Got You Babe" with a guy in drag, no beauty, as Cher. Alana said she and I should do Kenny and Dolly singing "Islands in the Stream." Lovely Alana, a former model, would have been great, and I at least looked the part. But mercifully, I didn't know it.

We all overnighted at the Riverwoods Field Laboratory in Cornwell on the Kissimmee River, where Alana had once worked in watershed education. In the Rookery, a handsome house under live oaks and Spanish moss, we slept to a concert of night noises composed of donkey, cow, wild pig, barred owl, Chuck-will's-widow, insects, frogs, toads, and I don't know what all.

Fresh-squeezed OJ from local orchards went down well with Linda's Irish soda bread and eggs for breakfast. Our day's objective was the great Kissimmee, largest remnant of the extensive prairies that once covered much of central Florida. Buck and Linda had written up the region's butterfly allurements as a "Definitive Destination" in the useful occasional series by that name in *American Butterflies*, and I was psyched to see it. They pulled out with Alana in their van, and I followed in single-seater Powdermilk.

We entered Kissimmee Prairie Preserve State Park to eastern meadowlark song through Bahia, a grass used for pasture on the biggest dry prairies. We drove the roads looking for tawny wedges on the native thistles, *Cirsium horridulum* and *C. nuttallii*. These proved up with big otter-brown palatkas, even bigger pumpkin-orange palmetto skippers, and Delawares as bright but half the size as the palmettos. Palamedes and palatkas supped together on one thistle, a pyle o' palamedes on another; a third thistle had three whirlabouts, a sachem, a Delaware, and four swallowtails of two species. A southern broken-dash (rich red) and a palatka (rich gold) sat side by side on the same thistle head. Altogether, as striking an assemblage as the year had yet provided.

These tawny skippers all graze on monocots—grasses, sedges, and the like—as caterpillars, so they are diverse and abundant in native grasslands such as this. Alana spotted a palatka ovipositing onto the sedge *Carex glaucescens*, its hemisphere egg the same turquoise as a great southern white's antennal clubs. Here and there Buck paused to give us looks at the lavender and white bells of pine hyacinth, actually a wild clematis, and rough green snakes whose green and yellow tails seemed convergently evolved with the tendrils of creepers. Giant cicada killer wasps with blue wings and yellow spots worked the sandy verges, and a loggerhead shrike dropped and got one before our eyes.

The Coopers called one wood lot Zebra Swallowtail Hammock, for reasons clear upon our arrival. Nearby, at Peavine and Milita roads, we found *Neonympha areolatus*! The Georgia satyr—a lifetime desire, satisfied. As a boy, I had been sent a specimen by a Tennessee researcher, in exchange for live hackberry butterflies I mailed for his studies. Coconut brown with coral red beads and hoops surrounding sea blue atolls with yellow shores . . . is it any wonder I'd always longed to see this rare Atlantic beauty in life? Now here were a number of them, alighting for good close-ups among the tall grasses. At lunch in a wooded campground, related Carolina satyrs skipped across the lawn.

Next came Metalmark Meadow, true to its name with lots of little metalmarks. These relatives of coppers, hairstreaks, and blues, hugely diverse in the Neotropics with just a few species in the North, draw their collective name from the metallic-looking markings many of them bear. *Calephelis virginiensis*, nectaring by ones and twos on fleabanes, glinted and shimmered *blue* like the blue-eyed grass all around. A sandy willow lane, traveled by otters and alligators when wet, now hosted a court convention of viceroys, queens, and pearl crescents on a jag, all courting, drinking, and jousting.

Bobwhites and wild turkeys—petite and moosy wild chickens—crossed the road. As we were stopped for them, Buck took a close look at Powdermilk and said: "You can't go anywhere on those tires!" I was shocked, and a bit embarrassed, to see the steel belts showing on the rear radials. I had no idea why, as they weren't that old.

Toward five, we drove to a short prairie with several species of *Polygala*, swamp milkweed, few-flowered milkwort, and the suggestively shaped queen's delight. On *Eryngium yuccifolia*, an umbel with narrow, spiny leaves, a twin-spot sat beside a tawny-edged skipper. I knew *Polites themistocles* as the common yard skipper in Aurora, Colorado, when I was growing up, but it has grown rare around Denver under the influence of lawn chemicals. The small spectacles of the skippers were magnified by big ones. A fresh-squeezed orange sulphur nectared on frogfruit, a mating pair of overloaded palamedes barely achieved liftoff, and a monarch exercised its rightful lèse majesté in an effortless flyover. To me, it seemed a heckuva butterfly day. We'd seen forty species, sixteen new, and some splendid natural history to boot. Yet Buck and Linda agreed that, of their many monitoring visits, this was one of the worst ever. "You've got to see it in October," said Buck, "when the Kissimmee is a sea of gayfeather and skippers."

Kissimmee and the Crooked Garden were hard acts to follow, but by all accounts, Sue Arnold's Butterfly Haven was up to it. So for St. Patrick's Day, I donned a set of green field clothes given me by Thea, drove up past Okeechobee, and found the place. Sue Arnold, a tall blonde of boundless energy and devotion, is well known and admired among Florida butterfliers and has long been involved in wildlife rescue.

Before any butterflies, she gave me a tour of Arnold's Wildlife Rehabilitation Center. Along with more predictable species, she had several cages of Florida panthers and other big kitties. Whether they were maltreated, abandoned, or otherwise unhoused, Sue took them in for shelter and rehabilitation and, in some cases, breeding. I was charmed to meet a caracal, with its long ear tufts, and a spotted serval, and to get to pet them. Like Sue, I'd far prefer that they were in the wild. But as a cat lover, I couldn't resist their broad, softly furred heads and big, deep purrs as I scratched behind their ears.

Like Jim at the Crooked Garden, Sue got into this devotion through the back door. On land that supported U-pick orange groves until a 2004 hurricane laid them down, she started small and found her visitors enchanted by the butterflies. With the help of many volunteers, over four years, she expanded Butterfly Haven into a half-acre garden with some two thousand plants. Twelve sections make up the shape of a zebra longwing, the Florida state butterfly. Visitors can see its form and watch the arrivals from a raised grandstand. Nearly sixty species have responded. "In summer," Sue said, "there can be three or four hundred at once." We walked into that fluttering horde. "The air shimmers with heat," she continued, "and sometimes people have thought there was an earthquake!"

There were butterflies here all right—scores rather than hundreds, but a lot: giant, black, zebra, Polydamas, and my first spicebush swallowtails; cloudless and orange-barred giant sulphurs; monarchs, queens, zebras . . . eighteen species in all. The bowered entrance supported host vines for *Battus polydamas* and *Agraulis vanillae* eggs and caterpillars, and the red cannas had been chewed up by Brazilian skipper larvae. I hated to leave, but Sue had endless work awaiting, and I had a date with a monk.

Several monks, actually. When I met Alana Edwards at the Jupiter Beach campus of Florida Atlantic University, where she works, she showed me three big monk skippers in their warm brown robes, nectaring on porterweed in her butterfly garden on campus. I'd been seeking *Asbolis capucinus*, around the palms its larvae consume, all week long. They were a treat to see, here in yet another garden grown out of someone's devotion to butterflies and those who notice them, or might, if they had a chance.

The next day, Alana drove me north from Boca Raton to Blowing Rocks Nature Conservancy preserve, a sea turtle nesting place with striking limestone formations. The Blowing Rock, where the surf sprays up through eroded limestone pavements, presents a stunning and wild beach scene with blue-green water and the nearest condos far to the south. The biologist Mike Renda, manager here since 1993, explained the huge twenty-year restoration project to reclaim the place from Australian pine and Brazilian pepper. "TNC wouldn't try such a thing now," Mike said, "but it can be done."

A smiling Deborah Galloway of nearby Tequesta joined us. A birder gone bad (as we call those who go over to butterflies), she discovered the Martial hairstreak here, in its northernmost known colony. We saw the uncommon beauty on *Bidens* as soon as we arrived. In a stiff wind, we prowled around a big stand of bay cedar (*Suriana maritima*), the hairstreak's larval host as well as a first-rate nectar source. Numbers of 'streaks, both males and females, perched on the yellow blossoms and basked out of the wind. Males streaked around and lit on overarching sea-grape leaves. Silvery gray beneath with clean white lines, a citrus patch, and long, wavy tails, night black with brilliant cerulean patches above, the Martials made for a magnificent blue sky, blue sea, blue butterfly day.

Back to Boca, then, for corned beef and cabbage and thick, rare cheeseburgers at Ellie's Diner with Alana's parents and husband, Rick. Her mom, Lana, had given moral support to Thea during her struggle with cancer. I'd met mother and daughter at a bird and butterfly festival at St. Petersburg, on the other coast. Coleading a field trip, I'd stepped into a fire ant nest in my sandals. The next thing I knew I'd ripped off my pants in the road and was slapping at my bare legs, to general amusement. Now I greeted Lana with a big hug and said, "It's been a long time since I've seen you both with my pants on!"

In spite of that, Lana presented me with a kind contribution to the Big Year from the Atala Chapter of NABA, of which Alana was president. Back at her house, we shared wine, her dad, Dave's splendid Key lime pie, and my inaugural episode of *The Bachelor*. I slept with the amazing one-eyed Skipper, a head-butting orange puss, dreaming no doubt that I had a caracal in my bed.

I awoke to Alana's soft announcement that a lovely, fresh atala was emerging in the backyard. I sat and watched that one slip its traces and begin to dry, as two more hung from the coontie, a dozen or more pupae awaited their turn, and a red trolley of a caterpillar propelled and pooped right beside the pupal cluster. And the adult! End on, from the blue-sparkled face, you see the red skirts of the hindwing open and enfold the red bum. The eyes black globes either side of the black palpi, the eyebrows, necklace, collar, and tibial muffs blue. Backlit, the blue flecks switched on, illuminated bulblets. I watched the original emergent climb to the top of a coontie and take her maiden flight. When Alana returned, she found me looking at a cluster of seventeen empty atala eggs with their exit pores, or micropyles, punched out. "I see," she said, "it's the macropyle checking out the micropyles. Come on, get up—it's time to go to Gumbo Limbo."

A City of Boca Raton nature center, Gumbo Limbo had yet another butterfly-full garden, where a Julia longwing crowded a ruddy daggerwing, the one smooth, the other scalloped and tailed like a swallowtail. This place was devastated by hurricanes; the first time, they lost strangler figs and tall trees, next time the lower paradise trees. Yet something survives, something comes back. And the strangler figs were not all gone: the spectacular caterpillar of a daggerwing dangled on a low one. Tiny larvae of a long-tailed skipper made their tents in leaves of *Clitoria*, a thusly shaped blue butterfly pea, and we found an evenly spaced triplet of fresh, live statira sulphur eggs on a coin vine near a spent pupal case. These counted, and it's a good thing, as I never saw the adult, unless maybe from a train several months later.

Back on the hammock, below the boardwalk, both fiddler crabs and giant land crabs ducked into their holes, the latter looking much like a big spider we saw rolled up in a fig leaf. I'm not sure which made the deepest impression on me—those crabs, the baby hammerhead shark in the display pool, or losing my *American Idol* virginity with Alana, Rick, and the one-eyed Skipper that night.

7. EASTER WITH ANDY

When the big dog leaped up on the back of Powdermilk for the third time, waking me from a sound sleep, I had to think hard to remember where I was. There were pines overhead. That helped. . . . Oh, right! Ocala National Forest! Eager to get afield on my own, with Marsha, in a great habitat. But some more sleep first. If that damn dog would only stop jumping on me. And if this heavy rain would only let up.

After leaving Boca on March 19, I'd driven back to Jupiter, then to Hobe Sound Beach, where a wade became a full-fledged swim thanks to a sneaker wave. All along Hobe Sound, great southern whites were moving north with the wind, and I followed.

Florida's Turnpike had swept me through Yeehaw Junction, through Tangerine; smaller roads took me to Mount Dora after dark, where I found McGregor's still open. I read Marc Minno's "Definitive Destination" article on the Ocala National Forest over local blues and a $2.50 pint of potable swamp water called Jeremiah Bullfrog's Ale. Stepping from the reek of the bar into orange blossom scent was almost overpowering. Once on the Ocala, I found a campsite after midnight at Farles Lake and settled in beneath a bright moon. Then this leaping hound, and the unnecessary rain.

The first day of spring came to the separate chuckles of red-bellied woodpeckers and sandhill cranes and a Carolina wren going "jeeter jeeter jeeter." Also to a time warp: all the other sites in this simple campground were occupied by a bunch of throwback hippies with modern add-ons—tattoos and piercings, buzzcuts and dreadlocks, robes and Florida Panthers blankets. One longhair grumbled over a sodden table that seemed to hold all of the supplies, "They left everything out, they left everything out." Others stumbled about dowsing for coffee. Babies carried on, and little kids ran about naked and muddy. Joe came over to see if his kids had left anything at my camp and apologize for his dog, an Akita-basset as it turned out, so no wonder. He said he was trading paneling from his old green school bus plus his big black Lincoln and $285 for a small Nissan RV that gets twenty-two mpg, to take his wife and kids and dogs to the Pacific Northwest when it heats up here. "We'll go via the Arizona 420 gathering," he said.

I asked if they were here for a Rainbow Family gathering. "No," he said, "they've got gatekeepers and a bunchadrunks." Some of this bunch had formed a little camp near here in the woods where they weren't noticed and stayed free for a while, then came here. Most smoked, and I heard several bad, hacking coughs. One difference from the sixties: one of the campsites had a Mercedes by the sprawling tent and tarps, another a Jaguar beside a green school bus. One camper was called Bubba—Bubba the Hippie! That's forty years for you—the hippies and the rednecks have merged, with their Jags and buses. Joe told me that, if you get into the woods, the chiggers and ticks are rife. "Put a white milk jug in there 'n' it'll have ticks all over it, both seed 'n' spotted." One black longhair in a Bud tee gathered cast palmetto fronds for kindling, a good way to get his daily dose of ticks.

The sun came out fitfully as I finished breakfast with a Riverwoods grapefruit, gathered from the ground. I was actually wearing a sweatshirt—it could be a spring morning in Washington—but a black swallowtail flashed by. By 10:30 butterfly time, the warming, sandy tracks came alive with loads of sleepy duskywings, waking up. *Erynnis brizo* is black and witchy like other duskywings but marked with warm brown and cool gray scales in beguiling patterns. Down by the crossroads, eight *brizos* furred a sheaf of wet Spanish moss in the sand, and a beautiful blue, yellow, and rust male parula warbler sang and buzzed my head when I pished at it. I wandered all the way to a naval bombing range in the middle of the national forest. Some pretty crusty hunters told me the road was difficult to the west, so I returned and took the 19 up the middle of the forest. The ditches were teeming with phaon crescents and sleepy oranges, and four species of swallowtails tippled at the roadside flowers. On

Marc Minno's tip, I tried Lake DeLancy Road for an eastern pine elfin but failed to find the right plum tree in bloom.

I was supposed to give a short talk about the Big Year to the North Central Florida Chapter of NABA in Gainesville. Loath to leave the splendid Ocala forest, I'd already dallied too long. I dashed over the Cross Florida Barge Canal to Kenwood and made the city with no time to waste. But waste it I did, foundering on the huge University of Florida campus. I got bum directions to the wrong natural history museum—there are two! I'd been where I was going several times before, but I got turned around and drove back and forth, now very late. It ended up just like the Essig Museum meeting at UC Berkeley, with me arriving just minutes before the end, only this time Jerry Powell wasn't there to make an acerbic comment. President Kathy Malone hurriedly reconvened the thirty-some folks, just breaking up, to hear my spiel. Considering I had been billed as a guest of honor, it's a darned good thing I wasn't two minutes later. My punctuality, poor at best, had dissipated with my other social skills after nearly three months as a butterfly hobo. Nevertheless, the chapter presented me with kind gifts for the trip.

Kathy Malone's beautiful home at High Springs displayed the top three Christmas card birds in the morning: cardinal, blue jay, and chickadee. In this case a Carolina chickadee was nesting, as were redheaded woodpeckers off her porch. We were definitely out of the tropics; the air registered 45°F at eight. But by nine, the first pair of baracoa skippers she'd ever seen mating in her garden were already affixed to each other's small golden reflection in the grass. As we motored toward San Felasco, the unsprayed roadsides hollered out with drifts of pink Drummond's phlox and blue lyre-leaf sage.

We met the UF biology professor Jaret Daniel at the San Felasco preserve. Jaret was conducting research on yucca giant-skippers here. The first novelty was a little wood-satyr, the larger, lilac-shad-owed southern subspecies *Megisto cymela viola*, sitting pretty among magnolia leaves. Carolina satyrs jittered through the undergrowth in abundance, like Viola's little sister. "A dancing meadow of satyrs," said Jaret, "is a memorable meadow." As we broke out of the forest, we saw my year-first great purple hairstreak nectaring high in a flowering crab apple, along with giant and pipevine swallowtails. Underneath the power line, clouds of purple Canada verbena covered a recent burn and clouds of spicebush and palamedes swallowtails covered it.

And then the giant-skippers appeared. These most robust of skippers are rarely seen by anyone. With larvae that burrow into the rootstocks of yuccas and agave, they occur in many desert and arid localities in the New World. But the adults do not come to nectar and may fly at great speeds—sixty miles an hour is often mentioned. I'd encountered them only a few times, ever. Now here were two black-and-cream males of *Megathymus yuccae*, swirling about us in Jaret's study site. One of the megs darted at a palamedes, like some battle of the Titans. Jaret showed us a yucca giant-skipper egg on the edge of a yucca leaf. It was *huge* for a butterfly egg—humpy in the middle and flattened outward, like a little brown mushroom pileus; uneven at the edges, like a handmade apple pie.

Jaret also pointed out old larval tents, three crusty gray-brown dildos sticking up at the centers of spent yuccas. The plants then sucker out and may actually be improved by the predation of the larvae. That would thicken the plot of this particular plant-insect coevolution tale still further, whereby many species of yuccas and agaves have their own obligatory species of giant-skipper associated with them. Jaret said he'll see up to eight eggs on a plant; we saw three on one leaf.

An adult male alighted for our inspection, his huge gray thorax like a rabbit-fur muff, and his white, black-tipped antennae thick as rods. Then a fiery red goatweed emperor flickered in and alighted. We watched the goatweed butterfly and the yucca giant in the same photo frame. A female *M. yuccae* with her lemon-drop forewing and hindwing borders perched and spread between two verbena flowers. I got up to a foot from her with my nose, and she audibly *whirred* off.

Thisbe herself, in the guise of a clearwing hawkmoth (*Hemaris thysbe*), left her midsummer eve to visit this spring verbena. From a whole different story, a Zabulon skipper displayed the mahogany spots on his golden fleece. Then a goatweed do-si-doed with a sleepy orange—"orange marmalade and butter," said Kathy. Sulphurs and swallowtails slathered themselves all over the verbena. We walked back past the tall crab apple again, an eastern tiger swallowtail on it now, and through the Glade of Satyrs, as a gray-cheeked thrush sang and blue-green skinks dashed across our path.

In the afternoon, I made my way to the lepidopterists' Mecca: the McGuire Center for Lepidoptera and Biodiversity at the Florida Museum of Natural History. The brainchild of UF Professor Thomas J. Emmel and largely funded by an endowment from the lepidopterist William McGuire, this purpose-built facility is the epicenter of butterfly and moth studies in the United States, and it employs the country's greatest concentration of distinguished lepidopterists, with the sole competition of the Smithsonian Institution. I met with my dear old friends Jackie and Lee Miller, the first curators of the phenomenal collections here, which originated in the Allyn Museum in Sarasota. The Millers had been major influences on American Lepidoptera studies and on the thoughtful direction of the Xerces Society.

Lee, drawn and thin, was afflicted with advanced cancer, but he was still coming in to the museum. I asked him if he had seen Jon Pelham's *Catalogue of the Butterflies of the United States and Canada*. As it was so important to my entire enterprise, I had been eagerly awaiting this tome. In fact, it had just been published, and Andy Warren, the book's editor for the *Journal of Research on the Lepidoptera*, had placed a copy in my hands just that day. Lee Miller had coauthored the previous monumental catalog, along with F. Martin Brown, my boyhood idol as author of *The Butterflies of Colorado*. With soft, labored speech, Lee said yes, he had, and he thought it was a good job. The nod was given, the baton was passed. I said, "He owes it all to you, of course."

Lee nodded, and just above a whisper, he said, "What a wasted life, huh?" Then he flashed his patented grin, one corner of his mouth lifted for half a second. I'm so glad I got to see him. When I returned to the McGuire in the fall, Lee would not be there.

I left the McGuire with Charles Covell, Kentucky butterfly guru, author of the Peterson Field Guide to moths and beloved friend and inspiration for more years than either of us could remember. Charlie was lured away from Louisville, where he taught for many years, to become a part of the McGuire team. As we stepped outside, a snout butterfly flew up and landed beside us. There would be about 7 billion later on, but this was my first of the year, and the only one I would see for months to come. We went to a barbecue for the land trust on Gainesville's famous Paynes Prairie. I walked the trail with the Miami blue biologist Emily Saarinen, gnawed on pulled pork and barbacoa chicken with Charlie, and went on my first hayride ever. Beneath the big moon, I pondered the connection between baracoa skippers and *barbacoa*, the Cuban word for "barbecue."

Saturday was cloudy, as befit a maintenance day, which meant new tires for Powdermilk. At the gracious old senator's house that was the Covell home, Charlie's wife, Betty, pursued her gentle activism on behalf of peace and the homeless from her breakfast nook nerve center. Outside, son Robert worked on a trellis in the ponded and bowered garden, which felt like a botanical cloister. CVC Jr. left with his new knee for a golf tournament. Meanwhile, Adrian and Amos changed my oil at Jiffy Lube. Daniel, Tyrone, and Billy installed two new twelve-inch tires at the Tire Outlet. Then some twenty African-American hoopsters washed Powdermilk cleaner than she'd been since her twenty-fifth birthday. We were made whole, safe, and pretty again, all right there within Charlie's green and leafy Gainesville neighborhood.

When he returned, Charlie took me out on the LaChua Trail. A fresh *Junonia coenia* basking at the base of a dock was gorgeous, a definitive, fancy-form big buckeye in all its exuberant color and pattern. Spanish moss hung from splendid oaks over a duckweed pond. Fifty or sixty alligators lolled by the shore, some of them twelve-footers and very big around. A few smaller ones lay right by the trail. Charlie said to a knot of UF guys, "Here's where you really have to say, 'Go, Gators!' " They laughed, as polite youths do at a prof's joke. As we strolled, we discussed records and range expansions. Charlie thought several species were expanding along the interstates, such as meadow fritillaries, the Jefferson County, Kentucky, record of which he nabbed with his driver on the links.

Andrew D. Warren, another member of the McGuire lepidopterist stable, was there on one postdoc while he held another at the National Autonomous University of Mexico. Growing up near Denver a generation and a half after I did, Andy parlayed his parents' enlightened indulgence of his passion for leps, and his own drive and intellect, into one of the most formidable butterfly reputations of our time, entirely deserved. While performing doctoral studies at Oregon State University on a DNA-based, higher classification of the skippers of the world, he wrote a terrific book on the butterflies of Oregon in his spare time. Andy was not only one of the young lepidopterists to watch but also a pal, and we were going to celebrate Easter together in the best way either of us could possibly imagine: in the field.

We headed first across to Florida's West Coast at Cedar Key, where, as promised, we found the two tiniest butterflies in the state: the eastern pygmy-blue and the southern skipperling. *Brephidium pseudofea* glinted bronzy in the glasswort, while *Copaeodes minima* skipped almost invisibly above the shore grasses. The two largest species, the eastern tiger and palamedes swallowtails, muscled over our heads. You could probably put a thousand *C. minimas* on one *P. palamedes*, yet they have the same level of organization. Wet spots were segregated by species. "Sulphurs are snobs when it comes to puddling," Andy observed. Many long-winged, white-dashed *Panoquina panoquin*, the salt marsh skipper, occupied the shore, though the related *P. panoquinoides* eluded us. When we saw the special Aaron's skipper but failed to net it, he asked what I'd seen. When I said, "The pale rays below," Andy replied, "That's what I wanted to hear."

We spent the long, hot afternoon working the roadsides of Goethe State Forest in a blur of butterflies, including two new cloudy-wings; both chocolate-chip and pepper-and-salt skippers, Alana's nicknames for the sometimes-similar whirlabout and fiery skippers; and a prolonged courtship of giant swallowtails in their sunlit dance over pink phlox. The Easter Bunny did not forget us: Andy found zebra swallowtail eggs on flaglike pawpaws in the woods, and we each detected eggshells of cofaqui giant-skippers on yuccas deep in the pines. Andy saw a live one, but mine were all spent, so I couldn't count the species.

One thing Andy and I have in common is a reluctance to quit.

Having gone hell-bent all this Holy Day long, neither of us wanted to let it go. Maybe we got this way from growing up in Colorado, where the shadows creep down the canyons and the clouds climb over the summits, putting the day to rest all too soon . . . never worse than on a Sunday, when school hangs over the morning. Easter Sunday must have been the worst of all, often the first bright, short spring outing of the year, which every young collector was utterly unwilling to relinquish. So these two Denver lads kept going. And so we should have, for we had another adventure to come, which we will always think of as the Satyrs at Sunset. Or, alternatively, as the Guy with the Badge.

ADW and I took our final detour along Wakahuta Road, where flights of Carolinas and a few silvery Violas flitted along the verge at last sun. At 7:15 P.M. we walked along the edge of a pinewood and investigated a caney opening. Andy spotted a third satyr, a cane-feeding southern pearly-eye. Marsha and I caught it to make sure, with an emphatic "Yes!" Just then, an older fellow strode toward us down the track, flashing his badge. "This is private property," he said, "and you're trespassing."

"It's not fenced, or posted," Andy explained. But the man said it was well known that all pine forest was private around there and didn't need to be posted. We followed him out. He was a farmer, and we never did figure out what the badge was for. When Andy mentioned his connection with the university, the fellow became more civil and ended up giving us directions to other canebrakes where we could hunt butterflies legally. Eventually he pulled away in his truck, and we worked the roadside a little longer, with dun skippers and still more little browns flying right up to sunset. The satyrs, it seemed, had no more desire to stop than we did.

Enodia portlandia turned out to be species number 100! The Big Year was alive and well. At a Mexican café on the way home, we consecrated that milestone with nachos and a Negro Modelo. Then we toasted the pearly-eye and the Guy with the Badge with another. "That was one fine Easter observance," I said.

"Indeed it was," Andy agreed. "Indeed it was."

8. BEACH LADY DAY

At the little sandwich stand on the outskirts of Gainesville where I bought a sixty-cent BLT for the road, the black woman at the counter called me "Baby," as MaVynee used to do. MaVynee, or Marvyne as I knew her, was on my mind anyway, as I was on my roundabout way to pay my respects to her memory in American Beach. Now, on my way north, I thought back to her.

MaVynee Betsch was no one you could easily describe. Let's say to start that she was completely unique in my experience, sui generis to everyone who knew her, and that this book would not be here if it had not been for her. Her history is tied up with that of American Beach, which was set up in 1935 by Abraham Lincoln Lewis and his six cofounders of the Afro-American Life Insurance Company. A progressive approach to insuring his people made Lewis one of the first black millionaires in Florida. He wanted to see a beach resort open to his company's executives, employees, and customers. As Florida's beaches were segregated until the sixties, American Beach became one of the few beaches in the Southeast open to African Americans. A. L. Lewis was MaVynee's grandfather, and she was an heiress to "the Afro-American," as she always called it.

Named Marvyne at birth, which was the name we mostly knew her by, she dropped the "r" out of contempt for Ronald Reagan and added an "e" and the middle name Oshun. She preferred, in any case, to be referred to as the "Beach Lady." MaVynee had an astonishing soprano voice. After studying music at Oberlin College, she became a professional opera singer, working mostly in European halls. When her grandfather was old and ailing, she returned to care for him until he died. Heavy, world-weary, sick of the European urban air, she was living in a small marsh house when a hurricane

97

struck and she suffered a heart attack. Marvyne told me that all she had for sustenance was a pot of honey. When she recovered, she dedicated herself to honeybees, butterflies, the beach, and all of life. Over the next couple of decades, Marvyne became the slender, beautiful, poised, and totally outspoken Beach Lady—the most formidable opponent that North Florida developers ever knew.

In the process, MaVynee grew her hair into a great, long, matted dreadlock that she carried in an African Kikuyu cloth. She also grew the fingernails of one hand to a spiraling length of thirteen inches or more, in the manner of an extinct tribe in the area. She kept the other hand trimmed, for writing thousands of letters and cards in support of her many issues. Somewhere along the way, she beggared herself in service to Nature.

Marvyne/MaVynee and I became acquainted when she wrote to ask me about the Xerces Society for Invertebrate Conservation, which seemed right up her alley. At that time the organization was all-volunteer and pretty close to the bone. Her support made a great difference to its early development. At the time I chaired the Lepidoptera Specialist Group of the International Union for Conservation of Nature and Natural Resources' Species Survival Commission, and MaVynee, eager to have butterflies represented in high places, funded my travel to a couple of general assemblies in distant locations. Later we became good friends, corresponding with great frequency.

When I left The Nature Conservancy and moved to the country to attempt a freelance existence, Marvyne lent powerful encouragement. A big tin of tupelo honey and a book she felt I must read might arrive by UPS and, in the mail, a pep talk full of faith in my effort, signed "Bee Sweet, Beach Lady." Her support of my early writing career, both moral and material, made all the difference for the completion of my first books; hence, as I said, this one. In recent years, our contact grew less frequent. Stomach cancer came and went, and when it finally took her, I was terribly sad to know that she was gone.

On my way north through pines and palmettos, the median strip was a sea of phlox and spiderwort. I didn't get far before stopping in the Austin Cary Memorial Forest, where zebra swallowtails appeared and disappeared through palmetto shadows, and one gray tree frog matched the damp gray sand. Fragrant azaleas made *Papilio* pubs, *palamedes, troilus,* and *glaucus* quaffing all together on the pale pink flowers.

That scene repeated itself the next day in Simmons Memorial State Forest, still farther north, except that I was naked and immersed in black water beneath the azaleas. I'd entered the forest in the morning, walking white sandy trails among burned and unburned pines and oaks, hoping to find frosted elfins near the southern limit of their range. I entered the recommended oak wood, leaned up against a big trunk, and right away a big, fresh *Incisalia irus* appeared and flew about the glade—biggish and slowish for an elfin. These small brown hairstreaks, spring flyers, are related to green hairstreaks and really belong in the same genus with them, *Callophrys;* but I prefer to use their subgenus, *Incisalia,* since they are all readily identified as such.

Perched on a live oak seedling, moving its hindwings back and forth like hands rubbing for warmth, it displayed a checkered fringe and cool frosting below. This so-called sawing serves to distract birds away from the body, toward the expendable bits. And it works: another elfin, bird-struck, had its tails removed. More elfins entered the glade, engaged with one another, and spiraled out.

Then my other desire here, a dusky roadside-skipper, materialized and alighted on the underside of a pale live oak leaf. Small, dark, and frosty like the elfin, it displayed a speedy, direct flight that told it apart right away. Not far away, across a white sandy square, in a dispersed patch of blueberry bushes, both sleepy duskywings and dusky roadsides sipped from the flowers. Back at my big oak, all three darklings were zipping around together. A fourth, a bigger Juvenal's duskywing, was attracted to something on an unfurling turkey oak leaf. I sucked the leaf and found it sweet.

The soft sand path was pocked like a battlefield with the inverted cones of ant lions. I tried to avoid stepping on them, but it was harder than avoiding the cracks on a sidewalk. As the white trail entered a dappled woodland, shadier and denser, I wondered if I might see a gemmed satyr. When a biggish brown popped up, *voilà*—Viola; a littler one was Carolina; and then a middle—I called

it for *Cyllopsis gemma*, and it was: soft doe brown with reddish striations and sparkly blue, yellow-rimmed eyes. New for the year, it
showed that gorgeous patch of mauve frosting and silver enamel
that gives it the name gemmel satyr.

Around four, I came to a primitive campsite on St. Marys River,
a broad, gently winding, blackwater river. Train whistles blew from
the Georgia side. I had a banana for lunch and spread out the peel
for bait. A bright green anole shuffled in the leaves beside an oak
log covered with conchs, then turned dark against the gray bark,
as if a green hairstreak became a frosted elfin. I soaked my sore
feet in the river; they looked amber in the shallows, then disappeared altogether. That truly black water, the steep, slippery slope,
and the possibility of unseen alligators and who knows what, all
argued against going any deeper. But it felt so good on my hot,
sweaty skin . . . so of course I stripped off and went in. Not as cold
as the Colorado River a month earlier but cold enough. When I
swam toward a bald cypress, the water looked like orange pekoe
iced tea steeped too long with too many bags. I stood on my knees
in soft silt, just my head out, looking up at azaleas with four species
of enormous elegant swallowtails hanging from them—spicebush,
pipevine, eastern tiger, and palamedes. Soft breeze and dragonflies
stitched the surface. This was what I'd dreamt of when I dreamt of
this trip. I rose, placed my bare little fanny on a tuffet of moss, and
just grinned and grinned.

Eventually I had to leave the water to the invisible gators. Back at
the campsite, I dried in the sun and the breeze. Holly leaves prickle
my feet when I walk barefoot at home too, but here the *Ilex* were native. I heard a flap, looked up, and a swallow-tailed kite was twenty
feet from my face with something in its talons. Back on with my
clothes and shoes, I headed out, wishing I were camping in there.

One thing I came to love along the small roads of the Atlantic
Seaboard was the presence of small fish houses, where you could
get a seven-dollar plate of fresh fish and greens, not even deep-fried.
That night, in Callahan, I had the sole dinner. Then in a campsite at
Cary State Forest, I barricaded against mosquitoes as a diminished
moon rose. The next time I looked, I found myself in grassy glade
overhung with tall bush blueberries, swallowtails and hairstreaks at

their breakfast. On my way out, I stopped for a mating pair of phaon crescents flying oddly. I found that the female was hauling about a dead male with inverted wings—this, minutes after listening to a "Morning Edition" piece on Viagra, with reference to men who died in flagrante, still tumescent.

For the hot drive to the shore, I dressed down to running shorts and sandals, then saw a meadow of white clover and blue sage that looked soft and inviting. Big mistake. As I swished among the grass with its many sachems and clouded skippers, something hit my feet and ankles that felt like fire ants crossed with nettles—yowee! Driving on, I raked at my screaming ankles. I figured out that I'd gotten into the loathed and storied little flies called, without exaggeration, no-see-ums. Eastward on the 92, I pulled into Pope-Baldwin Park and waded into soothing wetlands with clicking frogs. As my skin began to quiet down, I explored a wild wet lane haunted by white checkered-skippers and red saddlebags, a huge green-clouded swallowtail lording it over the end of the path.

Past the ferry *Jean Ribault* to Maytown, at Fort George Island, the sun dipped over the salt marsh estuary between two cooling towers for a nuclear power plant. It nuzzled into the curve of one tower, then shrank to a little peach slice from a fruit cocktail as tangerine clouds swirled into the nuke's plume. Running through cabbage palms and palmettos, the road ended at Kingsley Plantation, now the Timucuan Ecological and Historic Preserve. As the Daughters of the American Revolution's sign told me, "Jean Ribault and a party of Huguenots landed the morning of May 1, 1562, on this island. Here they knelt in prayer, beseeching God's guidance and commending the natives to his care. This was the first Protestant prayer in North America." That hadn't worked out too well for the natives.

Something amazing happened in the Sand Dollar Restaurant, where the oysters were inexplicably from Louisiana but the Tarpon Spoon beer from Jacksonville. At the next table over, three men were having a birthday dinner for one of them. I overheard him talking about rare butterflies and Say's spiketail dragonfly, which he surveyed for the Florida Division of Recreation and Parks! Of course I butted in, and found that Richard was friends with Kathy Malone. His pals were astonished, but no more so than I. I suspect it was good for them to see that their birthday-boy colleague was not the only butterflier in the world. We spoke of species and sites until his birthday cheesecake came.

As I passed through Amelia Island's ultra-affluence, I got another surprise: a big brown sign told me that I was on "Mavynee Betsch 'The Beach Lady' Highway," so designated by the Florida legislature in 2006. What a welcome for my visit! I camped at Burney Beach Park in American Beach, where I was awakened by the local gendarme. He said it was illegal to sleep there. I pointed out the sign headed "Camping Rules," and that it said "limited to 24 hours." He said you needed a county permit to camp there. I gave the policeman my card and mentioned my pilgrimage to MaVynee's beach. "She died a couple of years ago," he said, and that, since I wasn't a crazy kid doing drugs or breaking into cars (I was the only one there), I was okay, and he'd watch over me. I thanked him, scratched my bites some more, and turned back to sleep.

Morning in the park was sunny and mild. Micturating, I watched a six-lined racerunner creep beneath a long-tailed skipper at *Bidens*: nectaring blue-back over blue-belly basking. On the beach, folks surf-fished "for whities," both whities and blacks; and skinny women from Amelia speed-walked their iPods, every one. I waded. Just as the tattler had in Santa Cruz, a willet walked among everyone, as brown pelicans surfed the waves and dove offshore. I'd be leaving the Atlantic soon, so I did the same, much closer to shore. It was colder and clearer than the St. Marys, with rip tides instead of alligators, so I didn't stay in long or go out very far. I waited for the right wave, big enough and not breaking too soon, and bodysurfed in, which sounds more graceful than it was. Coming out, I picked up an open shell to remember Marvyne by.

On the boardwalk, watching a cardinal sing on a dune bush, I met Walter Houle. Tall, barefoot, my age or so, he'd known MaVynee well for a few years. He described the fine memorial for her here on Nana, her name for the Mother Dune she had managed to get saved between the immense condos to the south and north. Walter doubted that MaVynee would have succeeded, absent her eccentricities. He told me that her four-foot dread-braid, covered with conservation buttons, was saved to be placed in a historical mu-

seum to be built here. Her ashes were laid in Nana and given to celebrants to toss into the waves as recordings of her arias were played
along with her answering machine message: "If I'm not here, look
at the beach and I'll be a butterfly there."

"You know her color was orange," Walter said (I did: orange caf-
tans, orange beach house). "There were orange butterflies, and the
sunset all of a sudden came in orange—I never see an orange sunset
here, especially over *there*." Earlier, I had watched a worn, northing
monarch flipping among the interdune and playing with an orange
dragonfly; now gulf fritillaries swayed on the swale thistles, creatures that MaVynee will have seen almost every day. Orange is a
good bet here.

It had been close to thirty years since my former wife, Sally
Hughes, and I visited Marvyne here in American Beach, one of two
times we saw her in person. The other was at a memorable Xerces
meeting on Ossabaw Island, Georgia, where she sang her own
opera composition under Spanish moss embroidered with tawny
emperors. Now, I found it difficult to remember landmarks. When
she lived in her beach house on Gregg Street, Marvyne removed the
windows to let the wind flow through. Each afternoon, the instant
the wind changed from seaward to landward, she stopped what she
was doing to feel it. Of course, she had no use for air condition-
ing. Eventually, unable to pay the rent, MaVynee moved to a trailer
provided by her sister, the president of Spelman College. Displaced
from a vacant lot for "squatting," she finally lived in a small yellow
cinder-block cabin owned by supporters, farther back from her beloved shore. The insurance heiress had given everything she had to
the causes she believed in, and she died here, a beloved pauper.

Amelia Island once supported several slaveholding cotton planta-
tions. In 1862, Union forces captured Amelia Island, and the slaves
they freed founded Franklin Town at the south end of the island.
Today, the big, posh development to the south of American Beach,
which "owned" Nana and became MaVynee's biggest adversary (and
she the biggest thorn in their shorts), is named—incredibly—"The
Plantation."

Before I left, I walked a stickery way into a fold of Nana, watching
out for gopher tortoise mounds and their inversions, ant lion pits.

I said my words, shed my tears, for Marvyne up there. Cloudless giant sulphurs were northing along Nana's ridge like flying butter pats. From a little cove in the Mother Dune's side, I watched turkey vultures kettle above, dragonflies kettle in the lee of the dune. I thought of how this would be condos but for MaVynee Betsch. I wondered where I might be, if not for her. And I thought it was good to be here, on Beach Lady day.

9. LOST AND FOUND

Fernandina was steaming when I saw a sign for the Greater Fernandina Women's Club Butterfly Garden. Behind an old school, the women had placed a plaque designating a "Liberty Garden for 9/11." The plot, obviously planted for butterflies, had been little tended lately. That was fine, as it meant lots of beggar's ticks, better than most of the chosen plants for nectar. Neglected butterfly gardens often have more butterflies than tended butterfly gardens, unless they get a lot of informed care, as at the Crooked Garden or Butterfly Haven.

The monarchs and red admirables tussling about didn't mind the decay, nor did the rest of the ten species present, the brown thrasher, or the green anole running round the octagonal bench in the gazebo, pausing every couple of feet to do pushups and stick out his red gular flag. A kid named Zach Arsineaux, out walking Toby the poodle, was surprised to see me. He'd gone to that school and often returned. Now fourteen, Zach loved cars. He found Powdermilk pretty amazing. And why not? Onward, to Georgia.

In Woodbine, down a sandy back road through slash pine plantation and deciduous woods, I noticed a roughly hand-lettered sign nailed to a tree: "Mac's Place Honey Dipper—whiskey-beer-wine," pointing down an even smaller lane. I wanted to follow that arrow into the deepwood in the worst way, but the butterfly day beckoned. I came to a small trailer with another hand-drawn sign reading "Community Grocery," with several old black men gathered around. They stared, and I waved. Way, way back in, the rusty tin-roofed and cupolaed "Springhill Batist Church—John E. Bank, Pastor" rose out of the pines. I found my first northern broken-dash on the churchyard verbena, as big, blue-black, and very buzzy carpenter bees gathered on sweet white wisteria.

Reckoning the road might not go where I aimed to get, I went back to the trailer-grocery and asked for an apple. They didn't have any, so I bought some chips. I wanted to try their garlic crab, but it was only midmorning. Now there were two older men, two younger women. "What do you call this area?" I asked. They looked at each other, and one man rubbed his stubbled chin. "Around here," he said, "we just call it 'the woods.'"

I let that sink in. "Not too many mosquitoes," I observed.

"Not yet," he said.

"The swamp that way?" I asked, gesturing west, meaning Okefenokee.

"It's pretty much swampy all around," he said.

Back at the junction, zebra swallowtails and zarucco duskywings dug into the sunny mud. Several hungry palamedes frantically fed at a single white fluffhead of roadside thistle, and they were horny too—a trailer of three males followed one female across the road, and another harassed a mated spicebush pair, barely getting lift. Then, stopping at another promising site, I found my collecting bag to be missing. The little leather pouch had a couple of important voucher specimens in it. More than that, I'd purchased it in a Costa Rican market in 1978, and it was an old friend, like Marsha or my binoculars.

I retraced my steps to the grocery, where I asked if anyone had seen the bag. They seemed bemused, or possibly amused, but promised to keep an eye out for it. Back at the church, I netted a tawny-edged skipper, but I missed my tweezers, attached to the collecting bag on a cord. I looked farther. The loss took the edge off my pleasure in finding a wet ditch full of southern skipperlings and little metalmarks. Losing my collecting bag put a blot on the whole day,

Speaking of loss, when Roger Peterson wrote in *Wild America* that "all afternoon we drove through almost endless pine forests," he was speaking of longleaf pines in 1953. Half a century later those forests have found an end after all in sawmills and slash pine plantations. The virtues and decline of *Pinus palustris* have been movingly documented by the Georgia writer Janisse Ray. So the road into

Okefenokee National Wildlife Refuge, through a gallery of longleaf pines, gave a welcome sense of what went before.

A slender alligator swam slowly, barely emergent, so that its self and its reflection met in a bumpy line like some skinny caiman passing through the palmettos. Later, on the Swamp Drive, a six-footer lay by the shore of a pond. When I stopped, it crept out beside the car. Someone must have ignored the "do not feed the alligators" signs. It was remarkable to see all the working parts, sutures, and platy bits so well and so near.

At 6:00 P.M., palamedes courted over a grassy clearing. At 7:00, in hazy sun, many of the broad-winged swallowtails floated about the crowns of longleaf pines, then went to roost deep inside clusters of the long, graceful needles. They reminded me of monarchs bedding down, but singly, not in clusters. They flew around and around in the last sun, seeking just the right bower, as the frog chorus came up. They weren't alone up there: I saw a spicebush and a couple of tigers too, one of which settled on a bare twig. Saddlebags dragonflies circled in the sunbeams, and a turkey crossed the track and made itself scarce in the saw palmetto; I'd seen camouflaged men all over the countryside for the spring turkey hunt, but not in here. I slipped out at sunset, just before the ranger locked the gate. My initial visit to Okefenokee was bewitching if brief, almost driving the recent loss from my mind. But as the curtain of the southern dark fell, the dull ache of it returned.

I drove into Folkston and engaged a room at the Stardust Motel, another cheapie but goodie. There I received the message from Thea on my seldom-seen mobile. She read it to me, and I have listened to it many times since. "Mr. Pyle," the caller said, "this is Mr. Key in Jacksonville, Florida. I found something that belongs to you. Call me at your earliest convenience." I must have left my collecting bag atop Powdermilk and driven off—a bad habit of mine. I've lost everything from glasses and mugs to a freshly typed book manuscript that way. Never mind! In a much happier mood, I found another little fish house and celebrated with pollack. These dinners always came with fried okra and two hush puppies. The latter item was a lifer for me, and the former helped me confront my lifelong okraphobia, dating from when my Kentucky-born single father served us the glutinous canned kind. I was so happy my bag was found, I didn't even mind the okra.

Mr. Key called early in the morning in response to the telephone message I'd left for him. He indeed had my collecting bag, sounded very interested in what I was doing, and was eager to "restore it to your possession," as he put it. Things were complicated by his car being at the airport in Jacksonville. We agreed to meet halfway, back in Callahan in North Florida, as soon as he could get his car. Meanwhile, I booked the room for another night and set to work on things that needed doing while waiting for him to call. In a stroke of good timing, the day was drizzly, and cool enough for wool.

In the distance I could hear whistles of the many trains that poured through this rail-funnel town. When I went out, I saw the fancy train-watching park, full of granddads, excited tiny kids, and serious trainspotters. It's a big tourist draw. When I got back to my car from checking out the setup, a pretty cream tortoiseshell was ensconced on my sleeping bag, washing and looking forward to a nap. I hated to turf her out, and she looked forlorn when I did. I considered taking her with me, for about a second. But I reckoned she'd be happier as the trainspotting cat than the butterfly-spotting cat, maybe ending up lost in a rest area somewhere in Texas. And traveling with a live kitty would be complicated, turning the journey more *Travels with Charley* than *Wild America*. As I thought it over, Richard the trainspotter came up and said, "Her name is Chessie." He said that the train people bring food and leave it in a cabinet for her. I needn't have worried! Removing Chessie would have been catnapping. Rescue syndrome can be insidious, whether with kitties, baby seals, fawns, or folks.

I hung about the Stardust waiting for Mr. Key's call, which finally came. We found each other at the CVS drugstore in Callahan. Spontaneously, we embraced when we met. Mr. Kenneth Key, a good-looking man with short gray hair and a mustache, was a truck driver who hauled containers. "I was out on a drive with my lady," he said, "when I saw your article in the road." That must have been shortly after I'd lost it. Thank goodness I had some of my cards in it! Kenneth handed me my bag and said he wasn't going to be satisfied until he'd restored it to me.

With him was Eddie Williams, who'd taken him to the airport to pick up his car. Eddie said he used to love to see fireflies where he grew up in Whiteley, Georgia, but no more with all the lights and development. "I heard about it on late-night *tee*-vee," he said. And he seldom sees a butterfly—spotting a yellow-and-black one a week or so ago was an occasion. "I just watched and watched it," Eddie said, "until it flew away."

"My three grandkids love bugs," said Kenneth. I said mine do too, and that was what kept me working to conserve butterflies. Then it occurred to me to ask them if they knew about MaVynee—and yes, Kenneth said, he had met her! "How could you forget her?" he asked. They both knew about her work on behalf of American Beach, Nana, and nature. When he was growing up, Kenneth's family would go to American Beach, the only one where they were welcome. We spoke of those bad old days, and how far we've come in some ways.

"We may see an amazing day in January," I said, and they both smiled broadly.

"I have a feeling we'll be getting out of the bushes, after eight years," said Eddie. Kenneth said he just wanted it to be a better world for the kids.

Later that summer I would be reminded of our conversation when I read this propitious encounter from William Least Heat-Moon's *Blue Highways*, when he was talking with two black men in Selma:

"Lotta people in the project feel like they cain't be nobody," Walker said. "Me? I feel I can be President of the United States."

"Sheeit, man!" Davis said. "Force musta did your brain-housing group in."

"I know things ain't changed, but things gonna change."

Kenneth said he and his girlfriend were planning to go to the Redwoods this spring or summer, and I said maybe we'd run into each other—stranger things have happened. Eddie shyly accepted some gas money, but they wouldn't take a reward or let me buy them a meal (mine would be red drum). We parted with hugs and handshakes, and Kenneth said he had just one thing to request of me: "That you stay safe."

"Okefenokee Swamp 10 mi" read the sign, a big arrow with feathers. Someone had carved a bas-relief of gators, cattails, bald eagle, and woodpecker for the refuge sign. The Georgia Historical Commission plaque next to it, from 1954, expanded: "Okeefenokee, 'Land of the Trembling Earth,' was a favorite hunting and fishing ground for many tribes of Indians. General Charles Floyd with 250 dragoons drove out the last of these, the Seminoles, in 1838 ending Indian rebellion in southern Georgia. In 1937 the United States Fish and Wildlife Service acquired most of the swamp. Now a sanctuary for wild life, it abounds in rare species of birds, mammals, fish, and reptiles in a vast natural botanical garden. All hunting is prohibited; some fishing is allowed." I left the big alligator on Folkston's water tower behind me and headed back to the big swamp.

The lady at the entrance box told me that the pines with white painted rings were the ones in which they've seen the endangered red-cockaded woodpeckers. Looking around the pinewoods, I had no luck spotting the rara avis; just vocal red-bellies and a big pileated, dining, knocking slabs off a dead pine. Between them, these woodpeckers doubtless cause many visitors to believe they've seen the delinquent red-cockaded, whose advertised scarlet marking is barely visible.

The boardwalk trail crossed a fine sphagnum bog with white-polka-dotted, rusty-hooded pitcher plants. A green-clouded swallowtail flew over a green anole, displaying against fresh green cypress needles, its gular flag backlit neon coral. A side trail led to open water and a superb zarucco duskywing. Perched as it was on ferns, its brown patches stood way out. Rose saddlebags and blue libellulids, among the most colorful of southern dragonflies, hunted this odonatist's paradise.

I climbed an observation tower. After a nice but noisy French family left, peace was restored—only frogs clicking and harrumphing, big, blue, yellow-fuzzed mud bees buzzing, and the breeze. Tall oaks witchy with Spanish moss reared out of the swamp, and the rust-red flowers and needle bundles were just unfurling from the bald cypress.

A tree swallow dipped over the lake down below, my first for the year, and a red admirable basked beneath me on a shiny green leaf of one of the many deciduous trees here that I did not and would never know. The great swamp stretched out seemingly forever. The strange thing was that, with all the water below, I didn't see a single bird on, in, or around it—no waders or egrets, no fowl or gallinules, zero.

As I was walking back, I saw the bulbous-eyed face of a southern leopard frog poking out of the water in a gator crawlway by the so-called prairie, and a beautiful eastern indigo snake slid off the boardwalk into the water. Just then, with the sun still up and bright at about 70°F, as I was thinking there really *ought* to be a cool skipper out there in the sedge marsh, an orange skipper danced up and circled before alighting several times. I could not net it, of course, this being a federal refuge, but I was able to watch and draw it for a good many minutes, from several perspectives. A male, he perched on woody stalks, dead flowers, and sedges, often as close as I could focus.

A hesperiine, or monocot-feeding skipper, the handsome, white-faced insect was over an inch across, with broad brown borders on the pointed forewings; narrow, sharp black stigmata that didn't meet the border; and prominent orange patches on the dorsal hindwings. The underside was rich orange-tan with no rays, bars, spots, or white trailing edge; *but*—the lighter veins definitely stood out, and that, in combination with the habitat and other field marks, did the trick. This was Berry's skipper (*Euphyes berryi*), a highly local rarity of the extreme Southeast and a species few butterfliers have managed to see. Sight records, like the possible pair of red-cockaded woodpeckers that I saw on my way out, often carry a tincture of uncertainty. But this skipper was solid.

On April Fool's Eve, I was headed back to Gainesville—*not* what I'd expected. More and more bugged by how close I'd come to seeing the cofaqui giant-skipper near Williston, its type locality—or at least, its eggs—I'd decided to have another look. Andy had found a live one, whereas I had seen only shells. It occurred to me to lower my acceptance standard to recoverable DNA, but somehow I didn't think that would fly. So, before leaving the Southeast, though it might have been truly foolish, I was going to try once more for *M. cofaqui*. I arrived after midnight and camped in Andy's driveway.

After comparing notes and specimens with Andy, I returned to Wakahuta Road, where the many morning butterflies included my first question mark and southern oak hairstreak, a lovely fresh female with long, thin tails. The same patch of *Erigeron* held both a buckeye and an American lady, with their giant eyespots; the mise en scène needed only a common wood-nymph to make a completely confusing three-way target for birds. Right on cue, along came the same farmer with the badge. I assured him I was keeping to the roadside this time.

Molly Adams was the next person to accost me. Having taken the turnoff signed 316 into the main stand of yucca, I began looking up and down roadsides at the edge of turkey oak sandhills. I'd found five hatched *M. cofaqui* eggs on tender, young spikes so far when Molly approached. A local resident and gardener, she inquired of my business, as did several dogs. I was able to placate and even interest her in my search and its special connection with Williston. Said search was not, on the whole, turning out to be a whole lot of fun. Eight more eggs turned up, all with nobody home. Suitably called Spanish bayonets, the yuccas grew among poison ivy, brambles, fire ants, chiggers, and their own wicked points. It was close to 100°F on 159th Terrace. Plus mosquitoes. Itching like crazy, I was probably doing something like St. Vitus' dance when a local, paint-spattered father came at me and snarled, "We've got four girls, and I'm not real happy when some guy with binoculars comes poking around the neighborhood." I whipped out my card, and even the man who was rich in daughters, but not the dogs, ended up in my court.

Finally, at 2:45 P.M., a lovely breeze up with a bit of cloud, I found a live egg! It lay near two small turkey oaks but well outside the woods. Most of the plants in the yucca patch where I found it were old and tough. The only egg I saw in that stretch of road, it was on a tender, small yucca fifteen inches across, four inches up from the base, in the V of a leaf near the center. Like the *M. yuccae* eggs at San Felasco, it resembled a mushroom's pileus; but it was higher, almost hemispherical, with discrete edges rather than the mashed-down pie margins of the yucca giant-skipper ovum. It reminded me of the half-moon in eclipse, even in color—pearly but empurpled with the mature larva that I could just about make out within. The micropyle was dark with a pale areola, and I guessed it was quite near hatching. Two millimeters across, as measured by the scale on the edge of Klots's eastern Peterson Field Guide, it was one-third smaller than *M. yuccae*'s egg.

So twice in two days, I was graced by rarities. This one I had really worked for, even after all indications said to give up and go find a cold beer. The April Fools' joke on me, though, was that I seemed to have left my Klots field guide atop Powdermilk, and driven off without it. The 1954 Klots has been replaced in the Peterson Field Guide series by Paul Opler's excellent modern text, but the Klots is still a great classic that I frequently consult and enjoy. At least this was my paperback copy—not my hardcover Klots, the first book I ever bought with my own money. I would never subject it to the rigors and risks of travel.

"You've got to stop putting things on top of the car!" I told myself for the billionth time. A few years ago, I'd left my ancient wallet atop Thea's truck, on a California freeway. It returned to me two months later, and I still use it. And then there was Mr. Key and the collecting bag. But one is not always so lucky. If my Klots did not come back to me, I only hoped that Molly would find it and put it to good use it in her garden, or perhaps one of the many daughters of 159th Terrace.

One-quarter of the way into the year, the dearth of the West Coast winter was just a bad dream. In Madison, Florida, drifted in cream dogwoods and magenta rhodies, a café offered "gator tail & conch meat." Eschewing the local food for a change, I grabbed a mere hot dog. The flowery roadside park where I stopped for lunch throbbed with fifteen species of common butterflies. After Cherry Lake, crimson clover appeared on the roadsides. Camp time found me back in Georgia, along the Suwannee River.

In the foggy dawn, long tresses of Spanish moss touched their own reflections, suggesting the lichen *Usnea longissima* on our own rivers back home. This so-called moss is actually a bromeliad, or air plant, called *Tillandsia usneoides* (= "like usnea"). The mist lifted into a gorgeous blue-sky day for wending through Georgia. Crab apple blossom peppered with sulphurs and skippers stopped me long enough to notice the Twin Rivers State Forest and Wildlife Management Area. Though I'd been finding lots of northern and confused cloudywings, I'd failed again and again to discern a southern. So at the end of a walk here among longleaf and bunch grass, I was delighted to find my first unequivocal *Thorybes bathyllus*, smack in the middle of the trail.

Having once experienced a heavenly float on the Suwannee below its source, I hated to leave without seeing one of the great southern springs, so when I came to Blue Spring State Park, I ducked in. The round pool bubbles up next to the Withlacoochee River (Suwannee's "Twin" of the state forest's name). There were two scuba divers and a couple of watchers. I'd have loved to swim, but mosquitoes were legion, and disrobing sounded suicidal. I satisfied myself with dunking my scratchy legs and sweaty head. In an

accent I could barely understand, a well-liquored man in his thirties asked me if this was Blue Springs. I assured him it was. "But
it 'posed to be BLOO!" complained a woman with him, as if the
discrepancy were somehow my responsibility. "They say they's a big
cliff yoo can *dahve* off of," he said. "I wanna *dahve.*" The signs about
diving here referred to scuba, except the big one that clearly stated
"No Diving from Rocks."

Outside the handsome Quitman County Courthouse, prisoners
on a work crew wore comic-book black-and-white striped pajamas.
Along country lanes with names like Dew Berry Short and Old Egg
Road, lay bales of longleaf pine needles tied with orange twine.
Peanut and cotton fields stretched out between tall hedges of oaks
and great color fields of dogwood, white rose, rhodies, azaleas, and
flowering fruit trees. Hot and sticky in Pelham, Georgia, ("Founded
1881: A Special Place"), I drank a cold Jamaican Red Stripe Lager to
my truck driver friend Jonathan P. Pelham, a.k.a. Jamaica, author of
my running orders, the freshly published *Catalogue of the Butterflies
of the United States and Canada.*

In Camilla, unable to escape it and as sealed up as I could get, I
drove through mosquito "fogging." Intensified spraying since West
Nile virus surfaced has been rough on butterflies. One gardener
in Florida found dozens of palamedes larvae dying after the fogging truck passed. Just over the Flint River, I thought a palamedes
crossed my bow in cloud and light sprinkle. But then I realized it
must be a promethea moth, which (along with several of our black
and blue swallowtails) is a mimic of the distasteful pipevine swallowtail. The resemblance had duped me, as it was meant to dupe
the birds. The several species of giant silk moths each fly at a particular hour of day or night, to ensure that their similar pheromones
don't lead to useless hybrid matings. Now this promethea reminded
me of a faceful of scent that had hit me hard as I madly quartered
the UF campus in Gainesville, looking for the meeting. That blast
had been pheromones of a female cecropia moth calling, an aroma
I knew well from rearing the giant "robin moths" as a boy. Mosquito
"fogging," streetlighting, and parasitic flies introduced as biocontrol
agents have battered populations of all of these big silk moths.

In the south Georgia countryside, modern houses alternated

with dilapidated old cabins and shacks. Out of the dusk loomed the most amazing antebellum ruin of a giant-pillared and gabled plantation house. One of its pillars fallen like a redwood, this once-grand pile staggered beside a doublewide. I took a thirty-four-dollar room in the prefab Fort Gaines Inn Motel. Glum from the fogging and the overall sense of decay, I was further dismayed when I talked with Thea and she told me the results of her recent blood test. Her tumor marker had risen. I uttered a pagan prayer for her health à la Melville's Ishmael: Stand by me, hold me, bind me, O ye blessed influences!

Across the Chatahoochee River squatted the big plug of Walter F. George dam and its "lake," named for a local congressional pork-meister. In the visitor center, the Army Corps was forthright about double-crossing and land stealing from the Indians, less so about the displaced denizens of the dammed river. I crossed the dam into Alabama, buckeyes and pipevines hilltopping in the middle, the highest elevation I'd attained in a month. On mudstone bluffs below the reservoir, butterflies sipped minerals, while mud flats opposite hosted a great mass of birdlife and dozens of turtles, some the size of trash-can lids. A siren signaled a lock discharge, a great rush that washed all the cormorants into the roiled water. They came up with fish, looking for all the world as if they enjoyed the game. Maybe the Corps had something to offer the inhabitants after all.

Drag Nasty Creek Road. Cool Branch Road. Loner Lumpkin Road. This last I took to the Eufaula National Wildlife Refuge, hoping to find the little gray skipper *Lerodea eufala* there, but no such luck. A monarch gilded the crimson clover and eastern tailed-blue males shimmered almost unbearably blue on white clover. Even at 7:30 in the evening, there was one more butterfly to be seen. Beside a wildlife observation tower, sun about to go down, a form flew up from the sand, flickered about, and landed, again and again. Has to be a *Vanessa,* I thought, and it was *V. atalanta.* For half an hour I watched it rise, chase, and re-alight, spreading its shocking crimson bands to the last beams, then closing into a flake of wood ash. Promptly at eight o'clock it launched again and did not return. My relationship with red admirables goes back to fifth grade, when I first watched such a twilight spectacle by an old barn along a country canal. Watching this one was as good as seeing something new for the list, and it softened my funk from the previous eve.

Over a 10 P.M. breakfast at a Waffle King in Phenix City, I read Lucien Harris's *Butterflies of Georgia* and decided to bolt for Old Fort Mountain in north Georgia to escape the relentless heat and seek some springtime boreal species. Somewhere on the drive of half the length of the state, escaping Atlanta by a wide bypass, Powdermilk passed 365,000 miles. I salvaged the used up end of the night in a rest area beyond White. In the morning I learned afresh the meaning of one of the truest aphorisms, be careful what you wish for: it was fifty degrees and socked in. Over one of my more memorable breakfasts—white toast from the Waffle King, grape jelly, rancid peanut butter, and cold coffee—I watched a mocker on the drinking fountain, and six blue jays on the lawn finding some sort of nut. Like our western Steller's, they are beautiful birds, for all they are despised by some.

New Echota, at the head of the Oostanaula River, formed by the confluence of the Coosawatee and Conasauga rivers, was the capital of the Cherokee Nation—the seat of an effective self-government, economy, and the first Indian-language newspaper, thanks to the alphabet contrived by Sequoya. They were a sovereign nation recognized by the Supreme Court, the only American Indians with a republican form of government supported by a written constitution. But that didn't save them from the bogus treaty of 1835, under which the natives relinquished their land east of Mississippi. Seven thousand federal and state troops came and, on May 26, 1838, began the roundup, internment, and deportation of fifteen thousand Cherokees, driving them on the Trail of Tears to Oklahoma. Now the highway here is named the Trail of Tears Highway.

This was the fortieth anniversary of Martin Luther King's assassination. Had I gone west instead of north, it would have been through Selma, Alabama. You can't move about the South, or the United States for that matter, without running into the field marks of oppression and its aftermath. Plus, Georgia has some of the ugliest highway billboards anywhere. But the rain and cool felt like home, and the redbud in bloom was beautiful. Spring Place was certainly that: the trees just leafing out, with redbud, cherry blos-

som, and phlox banks all blooming in their own particular pinks. I
took a violet-strewn path down to an agate-built springhouse on a
sneezeweed-yellow and green brook with phlox swards under big
oaks. Yesterday in the sun it would have been a butterfly walk. Now,
it was just pretty.

Entering the Appalachians after Chatsworth, I traded the attractive but tame and crowded Piedmont for actual *mountains*. After
a month in Florida, that felt damn good to this Colorado boy. The
white-and-purple *Viola*-spattered roadside was worth the drive
on its own. In *Wild America*, Roger Peterson wrote that "North
America, with nearly 80 species, is abundantly blessed with violets."
Nowhere had I seen that better expressed. On a warm summer's
day that would also mean "abundantly dressed in fritillaries," since
they almost all depend upon violets. None today, in thick cloud that
might as well have been a bale of cotton. I was almost the only boll
weevil on the mountain. Another state park to the west was actually
named Cloudland. But the youth behind the desk at Fort Mountain
State Park told me it had been clear on top when he went up on his
lunch break. "Those clouds'll likely blow out," he said. So I paid my
three-dollar day fee and headed up the mountain, and the clouds
did clear out except for overcast.

I was about to hike to the top when the cloud mass moved back
in like a fist, the air darkened, the rain began to pelt, and thunder
rolled. It beat the hot, frantic, and overpeopled lowlands, except
for the absence of butterflies. I still hoped the sun would come—it
was only 3:00 P.M. butterfly time—and the orangetips, azures, and
elfins I sought here in the southernmost boreal would all pop out.
But time was the only thing that flew by. I decided to make a circle
through the higher mountains and return tomorrow if clear.

I reconnoitered almost to Georgia's crest at Brasstown Bald, then
dropped south. Last year's bleached leaves hung on the beeches at
Wolf Pen Gap, still in early spring at 3,260 feet, and laurels were
a long way from blooming. I dropped another three dollars for a
campsite at Lake Winfield Scott, where a family invited me to sit
by their campfire. I heard a long story of delivering cattle from
Georgia to Texas and back via North Carolina, with attendant adventures. Landon, cute in his garbage bag raincoat, thought I was

Santa on vacation, so I put the "be good" on him. In easy-on-the-ear Georgian, his folks asked, "Will yew be feeshin' in the mornin' when it clears out?" I said I'd be moving on. We agreed that we really loved camping, or we were all crazy, or both. They did not offer me a beer in that dry county, but the fellowship of their fireside was even better.

"Hallelujah He Is Risen" said the reader board on Mt. Lebanon Baptist Church. They meant someone else entirely, it's true; but I had indeed risen from my sodden camp, also from the south to the north, both botanically and seasonally. In a store for granola bars, milk, and coffee, I saw on TV that the whole region, from the Florida Panhandle north, was deluged; a westerly route might have brought no more butterflies than this. At Deep Hole on the Toccoa River, six men in camo and beer guts and one woman without the camo pulled in rainbows and bantered, "What yew *feeshin'* with?" Here in Deep Appalachia, I was keeping a wary eye peeled for old Clifton Clowers. But the national forest was pretty broken up, and much of the private land was getting prettified and tame, with the inholdings subdivided into river lots.

But this *was* still Georgia—if not Wolverton Mountain, at least maybe closer to 1950s Selma than to the Atlanta of today. Martin's Dixie Department Store, a modern log throw-up, had signs reading "Huntin' & Fishin' HQ," "Ammo-Lottery-Rebel," "Entering Civilization," "Confederate Owned," and "Jumbo Boiled Peanuts," all framed by Confederate flags. And a yellow reader board: "Bohica! Snafu! Fubar! Welcome to Obama's America. Eenie Meenie Minie Mo—You will reap what you sow." I could've used a warm-up on the coffee, but not there.

In unlovely Ellijay, Col. Poole's Bar-B-Q (the "Taj-Ma-Hog") had a Pig Hill of Fame. Dozens of pig-shaped cutout signs pixilated a giant pig on the hillside in blue, yellow, and white, bearing the names of pigs: Willis, B.A.D., Plenty, Bunker, Attaboy, Gropen Atta, Pollywatt; or those of pig farmers, all "Painted by Oscar Pig-casso." On the porch stood a dime-a-ride bucking boar named Piggy. The colonel's hefty son, Darvin Poole, a retired math teacher, welcomed me warmly and gave me a postcard, as the radio evangelist Charles Sims put a prayer in my other hand. From the walls, big pictures of George & Laura, George & Barbara, Pat Buchanan, Mary Kay, Miss America, all the colonel's pals looked down, with many commendations from admirers. I was tempted to give this place a pass too, but it smelled so good and I was so hungry and protein-starved that I fell for a Republican sandwich anyway. I'd passed many little barbecues, but never at mealtime. Over my named pig, I read my prayer. It included "May He accept your burnt offerings," which seemed just right for the Taj-Ma-Hog. It was still raining.

Back at Fort Mountain, I walked to the top, guarded by the urgent ejaculations of a gray squirrel in the gray drizzle. I walked along the 885-foot stone wall of the "Fort." An old interpretive sign headed "Mystery Shrouds Fort Mountain" related the builders and their purpose to sun worship, last-ditch defense by "prehistoric white people," bloody warfare between rival Indian tribes, defense fortification for Spanish conquistadors hunting gold, and a honeymoon haven for Cherokee Indian newlyweds, as well as an early European visit by one Prince Madoc of Wales. In the dim black-and-white light, the only ancient presence I could discern was one black-and-white warbler. Some sort of pupa huddled in the rocks of the fort, and a brown geometrid nestled in the stonework of the Loo in the Clouds were as close as I got to butterflies in boreal Georgia.

As I retreated into the dusk through green countryside, a pickup charged past me with no lights. Four troopers with full lights gave chase at seventy or eighty miles per hour. A little way on, in the outskirts of Villanow, I saw the cherry-tops at roost around a farmhouse, and then three more arrived. Not wanting to catch any stray lead, I veered away. This cannot end well for everyone involved, I thought. Then three sheriffs' cars passed me in the other direction. Even in little LaFayette, two local cops were all over a small pickup. It was a rough night in Georgia.

12. GOING TO GRACELAND

From the freeway into Tennessee, limestone benches were topped with peaking redbud and huge fireworks signs. I fled the big roads and wended back across the Tennessee River to the village of New Hope. A small sign caught my eye, pointing to the Shrine of the Virgin of the Poor. I took the little lane, through woods full of spring beauties, to a hilltop where sat the shrine.

It was an open, rustic chapel, in commemoration of the one in Liège for eleven-year-old Mariette Beco's Marian sightings in Banneux, Belgium. It had a handsome stone-built base and arch, a local limestone slab for an altar, and beautiful mosaics of Mary and Mariette surrounded by blue flowers and sun and moon faces in the corners. Wrought-iron leaves and tendrils draped river-stone pillars with the carved faces of human, cow, eagle, and lion. I made my devotions, especially to Sun and Moon. Aeschnids were hilltop-ping, and then the sun came out, and a big tiger swallowtail cruised and visited Easterish violets and dandelions. A black female tiger with its own blue mosaic, and a spicebush with its green, came to the phlox. I didn't see the Philenor they both mimicked, but it had to be around. Then two young men on loud dirt bikes roared up. I told them this was neither the place nor the time for their racket, on a Sunday, with people at their devotions. The first looked dumb-founded, or just dumb. He said, "We're just going through to the woods over there." Okay, then do it. They looked, came back, and then roared off with loud brays of their motors. But I didn't care. I was thrilled to be back in the warmth, having escaped the heat for two days of *cold*. "Amazing Grace" was on the Celtic show out of Chattanooga, the suns within and without were smiling, and I was back in the butterflies.

And in grace! Beside the little paved loop at the edge of the woods with the stations of the cross, up popped . . . yes! A falcate orangetip! Just the butterfly I'd hoped to find on Fort Mountain—a fresh male *Anthocharis midea*, tiny, about the size of a silvery blue. I netted, examined, and placed it on a violet, small, blue-purple and yellow-centered, where it was bound in the first place. He sat until I picked him up and held him in the sun, when he warmed and flew off to another violet and drank deeply. A female nectared on a periwinkle, then tried an English bluebell but couldn't figure out how to get in. A bumblebee hawkmoth arrived to show her how it was done, but she'd moved on to a chickweed. For several minutes I watched her on the left, him on the right, equidistant and partly spread. She dallied with a cress, but I could find no egg.

Then, as I checked a piney edge for pine elfins, lo! A larger white with a more robust flight appeared. I netted it—a flight-worn male, almost immaculate white, like a summer margined white at home— with very little scaling along the ventral veins. But the books (including my own) all say *Pieris napi* (= *oleracea*), the mustard white, gets nowhere near here—so it *has* to be *Pieris virginiensis*! The West Virginia white was my other great hope for the north Georgian diversion. This one was entirely new for me. I've wanted to see *P. virginiensis* ever since Dr. Walfried J. Reinthal sent me a pair from east Tennessee some forty-five years ago in exchange for live hackberry butterflies. I'd pored over those two, with the faint gray scales along the veins, over and over, until they were broken in some dreadful accident, and I could hardly bear to look at my inexpert repair of their damaged wings. But this was the butterfly itself—the real thing, alive, and right near the southern edge of its range. What word works but grace?

Four more four-wheelers charged down the woodland path from the east, but seeing where they were, they had the manners to turn around and go back from where they'd come. Again I had the shrine to myself, plus Mary, Mariette, and Marsha. And those two blessed pierids.

Having a bit of lunch on the rough-cut stone bench, Carr's water crackers, cheddar, tomato, and a drop of wine (for Mary), I thought about how *P. virginiensis* was my third year-butterfly with that specific epithet, none of which are confined to Virginia, as their shared name implies. But then *Lutra, Castor,* and *Cervus canadensis*—otter, beaver, and elk—each range well beyond Canada also. I thought too about how I had once again squandered much of the day near my starting point—but squandered it well.

On the lane below, more orangetips nectared on spring beauties and violets. Back down the road, a fresh tiger tried a dandelion clock, gave up, and connected with a daisy, as a monarch shot through New Hope, northbound: a biological definition of Hope.

South a ways, there was supposed to be a free ferry across the Tennessee River that would save me having to go back to the freeway. Somehow, I never managed to find it. But I did find—and this was just how I'd hoped to discover the best places, like the shrine, out of a combination of hunch and happenstance—a rich woodland on limestone benches running down to the road, which occupied the last level before the river. The spring green slopes burgeoned with spring beauty, a pure white anemone, and other flowers new to me. Right off I saw falcate orangetips, and then West Virginia whites—they were both here too, this time more whites than orangetips. I saw one or two dozen of them, working the roadside, rising up and dropping down the slope. They flirted with the anemones, a lovely pairing, but nectared exclusively on a white flower I didn't know. This place reminded me very much of slopes above the Columbia River near home, just as green but with different constituents: margined whites on ladies' smocks.

Farther south, I passed three lads coming up from tubing and fishing in the river. They gestured, just to say hi, and when I went back to see if they'd meant me to stop, one said, "Hi, Old Man." There was a brief misunderstanding that I had dissed them and then come back to hassle, but soon we all understood that we wished one another goodwill. We spoke almost different languages. It made my heart glad to see them *out* there, in a time when so few of the young ever willingly relinquish their built and wired world.

Sometime after midnight I saluted the Davy Crockett statue in Lawrenceburg's fine town square. His coonskin cap had no tail, unlike the one I got with box tops back when I was crazy about Fess Parker's Crockett on 1950s television. Somewhere between the Natchez Trace and Savannah, an armadillo shuffled along the centerline. There was a rare set of oncoming headlights, so I went back to shoo the animal off the road. The lights belonged to a trooper, who watched all this and stopped me. "Are you lost?" he asked.

"No, sir," I said, "I'm going to Graceland."

He was fine with that. "But don't worry," he said, nodding in the direction the armadillo had waddled into the brush. "We've got plenty o' *them*."

After driving all night across Tennessee and napping at two Wal-Marts (they've got plenty o' them too), and navigating horrid Memphis morning traffic, I arrived at Elvis Presley Boulevard at 7:00 A.M. When I had telephoned the 1-800 number, I'd learned that to visit Graceland, you had to take a tour, which I had no wish to do. Besides, for the price of the cheapest tour, I could see Scorsese's new Rolling Stones movie, with dinner and wine thrown in; not that I could afford either. "Ma'am," I persisted, "is there no way to pay your respects at the graveside without taking a tour?" With a clipped reluctance that was palpable over the telephone wire, the woman said, "There is a free hour between seven-thirty and eight-thirty A.M.," and hung up. So here I was, punctual for a change. For the King.

There was Heartbreak Hotel, there were his airplanes. The parking lot was not open yet—where to go for the free visitation hour? Then I saw a fellow loner, parked in an old van outside the very gate of Graceland, in a "no parking" bay for shuttle buses. But he told me that this was the place, and parking was allowed and free for the morning hour. Sunrise beside the mansion was a picture through the trees, a contrail shooting straight up between the house and the sun. The stone wall outside was covered with graffiti, mostly love notes like "Before Elvis There Was Nothing—KJN." The sidewalk bore a flight of butterflies, drawn by Paula, Zeus, Davie, Leigh Ann, Ashley, and Alyssa.

So at 7:30 A.M. I was in, for free, with just a reverent handful of other pilgrims and devouts, led by a redhead from Ontario. Toni had been here all week, taking the tours every day and taking advantage of this peaceful hour each morning as well. And it *was* peaceful. The tomb lay in El's meditation garden. There was a little round fountain and a pool behind the four graves (plus one empty space), the whole surrounded by a pillared bower with stained-glass windows in a brick wall, and a live mockingbird singing in a pruned tree with orange berries, through what arrangement I cannot say.

A big marble Jesus (with angels at his feet & PRESLEY on the plinth) *did* have E's mouth (I know: so do I) and a hint of the famous sneer. Elvis's grave, an eternal flame burning in a copper lamp by his head, was strewn with flowers and memorabilia. I duly placed a copy of *Orion Magazine* with my fellow columnist Rebecca Solnit's essay "One Nation Under Elvis" on the grave, as promised.

I remembered August 16, 1977, in the Davara Hotel in Port Moresby, Papua New Guinea, as hot as Memphis was going to be today, when I heard that Elvis had died, and how it made me cry. I'd grown up with his songs. I like what his father, Vernon, wrote for a plaque near the grave: "He was admired not only as an entertainer, but as the great humanitarian that he was; for his generosity, and his kind feelings toward his fellow man," et cetera. And he was no racist: *Blue Hawaii* and *King Creole* maybe weren't great films, but they were socially ahead of their time. Every one of the few of us present was reverent, quiet, and somewhat starstruck in absentia. I liked Elvis; but I think most of those folks were still grieving.

The house itself was handsome—surprisingly modest, tasteful, and unpretentious by today's megamansion standards. Friendly green shutters opened beside two lions, one rampant, one regardant, beside a circular drive under tupelo trees and azaleas. A white-throated sparrow sang over the leaf blowers, which I know damn well El would not have brooked. Robins and gray squirrels worked the pleasantly scruffy, unsprayed lawn. A yellow flurry over a low, swampy place near the wall resolved into dozens of goldfinches.

Toni and her pal Jean, from Liverpool, said goodbye on their way out. They said they'd seen a scarlet tanager yesterday and that there was a butterfly print hanging in the house. I saw no flying butterflies at Graceland, as it was a little early in the day for them; but there were at least two unidentified species there on the sidewalk graffito. Of course I was the last to leave, when they kicked me out at nine. I stopped at the Krispy Kreme on Elvis Presley Boulevard to find my well-hidden copy of Bryant Mather's *Butterflies of Mississippi* before striking off down the Delta. For a panicked moment, I couldn't find my collecting bag. And then I remembered: I'd put it in the cooler. Now that's grace.

13. DELTA BLUES

Mississippi at 11:00 A.M.: subdivisions, casino billboards, green fields, hazy air on a bright spring day. This black-soil, chemical-crop desert was dramatically *flat* land, rather like southwest Idaho's potato barrens. It was pesticide city; you could smell that much. I passed a big spray rig doing classic, old-fashioned, big-boom roadside spraying, right beside a wetland. Maybe that was the point—maybe it was for mosquitoes. I rushed to raise the windows and shut the vents. And then a crop-duster flew over.

Kenny Rogers was to appear at one of the many river casinos on April 17—if I hung around, I could score some autograph hits. At the Tunica visitor center, the young woman in a butterfly skirt said she'd had monarchs at her tulips the other day. A monarch northing up the Mississippi flyway made sense, if not the tulips, which lack nectaries. At the next welcome center, where Miss. 1 (the Great River Road) begins, I saw purple martins and house sparrows nesting together in the same three martin houses. Adult and young weaver finches sat at some doors, the big swallows at others—all together, quite companionably.

My third visitor center for the day came when I crossed the Mississippi River to Helena, Arkansas. Hostess Pam had butterflies all over and a poster for the Mount Magazine Butterfly Festival in northwestern Arkansas. Thea and I had enjoyed a fine visit there with the park naturalists Don Simons and Lori Spencer, author of *Arkansas Butterflies,* when I spoke at the festival. I'd have loved to go there now, but it was too early for Diana (the park's specialty), and I doubted I'd get back: just too many directions on the compass rose. Meanwhile, Pam's butterfly garden had the usual suspects, as well as a striking brown and yellow-striped nessus sphinx moth.

Tarpaper shacks lined dirt roads into the woods above, with a few hot butterflies in their gardens.

Downtown, John and Thomas invited me into the Delta Heritage Center. There was a radio setup, and they said had I been there earlier, I'd've been dragooned onto the air for *King Biscuit Time* on KFFA. The program originated in 1941, and since 1951, "Sunshine" Sonny Payne has been airing blues and interviews with just about anyone who comes through. I had my mouth harp too; I blew my chance to blow the "Xerces Blue Blues" on the same show that Sonny Boy Williamson, Robert "Junior" Lockwood, and Pinetop Perkins had played live.

Is the town as down as it seems? They said pretty much, but the blues festival still rocks. John and Thomas suggested I drive up onto the levee—the waters were as high as they'd ever seen them, flowing over the road and campground way above the river, right up to the town dike. I did, and the flood was indeed impressive. Mike, a teacher from Portland, Oregon, had walked his students up to see it for a field trip. The kids had grown up here, but they were wide-eyed. Later, from the bridge, I could really see how hugely flooded Old Man River was. Walden's Landing Casino was almost an island. But the floods can be worse. After months of rain, the Mississippi River broke the levee at Mound Landing near here on April 21, 1927, causing widespread death and destruction in seven states. This flood was raising eyebrows but not roofs.

On the bridge approach, a bright orange flash resolved into a goatweed emperor. It flew alongside Powdermilk for a hundred yards—what a remarkable thing to see it flapping, from above, for so far! It did not cross the state line but eventually headed back to Arkansas. On the Mississippi side, riparian strips of willow and bald cypress stretched across the flensed and flooded land like spider veins. Sleepy, I pulled into tiny Gunnison. Behind its sole street I napped, mourning doves moaning me to sleep in the moist, torrid air. Upon waking, I found myself in a butterfly and flower oasis— vetch, violets, and blackberry beneath nut trees in deep grass, with pearl crescents, checkered-skippers, monarchs, and orange sulphurs all over them. Red-banded hairstreaks sipped on blackberry, blue petticoats showing as they sawed their hindwings.

The Great River Road State Park was subaquatic, its fee station halfway under, the words "Great River Road" underlined by the Mississippi River, in which I dipped my foot. On the dike, a big orange fox squirrel leaped among flooded selvage across a slough, cardinals and hundreds of cowbirds at dandelion seed; that's lots of parasitized nests. In nearby Beulah, black boys shot hoops in a one-basket court opposite the old cemetery: the quick and the dead. It was the graveyard of General Charles Clark, Confederate governor of Mississippi (1863–65) and master of the Doro Plantation. What would he have thought of the hoopsters dancing on his grave?

The Mississippi sun melted into the big orange pool of a flooded slough, like a butter pat at the Waffle King. Then it morphed into a cherry and sucked the mosquitoes down with it into the pink punch of Ole Miss. It was good that I hadn't arrived in Memphis much earlier, or stayed any longer. The fortieth anniversary of Martin Luther King's death was marked with a mass event, including appearances by the presidential candidates; and tonight Memphis was playing for the NCAA championship. I was happy to be heading for a burger, a beer, and a bed in Greenville. It was also good that I didn't know Greenville had good blues clubs. I lacked the steam to seek them out, and I would have fallen asleep in my beer.

But first, since I was here in the Delta, I thought I'd better at least listen to Robert Johnson's "Cross Road Blues." At dusk I found me a likely crossroads and plunked in the tape. The raw guitar notes mixed smoothly with the peepers and crickets, the crescent moon hung over the river. Robert sang "Me and the Devil was walkin' side by side," and the odometer read 366,066.6, 066.6 miles. (Okay, I engineered that a little.) I saw neither Robert nor the Devil; I guess it's supposed to be at midnight, not twilight. But that's okay: this was one of the few days when I personally witnessed both sunrise and sunset, and it started and finished in the company of blues masters, Elvis and Robert.

Next morning, out by the levee, Rory's store was a great old place with Wall-o-Matics. Over a BLT, I met the wildlife biologists Rob Bellinger and Todd Davis. I told them I was searching for certain butterflies whose larvae feed on giant cane, Arundinaria. They gave me advice on finding a good canebrake: "Turn left at the round barn, then right on Nipper Road, after the big gin." I asked a grizzled fellow outside in a pickup for his opinion too. He used to make fishing poles out of the cane. "But," he said, "that cane is gettin' *scaice!*" I should have asked him where to find some Delta blues too; I suspect it would have been the same answer. He was listening to blues, but it must have been a tape: I couldn't find one bent note on the radio dial. I headed out, looking to raise some cane.

Along Nipper Road, past the big gin and an old, round, vine-hung barn, the cane was there as advertised. I thrust deep into the giant canes with Marsha, through thick poison ivy and mosquitoes, down to the edge of the flooded bayou: flared cypress butts and knees, a cacophony of amphibians and birds, great white egret floating over, lizards on the floor, branches falling into the black water. This was more like the Delta as I imagined it. One ghostly glimpse of a pearly-eye shadowed past into deep shadow, but I couldn't get to it through the dense "bamboo." I made it down to the edge of the oxbow, lined by yellow flowers, then retreated gingerly to the road through the poison ivy.

A red admirable came to Marsha and sucked sweat from her rim, bag, and ropework. As I walked up and down the road looking for cane satyrs and skippers, each time I passed the admirable came to me. Once it landed on my hand just as I had caught a goatweed. Picture scarlet-banded *atalanta* sucking sweat from my left hand as I open brilliant orange *andria*'s wings with my right. Here were both of the great, uncatchable High Line Canal barnyard butterflies of my youth at once—two birds in hand! As I released the goatweed, they both exploded. Back at Powdermilk I heard a flapping: another red admirable was batting around inside her.

Pulling into the Yazoo National Wildlife Refuge, I saw a fellow in uniform on a tractor. He stopped, took his earmuffs off, and introduced himself as Joe Fontaine, manager of the refuge. He showed me his butterfly garden, mostly milkweed, which had one pert zebra swallowtail in residence. Joe steered me to another canebrake along the forest edge, on the way to Swan Lake. I walked it until the sun hazed at five and the mosquito scream grew constant. No cane 'flies, but on the way out, something orange popped up—a painted lady doing its late-day bat-and-bask routine, a frantic folly that might explain the term "going batshit." My first eastern *Vanessa carkui*, it engaged a monarch, then alighted again and again at my feet—but not on my hand. It was larger, longer-winged than the little ones at Willow Beach in Arizona, maybe a second brood. And here was one to file with the sparrows and the martins: out on the far shore of Beargarden Lake, there was a gathering of two hundred plus white herons and egrets—the first heronry I was willing to call a rookery, because mixed in with the herons were scores of crows! A study in black and white. Speaking of which, the next town, Nitta Yuma, was largely big houses and big white men wrangling riding mowers; while the next, Anguilla, was all rickety trailers and black, like a refugee village in Angola. The gots and don't gots don't get much starker than deep in the Delta.

Past Rolling Fork, now that the day was almost done, I reached my day's target: Delta National Forest. The peeper chorus in a flooded slough of the Sunflower River was so loud and high-pitched that it almost hurt my ears. The public boat ramp on the Big Sunflower River was riverbed, and after Holly Bluff, there were toads in the road. This levee road went on seemingly forever into a black night full of frog song, mosquitoes, and water lapping at both sides. The road became nothing more than a narrow dike, and dikes had been failing daily around there. Finally the road overflowed, leaving barely a Powdermilk's width to get by. It would have been a very long way back, with no room to turn around, one hell of a place for a flat, or to get stuck. Headlights barely penetrating the murk, I tried not to imagine slipping off an eroding edge or driving off a broken road into the drink, to be found a few months later among rotting washup in a root-strangled slough. How in hell had I got here? But I finally reached Satartia. Then the highway, and dead Vicksburg, with nothing open but the many lurid casinos down along the river. "Only one thing I did wrong," wrote Dylan, "stayed in Mississippi a day too long." It was getting that way, so I crossed into Louisiana.

Rolling west, for once grateful for a freeway, I tried the radio for some Delta blues before I left the Delta behind. But they were scaice, to be sure. The entire dial, both AM and FM, back and forth, gave forth only corn country, old country, slick country, hip-hop, oldies, lots of milk of magnesia–cum–instant oatmeal schlock, lots and lots of religious, public radio pledge drives, hate and scare rants, idiot call-ins, and so on. There was something loosely called R & B, which had very little to do with actual blues. The closest thing I could find was a local program of black gospel.

I wish the reason for the blues had remained just as scaice. When I telephoned Thea to let her know I was safely back on the road, homeward bound, she had bad news. A CT scan had disclosed a tumor near her spine. I remembered the back pain she'd experienced at times in Florida. She would have to have an operation, as soon as it could be arranged, followed by another course of chemotherapy. I drove on, stunned. I was so hoping that Thea would stay well for the year . . . for good.

14. HIGH POINTS AND LOW

An overcast, muggy morn in Louisiana suited the mood. Back in the scary night, when I drove my Honda to the levee and the levee was wet, I'd passed a Mississippi hamlet somewhere out there in the flood with the perhaps unreasonably optimistic name of Onward. Thea told me that the last thing she wanted me to do was interrupt the Big Year, or plod on disabled with worry. The prognosis was good, as far as they could tell, and the surgery—complicated by the need for two busy doctors to cooperate in the procedure—wouldn't be scheduled before I could get back. So, though shaken, I resolved to carry on as positively as I could. There were many miles to cover and habitats to visit. I could not indulge the inertia of sadness and still make this work. Nor could I afford to lose momentum—one of my few scheduled lectures for the year awaited me in Denton, Texas, in just two days. So: onward.

Again I planned to make a national forest detour. After so many places where Marsha was not welcome, the national forests offered the freedom we both missed, as well as good, undeveloped habitat. But first, southwest of yet another Quitman, I stopped at a thistly roadside. The cool clouds gave way to hot part sun. Fully twenty-five species of butterflies tippled along the verge, including five kinds of massive swallowtails. A Virginia lady on crimson clover attempted a new definition of shocking pink. An olive-sided flycatcher invited me to "pick THREE beers," and I wasn't even interested.

And then something new and exciting, just what I needed to jack me out of my funk. It was nothing big, like the scores of swallowtails all around me; nothing brilliant, like the tailed-blues shimmering over the flowers. It was a definitive LBB—"little brown bird" to our friends, "little brown butterfly" to us. I had dropped down the bank into a roadside canebrake. Peering through the canes, I saw a thistly field open up beyond, fringed by a high windrow of longleaf pines. I couldn't get in, as there was a very serious fence in the way. But my eyes were drawn to a small brown wedge on a buttercup—*a buttercup!*, I thought, on which few butterflies ever nectar. I could see it very well, its sienna wings with a chestnut band and black-and-white zigzag dashes. There was no mistaking it: an eastern pine elfin. This mostly northern species flies only in spring, and I had all but given up on it. *Callophrys niphon* reaches its southwestern limit not far from there, so this really was my very last chance. It was a little tatty, but I didn't mind if it didn't.

Across the road, climbing up a deer stand in the pinewood, I surprised a green anole and a blue-tailed skink lolling together on top. Then, back at Powdermilk, I found a sheriff's deputy awaiting me to see what the deal was. He seemed to be on work release from the donut shop, or maybe a fried pie stand. I gave him my Xerces card, which he scrutinized with a frown of concentration, then turned over and over with his stubby but pistol-hardened fingers. After a significant pause, while he sized me up, the deputy looked me in the eye and spoke. "So," he said, "you're with this *exorcist* society?"

"No, sir," I said. "No exorcisms. Just butterflies."

In Bienville Parish, I looked around a junky, partially bulldozed area where red-dirt roads ran alongside pinewoods. I netted a gemmed satyr, then noticed a little larger satyr flitting along the edge of the woods. It alighted momentarily and I saw very well the loopy red pattern around the eyespots that only our three rare members of the genus *Neonympha* possess. Excited, I lurched for it but was repulsed (and impaled) by a wall of catbrier, and the satyr vanished into the shadows, as they are so adept at doing. Once I extracted myself from the claws of the *Smilax*, I found a way into the wood. But coming to a backyard that had *Deliverance* written all over it and a big sleeping dog, I retreated. I never found the satyr again. This was in dry upland pinewoods, which inclines toward the butterfly being the little-known helicta satyr. But the site lay within the range, if not boggy habitat, of the Georgia satyr. The third candidate, the federally endangered Mitchell's satyr, was known no nearer than central Alabama, so it probably wasn't that. Logic argues for *N. helicta,* but without a specimen or a photograph, there was no knowing for sure which *Neonympha* I'd seen. So that made one for two today; .500 is good in baseball, but I wished I'd caught that red-looped brown just the same.

I should have been southing, but seeing a sign for it and being near, I found my way slightly north to Driskill Mountain: the highest point in Louisiana. The trail up was a hot mile's hike through pretty woods with remarkable fringe trees in bloom, shed bits lying around on the ground like Silly String. Three species each of swallowtails, satyrs, and duskywings kept me company on the walk up. But what was that lime green swallowtail flying up the trail at a fast clip? Too pale for a *troilus,* tails too long . . . why, it was a luna moth, out in full daylight! Only the second I'd seen, since a tatty one in the meadow of the no-see-ums. A palmate-leaved shrub with bright red trumpet flowers lined the trail, but this held no attraction for the normally nocturnal luna: the giant silk moths lack functional mouthparts, living off fat and flesh laid down by the larvae.

The lofty top of dread Driskill, 535 breathtaking feet above sea level, was owned by two red-spotted purples challenging two giant swallowtails in a perpetual parade of colorful, circling gliders among the viburnums where Carolina satyrs nectared. Out of the bustle, in a quiet glade on the way to the Jordan Mountain overlook, a lone hilltopping skipper spread warm brown wings studded with brassy spots. When it closed up, the outer half of its hindwings showed silvery white. This was *Achalarus lyciades,* known as the hoary edge for those cool, frosty margins. For some time, I sat on the bench and took in the view over the green, leafy lowlands, an outlook I'd never anticipated and one I never expected to see again. How I could use a few weeks, I thought, to roam the recesses of this state, all the way from Bossier to Bogalusa and back up to Beauregard; but my two brief transects would have to do.

Downhill, the tigers and green-clouds had given up their patrols to tank up on the azaleas before dark. The hours had flown away like the luna moth, and it was already after six. Abandoning my national forest ambitions for the second day in a row, I left the very top of Louisiana and struck out for Texas. What followed, the long, slow trip to Denton, would prove the worst night's drive of the trip to date. I called Thea and learned I must be home by May Day for her surgery, sooner than I had planned. Then, plagued by the prospect of Thea's ordeal, I drove directly into a great line of storms with hail and tornado warnings.

The interstate, beset by never-ending hordes of semis, was badly grooved and potholed; it grabbed Powdermilk's tiny tires and threw us around like bumper cars. I took naps but still had a hell of a time keeping awake. Then the storm hit like a swat from some great seal, and the rain bucketed so hard I couldn't see the road. At 4:30, I took shelter beneath a freeway overpass east of Dallas, buffeted and drenched, and listened to the tornado reports just to the northeast. And then, for cripes sake, there was *Dallas* to dodge. Finally, gratefully, almost abjectly, I reached David Taylor's house in Denton, Texas, at 7:00 A.M., twelve hours late for dinner.

My good friend David Taylor, poet, essayist, and professor, had organized a conference called "Writing a Wide Land" at the University of North Texas, where he teaches. He'd asked me to give the keynote talk, present a workshop on nature writing, and visit with creative writing students. Fortunately, I was able to sleep for a few hours before a reception with the Texas Master Naturalists at an edge-of-countryside home. I borrowed Latte, the little black cat, for a lot more sleep that night and felt restored the next morning when it was time to go to work. It was difficult to spend two April days indoors on a butterfly Big Year, but the few jobs I had accepted were absolutely essential to pay some bills at home, and the time in Denton was pleasantly passed, to be sure. But when the morning of April 12 came, I was more than ready to get back into the field.

I did so on an outing on the LBJ National Grasslands northwest of Denton with David and his daughter Kory, much grown up from the little girl Thea and I had met in South Carolina a few years before. The grassland lies within the Cross Timbers region, characterized by post oaks, blackjack oaks, and heavy, brushy grass called broom sedge (*Andropogon virginicus*) that is not a sedge but was used for brooms. The LBJ was chopped up by private land and pretty dry, but it boasted several seeps and streams, a good dispersed bloom of purple verbena, blue sage, yellow crucifers and composites, and a few early shooting stars and big-petaled blue-eyed grass.

Spring was still early, the day windy and cool but sunny and warming. The Forest Service biologist Alfred Sanchez took us from unit to unit. Atop a sizable, beflowered hill, I soon tallied my first funereal duskywing zooming around—very black, and flashing its bright white fringes. In the early afternoon, in a broom sedge and native grass field surrounded by oaks, another big black skipper sped from verbena to verbena. It turned out to be a female dusted skipper—not only new for the trip but new in my experience.

David and Kory went crazy with the nets. She caught pesky gray hairstreaks, and he snagged hard-to-chase southern dogfaces. Kory laughed at the black poodle pattern on their bright yellow forewings. A day well spent finished with a Texas barbecue sandwich, Kory's volleyball game, then a second dinner at a fish house with crab cakes and crayfish. Over local beers—black lager and Kolsch, in keeping with the German settlement history—David and I talked of land, literature, and life for hours. And we pondered why, of all places, in the morning when I pointed west past Possum Kingdom, I'd be heading toward Lubbock.

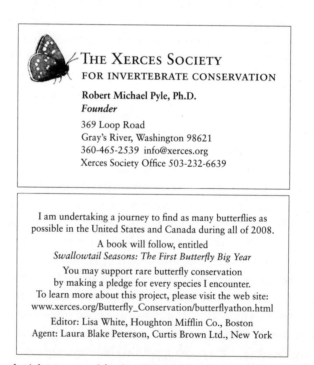

The author's business card for the Big Year, giving the original working title.

15. DESCENT INTO HOPE

Income tax day meant nothing to me. I'd taken care of mine when last I was home, and this year there was next to no income anyway. I did have a thought for my father, who would have been 94 in a couple of days, and his father, 120. I wondered what they would have thought of this caper, and I guessed that they might have approved: they both enjoyed a good road trip. They would have liked the chicken-fried steak at Sweetie Pie's Ribeye in Decatur, across from the turreted red sandstone courthouse in the central square, and breakfast the next morning in the Bobcat Cafe in Newcastle. They might not have been so keen about sleeping in the car at the Jacksboro library in between. But no one bothered me there, not even the librarian.

I was noodling along, enjoying the spring tones of paintbrush and the mesquite behind it, both the chartreuse of cockatoo plumes in the morning sun, when I realized I was on the wrong road. But it didn't matter, I had time, and it was a nice road going roughly the right direction. A few miles on, another little dirt road caught my eye and drew me south, and then another, left on white gravel. On the corner, I spotted a rare patch of green in the yellow-brown landscape—a tiny old cemetery shaded with oaks. This was at 10:30 A.M.; I didn't leave until 2:30!

Reynold Cemetery turned out to be where east, west, north, and south all meet. My first clue came when I looked up over the bank, through the fence, into a green meadow of closed white lilies. It was the greenest place I'd seen in Texas—it must have natural artesian irrigation. Next, I spied a white slice on one of the lilies. Could it be just the butterfly I most hoped to see on this swing through north Texas? It was! An Olympia marble. Talk about cockatoo chartreuse—the ventral hindwing was lightly marbled with that hue, infiltrated by a rosy wash. One of the dearest butterflies of my childhood, it was also one of the first extinctions I experienced, when the only colony in town was displaced by the very playing field where I threw the discus: dreaming dreams of hurling my platter in the Olympics someday, even as my own Olympia faded away. I'd been waiting almost half a century to see another one, and now here it was.

There would be more Olympias, but the next dainty whites I saw were actually more falcate orangetips, with their much denser, gray-green marbling below and petite corners of ripe apricot. The first bright orange butterfly was a gigantic Huebner's crescent, another old friend from the High Line Canal up north in Colorado; and when I thought I'd netted another, it was instead a silvery crescent, which I'd known only from the Rockies foothills. And so it went: new butterflies, right and left, as the day warmed and the lilies—false garlic by name—opened wide.

A little black number by the roadside was a scallopwing, though I could not for the life of me tell which of two species—it was very dark like the far southern mazans, but in the usual range of Hayhurst's, the other species—and it would be months until I knew for sure that these abundant mites were *Staphylus hayhurstii*, and even the expert would have to dissect one to be certain. This is why sight records are unreliable for some of our most similar species. Two more small, dark types proved to be roadside-skippers, one common and one Bell's. Among the many yellows appeared the first, fresh lyside, an extraordinary compliment to the white lilies: silky white wings, creamy yellow borders, cool green underside with a silvery ray, all matching the petals, stems, and leaves. And the list went on, with no sign of diminishing returns.

By the time I left, I had tallied twenty-five species, seven of them new to the year list, and seventeen of them new county records. All three numbers would have climbed had I stayed even longer. When at last, reluctantly, I stepped into Powdermilk after four or five "final rounds," the day was hot, the lilies were all open, and the graveyard meadow was not only alive but *teeming* with butterflies. Where have all the graveyards gone? Gone to flowers, every one.

Hundreds of cliff swallows milled around the bridge over the red and muddy Brazos. I thought of John Graves's incomparable *Goodbye to a River*, one of the most moving love songs ever penned to a river found and lost. The cattle brand "SM2" was spelled out on the hillside in twenty-foot letters of huge limestone blocks. "Sons of Hermann," read a sign, "Hob Kell Lodge." Cotton fields, then hot cows, and one black llama atop a red-dirt berm.

I shot the wind west to Lubbock over the long, hot, dusty miles, the air almost a dust storm, as tumbleweeds blew by. Finally the city appeared through the ruddy dust. I received a warm welcome and a fancy dinner and room as the guest of Bill Tydeman and his colleagues at Texas Tech University. I had no actual responsibilities here, beyond discussing and touring the remarkable Sowell Family Collection in Literature, Community, and the Natural World, a unique and invaluable resource that Barry Lopez helped to set up and Bill curates. After dinner, then Guinnesses and catch-up with my friend the fine young writer and faculty member Kurt Caswell, I retired to my hotel room for a couple of hours of specimen work and several more of hard, fully prone sleep.

The morning didn't seem dusty at all. I cut out, bound for the Guadalupes, after a few moments of pure terror when I couldn't find my day book and species book; but did. Out on the hot, flat griddle west of Lubbock, prairie dog colonies left their dead scattered along the roadside. I came to a place called Levelland, Texas—I guess to say! Oil wells pumped away through the windy murk, the dust up again. Pep, Texas; Whiteface, Texas. I was in the heart of lesser prairie-chicken territory, but they kept to themselves. A flock of seventy-five or a hundred lark buntings gleaned a blasted stubble field.

Many of the shacks and farmhouses had railroad cars tacked on as outbuildings. The Bledsoe Depot gas station consisted of an old Atchison, Topeka & Santa Fe caboose, its yellow metal bay window adorned by Prince Albert cans, and two boxcars. It was closed, but the Coke machine looked alive. The season's first lilacs were blowing in the wind, and amazingly, three sleepy duskywings (*Erynnis brizo*) nectared on it. How did they hold on in the thirty-mile-per-hour gusts? And how in the world had they found it? I saw no oaks, only elms, in that dead weed of a town. The school was boarded up, and the only people in evidence were two little kids on bikes. The girl blew over. Just west of town, two more duskywings clung for their lives to a tough, ladder-leaved, purple legume on the stubbly verge. Right at the border grew stands of a low, scrubby oak. Those west-of-the-Brazos *brizos* must have been drawn two miles by the powerful scent of the lilacs.

At the border it was 6:30 P.M. Texas time, 5:30 New Mexico daylight time, so only 4:30 butterfly time, really, since insects don't recognize daylight savings. The "Welcome to New Mexico" sign had a chile pepper theme. As it sometimes does at state lines, even biologically meaningless ones like this straight line in the desert, the landscape changed. The scrub oak increased and cholla appeared. There was more grass, less dust, and all of a sudden, a few miles west of the line, the first two pronghorns, a couple of does. Half a mile down a desolate side road lay the Bluitt Cemetery. If I was hoping for a repeat of the green and lively Reynold, I was disappointed: here was a graveyard that had *not* gone to flowers—nothing but dried weeds, yuccas, and the neglected stones. The only animate elements on the scene were a loggerhead shrike, a molting harrier, and one distant black cow. Elizabeth Jane Perkins lived here for ninety-eight years, in this wind, imagine. Her brother, Aristo Bulus Perkins, made it seventy-eight winters; his wife, Janice Amelia, lasted only forty-seven.

Just before dusk, a giant-skipper crossed my windshield, then sped into the waning sun and yuccas. It could have been either the already tallied *Megathymus yuccae* or *M. streckeri*—I would never know. A mustang was next to cross before me, then deer, then rabbits. The oval sun dropped into dust, a lone telephone pole etched against it, mourning doves moaning. Against the deepening dark, Hobbs glowed in a valley lit up by refineries and potash plants. With peanuts for dinner, I bedded down at the Wal-Mart in Carlsbad, New Mexico, a world away from the Cafe J and that fine hotel and good company in Lubbock.

Morning came on cool and dry as I climbed into Mountain Time, though a few plants were coming into copious bloom. Entering Lincoln National Forest, I hoped the year wasn't too young here for my purposes. Steve Cary's "Definitive Destination" article on Sitting Bull Falls described a high diversity in spring, including several species I hoped to find, especially the New Mexico specialty known as the Sandia hairstreak. The bowl already had a knot of folks at its green head, including two school buses of kids and a woman with a redtail on her arm. I tried to give them the slip, but one school group arrived up at the falls just as I did, so I detoured up a steep trail to where it burbled over a mossy lip. The Forest Service interpreter and school kids vied for volume down below, but the canyon wren's tumbling tremolo and the green-tailed towhee's notes worked their way through, and as I crossed rock faces slanting upward, the human sounds faded out.

Sitting Bull Falls were slender in the drought but high. I thought I saw bear grass, Sandia's host plant, all along the top of the falls. Pink-flowering Mexican buckeye sprang from the rocks. Water bubbled down, and I came upon a surprising wild place out of sight and earshot of all that lay below: a little bench land of limestone with springs burbling, running, and coursing as if there were no drought at all. All around the marshy spots and pools thrust big stands of what I'd taken for *Nolina* from below but were actually a large sedge: so, no Sandia hairstreaks to be had. But such pools! Ten by twenty, six by eight, grottoes rim-full of sweet, cold limewater tipping in and out through green runnels. They would make for a perfect dip on a hot day, but paralytic today, in the warm air but cold wind; and in any case I wouldn't want to disturb their life. So I just sat and watched, wrapped around by the terraced limestone basin. And I drank of the runnel, below a maidenhair wall—my first wild quaff of the trip—and it tasted better than any water since home. There were more and more pools and rocks and caves farther up. This Sitting Bull secret spot was one of the most enchanting places I'd seen all year, maybe ever.

I was early after all. At the head of easy navigation in a canyonlet with a sliding falls coming in, a white-fringed duskywing was the only butterfly for all the nectar. But on up the trail, as the air warmed, I did get into some butterflies. A tiny gold nugget on a rock became an orange skipperling. A bigger one settled into the year's first vesta crescent. At an oasis under oaks and junipers, a female dwarf yellow suckled at a little fleabane. About a mile up, the trail crossed the flow beneath a big white-barked madroña. Then Sitting Bull Spring, where the sweet, falling song of the canyon wren had no competition, ending on a buzz just to remind you it was a wren, not an angel, in case you thought there was any difference. I drank again at a watercress pool that I took for the head of the spring; then saw more flow upstream, crossed by deer tracks. "We'll see how that works out," I mumbled. A shadow turned into a northern cloudy-wing, a female full of eggs from a colony around the spring. The route down was way-marked by the brown berry scats of ringtails on rocks. Cat's claw acacia, hard enough on the legs, was worse than Louisiana catbrier on poor Akito's bag—the devil's own. Even still, he snagged a handsome new Rocky Mountain duskywing. Passing back through the chain of pools, I took one last drink from the fast, clear flow, just to make sure that, if I got giardia, I'd get it good.

Picnicking late at Last Chance Canyon, I made plans for the next stretch. For some reason lost to me a few hours later, I decided to drive the dirt-and-stone washboard Guadalupe Rim Road the entire length of the national forest, instead of the longer, paved route around the outside to the same destination. In the dim half-light, I surprised a pair of cow-calf units, as mother and child are known out on the range. They were the first of many, for this was surely the range: the Lincoln National Forest interdigitates with big private ranch lands and grazing leases. Way up on top of the lonely rim, an old rusty pump, gas motor putt-putting, squeaking and clanking its endless teeter-totter, raised water for a stock tank. I was already tired, and I was choking from the dust, Powdermilk's twenty-six-year-old rubber window seals no longer airtight. I guessed I was maybe halfway—ha!

Forest Road 67 turned into a nightmare passage, an ordeal of six hours plus. Two owls, one coyote in profile, and hundreds of remedial or suicidally depressed black-tailed jackrabbits accompanied the campaign. After many bone-jarring miles and an utter loss of confidence as to the correct route, I flagged down the only other set of headlights I saw the entire way. Inside the big, smoke-filled pickup sat a young cowboy and his girl. "Thanks for stopping," I said. "Say, does this road *ever* get out?"

He could probably hear an edge of exasperation, if not a quaver of terror, in my dust-laden voice. "Yes, if you keep going," he said. "Take a right down the draw, don't miss the detour, and continue on, and you'll eventually come to Highway 82 at Hope. You'd've hit pavement long before this if you'd taken that left back there a ways at the T."

Just as I suspected: a wrong turn, when the right way seemed to double back south, resulted in many more miles and an endless extra hour. I accepted his directions with thanks, followed them as best I could, and finally hit Hope at 2:00 A.M. Unable to go another foot, I put my seat back right there in the town picnic park, beneath tall cottonwoods. I'd just dropped off when bright headlights and a diesel rumble broke through my grateful haze.

It was the cowboy and his wife, not girl, and their baby, stopping by to make sure I'd made it all right. His family had three ranches up there, running about fifty cow-calf units per section—fewer than some, but then they don't have to back off as often. His buddies once talked him into riding a bronc off the Rim—"That was a ride," he said. After riding off the Rim in my own way, I could believe it. I asked if he rode rodeo, and he said, "No, I don't have time." I said he'd live longer and have less arthritis that way. "Oh, I'll get plenty of that in my everyday work," he said. We bid each other good night, and the young cow family drove off into the New Mexico night.

16. FROM HOPE TO HELL

Out of Hope, the southeast corner of New Mexico was a dried-out bone. The big event in Artesia that weekend was the BLM wild horse and burro adoption, not enough grass on the range for both them and the cattle. Nothing in bloom. Nothing, that is, until the Lincoln National Forest border, which was also the Otero-Chaves county line. There I saw what really *was* bear grass. The second of the droopy, grassy, thin-leaved *Nolina* I came to was in bloom—one of the few, of hundreds springing from the rim rock, that was. And there on the mauve club of tiny white flowers sat a small, tawny skipper. Still in the morning chill, it was *Stinga morrisoni*, which I call Morrison's silver-spike for the shiny white nail across its earthy hindwings. This uncommon southern Rockies denizen, my first in years, has to be considered a boon whenever you come across it.

Hiking up the rim on a deer trail, across the top, and down a piñon-juniper canyon, I found a colony of fresh, crisp Rocky Mountain duskywings, on Gambel oaks. They visited both the flowers and the glistening buds of the oaks, as well as cow-shat mud by the stream across the highway. A mourning cloak called on female flowers of pussy willows over the water. Along the weedy roadside flitted a yellow dwarf. I hoped it would prove to be a painted crescent, and in Marsha's gentle folds, it did. Just think, I thought—had it not been for Hope, I would have missed all these.

The great finds didn't stop there. In the nearby Mayhill Store, I scored local, *real* cherry cider, local jerky from local steers, and not so local but fresh coffee. Mayhill resident Dan Derrick, forty years with the Forest Service, oversaw fire prevention and control in this forest. He said the forest was so dry that this was his first day off in three weeks. I believed it when I reached James Canyon

Campground, where I had planned to camp before my long detour took the night. James Creek was so dry that two outdoorsmen stopped and, disgusted by the aridity, moved on. Even so, many duskywings of two or three species speeded up and down, as well as a zebra-striped marine blue. I walked the stony bed, enjoying the impatient traffic of the duskies and wondering what this crick would be like after a wet winter.

The road reached its summit at 8,650-foot Cloudcroft. I'd been here once in early fall, when the aspens quivered high above the white sands. Now the ski area looked like late winter. A few dandelions bloomed in the damp of recent snowmelt, and a tatty cloak powered through gray aspens. Aspens! What a tonic for Texas! On the dandies, fresh painted ladies showed neon pink, turquoise eyes as bright as I'd ever seen, so different from the citrus and sapphires of Annabella. Which I saw next: two newly minted West Coast ladies, the first since the Central Valley. Now I really was in the West. At a viewpoint over the defile once run by the Alamogordo & Sacramento Mountain Railway, a hilltopping nymph proved up as a faded but lively Milbert's tortoiseshell.

In tarted-up, touristy "Old Town" Cloudcroft stood a gift shop, The Copper Butterfly. I wondered why its sign depicted a tropical 88 butterfly instead of a local species. Later I discovered that celebrating a local species could have made the shop unpopular among the locals, because of their antipathy toward federal listing of the Cloudcroft checkerspot as endangered. According to Richard B. Stolley in *Time* magazine, "Cloudcroft residents . . . rebelled against the idea that the Federal Government, egged on by 'bug huggers,' was telling them how to manage their neighborhood." They think listing the butterfly will somehow harm tourism.

I'd have loved to find *Euphydryas anicia cloudcrofti*, but it was *way* early. I drove up to the type locality of the subspecies in Pines Campground, still closed for the season. Only the gold and silver of dandelions and dangling aspen catkins showed for bloom. A Steller's jay growled from up in a pine, much grayer and paler blue than ours, eyebrows white in place of azure. The campsites of Butterfly Loop encircled the primary habitat, a paddock protected by a cant-wood fence. A well-done interpretive sign illustrated the rare

Cloudcroft checkerspot and its life cycle, including the chief host and nectar plants, penstemon and sneezeweed. As I searched the paddock from outside for old pupal cases on stalks or fences, a little orange lep popped up, circled, and winged past me. It was no checkerspot, at that season. Someday I'll return and see *Euphydryas a. cloudcrofti*, whose name means literally "the beautiful dryad of the croft in the clouds." I'll always think of Cloudcroft that way.

Across the pass, white-throated swifts and violet-green swallows played over limestone towers above a gypsum base, which ran down the Tularosa to make the white sands below. At the bottom, White Sands National Monument was blinding to the south in the late sun. I think about half the sand was in the air. My nose was a dust bowl and my sinuses a wreck from the changing altitude and aridity. Almost out of gas, I had to coast down the big hill and was happy to find a Chevron right at the bottom. That meant I didn't have to detour into town, a bonus: Alamogordo looked about as pretty as Pahrump.

I struck north on the 54 in time to see the sun duck behind one of the Oscura Mountains sideways, then give a valedictory wink through a gap. I sank into a room at the first motel in Carrizozo, the pink and green, 1950s Sands, then crawled out for an alarming bowl of chili and onions at The Outpost, the only place open. At least it was filling, and the Alien Amber from Roswell was . . . well, it was adequately abducting.

West through Malpais, the Valley of Fires, and the Tularosa Basin with its black pahoehoe, the windblown volcanic soils were full of bear grass—but almost impossible to access, what with the yucca, cholla, other cacti, and tumbled, sharp-edged lava boulders. I settled for a scan of the purple peas lining the roadside, attended by Texas lupine blues. Before Bingham, I stopped for a pee and to prod the junipers. Across the arid Southwest, junipers have been cut, chained, and burned to favor grasses, which in turn favors cows over juniper hairstreaks. The "cedars" supposedly took over vast areas of grassland after heavy overgrazing, so this may be redressing the balance, but juniper-dependent birds and insects suffer for it. Fortunately, the hairstreaks are far from endangered. Lepists know that tapping the twisted trees with their nets will often put up the small, greenish brown butterflies.

I stepped around a juniper, looking up, when a sharp, loud rattle erupted at my feet. Instantly and perfectly, without benefit of rehearsal, the rattlesnake and I did our old evolutionary dance. It rattled; I leaped. Upward and backward, a vertical takeoff improbable for such a large terrestrial mammal. The buzzworm coiled tighter as I landed about three feet away. I admired the great reptile for some minutes, as my pulse returned to its normal low, and thanked it for doing what it was supposed to do. The previous year, making a movie loosely based on *Chasing Monarchs* with a German public television crew, I submitted to a large rattlesnake slithering toward me. The cameraman loved it, but the director freaked as I let it get closer and closer. I knew it couldn't strike, stretched out. But this one, even bigger, was fully coiled and could have had me in a blink.

After rounding the grove, hopeful of a longer and better look, I went back. I gave the spot a berth but then heard the rattle again. The snake slithered through the cured grass in front of me and disappeared beneath a juniper skirt. Some four feet long with five or more rattles, thick as my arm, and beautifully lined and dotted with a geometry of tan, brown, olive, and black, it was a western diamondback rattlesnake. Back at Powdermilk, I looked it up in R. C. Stebbins's *Peterson Field Guide to Western Reptiles and Amphibians.* He wrote: "Perhaps the most dangerous North American serpent, often holding ground and boldly defending itself when disturbed."

Rising from the Rio Grande, beyond Socorro, the Magdalena Fault divided the uplifted mountains from La Jencia Plain below. Those mountains were the Magdalenas. With a novel in progress entitled *Magdalena Mountain,* I had to come see them. As I westered toward the town of Magdalena, the sky gathered into a blazer worthy of an *Arizona Highways* cover. Driving out to see it, I was stopped by a police roadblock involving the county sheriff, town marshal, a state trooper, and a tribal officer from the Alamo Reservation. The big-mustached sheriff, checking my driver's license, liked my duct-taped wallet. He said his looked about like that and told me to enjoy the sunset.

I hadn't intended to take a room again so soon, but when I saw the knotty pine Western Motel, my kind of place, I fell for it. And when the next morning, clearing rubbish from around a grapey dwarf iris before the adobe wall so I could smell it without sticking my nose in the trash, I found a tenner, I knew it was a good choice. Armed with a breakfast burrito made right there in town and some more Carrizozo cherry cider, I headed up into the Magdalena Mountains.

Standing on the summit of South Baldy at 10,783 feet, I was just a bit more than 10,000 feet higher than the top of Mt. Driskill a few days before. Not so much standing, actually, as leaning against the insane wind. This was the highest point in the Magdalena Mountains; Magdalena Peak topped out at 8,152 feet. The way up here brought me through Water Canyon, where a huge mountain bike race was taking place. Fortunately, most of the riders were way uphill already. In the campground, a yucca giant-skipper had come down to the dry creek bed in search of moisture, its great bulk buzzing over what would be mud if it ever rained.

At Grapevine Curve, water appeared in the creek. New butterflies came in quick succession—a mylitta crescent, a "thoosa" Sara orangetip, a zephyr anglewing, and a spring white—a real one this time, with gray railroad tracks lining the veins underneath, new for the county. And then, a thrilling find—*Erora quaderna*, the highly sought after Arizona hairstreak, western counterpart of the early hairstreak, *Erora laeta*, a species of legendary mystique. The first one, sipping at the damp shore, really shimmered against the brown mud. It was much brighter than I expected, deep blue-black above, fresh grass green dashed with red jasper below. It looked like an animated piece of Indian jewelry, and I had to wonder if it had ever inspired such a piece. Walking the shaded creek, I saw a second one perched on an oak leaf, and a third, drinking at oak flowers.

Two well-met humans followed closely on these striking butterfly encounters. On the road, a man with a short gray beard stopped to ask what I was doing, and had I ever heard of Paul Grey? I certainly had! L. Paul Grey was the master of American fritillary studies for decades, and I had corresponded with him as a graduate student. My interrogator was Prescott Grey—Paul's son!—out for the day with his wife, Robin, from their home in Socorro. Then, just before Lone Pine curve, I met Dave Heft, district biologist for the Cibola National Forest. He filled me in on the Long-Term Ecological Research Program here. Dave was sweating in the heat. He had just released a beaver, having taken it a steep twenty-five feet downhill to water in a wheelbarrow, then pushed the heavy barrow back up.

Finally I hiked up to the top of South Baldy, where there was snow in the aspens, and the view was a helluva, if hazy—from the White Sands to Navajo Mountain. It was an ordeal in the ridiculous wind. The 35,000-acre Langman Research Site and observatory occupied the saddle below the summit. Hiking down in the lee, out of the wind but over steep, rocky tundra, I longed for midsummer and its alpine butterflies. Not that *Erebia magdalena,* the *spiritus loci* of my novel, could be found here. The black Magdalena alpine glides the high talus only in the northern Rockies; there would be other high-elevation summer specialties here. But that would be long after *Erora quaderna*'s jewels had turned to dust on the wind down-canyon: the perpetual paradox of this odd escapade.

From here I'd planned to bear due west to the coast. But that would mean giving up on Sandia, one of my major grails, and that was unthinkable. The Sandia hairstreak was one of the last full species of U.S. butterfly to be discovered in the twentieth century. It happened when a lad named Noel McFarland brought a 4-H insect collection into the university with an unfamiliar butterfly in it. Nor was this a minor variant of some well-known type: it was colorful, dramatic, and completely different from any other known species. Thus Paul Ehrlich and Harry Clench, describing it in 1960, erected not only the new species *mcfarlandi* but also the new genus *Sandia,* now considered a subgenus of *Callophrys* along with the elfins, cedar, and green hairstreaks. I heard Ehrlich present the new discovery at my first Lepidopterists' Society meeting at Gothic, Colorado, in 1961, and I'd desperately wanted to see it in real life ever since.

The only thing to do was to head north to Albuquerque, which I had planned to evade. Happily, the well-known New Mexico lepidopterist Steve Cary agreed to drive down from Santa Fe to join me in the search for *Sandia* in its type locality, the Sandia Mountains. I hoped at least that the urban immersion would lead to good Mexican food, but I got trapped in the hot tar of cruising youth in downtown traffic and had to settle for a green chile omelet at a Village Inn on the outer belt road. Well after midnight, I crashed at

La Cueva Recreation Area on Sandia Peak, in an area clearly marked for day use only.

In the morning, Steve found me enjoying my oat bran and banana under an oak on a monumental CCC picnic table with boulders for legs, beside a bear grass. He came just in time to share my hot coffee. Steve is one of our favorite people. I think Thea had a little crush on him, and I appreciated him forgetting his passport on an outing to Mexico, as I had the year before, making me feel less of a twit. The first thing Steve said was "You won't have to go far, you've camped about a hundred yards from the type locality."

The second, "You can't go anywhere on those tires—the steel belts are showing!"

Steve took me just tens of yards from where I'd camped, to a slope where bear grass abounded, and there was *Sandia*—a bright individual, perched on an oak seedling below a big bear grass. We watched it for minutes, until it flew to another oak. Several more darted about and interacted, mostly alighting on *Nolina* spears and old rabbitbrush. Removing one from the net, I was first struck by how beautiful it was; a half century of anticipation surely heightened the experience, as did being here with Steve, but it really *is* a gorgeous butterfly. Second, by how green it was below; I'd expected a more subtle olive, but it was as bright as the Arizona, though a yellower hue. Third, by the elegance of its crypsis. The white-lined, green underside blended perfectly into the stripy bear grass, and the bronzy tan ventral forewing and topside matched the older *Nolina* spears as well as the dead oak leaves among which they often perched. And since the bear grass is really two-toned, green and yellowy brown, the hairstreak's combo of colors is doubly adaptive. The butterfly's entire range is circumscribed by that of this grasslike cousin of yucca. I've never been more impressed by another instance of plant-insect coevolution, unless it be the famous case of yuccas and their yucca moths, which pollinate them from within.

After Steve returned to work in Santa Fe, I hung about a little longer, relishing the gift of the Sandias. Then I settled into the fancy, cool, and commodious Indian casino on the way down the hill, pulled up to a telephone with a roll of quarters, and commenced to dialing, until I finally corralled a pair of my rare twelve-inch tires.

With only fifteen thousand miles on them, the "old" tires should have been fine. I figured the rear wheel alignment had to be off, and that was likely why Powdermilk had slid all over the potholed road, so I had the alignment done too. As I was waiting, over the good garlic mariscos I'd missed the night before, I thought about how lucky I'd been. What a place that flooded dike would have been for a blowout, or that stormy interstate, or up there on the rim, or on the steep, rocky road to South Baldy. Had I carried on west from Magdalena as planned, one or both tires, ineluctably, would have given out, most likely in an awkward or dangerous place. The gift of Sandia, indeed.

Across Arizona by full moon, a dim sign in the night read Two Guns, another Twin Arrows. Hours later, in the bright clarity of Earth Day, the signs said Big Sandy Wash, Peach Wash, Holy Moses Wash, Black Rock Wash, and Rattlesnake Wash. There were gopher snakes and coachwhips; Great Basin whiptail, collared lizard, and leopard lizard. I had a picture in mind, tattooed there from an ancient *National Geographic*. It shows a bald man in plus fours bent at the waist below a saguaro. The caption reads: "A Collector Makes a Sideswipe at an Elusive Orangetip. Perched on a desert flower, near a tall cactus plant, is a specimen of the scarce *Anthocharis pima*, a resident of certain remote sections of Arizona . . . flying for only a few days in spring." This was my last chance for Pima, now considered a subspecies of the more widespread desert orangetip (*A. cethura*); I assumed I'd pick it up somewhere. But while I was in the Southeast, the Southwest spring had slipped past. Orangetips were absent from all the washes. For the pretty yellow Pima, those "few days in spring" had flown. I'd waited fifty years to see Pima; I guess I could wait some more.

The Havasu National Wildlife Refuge should be called the National Tamarisk Reserve. Here I found a gallery forest of the exotic saltcedar, some of them three feet through and fifty feet high, and not a sign of a lep in the furnace exhaust that passed for air. But the place surprised me. At Catfish Haven, I disturbed a dark thing that turned out to be a silvery Mojave sootywing. Then, checking out a yellow-flowered palo verde tree, I spied a blue or two darting among the myriad bees. When I went to remove them from my net, I found I had also caught the tiniest metalmark I'd ever laid eyes on. Nearby in a mesquite, I located a colony of Palmer's metalmarks, barely half an inch in wingspan, orangy gray-brown with white polka dots. A dozen or more were jerking all around at speed and alighting on leaflet, twig, fruit, and flower. Happy as a newt and hot as heck, I excused myself to the family of horned grebes at the dock and thrust my greasy, steamy head into the Colorado River.

Entering California at three in the afternoon, I could already see the great smog plume of L.A. sneaking up through the Mojave from the southwest, blanketing the Lanfair Valley. It stung my eyes, and I didn't want to go there. So I went to the Mojave National Preserve instead. I climbed a boulder-and-creosote hill, where a dozen butterflies in train swirled in a spectacular hilltopping display, playing tag endlessly, or at least until sunset: all gray hairstreaks. Mole gray, slate blue, jade green, they flashed paintbrush spots and mallow bodies. One male spread to show his blotchy stigmata, red topknot and mud flaps, tails blowing in the breeze. Somewhere up there, beguiled, I lost my forceps. The Trail of Tears it's not, but I have left a trail of tweezers across the West.

Back down, still stalling, I found a desert tortoise, maybe a foot long and six pounds. I played with it for a while, then moved it off the road and gave it some fruit. I would have been fine staying there with it all night. But I had a lecture to give in Long Beach the next day. I didn't even leave for Barstow until seven, and I had the whole damn L.A. Basin to cross. Let's just say it was one of the three worst night drives of the year, all of them in one week. I checked into the Ayres Hotel, Seal Beach, West Coast, at two in the morning, with 368,374.5 miles and 150 species on the meter.

17. TWENTY-SIX MILES, TAKE ONE

I really should have made that wake-up call for seven. Still, I maintain that the signage sucked. At least the exit was poorly marked, same as for Berkeley in the February rain. But then, I know for a certain fact that there exists a special school for interstate sign makers, devoted to maximum freeway frustration, with extra credit for getting motorists *almost* there, then dropping them flat at the critical juncture.

In any case, on my way to the Catalina ferry dock in Long Beach, I missed the exit from the morning lemming migration. The next exit took me nowhere useful, only put me back on 405 N. The next one allowed a reversal, but traffic was stuck at a green arrow that didn't work. I pulled out and went around, very nearly merging with a cream Cadillac. I whipped out my disused mobile and frantically asked the ferry folks to rebook me for the two o'clock sailing, to avoid forfeiting my fifty-four-dollar fare. But they urged me to try, bless 'em, so I did. I found the parking garage, dashed in, ran back out, and in the end, made the boat by two minutes, in a real state. My heart held up. Cheaper, I guess, than a hospital stress test.

And so to Catalina! The day was blue but hazy, L.A. a filthy smear beyond the derricks of the Port of Long Beach. There was the *Queen Mary*, where I'd last been in 1974, off a Greyhound bus. Leaving Long Beach, a bowed boom was a necklace of terns, with a cormorant at one end as clasp, a pelican at the other. I sat back in the bow spray, letting it cool me off, and read Fred Thorne's article "Collecting the Avalon Hairstreak" from an old *News of the Lepidopterists' Society*, never so happy for a five-buck Heineken. Two Mormon dudes on a mission looked over the rails. What a gig they've got, I thought, compared to the sorry ones I saw last year in Mexico City's miasma,

153

looking as if they'd been dumped at the very gates of Hades (unless, of course, they're actually based in L.A.).

So here we were on this little ferry, at speed. "Twenty-six miles across the sea," as the old song says, "Santa Catalina is a-waitin' for me!" The Nature Conservancy's Santa Cruz Island, where Don Meadows, Jerry Powell, and Charles Remington all collected, loomed long, tall, and in its short green season off to the right. But it was Santa Catalina that held the Avalon hairstreak, the endemic I was after. A skein of eighteen brown pelicans cut low toward us amidships, dropped back aft. The island loomed over the waves, bigger and higher than I'd expected. My stress was all gone, flowed out into sweet anticipation. We hit the dock at Avalon at 11:15 A.M. "Have a good one," wished the mate, in what had somehow become the universal American salutation in the past few years. I intended to do just that.

But I had only sort of a good one. For one thing, I lost things all day long and had to keep retracing my steps backward. For another, when I found the "Catholic church south of town" behind which Fred Thorne had located hairstreak habitat on his 1960s visit, I found it displaced by Sol Vista, a condo development surrounded by a wall-to-wall carpet of pink ice plant. The moisture source where he found fresh water and host plants was now a dry stone gutter. Then I managed to confuse the actual host plant, Channel Island silverleaf lotus, with a different species of legume that was hugely abundant up the side canyons, and fragrant like lemon curd.

When I realized my mistake, I climbed to a hilltop above town, where the sounds of roosters, quail, ravens, and children at play filtered up the canyon from the light industrial colony at the bottom. It wasn't a pretty hilltop—big tank, 'dozed top, burned not long ago. But lots of the actual lotus bloomed there, along with lupines and brodiaea. I hoped the Avalons would be active here, just like the similar gray hairstreaks on that Mojave hillock a couple of days before. But only painted ladies and swallowtails hilltopped, along with geometrid moths about the size and color of *Strymon avalona*. They flew differently but were superabundant and very good at springing false hope.

Fred Thorne had concluded that "all of my scientific approach was a waste of time. I believe that anyone can go to Avalon on any sunny day in spring or summer, and wander almost anywhere in the hills, and find *avalona*." But things had changed in Avalon. Some habitats he knew had been developed, others burned. I wandered for miles on Catalina, but as the sun dropped behind the island ridge, there were no *avalona* in those hills for me.

Not that the day was a dead loss, on that island that looked like Capri. I've never seen Capri, but that's how I imagined it. For one thing, I saw two fine new butterflies: just off the dock, the first anise swallowtail appeared against the cliff; and scrambling way up a canyon behind the condos, I spied a richly colored umber skipper. Plus, I found everything I'd lost, the last one on a particularly pleasing note.

The good steel thermos given me by my friend JoAnne had somehow, somewhere, slipped out of my day pack. I'd earlier visited St. Catherine of Alexandria to avail my heated brow of its shaded cloister and admire its beautiful enameled tiles of wildflowers and monks at a seaside mass, dedicated to Santa Catalina de Alejandría. So now I went back to inquire whether my thermos had been found there. Angelically beautiful Carrie in the church office had not seen it. She advised a prayer to St. Anthony. Never one to ignore knowing advice, I had a word with his effigy, as well as those of Catalina and Junípero Serra for good measure. Then I had an inspiration, glanced across the street, and saw the thermos beside a low wall where I'd knelt to sniff a flower.

To top off the half-full glass, Carrie told me about her friend Joey Hernandez, a "butterfly-mad guy" who worked at Van's grocery. Anna at Van's told me, "Yes, Joey's butterfly-mad all right. But he's on vacation. Right now, he could be walking anywhere on the island." I filed that away and dashed for my ferry.

Where I got a shock: the ferry was pulling out fifteen minutes early! I freaked out, but needlessly. That was the ferry to San Pedro, and I hadn't missed mine after all. "If there is any way," I told Santa Catalina as it receded, "I'll be back." Long Beach looked better by night, the lighthouse going red, blue, green.

18. CALIFORNIA BLUES

It was one of the weirdest places I'd ever been: a hill of solid blossom and weed—daisies, mustards, ice plant, elder, natives and not, all colorful—stretching away over hundreds of acres. All around sprawled massive tank farms with asphalted slopes, golf fairways, apartment complexes, a big green cemetery, and Little League fields. The Los Angeles Basin hazed away east across refineries and towns; the Santa Monica Mountains were either a dark smudge or a mirage, who could say? It was blazing hot, and presentiments were strange: huge flames shot from off burners at the tank farm, and a biplane passed over pulling a huge flying billboard for "The World's Most Refreshing Beer: Coors Light." If he'd made an airdrop, I'd've drunk it. That's how low I'd sunk on this hot, thirsty folly.

This leftover landscape just happened to have an endangered species living on it. I'd had trouble finding the Palos Verdes blue site until Jerry Fall at blessed BioQuip Products slipped me the coordinates. When I finally arrived at the San Pedro Naval Depot and Butterfly Preserve, I flashed my card at the gate. The guard joked about my being a butterfly spy and told me I was probably too late anyway. He'd had a blue land on his guard booth window three Sundays ago. You'd think I was seeking admission to Pelican Preserve to see the Crooked Garden or some such. In fact, hundreds of thousands of gallons of fuel were stored directly beneath us: the petrol supply for the Pacific Fleet.

Glaucopsyche lygdamus palosverdesensis was described in 1977 and federally listed as an endangered species not long after. A race of the widespread silvery blue, it was restricted to the Palos Verdes Peninsula. Most of its locoweed and deerbrush habitat had gone to homes and gardens of Rancho Palos Verdes, or something else more useful to humans than to specialized butterflies. When the last known colony was lost to a sports field through a snafu, the blue became the first taxon extirpated under federal protection—a head-rolling embarrassment, a shame, and a tragedy. The Palos Verdes blue joined its close cousin, the Xerces blue, on the sad rolls of Californian extinction.

Or so it was thought, until Dr. Rudi Mattoni, longtime authority on the biology and conservation of blues, rediscovered the butterfly on the San Pedro Depot. Since then a great deal had gone into its bolstering, breeding, and management, involving several agencies, many volunteers and professionals, and gang members miraculously reformed through butterfly nurture. I could have gone through channels and met all these people, but Rudi was in Argentina, and with my May Day deadline for getting home, I just didn't have time. The butterfly was the thing. But, as the guard said, I was probably too late.

I found patches of deerweed, but the flight was indeed over, after a huge emergence year. Feeding damage on buds and flowers of *Lotus* encouraged me to look for eggs, but that was worse than looking for deer ticks on a golden retriever. Tapping a robust buckwheat produced a gray hairstreak, and then two actual blues. I could see right off they were too small for Palos Verdes, and had orange aurorae like another endangered species in the region, the El Segundo blue. In fact, they were the closely related Bernardino blue, which has escaped the endangerment ax of so many California coastal blues by having a slightly broader range and niche.

A number of humpy "disaster shelters" brooded from the hillsides. Bunker 308 bore the sign "Storage and Care of Explosives" but had random pipes and pumps chucked in it now. The last one, 312, had a working beehive under its protective arch—the commander's pet project. Now, *that's* guns to butter! Checkered whites and skippers fluttered everywhere, and cabbages, but Palos Verdes blues were just a rumor to me.

Down in the butterfly garden by the project trailer, fiery and umber skippers sipped beside painted and West Coast ladies. Sam, Nellie, and Sonja greeted me at the butterfly breeding greenhouse. Mike Yavlick, director of restoration for the Palos Verdes

Conservancy, had heard that I was up on the habitat and tracked me down. He showed me around the facility. Even though the flight of the Palos Verdes blues was all over for the year, I was glad to see the captive offspring and the queer country-city habitat of this Lazarus butterfly, about which I'd heard so much.

When we left the Navy's big gas station and butterfly farm, since we were going the same way, Mike kindly offered to lead me to a couple of rare blue restoration sites up the coast. The first occupied a destination golf resort. The owner and developer, not to be named but known for his boorish hubris and bad hair, was required to provide public coastal access and habitat restoration on the site in order to develop a stretch of coast that had somehow, till then, remained open space. Gleefully and legally intruding upon the sanctum of the wealthy linksters, we walked the mitigation meadows. Only the acmon blue, a common coastal generalist but nonetheless new for the tally, showed itself.

The drive north ran through a pink tunnel of ice plant and bougainvillea above the blue sea, beautiful if ecologically barren. At Redondo Beach, Mike showed me habitat restored for the El Segundo blue right next to Highway 1. The thick sward of the buckwheat host plant ran down the slope almost to the beach. Protection of *Euphilotes battoides allyni* had been one of the first conservation campaigns of the Xerces Society. The Charles Eames designer Jeannine Oppewall, later an Oscar-nominated Hollywood production designer, led the early efforts, along with the young Xerces president, Larry Orsak. Chevron trumpeted the company's protection of butterfly-and-buckwheat dunes at their El Segundo refinery in a major magazine ad. Later, critical habitat at the end of the L.A. International Airport became the focus of a complicated chapter involving Rudi Mattoni's butterfly rearing laboratory, a proposed golf course, and way too many other elements to parse here.

The El Segundos weren't home, or they were but not as adults. This time I was too early instead of too late. (The bane of my year's existence! A little later, passing Malibu, I would have to acknowledge glumly that my window for finding the Sonoran blue this year had passed.) At least this visit saved me from having to stop at the El Segundo dunes proper, at the airport or the refinery, to see if the blue was out. We crossed the street to the handy Redondo Beach Brewing Company. Passing on the Coors Light, Mike and I improved on our California blues over a Pale Ale. I don't know another conservation arena as fraught with egos, bizarre twists and turns, rogue elements, quirky history, weird biology, and random battles—unless it be California monarchs.

I wasn't finished with the Golden State's endangered gossamer wings, but first, I had a date with an unlisted blue. At least I hoped I did. Few eyes had ever seen it, and no surprise when you figure that it's so tiny, it makes the other species look like condors. When I reached La Purísima Concepción Mission on Saturday, April 26, it was thanks to Debra Piot. From Redondo, I'd hopped up to Santa Barbara, where the Piots had a fine song for me that John had composed about the Butterfly Big Year, plus Debra's research results. On the Southwest Leps listserve, she had picked up that *Philotiella speciosa purisima* was on the wing. At last, a butterfly I was on time for! So I turned north past Lompoc, to the place for which the butterfly was named, where I'd once idled away an afternoon with Barbara and Mía. A lovely little mission, it is the only complete example in California. But it is a state park and, therefore, netless. The minute *P. s. purisima* is best seen in hand, so I went instead to the type locality: "Harris Grade at Burton Mesa Blvd., N. of Lompoc."

That intersection had one corner shot, a strawberry stand on another, but the other two were still good habitat. A path into Cal Fish and Game's Burton Mesa Management Area led right off to chalcedona checkerspots—my first *Euphydryas* of the year, "beautiful dryads" related to *E. a. cloudcrofti*. Beautiful, all right, checkered red, black, and white; but also *big*, the males over two inches in wingspan, the females near three. And they were abundant, hundreds of them clogging the pathways and airways among fragrant islands of buckbrush.

A low, fleshy buckwheat just coming into bloom must have been the host plant of my quarry. After looking around it at length, decoyed once by a pygmy-blue, at last I spotted the tiny blue sparks. I managed to net both males and females of *P. s. purisima*. They had to be handled with utmost delicacy to fully appreciate the sky blue male, the mouse brown female, both snow white below with bold black spots on the forewings. This jot of life, which barely covered my little fingernail, belongs to a species with the humble but wholly appropriate English name of small blue. Of the four subspecies, two are rare and local, one has been missing for many years, and one—this one—was only recently discovered. I hoped the tiny butterfly named for the lovely little mission would never become endangered.

A bigger blue named for a bigger mission, *Plebejus icaricia missionensis* was already endangered. I passed its best-known (and most contested) habitat, San Bruno Mountain, on my way north to San Francisco. I was there to join Liam O'Brien's Nature in the City field trip in the Sunset District. An experienced actor and artist, Liam combines photography with painting to create extraordinary portraits of California butterflies and moths in their native habitats. His "Green Hairstreak Corridor Project" seeks to restore and link habitat remnants for the rare coastal green hairstreak, once thought to be extinct in its type locality of San Francisco.

Driving up steep, steep streets from Highway 1, I found the group of fifteen Sunday devouts. Liam led us up and down hills in bright sun and cool breeze. He and his coleader, Deirdre Elmansoumi, showed us both intact bits of habitat on mossy balds and linear, "unused" bits of Department of Public Works ground that easily could be enhanced to serve both caterpillars and adults. Right away, coastal green hairstreaks appeared, now *Callophrys dumetorum* but once known as *C. viridis* for good reason. Everyone exhaled at once when we first saw it, and said *"Beautiful!"* Radiant blue-green, it was the biggest, brightest green hairstreak I'd ever seen. At Rocky Outcrop we watched a mating pair, a sharp white line across the female's rich kelly underside. Deirdre found eggs on the same buckwheat clump, and a male nectared on a nearby pompom of thrift. Liam's background as an actor showed well in his enthusiastic style as a field leader, practically a piece of street theater.

As exciting as it was to see a great rarity of surpassing beauty that seemed to be making a comeback, I couldn't help thinking of the Xerces blue. A distinctive and variable near-relative of the Palos Verdes blue, Xerces swarmed over the San Francisco dunes when Drake arrived. But as early as 1875, the San Francisco lepidopterist Herman Behr wrote to his friend Herman Strecker in Chicago: "*Glaucopsyche xerces* (Boisduval) is now extinct as regards the neighborhood of San Francisco. The locality where it used to be found is converted into building lots, and between German chickens and Irish hogs no insect can exist besides louse and flea." Last seen at the Presidio, the Xerces blue finally passed from existence in 1943. The lost butterfly lent its name to the Xerces Society for Invertebrate Conservation in 1971, becoming a potent symbol of butterfly diversity forsaken.

Liam really shook me when he pointed out that the Xerces blue and the coastal green hairstreak had flown here together. So extinction can happen. It need not happen again for the green, and if Liam and Deirdre and their adherents have their way, it won't. But it's too late for the blue. Or is it? The Pelham *Catalogue* adjudged Xerces a well-defined subspecies of the silvery blue. With part of the Presidio now restored as dune land, I have proposed that the nearest silveries, from up-coast in Marin, be introduced there. If they took, microevolution could be expected to bring the local morph back to something like the old form in time. I call this "resurrection ecology." So who knows? If the Green Hairstreak Corridor and such a reevolution both worked, the coastal green hairstreak and the Xerces blue might once again fly together in sight of the Golden Gate.

Now we crossed that Golden Gate, Liam with Deirdre in her *dumetorum*-colored RAV4, me following in Powdermilk. Over the bridge, we swung around to the Marin Headlands unit of Golden Gate National Recreation Area in search of still more rarities. There, warm and sunny where in February I was nearly blasted off the rocks, we walked up into a green bowl that was once a firing range. The ruins of the metal and wood contraption that moved the dummy targets up and down now rusted in the trench at the back. Along a south-facing slope, with thistles and mustards and more in bloom, we found the desired butterflies.

First, the celebrated mission blue. Several each of males and females glinted over the lupines they crave. These deep blue beauties remain a conservation cause célèbre in San Francisco, where they drive much of the habitat management debate. The whole habitat conservation plan (HCP) amendment, a major retrenchment for the Endangered Species Act, came about in order to palliate developers over this listed butterfly's requirements on San Bruno Mountain. It is still unclear whether the HCP will adequately protect it, and its San Francisco Peninsula habitats, in the long run. But today, at least, it seemed safe here on National Park Service land. Two years on, Liam would be featured in the *San Francisco Chronicle* along with the mission blues he'd helped return to Twin Peaks, after their thirty-year absence from the city.

Next came one of the most abundant butterflies in America, the common ringlet; but instead of the ordinary ocher type, what flew here were pale white California ringlets. The final entrant was another, larger white flier: the fresh cream and broccoli-streaked species known as the large marble. That common name seems silly in much of the West, where *Euchloe ausonides* is a smallish butterfly. But here, near its type locality, the subspecies *E. a. ausonides* really is substantial, twice the size of the Olympia marbles in that magical north Texas graveyard, which now seemed so very far away.

Before we'd left the city, Liam had told us that the green hairstreaks' habitat was underlain by the geologic formation known as the Franciscan Chert. I heard "Franciscan Church," not entirely inappropriate for that surprising Sunday in the Sunset. Now, in Marin, a wild red-chert bowl gaped from the greater green bowl of the valley, a natural sun trap. Dressed with lupines and served by mission blues in cerulean vestments, it could have been the type locality of the "Franciscan Church" formation.

Lying just across the hills from Muir Woods, the Marin Headlands are part of Mía Monroe's Park Service demesne. Now, sated spiritually and scientifically but corporeally starved, we repaired to Mía and Steve's ranger cabin for his BBQ chicken and beer. Man cannot live, after all, by butterflies alone. Basking there in the company of good friends and in the satisfaction only the field affords, with soft blues playing in the background, in the shadow of Muir Woods and the sunset of a very long outing, only one thing stood between me and home: the butterfly that is John Muir's very namesake.

19. DOUBLE SCOTCH ON THE ROCKS

Mía has always hoped that Muir's hairstreak might be found near Muir Woods. The small elfin was named for John Muir in 1881 by Henry Edwards, a leading California lepidopterist of his time. It has at times been subordinated under the Nelson's or juniper hairstreak, but the Pelham *Catalogue* recognized it as a full species, to my delight and Mía's. The *Mitoura* expert John Lane suggested that Mía seek it in a particular Sargent's cypress grove on Mt. Tamalpais in Marin County, just above the monument she manages.

Still consumed with the Muir Woods centennial, Mía couldn't come along. So Barbara and I met at Pan Toll in cool coastal fog and cloud and hiked up the Simmons Trail to Barth's Retreat, entering the cypress grove near the top of the ridge. We passed through splendid ferns and flowers in meadows and edges of Douglas-fir and redwood. Barbara knew all the wildflowers—*Whippleya* and *Pickeringia, Sisyrinchium, Sidalcea,* and *Sanicula,* the calypso and coral root. We noted *Perideridia,* known by the natives as yampah, the chief host plant for anise swallowtails before fennel came. The loveliest flowers to me were the wild irises, ranging from browny mauve through lavender to cream. Barbara's knowledge of the native plants was admirable, to be sure; but her delight in the plants, as in a golden-furred tiger-moth caterpillar on an iris leaf, was boundless, like a child's.

Up on top, Sargent's cypress grew dense, abundant, and distinctive, with its broad, fanlike fronds. We roamed sheltered coves of cypress among manzanita and madroña, tapping, tapping. It was wild back among the cypresses, but April was ending cloudy and cool, whereas March had been hot here. *Mitoura muiri* might be over with, for all we knew. At any rate, they never appeared. Down at the bottom of the mountain in the Pelican Inn, Barbara and I toasted our attempt, the hundredth anniversary of Muir Woods, and the fiftieth of the famous circumnavigation of Mt. Tamalpais by Allen Ginsberg, Gary Snyder, and Philip Whalen, described by Jack Kerouac in *The Dharma Bums*. The hike is still enacted annually, with Gary Snyder taking part sometimes. But the butterfly that bears the name of the patron saint of all California hikers has yet to be spotted on Tamalpais.

The next day, Mía and I met Barbara at the Sol Cafe in San Rafael, and our old trio proceeded to Miss Hallberg's Butterfly Garden outside Sebastopol—an absolute must for this year. It is a trip we have taken together several times before, always with a mix of joy and concern. Miss Hallberg, a.k.a. Louise, greeted us in a straw bonnet with a silver swallowtail on it, big dark glasses, a green silk blouse above her high belt, and a pretty field skirt with fronds, admirals, monarchs, swallowtails, and blues all over it. Right away we learned that her monarchs laid no eggs last year, and she saw just one buckeye; that her pipevines laid eggs densely on the flowers of the Dutchman's pipe, not the leaves, for the first time ever. Do freeze and drought render leaves of poor quality, she wondered, while the more succulent flowers retain their chemical cues? She has released thirteen pipevines so far this year, and there are more coming. All the essential news dispensed, we finally got a hug.

Louise Hallberg has run this butterfly garden on a fertile corner of her family's orchard land for some twenty years, hosting thousands of students and other visitors. Now ninety-three, with limited vision and hearing, she carries on. More and more, she says, school groups have docents, so she doesn't do as much teaching, and she feels somewhat extraneous. I said she seemed to be in good spirits, and Louise said, "Well—it's okay." She smiled and chuckled a lot, while deploring the loss of this or that particular change. Mía and I exchanged a smile; Louise is still the miracle we have come to know and love.

Louise's brother-in-law and steadfast helper, Haven Best, dropped over to join our walk around the place. It was *Papilio* city at the old rock-rimmed spring—anise, tiger, and pipevine swallowtails all zipping and zooming over juniper, Japanese maple, lilac, and rhododendron, and coming down to nectar on purple wallflowers, beneath an overarching white oak. Five 'tails circled together through the heat of the glade. Louise can still make out the swallowtails, and with her glass, we showed her the sawfly larvae that were eating up a willow. In the meadow, green and flowery and breezy, not a lot was flying.

Back in a shady bower for lunch, we looked for Lorquin's admiral, which had been around. Louise so wanted us to see it, as it would have been new for my year, but it eluded us. A pair of mournful duskywings appeared, *Erynnis tristis* trysting on peach twigs. We spoke with her helper Catalan, an endless source of energy and quiet aid, and asked after Wintress, her longtime assistant, who has one of my favorite names ever. We all wish we could do more to help this bent and ancient dynamo, who has been about the best butterfly ambassador any of us has ever known, and who just keeps going. It's difficult now for Louise to maintain her notes, voluminous over the years. Yet she goes out for hours with the groups, and loads of school kids are booked for May. It was time for her nap, and for us to go. With a hug from Louise expressly for Thea, we took our leave from Miss Hallberg's remarkable garden.

Unready to give up on Muir's hairstreak, I called John Lane, who vouchsafed me a location in the Coast Range east of Clear Lake. On the last day of April, I struck north through Napa, stopping to stretch at the old Bale Grist Mill. At thirty-six feet, it is the largest overshot water wheel west of Mississippi, where I'd somehow missed the bigger one. Above the cool, shady millstream, a silver-spotted skipper tapped a red spicebush flower. One whiff transported me back forty years to Sequoia National Park, where spicebush around the mouth of Crystal Cave enveloped me in a cloying warmth when I emerged from ranger walks underground. There are no spicebush swallowtails in California, but a pipevine's pupal shell hung from a purple vetch. Half a dozen new butterflies streamed down a dry tributary in quick succession: Propertius duskywing, northern checkerspot, both western and pale tiger swallowtails, a California sister circling over the streambed, and its mimic, that Lorquin's admiral we'd never found at Miss Hallberg's. Both species flashed their blazing orange wingtips, the lesser Lorquin's an evolutionary mirror of its big sister.

Beyond Clear Lake, east of Wilbur Hot Springs, I drove straight up Bear Valley, then turned back westward up to serpentine Walker Ridge. John had said that Sargent's cypress grew along the creek below, while MacNab's cypress occurred on the ridge. *M. muiri* uses both. The canyon lay in shade, and I didn't see any cypresses down there anyway; but the top was still in sun when I made it up to the ridge at six PDT (five, PBT). An exhaustive search on foot, through tough walls of manzanita, produced little cypress—until sunset, when I discovered loads of it in the other direction on Walker Ridge! I'd neglected to ask John which way to turn once I got up there. Frustrated to the max, I knew I must stay, camp, and check it out in the morning, despite the time crunch.

So I settled into a cove among the cypresses, off the ridge road. The night cooled off fast. As I cooked my noodles, brilliant planets and stars, lots and lots of them, came out, unwrapping a night sky such as few I'd ever known. When Barbara, Mía, and I had left Miss Hallberg's, we'd stopped at a bee and honey store in Sebastopol that they both love. I resisted at the time but later kiped one of Barbara's jars of poison-oak honey, which she refers to as California sumac. Now I spread my new *Toxicodendron diversilobum* honey on Carr's crackers for dessert with an Anchor Steam beer and wrote in my journal, listening to Beethoven's Fifth on the radio. As of today, I noted, one-third of the way through the year, I'd tallied 167 species. Multiply that times three, and you get 501—one more than my goal of 500 species. I was very tired; it was good that I didn't try to drive those tough roads all night long. Besides, I told the stars and the nearest MacNab's cypress, I didn't come this far just to blow kisses at John Muir.

May Day at 7:30, bright sun was pouring over the ridge and porridge steaming, as the cypresses and cypress bugs warmed up. "Mr. Muir and Mr. MacNab!" I intoned. "If ye be here, ye maun kindly consaider comin' *oot!*" I set forth at ten, walking up and down Walker Ridge road, checking nectar. Pink grass widows, yellow *Calicortis*, a beautiful big blue *Penstemon*, and a striking maroon sessile lily all decorated the serpentine. Ducking into a sheltered cove of cypresses, I yipped my appreciation as the first Muir's hairstreak materialized and basked on manzanita for a good look. Hairstreaks hold their wings closed, so you see the underside: in this case the forewing coppery, the hindwing based in grainy purple-slate, grading out into lilac, rust, and a sparkly blue rim, all crossed by a zaggy white line. John Muir would have no complaint with his patronymic.

Another Muir's appeared on an exposed road slope on a yellow composite, then more on a small white borage called popcorn flower. Along with superficially similar brown elfins, they also employed the tubular white flowers of a shiny, low shrub called yerba santa. I was surprised that their tiny proboscises could get in there.

Topping the ridge, I dropped down to a small valley. Its creek was mostly dry but held puddles and trickles running over serpentine through gray pines and MacNab's cypresses. I gasped as I came upon a crowd of Scotties at a patch of popcorn flower about the size of a kiddie wading pool. Literally dozens of John Muir's own butterflies clambered over, dug into, and streaked about the white bed of borage. I watched, and netted, and studied for a long time, just shaking my head.

And that wasn't all. First, I found my first *Ochlodes agricola*, a small gold triangle in the dried yellow grass. Modern books call it the rural skipper, but I prefer its old vernacular—the farmer. Then, tipped off by a whine that I first took for a mosquito's, I looked down and saw that it came from a middling black robber fly on the rocky bank. It was perched near another, larger one, doubtless the female. When she flew, he followed and hovered just behind until she alighted, when he again settled beside her, over and over, until one flight finally took them out of my sight. I wondered if they ever succeeded in hooking up. With all the false starts, it's amazing everything isn't almost extinct, like the nonreproducing Shakers. For me, following that buzz confirmed Gary Snyder's advice in *Tamalpais Walking*: "Attention to the particular is never in vain."

Back on the ridge road, I met a bright male Edith's checkerspot of the race *rubicunda*. Studied in every aspect of its ecology and population biology by Paul Ehrlich and his Stanford students and colleagues, *Euphydryas editha* has become one of the best-known insects in the world. Its contraction northward, as shown by the scientist Clare Parmesan, is considered a bellwether of climate change.

At noon, it was time to leave this Brigadoon before it vanished beneath me. I crossed valley after range after valley, through a sea of yellow lupine. The McGarrigle girls, backing up their countrymen Muir and MacNab, came staticky out of Nevada City, singing "Talk to Me of Mendocino"—well, I was in Mendocino National Forest, after all. Then, as I was crossing Leesville Gap, the song on the radio talked about crossing a gap, on the way home, at the end of a long, long ride.

After the last valley and ridge, I came down to pecan groves and oats, and finally the 20, just twenty hours after I'd left it. I-5 came at Williams, six hundred miles from home. And when I reached Thea by telephone at five, I'd made Willows. As I guessed, she supported my decision to camp among the stars and the Scots.

Twenty hours later, as I came off K-M Hill into green Gray's River Valley, Thea was coming the other direction on her way to work in Skamokawa. We both stopped, and we embraced on the roadside as log trucks hooted. From the forget-me-not bed in our backyard, an echo azure fluttered up to welcome me home (as I flattered myself), flashed sky blue, then settled back among the sky blue blossoms. Somehow, I'd been lucky enough to miss it so far, all this way.

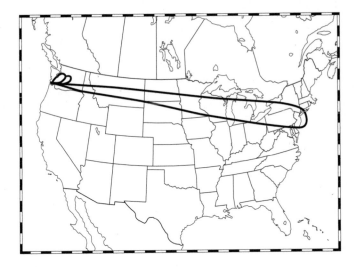

Hunting for Hairstreaks I

I connected the blue marks on these maps mentally, imagining possibilities, not planning a route as a military man would, but feeling my way towards the places that most aroused my curiosity, more like a prospector.

—Roger Deakin, *Waterlog*

1. OBSCURA

"This is a nice little glass," said Mr. Close, looking out his window and turning the screw. "A *nice* little glass."

Before I left Seattle, I went to see Mr. Howard Close at Close Scientific Instruments. Just as Dave at Stirling Honda has kept Powdermilk on the road for decades, Mr. Close has maintained one of my other major tools: my binoculars, which I have had even longer than the car. This small, light pair of Leitz 6X24 Trinovids has been with me all over the world, from New Guinea to New Jersey. My beloved binos have parted from me many times, on planes, trains, security checkpoints, and mountaintops, and through grace, goodwill, and good luck, have always come back to me. Many birders would consider six powers of magnification too small, and modern butterfliers use binoculars that focus more closely. But my 6X24s are exceedingly clear, gather good light even at dusk, and serve beautifully as an all-around optic. Fitting my hand like Marsha's net stick, they've become a part of my body, just as much. I feel not only naked but blinded without them.

Mr. Close had recognized their measure when I first took my binos to him after a bad bump had misaligned them: "A *nice* little glass." He's said it every time I've gone in, for cleaning or a new strap or a jury-rigged eyecup. In a casting call for Geppetto, Mr. Close would be a shoo-in. His old shop on Fourth Avenue is stuffed with splendid if obsolete confections of glass, steel, brass, and leather, as well as modern instruments awaiting his attention. I like going there whether or not I have need of his expertise.

Now, the specks in the left ocular that had been mildly bugging me, no big deal really, made a good excuse to drop by on my way out of town. Mr. Close said he couldn't see any specks and recommended that I just use and enjoy my nice little glass. I told him I certainly do, every day of my life, and thanked him. On my way out, he said my beat sandals were in better shape than his. I challenged him on wallets; his wasn't bad, but it didn't match my well-traveled, lost-and-found, duct-taped billfold.

A couple of days after I'd gotten home from the last leg, Thea and I topped K-M Hill again, this time together. We had just enough time for a Columbia Gorge butterfly-and-wildflower field trip before heading north for the operation. Margined whites and echo blues crossed sunny patches in the road. At the Kalama Bluffs south of Longview, Sara orangetips flicked over the ditches. Their orange apices looked disembodied, like fire-colored fireflies operating on their own. Silvery blues lit up the verges everywhere we stopped, from Kalama to Washougal Oaks to Beacon Rock and beyond, this northern subspecies in none of the hurt of its at-risk cousin in Palos Verdes.

In the afternoon, we drove up Blue Lake Road above the Columbia. There, in a clearing off Oak Lake Road, we found what we'd come for: a two-banded checkered-skipper, spreading its wings in a nettle patch. Its clean, ivory-on-charcoal speckled pattern stood out sharply at rest, unlike its buzzy gray blur in flight. Later, at the Walking Man in Stevenson, the umbrellas in the beer garden were labeled "Butterfly Freedom."

"Appropriate name for a western Washington bumbershoot," I said, "when you think how many days here are butterfly-free."

"But not today," said Thea.

Late in the warm day, across the Bridge of the Gods at Wahkeena Falls, we stood on a stone bridge, mist full in our faces, in infinite green and freshness, the antithesis of the desert in drought. We were looking for green hairstreaks on a friend's advice, and didn't find them. But that was okay. We never got far enough up the gorge for the drier east-side flowers, but we enjoyed the wetter west-side ones in full glory—larkspurs, tellinas, meadow rues, sorrels, and more—their rich, warm, sweet fragrance filling the air. Just what Thea needed to see her through what came next.

On the sixth of May, as Thea checked into the Seattle Cancer Care Alliance for preop tests and preps, I took the South Lake Union Trolley (lovingly known to its fans as the SLUT) directly to

Dr. Branch's office downtown. It seemed wise to investigate the shape of my oral minefield, which had been sending bomb threats again in recent weeks. David confirmed that Dr. Rembos had saved me some real grief, as well as given me such a great butterfly tip, back in Florida. But the original crown that fell out in January (not one of his) needed replacing; and tragically, the tooth beneath a real beauty of a crown he had laboriously installed not long ago was cracked and dying. That crown even had a butterfly on it—the inspiration of David's assistant Heidi—though I never got a good look at it until, sadly, it was unseated. But wait, there's more: one of my two remaining wisdom teeth was ticking to detonate too, and it needed to come out pronto.

So what began as an exam became an emergency extraction. David's oral surgeon colleague, Dr. Maring, said he could do it right then and there, or else in a month or so. He advised me that, with my old guy's dense bones, he'd probably have to cut and chisel and said that I could expect quite a lot of pain for a week or so. This alarmed me, not least because I needed to be alert to take Thea for her surgery early the next morning and to support and care for her later. If it meant we were both out of commission at the same time, I wouldn't be much use for Thea. But there was nothing for it.

So the surgery buddy went into surgery himself. I leaned back in the chair and girded my oral loins, as it were, for agony. But amazingly, Dr. Maring had them both out whole in five minutes. I felt next to no pain . . . and never did. I took an ibuprofen or two for swelling but never touched the Percocet. My one disappointment was the nitrous oxide. He gave me quite a dose, but it failed to register. I'd never had it before, and in view of my pallid drug history, I was looking forward to a bit of a legal buzz. Nothing.

Thea's operation, however, was not nothing. The tumor was in the psoas major muscle in her back but too near the spine for safe removal from that side. Access from the front meant massive abdominal surgery—the third in Thea's five-year adventure in cancer. Her oncologist, Dr. Swensen, was joined by a soft-tissue surgeon at the University of Washington Medical Center for the operation. Meanwhile, my stepdaughter, Dory, and I walked across the sunny and flowery UW campus. I showed her shrines and historic sites for her parents, me, and her virtual aunt and uncle, JoAnne and

Fayette. This was the habitat we'd all haunted together in the sixties. It helped take our minds off our fears.

The operation went well. Back in the hospital, Thea's room was full of flowers—forget-me-nots picked by Dory, red alstroemerias, purple campanulas, and many others from Thea's concerned friends. And when Dory's brother, Tom, brought his family for Mother's Day, little Cristina Linnaea came dressed in pink and carrying a big jar of pink tulips. I placed Thea's wedding ring back on her hand. Out her window in 7SE, violet-green swallows swooped over the Montlake Cut and Portage Bay, where Tom used to cox the UW crew, and a gold light settled over spring cottonwoods along the shore.

While Thea was on the mend, I met the journalist Eric Wagner for a day trip to Hood Canal and the southeastern Olympic Peninsula. He had assignments to write articles on the Butterfly Big Year for *National Wildlife* and *High Country News*. I was hoping for Johnson's hairstreak, a rare, old-growth obligate species that Jon Pelham and I used to find at Staircase in southeastern Olympic National Park. We took the big ferry to Bremerton, then drove north to Lake Cushman. The day, supposed to be sunny, was cold and cloudy; and the Lake Cushman Road was closed by winter landslides in any case. Late-afternoon hunts for Moss's elfins, pine elfins, and green hairstreaks with the crack butterflier, Idie Ulsh, all bombed. At last up at Mt. Walker, a spurt of thin sun brought out two shimmering echo azures for Eric to see, so we were not completely skunked. The outing might not have gone just as I'd hoped or he had anticipated, but at least it gave him a good sense of the challenges I faced every day.

With Thea comfortable, now out of the hospital, I went to see Mr. Close and then made one more nearby excursion. Fleeing I-5 after Olympia, I ducked into Scatter Creek Wildlife Area, one of the few remaining glacial outwash prairie preserves in the south Puget Trough. These remnant grasslands hold several special butterflies otherwise excluded from Pugetopolis by either forest cover or development. At the North Unit parking lot, a sign announced that catch-and-release of butterflies was prohibited, as well as collecting, never mind that there was plenty of hunting, with shotgun shells lying about, dogs off leash, and so on. This was the first time

I'd ever seen a net-and-release rule on game land. But pals of mine were responsible, and I knew their rationale was protecting certain rare prairie species under restoration. I walked among the camas, fescue, violets, and shooting stars, and saw one of those species—I think—a small yellow-orange bit, almost certainly a mardon skipper. This is one of the few places the narrowly endemic, disjunct *Polites mardon* survives, but it disappeared without alighting. It would take a better sighting than that to count it.

Striding across the prairie, I came upon a big, very yellow female margined white, drinking deep from a blue camas lily—such a sight! Then a female echo blue, spread, showing her charcoal hems and chalky ocelli; and two clear azure males at mud on the shore of slow Scatter Creek. On a fescue mound appeared the only ringlet, richly ocher, not at all like the white ones of the Marin Headlands; something chased it, possibly another mardon.

And then came the new check on the list I was hoping for: a hoary elfin, very fresh, warm hazel above, dark chestnut at the base, with a broad, cool, frosty band, the "hoary" bit, on the outer half below. Many elfins rose and bounced around like jumping beans, all over the numerous kinnikinnick patches and mounds. So if I had so far missed the other spring *Callophrys* I'd sought—*johnsoni, mossii, eryphon, perplexa*—at least *polios obscura* had checked in. On the way out, I met Mary McCollum, a former student of mine, fine naturalist, and hired net for Fish and Wildlife, conducting a mardon skipper survey. She told me that mardons were recorded last season in both the locations where I thought I'd seen them.

I was more than reluctant to leave Thea so soon, to prepare for the next journey. I hated saying goodbye again for a couple of weeks, and I did not feel good about being away at such a time. But Thea was sure and encouraging about it. "Get back out there," she said, the color back in her cheeks. She was recovering well at Fayette and JoAnne's apartment by the Ballard Locks, with plenty of good care from friends. I left knowing that this unwonted (and unwanted) but unavoidable detour in our lives had gone as well as we could have hoped. Thea had done this before, and we knew she could do it again. I knew, too, that she would be well again soon.

2. HESSELI

In the months of wending, I'd forgotten just how sick and tired I was of airports and air trips. Dory took me too darned early to the Portland airport, and I flew off toward Philly, and remembered. Most of the successful birding Big Years had depended on a great deal of air travel, with the notable early exceptions of Peterson and Fisher, and Kaufman. Not only had I no desire to fly after the butterflies but I could not afford it. I would make a few flights during the year but in every case either through redemption of frequent flier miles or patronage. This time I was being flown to Connecticut to receive an alumnus award from the Yale School of Forestry and Environmental Studies.

As part of the festivities, I took an alumni field trip to Yale Myers Forest in central Connecticut. I had a fine time riding in the van with old friends from forestry school, hearing everyone's Lyme Disease stories, and catching up on thirty-plus years. The singing and displaying redstarts and red-eyed vireos, the eastern chipmunk scampering over the rock walls, and the walk to salamander research sites were all very fine. But this really *ought* to have been my day for eastern mustard whites and spring azures. Instead, the clouds gave way to a pelt of rain, and I saw no butterflies whatsoever.

I spent much of the remaining time in New Haven with Ellen Mahoney, widow of my late, lifelong mentor, Charles Remington. With the sky a bit lighter, we explored a beechwood preserve in Guilford, where flowering dogwoods alongside a grassy meadow promised azures. But even the violets, asters, and strawberry blossoms were innocent of insects. We climbed up to a rocky ledge among the beeches, but the best we got was a fine gander at a male scarlet tanager. We drove to the traprock ridge of West Rock, a favorite place of Remington's. I'd done a project on its conservation history and was glad to see that it was better protected now than ever. Charles had long studied the butterflies there, contending it was the richest butterfly locale in New England. But in the steady rain, you'd never know it.

I was both honored and deeply moved to help Ellen spread some of Charles's ashes under a sassafras sapling planted for him at the Eli Whitney cotton gin historic site and waterfall in Hamden. We dug some soil away, seeded in some ashes, cried, laughed, and covered them. The white powder clung to the soil, the shovel, our hands. I tasted it—limy and bitter, like hops. Then Ellen and I walked the Yale campus. We came to a small gray clapboard house with slate roof and gable windows, where Sally Hughes and I had once lived rent-free in exchange for watering plants in university greenhouses. A sign at the door now read "Beware of Bees/First Floor." A friendly, big tabby rubbed and wanted in, but I had returned my key thirty-four years ago. I turned to point out to Ellen the room where I began *Magdalena Mountain* upstairs, and just then a cabbage white flew over the slate roof and disappeared among white flowering dogwood blossoms.

It was funny that cabbage whites were my sole New England butterflies on this visit. In my 1976 doctoral dissertation, written under Charles Remington's supervision, I made the following acknowledgment: "Lastly, I wish to thank the forgotten (never known?) person(s) responsible for the introduction of the European Cabbage Butterfly to North America: during the final days of this undertaking, *Pieris rapae* gave me certain knowledge that butterflies exist, other than on paper."

When I lived in New Haven, the train station was the meanest of shabby Amshaks. Since then, the magnificent terminal portrayed in any number of Ivy League books and movies from the thirties and forties has been superbly restored by Amtrak. Driving me there on the morning of May 19, Ellen passed Merwyn's Gallery—where Sally bought my "nice little glass" for me in 1975.

The flexibility I so jealously guarded for the year was now coming into play. The dates in New Haven were fixed, but my plans for the aftermath evolved as I went. I had anticipated traveling north after the Yale festivities, deeper into New England. I thought this would be my best chance to find the early hairstreak, the storied congener of the Arizona hairstreak I'd seen in the Magdalenas in New Mexico. All lepidopterists of my generation grew up with the small blue-green *Erora laeta* as a lifetime desideratum. It was considered so rare, so hard to find, that it achieved mythical status out of all proportion with its appearance. No one seemed to be able to locate it with any regularity. In more recent times, *E. laeta*'s association with the forest canopy, and with beech trees in particular, made finding it a little more tractable, with certain sites considered almost reliable. Chief among these was Mt. Greylock in northwestern Massachusetts.

My plan involved driving to Greylock by rental car, then coming back through upstate New York to hunt other northeastern spring specialties with Robert Dirig of Cornell. Robert, one of the earliest leaders of the Xerces Society, was also a pioneer in Karner blue conservation and is a definitive New England field lepidopterist. Then I was going to make my way back to Florida, by rail or bus. Back in March, the Coopers had invited me on the annual butterfly count at Key Largo in early June. If I could join them, it would mean a chance to see the federally endangered Schaus's swallowtail. I had talked the airline into flying me home from Miami instead of New York, so everything seemed to be a go for *Erora laeta* and *Papilio aristodemus ponceanus*.

But that plan came unlaid. First, I learned that the road up Mt. Greylock was closed for the next *two years* for rebuilding. I would have been happy to take my chances in similar beechwood habitats, but then I heard that the long-term forecast for New England was, in a word, crappy. The last nail was advice from lepidopterists that the spring emergence was way behind, because of the weather. So, scratch New England for now. Then, as for Florida, I just couldn't brook being away from Thea so long during her recovery, in order to (figuratively and maybe) bag the Schaus's. So I asked the good people at Yale to rebook my return from Philadelphia, at a cost that would barely be noticed against the interest on my college loans, only recently paid off, and they kindly complied. So I decided to pass on *ponceanus* as well as *laeta* and to bail on this trip much earlier than I'd originally planned. What remained was just to figure out how to spend the last few days of the journey. Where would *you* go at such a time but New Jersey?

Amtrak took me south to Philadelphia, where Jane Ruffin collected me at the huge-pillared 30th Street Station. A veteran butterflier and distinguished photographer, Jane is an incisive Englishwoman who suffers no fools and is second to no one I know for her mordant wit. The last time I'd been here was to see the eighteenth-century botanist John Bartram's Garden; I was hopeful of seeing his namesake hairstreak before the year was out. But the hairstreak of current interest was one I'd seen only once, with Jane, a few years ago: *Callophrys (Mitoura) hesseli*. Hessel's hairstreak is more closely related to John Muir's hairstreak than to John Bartram's. On the way out to Jane's house, we reprised the day when she took me to see my life Hessel's in 1995. She reminded me that I had also achieved my life Big Day for ticks: three species—wood, lone star, and deer—all embedded.

This time Jane was otherwise engaged, but she got me back to the station, and I took New Jersey Rail to Egg Harbor. Jack Connor of Stockton College and the author Pat Sutton met my train. Our trip into the Pine Barrens was my first. Pygmy pine forest painted the wet, gray day in the colors of golden-heather, white sand myrtle, pink sheep laurel, ivory leatherleaf, and various blueberries, all in bloom. Scrub oak and blackjack oak interleaved with *Pinus rigida* on fire heath where the vegetation shot up after last year's flare-caused blaze, from a drop that missed the nearby bombing range.

A woodcock hunched sodden but exquisite in the rain. We were sodden too, and anything but exquisite. Chilly and hungry, we took shelter in Lucille's, a crossroads café famous among all Pine Barrens butterfliers and other natural history pilgrims. We downed good old toasted cheese and BLTs as we made friends with Lucille and her daughter, the waitress. The locals were used to birders and wildflower types, but these butterfly people, out hunting some goddam streakhairs in the rain, well. . . .

Back out on a bog boardwalk, pixie moss and curly grass fern twined subtly over the sphagnum. The wealth of insectivorous plants—round, spatulate, and long-necked sundews as well as purple pitcher plant, with its big, round, maroon flowers—would have you believe there were insects here, but the insects gave no evidence of it themselves. Certainly there were no Hessel's attending the masses of white sand myrtle, putatively their favorite tipple. I let my eyes settle on the amazing dragon's mouth orchids—orchid pink, flame-mouthed, fine enough for any high school corsage—bursting out around the bog. Just for form, we looked and looked and shook and shook the ranks of Atlantic white cedars. Actually cypresses, these coastal bog conifers offer the sole, obligatory host for Hessel's. We put up a few handsome fawn and rust geometer moths and got soaked through for it. Our eyes meeting through the shower-stream, Jack and I burst into giggles at the silliness of mission versus reality, as Jersey water poured off our slickers.

After the bog, all of us soaked and chilly, we squished back down the Garden State Parkway to Jack and Jesse Connor's for restorative hot chocolate and a look at their wondrous garden, which gave meaning to the state's slogan. Then all back to the 1840s, two-story clapboard that Pat shares with her husband, Clay, in Goshen, for a memorable naturalists' supper including my good friends Mark Garland and Paige Cunningham from Cape May. Mark and I made plans to meet in Alaska. After a productive (but no new record) tick check, Clay cooked us up a fine mess of drum he'd caught. And in the night, the storm washed away all the rain.

So, *sun*, for my last Jersey field day! Another Cape May butterfly friend, transplanted from Montana, Will Kerling, joined the Suttons, the Connors, and me for an expedition back to the edge of the barrens. When Will had to leave his beloved Missoula, where he had found nearly a hundred species of butterflies on one mountain, he adopted an ingenious way of compensating. His new passion was finding one or more butterflies on the wing on as many days of the year as he could at Cape May. The famous birders' mecca at the tip of New Jersey, where monarchs congregate along with feathered migrants before crossing Delaware Bay, has a mild climate; even so, Will has surprised even local butterfly experts with his early and late dates for various species. Now we walked the Old Robbins Trail to see what we could see. Butterflies, absent the day before, materialized in force: spicebush swallowtails, Zabulon skippers, red-banded hairstreaks, singletons of worn Henry's and eastern pine elfins, for starters.

Then just after noon, Hessel's hairstreaks came out! My raison d'être for this whole Jersey caper, *C. hesseli* is another species, like *Erora laeta*, whose very name conjures romance and rarity in the ears of butterfly lovers. Restricted to white cedar bogs on the East Coast, and only a fraction of those, guarded by legions of ticks and squadrons of mosquitoes, Hessel's is wanted much more than spotted. Yet few of the seekers, I suspect, have a sense of the man who lent his name to this sought-after animal.

Sid Hessel was a successful banker who used to watch monarchs sail past his skyscraper window in the city, then commute back to his peaceful country home in Connecticut. A good friend of Charles Remington and productive volunteer at Yale Peabody Museum of Natural History's entomology department for decades, Sid was a friendly face behind a pipe when I was a curatorial assistant in the museum. With distinguished collecting pals including Cyril dos Passos and Alexander "Bill" Klots, Sid often visited Lakehurst in the Pine Barrens for its excellent insects. He noticed that the "olive hairstreaks" in the white cedar bogs, unlike the ones common around old-field red cedars, had a bluer, grainier scale pattern and various other subtle differences, as well as an utterly different ecology. In 1950, George Rawson and Ben Ziegler described the new species, naming it for their perspicacious friend. Sid Hessel was the quintessential *amateur*—"one who loves"—and out of love, looks closely, and learns much.

Jack spotted the first one, a fresh female with big abdomen, and we watched her at length. She had the most extraordinary false head, with white-tipped tails at a forty-five-degree angle and bulging black spots looking uncannily like eyes below antennae. In the next half hour we saw ten or a dozen *hesseli*, three or four on a single shrub. Perched on federbush, they appeared to nectar from bee-bored holes at the bases of the white bells lined up along the stem. The punctured flowers smelled like honey on the air. As lovely as Muir's, they were differently colored, like green leaves with chocolate drops. The Hessel's were compliant—easy to approach, watch, and photograph. One worn and bird-struck example and other fresh ones flew high up into a white cedar, a new behavior in Will's experience.

The black water of the white cedar swamp lapped either side of the trail. Prothonotary warblers and green frogs sang out of the deeps. One sad note intruded. Back in the bushes, a dreadful stink gave away a gruesome trapper's larder of flayed carcasses, mostly otters and beavers. We'd noted otter spraint not far away. Their tortured yellow grins haunt me still. Butterflies often come to carrion, and one spicebush swallowtail blessed this grisly bone pile, but no nymphs or satyrs. Poached or legal, I don't know how they do it. Others might feel the same about the voucher specimens I take, still others about the mosquitoes people swat, or the animals they eat. We all make our own personal accommodations with killing. But knowing that doesn't make me any happier about those otters.

In the afternoon we hiked the abandoned railroad tracks on the Dennisville-Woodbine line, communed with great crested flycatchers, solitary sandpipers, Fowler's toad, and a spectacular five-foot pine snake that slithered across the rusty rails like so many cars derailing. Among the many Juvenal's and wild indigo duskywings, a fresh frosted elfin perched on the earth for a good look, less frosty and much pinker than the Florida ones. We were hoping out loud for the cobweb skipper when a female alighted beside a shard of white porcelain insulator between the rails. Her striking pattern showed off well against the ballast as a tiny red mite ran around her tarsi. A second cobweb came and clung next to her, then by short hops, found ground bramble blossoms. A worn male alighted beside a tie. As a surprising bonus, three common roadside-skippers turned up. Hardly common in South Jersey, no more than singletons had been seen for fifty years until then.

Pat took me to Beaver Swamp to look for spring azures in the afternoon. A hen turkey with eight polts scratched in the verge, and gull-billed terns with their heavy black beaks hawked for frogs in the lily ponds, but we couldn't find *Celastrina*. Along the woods lane ants tended aphid-curled cherry leaves and woolly aphids on alder leaves, and we thought of harvester butterflies, whose own larvae prey on woolly aphids. Searching for them and for emperor larvae on hackberries, I managed only to alarm a woman out walking her squeaker dog as I burst from the foliage like some second coming of the Green Man.

The kind Suttons drove me all the way to Lindberg Field in Philadelphia at 3:00 A.M. to make a dawn departure for Portland. Before we sank into the heavy clouds over western Oregon, I glimpsed the Cascades stretching away north from Mt. Hood—a pearly string of peaks perching on the fleece. If I could have seen about that far into the future—past the first Swainson's thrush song, lilacs, and the joy of being at home in May with Thea; past the banana slugs chowing down on the petals of poppies and columbine—well, I might have spotted myself down there, pursuing the next chapter of the hairstreak hunt.

3. PERPLEXA

The first time I'd slept at Stonehenge, it was in a twin bed set crosswise just inside the rear door of a Ryder truck. I'd awakened to
the basalt breaks of the Columbia Gorge laid out before me, like
breakfast in bed for the eyes. After all these years I'd expected a
fence, or at least a stern sign. But no, so here I was again encamped
at Stonehenge, avoiding the stiff fee at the state park below, steeper
still at the motels across the river.

This stone circle was not in Wiltshire but at Maryhill, Washington.
Sam Hill, Quaker pacifist road builder and booster, built this version
of concrete and pebbles and dedicated it to thirteen young Klickitat
County men killed in World War I. The standing stones bore brass
plaques for each. When Sam saw Stonehenge in the teens, he was
told it was for human sacrifice. He said, "After all our civilization,
the flower of humanity is still being sacrificed to the god of war on
fields of battle," and he dedicated his henge to peace. He built it just
a standing stone's long sunrise shadow away from his lonely mansion folly, just above the cherries, peaches, and steeple of his model
village on the river.

Before retiring, I did handwork in my lantern beam: making
mini-butterfly triangles from Zig-Zag papers, sewing up a hole in
Akito's net bag, knitting up the rent leather seam in my collecting
bag. Listening to hymns, then oldies, then George Noory on *Coast
to Coast A.M.* about extraterrestrials and angels. Looking out at red
and amber lights of semis tracing the black canyon, and the bright
beams and loud horns of trains cutting through the Columbian coffee midnight.

Running that black and green slot to get here, I'd found the first
juba skipper not only for the year but also for my thirty-year study of

Lower Columbia butterflies. Then much farther up the gorge, on a mossy flat below Dog Mountain, Columbia dotted blues courted and mated around the puffy heads of northern buckwheat. Windsurfers and paragliders bounced about the surface of the Big River like so many aquatic butterflies. And so, to Stonehenge; and so to bed. I slept well, and though on my little inboard pallet instead of a made bed, I was open to the entire gorge just the same as before.

I awoke to meadowlark song and the sweet smell of . . . rain. The weather forecast said brighter by Thursday to the north, so I forsook the flowery gorge for Goldendale and Satus Pass, hoping for sucker holes along the way, if only to humor this sucker. My nets were ready to go—I'd reinforced Marsha's oft-broken pole, and Thea had even made me a new bag for my little hand net, Mini-Marsha—all we needed was the sun!

Stopping in Goldendale for coffee, I ducked into a secondhand store. They had books, and I needed one for the road. The moment I spotted a paperback in a neat maroon leatherette jacket, I knew what it had to be, and it was: *Blue Highways*. Rereading it over the coming months would bring nods of recognition, and surprises too—not least being the fact that William Least Heat-Moon had camped at Stonehenge! Just the book for this sucker looking for blue skies on small roads. Sucker spots were, indeed, showing to the north. And when I reached Satus Pass and turned up Ski Area Road into balsam and lupine mixed with running water, the sun emerged from one of the small blue holes.

Then, as if I'd scripted it, cow pie lotus appeared alongside the road. And on a single patch of lovage nectared two brown elfins, an echo blue, and two beautiful fresh bramble green hairstreaks—just what I'd come here for! They were almost as emerald as Liam's greenies in the Sunset District of San Francisco. Through taxonomic prestidigitation, the name *dumetorum*, which means "of the bramble," has come to apply to that SF species, known in English as the coastal green hairstreak, formerly *C. viridis*; while the common name "bramble green" has stuck with the northwest species formerly considered *dumetorum* but now assigned the specific epithet *perplexa*. This is just one example of how the muddy science of greenies "the dull brain perplexes," in Keats's words.

This habitat lay on the very border of the Yakama Indian Nation and Gifford Pinchot National Forest, as close as I was allowed to get to the reservation. Farther on I looked longingly into Kushi Creek, a famous butterfly locality now off-limits, fenced and posted by the Yakamas. At a pullout I'd used just last year, a tribal officer stopped and told me I couldn't be anywhere off the highway. Then the long, truck-grinding grade down to Toppenish, where I dowsed a Yakama milk shake from a onetime A&W.

Turning up into the foothills toward Wenas, I scanned an alfalfa field full of clouded sulphurs. The landowner lady stopped to see what I was doing. To her, they were hay pests, and she was right; but she liked the butterflies anyway. My first true fritillary of the year, *Speyeria coronis*, rose from a barren, littered ditch by another alfalfa field across the road from beat-up sage land. Sulphurs, frits, and skippers were all over the dusty margin, lapping at the drippings from the giant irrigation booms.

For many years, Washington Audubon Society members have gathered in Wenas Canyon for an annual campout and birding weekend, sometimes including a starling barbecue. I used to attend these forays long ago and thought I would come back for a look. I arrived at Wenas well before sunset. Vaux's swifts and swallows nickered and flicked through my campsite, a long loop of stream bank. The eve was extraordinarily peaceful. A fledgling spotted sandpiper chased its mother up the stream, rock to rock, then along the bank downstream, learning to hunt and peck for itself. *This* bird, with its high call, inky breast spots, and watery haunts, might better be called "water thrush" than the warbler that bears the name.

In the morning, I walked up a lithosol ridge bright with four species of buckwheat and masses of bitterroot on top. *Lewisia rediviva* was so named both for Captain Lewis and for its seeming immortality, reblooming each spring from vanished vegetation. Its display, like so many pink tutus tossed across the rocks, brought to mind the pink ice plant of Avalon but softer, in both petal and hue, and *native*. In a stunning pairing, a large mother-of-pearl spotted female juba skipper tanked up from bitterroot to bitterroot.

Butterfly hunters know that roads often furnish excellent territory. This fact owes partly to their edge quality, with woodland vegetation meeting the sunny opening of the cleared roadway. The wildflowers and other low plants growing in the verge offer plenty of nectar as well as caterpillar host plants. Roadsides' other important quality is moisture. Seeps, creeks, and waterfalls flow down to roads and the ditches that line them, carrying rain and meltwater, pooling, and saturating the gravel, sand, and soil. Male butterflies visit these damp spots, seeking not so much water as mineral salts dissolved in it.

Mud-puddle clubs may have hundreds of swallowtails, skippers, blues, and others. Preoccupied, they may be approached closely by a deliberate watcher, but one net swing sets up a swirl of wings that takes minutes to resettle. Thanks to mudding, checking out roadsides can be highly strategic; it was for me as I climbed toward Ellensburg Pass. My first happy find among the masses was Moss's elfin, one of the species I'd missed on Hood Canal. One old example kept company with brown elfins at the moist sand, a save for a species I'd thought past. Ditto for an indra swallowtail and a sagebrush checkerspot, both worn females—surprising, since females rarely puddle. A small white surprised me by being a Becker's, usually bigger, with parallel vein tracks of kelly green.

The next few novelties came in unmatched pairs. First, two successive mountain sulphurs that you can't find in alfalfa fields, one western and one Queen Alexandra's. Then a pair of coppers—purplish and lilac-bordered—the first shimmering amethyst above if sunshine strikes the right angle, the second adorned as its name says in any light. Next, the trickling ditch doubled up on new blues, as I put up a cloud and swept it. Releasing half a dozen species from Marsha's bag back to their pubbery, I noted the first arrowhead blue, our largest kind, blazoned with not just one arrowhead but a whole quiver full, and a new buckwheat blue awaiting a name.

Rotating over a lush stream bank and under a ponderosa pine, a pair of brown mites resolved into western pine elfins. Another one visited desert parsley, while one more, just out of its chrysalis, hung purplish and pendent from *Poa bulbosa*. This ubiquitous introduced grass nods in the breeze, faking butterfly shadows to the suggestible peripheral vision; now here it was with a real butterfly on it. The western pine elfin looked almost like the eastern, with their shared zigzag patterns, but it was a long way from that Louisiana buttercup to this Cascadian glade.

Just over Ellensburg Pass, the road crossed a high expanse of rocky ground covered with rounded mounds and broad intermounds of red-and-black basalt pebbles. The mounds had bunch grass on their slopes and basin big sagebrush on top, the whole thick with wildflowers. Mount Rainier echoed their form, shining to the southwest across the Goat Rocks. Having found two of four green hairstreaks—one in San Francisco, one on Satus Pass—I wondered if either of the missing greenies might be hilltopping here. I checked atop mound after mound, and from one a dark little butterfly shot up into the air after a checkerspot, then dropped to nectar on a buckwheat. I bricked it, then got one more chance at another in the lee of the same mound. This time I got it: *Callophrys affinis*, the western green hairstreak. Three down, one to go.

Few folks lived way up there. One fancy glass-and-pine edifice was where a European blonde was headed when she stopped to ask, "Vat are you catchink?" Her eyes popped at the bagful of blues I released for her. A sign by her gate said, "No light beer—no video games"—my kind of place. But most of the houses around were for western bluebirds. Every time I paused near one of them, a parent protested my trespass.

Yakima Valley Audubon's blue-roofed bluebird houses, all 118-plus of them, led me down to pavement. Down into a cold wind that seems to be almost a permanent feature in Ellensburg. Camped in the rest area east of the town, my car rocked in that wind, as well it might out there among the wind farms. Doing meticulous specimen preparation was difficult enough under the cramped circumstances with dim light and the atabatic rock 'n' roll, when I discovered that I had an ant in my pants and could do nothing about it until I finished. Then when I got to sleep at last, a car with its lights on pulled up between me and another sleeper. The driver got out, left the engine running, did a deal with a trucker, and pulled away again.

Next morn, up the Old Vantage Highway, the desert was already burned out with the advancing season. Phlox was over, but two brand fresh dark wood-nymphs nectared on sulphur flower and danced among the purple sage. A rock wren sang from a wire, flashing its buffy outer tail tips; then, as if remembering its name, it dropped the Leonard Cohen routine and flew down to a rock. At the entrance to the Whiskey Dick Wildlife Area, the wood-nymphs' cousins, bright new ocher ringlets, scattered all over some yellow daisyettes. They weren't new, but they were as pretty as anything, and they reminded me of my determination to resist contempt for the common.

Hazel Wolf was the centenarian doyenne of Seattle Audubon and the Queen of Wenas for decades. As Hazel put it, common things tend to become "justa birds." I remember how she was appalled on one trip when burrowing owls became "justa birds" for her. I also recall the thrill of finding my first ringlet, tatty as it was, on a family trip to Mt. Evans in Colorado. The challenge would be to bring that same attention and appreciation to every one of the uncounted thousands of ringlets I would see over many a grassland this year, and many a year to come. It was easy here, with these fresh beauties.

Shooting south down the Yakima River Canyon, I took the footbridge over to the Umtanum Recreation Site of the BLM. "Hot" was the operative word, at almost five post meridian. A sweaty hike up a steep side trail opened to a sight across the mouth of the canyonlet that made the effort worth it for sure: a duo of doubletails— two immense two-tailed tiger swallowtails, nectaring together on tall blue *Salvia* in deep shadow. Their same hue of brilliant yellow echoed down from the top of a cottonwood, set off by blue-gray, as a Nashville warbler sat still in the sun and sang for minutes on end.

Before I recrossed the footbridge, I wondered what it would be like to be under the overpass when a freight train came. Just as I stepped down the bank, the train appeared. I stood by the track and waved, and the engineers waved back, relieved that I wasn't going to be a jumper. But it was very strange: the big BNSF engine came right at me until the last second, when the track swung it round. That's what it would be like, and you'd know no more. Then I popped down and felt and heard the rest of the train pass overhead, just inches from my skull. So rare to feel such power! Out the other side, I watched the wheels strobing the sun through the ties, rails, and girders, all bending under the great weight. How quickly quiet resumed after the last car rolled by, as an eastern kingbird hawked the masses of glittering caddis flies swarming in the late sun.

On the last morning in May, in Willow Campground on the Tie-
ton River, I thought back to the summer of 1967, when I attempted
to teach my first butterfly class. The only one interested was a gan-
gly high school kid named Jon Pelham, and he knew as much as
or more than I did. We dropped the pretense of the class and got
his mother, Elizabeth, to take us collecting. These decades later,
I was conducting a year of my life according to the contents of *A
Catalogue of the Butterflies of the United States and Canada*, authored
by the one and the same Jonathan Pelham. This morning I would
revisit Bear Canyon, that first place Jon and I had ever gone afield
together, thanks to his mom.

As I arrived, a nighthawk peented and boomed overhead. The
sky was clear to the east, black to the west, and I was right on the
line. Half a mile up, foamy drifts of red-stemmed ceanothus backed
the soft green new growth of Garry oak, Douglas-fir, and Douglas
maple. A ten-inch southern alligator lizard sunned in off and on
beams on the dry streambed rocks. Water appeared in the stream,
and raindrops on my glasses. A gorgeous pale tiger swallowtail
sucked on long cherry spikes, and an azure glinted over the ceanothus—was it Lucia's blue, the special object of my day's search?
Entering a sea of creek dogwood, I came to a heap o' steaming horse
apples. A bright blue flew up from the equine offering, I netted
it, and it was indeed *Celastrina lucia*, just where JPP advised me I
should find it. A shrubby smorgasbord of cherry, ceanothus, ocean-
spray, and creek dogwood lined the trail, the buds and flowers of
any of them suitable larval medium for the male and female Lucia's
dancing through sunbeams and raindrops.

Hopping rocks back down the canyon, I saw an orange something coming toward me that didn't fly like a frit—a great arctic!
The sizable satyr, alighting on a gray rock, tilted its wings at an
angle to catch the coy sun. White, frosty patches with sienna striations made it cryptic against mottled basalt with a lichen or a mineral stain for every one of its colors. A bit of mountain lion tawny
and one good bull's-eye showed on the forewing, mostly hidden
under the hindwing. As clouds cooled the air, the arctic flattened
itself against stone, white crenels on ruffled hindwings sticking up
like mini mountains.

Oeneis nevadensis, named for the Sierra Nevada mountains rather than the state, was formerly known as the Nevada arctic. Since it does not occur there, and our subspecies is *O. n. gigas*, it became the great arctic; another old vernacular is "great grayling." By whatever name, this one sat so compliantly that I attempted a rare drawing. When it finally flew, its small cousin the ocher ringlet popped up, along with an orangetip, and the three of them performed an impromptu pas de trois.

South then to Klickitat, in search of the final greenie, called Sheridan's. I was too late to reach Glenwood, where Thea and I had found *Callophrys sheridanii* last year, so I dropped down the inverted worm can of the Klickitat Grade to a known site at the old ice plant at Klickitat Springs. Propertius duskywings love the feral lilacs here, and Vaux's swifts roost in the square brick smokestack, but the hairstreaks checked in absent. An old pickup pulled in next to me. A Levon Helm look-alike, friendly black Lab on the seat next to him, leaned out the window and asked, "Lookin' for swallowtails?"

"Little green ones," I said.

"I'd try the Appleton Grade," he said. "There're loads of butterflies up there."

Having learned that you don't take local advice like that lightly, I followed his tip. Indeed, the early part of the grade did have great stands of *Eriogonum umbellatum* in the sun, one of the proper hosts. It harbored Columbian dotted blues but no sign of greens. But the Appleton Grade panned out just the same. It brought me from the deep, dry Klickitat up to lush forest of grand fir and ponderosa pine; to wet meadow of cinquefoil and starflower, horsetail and hermit thrush, smelling of mint. Right off I saw a butterfly—a Boisduval's blue roosting on timothy. Then a mated pair. But no—it was a Boisduval's and a silvery, perched so near that I took them for being *in copula*. In all, six blues roosted in the timothy together, three of each, beautiful against the purply heads.

Never mind the green hairstreaks; two out of three wasn't bad, and Sheridan's might turn up later, higher. Even without it, May concluded with two hundred species, give or take, and with that indelible vision of blues gone to roost in timothy at day's end.

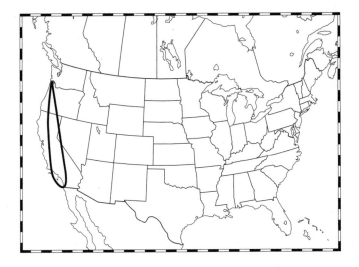

Hunting for Hairstreaks II

With wild times, the wild habits have returned.

—Richard Jefferies, *After London*

1. HERMES

On Sunday, the first day of June, Thea and I drove to the beach to see Dr. Law at Ocean Beach Hospital, in preparation for her chemotherapy. By having it closer to home, she would not have to arrange for rides to Seattle. She was able to take a gentle walk at Black Lake with me, where we saw an echo azure on pink salal blossom in the cool maritime sun. Over the next few days I tried to care for Thea, who felt alternately well (thus overdoing it) and ill (losing her good lamb chops); to pack and plan for future travels, and to sleep a little. I felt close to chaos, and then my glasses fell apart. This was prime butterfly season in many states, but at home the season was cool, wet, and subtle, and our violet-green swallows were failing to nest for the first time in memory.

At last, on the fifth, I got away, leaving Thea somewhere between a PET scan and a Port-A-Cath installation. I slept a couple of hours before dawn at the designated wetland economy parking lot at Portland airport. After reaching the terminal at 5:00 A.M., I found I'd left my Kleen Kanteen in Powdermilk, went back for it on the shuttle bus, and nearly missed my flight when the checkpoint backed up for a security breach.

I was supposed to be flying to Alaska. My adviser there, Kenelm Philip, had told me all winter that I had to come to Alaska *early*. With each season coming warmer and earlier, the flight seasons had speeded up, and I'd miss key species if I waited until July, as used to be the norm. So I'd booked the Alaska flight for now. Then Ken called: "Bob, you're too early," he said. "The season's late—better hold off a week if you can."

Fortunately, Alaska Airlines let me shift my frequent flier ticket. And there was a built-in boon to this: Debra Piot wanted me to attend her dissertation committee meeting in Santa Barbara the same week. Delaying Alaska freed up a week so that I was able to do so—and in the process, hunt some hairstreaks and others I surely would miss otherwise. So instead of to Fairbanks, I was heading back to Southern California, courtesy of Debra's university.

Unlike my first visit, San Diego was warm and clearing. I left the airport with a rental car, a red Hyundai Elantra that I named Hermes, very excited and very sleepless, to meet Mike Klein at the Mission Gorge Road Jack in the Box. Mike is an independent conservation contractor, one of the gypsy biologists who have collectively done as much to protect diversity in this country as all the academics and agency officials with portfolios. We next met Kojiro Shiraiwa at Mission Gorge park. A handsome young Japanese businessman stationed in California, Koji has become one of the most knowledgeable amateur lepidopterists in the area. He would soon publish an impressive book on the butterflies of San Diego County based on a successful Japanese approach, but in English. This was my first meeting with both of these fellows, and we hit it off right away.

In the park, above one of the oldest dams in the country, we soon encountered Bernardino blues and the silvery desert form sylvan hairstreak around its willows. Western tigers and mourning cloaks use the same willows, and they were present too. All the water brought in giant darner dragonflies and California dancers, a stunning blue damselfly. But in spite of good stands of their own required plant, spiny redberry (*Rhamnus crocea*), we saw no Hermes coppers here, and so moved on.

Next we drove to Wright's Field, behind Joan McQueen Middle School in Alpine. This Back Country Land Trust site with more than four hundred acres of native grassland and other endangered communities held fourteen vernal pools with spadefoot toads and one of the largest stands of Engelmann oak in Southern California. An old ranch, this stupendous habitat nearly fell victim to sports fields, until the land trust sued to prevent that fate. Then Mike discovered Hermes coppers here. That clinched the deal, and the county too got behind a conservation plan. Now Mike does mark-release-recapture studies of the coppers with students from the adjacent school. Crossing the meadow, we encountered a bright female Behr's metalmark, mottled orange and brown with white dots, on a California buckwheat—a nice surprise. And then we saw *it!*—Hermes copper. Two fresh males alighted on sugar bush, the leaves and butterflies both flamelike, backlit.

Hermes is no hairstreak but a copper. Nonetheless, we may call it an honorary hairstreak, or at least a convergent hairstreak, for it has tiny tails projecting off its hindwings just as many theclines possess. As we have seen, tails have arisen numerous times in butterflies not closely related, through convergent evolution. When something works well in nature, it happens over and over, like "ears" in moths and mimic wasp bodies. So we find coppery blues and hairstreaks, coppers and hairstreaks that are blue, and tailed-blues and coppers. In North America, only two species of coppers possess caudal tails. One is actually called the tailed copper, and Hermes is the other. These before me, my first ever, were incomparably lovely—dusky brown and gold above, sunny yellow below. Not far off, that yellow found its like in Dunn's mariposa lily, very hirsute, in the grass. Such a *neat* little butterfly is Hermes, in any sense of the word you wish to apply.

No viewer escapes the enchantment of Hermes. John Adams Comstock's classic *Butterflies of California,* in the innocent ornament of 1920s American, dubbed it thus: "It is a fascinating sprite as it darts about in the sunlight, or sports its showy colors while balanced on a tuft of wild buckwheat." Hermes was one of my most desired grails and now, by rights, most satisfying sightings. There was no question of catching it. Though unlisted, it deserves to be, maybe more than any other unprotected American butterfly.

Not only is Hermes evolutionarily unique in the strictest sense but it is also extraordinarily limited in range—entirely restricted to San Diego County and a bit of adjacent Baja California in Mexico. And tragically, within this narrow range, Hermes has experienced grave reduction and ongoing risk. Much of its potential habitat lies beneath housing, shopping, or pavement; much of the rest has recently been burned in explosive wildfires; and all that remains stands in jeopardy of burning or bulldozing. Even in 1927, Comstock wrote of Hermes: "It will always be a rarity, and may, in fact, some day become extinct, if San Diego continues to expand at its present rate." And Comstock didn't have a glimmer of future fires, as a bloating population meets the tinder chaparral in this warming, drying climate.

As Koji maneuvered for photos of Hermes and I simply watched it (which I could do forever), Mike said, "This is my religion, this butterfly." I believed him. Its image adorns his business card, and its fate preoccupies his mind, after thirteen years studying the species on the steep, sandy hills where its redberry grows. Mike told us about the ecology of *Lycaena hermes* and the dangers it faces. The Crestridge Ecological Preserve, for example, had a population of over a thousand Hermes—all burned! Mike was sick about it. I tried to assimilate all this while ogling the sheer beauty of form, color, and adaptation as a pale, pearly male sat and nectared for many minutes.

This need to honor the plight of rare butterflies at the same time you admire them creates a cognitive dissonance, like acknowledging evil while giving oneself over to love, not a job for weaklings and children. Or maybe, especially for children. Many's the time when I wished I could go back and see these creatures through a child's eyes. Or, as Bob Seger put it, "Wish I didn't know now what I didn't know then."

As we retreated from what should at least be one safe harbor for Hermes, we strode among lots of Bernardino blues, a female western pygmy-blue, a gray-form buckeye or two, a California sister, a pair of orange sulphurs *in copula*, and then we actually observed a pair of checkered whites link up and fly—so it does happen! Next, a female California dogface flew past us, giving a pretty fair and unequivocal look. I didn't know it then, but she would turn out to be the only example of California's official state butterfly that I would see; the amazing male, with its orchid purple neon sheen, never showed himself.

But Hermes, thank the gods, had shown for us, and shown well. Hermes was also known as Mercury, father of Pan and Silenus, helper of Perseus, guide to Persephone, and messenger of the gods. Mentioned in the myths more than any other god, he came and went on wingéd sandals. Long may Hermes fly.

2. THORNEI

I took a new toll road south from the clotted 8 at Alpine and had it all to myself. At the appointed hour of 9:30, I met Koji at Otay Mountain, on the border east of San Diego. He led me into the hills by the back way, through an industrial plant. Up on the first pink granite cobble-and-boulder eminence, worn but energetic Comstock's callippe fritillaries were hilltopping in numbers. It didn't take long to locate our special quarry for the day, Thorne's hairstreak. *Callophrys thornei*—my third rare, patronymic hairstreak in three weeks, all in the subgenus *Mitoura*. Unlike the honorary hairstreak of yesterday, these elfins were named for no gods, although some would gladly extend that status to John Muir, some of Sid Hessel's qualities were at least saintlike, and Fred Thorne was considered by all to be a heck of a nice guy.

When scientists describe new species, they may name them after whatever they choose—the host plant, the terrain or location, physical attributes, or a person. Early lepidopterists, possessed of classical educations but seldom much intimate knowledge of the organisms they were charged with naming, often selected gods, goddesses, Native Americans, or figures from history or mythology—hence Hermes, the Zabulon skipper, or the Xerces blue. More modern patronymics have tended to honor famous or revered figures (John Muir, John Bartram) or lepidopterists involved in their discovery or study (John Comstock, Sid Hessel). In this case, Fred Thorne was an admired Southern Californian butterfly man who studied the hairstreaks that fed on cupressaceous trees. When John Brown separated and named the species, only in 1983, it was to commemorate Thorne's many contributions. We last met him on

Santa Catalina, when I followed his, now sadly obsolete, directions from a successful hunt for Avalon hairstreaks.

Now Koji and I were seeking Fred's butterfly namesake, like *L. hermes* restricted in the United States to San Diego County. But *C. thornei* is even more narrowly endemic, flying solely in the San Ysidro Mountains on the U.S. side of the border, where its host plant, Tecate cypress, grows; the tree laps over the border, but *thornei* isn't known in Mexico.

Like *C. hesseli* and *C. muiri*, *C. thornei* is considered a full species, unlike the many regional components of the juniper hairstreak. It makes sense that the cypress-feeding hairstreaks of the *Mitoura* group, with their highly segregated host plants, would maintain their specific integrity while those feeding on widespread cedars have been lumped because of frequent intermixing.

The first we saw was a somewhat worn female, getting ready to lay eggs on top of a five-year-old Tecate cypress on a summit that last burned in 2003. As Koji pointed out, it is good that they will use younger trees. He rears a lot of them and has observed them ovipositing from the top of the tree on down. This Thorne's hairstreak was bronzy-greeny-purply, very comely though not quite fresh; brassier than *C. muiri*, not nearly as green as *C. hesseli*. Then a superb, newly eclosed male appeared, of which Koji got many pictures. Its underside shone a truly beautiful fawn and bronze on the forewing, gray-violet across the hindwing. When I contemplated the sheer pulchritude of these diminutive hairstreaks I'd been hunting, versus the vanishingly small number of people who have ever beheld them, it seemed to me nothing less than tragic. All those people reveling down there in the hollow, pallid blandishments of the cities on the plain—and this, right up here, unseen but by us. Well, it's just a particular of the general condition.

Big tarantula hawks hunted from burned cypress tips. A pair of farmers, several funereal duskywings, and a marine blue all drank side by side on a buckwheat. (As I read that now in my notes, it suggests a joke: "A farmer, an undertaker, and a marine all went into a bar . . .") A male russet hairstreak nectared obliviously as a yellow jacket consumed his female counterpart above. We saw several more Thorne's, and with Koji's permission, I vouchered a male for the Burke Museum in Seattle while they were numerous and it was still legal to do. (Removing extraneous males, to a point, affects most populations very little, since all the females will be mated as long as a few males remain.) We were buzzed by an official helicopter but not, I think, checking on the well-being of the hairstreaks, rather because we were right next to the international line.

Koji asked me what else I needed to see. I named a couple of skippers, and he swept me off across San Diego to Famosa Slough, right in the city across the river from SeaWorld. Glasswort and salt grass lined the estuary, the former with its expected western pygmy-blues. Thanks to the salt grass, we soon saw sandhill and eufala skippers sitting on salicornia in the shade; and then a nice, fresh wandering skipper, basking on a white flower. With its long panoquin-type forewings and prominent vein-and-spot pattern below, there was no question this was the southwest seaside counterpart of the salt marsh skipper I'd seen in Florida with Andy on Easter. All three of these were new for me, the last a lifer. What a fine little in-city habitat this was, right under the airline flight path but chock-full of skippers. And what a find Koji was!

The day was not over. We headed out of town on I-8 east again, back to Guatay. Koji had first taken me to Guatay, at 3,600 feet in Cleveland National Forest, after we parted from Mike the day before. There we had found the large, drab relative of Hermes known as the great copper, and a bouquet of distinctive Laguna Mountains varieties of blues with appealing names such as *evius, monticola,* and *paradoxa*. Several of these were associated with *Lupinus excubitor,* or grape-soda lupine—when I sniffed it, it really *did* smell like grape soda, and it was that deep purple color too. Next we drove to Noble Canyon off Pine Valley. At a high view, we watched lots of *Satyrium auretorum*—gold-hunter's hairstreaks, first collected by Pierre Lorquin, an actual gold hunter—flashing around their host scrub oaks, while we listened to black-chinned sparrows and ash-throated flycatchers singing.

But we hadn't seen everything possible, so today we'd motored up again, to the Laguna Mountain Recreation Area. First, Koji netted *Limenitis lorquini powelli,* a subspecies of Lorquin's admiral named for Jerry Powell, in the same grove occupied by its model, a California sister. Then, as I walked ahead on the trail, something flat and orange glided past me. I caught it with Akito—Marsha does not fly in these days of TSA—and found in his bag a Gabb's checkerspot. By this late date, I'd all but given up on this handsome, springflying California coastal endemic.

As if this weren't enough novelty to absorb, at the next pullout we saw two Harford's sulphurs fly right past our faces. These look very much like the clouded sulphur that throngs the alfalfa fields and clovered roadsides of North America. But *Colias philodice* omits southwest California from its range, and *C. harfordii* occurs only there. At another site among Jeffrey pines and boulders, yellow composites and Wright's buckwheat filled the big meadows. On both, numerous small orange butterflies sucked and darted with different styles: a separate subspecies of Behr's metalmark from the one at the Hermes site, and lots of Leussler's branded skippers. Laguna was good to us, and in two days, Koji, Mike, and I had seen forty species.

Koji and I parted only after we each had a first-rate slice o' pie at the Julian Pie Company, his apple, mine apple-cinnamon. We didn't know it then, but I wasn't through with him for the year. For now, I carried on up the Mount Palomar Road. The La Jolla Fire of October 1999 had burned right over much of the chaparral and incense cedars hereabouts. Some memorials recognized firefighters who'd lost their lives, others celebrated the Penny Pines program for reforesting the crisped hills. Up on granite outcrops below the observatory, big, fresh and shrimpy, worn painted ladies gamboled and sallied together in the late sun through the usual haze.

I spoke with Thea, who was subsisting in cold rain, and sent her Laguna sun from the side of Palomar Mountain. Later, if only to assuage her envy, I spent a few hours in San Juan Capistrano at a Denny's, where you can work on your notes and nurse your coffee under bright light all night, if you have a mind to. The last time Thea had dined at a Denny's in Southern California, in 1970, she'd been sick for a week.

3. *AVALONA,* TAKE TWO

Unwilling to relive my close call of last time, I arrived at the San Pedro–Catalina Island Terminal at 2:30 A.M. for the seven o'clock sailing. Thanks to Alaska's late spring and Debra's committee meeting, I was taking one more crack at the Avalon hairstreak. There in the terminal parking lot, to heavy sounds of cranes moving containers and trucks bumping across the bridge above, I slept behind the wheel of Hermes, the red Elantra with the wingéd feet.

On Saturday, June 7, at 7:40 A.M., I was well under way on my second sea voyage to Catalina Island. The sun peeked out of overcast, shooting godbeams over the water, and I had faith the day would clear. Hundreds of cormorants made a solid whitewash on the long jetty running south toward Long Beach, many backs, or cloacae, bent to the job. A sooty shearwater flew beside us for a long way, going the very same speed, about thirty-six knots, until it decided to overtake us. It sheared the water all right, like a big swift or bat.

Most of the passengers were in couples, taking that twenty-six-mile ride to "the island of romance, romance, romance, romance," for tryst, honeymoon, or trying to get it back. There were also families aboard. How many of these kids were conceived over there? I wondered. Dressed in shorts, flip-flops, and T-shirts, most folks abandoned the cool breeze of the rear deck for the indoor saloon. Sun buttered the eastern slopes of Santa Catalina, which we now approached, my romancing of Doña Avalona about to resume.

I dropped into the Catalina Island Conservancy for maps, but they were coarse and disagreed on road names. The expensive one looked no better than the freebies. The desk person, who used still different names, had never heard of the Avalon hairstreak. I pointed it out on their own brochure of Catalina endemics and quoted Comstock: "one of the world's most restricted species." Along Clarissa Street, a riot of roses and bougainvilleas, a pale Annabella studied a crushed nasturtium petal on the sidewalk. One perfect purple iris linked me with home in the northwest rain. A brick-arched niche in an adobe wall held not a saint but a tile of brilliant tropical reef fish; a jogger wore a short skirt instead of shorts, and the streets, empty of cars, were full of noisy golf carts: such was Avalon.

Up in Avela Canyon, the sun was coming on strong, as was St. Catherine's lace, the massive, frondose *Eriogonum giganteum*. A monster lantana hosted no one that I could see. Then, an anise swallowtail on an elderberry! That was news, as butterflies never seem to nectar on the elder's sweet and abundant sprays. Nor did this one: she was only basking, and there was fennel all over. At eleven, I thought I saw *Strymon avalonas* flying around and alighting on coffeeberry—they looked dove gray, not blue—but this was just wishful thinking. The first I netted was a male echo blue, pale here, with grayer females. Besides, their flight was far less direct than that of the speedy 'streaks would be.

On Mike and Koji's advice, I'd contacted the lepist Doug Aguillard. He had seen *S. avalona* a year or two ago in the botanical garden, so I continued up-canyon to find it. But the garden was dead bone dry, with not a lot in bloom, nothing to draw hairstreaks down from the hills. I continued to the Wrigley Memorial, with its Blue Mosque–like tiles (made on-island), lion, Green Man, and early Deco arch and cast-concrete work. The edifice was "Dedicated as a memorial to William Wrigley Jr. (1861–1932) who in 1919 recognized the potential of Santa Catalina Island as a nature preserve and took the initial steps needed to save and protect this beautiful island, its wildlife, and its historical artifacts for posterity." He did more than make gum.

I had also talked with Joey Hernandez, the butterfly-mad young man whom Carrie at the church had told me about last time. He had to work, but we agreed in principle to meet up at the end of the day. From Joey, I knew that my best chance for butterfly diversity lay in the interior, protected first by Wrigley, now by the conservancy. As J. A. Comstock wrote: "One must seek this little rarity on the rugged slopes of the Catalina hills, where collecting is not an easy matter, and every capture is an achievement." I'd considered taking the bus to the airport, up on top of the island, but there wasn't time. Now I decided to try the trail from the memorial uphill to the Divide Road. As I started up the steep, rocky track, dry and slippery and dusty, pale violet datura bloomed by the edge. Lots of coffeeberry lined the canyon, with echo blues all over it.

Atop the ridge, the necessary lotus framed a wonderful view of both coasts. Turquoise lagoons opened to the west. Along came a truck driven by Stephanie Jijon, monitoring bald eagles for the conservancy. She showed me a much better map, made for fire control. I thought I would return the way I'd come, or take a smaller, steeper trail around the ridge to the north and then cut down to the botanical garden. She told me that both ways would be dry, recently burned, slippery, and not very interesting.

"If I were you," said Stephanie, "I'd go all the way around the south end of the island to Renton Mine Road, and back into Avalon that way. It's a good hike, but worth it. No one ever takes it. It hasn't all burned, and the habitat will be much better."

"Do you think I can make it in the time I have?"

"Oh, yeah . . . you've done most of the work already," Stephanie said. "It's just a little more *up*"—she waved vaguely off toward the long, steep pitch she'd come down—"and then it's mostly downhill."

It looked like a long way, and me with no decent map, for the maze of fire roads. But I knew "Renton Mine" as an old *avalona* site from Fred Thorne's article. And a metallic taste had come into my mouth: a fear of leaving disappointed a second time. This seemed my best, or only, chance to avoid that unhappy fate. "As long as I'm already up here," I told Stephanie, "I might as well." I thanked her and took off up the ridge. I had to give this my best shot. After all, that's what I came for.

The plants were lusher over there, out of the burn. The St. Catherine's lace came on stronger, some in bloom, and *Lotus* trailed nearby. A checkered white nectared on star thistle. It was good to see a native white, not only the cabbages that fly like summer snow down in Avalon, even if it was on an exotic flower. A side ridge branched off to the west, punctuated with successive hilltop clumpets. I veered to check it out, as sea mist moved in on the clear day. I asked Sun to please hold it off. "Or, as an option," said I, "perhaps deliver up the hairstreaks soon."

"Which would you prefer?" Sun asked back.

"Hairstreak now," I said. "Please."

"You got it," said the sun. Then there was a small, dark flight most unlike the floppy blues, which I recognized at once as being theclid. A pert dun hairstreak alighted on the first hilltop thicket of a manzanitalike leatherleaf, right before my eyes. Akito netted it. "Quite an accomplishment," I saluted Akito, quoting Comstock, as I gingerly removed it from his bag. For about half a second I thought it might be a gray hairstreak, as the slate wings were darker and richer than I expected. But the median line beneath was vaguer and interrupted, and the red and blue "thecla spots," though brighter than on pictures I have seen, were lesser than on *Strymon melinus* for sure. It was most certainly the butterfly that W. G. Wright named *Thecla avalona* in 1905. Glory be, all three of the extreme Southern Cal endemics, all new to my experience, in three days! Thank you, Sun!

As I watched other individuals, even nose-to-proboscis with inverted binoculars for a hand lens, I learned how distinctive they truly are. I saw why, with recent DNA evidence, *S. avalona* and *S. melinus* are no longer considered sibling species, as was long thought. In fact, we used to be worried about the appearance of grays on the island, that they might swamp the Avalon through hybridization, and a plan was even floated to introduce *avalona* to a distant island for the sake of insurance. The greatest generalist of all American butterflies and among the most widespread, the gray hairstreak feeds on everything from beans to hops, while the lotus-eater Avalon hairstreak lives only here, so the concern made sense. But now that we know they are not even closely related, that particular worry may be put to rest.

The real risk, I suspect, is fire. *Strymon avalona* appears to be highly fire-sensitive—just like the Hermes copper and Thorne's hairstreak. But here, where fire has not reached, the hairstreaks popped up all along the unburned side ridge. From the last knob before the cliffs, I could see fishing boats offshore. I heard only the boaters' voices far below, a raven, and wind.

Even though I'd met my grail, I continued the long walk around instead of going back. I figured I must be nearly halfway. The day had grown wildfire hot.

Back on the original bush, two hairstreaks were zipping about, just like the Mojave *melinus* madness. One beauty, sawing her hindwings on a lower bush near the main trail, looked like a fresh female. A nearby male's tails were neatly bird-pinked. A real stunner perched one-third open an inch off the ground, her abdomen pale salmon pink, like a fresh brookie, not the Copper River Chinook of the male gray hairstreak's tip. One Avalon basked on a prickly pear; apparently they're not picky about substrate. But none went near what had become waves of St. Catherine's lace, its tall white fans spreading over the slope like umbrellas, supposedly the butterfly's favorite nectar source.

Back on the spine of the island, a panorama of Avalon opened out to the east. Many more boats bobbed in the harbor on this side, and much larger ones. The big, round, red-tiled casino guarded the harbor and its vessels like a Martello tower. The cries of revelers rose up to me. Ye gods, it was good to be up there away from the holiday hum and those nasty little golf carts. I wouldn't trade one second of my day for the entirety of any of theirs.

More Avalons appeared as I was "coming down." Flat-spread, white-fringed—what a lovely little mouse of a bug, in the best sense: wee but not tim'rous, mouse gray but not mousy, this was the true *fledermaus*. Over one coffeeberry, an echo, an Avalon, and a damselfly circled together. When it settled, the 'streak's red spot was set off against the leaf's red rim. A crisp, coifed pair of California quail fluttered up, perched right above me, and whirred off as I carried on—back uphill again. From there, the way went up and down and up again, over and over . . . much steeper and far longer than Stephanie had suggested. But then, she is young—and has a truck. Just before five, I crested the shoulder of East Mountain.

A huge and brilliant American lady owned the top. She did a turn with an Avalon, then two, then a train of three *avalona* followed the lady together, like fireworks over Catalina. All four perched side by side; then, all up again! Almost unbelievably, a rufous humming-bird joined the conga line. All the while, a mockingbird sang and shrilled every known song, as white-throated swifts and barn swallows cleaved the freighted air.

Past 5:30 I passed a sign that said Wrigley Terrace was still *three miles* away! Thanks to a much longer route than I had supposed, and to some of the best butterfly watching of my life, I was now in trouble. I began jogging around the many switchbacks. After I met Renton Mine Road, they curved beneath giant eucalypti, whose menthol scent would have been pleasant if this were not such a frantic haul. Curve after curve I jogged, stopping only to pull pebbles out of my hiking sandals—fine for the walk but not so hot for the run. It seemed I'd never get down. I finally hit pavement at 6:30—and the road went *up*, for cripes sake! I would even have hitched a lift on a golf cart, but either they were full of large people or they didn't stop, though I was obviously under duress. I was right above the harbor, but there were no freaking stairs! I had to loop way back into town and out again to reach the water.

Ran more, round the big condos that displaced Fred Thorne's habitat; passed my canyon from last time, passed Caterina's church. I'd hoped to stop in to see beautiful Carrie, and there was no time to meet Joey, either. *Run!*

I made the dock in a lather at ten or eight minutes till seven and presented myself at the ticket window. "Your ferry has already gone," the woman said.

"*What?*" And then I remembered last time, when the ferry I thought I was missing was actually the one to San Pedro. This time, I was *going* to San Pedro. Again I had confused its time with the later Long Beach departure. Mine left at 6:45, not 7:00! After all that.

I thought I was doomed, stuck on the island, and started to conjure scenarios of charter planes, or speedboats, or whatever . . . Debra's meeting, which had grubstaked this whole trip, was the next morning, and I *had* to be there. And anyway, where would I stay here? I was desperately in need of sleep, and I couldn't afford the meanest coat closet, even if there had been any vacancies. They don't take kindly to people sleeping rough on Catalina.

Then the ticket woman, seeing my crushed and florid face, re-minded me that there was still one more ferry off the island—it was just that it went to Long Beach. "But you'll have to hurry," she said. "It's about to leave." She accepted my ticket for it, which she was not obliged to do. I ran again, up the gangplank, and collapsed in my old place in the stern.

I'd have to take a taxi from Long Beach to San Pedro, and then drive half the night to the Piots' in Santa Barbara. but I'd get there. Tomorrow I'd meet my way-back Yale pals and fellow Remington students, Francie Chew and Larry Gall, along with the eco-philosopher Joe Meeker, for Debra's committee meeting. We would gather by the canyon outside the Santa Barbara Museum of Natural History, where in 1962 I'd actually met John Adams Comstock, the grand old man of California butterflies, who wrote so well of this "inconspicuous little butterfly," *Strymon avalona.*

Once safely onboard, I called Joey and made my apologies, and then Thea. Face washed and pulse down, again I ordered two chilled Heinekens, maybe even more welcome than last time. I toasted the grand slam of extreme Southern California endemics, then settled back in the backwash wind. Lots of folks were wearing wacky woven hats and bumper stickers on their backs, butts, or heads, saying, "I got my wiki wacked at Luau Larry's." I don't know what everyone else had been doing, wiki-wise. But it's safe to say I'm the only one who got my wiki wacked by the Catalina Divide in a successful but-terfly hunt and lived to tell about it. And, that I was the lucky one.

But really, who am I to feel superior? Much of this stern con-tingent leaped up, wowing and pointing, when we passed a large school of leaping porpoises, just after sunset on the Pacific Ocean. Maybe they would have liked the butterflies after all. Maybe some of them would even prefer to have their wikis wacked up there on the high ridge by hairstreaks, Hunter's butterflies, and humming-birds. I'll never know. Neither will they.

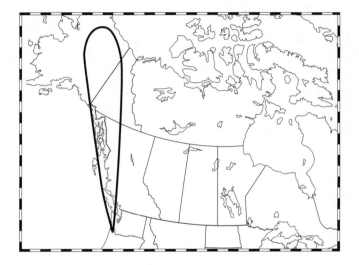

North to Alaska

I relive each day the ancient expectation of the
hunt—the setting out, and the trail at dawn.
What will we find today?

—John Haines, *The Stars, the Snow, the Fire*

1. MURPHY DOME DAY

Flying over the Inside Passage, I had a Glenlivet, an Alaskan ale, and ice water before me, in glass glasses—and a *meal* to come! When I had to pay a bit to change my frequent flier reservation, Alaska Airlines for some reason made my new booking first class—my second or third time ever. I was excited to be Alaska-bound, and grateful—above all, that Thea was getting well. Her first infusion behind her, she was recovering in the damp gray of Gray's River, which was frustrating our swallows but was not bad for healing. I earnestly hoped it would not follow me to Alaska. Many have been the Alaskan butterfly expeditions when the midnight sun (and butterflies) might as well have been under a basket.

After this midnight, amazing glaciers and snow stripes showed below the moon, and the night grew brighter as we powered west and north. We'd traveled back in time when we descended over braided rivers and a million mosses, spring birches, and skinny spruce, potholed blue and green waters, and great muddy loops of the Chena. The half-moon had been with us all night long. And there I was in Fairbanks, under skylight, amazed. What would I see in these ten days?

I'd made no arrangements for transportation. I'd tried, but no one would rent a vehicle for the roads I wanted to travel except for big 4X4s at usurious rates. Everyone I asked told me the same thing: Just lie—and then don't get stuck up there! So I went to the first rental car booth, prevaricated a bit about my probable route, and had a little red Ford Focus before my luggage came. My rental had to serve as camper too, since the luggage limit precluded bringing along a tent and other gear and there wouldn't be time for proper camping in any case. I would pretty much be traveling, butterflying, and catching a little sleep when I could before taking off again. The Focus had a nice fold-back front seat.

I slept outside Gulliver's bookstore, bought breakfast and the Alaska DeLorme atlas and gazetteer when it opened, shopped for a week's food at Fred Meyer's, and lit out for the field.

At noon, I arrived at the Bonanza Creek Long Term Ecological Research site with Kenelm Philip. Many years ago, I'd hatched a plan to do graduate work with him on the butterflies of the Yukon. That never happened, but we'd become friends over the years. Ken had worked for the Institute of Arctic Biology and ran the Alaska Lepidoptera Survey (ALS) on the side. When he retired, the survey became full-time. Putting nets and supplies in the hands of Alaskans all over the state, from fishermen to natives to pipeline workers, Ken built an invaluable reference collection and a rich database on the Alaskan fauna. He is close to publishing his long-awaited work on the butterflies of Alaska. Ken had helped me plan my Alaska jaunt, and now he took me out for the initial outing.

My first Alaskan butterfly, as we rolled down the dappled Appalachian-like road listening to Vivaldi on Ken's iPod, was a beat-up Compton tortoiseshell. We would see many of these overwinterers, larger than the somewhat similar California tortoiseshell that had started off my year in the woodshed. More of them rose before us as we walked the road to the bog, under a hill of aspen whose leaves all shone silvery with the serpentine paths of aspen leaf miners. Comptons occur all across the Canadian Shield, following birches well into the Arctic, the same pattern shown by the next one to appear: *Papilio canadensis*, the Canadian tiger swallowtail. A big beauty sat on *Mertensia* the color of my blue pencil, crawling from panicle to panicle. Another had its left hindwing cleanly halved by a bird, revealing the topside orange that sets it apart from a western tiger. The slope above us opened to a steppe of artemisia with spent pasqueflower and pink roses.

Rain came on as we crossed the bog, where lots of western tailed-blues nectared on blueberry, and a couple of dark Persius dusky-wings rode their broomsticks. We all retreated from the rain, then came out again as the sun did the same. Northern bogs hold several species of lesser fritillaries in the genus *Boloria*, many of which were named for Norse goddesses. The first of these to show, Frigga, flew fast and alighted briefly on the bog road. We both saw three or four and knew what they were, but the first and only one I had a chance to net, I missed out of sheer eagerness.

A faun anglewing (a.k.a. green comma) and then palaeno sulphurs popped up from the Labrador tea, and we each netted one palaeno. Ken kept one to photograph alive for his field guide. Mine was lovely and fresh, densely dark-scaled green below, with rounded wings, broad black borders, a bright pink fringe, and an oystery white cell spot. The rain resumed in earnest, and we got soaked. The drive back to Ken's house in his electric yellow camper truck with its ALS sign on the door was rainy and muddy but happy—eight species, six of them new already. A great start, despite the rain.

Over our oatmeal the next morning, Ken recited Ogden Nash. Our second field trip fell on Friday the thirteenth, a fine, fair day. Ken decided we should go to the Chena River Flood Project to photo *Erebia epipsodea*. This time, on the way, we listened to *Lautenwerk* music. We entered a locked gate onto the dam, then two more; Ken had the keys. We parked by a clot of kid archers, very interested in what we were doing: "There's one!" Later, at the pond, we saw them canoeing among brightly plumed red-necked grebes.

Our way lay along a dirt track lined by cottonwoods and firs growing on a grassy dike, then through birch woods to the river. As Air Force jets roared over, the first *Erebia epipsodea* flip-flopped silently through the tall grass. Another special Alaskan genus, and my most anticipated, was *Erebia*—the alpines. I love their soft colors, as beguiling as any tropical brilliants. I'll never forget catching my first alpines in a wet meadow after a cool Colorado rain, as GrandPop visited a lady friend in Idaho Springs. Then, as now, the species at hand was Butler's alpine—three square inches of rich, dark chocolate wings with cinnamon bands and sugar-centered, licorice eyespots—the archetypal *Erebia* pattern, on which I would soon see several variations.

Here came a couple of large marbles, my third far-flung western variety of this species in the past few weeks. As I tried for one, Akito's spring-steel rim broke. What a fix—here, I had no backup except the little hand net. Later, back at his place, Ken repaired

Akito. His house, a rambling warren of rooms full of books, magazines, and other papers, includes a well-equipped shop, even down to the necessary drill for hard steel. Ken has made many wonderful wooden pieces of furniture, his own specimen cabinets, and various clever labor-saving gadgets. I am always awed and a bit appalled by the sort of lepidopterist who can do these things, and I've known several; their skills and inclination seem to go along with the meticulous facility that suits specimen work too, and their collections—Ken had a whole big room for his—were always the most beautifully curated. I don't have such a touch, but Ken does, and now he put me back in business.

I drove back to Bonanza Creek, hotter now, breezy, and mostly sunny. Only one Frigga fritillary showed, and I missed it too. Arctic skippers ping-ponged in and out of the edges, a Holarctic species with an extremely handsome pattern of gold spots on top, silvery orbs on the bottom. I remembered them dripping like gold nuggets from the deep green grass of Katmai, on my first Alaskan trip ever. On my way out, one *Erebia* flew up from the bog road, and I netted it—*E. discoidalis*, the red-disked alpine—namesake, I decided, of my red Ford Focus, home for the next week. On this kind, the cinnamon scales smear all over the chocolate above. Below, the subtle but intricate mix brought to mind rust and cloud on peat and loam. It was just the creature I'd hoped for here.

The evenings are long in Fairbanks in summer, and Ken and Betty Anne Philip retire late. They took me to the old Chena Pump House restaurant, then back home for engaging talk until one in the morning. Betty too had worked at the University of Alaska, in chemistry. Since she'd suffered a stroke, her mobility was somewhat limited, but she lives a very full intellectual life with Ken and good friends such as Mary Clench, widow of Harry, the codescriber (with Paul Ehrlich) of the Sandia hairstreak. Ken and Betty Anne are both prodigious readers, of everything from science fiction to science and many stops in between, and their eclectic library makes our rather large one seem like the used book shelf at our local library. Each night, Betty Anne and Ken observe "coffee call" at about midnight, with coffee, ice cream, and conversation. Their chat was spiked with jokes and stories alternating with many a book review and recommendation.

So it might have been tough to get up the next morning, except that it was a Murphy Dome Day! Ken had advised me that the best Arctic collecting close to Fairbanks was to be had on a mountaintop called Murphy Dome, which rises above timberline and therefore matches conditions farther to the north. "But," said Ken, "don't try it unless you have a real Murphy Dome Day."

"And that is?"

"Clear and sunny, horizon to horizon. Or else you're bound to get caught in the afternoon clouds, and very likely an electrical storm—and you don't want that, up there!"

This was just such a day, when (as Cervantes saw it) "the earth was joyous, the sky unclouded, the air limpid, the light serene . . . the day which was treading on the skirts of morning was to be bright and clear." It was also my last day in the Fairbanks area. I walked up to the big white golf ball of the USAF's Murphy Dome Long Range Radar Site to look for *Papilio machaon* hilltopping, and one flew right up to me. This is the insect known in England as *The swallowtail*, in the United States as the Old World swallowtail, and it is probably the ancestor (or close to it) of all of our big black swallowtail group in North America. Thea and I had seen *P. m. britannicus* on the Norfolk Broads, and it was quite similar, but the smaller *P. m. aliaska* was brand-new for me.

Two males claimed the summit, dropping now and then to bask in the ring of stones in the middle, oriented toward the sun. Their wings tipped in the breeze like light planes on a windy runway, before they flew out at flies and swallows and each another. Moose Duds lay about in the circle of rocks, and a male western white basked, displaying his crisp black-on-white pelage, then flew and put up a swallowtail. A fresh female *machaon* came up the hill and engaged with the nearer of the males before they sky-tumbled off into the alders. I thought, I just saw hilltopping *work*! I netted the remaining male to examine him in hand: those big, clean, persimmon tail-spots, orchid running into orange, a broad blue galaxy filtering out from them into the black night of the wing, his pheromones light and sweet like lemon verbena on a gentle upwind breeze.

I headed down the first rocky little road into alders and willows. In a fragrant swale of marsh marigolds, I netted a Freija fritillary, with her distinctive pearl spearpoint underneath. One beautiful, dark, fresh *Erebia discoidalis* disengaged from the black earth, and soon they became frequent. At puddle mud appeared a cloak, a Persius, and a hoary elfin—one large and two small darklings. A very beat Compton and a not-so-beat cloak did a *Nymphalis* pas de deux, and a tiny moth extremely like a metalmark allowed me to entertain the briefest of fantasies of a new species for Alaska.

At the Y on Ken's map, a bigger, stronger *Erebia* flew toward me, six or seven feet off the ground. Akito swished it up, and it was a stunning *Erebia fasciata*! The banded alpine, not surprisingly, has prominent gray-felt bands around the hindwings instead of the frosting of the red-disked. Another showed me just how large they really are—strong too, but they hang on the air and give you a chance, unlike speedy *Bolorias*. And such iridescence! All *Erebias* show green and purple glints when really fresh.

Down the left fork an arctic flew up and then lit. Closely related to alpines, arctics sport striated grays and tawnies rather than dark browns and reds. This one, *Oeneis bore,* has a broad mesial band, much like that of the banded alpine, and stand-out white veins that give it its English name of white-veined arctic. Many arctic butterflies are biennial, taking two years to develop and flying only in even or odd years in a given district, so certain species I would simply not be able to find in 2008. Of the even-year species, at least two more arctics are known from Murphy Dome. I climbed to a breezy, south-facing *Oeneis* bank meant to have *O. melissa* and *O. polixenes*. In the intense scent of pink saxifrage and marsh marigold carpeting the top, I almost failed to notice their absence. Striding back and forth along the bank, over its screes and lichens, I saw no arctics. I did see Denali (Mt. McKinley) and its range, hulking over a drift of *Dryas* through a blue haze off to the south. I had planned to go there, but Denali National Park's net-free status, the difficulty of getting high up in the park, and Ken's advice all steered me north instead. So I was glad, at least, to see Denali's face. Many pilgrims to this coy crown of the continent have to take its existence on faith.

Below me stretched a low, porous rim of alder, fir, and willow. Ken told me that the arctic white, *Pieris angelika,* might be here. I saw some right away and then saw *why*: a large mauve crucifer bloomed all along the edge of the copse. Parry's wallflower makes a good host plant for this far northern species of mustard white. They ducked facilely back into the brush. Spotting fresh moose pellets, I declined to follow them into that opaque green labyrinth. It would be a good place to meet a moose or a bear face-to-face—or a bad place, depending on how you look at it. I veered around by a mosquito-filled pothole instead and met another moose of a white-veined arctic.

I made my way over to the Tor, a schist horn poking out of the tundra lawn, split down the middle. Up on top, I considered leaping across the gap. I knew that I could, but I also knew that I needed to be more careful than playful this year. A broken leg, way out here, would mess things up good. I climbed down and split the cleft at the bottom, much as I had a similar slit in the earth in Tajikistan's Varzob Mountains a couple of years before. Then I went back up and leaped the gap anyway, but the safer way, from higher side to lower. On the windy downhill side, dryas petals blew over the edge like summer snow. Banded alpines floated down the birch, willow, Labrador tea, and lichen slope. A giant female flopped by so slowly that I could see her cocoa banding, even on the wing. Another alighted, permitting a near look with the binos. This *has* to be one of the most beautiful *Erebias* of all, I told the bear in the willows; ergo, one of the most beautiful of butterflies.

Coming back up the far track of parallel quad ruts in the tundra, I netted a white that was a fresh *P. angelika*, so I saw it in spite of the moose guarding the willow maze. Back at the Red-disked Alpine I downed a bucket of water and a Gala apple. Then, before leaving, I walked back to the top of the dome again. A bright male *machaon* was calling on the pussies of dwarf willows, assiduously and at length, and preening his proboscis. He experimented with different trees and flowers but kept coming back to the original shrub. As I headed down the mountain road, I gave similar devotion to the scent and color of wild roses lining the verge beneath the birches. It was still a Murphy Dome Day.

Eagle Summit loomed before me, a great multigrained tundra loaf. For years I was envious of my friends who had come here for the 1979 Lepidopterists' Society meeting organized in Fairbanks by Ken. The main field trip had been to Eagle Pass, and it pained me to miss it, its arctics, alpines, and others. Now, I was here!

Both sets of kids and grandkids called me at the Philips' for Father's Day. I also spoke with Thea, who was feeling better and better. Outside Fairbanks, I stopped at an Alyeska Pipeline interpretive sign where coach tourists and RVers gawked and snapped at the instrument of their extortion. I finally struck the Steese Highway at 5:30 P.M., which would mean the day was running down most places but meant no such thing here and now.

A red fox crossed Highway 6 between mountains of hydraulic mining tailings and innumerable birches. Whole mountainsides of aspen and skinny little spruce were dead from fire and pine beetles, exacerbated by the warming trend. Still-living aspen on the left were silvered by leaf miners; spruce on the right, blackened by fire. The pavement changed abruptly to dirt. Though banned for rental cars, the road remained smooth. People drove fast, but the gravel was small; you just closed your windows for the dust and waved. Or, as the locals did, just put up one finger (index).

Orchid pink vetches lined the roadside, snowbanks appeared along the creeks, and Arctic hares nibbled at the minerals in the road. Tundra came at Twelve Mile Summit. With all the snow in Willow Creek, it was hard to believe that I wasn't too early, but the bloom was well along. Parry's wallflower spattered the turf with purples both grapey and pale. Dryas blew about in the considerable wind on the summit. No one was still hilltopping, but I found the perch of the peregrine that was cutting the air above—a small cairn on top, well whitewashed. Then Bear Creek, Fish Creek, Ptarmigan Creek, and the climb to Eagle Summit, where I was met by my friend Ann Zwinger's quotation from *Land Above the Trees* on a BLM sign: "The alpine tundra is a land of contrast and incredible intensity where the sky is the size of forever and the flowers the size of a millisecond."

After dinner, I read *Blue Highways* in full sunlight after eleven. Two lads, Drew and Evan, came over to say hi. They had skied, climbed, biked, and finally paddled 130 miles of Birch Creek since coming here from Bozeman. I offered them Alaska IPAs, happily accepted—after all that, they were ready for a beer. Drew was reading *Blue Highways* too.

It appeared to be almost sunset at 12:47 A.M., but at 1:26 A.M., the sun was still sitting on the ridge, where it had squatted for an hour. Then at 2:49 A.M., it was rising again, never having gone all the way down. The BLM explained how that worked. The midnight sun is not normally seen south of the Arctic Circle, about fifty miles farther north. But because of the altitude here, greater than 3,600 feet above sea level, refraction makes the sun appear to be above the horizon even though it really isn't. Seeming to sit for so long on the horizon, it was actually skipping along it. Supposed to occur at Eagle Summit from June 17 to 24, this phenomenon manifested for me one day earlier.

I awoke at 5:00 A.M. to see the sun higher, yellower, farther north, and heading east. Before I went back to chilly sleep, filmy clouds came from behind me and took over. When I awoke again, farther down in my Volcano bag, I saw it was no Murphy Dome Day. By 7:00 it was downright cold and cloudy with a stiff wind. At 9:00 I turned the engine and heater on and fetched warmer clothes from the trunk. Then I sat and waited for the sun. Blue in the west seemed to be spreading, and bits of sun swept across, but not enough to warm things up, and the wind persisted. Noon was no better.

Then at 1:00, an American pipit popped up on the parking lot berm right before me, shaking me out of my lethargy. It pecked at something, then started bashing it on the ground with its bill. It appeared to be an *Oeneis*. I *wanted* that arctic! I thought, stupidly, that if I disturbed the bird, it might just drop the butterfly. So I opened the door, and of course the pipit just flew off with the prey in its bill. Damn, why didn't I just watch? I cursed. But then the wings likely would have blown away or been swallowed. Well, if the pipit can find a butterfly, I thought, maybe I can too. I had to get out.

I pushed through the wind to the southwest base of Eagle Summit, then climbed up through the black-lichened, rock-striped scree to the flat top. I crossed it to the north rim, circled back, and dropped back down. The scree was fairly stable, and the tundra not too wet or tussocky except in potholes. Early in the walk, I kicked up an *Erebia*! Unable to fly far in the forty-some degrees, it resettled among the turf: a fine *fasciata*, one thread in the exquisite embroidery of the Arctic. It was the only butterfly I would see at Eagle Pass, outside a bird's bill—no *Erebia mackinleyensis* on the rocks, no *Parnassius eversmanni* on top.

In a little bit of lee, I could hear the high, two-note calls of Lapland longspurs. They sounded to me like "Siree! Siree!" James Fisher, when he and Roger Peterson reached the Alaskan apogee of *Wild America*, described the Lapland bunting's voice like this: "tirraleeo-traleeo-tirralee." Well, we agreed on a couple of syllables, and that the song was a lovely one. Both males and females called back and forth to keep in touch. They seemed curious, landing near me, the males striking in black cap, chin, and bib, chestnut nape, and starched white coat. A horned lark's devil horns wiggled in the wind, and a big long-horned beetle sheltered in a borehole in a wooden block.

On my way back to the car, I investigated the Central Lions Club emergency shelter, a fiberglass pod set up beside the pass. I could have used it, made a fire in the wood stove, stretched out on the old, mousy mattress. There were even tins of food to be cooked. But all that was for folks in serious need. I had sardines, crackers, and ale, and I was happy in my crimson corpuscle in the midnight sun, due in one hour and six minutes. I had copied a poem taped up to the wall of the emergency shelter:

> Windy Trail:
> Scat scattered on a windy trail
> A yellow flower from a rainy veil
> The alpine ridge proves life frail.

Summits seem to sing and wail.
Windy voices, telling a tale?
Or nature's reminder it will prevail,
Every time I'm on this windy trail.
—Friday, Aug 13, 1993. GSM.

As if in illustration of the near-anonymous verse, four guys in a small SUV pulled in and got their stuff ready to go backpacking—in this chill wind and spattering rain, at 44°F! Better them than me. I'd like to say younger too, but I doubt I ever would have done that. They'd have sunlight anyway. Two of the kids went Yellow Brick Road–skipping across the tundra, one beer between them, arm in arm. When they came back by me, I asked how far they planned to go, and one said, "As far as we want—that's half the fun of it." That reminded me of something . . . and then I remembered: "I've got from now on!"

Refraction or not, Eagle Summit lay in brighter light at the midnight sun than when I'd been up on top by day. The lads took off, and I wished them well. That left me alone up there for the night. Last night there'd been a small trailer with a Fairbanks doctor, his wife, and their daughter, but they gave up and pulled out while I was up on the mountain. I read some Heat-Moon and some Vargas Llosa with my sardines and beer and jazz from Fairbanks. And so to bed, hoping for sunshine in the morning—not that the morning would be remotely distinguishable from the present midnight moment.

Actually, it was. I'd retired with half the sky blue and the tundra-skipping sun bright beneath my eyelids, and I awoke to a pale gray scrim over everything, rain pelting, and the car rocking in the wind—more like Gold Beach in January than Murphy Dome two days ago. Eagle Summit was invisible, as were the road and the emergency shelter. I was inside an Arctic cloud, fog blowing across the tundra. With the weather forecast even worse for the North, I decided to follow the Steese to its terminus at the Yukon River.

At Central, the Steese Roadhouse was the last place open. The proprietor and waitress, Diane, told me there were around two hundred folks about, not counting summer prospectors. The school was hanging on with ten students. Big festivities were coming up for Solstice, when they were supposed to get better weather. I had a good BLT for ten times more than the sixty cents I paid for the one outside Gainesville. A menagerie of furs hung on the wall: two wolves, two martins, a mink, and a lynx with its giant soft paws, long claws, black tufts, and long legs.

Diane told me about the boon of Central Services, whereby two "great ladies" at Fairbanks library make up magic red bags of books and movies for you with always-suitable choices and send them out via the daily mail plane, for a two-month loan. "It's like Christmas, every time!" said Diane. A lively place, the roadhouse was essential for the locals, like our café in Gray's River. A sign at the door read: "No Guns or Large Hunting Knives." Having lamented my lack of a stocking cap in the wind, I spotted the perfect one in a case of furry winter hats: red fleece with black moose and conifers for ten bucks. I bought it but hoped I wouldn't need it anymore.

I pushed on to Circle, which isn't on the Arctic Circle but is on the Yukon River. Driving toward this largely native community, I listened to an Indian station on AM, out of Porcupine. It was holding a fundraiser—*not* a pledge drive but an auction benefit for Hannah Paul. The DJ was taking bids on cupcakes, a winter coat, five gallons of gas, two-stroke motor oil (the donor of which wanted her can back), and bags of dried meat. Two ladies were in a bidding war for a black beaded bag; Ruth got it in the end for $125.

Wild roses and mertensia lined the gravel road, and there were very few cars. On a long, steel, wooden-decked truss bridge over Birch Creek—wouldn't you know?—I met three trucks, as many as I'd seen all the way from Central. A beautiful slope of a big-flowered purple penstemon and artemisia and aspen looked right out of Wyoming, and like it ought to have checkerspots. A lapis blue Jacob's ladder bloomed at the base of the sage slope, and white-winged crossbills flew up from the road, alighted in spruces, and cracked cones.

The big sign, two moose above, two salmon on either side, said: "Welcome to Circle City—Established in 1893 as the Hub for supplying Interior Alaska's Oldest Major gold camps. Population: 73. Elevation: 596 feet." On its lower left, a map of Alaska, with a "You are here" arrow, and on it, "Yukon River: 1979 miles in length/1866 miles navigable/4th longest North American waterway/5th largest river in world capacity." At the bottom, "THE END OF THE ROAD," with a stop sign. Beside it, a faded plywood sign said "BOAT RIDES MIGHTY YUKON RIVER contact Albert Carroll Sr."

Much of the town was boarded up, like the tiny Calvary Mission. A two-story log home signed "The Outfit of the Carroll's" seemed occupied, and a boat by the launch looked capable of small tours. Another, a long, low-draft aluminum pirogue, had two dog kennels and a steel folding chair on it. On the river bank, someone was constructing an elegant, double-bow fish trap of peeled willow poles and steel mesh. Older traps lay about rotting in the long grass.

This was the edge of the Yukon Flats National Wildlife Refuge—8.6 million wild acres—the third largest refuge in the country, created as part of the Alaska Lands Act of 1980, as many of the federal reserves up here were—Jimmy Carter's finest legacy. Geese gabbled upstream, ravens prospected the shore, and swallows worked overhead, or there would have been even *more* mozzies. The river was big and broad, flowing strong between green balsam flats. I washed my hands in the river, and they came out brown. Permafrost showed in muddy ice shags sticking out of the eroded shore. I broke off a dirty piece, washed it in the river, sucked it to nothing: it tasted sweet. How old? There was a pleasing willow and cottonwood scent in the air, and maybe that had made its way into the ice. I'd read of Yukon villages falling into the river or horribly flooded because of melting permafrost. A gauge showed a high-water mark at 28.5 feet, a foot above the Alascom dish, four feet above the power plant, five feet above the fire hall. Even so, a red plastic bin contained forest fire–fighting gear: with warming, the flip side of spring flood is summer fire.

I gassed up back at the Steese Roadhouse, still open at eleven. Inside, with no provocation, John Brown bought me a Crown Royal. He said he'd been "after marlin in Puerto" but a week early, so he didn't get any. I told him about Eversmann's parnassian at Eagle Pass, same deal. A third-generation gold miner out of Telluride, John lamented times when "gold was high and fuel was low." That quotient has flipped, but he still mines gold. "Why would I do anything else?" he asked. "Nothing else makes any sense."

He told me about Harvey Wheeler, lying dead in the bar at Circle Hot Springs. The bartender said, "He needed shot." In the morning

Harvey got up and walked away. About Harold Emory, "the only outlaw the Mounties didn't catch," whose great-bearded portrait hung on the wall. "Gwitchen Indians smashed the glass out of Harold's International because he was 'going Carrolling,' " John said. "Carroll girls were cute!" And about going fishing with Albert Carroll, Sr., both a traditional and an actual chief. "Albert would take me to fish camp, saying, 'We'll come back tomorrow'; and that'd be four days."

I bought the next round. Diane offered me a room for seventy-five dollars. John offered her as part of the deal, saying, "You ought to take it. Can't find a girl around here now with a search warrant, but we used to stack them like cordwood." Diane just rolled her eyes. I thanked her for the offer of the room but declined. Instead I pushed off into thrush song and birch smell, sweet after all the smoke, talk, and whiskey.

As I drove west, I recalled a remarkably parallel exchange from *Blue Highways,* when a man leaning on a rake asked Heat-Moon: "That your honeywagon?"

"That's my truck."

"I 'spect you can stack the ladies in there like cut cordwood."

"Haven't done any stacking," I said. "Been movin' along." I did the same.

Past Stack Pup Creek, hares lined the road and tried to commit hare-a-kari under my tires. A cow and two-calf unit of moose crossed the road before me, dark and glossy, as I listened to Loch Ness and Bigfoot on George Noory's *Coast to Coast*—perfect for these specters in the mist. I entered the cloud, in the Land of the Midnight Fogbank. Back at Eagle Summit, I shoved through the densest fog I'd seen since the Brussels sprouts fields of Bedfordshire. The young hikers' truck was still there; I left a note with my card under their wiper, asking them to let me know that they got out okay.

Sometime later, I received this message from Chris Benshoof of the U of A:

Dr. Pyle—We were surprised to get your card after our
return from the Pinnell Mountain trail, but are happy to let
you know how it went. We ended up hiking about 7 miles

Monday night. We made camp about 3:00 in the morning that night and slept for a good 12 hours or so. When we awoke the clouds had moved in and while the winds were still very high, the rain had not yet started.

Tuesday afternoon we hiked another 11 miles, stopping at the second of two shelters for the night. Wednesday we fought off a small band of marmots attempting to infiltrate the shelter, and later finished the last 8 miles of the trail in clear weather with manageable winds. Overall we hiked the 27.5 miles in about 14 hours and slept/rested for about 28 hours . . . not the most efficient travel, but none of us are complaining.

We hope the rest of your travels this week have gone well. We thought back to our time on the trail and could not remember seeing much of any invertebrates during the hike—let alone butterflies—but we weren't on a focused search, either. . . .

3. OVER ATIGUN

In midmorning, under full cloud cover, I pulled onto the forbidden Dalton Highway. The only road to the North Slope, it came about as the Haul Road for the construction of the Alyeska Pipeline, which would accompany me all the way. I crossed the pipeline just past pump station number 6, and then the Yukon River, where I stopped into Motel-Restaurant-Gifts at noon for a good basic breakfast. Gassing up at $5.199 per gallon recalled another prescient prophecy from *Blue Highways*. A wistful waitress, looking out at Heat-Moon's truck, said, "Time I get the nerve to take a trip, gas'll cost five dollars a gallon."

Northward, nuggets of sun brought fleeting glimpses of a Compton tortoiseshell and a Canadian tiger, but at the Arctic Circle, rain sprayed the monument like a car wash. Four young Circle crossers from Hong Kong asked me to take their photographs and vice versa. I showed Lucia a field guide photo of the blue that bears her name.

As I descended into the Koyukuk Valley, the Brooks Range parted to receive me, a broad green apron of spruce and poplar like a landing pad for the Arctic. In *Two in the Far North*, Mardy Murie wrote, "We stood there for a long time, just looking. This might be our farthest north, ever. If we could only take a giant step and see the Arctic Shore; we were so near. . . . In a tiny birch tree, a white-crowned sparrow, the voice of the Arctic summer, 'you will remember, you will remember,' he sang." And so I shall.

Coldfoot, on the other hand, could fairly be called forgettable, so I shot through. On up toward the pass, a cow moose feeding in an oxbow of the Koyukuk wore a radio collar, and the speculum of a green-winged teal looked huge in a momentary sunbeam, doubled on the limpid surface. A great horn stuck out of the cloud ahead. Getting out to see it better, I heard that the Brooks Range in the evening rain was full of hermit thrush song. On the steeply tilted way up Atigun Pass, a wind-sanded sign said: "Entering the North Slope Borough—The World's Largest Municipality." Another, "Dalton Highway patrolled by North Slope Borough POLICE—next 180 miles." To which I mumbled, "I'll bet not *often!*"

The slopes had grown largely treeless. At this point, white spruce reached its northern limit; black spruce, one mile south; paper birch, twenty-five miles; quaking aspen, fifty-five. Great, broad Arctic flats spread out to the east. A knot of sandhill cranes was flying way off across the Chandalar Shelf, and a long-tailed jaeger perched right beside the road—a hefty, raptorial tubenose, black-headed, white-breasted, swallowtailed.

Atigun Pass straddles the Continental Divide, between the Arctic Ocean and the Yukon Drainage to the Pacific. Attaboy Pass, it ought-tabe called, for anyone who makes it up there: incredibly wild and immense, in the strictest sense of all three words. Though some would quibble with the word "wild" where a road and a pipeline are involved, and sensibly so, their temporary imposition is like scratches on a rhino's hide that haven't been there long and will be sloughed off in the short time left for the species that made them. Or so it seemed, to me, up there.

The way went right through the rockslides, avalanche zones, and vertical walls of moss, lichen, rock, snow, and ice that made the headwaters of Atigun Creek. Then it leveled abruptly onto fields of yellow dryas. Ahead, a sunny sky showed over the North Slope, and the valley stretched away toward the Arctic Ocean, just a hundred miles away. Who knew you could drive here in a Ford Focus?

The guardrail near the top was battered, with big holes and gaps. I came to a pullout just in time to avoid a juggernaut truck bounding down the grade. It is those trucks, and the rocks they toss, that most concern the rental car companies. I discovered that if you crowd the trucks and pass them at speed, as I saw some drivers do, why yes, they will speed too and kick rocks like crazy. But if you pull over for them and get as far out of their way as you can, they invariably slow down, salute, and pass at a safe speed. The Red-disked Alpine never caught a rock to the windshield or her pretty red finish. I couldn't imagine making that run time after time, especially in winter; but one driver told me he preferred winter, because the surface of the road was so much smoother.

I arrived at Galbraith Lake for the Midnight Sun, which was at least semi out, and no refraction this time—this was the real Arctic. Ken had recommended this destination as offering the highest butterfly potential for the ridiculously short time I had. The tundra here was fuchsia purple with Lapland rosebay (*Rhododendron lapponicum*) and windy. Arctic ground squirrels—sicsics—scooted all about, almost as big as marmots. There were three rigs here, and one tent; I took the last campsite. A vast, double-peaked pyramid loomed out of the cloud, just one of a boundless roundel of mounts: alpine eminence and immanence such as I had never beheld outside an airliner. The high peaks up toward Atigun Pass came into full sun by 1:00 A.M. I retired in bright sun, hoping beyond hope for the same on the morrow. Or, since it already *was* the morrow, when I awoke.

But I was too excited to sleep. If I hadn't been beat by a three-hundred-mile day on the Dalton, after little sleep the night before and the night before that, I don't think I would have even tried. Cloud tongues slipped down the throats of valleys. The mountains were again befogged, but the sun behind me was fully out and the tundra shone like an outfield under lights. In front of me, a faint but full rainbow arced. Its right end came down plunk on the brook side where Ken told me to seek the special butterflies of Galbraith. I had to get out to pee and to take it all in once more. The couple in the tent behind me poked their noses out, afraid I was a bear. When they saw the rainbow, they came out to behold it too, their arms around each other. I couldn't believe I was where I was. Overwhelmed and suddenly exhausted, I slept the sleep of the winter marmot.

In the morning, I met the couple who'd hoped I wasn't a grizzly. Keith and Katrina Andrews were exploring the natural history of the North Slope with their guide, Dan Wetzel. I showed them a gritty, dark gray silvery blue, utterly different from the bright ones along the Columbia, let alone the pale, white-spotted Xerces. I released it onto Katrina's nose, where it remained for some time, whether for the warmth or for the company. Before they went afield, Dan turned me on to good spots for wheatears and Alaska marmots, both of which I hoped to see.

I made sure to visit a key landmark that Ken had said I must see here at Galbraith: the Outhouse of the Midnight Sun—the last loo on the Dalton before Prudhoe Bay. A handsome wooden structure it was, unassuming but indispensable. As I came out, a poppy yellow pickup pulled into the campground. It was Ken! I knew he had been planning to head north, but we'd made no plans to meet up. He'd been blanked too and had just got up here. We walked upstream to his favorite spot: a sunny, south-facing bank, orchid and ivory with white heather and rosebay, with a notch that Eversmann's parnassian liked to fly up and down. Not much flew now but fresh Freija fritillaries.

It was early yet for butterflies, and maybe the rain had knocked things down. But Ken caught an *angelika*, and then I spied an *Erebia*. The chase—the catch—a gorgeous, fresh *Erebia rossii*—a lifetime desideratum! Ross's alpine has smaller ocelli than Butler's, a double iris in a yellow patch on otter pelt brown. Ken said, "That's a good bug. Poor Don Eff always wanted to catch *rossii* but was frustrated and never did. He was always rained out here." Don was a boyhood mentor of mine, a gentle postmaster from Boulder, a coauthor of my bible, *Colorado Butterflies*. If it could happen to him, it could happen to me, as it did up on Eagle Summit. This was starting out better, so far. Ken took up a perch on a rock where he likes to just sit and see what comes along, while I hunted upstream.

I hiked up to a pingo on the tundra. Three long-tailed jaegers hunted the high ridge, recalling the swallow-tailed kites of the Big Cypress; tiny shooting stars appeared in the tundra, a throwback to Malibu Canyon. But this lonely land had nothing to do with California, even less with Florida. Could it really be June already? I was musing, when Akito broke again! All the twisting, flailing, and high winds had stressed the metal. Absent Ken's shop, I repaired it as best I could with dental floss, some copper wire I'd found at Coldfoot, and a Band-Aid. The expression "Band-Aid fix" is supposed to be a metaphor, but this was for real. My glasses too were patched up with floss and tape and superglue. Then I lost my watch on the tundra, one with a broken band that Thea had found and given me, since I haven't worn one for years.

I was falling apart here, but I was happy. Ken and I decided to check another favored habitat of his. Driving out the road past the small Galbraith Lake airport, I noticed alpines bobbing over the wet tundra alongside. One flew out in front of me, and I struck it, thereby collecting my first-ever disa alpine with the fender of the Red-disked Alpine. Endemic to the North Slope, *Erebia disa* has four ocelli in a row, embedded in rich russet, with diagnostic white spots beneath. Our quarry was the smaller *Erebia occulta*. Ken had found a colony of this small species, the Eskimo alpine, north along the pipeline. Around the base of the scree, we caught three species of *Erebia*—disa, Ross's, and banded alpines—in a quarter-hour that I would have traded half a summer for at age fourteen. But our object, *occulta*, seemed to be absent.

Up on the steep scree proper, I caught an *Acsala anomala*, an orange-collared, smoky-mica-winged tiger moth that feeds on lichen. As the name implies, it is indeed anomalous among the colorful family Arctiidae, with its drab, shiny wings. It reminded me somewhat of a mysterious, primitive Andean butterfly of isinglass wings that bears the sinister if wonderful name *Styx infernalis*. Ken said this was the first record of *A. anomala* ever for the Dalton! Thus encouraged, I continued toward the top of the ridge. Ken had seen *Erebia mackinleyensis* on the summit, so I headed up there, over scree, fell-field, and boulder pile. A red fox loped downslope in my direction but apparently never saw me. I watched her well at close quarters before she ducked into her den beneath a great slab of granite. She had the biggest brush I've ever seen. I missed one foxy *Boloria* (in both senses), caught one more *E. rossii*. Then on top, a big black *Erebia* sailed up over the lip, floated down a small scree, and vanished from my sight. The habitat, behavior, and looks were all just right for the Mt. McKinley alpine, sister species to my beloved Magdalena alpine of the Colorado talus and a huge grail for me. It should have been on the rock stripes at Eagle Summit, and perhaps it was, but in cold storage. Had this one been a McKinley? That would remain a fat, tantalizing *maybe*, since it never showed again, and there were two or three other species of big dark alpines up there, all of which sometimes visit rockslides.

We had a tailgate lunch beside the pipeline—KWP, cheese san with milk; RMP, cheese and PB san with beer. Then we returned to the bank above Galbraith Lake. As I checked my banana bait by the creek side, finding nothing on it, an *Erebia* flew right over the bait, totally ignoring it. Then a marble materialized out of the white glacial rocks: my first *Euchloe creusa*. We netted one each and laughed at ourselves as we comically missed others, solo and in concert. The northern marble was more densely mottled with green than the creamy large marbles I'd been finding from San Francisco Bay to Fairbanks. By the stream, tall willows issued puffs of cotton from erect catkins onto late snowbanks, mimicking both of our beards.

An arctic white perched like a swatch of pale linen in a drawer lined with white heather, lichen, and moss. All this was very fine, but I kept watching for the parnassian that declined to appear in its notch. Parnassians are large swallowtail relatives with waxy white wings and coal and cherry spots. Only one species is lemony yellow, the far northern Eversmann's. It was a life's ambition of mine to see it, and this should have been my best shot, after the fogged-out Eagle Summit. Looking back, I saw Ken perched on his special sitting rock: red, white, and black plaid jacket, trademark black slacks and blue shirt, safari cap with earflaps, and English net with short wooden handle, teardrop hoop, and dark bag. Eversmann's or no, I was tickled to have swung nets here on the North Slope with the First Dude of Alaska Leps.

We parted at our cars, happy for our lucky "hail fellow, well met." Ken was off to a field station a little way north to give a talk and to check out Oil Spill Hill for *Oeneis excubitor*. He'd have taken me, but access was by invitation only, and my time was short. I wished that I had a week here. The stream rushed with glacial water. Aufeis poked into mostly frozen Galbraith Lake, layered and blue like a mini–Glacier Bay. A red-capped sparrow flitted willow to willow over the pools by the road, hopped on the ground, leaped up and grabbed things from the willows, singing "DudleyaduhduhWheep!ooh." The bird's breast spot finally twigged for me: it was an American tree sparrow.

A little before the highway, a rill cut through the willows, lined by boggy grass and spattered with blue and pink corydalis. I saw *Erebia*—the swale was teeming with them! I spent a precious hour, one of my last on the North Slope, pacing carefully back and forth in this Arctic glen among flowers and alpines. I found nothing new, but the sight of both disa and Ross's alpines paired elegantly with coltsfoot justified, nay, *sanctified,* that hour.

I'd seen plenty of sheep scat and mires on the heights. Now here were fourteen Dall sheep, four-legged white specks climbing a canyon to the south end of the mountain on whose north end I'd earlier stood, watching the mystery alpine. I saw no live caribou, but various parts of them lay about Galbraith Lake—a pelt on the tundra, a skull with antlers in camp, bones up by the butterfly bank. Vast caribou migrations used to range through the Steese and Dalton areas. Olaus Murie estimated 500,000 animals in one Steese movement; now that herd registers fewer than 5,000. Though herds normally fluctuate, managers and trophy hunters often blame predators for the decline of game. Hence, the revival of aerial wolf shooting under Governor Palin, then about to be nominated for vice president. A public meeting on this volatile subject had been held just the night before in Fairbanks.

I walked along the pipeline to peer into Atigun Gorge, an amazing array of teeth, horns, folds, spikes, hoodoos, ledges, and ramparts, with massive rockslides rolling down to tussocks along the river. This was the edge of the Arctic National Wildlife Refuge, where the Porcupine caribou herd still ranges in its vast numbers. Tiny icebergs flowed down the inside curve of the Atigun River toward the gorge, beneath the pipeline bridge. There was a lot of sicsic action in the silty banks here and an Institute of Arctic Biology research project in place to study them. A Lapland longspur and an American pipit perched and sang atop the pipeline. I laughed at the peristalsis of the big tube, its burps and gurgles. It occurred to me that the pipeline and its haul road form an almost closed-community ecosystem: oil down, trucks up, crude down, diesel back up—and that most of the oil used on the Dalton is in service to the oil traveling alongside it in the pipeline.

Heading up the pass, I pulled over and saw wheatears right where Dan said I should, though the Alaska marmots sent their regrets. Across the eye-popping pass, I stopped to poke about in a stony cirque. It was then that I realized my mistake. This was just like a perfect place for *Erebia magdalena* in Colorado, and I knew for a fact that *mackinleyensis* would have been there earlier in the day. I tried to expunge the word "should" from my vocabulary many years ago, but now and then I allow myself a big fat one, as when I frightened the pipit with the arctic in its bill. I damn well *should've* shot right up here when Ken and I had parted, or at least after the alpines' swale. Instead, I had dithered about a seductive, purpled slope well stocked with evasive Freija frits but nothing else.

Now it was too late and cold for alpines on the pass. I could have camped there until morning, except I no longer had time, unless I wanted to speed all the way back to Fairbanks. Besides, had I stayed, I would have missed what was yet to come: always the enigma of the entire trip. As I released the brake and rolled down the south side of Atigun, my sweet satisfaction was spiked with a dash of the bitters of disappointment.

It didn't help when I called Ken before flying out and he told me that he'd found the Mt. McKinley alpine, Eversmann's parnassian, and the Melissa and sentinel arctics, *all right there*, the very next day.

4. DOWN THE DALTON

Southward from Atigun, Roche Moutonnee Creek squirted out of a canyon that could have had Bhutan at its head, or Tibet, or Nepal— or maybe the Brooks Range. Fairbanks was 321 miles away, Coldfoot 67, and my instruments told me that I had 77 miles until empty. That seemed a bit close for comfort. I drove very conservatively, coasting where I could. I heard a varied thrush, a.k.a. Alaska robin, singing from a sprucewood beneath even grander Grand Tetons; down-valley looked like Glacier National Park, squared.

When I arrived at Coldfoot, the gauge said 39 miles to empty, so I'd made up almost 20 miles by coasting. Old Coldfoot Camp was a fin-de-siècle gold town. The present one, called "temporary," was built in 1970 to accommodate 260 workers on the highway, then 450 for the pipeline. Slate Creek Inn (formerly Arctic Acres Inn) consisted of pushed-together trailers. The record low was −82°F, the high +97°F, and the winter of 1989 had seventeen consecutive days below −60°F. The place is pretty much a big, broad dust flat full of trucks and old trailers: a fairly grim tourist experience, but the ones I saw kept up a brave face. The staff bunkhouses were small metal cubes on risers, and I guessed people drank a bit here, and perhaps rutted as well.

Gas cost an arm and a leg at Coldfoot, but the camping was free. I woke up hot and sweaty, with both an *Erebia* and a *Boloria* out my window among a solid mass of mosquitoes, and Akito broken good. Wondering what the heck to do about it, I experimented and discovered that Mini-Marsha and Akito could be grafted together. The aluminum sleeve of the small hand net just fit over the long pole, and the mounting screw was the right gauge. This made for a teeny net hoop and bag on a long pole—funny-looking but functional. If

236

I could see anything. Almost simultaneous with Akito packing it in, my cobbled-together glasses gave up the ghost for good. I was down to a pair of oldies with an ancient prescription. Still, I think I saw a lone painted lady working the dandelions around the camp, way up here, a long way for a butterfly that cannot winter within two thousand miles.

Walking the gravel path through woods behind the interagency visitor center, I saw a large dark arctic landing on trees. I expected it to be *Oeneis jutta* and got all excited. But nabbing it with the hybrid net, I found it was *Oeneis bore*, acting like Jutta in Jutta's kind of habitat. Thus the importance of checking closely rather than making a sight call based on expectations—especially with Franklin-era specs on my nose.

When the Alyeska Pipeline was proposed, in the 1970s, I harbored reservations about it and opposed its construction. Of course it was built, and I have to say, oil aside, it offers the naturalist on the Dalton a handy service. Every few miles, a pipeline access road leaves the highway. While you mustn't block these lanes in case of emergency, they are not posted against entry. You can pull off on any of them, stash your rig off to the side, and use the right of way to investigate the habitat. Since it is difficult to park along the main roadway, given its narrow shoulders and the zooming haul trucks, the access roads make the territory far more easily and safely approachable for butterfliers and birders.

On the first pipeline access road south of Coldfoot, purple with vetch, I netted a male palaeno sulphur. The mosquitoes were almost insupportable around here, and I got out in a hurry. But at another access point some miles south, the mozzies weren't so bad, and a puddled track paralleling the pipeline through a weedy woods edge proved remarkably productive. Three types of blues, including the first greenish blues of the year, the first field crescents, and several other species all welcomed the sun.

A sulphur flew at me, and then another, and even with the small hoop and legendarily evasive yellows, I managed to net them both. They weren't palaenos, or any other *Colias* I personally knew. One was heavily dusted with dark scales beneath; the other expressed an odd two-tone pattern, with orange forewings and yellow hindwings.

Uncertain of their identity, I thought it best to collect samples. It's a good thing I did. Back in Seattle, Jon Pelham determined that the first was the small northern subspecies of *C. gigantea,* nothing like the giant sulphurs I'd known in Montana; and that the other was Booth's sulphur, *C. tyche thula*—according to Ken, the first ever recorded south of the Brooks Range!

I jogged the gravel pipeline pad through black spruce bog at the third site, which may have had the worst mosquitoes I have ever encountered. Without stopping, I caught a hoary comma, confirming an earlier sight record. Still another side road to a rock pit had no mosquitoes, because no plants, thus no butterflies. But it did have fresh bear scat and big gravel piles for bears to hide behind. Again I recalled the Alaska author Richard Nelson's conclusion, upon dipping a finger into a fresh brown bear brownie and finding it still warm: "that information like this should never be taken lightly." So I scatted.

Finger Peak was dry tundra, where it seemed I could look for *Erebia youngi* since the sun was out and it was only 9:00 P.M. on the longest day of the year. But it was burned-over rocky bogland teeming with mosquitoes. Something that felt just like a hypodermic needle bit my shoulder through a thickish shirt. Back rolling in Red, I spotted a red vole or lemming as it crossed the road, and a short-eared owl hunted alongside me. Then a large marble shot across at 9:40 P.M. I thought that was late. But a few miles on, I stopped at a sandy spruce hem to see if there was still any action and beheld a perfect, fresh *Papilio machaon aliaska* nectaring on a sunny stand of Labrador tea.

Careful not to get too close or to cast my mile-long shadow on the swallowtail, I watched and watched and watched, *almost* oblivious to my pelt of mosquitoes. When it shivered its wings, the whole inflorescence of *Ledum* shivered. He dug deep! I retired to the car to watch; it was full of skeeters too, but the blower helped keep them off. I must have had dozens of bites, hundreds maybe. But what a wonderful way to wrap up the first half of the butterfly watching year, which began around the Winter Solstice with a California tortoiseshell, beholding this quintessentially circumpolar butterfly engaged with this definitively Holarctic plant, at 10:23 P.M.

on the Summer Solstice! I was sorely tempted to see how long it would go—maybe I could still be butterflying here at the utmost midnight sun?

It was a tough call, but there was a piece of pecan pie with my name on it waiting at Yukon Crossing, and I doubted they would stay open till one. Anyway, I was relieved of the decision, for at 10:28 he rose, flirted around the stand, circled the car, and then, perhaps with his crop running over, flew off into the forest. I smelled, then tasted the *Ledum,* got a hint of the sweetness that brought him down, and then of the astringency that makes it a favored tea among boreal peoples. On to that pie!

Or not. Motel-Restaurant-Gifts at Yukon Crossing had closed at nine—on the Summer Solstice! Luckily, there was another establishment up the road in the woods, a hodgepodge of prefabs, gifts, bygones, and burgers. My cheeseburger was the size of a tire. I told Theresa I thought her place should be crowded tonight. She said custom was down because of the price of gas. Feeding the folks on Princess tours was saving her for now, but next year *their* prices would climb. She told me that she spends $120 *per day* on generator fuel! I wondered if she'd considered just tapping the pipeline.

The Solstice sunset on the Yukon River was all rosebay purples and dryas golds amid Swainson's thrush song. I'd been spoiled by sunsetlessness on the North Slope and the High Ridge. Here, near sea level, even on this shortest night, the sun slipped beneath the far hills' horizon, leaving the night far from dark. And so fragrant, what with the fresh vegetation, the river, the rising moisture, and the wild roses all around. But wait, I'd been mistaken—the sun *was* still above the hill, behind a narrow purple cloud. And at the stroke of the Summer Solstice, near enough (12:40 A.M.), it peeked out again, and the whole northwest sky went the color of those roses mixed with mertensia blue, with painted lady rays and swallowtail-spot persimmon. What it really looked like was an Aurora Borealis. And it might have been, for all I knew.

I crossed the high, wooden-decked Yukon bridge and back four times, since the only security guy I'd seen for my whole time in the North came along and told me to move on when I parked in the middle to watch the sunset. The bridge over the pipeline was twice as high and brought me down by a quiet pond where horned grebes fished and ring-necked ducks displayed, turning out from the middle and then stretching their heads forward, all three drakes in succession.

Much farther on, in a pair of little ponds below the road, I stopped for a ripple and saw two parent beavers and two babies. The flat tail of the larger adult dragged behind it as it climbed out and walked through tall sedges to the other pond; the smaller fed and dove and swam, emerged, hunched, ate, and pushed out, nose up, and dove again, over and over. The mom's fur parted in broad, slick furrows when she hunched to munch, or on her back as she swam; the furrows and the water ripples, the beaver and the pond, were extensions of each other. She paid me no mind whatsoever. I could watch all night—except there wasn't any night. The sunset was grading directly into sunrise, at 2:52 A.M. I needed sleep, but it was hard to leave—this was my best beaver watching ever. Here came one of the young, its tail going like a beanie propeller, but the adult seemed to chase it away. Its cheeks were whitish, gnawing off rushes, and—oh, its tail was flattened sideways—it was a muskrat! There weren't any baby beavers after all. Well, cool—both species feeding together. The muskrat dragged a big sheaf of grass across the pond to its lodge, dove to deposit it, and swam back toward the beaver. It was instructive to see their ten-to-one size difference, side by side.

I was glad I'd had my coffee thermos filled, the one recovered at Santa Caterina's. "Over the Rainbow" came on the jazz station out of Fairbanks as the sky became a bumbleberry pink-and-purple flock and a big, juicy sunrise got ready to pop just a few degrees east of the downer. At 3:22, I hit the intersection with Highway 2, and the end of the James W. Dalton Highway, at the start of the Elliott. I'd had it all to myself, all night, but for a few truckers who waved (it is still the Haul Road), that one cop, the wildlife, a few bazillion two-winged insects, and a few with four. And here it was—the sun, fully up at 3:44 A.M., all rested up for its big trip south.

5. ARCTIC SOLSTICE

It was my last day in Alaska. I'd stopped to net some z's at 4:00 A.M. at Tatalina River, a pretty birch green, rose-pink, riffling water place. Up at 6:30—not much sleep, even for me, even for this year. Coffee still hot in the thermos, thank goodness. From the old bridge over the stream, chickadees called—black-caps not boreals. A white crossed the road before Globe Creek at 8:25, ten hours since yesterday's last butterfly. If it was a large marble, that species was the last but one of the spring and the first of the summer.

At 11:11, I arrived at the Wickersham Dome trailhead for its excellent Outhouse of the Seventh Solstice, a requisite short nap, breakfast, a change from my filthy clothes, and contemplation. I made up my mind: I would not attempt Eagle Summit again—it was just too far for the time, too much driving for my woozy head, too risky to make my plane. I would save Eversmann's parnassian and Mackie's alpine for some future grail quest. Instead, I would hike and search here, then repack before meeting Mark Garland in Fairbanks. The city was certain to be a hot mess today, and a zoo for the Solstice; whereas I had Wickersham Dome all to myself, and no mosquitoes for a change.

There were butterflies from the outset—Persius and arctic skippers, a Canadian tiger, and a silvery blue in the parking lot, and a bright orange sulphur coming down the trail. I chased it out to the highway, where it dallied briefly with the roadside dandelions before the wind carried it off. I figured it was probably the Canadian sulphur, my chief object, which Ken said occurred here. Walking up the trail, I put up small fritillaries, commas, white-veined arctics, and a yellow sulphur, all fast and evasive. Butterfly sport on all sides—and then, out of one tiny, fertile cloudlet, heavy clouds fattened to cover the sun, making a mess out of the Wickersham Dome day and shutting down the action like a raid on a sporting house.

Up on a shaley hilltop with pink paintbrush and arnica, I thanked the water, air, land, and fire, the sun, the plants and animals, and Alaska—for the day, the week, and all the rest—and importuned Sun's kind return.

It worked, at least in dribs and drabs. Persius spread on the trail for the rays, and a Ross's alpine, which Ken had not found here. I passed the first knob to climb to the second, where a lazy *aliaska* flew up, as it *should,* in such a place. Now it was raining lightly, but the sun was finding gaps. Another big black cloud was coming, but blue jay sky showed to the south. On the cairn, neat spiders skittered and basked like long-legged ants, but they *were* spiders, not spider-mimic ants. The sun came through, and a *canadensis—Papilio* not *Colias*—did a flyby past the cairn as another hilltopped. With both Alaskan swallowtails here, why not a yellow parno? But that was asking too much.

I walked down, around, and under the bank of another knob, where I understood Ken to have meant the *C. cans* to fly—and there was a big white female sulphur flying up the slope, then fluttering over the top. In sulphurs, the females are often dimorphic, either yellow-orange or white, while the males wear just one main color. In this species, the males are bright orange and the females usually white. I was about to go up when a male came off the first *Ledum* bush to my left. I ran, intercepted it, got two or three swipes with my little net, but missed. Then the clouds came heavy and cold, with thunder, so I abandoned the top and walked down the trail to the spruce bog boardwalk. I walked it to its end, maybe one-quarter to one-half mile, new boards running into the broken and rotted old ones, lengthwise versus crosswise. The habitat looked good for Frigga and Jutta, but the air was too cold and dark. I attracted those other noted Nordics, gray jays, but that's it.

I sat on a rock on the upper lip of the *Colias* bank, in light rain and breeze, flies basking on me. I'd been working the dome top, and then it occurred to me that perhaps I shouldn't be standing on the highest point around with a thundercloud overhead and a lightning rod in my hand. The cloud shifted, so I ran back up, netted a Lucia's blue, then saw a female "*Colias*" at the bottom. Clambered down the rockslide, caught it, found it was actually a clotted-cream female of an arctic white. Then a dark "*Erebia*" on the rocks got me all excited for *mackinleyensis* . . . and it was an unusually smoky *Oeneis bore*. I was getting tired of being faked out, and questioning my sleep-deprived perception.

Then all of a sudden, full sun! So I finally caught a pale orange sulphur on top, and it was indeed a female Canadian. That found, I walked the boardwalk again, now alive with small fritillaries—what a difference a sunbeam makes! But every *Boloria* I caught was a freakin' Freija, no friggin' Friggas. *Erebia rossii* too grew common in the sunshine. Coming back, just as the cloud came back too, I netted a *white* female sulphur in the trail, showing the dimorphism of *Colias canadensis*.

Coming down the trail, I was feeling very happy about finding the butterfly I'd come for but wishing I'd caught that male—we're never quite satisfied, after all—when an almost unbelievable piece of luck fell literally in my path. Striding along, I spied a bright bit by the trailside. I bent to pick it up with my forceps, and my jaw fell so far I had to pick it up too. The bright bit was a brilliant, perfect, but dead male *Colias canadensis*! But *how*? Then I realized that the weird spitting noise I'd recently heard had been a dirt bike—and here were the fresh knobby tire tracks on the earth, grass, and moss. The sulphur was a roadkill, on a pedestrian-only trail! Just the butterfly I wanted, and I just happened to see it: this is what I mean when I gabble on about the glory of happenstance.

I heard the two guys with dirt bikes burping and bragging in the parking lot before I got down. Big sign: "No Motorized Vehicles Permitted on Foot Trail," plus a red-slash symbol in case they were illiterate as well as idiots. The scofflaws cut out before I reached them, saving me from a confrontation that would have detracted from the day. I am possessed of the atavistic affliction of rangering such jerks, in and out of uniform. Once, leaping out in front of one dirt biker in my bona fide National Park Service Smokey hat, Marsha held aloft like Little John's staff or Beowulf's broadsword, I'm pretty sure I caused the offender to go pedestrian if not Sierra Club; or maybe it was just cardiac.

On my way down, one more small fritillary had appeared on the trail. Seeing that it wasn't Freija, I pounced and caught it—my last Alaskan butterfly. I ID'ed it as *Boloria alaskensis*, a lifer, and an apt climax for the trip. A few months later, Jon Pelham would determine that it was actually the odd little Alaskan version of *Boloria eunomia*, the bog fritillary, not much at all like those I knew (but would brick) in Colorado. The two differ mostly in wing shape. But nothing lost to the list and, either way, a fine finish. A sweet segue too, because tomorrow afternoon Thea and I will visit a sunny forest corner near home that we call Boloria Junction. We'll no sooner drive up than Thea will say, "There's one!" and indeed there will be a western meadow fritillary fluttering before us. To finish Alaska and pick up at home with new *Bororias*: not bad.

In Fairbanks, I found a car wash and cleaned off the evidence of my perfidy: the Dalton Dust, a special coating that tells the rental car company exactly where you've been, where you promised not to go. Then I negotiated the sprawling Solstice Fair and traffic crush of Fairbanks to find Mark Garland and Paige Cunningham's hotel, the Bridgewater. At our post-*hesseli* dinner on Cape May, we'd agreed to meet here and, though we couldn't manage a day afield together, lift a glass to the Solstice. I was also planning to use their hotel shower. This was critical: I hadn't bathed for a week. But they were out at the Pump House with Mark's birding tour group for dinner, delayed in getting served and back to town by the holiday crowd. In Fairbanks, there is no holiday like the Summer Solstice.

While I waited, I found a barstool at Big Daddy's BBQ and gnawed on burned ends washed down with Sockeye Red IPA from Anchorage's Midnight Sun Brewery. Outside in full sunshine, in the eighties at 11:00 P.M., there were bands, dancers, and a street fair. In my near-catatonic state, looking out at folks strutting by in shorts, halter tops, and bikinis, everything but thongs, I thought I was back in Malibu, Miami . . . anywhere but Alaska.

Mark and Paige didn't made it back before I had to leave. I was sorry to miss them but, to be brutally honest, even sorrier to miss that shower, and sorriest of all for the people who had to sit next to me on the plane: it wasn't first class this time, so we'd be packed in. I returned the car with the rental folks none the wiser, made the airplane, and settled in for the long flight south. I left Alaska feeling battered, knackered, and with mixed emotions: hugely gratified, but stung from barely missed grails. Outside the Airbus, the midnight sun dazzled the great land. But it wouldn't be that way for long. This was to be one of the rainiest Alaska butterfly summers in Ken Philip's memory. Eversmann's or no, I'd been one lucky lad.

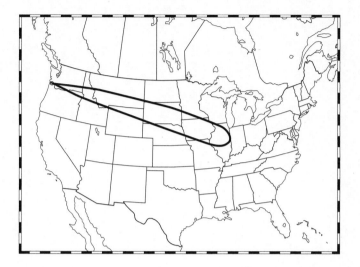

Land o' Lincoln
(Wending with Wiker)

Here was no service to science, no naming of unknown
animals, but rather—we liked it. We liked it very much.
The . . . sea, the beer and the work, they were all one
thing, and we were that one thing too.

—John Steinbeck, *The Log from the Sea of Cortez*
(with E. F. Ricketts)

1. BALTIMORE AT LAST

If this was any sign of how our next few days in the field would go, I was in for it. Jim Wiker showed up at Pett's Victorian Veranda B & B with a devastating growler of Humulus Lupulus IPA, and we talked until 3:00 A.M. I thought maybe I should just dispense with sleep for the duration. I'd flown from Portland to Chicago and bused to Rockford, Illinois. On the morning of Friday, June 27, Jim and I struggled up to our hostess Ret's apple lasagna and coffee and got ready for our butterfly gig at Severson Dells Nature Center. Don Miller, the educational director at Severson, came for us. I'd been here once before to speak and lead walks, and I liked Don and the place so much that I accepted his invitation for a return visit during the Big Year. Jim, one of the top Illinois lepists, had kindly offered to help out and to usher me about some productive habitats afterward.

Once at Severson Dells, a great limestone prairie preserve and education center, we walked the paths into a cloudy-sunny-muggy day. Richard, Kathy, Dan, and Betsy, a covey of Severson naturalists, joined us to check what was on the wing. We hadn't taken many steps before a passel of new species joined the list, not surprising for first immersion in a new region, and they came in pairs. Several commas darted about, the anglewing whose silver mark suggested the name *Polygonia comma*. One gray comma (*P. progne*) played among them. I thought I saw hackberry emperors in the swirl of fast brown butterflies, confirmed when an *Asterocampa celtis* lit on my sweatband to suck at its copious load. Then, just as Richard was looking at its picture in Opler's Eastern Peterson guide, a tawny emperor (*A. clyton*) came and lit on his thumb!

Both blue male and chalky white female summer azures flicked on and off around the wooded edges. Eastern tailed-blues flitted below, as if reflecting the azures. The final pair doubled up on fritillaries: clip-winged meadow fritillaries—where else but in the meadows?—and great spangled fritillaries lording it over the milkweeds. It would take the wings of three or four *Boloria bellonas* to cover one great female *Speyeria cybele*.

We set off east over the flooded Rock River, through Loves Park, to the Harlem Hills. Illinois's largest and finest remaining gravel hill prairie, Harlem Hills Nature Preserve lies on a gravel terrace that extends along the Rock River from Wisconsin to the mouth of the Kishwaukee River. We found it green and pink with lush grass, wild rose, and coneflower, the roses transporting me back to Alaska, so recent, so far. Jim, spotting a borehole with frass in a coneflower, stripped it to find what he knew he would—the striped, greenish yellow larva of a moth in the genus *Papaipema*, probably *P. nelita*. The handsome "paps," as they are known to their devotees (of which Jim is one of the most knowledgeable) grow up in the stems and roots of specific plants. Jim has reared many species, having found that any pap plunked in a hole bored in a carrot is a happy pap. Over the next few days, I would conclude that Jim could pull a pap out of a garden hose if he wanted to.

Harlem had the advantages of a nice cool breeze and lots of big, purple-flowered Hill's thistle, a native. There was plenty of leadplant, a lep-rich herb, and indigo very heavy with seed. But there were no butterflies. "Probably too much fire, too recently," said Jim. "There used to be hundreds of Ottoe skippers here, and now there are none." I would find this sad contradiction in midwestern prairie management coming up again and again. On the way down we spotted a common wood-nymph, still soft, just out. Because of its big "eyes" on Illinois loam–brown wings, an old name for it is ox-eyed wood-nymph. It was easy to see why the archmapper of butterflies, Ray Stanford, calls them "flip-flops," for the way they flit among tall grasses. This grazing generalist, *Cercyonis pegala*, returns fairly soon after fires, unlike scarce, specialized skippers that become hopelessly fragmented.

At the Kieselburg Forest Preserve in early afternoon, another eye-spotted beauty abounded. Lots of the cocoa-colored eyed browns flip-flopped through the rich sedge marsh full of Indian hemp and lotus. Graced with a doubly mythic name, like many satyrs, *Satyrodes eurydice* was a quiet presence among the tall sedges, grasses, and rushes. Early lepidopterists saw them as being on a constant bacchanal and named them accordingly. They were right, as drinking and mating chiefly occupy these satyrs' days.

But we had to hurry back to the Victorian Veranda, so we could relax on the eponymous porch with my old friend Scott Russell Sanders and his wife, Ruth, who had arrived from Bloomington, Indiana. One of the finest of American essayists, Scott teaches there at the University of Indiana. Don had brought us to Severson to give a joint reading that evening, part of his initiative to commingle the literary arts and nature. It was a comfy fit for Scott and me, as we'd read together many times on the Orion Society's Forgotten Language Tours. Not since one of those tours had simmered in the waters of Sanibel among galaxies of *Noctiluca* had I witnessed such a burst of bioluminescence as we saw this night at Severson Dells: thousands and thousands of fireflies lime-lighting the grass. After that, it was only natural that the rest of the Humulus Lupulus came out, as art and biology mingled well into the night.

On Saturday, following the redoubtable Ret's French toast and blintzes, Jim and I led our butterfly outing for families on the Severson Dells meadows among eastern tigers and monarchs, red-spotted purples and bunches of *bellona*. The keen children—Jacob, Sean, Joseph, Bryan, Elena—loved the chasing and the catching, and asked good questions. No "last children in the woods" these. Give a little kid a camera, and he'll drop it in a flash, but give her a net, and watch her go!

Then back to Kieselburg with an adult group. As we gave an introduction using Jim's fine cases of specimens, a black cloud came over, and then a great thumping storm. We had a good picnic shelter for carrying on the butterfly talk during D-day thunder and ricocheting rain. When the sun came out, so did the butterflies: they're great that way. We marched out through the sedge meadow among the eyed browns and great spangleds, both crowd pleasers and easy treats to teach. Jim and I did something of a tag-team act, or Costello and Costello as I put it, considering our statures. As I was earning my blintzes and pumping up the gas fund, Jim caught goodies on dogbane and saved them for me to release for all to watch as they resumed nectaring on the Indian hemp: perfect striped and banded hairstreaks, a snazzy little male mulberry wing, and a gigantic female viceroy, even bigger than your average monarch, which sailed through just then as if to prove it.

After we discharged our day-trippers, Don and Jim and I continued on our own purposes, which were my purposes, thanks to them. We had something special in mind. For every naturalist, certain organisms now and then achieve mythological status, after so many unsuccessful attempts at finding them in seemingly suitable times and places. The snowy owl was like that for me for decades, and the tailed frog still is. Several of my butterfly grails this year fit the category well, none more so than the Baltimore checkerspot: state butterfly of Maryland for its colors, the same as Lord Baltimore's and the oriole's, more or less, though really redder than either. I'd tried and tried in known localities and just couldn't find it, whether because of weather, early or late seasons, or funky luck. So we'd come out today under the guidance of Brian Russart of Brookfield, manager of nine thousand acres of county nature reserves for the University of Illinois, loaded for Baltimores.

Our focus was a horse farm on Kinnikinnick Creek in Boone County. Massive presettlement burr oaks burgeoned downslope, away from the owners' expansive house. We walked down to the wetlands that their farm preserved. After we'd looked about the meadows and creekside for some time, Jim found a caterpillar of *Papaipema harrisii* burrowed into a stem of *Angelica*—a life pap, and his own highest hope in coming here. Though I was happy for him to be sure, I was churlishly wishing it had been a *Chlosyne harrisii* instead, the Harris's checkerspot that I so coveted this year. So I didn't deserve it when Jim yelped out from under the thicket of his red beard, "Baltimore!"

And so it was—there, right in front of us, down in a little swale: an immense female Baltimore checkerspot, sitting on a common milkweed. She drank like crazy, backlit by a sun that was on its way down and would be long gone by midnight. Her red- and black-checked gown spread broad enough to play pocket checkers on, accessorized with snappy orange: legs, palpi, antennal clubs, even the milkweed pollinia stuck to her feet, all in the same bright shade of citrus. Sated, she took wing, flying languidly out over the burbling, willowy country brook—an impossibly romantic scene from a child's dreams of a hundred years ago—or, in my case, only fifty.

And so Jim and I had each found a grail in this idyllic place. I saw one other Baltimore, so big and bright I thought it was an Aphrodite fritillary at first. But it dropped into the grass and stayed there, invisible, just as the other one had, after flying. Lucky for us that Jim had spotted it first at sup. This expression is *Euphydryas phaeton phaeton;* Jim says *E. p. ozarkae,* in southern Illinois, is altogether different, smaller, and flies fast and erratic in open, sandy woods. Waves of wind swept across the sea of sedge. We felt as if we could catch it and bodysurf it, or at least bottle it to take home. We whooped with the sensations and highs of the afternoon, and that was without the ale.

But we didn't have to maintain such a state for long. The mood continued into the evening, when Don took us all into Rockford for dinner at the Carlyle Brewpub. Rockford was in festive mode, just like Fairbanks. As we stood on the bridge in a light rain, looking across at the lighted canopy of an outdoor concert, the strains of Dicky Betts's guitar floated over the high water of the Rock River, and I knew for a fact that I was doing something good here.

2. FRIT CITY

It was a heck of a butterfly day, the first of three. Breakfast at Nance's Cafe came with eggs, bacon, pancakes, and a snarl from the democratically surly waitress. Then we drove down gravel roads, their lush ditches full of cabbages and sulphurs between bumper cornfields, toward Havana, and on to Revis Hill Prairie in Mason County.

On Sunday, Jim and his wife, Sally Agnew, had brought me south from Severson Dells to their house in rural Greenview, Illinois, north of Springfield. Over local white wine, we'd stayed up too late again in Jim's amazing collection and library. He has an extraordinary assemblage of almost untouchable old Lepidoptera works—Seitz, Edwards, Scudder, Cramer, Boisduval, Hübner, many more—as well as contemporary literature, back runs of many journals, and on and on. We played with several texts over arcane questions. Jim is no high roller but a working man in health care. He has just carefully marshaled his available resources to create the most remarkable private lep library I've ever seen.

Now we rolled under Revis Hill. Zebra swallowtails, bigger and with longer tails than those in Florida, floated with black- and green-clouded swallowtails around vervain. Old, flat roadkill furnished a smorgasbord for ladies, hackberries, and a beautiful tawny question mark. Its polygonal wings and clear silver "?" underneath made it clear why it owns one of the most suitable scientific names of all: *Polygonia interrogationis*.

Jim led me up onto Revis Hill Prairie, the original purchase for the state nature preserve system. "And it's the largest, so it's taken the most time to fuck it up," said Jim. The uncommon arogos skipper, once regular here, was last seen in the state in 1989. The large

Ottoe skipper, a prairie icon, used to be abundant at Revis. "There were hundreds," said Jim. "We'd see them on every knob; but they've declined since 2002." Jim saw one example on a good day's looking last year. He'd see other skippers too, and now virtually none. We saw no grass-feeding skippers at all along the hems of the hills, hard up against the cornfields. Jim suspected that Bt corn may have done in these skippers, just as it has been shown to affect monarchs in other locations.

Bt corn is maize that has been genetically altered to express the toxins emitted by the bacterium *Bacillus thuringiensis kurstaki*, lethal to corn loopers and other Lepidoptera that come in contact with it. This clever ploy might be fine if it affected only the pests of corn. But the toxins also occur in the corn's pollen, which may fall on milkweed or other host plants, and kill the larvae that feed upon them. "The southwest wind that created these loess hills can also blow pollen all over them," Jim said, gesturing off toward the seeming infinity of Bt cornfields across the south and southwest.

Up on the loess knobs, overlooking those forever flats, the purples and grays of leadplant took over the green grass sward along with the fuzzy rods of pink prairie clover. A big rare dragonfly, *Erpetogomphus designatus*, flashed its golden abdomen and costal spots. Something even larger flew a loop around me. Monarch, I thought, but the contrast was too great between the primaries and secondaries. Of course—regal fritillary! A gorgeous male grail, *Speyeria idalia*. A fraction of its size but just as striking, the yellow, orange, chestnut, and sienna flower moth *Schinia jaguarina* hovered over its host *Psoralea*, prairie turnip.

"I've got one!" called Jim, and I rushed over. He'd found a male Ottoe. Pointing it out affrighted it, and I got only a quick but diagnostic look before it flew. We cast about for more for quite a while, and we each got a couple more likely sightings, but only wing shots. "Fifteen years ago I'd have never thought it would come to this," said Jim. "I could always bring people here and show them *ottoe*." Coauthor of *The Skippers of Illinois*, he takes these things personally. Now he worries that the site may be subjected to intentional burning, finishing the skippers off. The ravines, with thick, invasive scrub, could use burning, he explained; but the beautifully intact prairie up here—with the fire-vulnerable leadplant and listed pink prairie clover—*needs* no fire. Burning leadplant is lethal to three species of caterpillars, including another flower moth. On the way down, we briefly detained a pair of enormous gray coppers, with their ermine undersides and fire-engine zigzag borders, even larger than their sister great coppers I'd seen with Koji. But Jim had Ottoe on his mind. "That might have been the very last one," he muttered.

Next stop was Witter's Bobtown Hill Prairie, in Menard County. The thick-stemmed leadplant on this hill showed that there had been no burning for some time, but exotic white sweet clover covered the top. One darkish, biggish skipper that merely flirted with a pink prairie clover could have been a female Ottoe. Jim caught a fabulous four-inch female regal fritillary for my examination. At just the right angle to the sun, she showed *blue* like a morpho, and all of a sudden I could see how the blue female Diana fritillary evolved. Released, she shot down the path past a silvery checkerspot basking backlit on a sycamore leaf.

In *Wild America*, Roger Peterson and James Fisher fueled their far-flung travels across the continent with gallons of cold Coca-Cola. I discovered that Cokes were Jim's poison too, and none of those little nickel bottles that Peterson and Fisher guzzled. I'll bet they would have been equally enamored of Big Gulps. I'm no soda swigger, but I got just as thirsty as Jim in the muggy oven of southern Illinois. At one of the little stores we stopped into, I tried for a nonalcoholic beer in the attached saloon. Jim thought it was a fool's mission in that country-music beer parlor, but by gum, they had one for me.

The Sand Prairie–Scrub Oak Nature Preserve was where it really got good. This extensive milkweed meadow hopped and crackled with butterflies big and small: clouded sulphurs, silver-spotted skippers, little glassywings, American ladies, and bags of others. But get this: there were *hundreds* of *Speyeria idalia*! The regal fritillaries mostly mobbed the milkweed, both males and females, easy to catch with forceps or fingers at milkweed to examine, as the nets had to stay in the truck here. With its fiery forewings and white-spotted black hindwings above, olive-bronze underneath, Idalia looks like no other silverspot. At their greatest, the females are the biggest frits in the world—only Diana and Cybele can contend. And those silver blades below! Like a wall of polished halberds in the Tower of London.

They floated all around, those generous regals. The males flew low out of the grass, the females down into it for the small host violets, then they mingled on the milkweed to drink. A lifetime desire met, to see such a thing! Idalia is a rare butterfly overall, nearly extinct in the East and gone from much of the Midwest, owing at least in part to overzealous burning of its prairies. But here, they were blessedly abundant. Along with the monarchs of Santa Cruz and the swallowtails of Kissimmee, they were surely the greatest butterfly spectacle of the year so far; it was hard to imagine what could match them. I lingered and lolled, mind-flying through this city of frits, watching and wondering for a long time.

But we had still more to see. Hot and steamy Sand Ridge State Forest was a savanna graced with many stands of butterfly weed. Few flowers attract butterflies better than this flaming orange milkweed, hence its common name. Patches of *Asclepias tuberosa* scintillated with American coppers, scattered like cinders in the flames. A popular butterfly portrait for magazine covers, even before the digital explosion, has been that of the coral hairstreak tucking into butterfly weed. Hairstreaks love *tuberosa,* and the flaming red marginal spots of *Satyrium titus* arrayed against the lurid milkweed amount to visual ignition. Now I actually got to view this canonical placement, with an enormous egg-filled female coral at that. Not enough? How about a nice *Satyrium edwardsii* nectaring on *A. tube.* too, right beneath its larval host, post oak. The neatly marked Edwards's hairstreak was a life butterfly, as well as one for the year.

We walked around a little pond nearby. There were few butterflies left at 6:30, but gray tree frogs croaked in the trees and little clickers in the water. "It's like they've got a crusade against milkweed around here," said Jim, sweeping his arm at a stretch of road that used to have a lot and was now buzzcut. "But they let *that* grow." He laughed, flicking a big marijuana plant on the verge as we passed by.

Home through Forest City—no forest, no city—past Whitaker Farms, endless acres of ears destined for popcorn, and a city of silos and round metal grain bins to hold them. "I wonder what would happen if they got too hot," said Jim. Silly with heat, hunger, thirst, and overstimulus, we both cracked up at the prospect of Bt popcorn spilling out of the bins, filling up the countryside.

Constitutionally incapable of quitting, just like Andy and me on Easter, we walked Jim's back pastures after eight o'clock. A little before sunset, we put up a meadowlark from her nest and an eastern tailed-blue from white clover, the final butterfly of the first half of the Big Year. Only the prospect of a shower, a pizza, and a beer to toast the first six months finally brought us in.

I scrubbed off the sweat and stickers and cactus spines and poison ivy and ticks—I had only five or six immature lone stars—and counted them small price to pay for such a day: forty species, seven new, including all those amazing regals—the stuff of dreams.

And so they were, all night long.

3. GARDEN PARTY OF THE GODDESSES

On the first day of July, Wiker and I struck northeast out of Menard County, bound for Iroquois County. He stopped by the roadside to show me a caterpillar of *Papaipema circumluscena* (= *P. humuli*) in a hop vine—the true *Humulus lupulus*. I've long been aware of several leps that feed on the noble hop: the comma, also known as the hop merchant; the gray hairstreak, which can sometimes even be a pest on the hop crop; and the hops azure, a *Celastrina* discerned by James Scott as feeding on wild hops in the larval stage. But this pap was a new hop lep on me. It spends its whole life as a larva in about two inches of vine. Sounds bleak, but it's a good life, really, lived as it is in *that* vine. Now it is bound for a carrot instead; a pallid substitute, I should think. Imagine carrot-flavored beer.

We arrived at our morning's destination, Iroquois County Conservation Area. On the way into the preserve, we checked a sandy hillock where *Hesperia sassacus*, the Indian skipper, has been found in the past. Most of the nectar plants, a yellow composite, and the flight period were already past. We did see a hesperiine skipper up there, but it didn't quite alight and then shot off. We suspected it was an Indian but couldn't prove it.

On a gentle, shady woodland ride, escorted by little wood-satyrs, we met red squirrels, the only ones in Illinois. The path led through a brake of oak, sumac, aspen, and royal fern, then opened out into the meadow of the meadow fritillary, carpeted in ripe blueberries and tall white orchids, on which *Boloria bellona* was at its morning nectar. First blood, so to speak, was a greater fritillary known as Aphrodite. Along with red squirrel and aspen, this mostly northern species gave a boreal cast to the place. We had indeed shifted a notch north ecologically as well as geographically. Spotting a

259

patch of a tall pink phlox, I said, "There ought to be something on *that*," and there was.

"Hey," said Jim, "it's a regal! First one I've seen here in ages!" Idalia rose, then floated off across the royal ferns.

Entering a sedge wetland, now dry, we came to a patch of Indian plantain (*Cacalia tuberosa*). Jim deftly netted and I looked over a *Euphyes bimacula*, not surprisingly named in English the two-spotted skipper, one of the special wetland butterflies we were hoping for here. Its white, trailing edge, long, pointed wings, and tawny forewing cell split by the stigma within broad black margins were distinctive for the male; it's the female that has the double white spot on the dark forewing. Then came *Euphyes conspicua*, the related black dash, but I barely saw and missed it. I didn't have time to worry about it before a beautiful little mulberry wing, *Poanes massasoit*, darted around the hems of a willow, leading me on a merry chase. A dark and rounded mite, it should have had a yellow crossbow on the russet underside according to Kaufman and Brock, and it did, here at the southernmost edge of its upper midwestern range. The deeper we pushed into the wetter marsh, the more skippers appeared. Another sharp black dash jumped up, and I nabbed it temporarily—*big* black stigma, golden spot band with the central one elongated—check. Another two-spot landed on tall stalks, its sheer white veins really prominent—check. This was like a fashion runway for wetland skippers.

We were in the western edge of the Grand Marsh, south of Lake Michigan—400,000 acres in the nineteenth century, then drained, tiled, and cultivated. It is told that the stench of rotting fish and dead ducklings was intolerable. The story of the Grand Marsh parallels that of the Limberlost Swamp in northeast Indiana and its loss, so poignantly described by Gene Stratton Porter in *A Girl* and *Moths of the Limberlost*. One of the last two remnants of the old marsh, this place still seemed huge to me as I gazed out across the phloxy, shimmery green expanse stretching away to woods in the distance, over waving plains of sedge, spattered with white, pink, yellow, and blue. I really didn't want to leave. I had never expected to see a place as bewitching as Alaska in Illinois.

And as for that, several territories' worth of yellowthroats were all singing "Witchety, witchety, witchety" for the wetland skippers known collectively as "the five black witches." We'd seen a few of them, but "finding all five species out here would be like finding a kid lost in the woods," said Jim, and he's the expert.

Back near the woodland edge, we came to a rich, drier meadow full of the tall white orchids. There were two Idalias nectaring on them, as well as Aphrodite, Cybele, and Bellona—it was a goddesses' garden party! Ida, who cared for the infant Zeus; Aphrodite, the goddess of love and beauty, who beguiled all; Cybele, the Great Mother; and Bellona, the unfortunate goddess of war. All those expansive, ink-spotted orange wings would have taken yards of Danae's golden fabric to fashion. Their scores of silver orbs reflected the porcelain nectar pitchers of the orchids. On one stalk, the unopened buds curled against Cybele's hindwing, and they seemed wrought from the same material. I'm not sure the ancients—those venerable authors in Jim's library—named these fritillaries for the feminine deities simply out of convenience. It seemed, looking at these, that they must have taken into account their rustic habitats, ambrosial habits, and pastoral ways, and of course their unimpeachable beauty.

A few more goddess types greeted our reentry to the forest. Red-banded Atalanta spread at the wood edge, and yellow-banded Antiopa guarded the dappled path. It is difficult to carry out this business and not feel *accompanied;* I guess that's why I never got lonely, except sometimes on the road. When we came to the woodland marsh, right where Jim said we should look, we put up several Appalachian browns among the many little wood-satyrs. The differences between *Satyrodes appalachia* and the *S. eurydice* we saw at Kieselburg were subtle but clear. Then a humongous red-spotted purple glided by, followed by a gargantuan viceroy, the two so different in appearance yet capable of hybridizing. Seeing me gawk, Jim said, "Yeah, we grow 'em big here."

We gorged on blueberries. When Jim decided to pick a bunch for Sally, I went back to look for the Indian skipper. On my return visit to the sandhill, I found a good stand of the yellow nectar plants, but they were vacant. I had no further luck with skippers. So that species was relegated to the category of tantalizing maybes, and my monkey mind would often return to it as one of the ones that shoulda been. But I did find a patch of luscious blackcaps, a native black raspberry, to add to the berry harvest.

Now we walked a willowy track down to the end of the preserve, hard by the Indiana border. The wet ditch was rich in mosquitoes, the path with common sootywings on white clover. A bullfrog coughed. Across the ditch (wet feet!) lay a tall marsh of big sedge, small willow, reed canarygrass, cattail, dogbane, and dock. Jim made it over there first and saw an Acadian hairstreak. So I worked the willows around and around the marsh, looking for another to dart off a top twig, but it never did. Jim also caught a Dion skipper, which we examined and watched well as it sucked sweat on my finger—big, double-yellow-barred, rich colors—until it flew, nicking my hat. It was my second one ever. Now the bugs were coming hot and heavy. A fine female bronze copper spread on her dock leaf host plant. I'd seldom seen this butterfly since the Lutherans paved their marshy parking lot, thus eradicating it in Aurora, Colorado, when I was a small boy.

I slogged all over the marsh to the songs of mosquito and indigo bunting. Meadow fritillaries led me to nectar, but no one was drinking. A little way off, Jim chased and apprehended a dazzling *Boloria selene*, the moon goddess, come late to the party. The silver-bordered fritillary is the only one of the lesser fritillaries with silver spots below such as the greater fritillaries possess. I watched it spread, then settle silvery in the late afternoon's slant sun. In the hot, sticky, buggy bog, a regal fritillary nectared on a milkweed above a peaceful pair of coral hairstreaks in tight copulation. We watched, rapt, and disturbed none of them.

On the way back out, in the shady edges of the slough, another Appalachian eyed brown perched on a birch branch, as a little wood-satyr alighted on an aspen and spread its Hershey's bar wings and baby blues flat to the western sky. The mosquitoes here were heroic—practically Alaskan. In sweaty satisfaction, we drove home over the "whole lot of nothing" fields, as James put it, lamenting how it all was before. Though we arrived hours late for dinner and didn't deserve it, the excellent and patient Sally had a delectable meat loaf and local wine awaiting us. I have to say, that Jim's no dummy—the blueberries did the job. I like to think the blackcaps helped.

At breakfast at Nance's the next day, Sherry was slightly less rasty than last time. At least she spoke. When Sally ordered the hash browns from the menu, Sherry growled, "We don't have hash browns." Then, "I guess I could cut some potatoes into cubes."

One last time, we headed north on back roads, gassing up in San Jose, pronounced "San Jōz". A probable wild indigo duskywing flew past the windshield, at a point where crown vetch covered the verge. This once quite limited species has spread dramatically thanks to the exotic pink pea's proliferation along the interstate system, creating an ideal network of expansion corridors. "Dwight, Ill.—Home of the Illinois Bassett Waddle."

We reached Goose Lake Prairie Nature Reserve, southwest of Chicago, in the cloudy, cooling afternoon. A mesh enclosure signed Butterfly Barn had a monarch and a Hunter's butterfly within. The mowed path led out to a mere with bulrushes and tall sedges around it, and a boardwalk to a broken bridge. This is the spot Arthur Shapiro designated in 1971 as the type locality of *Poanes viator,* the broad-winged skipper, since Edwards's 1865 description contained only the vague designation "Illinois to New Orleans."

As soon as we arrived at the marsh, Jim spotted one skipper, and then we both saw one fly past us, huge and dark. We split up, and Jim saw two or three more skippers. I did not. One was definitely *P. viator;* but he also saw a black dash, casting the ID of our initial flight sighting into doubt. Then he caught one and we thought that would settle it, but it turned out to be a Dion skipper! We took turns walking the boardwalk versus charging through the marsh, but no *viator.* We kicked up some more skippers, but they never settled for a look. Clouds grew heavier, the day later, then rain. We finally had to give it up. The broad-winged skipper joined the Indian skipper on the growing list of mightabeens.

That night, in a motel in South Beloit, I found a bedbug on my pillow, to go with my several ticks and many chiggers. But in the morning light with binos, it turned out to be a wee tim'rous beetle. I released it to the habitat outside as Jim snored on. He'd earned it, helping me to see sixty-two species, twenty-seven new. Plus, paps! That Wiker—what a good guy.

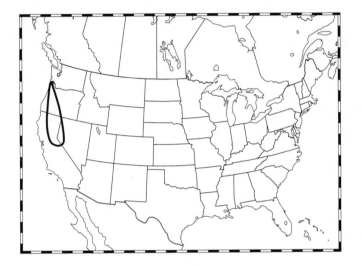

Yosemite Run

The highest enjoyment of timelessness . . . is when I
stand among rare butterflies and their food plants. This
is ecstasy.

—Vladimir Nabokov, *Speak, Memory*

1. LEONA

Up on Salme Hill, the first parnassian was flying. When I returned from Illinois, I found Thea feeling punky. After a hitch with her last chemo session, she'd required a transfusion of two units of blood. Dr. Law said her low blood count was evidence that the chemicals were doing their job, but they left her depleted. Fresh strawberries helped, and she felt nearly normal the next day, good enough to take a Fourth of July field trip with me to Fossil Creek and Salme Hill. We found a patch of sun and six species of butterflies—a respectable total in Wahkiakum County anytime but especially this sodden summer—including two new ones, Sonoran skipper and Clodius parnassian. They put me around 270 species, well ahead of the target of 250 for June 30. I loved this coming home and finding new year-butterflies with Thea right on our home ground.

The next day we met our kids and grandkids in Castle Rock for a holiday trip to Mt. St. Helens. I had hopes of finding the first snowberry checkerspots, and though we passed plenty of snowberry bushes, the weather augured poorly. We stopped to picnic at a meadow of lupine, lotus, thistle, and hawkbit, and everyone began running about with nets—a little pink one for Cristina, green for David, Tom's old BioQuip special, and I with Marsha—catching ocher ringlets and grass moths that struggled out in the thin sun. Francis was too small for a net, but he trailed behind his bigger cousins, right through the stickers—I knew he'd be a good chaser one day.

We drove on up into cloud, Francis singing "Old MacDonald" and the Barney song behind me. The moist forest edge glowed with the pale faces of *Trillium* and *Lilium*. Johnston Ridge stuck out of the mist, daubed with the purples and reds of other checkerspot hosts, penstemon and paintbrush. Loowit was only partly obscured, her great shattered crater with its growing lava dome naked to the rain. Which put pay to any more butterflies, but thanks to the little grass ringlets, we hadn't been skunked.

Back at home on Sunday, there was a baby raccoon falling from a tree hole and getting back up, a mink and its two young crossing the county road, and a coyote over the highway; the butterfly-themed geocache found beneath the covered bridge; sticks thrown for Lucy the dog; and stones skipped in the river. And when the sun emerged Monday, swallowtails and whites to chase. Dory, Francis, and Lucy returned to Portland, and Tom and Iliana, Cristina, and David took Thea to chemo at the beach while I packed to head out again. If all of this seems mundane, it was anything but, for us. Tom and his family would move to Mexico in a few short weeks, and Thea's health was uncertain. The rain resumed. After everyone left, I bawled my eyes out.

Southbound into Oregon, I was aiming for Mt. Ashland. But by Roseburg, I couldn't take hot, smelly I-5 anymore and abandoned it for the Diamond Lake/Crater Lake Road. The cooler, greener North Umpqua beat the heck out of the freeway in every conceivable way. I had it almost to myself after Bug Farm Road in Glide. Colliding Rivers, Susan Creek, Bogus Creek, Steamboat Creek, the Narrows—all cool, green, and wet. Pink wild sweet peas attended by triplets of tigers advertised that summer was well here.

Once I got into the Umpqua National Forest, butterflies came out like candy from a broken piñata. On a nice stand of naked buckwheat, a chunky dark checkerspot reclaimed the St. Helen's foray with that rainy day's desire: *Euphydryas colon*. At Steamboat Inn, I gathered up a female great arctic, road-struck. As I was about to voucher her, she grew lively. I noticed that her abdomen was immense with eggs, so I released her onto grass up a quiet forest road. Later I hit another big *Oeneis nevadensis* and killed it outright, so I vouchered that one instead. Highway 184 sparkled with auto-struck tigers and checkers of several kinds. Butterfly roadkill is a sad aspect of this work, but it seems inevitable. I braked for butterflies a thousand times. But the trucks slaughter them wholesale, and even the most devoted optics-only watchers smack the objects of their affection on the way to the habitat. Recovering them as museum-bound, well-labeled specimens is a way of honoring their lives, and maybe redeeming their downfall.

Even up at 2,000 feet, the day approached 100°F as the sun passed the meridian. At 4,500 feet, off the Windigo Pass Road, where small pink phlox and delicate white iris spiked meadowlets among lodgepoles, the Persius duskywings were just half the size of the ones I'd found much lower. Then, at Diamond Lake, I beheld one of the most remarkable visions of the year: *hundreds* of bluet damselflies, lined up on grasses and sedges by the shore. I'd often seen dozens, or scores, but never *this* many. The bright blue and brown bodies lined up perfectly with the bright green blades: seemingly so out of place, they were, of course, completely in. Tiny swarm flies hummed in discrete cumuli. Some of the damsels flew through the swarms, like falcons plucking off bats in a Texas fly-out, then returned to the cluster. Many pairs were in hoop or still connected by the male's claspers to the female's "neck." I watched a pair complete the wheel, that pretty blue heart known to observant pondside fishermen everywhere. But no one here at the boat launch noticed at all, except two children playing Mole and Ratty in the shallow water.

Spiky Mt. Thielsen oversaw the scene across the lapping lake. I cooled my head in it and drank gallons of water as the day grew less diabolical by measures. The road up to Crater Lake was still snowy, and too long. So I dropped down across the north flank of Mt. Mazama (or what was left of it: like St. Helens, it's not the mountain it used to be) to the busy east-side truck-and-tourist pipeline of U.S. 97. Then north to Chemult, where I got a sketchy meal of a microwaved burrito and Fig Newtons at a truck stop before crashing in a rest area: imperfect, but better than the previous night along I-5.

The first days of each outing were always hard. I'd been down about the kids leaving for Mexico, fear for Thea, short funds, and the daunting six months ahead. Following my whim, I'd deferred Mt. Ashland in favor of a try for Leona's little blue, over here on the east side. That beautiful drive and the burst of bluets had improved things, as would sleep, if hot and mosquitoey. Also on the plus side, a stash of a good Thunderhead IPA in seriously marked-down twenty-two-ouncers at a small Chemult store—such a good deal that I went back for two more flagons for the days ahead.

I got out early to look for Leona. At 9:00 A.M. the air was already warm in the sun, cool in the pine shade, but not as stinking hot as when Thea and I had first been here. Leps were getting up and moving: anise swallowtails and desert checkerspots, lupine and Oregon dotted blues. Behr's hairstreak showed off its bright tawny uppersides in flight. Watching it at rest on its host plant antelope brush, sawing its hindwings, was like peering into the barely opened door of a firebox as it gave a glimpse of the flame within. Mostly it showed the Morse code dots and dashes of the gray-flannel underside.

The butterfly I sought would be half the size of the hairstreak, easy to overlook. In fact, everyone overlooked it until 1995, when the Willamette Valley lepidopterist Harold Rice and his wife, Leona, came collecting here in July. The Mazama Ash Fields east of Crater Lake, created when the caldera blew some six thousand years B.P., were already well known for a distinctive fritillary. Harold Rice, a big, bald, and jovial hazelnut farmer, is a master netsman who had discovered new blues before. This unknown butterfly did not get past him. To their surprise, the Rices quickly found several minuscule blues. They seemed to be the small blue *Philotiella speciosa*, to which the blues I'd found in April at Purisima Mission belong, but that species was not known to occur nearer than 250 miles away, in northwest Nevada. David McCorkle and Paul Hammond examined the catch, found it distinctive, and described a new species: *Philotiella leona*. For *The Butterflies of Cascadia*, I had the happy privilege of giving it an English name: Leona's little blue.

It didn't take long to find it. Walking a dirt track through the pines where Thea first spotted it for us, I saw a bright male Leona flicker in a buckwheat cove, then another fly out at a hairstreak. I netted a female. Just a titch bigger than *P. s. purisima*, the males are clear pale blue or blackish blue, the females brownish gray or black, both chalky white below with crisp black dots. It's hard enough to discern the moving targets of the blues, but the dinky flowers of reniform buckwheat, their host, almost need a hand lens to make out. It's hard to see how they provide enough biomass even for these peewee lycaenids. Their favorite nectar plant, a fireweed, is impossibly tiny too. The three of them make up a world in miniature.

At the other end of the size scale, elegant day moths (*Hemileuca eglanterina*) flapped about by the hundreds. These three-inch diurnal silk moths fly high and crazy, causing false alarms for large fritillaries until their erratic flight pattern gives them away. I'd never seen more than a dozen or two in a particular place, but here they were on every side, every moment—milling like day-dispersed monarchs on their wintering grounds. A few were clear tawny orange all over, others black-patterned on an orange and orchid-purple background, while still others had the orange all shot through with pink or were solid magenta. The day moths' polymorphy impressed me as much as their remarkable abundance. You'd certainly never get these out of that minute buckwheat. Like the snowberry checkerspot, they feed on *Symphoricarpos* bushes, an abundant fodder.

After the pleasures of the field, the penance of the road. The 97 was a madhouse of interstate trucks. Again I made an escape, this time onto small roads up past Klamath Agency to Fort Klamath, then west toward Rocky Point and Lake of the Woods. The sweet smell of irrigated clover meadows and the brimming ditches belied recent battles between Indians and whites over Klamath Basin water. This pleasant paved road was no penance, and it seemed made for me alone. Then it got better. A fritillary crossing the road led my eyes onto rich meadows and marshes full of penstemon, cinquefoil, and sneezeweed. Such a display, plus a pretty wimpy fence, sucked me into 7 Mile Ranch, where butterflies fairly abounded.

The silverspots were the unsilvered race *dodgei* of the northwestern fritillary. Edith's coppers, known by their big putty spots on beige, engaged fully with the penstemons. The dominant butterflies, in numbers I hadn't seen since I was a boy in high Colorado clover meadows, were Sonoran skippers. I was glad that Thea and I had found the first Dog Star skipper (race *siris*) on Salme Hill. But these *Polites sonora sonora* were something to see in their legions. The meadows ran down to a shallow stream with bridges of monkey flowers and lupine-covered logs. Greenish blues and field crescents flittered by the score. In sheer sublimity, this stream echoed the Illinois brook of the Baltimores. I soaked my overheated head in it, but the ferocious mosquitoes drove me out all too soon.

Just east of Lake of the Woods, the Great Meadow also shadowed back to the Grand Marsh in Iroquois County, Illinois. But on this expanse of water, rush, sedge, grass, and sea blue camas lilies, all the goddesses had decamped. I crossed the Pacific Crest Trail on the Dead Indian Memorial Highway and hiked a ways along it, far from my last nibble of the PCT in Anza-Borrego. It does have a way of leading you around that next bend. In the day's last meadow, at Old Baldy Road, elephant's head bloomed alongside stupendous orange leopard lilies, but the butterfly day was over and done except for one western meadow fritillary.

Toward Ashland, lavender three rows deep lined a quarter-mile, serpentine driveway to a farmhouse: instant aromatherapy. Among the thousands of honeybees, bumblebees, and other pollinators visiting the millions of purple spears, I thought I saw the flickers of a skipper and a lady, but I couldn't be sure. Earlier, there must have been loads of butterflies along that lavender lane.

Down in the town, Chevron didn't have my gas cap they stole on my last trip through. I camped on a dark and quiet street, except for the cell-phone crazy who strode up and down the pavement after midnight, shouting and swearing into his unit about being stranded in Ashland by a perfidious friend. He finally drifted away to his own despair, and I slept away mine, much lifted by the day's gifts.

Mt. Ashland rises across the valley from the Cascades, a high outlier of the Siskiyou Range, where many plants and a few butterfly subspecies occur exclusively. Mt. Ashland is the one place where you can get high up in the range with ease, and thanks to snowmelt, moist conditions and flowers last into the summer. In the last mile below the small ski area, Hoffman's checkerspots visited the thick roadside flowers. Up in the subalpine meadows, five species of blues tapped the damp gravel by a puddle. Two of them were new for me—chalky Anna's blue and the endemic race of the Sierra blue known as *Agriades podarce klamathensis*. One cool-blue male basked open on a marsh marigold leaf, until another bumped it. As the morning warmed, both species rose out of steep, wet meadows of bistort en masse.

Up on Siskiyou Gap, a zephyr anglewing strafed a high pumice slope of prostrate lupine and pussy-paws. From Meridian Overlook, I took a long, hazy look over the high, hot Kalmiopsis-Biscuit country, so plagued of late by fires, and then by those who want to log the scorched roadless areas.

Coming back down, I stopped below the one holdout snow patch. I was watching dozens of iridescent green tiger beetles skittering over wet sand at the melting edge of the snowfield when one of them got up and flew. Beetles fly, but this was funny flying for a beetle, especially a tiger beetle, whose flight looks like a long hop. When this odd cicindelid perched on the ground, the fully restored Akito caught it. It was no tiger beetle, though it was just as shiny green—but *Callophrys sheridanii lemberti*, the missing species of green hairstreak! Quite worn this late in the season, the Sheridan's still showed its white ventral line and was more than adequate— the last of the true greenies for the year.

Attending to a fresh hatch of California tortoiseshells at a moist slope, so dark they looked like alpines, I saw two smaller dark stars fly up. For their species, they were mooses: my first (and only) sooty hairstreaks. Untailed and rounded, the mole-pelted sooties look more like female blues than hairstreaks. Next, their exact antithesis—a lilac-bordered copper so brilliant that I first thought it was a ruddy copper.

Near the bottom, I braked for spreading dogbane. No self-respecting butterfly tracker passes up a patch of *Apocynum androsaemifolium* without a look-see. Nothing short of butterfly bush or butterfly weed draws them in quite like these pale pink bells. This stand made no exception, with an array of at least fifteen species in attendance. Two endemic fritillaries, Mattoon's Great Basin and Elaine's callippe, made their debut on the list. I could not, however, scare up the lovely Leanira checkerspot, here at its type locality.

Way short on time now, I dashed across the valley, over I-5, and up the winding mountain road on the other side to the Green Springs, before the day shut down. Green Springs lies next to the Cascade-Siskiyou National Monument, set aside by Bill Clinton on his way out of office. An article in the Ashland paper, reporting on a plan to reduce grazing on the monument, mentioned the butterfly diversity of the area as a factor in its preservation. Fully 111 of the 162 Oregon species have been found in the Cascade-Siskiyou, largely thanks to the work of Eric Runquist. Eric, now a graduate student in butterfly ecology at UC Davis, grew up in Ashland, the son of a couple who reared monarchs for schools.

Fortunately for me, netwise, Little Hyatt Reservoir is Forest

Service, outside the boundaries of the monument. I waded like a bad dream through deep gravel on the side road to the lake, then plunged into the meadow below the dam for the last twenty minutes of sun. Moments later, I found the single, worn but certain male mardon skipper I was seeking, to confirm the shaky spring sighting from Scatter Creek. This rarity has one of its three centers in the Cascade-Siskiyou. Though I looked and looked, the only grass skippers I found after that were duns, as shadows drew across the meadow. I was extremely lucky to count coup on mardon, after dawdling so.

Uphill, the road passed a small and mossy old stone dam. Along the still-sunny shore beyond, on a flower above the road, sat a single, dull white butterfly. Could it be? Yes! My other great hope for the Cascade-Siskiyou, a nice male gray marble. Actually an orange-tip, *Anthocharis lanceolata* has neither orange wingtips nor green marbling below but a fine, reticulated gray pattern. What a thrill.

On the way back down, I hailed four fellows who were relaxing by their trucks after work at a nearby resort. I asked, only half in jest, if they had an extra beer they would sell me. "No, we won't sell you a beer," growled one of them. "But we'll damn well *give* ya one!" I expected a Bud Light, but he handed me down a Sierra Nevada. Never has a beer been so welcome to a hot, sweaty, scratchy, thirsty, and tuckered-out butterfly wrangler.

Back down at Powdermilk, watching a female western sulphur float down from the pinewood, I could hear the men up above talking about me. I heard "butterflies!" and soft laughter, but at least it wasn't the usual "fucking butterflies!" And then one of them said, "Well, let's go down and ask him!" and down they came.

"What's the big deal about the butterflies around here?" asked Rodney, and it went from there. Pete was a microbrewery distributor, hence the decent beer; Rodney and George both worked at a resort on Hyatt Lake. Young Travis was a cowboy and Rodney's son-in-law. All any of them wanted was to live up here at the Green Springs and be left mostly alone. We found plenty to talk about, and in the end, against my stringent protests, they prevailed upon me to take two more Sierra Nevadas with me.

2. FANDANGO

The 2008 Pacific Slope Section meeting of the Lepidopterists' Society got under way at nine on Saturday, July 12, in Alturas, California. I've belonged to the society since 1959, and I wasn't going to make the national meeting in Mississippi this year (been there . . .), but I hate to miss the small, intimate Pacific Slope gatherings. Most of the attendees were old friends, some for forty years. Though I'd been in town but seven hours, I got there on time, so Jerry Powell couldn't make a crack. Several of the folks who'd already helped me, including Liam O'Brien from the green hairstreak walk in San Francisco, gave talks.

When it came time for my own contribution, a ramble on the Big Year to date, I was able to report some 280 species more than the handful I had when I'd met with much the same group at Berkeley in February. Later, Jerry told me that he hadn't expected me to pursue this year with so much energy. That meant a lot to me, because Jerry is one of bluntest, most honest people I know. I doubt a word of false praise has ever passed his lips, which always seem to waver between a frown for fools and a hearty laugh. Jerry was my first editor, when I submitted callow pieces to the society's journal in the sixties, and he has been the godfather of the Pacific Slope Branch for many years.

For the field trip to Cedar Pass in the nearby Warner Mountains, I rode with my old friend John Lane, donor of the Mendocino monarch tips. We saw a good many species, though none new. Ben Warner blues, the subspecies of Anna's named from here, were the color of the California sky that summer: clear blue with a hint of white smoke. The next day I returned to the Warners on my own. I was checking roadside buckwheat, having just found my first

California hairstreak, when a car stopped. It was Paul Opler and his wife, Evi Buckner, who had spotted Marsha in action. Paul wrote the eastern and western Peterson Field Guides for butterflies. He and I have collaborated on butterfly conservation for many years, and I leap at any chance to be in the field with him. Paul and Evi led me on a long, dusty road to a site for Lindsey's skipper. We quickly found females of *Hesperia lindseyi* on thistles, and they went on their way, Montana-bound.

I watched the handsome gold and silver skipper for some time. Then, backtracking along the road on which we'd come, over Lassen Creek, I drove through clouds of snowberry checkerspots, all over the yarrow and even on St. John's wort, which almost nothing ever visits. Buckwheat was plastered with two homonymic hairstreaks, *S. behrii* and *C. g. barryi*. Among them, but far fewer, showed two exciting coppers. The tailed copper is the only one besides Hermes to sport little tails on its hindwings, but larger, and its swirly pattern is unique. The gorgon copper, at almost twice the size of most other coppers, was not only gigantic but really flashy in flight—what a beast! Three branded skippers—Colorado, juba, and Lindsey's—abounded on roadside gumweed.

Fighting my way back through the dust one more time, I turned east up Fandango Pass. For one mile the road was blessedly paved, then returned to dust. Fandango Pass was very dry. I made an advertised *Apocynum* patch in time for a twenty-minute gander before the first clouds in days took the sun. Maybe dogs don't like it, but scores each of hydaspe fritillaries, snowberry and desert checkers, hordes of hairstreaks, and several fancy black and white bluebell moths were all crazy about the dogbane.

I'd last been over Fandango in late October 1996, coming home from the autumn's monarch chase. I found the last one, a poignant pupa frozen just the night before, on a showy milkweed on the muddy road up, and that night drove through the worst blizzard of my life on the way across the Cascades. It was hard to imagine that now, in the upper eighties. But the milkweed was still there, and near where I'd found that sad chrysalicicle, I now saw one live caterpillar and one adult monarch tilting over. The playa smelled like rain as I dropped into the cool evening of the Surprise Valley.

Everything, including my alveoli, was gritty with the dust of the Warner Mountains.

My rear (actually Powdermilk's) had been fishtailing all over the washboard. So back at my room at the Hacienda in Alturas, I called Dave at the Honda shop. He said it might have to do with a worn bushing and/or the extinct shocks (struts) and that I'd better baby her in to him or she could pack up on me deep in the Great American Desert.

On the way out, I gassed and washed off the dust at Chevron. A fellow from the motel, whose bashed-nose white Caddie was parked there, and who looked like an older, paunchier me but Hispanic, came along with a load of cans. He gracefully accepted my recycling. Me: "Are you collecting cans and bottles?" Him: "Yeah, let me see—they take them all; thank you." I thanked him too. Then he passed me at the pump, twinkled, and said, "Actually, I do not collect them—I *sell* them!" "Much better," I said. I could see myself there, without much trouble.

I added up the mileage: Alturas to Tioga, about 311 miles; and reckoned I could do it overnight. Needing calories for the road, how could I resist Harold's Frosty, with the Best Burgers and Fries in the West? No fries, but my chocolate shake and cheeseburger were at least the best in my car.

The night was Likely, CA; Likely General Store; inevitably, the Most Likely Cafe. Sagehen Summit, with few cars. Saturn and the Moon. Madeline Valley—another name for Magdalena. Termo. Ravendale. A good traveling night and road, mild and fragrant, except some of that was smoke and it stung my eyes and hazed the hills thickly in the moonlight. Across California, 288 fires were burning, and Arnold Schwarzenegger declared an emergency. Halfway to Reno, a young jackrabbit darted out, crossed my path, and though I veered, I couldn't avoid it. I closed my eyes and awaited the awful thump, and it came. I placed the hare, its huge ears clotted with ticks, in the sage.

Reno was just a flash of bright lights in the night—including flashing red and blue ones in my rearview. The policewoman stopped me and stomped over to my window. "How much have you been drinking?" she snarled.

"Coffee and lots of water, ma'am. That's it."

"Well, your driving is *terrible!*" she spat.

The freeway was concrete with seams, and every seam made me swerve. I told her about my fishtailing rear end on a rutted road like this, and that I had a date with my mechanic to replace the struts, but I had to go to Tioga Pass first to see Behr's sulphurs. She ordered me out, checked my license and my eyes, and made me walk a straight line. "Well, I'm just glad you're *not* a bad drunk," she said, still pissed. "I'm getting off in twenty minutes, and you would've messed everything up!"

I said I was a little sleepy too. "Well, hopefully this woke you up!" she barked and pulled away. It had.

After three, nearing Topaz and the Cal border, I floated along on Mexican music and the scent of sagebrush. The trusty tape player had gone belly-up after twenty-eight years. I turned the radio dial and found *Coast to Coast A.M.*, which was doing the Dead Sea Scrolls. Dawn came at Dogtown, site of the first gold rush in the eastern Sierra. A dead raven lay in the road; two others were circling, keening. I laid it back in the sage.

There were flash-flood warnings in Santa Barbara, and there'd been rain here—the damp steppe smelled fine. Much cloud, much snow up in the Sierra, where I was bound—but the clouds were broken, and the snow was patchy. "Tragedy," sung by the Fleetwoods, which I remembered trying to dance to with Pam Walker at a preteen party in sixth grade, came on an oldies station: "Blown by the wind, kissed by the snow . . ." That's how things looked. Then at sunrise, just over the Conway Divide, Mono Lake opened out across the plain.

3. TIOGA

If you were a kid lepidopterist and someone put an article from the *Geographic* in your hands called "Butterflies: Try and Get Them," and you were reading it for the 417th time and skipped to your favorite part; and then if you read this, your net hand twitching, your wanderlust itching: "Some years ago a man sold quantities of the small green sulphur butterfly that swarmed near Tioga Pass, above Yosemite Valley. This butterfly, *Colias behrii,* is a rarity that flies only for a few days in any one locality. There is a legend that Indians killed this man!"; well, then tell me, what would *you* do? You'd set your cap for Tioga Pass, that's what, same as I did fifty years ago. Now I was there.

Not that it took me half a century to get to Tioga for the first time. I'd driven across the pass probably half a dozen times over the years—but always in snow, autumn straw, rain, dark of night, the thrall of others, or a rush. Never, anyway, during those "few days" when Behr's sulphur might be observed, though I'd certainly tried. So here I was at last, on a plausible day. John Lane thought I just might be early. All I could do was try. I felt that familiar twitch as I stepped from Powdermilk, Marsha firmly in hand.

I could barely contain my excitement as I ascended the Range of Light, and it wasn't the coffee. I'd almost forgotten those amazing sugar stone roadsides from my ranger days in Sequoia. At 9:00 A.M., winding my way up the pass, I checked a pullout. Right away, a brilliant male lustrous copper alighted outside my driver's window on a rock and spread itself wide. Fire, fire on the mountain! It flicked off like a cinder on the wing when I opened the door. Then an Edith's copper settled on alpine goldenrod. A bit farther up, I pulled over again for a pink-and-white puff of nude buckwheat on the verge.

A couple of years before, Thea and I had found a new butterfly for Washington when we answered Andy Warren's challenge to examine stands of *Eriogonum nudum* for the enoptes dotted blue. We'd located the plant, and bingo, there was the butterfly. Now I hoped to find it here. Double bingo: a perfect pair, the female on a cinquefoil, the male on the buckwheat.

The Adopt a Highway adopters from Tioga Pass Resort were called "Butterflies & Rainbows." I was seeing more sparkles than rainbows. Between high excitement, high elevation, and sleep deprivation, I felt quite woozy. I reckoned I'd better get used to the altitude, as I'd be up at thirteen thousand feet plus in a few days. I parked below the pass on the east side, above Tioga Lake, at ten—nine o'clock Butterfly Time, already at my day's destination—now *that* was notable. Sandhill skippers and greenish blues diddled about the car. I checked my sun cream, water, wallet, net—I was on the USFS side of the line and loaded for Behr's—and finally entered Tioga Meadows, just fifty years late.

I strode off across the near-timberline meadows, picking my way between willow clumps and delicate wildflowers that I did not want to tread on. Right away, a *Colias* came to the ground before me. It was a small alfalfa butterfly, greenish below but Union Pacific orange above. Abundant in the agricultural lowlands, *C. eurytheme* invades the high country each summer. I was thinking of the various arctic-alpine butterfly groups that are absent from the Sierra Nevada, or nearly so—*Boloria* (1), *Oeneis* (1), *Erebia* (0)—when one of the few first truly alpine species that does occur here suddenly appeared.

It flew up and over a willow . . . looked greenish . . . *Colias behrii?* I thought so . . . and then, *yes!* There it was for sure—Behr's sulphur! I nearly burst open with delight. I didn't want to net that first one, just watch it—that beautiful, improbable, lime green wedge on an alpine daisy, just as I'd always imagined it. Many sulphurs, even the common clouded sulphur of the farmlands, show green beneath. But apart from the far northern Labrador sulphur (*C. nastes*), none of our species are colored green on the upper surface, and this one was much more so than *nastes*. The green was more bluish below, more yellowish above. One white dot adorned the cell of each hindwing, top and bottom.

Then came another, in perfect condition, an impeccable, impossibly beautiful thing. This one I netted, and reminded myself with my inverted binos that there really is no green here at all: it is an illusion caused by the pixilation of black and yellow scales together, just as with the "green" marbling of marblewings. But to our eyes, the hue before us is inarguably *green*. More and more appeared. I was close to being there too early, as John feared, since the males were all fresh and the later-emerging females were yet very few. I did find one. It looked much like the male, only its black border was more nebulous, and the green upperside had a paler, yellower tinge to it. John Muir knew this butterfly.

Rarity is relative, and this noted rarity was common there that day. The man who, according to Laurence Ilsley Hewes in the *Geographic*, "sold quantities" of it, wasn't necessarily evil; many plant and animal explorers collected commercially in those days to support their studies, just as Doc Ricketts did as portrayed by his friend Steinbeck in *Cannery Row* and *Log from the Sea of Cortez*. I collected myself for a New York dealer when I was in high school, to earn money for college, until all their little deaths began to overwhelm my pleasure in the insects. Few had ever seen this butterfly alive in the late 1800s, and the demand among museums and collectors was likely high. I can see how "that man" became greedy at such a flight as this. I can also see how the Indians—when they were still in these mountains—could get exercised over a white man plundering even this small verdant bounty, as if all the rest wasn't enough.

One of the most dramatic endemics anywhere, Behr's sulphur flies only in a short, narrow band of the High Sierra. In fact, the common name for it in Kaufman and Brock is Sierra sulphur. I introduced that name in my Audubon field guide, but now I prefer the old moniker "Behr's sulphur," because it takes me back to that *Geographic* article where I first met it. Herman Behr was a major student of the Lepidoptera in nineteenth-century California. His name affixes also to a hairstreak we met along with Leona's little blue, and to a parnassian recently reseparated as a full species. A High Sierran specialty like Behr's sulphur, Behr's parnassian was another item on my wish list for that day.

Sensations came fast up there. A Mexican cloudywing basked

on granite before me, black on white, but took off fast. *Thorybes mexicana* was much smaller, paler, and had proportionately bigger glassy spots than the three cloudywings I saw in the South. The turf was rich with pussytoes, lupines, asters, cinquefoil, and a bloomed-out *Allium* whose leaf bunches looked just like those of daffodils. A pair of lustrous coppers courted. I was stalking a *Colias behrii* when a *Parnassius behrii* appeared, or what I believed must be that, up there. The sulphur flew up at the parno, and they actually did a pas de deux de Behr on the wing! I had a shot at catching both in the same net swing—how cool would that have been?—but of course I swished Marsha's bag right between the two, and they scattered.

Then a glittering greenish blue swam through a spray of tall forget-me-not, came back, and nectared on it, too blue to be true. I had just missed what I thought was a Lembert's green hairstreak, the same race of Sheridan's I found on Mt. Ashland among the green tiger beetles, when a brilliant green buprestid beetle alighted on my net. These greenies stick together, butterflies and beetles. I crossed the bogs to drier, north-facing rocks and a piney slope; not much there. As I crossed back, yellow sandhill skippers thronged the sneezeweed. I recalled their abundance on a little pink clover up at Tuolumne Meadows one Fourth of July, when having gone to Yosemite Valley out of necessity on that date, Thea and I had expected the worst. But everyone else thought the same, and we had found it uncrowded after all. Here, I was entirely solo.

And in a species of heaven. If, like that unfortunate collector who paid dearly for his cupidity, I were to forfeit my life up there, I could think of no better resting place. For a molecule or two of me, well distributed by coyote, raven, and vulture, to end up in a Sierra sulphur coursing over this sward, green on green, would be just fine by me.

But I didn't croak up there, nor could I stay forever, after all. I returned to Powdermilk at 1:30 P.M. and drove up toward Saddlebag Lake to seek more parnassians. But first, I tried a drier old gravel track, across the highway and uphill, toward the high fell-fields and cliff slopes. *Cassiope mertensiana*, red mountain heather, was all about, and I wondered whether the lately discovered blue known as *Agriades podarce cassiope* might be here. This old road ran right

under the fell-fields. Two brightlings lasered out from under willows by a creek, and I caught one—a male ruddy copper. New for
the year, it's the only other copper as brilliant as the lustrous, and
that was here too. Imagine—*Lycaena rubidus* and *L. cupreus* in the
same place! The ruddy, clear molten copper, the lustrous black-
spotted and even hotter, redder . . . a guy could go blind if he looked
too long at both at once. With Edith's and lilac-bordereds flitting
about as well, there were four species of coppers up here. And talk
about blinding—just then two male lustrous coppers spread their
wings at the feet of a fully spread female, all three of them fresh out
of the forge.

From the old road, I easily gained the rocky fell-field, where parnassians were lunking all about. There was plenty of *Sedum* too, the
yellow, succulent stonecrop upon which the larvae of Behr's parnassians feed. But the first two I caught were female *Parnassius clodius*!
These large, rounded, white, swallowtail relatives with black and
red spots possess a visible sphragis in the female—a waxy plug that
the male implants in coitus, which prevents future mating for her,
thus ensuring his genes are passed on. The big white sphragis and
all-black antennae, with red spots only on the hindwing, militated
against *P. behrii*. What a surprise! Clodius normally occurs at lower
elevations, where its larvae consume bleeding heart foliage. So they
must *both* be here, I thought; but every one I managed to net was
a Clodius, if smaller and darker than the ones in our backyard at
home. I have to conclude that I never saw a Behr's for sure. They
must occur higher yet, way up on the out-of-reach ridges that were
probably still under snow. The bleeding hearts or steersheads that
provendered all these Clodius remained hidden from my eyes.

I came down a red-heather rivulet headed by a mossy rock wall.
Lush, sweet, fragrant—I love that mountain heather smell almost
as much as the real thing in Scotland. But no cassiope blues. I took
a fall when my foot went out on a slick bog slope, landing well with
a wet butt; but a steep rockfall lay not far below. You can self-arrest
with a net pole as well as an ice ax.

Eventually I got to gravelly, dammed Saddlebag Lake, a small resort with many fishers. This was supposed to be a classic butterfly
site, but all the attractive habitat seemed to be way around the other

side of the lake, and it was late. I didn't mind. It would be hard to beat Tioga Pass today, just off the highway.

As rain started spitting at seven, I set out for home, via Bartle. Forty minutes later, well into Yosemite National Park at the sugar cone of Lembert Dome, big thunder struck to the south. Lots of people were angling for unprotected vertebrates, but many of them (and all the rangers) would take exception to me netting bait, if it had four colorful, scaly wings. Everyone was swatting the aggressive little mosquitoes too, but if I were to pin one and give it a data label, I would be committing a felony. Over and over, I thanked the geographer gods who drew the federal jurisdictional lines where they did, right along the top of Tioga Pass! I worked with Marsha in hailing distance of the NPS ranger's hut but soundly, safely, and legally within the national forest.

Mind you, I love both the parks and the forests and wouldn't want to live in a country without both. I just think the national parks could be more open to entomology, to their own advantage. It is always better to know more about what you've got, as Great Smoky Mountains National Park has proved with its exemplary BioBlitzes. I also love the wilderness areas, if they sometimes concentrate too many people in too small a part of the vast park. It's not hard to avoid the masses by going where no special designation bids you to go. The butterflies often lead me to such places. When I reached the John Muir Trail parking lot, it was jammed full of vehicles belonging to backpackers bound for wilderness with all the others. There was no one on my anonymous trails today but me and a few thousand scaly-winged insects, some of them green.

Outside the Tuolumne Meadows Store, a couple of tanned young hikers had OD'ed on jellybeans, which they were washing down with Sam Adams Boston Ale. A young woman had given them a big jar of jellybeans, and now they were trying to offload them on someone else. They offered me some, but I declined. I came out instead with a bottle of local 395 IPA (named for U.S. 395, and which I wouldn't drink until I got home, or I'd never get there), a pint of milk, and Fig Newtons—a far better combo, we agreed. "Whoooa, dude!" said the young clerk, "check out your total!" It was $6.66. Whoooa, indeed.

Out on Tuolumne, a four-spike buck in velvet and a doe crossed the meadow and the road together, a perfect Bambi postcard. A caravan of cars braked, and a cordon of cameras and cell phones clicked. A few miles on, I braked myself for a hairy woodpecker in the middle of the lane. It was alive and alert but had a broken wing. I herded it off the road, and it climbed right up into a fir, like the baby raccoon the other day with the grandkids. It occurred to me that it might have a better chance of surviving than most broken-winged birds. It could feed, at least, perhaps until it healed, even if it would not fly again. But all across the white stone wonderland, the whole solar-paneled roof of the Yosemite, there was not one road-struck Behr's parnassian for me.

I grew sleepy, and there were too many large things to run into, so I caught a nap between big firs and big boulders, seventeen miles by trail from Hetch Hetchy. I drifted off to the notion that Hetch Hetchy was to John Muir what Glen Canyon was to David Brower: the loss that defines what you managed to hang on to. Or you could say, you win some, you lose some. Some Behr's you bag; some Behr's get away. When I snored myself back awake, refreshed, I just sat and listened to the silent night, the moon and its companion Jupiter right outside my window. It was almost like camping in Yosemite except it was free, and I was alone, while every campground I saw was crammed like a camp meeting. I was sorry to leave the park. Unstaffed at both ends, it never even let me use my annual pass.

At some point I entered Mariposa County—pity it was in the dark—and took my big sleep of the night from 1:30 to 4:30 A.M., in a parking lot in Stockton, off Mariposa Road. My Mariposa Road had taken me Stockton to Stockton in five months, with nigh onto three hundred kinds of butterflies in between.

4. MCCLOUD

Only one more objective lay between me and a brief touchdown at home: McCloud. The name had been a mental magnet to me ever since my Nature Conservancy days, when the McCloud River Preserve was created to protect the golden trout. It bespoke cool, green forests and waters, high above the blasted valleys, at least in my imagination. Now it meant something else as well. When I told John Lane I was especially desirous of finding the uncommon California crescent, *Phyciodes orseis*, he recommended a certain campground on the McCloud River where a number of captures had been made. It seemed the only likely locality for the species that I might be able to reach on my way north and still make it home in time.

But to get there, I had to shoot the 5 north again, much hotter than last time after the Muir's hairstreak caper, with Powdermilk's butt swimming all over the road. I couldn't wait to get off the painfully hot and smoky freeway. I could barely see Castle Crags when I was right beneath the spectacular landmark. I hadn't seen a flower besides St. John's wort, star thistle, and oleander for a hundred miles. Northern California was burned out, both ways. I was dangerously sleepy and my eyes burned with particulates, but it was too hot to nap, and I was behind schedule. This was pure hell, particularly after cool, clean Tioga. I could only hope McCloud would be better, even if it didn't match my long-held ideal. When I finally reached the McCloud exit and rose rapidly into the foothills, at least there were butterflies and bluebell moths on the buckwheat.

I saw no sign off the highway to Algona Camp. I obtained directions in Bartle, which is next to nothing now but once had two hotels, a train station, a newspaper, a blacksmith shop, and a sporting house, as E Clampus Vitus Humbug Chapter 73 told me. The deserted campground was just a flat with a few sites below a bridge, along a small national forest road. Two Lorquin's admirals, a western tiger swallowtail, and one of the biggest, freshest mourning cloaks I'd ever seen were there as my welcoming party, all the big willow gliders together in this one grove.

I tied up Powdermilk in a shady glade beneath a tall ponderosa pine, with a little breeze and the burble of sweet McCloud River water. Along the shore grew the umbrella plant (*Darmera peltata*) that Thea and I had once marveled at along the Illinois River in the Kalmiopsis Wilderness, and the giant orange leopard lily. A spotted sandpiper whistled its way to work along the cobbles. Various blues, of course, frequented the shore and the moist green meadow above the bank, with many other butterflies. The cloak perched, sucked something I didn't want to know about on a picnic table, and spread its wings. It looked delectable, with dark chocolate inside, French vanilla topping, and blueberries. Nabokov called it the grand surprise, for the way the upperside shocks anyone who has seen only the ashen underside. This one could have been a contender for grandest surprise of all.

But I was here for smaller game and went at it in earnest. I swung too soon at a possible *P. orseis* in the campsite and missed it, then caught a female field crescent. In the lush riparian meadow, with Oregon branded skippers and western meadow fritillaries, were more *Phyciodes*. Two bigger, brighter ones gave me fits and would never settle. But all of these so far were field crescents, quite similar to the California crescent except for subtle distinctions, and much, much more common and widespread. This butterfly has borne two former specific epithets, *campestris* and *pratensis*, both of which translate to "field." But the current name is equally suitable: *pulchella*, meaning "beautiful," which they are, with intricate patterns of beaver brown on marigold, and those shiny crescents.

I tried under the bridge, along the river cobble. It was difficult to stay on task in view of the circus of Anna's blues and sylvan hairstreaks under way. Maybe twenty 'streaks jetted all around and perched on the willow tips in a perpetual motion of mating and trying to prevent others from mating. One or two crescentspots kept popping up and eluding me. I had a good shot at a pair fooling around with each other near the rocks and caught the worn-out male, but missed the female. The escapee teased me several more times before I left. By others' accounts, California crescents could be fairly common here; I was probably at the tail end of their flight period, with fields taking over.

But I was lucky: among all the colorful crescents of McCloud, this one beat remnant was the only sure Orseis, as it turned out, and the only one I needed to see. Before leaving, I bathed in the freezing McCloud, just as refreshing as my fantasy of it all these years. Looking up, I saw a dipper hopping along the shore past me, paying me no never mind, as if I were just another cow elk. With all the rivers I'd been on, this was the first water ouzel of the year.

Driving out, I found the McCloud River Loop Road weirdly deserted at only 5:00 P.M. CDT, 4:00 BDT—buckets of roadside nectar and not a butterfly to be seen. I concluded that all the smoke in the air reduced the effective albedo and sent them to bed early. When I got back to I-5, the forest-fire ash outfall was as thick as a snowstorm.

I tried the star thistle on Siskiyou Summit in the last rays of sun, but nope. Back in Ashland, where I always seemed to leave something behind, I rescued my credit card at Standing Stone brewery. I'd left it there when paying for my buffalo burger on the way south. But let it be recorded that I merely ducked in and out again, taking on no alcohol for an awful, all-night drive that needed no further inducement toward total coma. The best I could do was to saltate from rest area to rest area. After Longview on the Columbia, cold and cloudy, the air finally came clear from the smoke that seemed to smother the West. And in Skamokawa, certain cottonwoods were already going yellow.

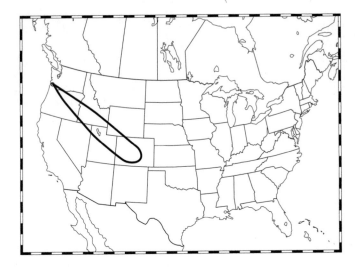

⊱I RAY EIGHT I⊰
Colorado Kid

. . . purple flowers clouded on a stem, and the yellow
butterfly folding light and shadow where it flashed.

—Kim R. Stafford, *Lochsa Road*

1. UP TO UNCOMPAHGRE

Scott was nail-biting nervous when I boarded the plane, moments before takeoff.

At the beginning of the Tioga trip, I'd met Scott Black southeast of Portland for a quick field trip at the Larry Everson Memorial Open Space on the Clackamas River. Scott is the executive director of the Xerces Society. Larry was a loyal Xerces member and fine butterfly photographer, gone too soon, who discovered here that snowberry checkerspots use Oregon ash as a host plant as well as its namesake shrub and scrophs. *Euphydryas colon* sometimes swarms at this preserve. Having missed it with my grandkids at St. Helens, I was having a vain go at it here, and a rare day out with Scott.

Over the inevitable beverage afterward, at a crusty riverside tavern, Scott tendered an invitation. "Bob, you've done so much for Xerces with the Butterfly-A-Thon," he said. "Why not let Xerces take you to Colorado with me, and we'll hike up to see the Uncompahgre fritillary, as we've always said we would?"

I had been planning to swing down through the Sierra, across to the Rockies, and back up and around: a marathon mountain loop. Accepting Scott's seductive offer would probably mean skipping the southern Sierra altogether and missing some remaining California endemics along with one of my favorite lepists, Ken Davenport. After this it would be too late down there. On the other hand, Scott's scheme would save me thousands of miles of driving across hot, dry country, lots and lots of gallons of four-dollar-plus gas, and precious time that could be applied elsewhere. It was beginning to dawn on me that my original fifty-state, dozen-province ambit would suffer some triage.

So after the second beer, I said yes—not the first to do so in that old tavern, I'll bet. But it would mean a real boogie to Tioga and a mad dash back from McCloud. After all that, I enjoyed Swede Park for less than fifteen hours before amazing Thea, so recently on her back, woke me with coffee at 3:30 A.M. and drove me to Portland Airport, where I barely made check-in. It was a nervous and beaming Scott I high-fived as I passed him in the aisle of the 757.

The lines at the rental car agency at Denver International Airport were so long that the agents pacified the customers with hot dogs. Eventually we pulled out in a Jeep Liberty; what a luxury to be driven. I slept until Scott pulled off at Evergreen for sandwiches. I swished the net over a flowery slope crowded with female Queen Alexandra's sulphurs being harassed by male orange sulphurs. Across Kenosha Pass in South Park, in High Creek Fen TNC preserve, blue spruces spiked a peat fen full of shooting stars, tall white gentians, and orchids. Scott hoped to find Susan's purse-making caddis fly, recorded from here, but Susan wasn't as eager to see Scott. In the chilly clouds, the only butterflies were three painted ladies flying crazily around a south-facing bank beneath a crying kestrel's nest. The type locality for the rare caddis, on Deer Creek, was also vacant, battered by cattle drives and eutrophied. I snoozed again to Gunnison, then on to Lake City deep in the San Juan Mountains. In Cabin 14 at G & M Cabins, we had a beer and a Baby Ruth each and hit the sack for our big day tomorrow. I slept the sleep of the very grateful dead.

Saturday, July 19, my sixty-first birthday, was a fine, bright, Nabokov's Blue Day in Lake City. On the Cinnamon Pass road toward Red Cloud Peak, we slowed for the first Weidemeyer's admiral. This spectacular coal black giant with milk white bands accompanied my boyhood days afield on the High Line Canal, which we'd crossed after leaving the Denver airport. The Silver Creek trailhead, at about 8,500 feet, produced the first chryxus arctic. And then as we started up the trail, the first of a zillion arctic blues rose to meet us—number 300 for the year!

Of the many blues that followed, the next up were the aforementioned Nabokov's blue, *Lycaeides idas sublivens*. It was in search of the first females of this subspecies that the incomparable novelist-lepidopterist Vladimir Nabokov came to Telluride, some thirty miles to the west of us. He took away not only the specimens he sought but also the final scene in *Lolita*. The penultimate paragraph, evoking the far-off voices of the children of Telluride, ties with the final paragraph in *On the Origin of Species* for the most moving passage I know in literature.

As we climbed up the steeply broadening canyon, the new butterflies just kept coming. A slopeful of courting, playing, nectaring, and dodging Uhler's arctics led to a stream of blues, which led in turn to an improbably brilliant blue copper, bigger and brighter than any of the true blues. A ruby-spotted mountain parnassian, closely related to the Behr's I missed at Tioga, flew off across an avalanche that blocked the trail. We clambered over snow covered with smashed fir debris that released powerful terpenes onto the high air, a scent blending Christmas with junior high wood shop. And then came the fine little high-country skipper called Draco, the dragon, perhaps for the sharp ivory tooth crossing the spot band below. I saw several, and Scott, handy with a net, nabbed one.

The butterflies left no time to think about the considerable exertion as our eager feet ate the elevation. A rockslide came down to meet the trail from the left, and I knew what that meant. In minutes, most of the guild of rockslide specialists checked in—first several Snow's lustrous coppers, deeper red than the Sierran subspecies; next my own dear Maggie, a big black Magdalena alpine, of which more later; and finally a rockslide (or damoetas) checkerspot, with its odd, greasy-brassy cast. As the valley narrowed, Colorado blue columbines, Parry's primrose, and purple phacelias all increased beside the meltwater of true-named Silver Creek. Buttery Scudder's sulphurs skimmed their host willows.

Another Magdalena crossed the path, followed by a couple of nothern grizzled skippers. And then, three beauties in quick succession: another *Erebia* about a third Maggie's size, the diminutive Colorado alpine; a burnt-orange-and-lime Mead's sulphur, and an arctic fritillary. Both *Colias meadii* Edwards and *Erebia callias* Mead (the author's name is affixed last) hearken to one of the great adventurers in Colorado butterflies. Hoping for his daughter's hand, Theodore Mead came west to collect for the leading lepidopterist of the day, W. H. Edwards. Traveling by stagecoach and horse in the summer of 1871, under threat from both hostile Indians and drunken miners, he discovered several new species, including these two. Later he named Edith's copper for Edith Edwards, whom he indeed wed, then took to Florida to raise orchids.

Scott and I had arrived not by stage but by air-conditioned Jeep, and we came under no fire, at least not yet. But we did climb most of a mile in elevation (around 8,500 to 13,500 feet or more) in five or six miles. The habitat we were heading for seemed to keep on receding around each new mountain, and we worried about the notorious Colorado clouds closing in. But when we arrived at the site, just a few small fleecies gamboled overhead. We stood in a great green bowl, a glacial scoop out of the side of the summit of Red Cloud Peak, just below the ridge that separates Silver Creek from the next drainage south. Two young women hikers came along, the first we'd seen. Kerry and Tara asked us about the flower names and the Uncompahgre fritillary, which is fairly famous in these parts.

In 1978 two graduate students, both serious lovers of leps, hiked up to Uncompahgre Peak near here. Larry Gall of Yale and Felix Sperling of Stanford would each serve in later years as president of the Lepidopterists' Society, but that fact probably did not owe directly to (or derive from) their remarkable discovery that summer. In the footsteps of Mead, they brought down a butterfly new to science. They described it as a new species, *Boloria acrocnema*, the specific epithet cleverly combining "acro" (top of) with "chemus" (mountain slope, changed to "chema" for gender agreement) into an anagram of "uncom's race." Later workers subsumed the butterfly under the Arctic *Boloria improba* as a subspecies, along with another dramatically relictual population in Wyoming. "Postglacial relict" is the term for such organisms left behind in high places by the retreat of Pleistocene ice. In the meantime, *B. (i.) acrocnema* became federally listed as an endangered species. It has only ever been found in a few high basins of the San Juan Mountains in Colorado, always around or above thirteen thousand feet, where its host plant grows. One of the few fritillaries that doesn't feed on violets, it uses instead prostrate snow willow, *Salix nivalis*. Sheep grazing, commercial collecting, and global warming have been cited as threats. Long before he became director of Xerces, Scott worked as a field monitor for this species. Intimate with its habitats, he had brought me here to see it for my birthday and for my Big Year. I'd once hiked up to Uncompahgre Peak itself in an attempt to see the insect, but too short on time to reach the necessary heights, I came away without a look.

Now, near a cairn just above a snow willow slope and ravine, we both spotted the first Uncompahgre fritillary simultaneously. Happy birthday, Bob—number 310 already! It settled down, and we watched it closely for several minutes. (Scott made me put Akito away well before we got here. It wouldn't do for a couple of Xerces guys to be mistaken for collectors of a federally listed butterfly.) Several more of the small, drab insects popped up, though they were not abundant. It makes sense to be dark in the alpine, the better to collect solar radiation, but it's still a surprise to see a frit so dull; in fact, the usual common name of *Boloria improba* is the dingy fritillary. Spectacular nonetheless!

After lunch, Scott stuck with the Unc. frit, as monitors call it, while I traveled across the cirque to the bottom of a gargantuan scree and an absolute avalanche of Colorado columbines, their blue and white imitated by the stripes on the state flag. I found a flight of *Oeneis* in a swale, and I was hoping for polixenes arctics, but all turned out to be chryxus, and the *Boloria* were all the same Freija frit so common in Alaska.

Up in a moist cinquefoil swale bound by rocks and snow, somewhere between climb and cloud, a pika geeked at me and a hoary marmot humped up the slope like a fast, furry slug. Then it posted like a hoodoo, looked back, and started working its way down toward me, munching bistort and cinquefoil all the while. It paused, resumed, but didn't stop until almost on my feet. I placed Akito between us in case it wanted to bite my boot. As big and golden as a year-old retriever, it really seemed to want to climb my leg. Meanwhile, the boulder bunny geeked on and showed its terminally cute face just above a snowbank. I went down onto my belly and drank deep of snowmelt coming off the bank; perhaps this was stupid, as the marmots and pikas were up there peeing, but it tasted better than anything I'd drunk since Guadalupe, except for Gray's River water.

Then I hiked the mile down, across, and back up to Scott. He'd seen only about a dozen Unc. frits, and that concerned him. The whole bowl of the habitat lay above us, the largest of fewer than ten known colonies in all. The suitable part, in terms of willow cover, snow cover, and exposure, was not very big. It seemed odd to sense fragility in such an overwhelming scene, but there it was. Two University of Nevada ecologists published a prediction several years ago that *B. i. acrocnema* would be pushed right off the top of the mountain, one of the first extinctions due to climate change. This jeremiad has not yet come to pass. As a strange, sleety rain began to fall in fits and starts, all we could do was hope that it never would. For as the Uncompahgre fritillary goes, so goes the rest of our arctic-alpine butterfly fauna.

Reluctantly, we started down. Scott pointed out stringers of white marsh marigold hugging the rivulet, mirroring snow stripes along the mountain flanks, as in cliché calendar pictures of the Maroon Bells. Crossing the snow, we glissaded. Then on the muddy rocks, I went down—bloodied a hand, bruised my butt, pulled something in my shoulder—but I felt fine. My birthday butterfly list was thirty species, half of them new, including many old friends, thanks to Scott, Xerces, and Red Cloud Mountain.

And that wasn't all. Back in Lake City at the excellent Cafe Luna, Scott treated me to a special birthday dinner. I thought it a little odd that the splendid rack of lamb came from New Zealand when we were in the middle of Basque sheep country. The friendly proprietor did her best to explain the weird economics of that irony. So we chose a New Zealand pinot noir to go with it, and if you'd told me it had actual raspberries in it, I would not have argued. But it might have been just the sweet aftertaste of the toughest hike of the year, the most challenging butterfly of all well seen, and One Darn Fine Birthday. Cafe Luna comped our dessert, and I didn't mind a bit the lack of sixty-one candles.

2. GOTHIC TALE

For me, two great things came from my father's second marriage. For one, my stepbrother, Bruce Campbell, invited me to go insect collecting one day. Bruce soon gave it up for other interests, but I did not, and here I am. For another, Gothic. My stepmother Pat's family owned an old cabin in Crested Butte, then a crusty, dusty coal-and-cow town where the dancers at the Saturday night polkas had no clue of the coming ski-town glitz. My dad and I, escaping the perpetual smoky bridge games in the cabin kitchen, went fishing up the nearby streams. While he flicked his dry fly over the clear water, probably as happy as he ever was, I drifted away with my butterfly net into high, clovery meadows full of silver-bordered fritillaries and other small glories.

One day on the meanders of the East River, I climbed a ridge and beheld an amazing sight: a field full of butterfly nets. Overcoming my intense shyness, I went down to see what was going on. The nets belonged to the young professors Charles Remington of Yale and Paul Ehrlich of Stanford, conducting a mark-release-recapture study on Mormon fritillaries with their students from the Rocky Mountain Biological Laboratory, situated just up-valley in the remains of the old silver mining ghost town of Gothic. As one of its youngest members, I knew of Dr. Remington as founder of the Lepidopterists' Society. These two Lepidoptera gods would encourage me over the next several summers. Eventually I went to study with Remington in New Haven, came back to Gothic as his graduate student, and again with Thea in 1984 to teach biological conservation. Now I wanted to return to Gothic not just for old times' sake but to seek a particular creature. Scott Black had his own history with RMBL, and his own target insect.

So, leaving Lake City on a cool, clear morning, we bordered Blue Mountain and Curecanti National Recreation Areas northward, picking up the russet skipperling and the peculiar, mothygrasshoppery, lightning-streaked Ridings's satyr on the way. Out of Gunnison, we came in view of Crested Butte itself, one of the most distinctive mountains I know and one of the great landmarks of my youth. But it broke my heart to see the meadows outside town taken over by people with too much money and an Edifice Complex.

Climbing the eight miles from Crested Butte to Gothic, we passed through the ski-fed mess of Mount Crested Butte, now a small city and not a very nice one, full of concrete and dust. The famous wildflowers, which have their own summer festival here, were still fabulous, but the development had crept to within three miles of Gothic. The East River still meandered across the valley below, but whereas back then Dad just asked the rancher, now you'd have to buy into a syndicate to wet your line there.

But wonderful Gothic still felt the same after all these years, a confabulation of time-blackened old cabins, fragrant willow bogs, and flower meadows, albeit with a few newer and restored dorms and labs tucked in these days. All this sits in the lap of Gothic Mountain, higher than anything else around, like a *Stegosaurus* at rest. We managed to find the renowned pollination biologist David Inouye, about to be interviewed, for a quick visit. I knew him from my grad student days here, and Scott wanted to ask him about a habitat he had found for the almost-vanished western bumblebee. Then we located the Stanford biologists Carol Boggs and Ward Watt in their South Gothic cabin. Ward too had been a Remington student, and he and Carol were mentors of Larry Gall and Felix Sperling when, as students here themselves, they discovered the Uncompahgre fritillary.

Ward and Carol received us cordially, even though they were preparing a National Science Foundation grant application against a deadline. We heard about an Arctic expedition they'd taken with my grad-school lab mate Francie Chew of Tufts University. Their findings in the Far North will have major implications for the worldwide climate discussion. Ward has built his body of science

around *Colias* sulphurs, Francie studies *Pieris* butterflies, and Carol
has worked on checkerspots, blues, and fritillaries, among others.

I said, "So, Carol—where are the *gillettii* when they're at home?"

She pointed out of their picture window at an aspenish beaver
marsh about a quarter mile away, across the road. "Right there," she
said. "My students were working on them this morning, but it's a
little late and cloudy, and I can't promise you'll see them."

We owed this chase to Paul R. Ehrlich, Carol and Ward's illustri-
ous Stanford colleague, frequent guest on Johnny Carson's *Tonight
Show*, and codescriber of the Sandia hairstreak. Author of *The
Population Bomb* and, with Anne Ehrlich, of many important conservation books since, he studies population biology of butterflies
as well as humans. An *Erebia* freak like me, Paul named a subspecies
of Butler's alpine after his Gothic neighbor and cofounder of Zero
Population Growth, Charles Remington.

In 1977 Ehrlich and his graduate student Cheri Holdren introduced Gillett's checkerspot to suitable habitat at Gothic. The exper-
iment asked whether this northern Rockies endemic was excluded
from the southern Rockies by the geographic barrier of the Red
Desert or by ecological factors—was there an empty niche? When
I'd seen Carol at Yale the previous fall, I asked how the checker
was doing. After barely ticking over for years, she told me, it had
exploded just that year, with thousands on the wing.

Such boom and bust cycles are characteristic of checkerspots.
Populations crest, crash, and not infrequently flicker out—not a
problem if there remain other colonies nearby to recolonize but
leading to endangerment when habitat becomes too fragmented.
Euphydryas also vary year to year in flight period, subject to moisture and weather. In spite of many attempts, I'd never managed to
find Gillett's checker in its native northern Rockies. I'd hoped to
bookend this lifetime grail with its relative, the Baltimore, recently
seen at last in Illinois after a similar string of failures. Since it was
so dodgy on its home territory, I wanted to try for the recently exploded population here at dear old Gothic. We thanked these great
supporters of Xerces, the Lep Soc, and RMBL, my three favorite in-
stitutions, and went forth to see if we could indeed find *Euphydryas
gillettii*.

Scott and I crossed the East River and took the tiny track that led up toward the habitat. Then we walked to the willows around the beaver pond. Carol had told us to take care not to step in any rivulets, since another old friend, Bobbi Pekarsky, had research going on in the water. We poked about a bit, and so did the sun. The host plant that Ehrlich had rightly observed as abundant here, twinberry, twinkled with raindrops.

Then the sun came out in full, and with it so did *Euphydryas gillettii*! Several stunners arose and basked well and long for Scott's photographs and my delectation. With Carol's permission, I netted one for a good, close look, then released it—"B12," it was marked. Smaller than the Baltimores I'd recently seen, it was just as radiantly black and red; but on *gillettii*, much of the scarlet scaling is arranged in dramatic submarginal bands against the black—almost like a red admirable. So I found my thrill on checkerspot hill, redoubled by having so recently seen its Baltimore cousin for the first time too. Both checkerspot grails: check!

Now it was Scott's turn to look for the extremely rare western bumblebee, once common over much of the West and now, unaccountably, almost gone. We dropped down to the Slate River, where I used to fish and swim with my stepfamily, and where David Inouye had seen the bumbles on *Ipomea*. Scott, slim and fit at forty-five, ranged all over the mountainside and found other cool bees. But the enigmatic western BB lived up to its recent reputation of absence from known habitats. Butterflies did better. Mead's callippe fritillaries mated on a helianthella, female open-winged and shivering, male closed above her, cupric green disks flashing big silver orbs. On the hill, blue and ruddy coppers sparked like diodes, mirror images but for the color their scales refract from the sun. Nearby, a lilac-bordered copper, the brightest purple on yellow ever—pure Easter eggs!

Down below, on the marshy shore of Nickelsen Lake, I hoped for silver-bordered fritillaries. There were flashing frits in the tall sedges, but they were Mormons, the same species Remington and Ehrlich had been marking in my long-ago ambush and the subject of Carol's new grant proposal. Dozens of them were going to communal roosts in the sedges before evening, in groups of four and five. I was entranced, when a rather nasty man drove down from his house to kick me out. I pointed out that there was no fence. Then I tried out Woody Guthrie's brilliant but lesser known lines from "This Land Is Your Land" ("But on the other side it didn't say nothin', that side was made for you and me"), saying I couldn't see the words "No Trespassing" from the other side of the sign. He didn't laugh. Scott stayed out of it. After other words, best forgotten, I thanked the man for his courtesy, of which he had no more than he did irony, and we left.

Once back in Crested Butte, Scott and I took a room at Elk Mountain Lodge, where my mother, brother Bud, and I had stayed forty-four years before. We found the old town less ravaged than the meadows outside and the snow-sports ghetto. Walking around after dinner, I showed Scott landmarks of my adolescence: Tony's gas station, Tony's hardware, and Tony's bar; the movie house and polka ballroom; where our cabin had been and coal shed still stood, and the log cabin from which I heard an electric guitar that vibrated right through my gonads (just as Tipper Gore says); where I kissed Marcia Stephanik when I was fourteen, she sixteen, and where her twenty-three-year-old cowboy boyfriend from Gunnison punched me out for it. "You're just lucky you didn't get another knuckle sandwich today," said Scott.

On Monday, the Jack's Cabin cutoff took us to the Taylor Park Reservoir, and beyond that sagey dust bowl, up under aspens and lodgepoles to Cottonwood Pass. One thing I'd sacrificed for this trip was my fantasy of visiting Cumberland Pass, with days to wander the trackless alpine. In reality, I doubt I would have had those days, and the alpine isn't so trackless anymore with all the quads and dirt bikes out there scoring the tundra. But Scott and I both loved Cottonwood Pass, and though more populous than either of us remembered, it still framed the whole central Continental Divide as well as any vista. A Magdalena floated down a rock chute, and what I took for Melissa arctics but didn't manage to net ghosted along an old gravelly track across the fell-field near the summit.

Down the other side, beyond Buena Vista, we crossed again the high, wide expanse of South Park, with just enough time to visit the fen once more. This time, in sunshine, butterflies flocked the yellow

composites by the entrance: many pretty little bronze bits called garita skipperlings, and a few strikingly white-veined uncas skippers.
Counting these two, the trip yielded fifty-four species, twenty-two
of them new, and two elusive grails, if neither Susan's purse-bearing
caddis flies nor western bumblebees for Scott. But when he boarded
his plane, I'll bet he was just as refreshed for his work as I was for
my play. And when he returned to the fen the very next summer,
that fancy caddis was waiting for him, designer bag and all.

3. DEEP PURPLE

Janet Chu and I went way back. She and I had taught at National Wildlife Federation's Conservation Summits for many seasons, during which Jan, her late husband, Ray, Thea, and I became good family friends. A longtime Boulder biology teacher of distinction, Jan had been surveying the butterflies of Boulder County Open Space for several seasons. Now, with daughter, Amy, and friends Larry Crowley and Jean Morgan, we'd come to Heil Valley Ranch preserve. It was alive with orange and clouded sulphurs, variegated and Aphrodite fritillaries. Near a fine stand of big bluestem grass, we found what we'd come for: a lone, beautiful female arogos skipper, clear orange, on the last blooming bull thistle. By checking the county vegetation maps to see where the bluestem was, Jan had come here with Larry and found the rare skipper, as hoped. They'd seen multiple males and females a fortnight before; now, with the weather hot and dry, the tail end of the flight period was at hand. A good find, arogos, one Jim Wiker could no longer show me in Illinois.

Buckingham Park on James Creek was Skipper City. Eight species thronged purple lucerne, three new: afranius duskywing, the hefty, polished-brass taxiles skipper, and the smaller, tawny woodland skipper. Since the woodland is our most abundant butterfly at home in late summer, I was hoping it would hold off to be another species first found in Gray's River. Larry and I dangled over the canyon to watch fifteen northwestern fritillaries and a northern crescent on black-eyed Susans flicked by the bouncing stream.

Jan helped to set up the Cal-Wood environmental education center, and she now runs a butterfly count on its extensive mountains and meadows every July. In 2007 we'd found lots of Snow's skippers. *Paratrytone snowi* restricts itself to the higher Rockies, where it is seldom numerous. As at Heil Ranch, again we proved lucky in Geir Meadow. Last year's good flight of Snow's skippers was absent this time; but Jean spotted a single bulky female that I netted and released—rich russet, with a high-wattage white spot on her dorsal forewing that flashed as she flew away.

In the process of finding Snow's, two other newbies turned up. First, a beat-to-heck mystic skipper, a.k.a., the only one I would see for the year. Then serious spectacle, as Akito snagged an Edwards's fritillary. The largest western silverspot and the only one not broken into subspecies, *Speyeria edwardsii* combines copper-green, quicksilver, Popsicle pink, and puma tawny in a three-inch package. Of all the butterflies named for Theodore Mead's father-in-law, this must be the grandest. Lemon and lime Alexandra sulphurs—named by Edwards—fussed over fiery *Gaillardia* and lavender *Monarda*. I cannot say if they inspired the superior Key lime pie that Jean served us later, back at the House of Chu.

The next day was to be our day in the alpine, but it was cloudy up high, so Jan and I went east instead. Sometime this year, I had to visit the place that made me a naturalist and where I learned my butterflies, so why not now? The High Line Canal runs 66 miles from the Platte Canyon southwest of Denver out onto the plains, winding as it goes through the neighborhood in which I grew up. My brother Tom and I escaped the grid of our Aurora subdivision to the wet and winding possibilities of the ditch, and it became our constant haunt. Over the years I found nearly a tenth of U.S. butterfly species along the canal.

Jan drove us to Tollgate Creek, an open space where I had often found Acadian hairstreaks among dense willows and thistles in the flood zone. Since I had missed *Satyrium acadica* with Jim in Illinois, this was my last chance. I worked hard, thrashing through the willows and reeds in sweaty, stickery heat, at one point losing and frantically finding my notebook that covered the past several weeks. But the hairstreaks never appeared; in fact, almost no butterflies appeared, aside from about two bozillion cabbage whites. A Fourth of July Butterfly Count had taken place on the canal most years since the counts began in 1975. Since it might not happen otherwise, Jan and I made this visit a 4JBC. We sampled a few of our classic habitats, including a nearby city garden with great nectar, but few butterflies. In the end, we reported just eleven species and 105 individuals, 91 of which (I overestimated above) were cabbages. "Fauna seems to be collapsing," I summed: a sad statement about the place responsible for my life as a lepidopterist.

Before leaving, we visited the site of the old hollow tree that saved my life and my brother Tom's in the violent hailstorm of 1954. I told this story in *The Thunder Tree,* my portrait of the canal as one person's special place in the context of uncontrolled human expansion and the western water wars. Each annual count begins at the hollow tree with a group photo. We asked Christine, a mom picnicking in the adjacent Del Mar Park with her kids, to take our picture. Christine, seeing our nets, said that her family walks the canal all the time, looking at things. Hannah, nine, loved butterflies, and six-year-old Vincent liked bugs, though Henry, eleven, was indifferent. Christine said, "You know where there's a lot of butterflies? Over in that canal!" Yes, I wanted to say, that's what I found fifty years ago, and that's why we're here. But I just smiled and thanked her, happy that someone still noticed.

I hope I was wrong in my assessment of our meager count, that it was just the drought (the fourth driest year on record), and maybe the later date than usual. Even as I looked down in the lateral ditch at a bleak scene of mowed weeds and plastic trash where silvery blues and purplish coppers used to fly in the lush growth of summer, I took hope in Christine's family. After all, they didn't know how it used to be, several hundred thousand people ago; they know how it is now, and they still walk here, and still look for things. I hoped that Hannah could still find what I found along the old ditch, under the grand old cottonwoods that remain, even if the butterflies are fewer and different.

We fled to Castle Rock and east into Gambel oaks, along dirt country roads. Tapping those oak copses, we put up a number of banded hairstreaks. But just as we found perfect habitat for Colorado hairstreaks, our special objective, a Colorado thunderstorm struck and drove the butterfly day to an early finish. We took shelter, lemonade, and garlic bread at a little place in Larkspur during the downpour. Afterward, in the cool fragrance of rain on dust, we traced a circle through Elbert, Elizabeth, and Franktown, then Sedalia, Golden, and back to Boulder, evading most of the diabolical Denver traffic. With Amy, we watched a stunning rainbow from Jan's garden deck; and after dark, one of the rare, westernmost-in-the-country Boulder fireflies flashed for us.

After the storm came a Murphy Dome Day! Jan and Amy couldn't come out to play thanks to a pussycat crisis, so I drove Jan's car directly back to Lake Gulch Road, where we had found the best oaks, by freeway this time. Hairstreaks met me right out of the car—and such hairstreaks they were! *Hypaurotis crysalus* was an object of high lust for me as a young collector. It graced the cover of Brown, Eff, and Rotger's *Colorado Butterflies,* my gospel, in full, glorious color. That color was *purple*—a purple of such amethyst shine and iris depth as to be found in no other butterfly I know. In high school, my friends and I built a make-out pad in my attic that we dubbed "Deep Purple Penthouse." We said it was named after the Nino Tempo/ April Stevens version of Hoagy Carmichael's classic love song, then popular; but I think it was equally inspired by the butterfly.

A dozen different butterflies fairly dripped off the mauve *Monarda* and crowded yesterday's damp sand, but I couldn't keep my eyes (or net) off the hairstreaks. Their silvery gray, blue-and-red-medaled undersides showed well in the dappled sun. The uppers looked black in the shadows, but in hand, held ever so lightly and opened with forceps, they cast their ultraviolet spell. I could see why the Kings of Tyre kept secret the recipe for royal purple dye, from a gland in a *Murex* snail, upon pain of death. Just think if they could have distilled this richer purple for their garments. Though butterfly scales have been transferred into books (you can see them in Jim Wiker's library), and Montezuma arrogated the plumes of the resplendent quetzal for his own robes, the fugitive colors of butterflies have never been captured for any king's new clothes.

In a favorable year, *H. crysalus* abounds in thick-clumped oaks about ten feet high, and this was such a year. They flew just a little way when disturbed, often alighting right in front of my face. Females, easy to tell thanks to dimorphic black markings, dominated. Along with bandeds, they visited glistening buds, from which they obtained some sweet exudate. Not much later I would emulate them, making plans with Amy, Jan, and Larry for the morrow's expedition to Loveland Pass. Larry and I had discovered a mutual affection for Dale's Pale Ale from Lyons, just up the sandstone hogback from Boulder.

But first, on the way back, I drove through the fluted white sandstone walls of Diablo Canyon. The ruin of old Castlewood Dam under oaks and pines brought back bicycle expeditions with Tom, woodsies with other high school hornies, and, especially, my lifesaver: Ed Butterfield's Aurora High Ecology Club. Field trips to parse the natural history of that little gorge on the plains invested a closet pleasure with the respect of recognition. I recalled a chilly spring trip on which I pulled a pine elfin out of a ponderosa, and the excitement it created. Because of summer vacation, we never went there in Colorado hairstreak season. But if we had, I could just imagine (as I passed Diablo these many years later) the faces of my fellow ecology geeks at the sight of that improbable insect.

The sun held for Friday. To Idaho Springs, where we met Larry and his friend Skeet at the Steve Canyon statue. Then up old U.S. 40, over the top of the Eisenhower Tunnel of I-70, to Loveland Pass. This easy-access but very high route (11,990 feet at the divide) has always been one of my favorite entries to the arctic-alpine. Right off the bat I fouled out on a small fritillary in the willow bog near the lake, missing it twice, and we never saw it again. I was pretty sure it was a bog fritillary, *Boloria eunomia,* but there was a chance it could have been *chariclea,* or even late *freija* or *frigga.* This irked me for months, until I learned from Jon Pelham that what I'd taken for *B. alaskensis* in Alaska was actually *eunomia,* very different from the Colorado bog frits I know.

We headed up the rockslide, for a good time watching and catching black Maggie. I placed one on Amy's nose, as I had when she was a girl. The others didn't let me forget the summer when I was investigating the behavior of *Erebia magdalena* on this very rockslide. Replicating Niko Tinbergen's famous experiments with graylings, I'd fashioned a low-tech model Maggie out of black cardboard, which I flew down the talus on a monofilament fishing line. The male Magdalena alpines freaked out at the superfemale model, as did pikas that mistook it for a raven or an eagle. But my field assistant, David Shaw, defected on me after his third trip up to the top of the rocks.

Which is where I went now, after we wandered all over the meadows, bogs, and hilltops, with little flying but Colorado alpines, with their natty, gravelly gray venters. I climbed to the ridge and pulled myself over the top, way up and above the pass, to where the others became tiny to me. I emerged into a fresh flush of *Plebejus shasta minnehaha*, just what I'd hoped for up there. The shasta blue is a tiny, dusky one, with glittering scintillae just the same. "Atlastashasta," I said and then struck off up the tundra ridge to where the few other hikers quickly fell away. This was more like the real thing—a Colorado alpine assemblage, with most of the constituent species a-wing: Mead's sulphurs blazed, and Bruce's anicia checkerspots, tiny and aggressive, hilltopped on rocky knobs.

Finally, on a steep slope scored with soliflucting rock stripes, I entered a flight of the euphonious *Oeneis melissa lucilla* and confirmed the Melissa arctic I thought I'd seen on Cottonwood Pass. A nonlep movement surprised me, becoming a mother willow ptarmigan and her three chicks. She'd be easy to lose in her elegant brown and white crypsis, if she didn't keep making sweet, quiet clucks to keep them together. At the high point on the ridge, I could barely make out Janet waving way below. She shot a photo of me up there in the rocks, in which I am no more than a flea on a big gray pika.

Up and down through alpine gardens of moss campion and forget-me-nots among the rocks, I came to a recent snowmelt bowl with a flat slab of pink granite at one end, snow at the other. I lay back against the boulder, looked out at the high peaks, the Mount of the Holy Cross off to the west, the Jackson Pollock tundra all around, and felt quite whelmed. The butterflies were nice, but this was what I came for.

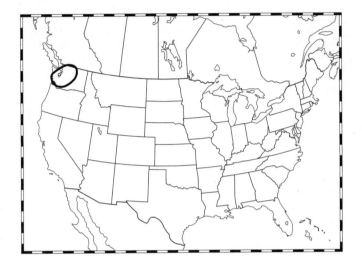

⤐ RAY NINE ⟻

Close to Home

It invariably takes longer to "write up" an incident than to experience it. Every naturalist who writes needs ten days to sort out one really productive day in the field.

—James Fisher, *Wild America*
(with Roger Tory Peterson)

1. OLYMPICA ARCTICA

The day after I returned from Colorado, I drove Thea to Iwaco for her chemo infusion. While she got hooked up, I parked on the end of the pier to catch up on my notes and checklist. Two young women from Washington Fish and Wildlife were waiting to check fish catches and not getting much business. When I checked back in on Thea, I was shocked to find her flushed and on oxygen. Her blood pressure had dropped dangerously, in allergic reaction to the carboplatin. She'd come close to anaphylaxis before stabilizing. I'm not sure who was more shaken, Thea, the nurses, or I.

When it was clear that she was okay and resting, I motored a few miles north up the Long Beach Peninsula toward Leadbetter Point. Lorquin's admirals dallied in the sun at Loomis Lake, and on Stackpole Road, thirteen margined whites bounced over the verge as the country swing show on KMUN played "13 Nights." One nectared on *Bellis perennis,* its pink iridescence exactly catching the pink of the daisy, as another spread to bask on bracken fern. I tried to enjoy them, but I was torn up over Thea's reversal.

Doctor Law said no more carboplatin, just the gemcitabine, which she took all right. That brought a new concern, since it was the carboplatin that had reduced the tumor so effectively last time around, along with Taxol, which she wasn't having this time either. At least she'd keep her hair, a minor concern compared to the cancer, but a gift just the same.

Back home, I scrapped plans for a long Amtrak trip to Maine and the Carolinas. While I was at it, I all but bagged Canada altogether. My original vision included every state and most provinces. First, the Yukon fell off the map when the fabulous Dempster Highway proved too costly to organize in both time and money, leaving me to settle for the Steese and the Dalton. Next, the Canadian Rockies dropped out of the picture as the calendar contracted, and the map seemed to grow. Given recent tales of border harassment of entomologists with nets and specimens, and the summer's poor weather across the North, I reconciled all that; there weren't so very many unique species involved after all.

But I continued to hold out hopes for one great Canadian grail: the beautiful short-tailed swallowtail (*Papilio brevicauda*), wholly endemic to the Maritime Provinces and one of my oldest and deepest desires to see. Those hopes grew dimmer as I canceled that train trip to Maine, the jumping-off point. But the upside to these retrenchments would be a more thorough examination of our backyard habitats, where many species remained to be found. Thea feeling fine the next day, we drove to Boloria Junction for a walk on the exotically flowered logging roads. *Boloria* were all gone, but the woods were littered with Clodius parnassians blowing about like scraps of paper escaping the transfer station on K-M Hill. One male spanned three inches, and on a fresh female with lots of cherry red, the milky sphragis was pink-tinged, like the pink-flowered clone of blackberries we found her on. As she shifted to a hawkbit, her transparent wings arrayed over its lemony ray flowers, I had the delightful surprise of beholding a bright yellow parnassian after all! Who needs Eversmann's?

Thea insisted I get going, so I picked up my new glasses in Cathlamet and pointed Powdermilk toward the Olympic Mountains. The wet, green drive beyond Gray's Harbor shot corridors of clearcuts. The Department of Natural Resources had placed Burma-Shave-type signs for its trust lands: "We cut some trees / to help the county / we plant some more / for future bounty." At least it scanned. The stumps and doghair gave way to tall-tree alleys in the Quinault. Magenta patches of fireweed and foxglove announced High Summer, never mind pot metal skies and 55°F. Few automobiles plied the 101, very few RVs for July, even fewer log trucks, with gas up and log prices down. Up past Queets, through witchy ranks of dripping, drooping hemlocks. La Niña fog squatted over the still lagoon at Kalaloch, where a damp rufous hummingbird searched for any undiluted nectar; welcome to July in the rainforest! It was becoming my second zero butterfly day of July.

In Forks for fruit and peanuts, I bantered with Willow Roundtree, the black clerk (that in itself notable in Forks). I complimented her lovely name and asked whether her sister also had a tree name. "No," she said, with a smile and a pat on my hand, "but my daughter is named Amber Michelle—I figured since I was the tree, she could be the sap." I recorded just as many vampires as butterflies.

In campsite 103 at Heart o' the Hills campground in Olympic National Park, I listened to the CBC and studied my own book *The Butterflies of Cascadia*. The forecast from Victoria called for cold and cloud, but the stars were out, and I anticipated *Erebia vidleri* in high Olympic meadows as I lay down beneath old-growth Douglas-firs. A chipmunk woke me up at 7:30 A.M., chilly enough for sweatshirt, gloves, and my red fleece moose cap from Alaska. I found *Linnaea borealis* blooming next to my campsite, namesake not only of Carolus Linnaeus but, thanks to her plantswoman mother, of Thea Linnaea as well. I wondered if Willow Roundtree's mother had been a gardener too.

The national parks change less than other places, but nowhere is static. I saw differences since 1975, when I studied the ecology of the valerata arctic here, but they weren't all bad. Some of the giant trees had blown down in Heart o' the Hills, but the Elwha Dam was due to come out, and fishers (the mustelid type) have been reintroduced. Hurricane Ridge Road was being rebuilt, making for a slow passage up the mountain. Hurricane, one of only two places you can drive into the high Olympics, is as good as anywhere for viewing the valerata chryxus arctic and the Northwest endemic Vidler's alpine. I hoped to see these two here, as well as Hulbirt's branded skipper, another Olympic specialty. Following a pilot car, I couldn't stop at a favorite seep on the way up the hill, but a thick mist enveloped the mountain anyway.

It was 10:30 when I reached the Hurricane Hill trailhead and got my boots on. The sun, off and on, raised the temperature into the sixties. My new photogray glasses went almost too dark in the snow-reflected UV, like car windows these days. But they did concentrate the colors of the stupendous Olympic tundra flowers: harebells, bistort, woolly sunflowers, Columbia lilies, starflower, paintbrush, red heather, pink ram's horns. A few bumblebees and flies called on them, and ants plied an old trail, many yards long and deeply incised into the thin turf. But not a single butterfly flew, even on a flower-strewn hilltop in the sun. One black-and-rust zerene fritillary caterpillar crossed the trail. Otherwise, the summer Olympics, normally rich and prolific, were utterly butterfly-free.

I had a hot dog at the visitor center and watched the many Germans, Japanese, and other tourists with rented campers and digital cameras take pictures of a few tame does with one fawn between them and fog, as the Olys, snowy, cold, and shrouded in cloud, peeked out. I might as well have been back on Eagle Summit, with that Arctic Prospect. Down in Port Townsend, waiting for the ferry, I rubbed in my one-caterpillar day with a pint of IPA called The Bitter End, a short pour from a snippy young barmaid at that. Consolation is where you find it. Not that I really needed compensation for the Heidi-like blooms of Hurricane Hill. Or for watching, from the *Steilacoom II* to Coupeville on Whidbey Island, tufted puffins with their bills full of fish.

The last day of July felt more like October. I awakened beneath Doug-firs again, but they were far from old-growth and they grew among paper birches. The air was dry but cloudy and cold; and when I arrived at the power line cut east of Blaine, raining. This was the very spot where Thea and I had recorded the first European small skipperlings in Washington. One of only two widespread introduced species in the forty-nine mainland states, *Thymelicus lineola* is known as the Essex skipper in its native England. Since its larvae love timothy, a common pasture and hay-field grass, and the eggs overwinter, the bright gold mite is a natural for easy transportation and multiple introduction. We'd been monitoring the state's borders and finally found it on this weedy power line right of way less than a mile from the Canadian border. This was Thea's third state record: she had earlier discovered the first *T. lineola* ever noted in both Idaho and Montana. I'd taken to calling it "Thea lineola," or Thea's skipperling.

The weather called for a time-honored insect-collecting technique that is very seldom used for butterflies: sweeping. Just as it sounds, this method involves swishing the net back and forth through the vegetation to see what's lurking there. Along the power line road, I swept tall, wet grasses, bird's-foot trefoil, clover . . .

twenty minutes of this activity yielded a soaked and seedy bag for Marsha, crawling with droves of spiders, caterpillars, grasshoppers, crane flies, beetles, bugs, and others. One more sweep on *Lotus*, and . . . "Holy shit!" I said. "It worked!" A fresh Essex skipper clung to the mesh. "Lucky me," I told the Border Patrol helicopter overhead. "That's all I needed. We're out of here."

That evening, I met Jon Pelham at Hale's Brewery in Ballard. After we made a dent in a pitcher of Hale's Pale (not to be confused with Dale's Pale from Colorado), I pulled out my stash of voucher specimens for Jon's expert evaluation. Itching to see them, he confirmed nearly all of my species IDs from Alaska and added a couple of sulphurs I had not yet discerned, and an Atlantis fritillary from Colorado. I put them back in the container and set them aside while we dined.

Afterward, Jon and I went over to David Branch's house in Magnolia. The single malt came out, and the stories from the field flew like skippers from place to place—Okefenokee to Iroquois, Guadalupe to Catalina, Atigun to home again—as the lads filled my glass and egged me on. Under their influence, I might have drunk a dram more than was strictly necessary.

2. DUMPSTER DIVE

The single malt notwithstanding, David Branch and I welcomed August early. Heavy clouds and rain rode all the way up Snoqualmie Pass with us, then dropped away over the top, just as they are supposed to do. We breakfasted at the Cottage Cafe in Cle Elum with unsuccessful but chatty bear hunters who wished us better luck than theirs. First signs were unpromising, when Swauk campground, in good sun with fair nectar (goldenrod already!) had zero butterflies, just like the Olympics, which was just *weird*.

We crossed U.S. 2 and the Wenatchee River into the Chumstick Mountains, where we'd first met on a butterfly class and butterflied together a great deal over the years since. Up Derby Canyon, the first butterfly showed up in the form of a western tiger swallowtail as we gleaned apricots from a roadside outlier of an abandoned orchard. David's Expedition's thermometer read 77°F. I don't know how we got lost after so many trips, but the Chumsticks are a maze, and we did; but it didn't matter, all roads eventually go up into the national forest. When we entered the woods, David saw a nice fresh pine white. This primitive pierid with its floppy flight, pen-and-ink veins, and dash of scarlet actually recycles pine needles into itself through the larval change machine and doesn't fly until late summer. It made a nice addition, even as it heralded the waning season.

I decided to investigate a little hilltop among ponderosa pines. Shreds of dogbane and fleabane remained in bloom—good combo, I thought, and it seemed to work, as I was bothered by neither dogs nor fleas. There were some butterflies, however. Besides woodland skippers, ubiquitous for the rest of the summer, several hairstreaks hopped around the sparse blooms. Let's see—there's a hedgerow hairstreak, a few nootkas . . . and what's this? Aha! One worn fe-male of *Satyrium semiluna*, the newly split-off segregate of the sooty hairstreak with the obvious and too-beautiful-not-to-use common name half-moon hairstreak. Seeing my grin, David asked, "Get a good one?"

"Heck yes," I said, "just the one we were looking for!" I think he said something about that calling for a scotch later, but I ig-nored it.

We both found it odd to be running our usual Fourth of July Count route without the other folks or the usual hell-for-leather regimen. But though we missed our sweeties, it was pleasant to be more casual about it. Being later than usual made for a very dry passage to Chumstick Mountain, the count center, where all the count groups coming up different canyons traditionally converge in the afternoon over watermelon. The late date also meant far fewer butterflies than on the usual June count but also allowed for the possibility of later-emerging species, such as the pine white.

There have been many fires in the Chumsticks in recent years, and the road we thought was the main one died in the burn, send-ing us back. But just there we saw an amazon of a female *Speyeria cybele leto*. In its colors, chocolate and undyed cheddar, our race is hugely different from the orange Illinois *cybele*, yet both are consid-ered great spangled fritillaries. Then David, an ace netsman, finally apprehended a zerene fritillary, candidates for which had been teas-ing us all day.

When we finally made the ridge, the paintbrush and penste-mons were largely over, but we found it pasted with pale purple asters. Big anicia checkerspots crowded the asters so that we barely noticed the year's initial mariposa copper, a small brown triangle among showier purplish and blue coppers. This check mark felt especially significant, as I had years ago found a striking new variety of *Lycaena mariposa* in Olympic coastal bogs and was working on a revision of the species with Jon Pelham so I could describe it. One more milestone along the Mariposa Road.

The densely flowered meadows running up to the summit might have been teeming with butterflies had we arrived earlier in the day, but then we might have missed the half-moon hairstreak. We made the top of Chumstick Mountain, where over the years we had known everything from snowstorms to butterfly swarms at five. This time, a fierce wind off the Columbia sent us downhill in a hurry. David took me to the top of Sugarloaf Mountain, where I'd never been, as it's just outside the count circle, and if the day hadn't fled, we'd have been flailing away up there yet. We'd had a high time, even more fun than all our good hours together at his dental chair. But as David had noticed, I'd been somewhat distracted all day. "What's on your mind, Heap?" he asked. "Are you thinking about Saint T.?"

"Always," I said, "but she's doing well. Fact is, I'm worried about my vouchers."

That morning, packing up at David's, I couldn't find the specimens that I'd shown Jonathan at Hale's the night before. As my slight overhang dissipated with the clouds over the Cascade crest, I had to face the fact that I'd probably left them on our table at the brewpub (although Jon thought sure we'd cleared the table). Now, heading back, I called Hale's from David's mobile. My specimens weren't to be seen among the lost and found. The fellow I spoke with asked me what they looked like. I told him they were in a yogurt container. "Aw, dude," he said, "they would've gone out with the trash, for sure."

"When does the garbage truck come?" I asked.

"Monday," he said.

When we got back from Chumstick late Saturday night, I told David I was going down to Hale's. I knew if he thought I was actually going to look for the specimens, he would have insisted on going with me. But it was his grandson's birthday in the morning, and he had a date with young Nicolas. So I told him I was just going to case the joint.

It was after midnight, and the pub was closed when I arrived. I found the jumbo Dumpster next to the alley out back. Neither the pen nor the Dumpster was locked. I opened the massive lid, fortunately plastic and not steel, the regulatory result of mashed Dumpster divers in the past. Behold, Gentle Reader, and tremble: some twenty or thirty supersize Hefty bags lay within that ghastly hold, and the gods know what horrors seethed beneath.

I thought the bags would be light, full of napkins and paper. But they were heavy—twenty pounds or more—stuffed with castoff food: rotten old burgers, catsup, pickles, salsa, fish, fries, sloppy salads, and myriad other delights in various states of decay, as well as all the smeared and crumpled paper. And though it's a no-smoking establishment, still there were the kitchen staff's stinky butts. I estimated where Friday's sediments most likely lay among the fetid strata. Then I rolled up my sleeves, assumed my best Elvis sneer, and dove the hell in.

The horror I felt was less with the task itself, as repellent as it was, as with myself. Of course, it's just my old stupid game of shedding my possessions everywhere I go. It wasn't the first item I'd jettisoned during the year, and it wouldn't be the last. But the *specimens*! Not only were they of scientific value. Not only were they essential for establishing the reliability of my claims for some difficult-to-identify species. Not only did they represent many hours of labor in their chasing, catching, labeling, and careful curating. No, not only these. It was "all those little lives," in the poet John Haines's words. I don't *like* killing butterflies! I don't know any entomologist who doesn't feel some compunction over the necessary act of dispatch, no matter how blithely we justify it to ourselves and others. Every human kills to live, and we each make our own accommodations with causing death. Fair enough: this is one I choose to make, on carefully chosen occasions. But, damn! For them then to end up in a *Dumpster*—and then a landfill? *That* was insupportable!

I held the lid open with my right hand, in which I also held David's flashlight. Then with my left hand, I lifted the bag to face level, balanced it on the rim, tore it open, and excavated. The first was pretty disgusting; I was grossed out and depressed in equal measure. What chance, what chance? I hefted the second bag, feeling all but hopeless. I was not sure whether I would cry or vomit first. Or be pinched by the police, since I was perpetrating this act in full view of all who passed by on the Burke-Gilman Trail and the small road beside it. The second bag was so gloppy that I just set it aside; I couldn't face it yet.

And then, just a little way into the third bag, out popped a yogurt container with the lid still on. I couldn't remember what mine was like, and I was not at all sure this was the right one. I was afraid to think so. It was smeared with food bits. I thought that might be it. I picked it up, shook it . . . it sounded right. Opened it, and—yes!—it *was*! The blue Greek yogurt cup that Thea gave me, and with all the specimens intact. I nearly wept, and couldn't stop yipping. I was *so* happy, unspeakably relieved. This was better than any several other finds combined: it was the best catch ever! I whooped with sheer joy, alarming a bicyclist out of his nocturne.

Wiping my southpaw on somebody's used napkin, barely touching the steering wheel, I whipped back to David's, washed me, washed the yogurt vessel, and then put it out for David to see on the table when he rose in the morning. I affixed a new sign to it, on my XS/BBY business card: "Important Scientific Specimens! *Do Not Discard.*"

When I next saw Jim Wiker, among the many stories shared of adventures in the field, he told me this one: following a major moth-collecting trip into the North, the three lepidopterists spent the night in the same Knights Inn where he and I had lodged in South Beloit last month. The next day, hundreds of miles south, they noticed that their large canister of valuable research specimens was missing. After a long drive back, one of the guys recovered the cache in the Dumpster out behind the motel. How happy I was, considering how it all came out, to reciprocate with an all's-well-that-ends-well horror story.

So maybe I didn't get to travel the Dempster Highway in the Yukon. But the Dumpster Highway—now that one, I've done!

3. ASTARTE ARISING

Up the Arlington–Darrington Road, big salmon letters on a gray metal barn read "HAY." It was that season already. Another said "Fresh Blueberries"—that season too. Tired big-leaf maples hung over the road on the left, fir and cedar on the right, as I ascended the Stillaguamish River. "Thieves go to hell" was hand-painted on a garage door; a bluegrass festival was coming to Darrington with seventeen bands.

The towns get progressively prettier as the North Cascades Highway ascends, as do their names: Concrete, Rockport, Marblemount ("Gateway to the American Alps"). Winding up the wonderful Skagit River, I'd have loved to stop and see my friends at the North Cascades Institute's Environmental Learning Center, but there was no time for that. Mountain chickadees called at yet another Pacific Crest Trail crossing. I skipped it this time, eager to reach the hot east side to hunt summer species of the northern range. I crossed over at 6:00 P.M. at 4,855-foot Rainy Pass. As for "American Alps," between there and Washington Pass, I'd hold them up to any in Austria or Switzerland. I remembered why Thea and I had testified on behalf of our student conservation club before Senator Scoop Jackson in favor of the North Cascades National Park some forty years ago. And though I was driving the highway now, I was glad that most of the park was unroaded wilderness.

About half of the light traffic on Highway 20 this evening was motorcycles—loud Harleys, fast racers, and a few quiet Gold Wings. A pack of four speeding sports bikes, tightly bunched, was coming toward me. Just before we passed, a snowshoe hare bounded out across the road between us. The lead cycle didn't miss it by more than six inches at sixty-plus miles an hour. Had he hit it, he might well have flipped, the ones behind running into him and any one of them sliding across the centerline into me. Or it could have been just the hare. That was a close call, at least for the snowshoe, and likely for the rest of us. As I passed 375,000 miles on Powdermilk's odometer, I couldn't help but speculate on luck, chance, and circumstance. And a good drivers' education teacher in high school, who took my buddies and me out cruising on the high plains east of Aurora for the best hour of the week, as he drummed defensive driving into our rash young skulls.

Klipchuck campground in full sun, granola and coffee, western tanagers and western wood-pewees, the soft voices of tenters at breakfast. Chickarees dashing through the shade. I hoped to find thicket hairstreaks here, as I had before with classes. One of two Cascadian hairstreaks whose larvae consume mistletoe, in this case on pines, *Mitoura spinetorum* fluctuates in numbers. But nectar was sparse, the season advanced, and one way and another, the bug blew me off. So I walked down to the Klipchuck River bridge, where a morning's worth of frits, 'streaks, and nymphs flitted about. A woodland skipper alighted on my brown arm and tried to suck sweat but couldn't get his proboscis through my pelage. I put out bananas for bait. A satyr anglewing basked on thimbleberry and currant below the bridge, and a faun anglewing soon lit between the bananas and a pat of bearberry scat next to them, unable to make up its mind, like a kid in an ice-cream shop.

Then a really big nymph did a flyby. Could it be a Compton tortoiseshell? It landed in the road, enormous, then alit on a bare branch at eye level, wings shut, its two-tone hindwings and unique silver J showing clearly. This was only my second *Nymphalis vaualbum* ever in Washington, in much better condition than the overwintered rags I'd seen in Alaska. Later, I spotted the Compton fully spread on a moist, sunny bank. I saw its four white spots, one on each wing, and the broad golden border around the trailing edge of the jagged hindwings—a simply stunning butterfly, one of the best sightings of the year. As if for comparison, a California tortoiseshell flew down and spread *its* wings, with just the two white spots. It put up its larger congener—headline: "Spunky Cal Tort Routs Compton"—but then the heftier Compton returned and reclaimed the prime basking space.

Nothing bloomed at Early Winters campground, where I turned to follow the Methow River up toward the crest. I stopped at Mazama Store for a slab of sharp cheddar and a copy of *The Methow Naturalist*. Then up past the steep rock Goat Wall, like a mini–El Capitan. The farther up the steep dirt Methow, the narrower the road between cliff and precipice, and the moister and more flowery the roadsides. Between Harts Pass and Slate Peak, blues, checkers, frits, and parnos grew so thick as to practically halt my progress.

I arrived at the top of Slate Peak Road before three, in patchy clouds. Thrust up between North Cascades National Park and the Pasayten Wilderness area, Slate Peak is to the North Cascades as Hurricane Ridge is to the Olympics: the easiest place to get into the high country. But Slate, in national forest unlike Hurricane, is conducive to nets. This circumstance brought many entomologists over the years and led to some notable discoveries. The mountain became known as the most reliable and accessible place to find several butterflies rare in Washington. On this visit, I wasn't going to hike to the top to look for lustrous coppers, as I'd seen them in both California and Colorado. My objective was the fabled Astarte fritillary, biggest of the *Bolorias*, represented in the Lower 48 only in the Montana Rockies and the North Cascades. One of the biennial species, Astarte flies here only in even years. In 2006, on my fifty-ninth birthday, Thea and I had seen a few fly by us here; but I'd never observed Astarte well and up close.

As I began down the West Fork Pasayten River trailhead, the clouds closed in, the day cooled, and I feared for my prospects. Then I descried a person, prone, a couple of switchbacks down. I thought he might have fallen. But when I made out that he was alive, examining plants, and had a net, I knew in a flash that he must be St. Dave—Nunnallee, that is; unless he was Dana Visali, editor of *The Methow Naturalist*. He didn't notice me till I'd tiptoed down the steep, rocky switchbacks and was upon him. With startling originality, I said, "Dr. Nunnallee, I presume."

Talk about a happy "hail fellow, well met!" Up here on the remote rockslide yet. A retired state ecologist, Dave became enamored of the immature stages of our butterflies and had been rearing them with zeal and photographing every stage. A state entomologist named David James, who works on biocontrol in vineyards, shared a passion for this work. The two Daves were close to completing a photographic record of every Washington species' development, from egg to adult, for what will be a stunning book. Already today Dave had found three arctic blue eggs on spotted saxifrage. That's the same plant Astarte uses, so we both trained our attention on the rockslide, in hopes of seeing one.

When the sun came back, we began to see Astarte coursing down the rocks, big, bright, and like nothing else. I would have been content with that, but Dave said, "Look!" and there was one alighted thirty feet away on a yellow daisy. I got great bino looks, first of the dorsum, with its unusual, salmony orange; and then the ventrum, both in direct light and as backlit stained glass, with its utterly distinctive mosaic of cream and rust. Astarte arose, then flew nearer, alighting in a classic position on the yellow flower smack between two rocks, eight inches apart. It was very beautiful, and a very difficult net shot. But with Dave's consent, Marsha made the attempt and *got* it! So Dave and I were able to examine Astarte in hand, a perfect big female. Dave took some excellent pictures, both before and after we set her loose. In one of these, she perches with a rock for a backdrop that looks in the image just like a major mountain rising behind her.

So then I needed to see *Erebia vidleri*, having bombed out on it in the Olympics. This was a scary situation: since the day and the flight season were both almost over, there would be little more opportunity, and I could not imagine our special Washington alpine absent from the list of the year's encounters. Dave thought the best chance for it was down in the meadows toward Harts Pass, in the salad bowl of a valley above the horse lot. I remembered that green glacial cirque as a piece of paradise. The two of us dropped down the loopy road to tramp those meadows for a late-day hour.

The wildflowers were superb. Little flew so late, but we were having a fine time talking butterflies and perambulating one of the most scenic alpine settings in the world, or anywhere else. Then I kicked up a Vidler's and cried, "There's one!" Dave spotted another, and there might have been a third. Mine settled, and I binoed it beside an *Elephantella*: round brown wings, yellow-orange eye-spotted patches, frosty band and white dash, huddled right up to a pink baby mammoth. It brought back an August day in 1970, up on Mt. Baker, when I finally got my photograph of Vidler's alpine for *Watching Washington Butterflies*—also at the very last chance. So, once again, the neutron-butterfly-bombed Olympics notwithstanding, I didn't miss out on what Pyle (in *The Butterflies of Cascadia*) called "the most striking of American alpines."

As we walked down at almost 6:00 P.M., the sun again emerged, and butterflies erupted from the floral array—tiny Mormon fritillaries, both silvered and unsilvered, plus Anna's blues, a single arctic fritillary, and finally a bright little mariposa copper on wet sand by the brook at meadow's bottom. Dave said, "Where are you staying tonight? I've got a room with two beds at the Methow Country Inn." *That's* where I was staying, as it turned out. Dave also treated me kindly to a fine dinner and breakfast, in support of the project. I sang for my supper with the story of (and a peek at) the Ballard Dumpster butterfly fauna.

Next day on the Loup Loup road, I crossed from the Methow to the Okanogan River. These Cascadean valleys have farms at the bottom, timber at the top. On the way up I passed alfalfa fields dancing with whites, sulphurs, and Melissa blues. Soon I entered pines and found JR campground bursting with butterflies. Sulphurs proliferated, but rather than the orange and clouded sulphurs of the alfalfa fields, these were montane specialists on native legumes (Queen Alexandra's sulphurs) and blueberries (pink-edged sulphurs). You haven't seen a thing until you've looked *Colias interior* in its chartreuse eyes and regarded the deep rose borders of its buttercup wings. *C. alexandra* females, absent of black borders such as the males possess, come in both white and yellow forms. A yellow one flirted with Powdermilk; a white one wraithed sheetlike through the pines. But when I first swung at one, I got the torque wrong, and Marsha snapped in half at the site of an earlier injury. Darn! Akito came out.

On a little track off the end of Forest Road number 100, butterflies teemed in a large, moist meadow. The most common of twenty-five species present was the northern blue. Like Nabokov's blue in Colorado, this Okanogan race has converged with Melissa's blue of the lowlands so that their chief distinction is ecological. Both

Lycaeides idas and *L. melissa* display orange lunules that Nabokov named aurorae, backed by blue sparkles he called scintillae. The two blues divide their worlds between high-country specialization and low-country generalism. Private and public ownership patterns allow each to thrive in its preferred home of farm or forest. Now I returned to the alfalfa fields to find a Melissa to compare with its nearby northern look-alikes. By walking along the fenced fields and flicking the sweet purple plants with Akito, I put up one roosting male—the day's last butterfly, of thousands.

Down in the Methow Valley, it was still very hot at 7:30. Outside Twisp, I was compelled to stop for an amazing spectacle: a mass hunting party of nighthawks, perhaps fifty of them. They flew back and forth in circles and swerved over the fields on either side of the highway and across the road itself, hawking some hatch or other. I stood among them, and they carried on all around me, nearly flicking my face several times. There were many midair near-collisions, but they always just missed or tapped and shot on, showing their big white wing patches. When they spread their tails to brake, white spots showed up in that dark fork too. I could see their grays and browns and handsome striations in flight, everything but the vibrissae around their great gapes. People are so unobservant and drive so damn fast. I tried to slow them down. Some did, and nodded, others sped up. But the caprimulgids did a good job of avoiding the speeding trucks and SUVs, seeming to play with them before dodging. I saw no roadkills, though many close calls. Those sicklewings changed direction on an air dime.

The spectacle thinned out. A killdeer called, cows grazed, sprinklers sprinkled. Shadows grew huge and long in the lowering sun.

4. OVER THE MISTLETOE

Some five hundred miles after the suicidal snowshoe hare incident, I made home at 7:00 A.M. I slept until noon, then unpacked, repacked, attended to the cat, and watched wood-nymphs, swallowtails, admirables, and azures in the garden with Thea. In late afternoon, we drove in caravan to Longview, where I placed Powdermilk in Dr. Dave's gentle hands for her strut transplant. Then we drove in Thea's green Forester up the Washington side of the Columbia Gorge to meet yet another Dave. Dr. David McCorkle had a room for us at the Econo Lodge in Stevenson, where he was staying with Ray Davis, forest biologist on the Umpqua National Forest, where I'd lately been. Tomorrow—to the canopy crane!

If Dr. Jerry Franklin had gotten his way, the canopy crane would have been erected near Forks, outside Olympic National Park. Franklin, the preeminent northwest old-growth forest ecologist, had long envisioned a facility that would lift investigators into the very treetops to study the wilderness of the ancient forest canopy. But this was the height of the timber wars of the eighties, when the jest of spotted owl on café menus betrayed the very real fear and frustration gripping timber country. Never mind that the spotted owl was mostly a scapegoat for a panoply of problems afflicting the logging economy—among them overcutting, foreign log exports, automation in the woods, broken unions, and changing mills and markets—the canopy crane was seen as one more threat.

Franklin was burned in effigy in Forks, and the crane project got the boot from Jefferson County. Poor Forks, with its ravaged economy, would have to wait twenty-five years for another such boon, when Stephenie Meyer's immensely popular teen vampire books and movie *Twilight* came its way. Meanwhile, Carson in the southern Cascades got the crane and hasn't been sorry. Thea and I had long talked about visiting the canopy crane, and I'd had many invitations from its former director, David Shaw (no relation to the David Shaw who ran after my model Magdalena on Loveland Pass). We'd never gotten around to it. Now we had a specific reason: to hunt for the eggs of Johnson's hairstreak.

Of the two species of hairstreaks that utilize mistletoe in Washington, apparently I'd missed out on one, the thicket hairstreak of pinewoods. The other type, Johnson's, employs dwarf mistletoe (*Arceuthobium campylopodum*) infecting hemlocks. In Washington, it occurs solely in a few remaining stands of old-growth western hemlocks. Since that kind of forest has been all but eliminated, few colonies are known to exist. Johnson's may be endangered in the strict sense, though it is not listed as such. This was the butterfly I'd been seeking with the writer Eric Wagner when we tried to reach Lake Cushman in the southern Olympics back in May but were frustrated by weather and slides. It seemed at that time that *Callophrys johnsoni*, like *C. spinetorum*, would be absent from the Big Year roster.

But then I had an idea. A few years ago, I'd found the first Skamania County record of Johnson's along the edge of the Big Lava Bed, a few miles north of Carson. When I mentioned the find to David Shaw, he told me that the insect might have been seen by workers on the canopy crane earlier that spring, but he couldn't be sure. So why not go up and have a look? I ran the idea past Dave McCorkle, and guess what—he had a date with the canopy crane crew to go up and do just that! Calls were made, we were included on the manifest for the day, and now here we were.

Early in the morning, the four of us drove to the old forest nursery and research station above Carson. There we met the rest of the crew for our ascent: Ken Bible, the canopy crane site director, and the research scientist Matt Schroeder, both of the Pacific Northwest Research Station, run jointly by the University of Washington and Oregon State University. We met in the kitchen to hear about the research here and to discuss butterflies and climate change. For example, we wondered how *Callophrys johnsoni* would respond to cold, wet springs such as this one. Ray was developing a habitat predictive model and regional inventory strategy for Johnson's hairstreak in the Northwest. Standard measures here at the crane site included carbon dioxide flux, invertebrate pitfall trap samples, soil conditions, and total ecosystem qualities. Any of these or many other factors might affect the insect. But so far, no one knew for sure whether Johnson's hairstreak even occurred here at all.

As we walked out to the canopy crane, very excited, I thanked Dave for including us. He and I had both studied with Melville Hatch, who taught entomology at the University of Washington for nearly half a century. We'd met in 1967, when we were among the few American voices speaking up for butterfly conservation. A few years earlier, Dave had worked with The Nature Conservancy to protect Moxee Bog near Yakima for the silver-bordered fritillary; it was arguably the first butterfly preserve in the country. Later he did research for the Forest Service on mistletoe hairstreaks and their impact on their host plants, considered a forest pest in commercial stands. For many years he has organized a Halloween gathering of northwest butterfly and moth folk. Dave is well liked as a genuinely kind and thoughtful person. I could think of no one with whom I'd rather stand in the lofty treetops.

Except Thea. We had our own special reason for seeing Johnson's together. The butterfly was named for Orson Bennett ("Bug") Johnson, professor of natural science at the University of Washington from 1882 to 1896 and founder of the Young Naturalists' Society in Seattle. Johnson's protégé C. V. Piper, later a celebrated botanist, brought in the larvae from mistletoe he had shot down. The professor, of course, got the patronymic, as well as the zoology building named for him. Thea and I met in a mushroom class on the fourth floor of Johnson Hall, in 1967.

Now, as we approached the full-size construction crane beneath the monumental, sky-high trees, Thea wasn't at all sure she wanted to go up. She thought she might be content just to watch from below and see what we'd found when we came down. But I didn't want her to miss this, and I knew we'd need her sharp eyes up there. The question was settled when handsome Mark plopped a bright orange hard hat on Thea's head and strapped her into a full body harness.

We all locked on to the sides of the gondola with double lanyard clips. The gate shut with a clank, gears whined, and then we rose. Up past massive trunks, then the first heavy branches. Up through the dark walls of foliage, kelly green hemlock, loden green cedars. Up, up, up, silently. Up at last into the bright zone, as branches and needles thinned. And in moments, there we were—in the canopy of the ancient forest!

At once I could see Jerry's vision, and what brings canopy scientists such as the Evergreen State College biologist Nalini Nadkarni to the treetops over and over, with ropes or elevators or whatever it takes. When I met Nalini in New Guinea in 1977, she was in the early stages of her passion for woody heights. Soon after that, she made revolutionary findings in the mossy Olympic greenwood. Since then, she's had everyone from students to prisoners, from musicians to blind folks, on top of trees. Looking out over these green fields of needles, I could see why people come here. For us, today, it was for one particular thing.

The operator of the crane was a master at his controls. He set us right into the spots requested. Ken or Matt or Ray would speak into the telephone, and say, "Five up, eight right," and that's where we'd go. We dropped into a heavy mistletoe area, where Ray's traps were baited with fresh thistle bloom. Once there, we reached outside the open-sided cab and checked clump after clump of mistletoe by hand and eye. It didn't look like Christmas mistletoe in the store but rather like fat, fleshy cedar fronds.

Soon we found several *C. johnsoni* eggs. Thea found one of the first with her binos. She always finds the best stuff. After a while we'd all seen eggs, and we collected several mistletoe clumps for examination back in the lab. Many caterpillars eat their eggshells, but not these apparently. From small holes, we could see that some had hatched. Others, we hoped, were yet unhatched. We found no free larvae on the mistletoe, but I thought I saw the head of a first instar caterpillar protruding from one of the eggs I'd spotted, mighty tiny, before it was tucked into the collecting bucket with the others.

Being up there in the canopy was every bit the immense rush I'd always expected it would be, more so for having Thea there too. Of course it brought to mind being up in the canopy of the giant karri trees in Australia the previous year, when I'd climbed that dodgy spiral ladder to ninety meters. Here, the crane had lofted us to forty-five meters, but much more securely. A Douglas squirrel popped up beside the gondola at our apogee, no problem.

Once we regained the ground, all too soon, we saw pine whites floating up in the heights where we had just been, though none showed while we were up there. Their exact negatives, common wood-nymphs, zigged and zagged, hugging the long grass. They would never see the canopy. The crane operator, Mark Creighton, joined us. A local man, thirteen years on the project, he came to it from construction cranes in the city. I asked him why the shift. "It's a better commute," he said, "and definitely a better view from the office."

We said our heartfelt thanks and bid our goodbyes to all the lads. But we weren't finished with the day, as another of Washington's rarest butterflies lived just miles away. At Cook, we turned uphill from the Columbia. Mormon Curve, although too early for the fall-flying Mormon metalmarks, had a remarkably late Propertius duskywing nectaring on puffs of blue gilia. Hydaspe fritillaries visited dogbane on the way to Willard. Our destination: the toe of the Big Lava Bed, the only locality north of the Columbia for the golden hairstreak and one of only two for its host, golden chinquapin. As this small chestnut is common in California and much of Oregon, so is the butterfly. But one must come here to see this toasty gold butterfly in Washington, against leaves of the same hue.

We found the site largely grown over by small firs. Most of the few small chinquapin trees were in the shade, but a few were kissed by the late-afternoon sun. About to give up, we checked a small clearing where we'd once camped, and there was *Habrodais grunus* after all. The golden hairstreak flew back and forth, as big as the purple Colorados of my recent viewing. The flybys gave us good-enough looks. Then, on our way out, Thea spotted a shiny chinquapin in the sun with two hairstreaks zooming about it. They perched on dogwood, huckleberry, and ocean spray. I netted a male on a fly-out for close examination in hand and then released it back to its other encounter. Metallic silver crescents shone against warm gold unders, leading the eyes of birds down toward the pert tails. Among the hunters, nighthawks boomeranged over the Big Lava Bed. Unlike the feeding frenzy at Twisp, these were solo birds—peenting, diving, and bull-roaring as they pulled up at the bottoms of their arcs, just above the jagged black lava.

And so, as we motored back to Gray's River, we did so in the warm satisfaction of a two rare-hairstreak day. Actually, we were not yet certain we had any living material of *johnsoni*. As in Florida, before I finally found that living egg of the cofaqui giant-skipper, I now wondered whether I could get away with "recoverable DNA" as a finding criterion. We'd just have to wait and see what turned up in the lab.

Only a week later, calling Thea from Montana, I would learn that Matt had indeed found larvae among our mistletoe samples at the canopy crane lab. And come Mother's Day 2009, a happy stork message arrived. Ken Bible wrote the simple message: "The first one's emerged. Do we have *johnsoni*?" And Ray Davis replied, "Well! Looks like you are the proud papas of a Johnson's hairstreak!" There in the accompanying JPEG stood the butterfly, chestnut wings a-gleam, awaiting its return to the canopy, somewhere over the mistletoe.

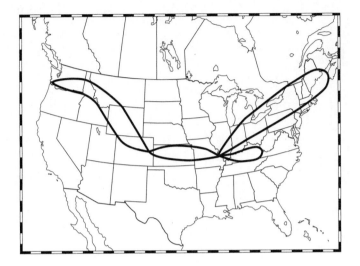

To Kingdom Come and Back

If we had a keen vision and feeling of all ordinary . . . life,
it would be like hearing the grass grow, and the squirrel's
heart beat, and we should die of that roar which lies on
the other side of silence.

—George Eliot, *Middlemarch*

1. LOCHSA ROAD

The pleasant chap at the United Airlines frequent flier call center in Mumbai told me it was raining there in India. Sister-in-law Mary in the Springs testified to rain there too. It seemed to be a general condition. Gray's River made no exception, with rainy days at home in preparation for the Next Stretch. I wasn't having any fun trying to work it all out, so I decided just to bag New England.

Then Debra Piot called from Maine, where it was raining, and offered to bring me back with their frequent flier miles. So I reinstated Maine but, sadly, not Vermont or New Brunswick, in spite of kind offers of assistance on the ground. It was getting late for Harris's checkerspot and *Papilio brevicauda* anyway, except maybe larvae; and besides, it was raining there too. Once I'd settled all this, as if in mock, the clouds parted, and the backyard became a flurry of skippers grabbing some nectar while the sun shone.

On Sunday, the tenth of August, the new-strutting Powdermilk rolled up the Columbia Gorge again. The poison oak was already dusty red, but somewhere east of Stonehenge, virgin's bower cascaded over windbreak poplars that still hinted of spring's sweet balsam. On a scratchy sashay through a field of salsola, sunflower, and milkweed, I reminded myself that I wasn't just chasing monarchs, however this felt like the fall when I did just that.

Even so, I had to pause briefly at the Fish Patch, as I christened a Columbia backwater marsh and windbreak locustwood where monarchs abounded in '96. David Branch and I tagged monarch number 00727 here, and it was recovered near Santa Cruz one month later. There was even more milkweed in the swale than before. So where were the monarchs? Well, it had been a crummy winter for them in California, as I well recalled, and a crummy spring for their coming north as well, though you wouldn't know it now, in the August heat.

A scrap of Walla Walla onion skin, flapping on the wind in a spider's web, gave me a false alarm for a northern white-skipper, one of my main hopes for this outing. I gleaned a couple of whole Walla Walla sweets from the road to have with dinner later. There was also corn, but I didn't want to have to cook it, so I left it for the crows. The onions smelled good behind my seat as they cooked in the heavy heat of Umatilla. Wrapping around Tri-Cities, I passed asparagus, alfalfa, and corn, which spread out like palms in an untended field. Stubbled uplands of loess ran on forever, giving altitudinal relief but biological monotony. Beyond the Juniper Dunes Wilderness, a peeling white clapboard schoolhouse languished in the middle of a wheat field.

In Kahlotus, elevation 882 feet, population 225, the school had a mural of baying coyotes for the Kahlotus Koyotes, and the alma mater, "OAHE": "Barren hills so rich with promise / Boundless as the sea / Land overarched by heaven's beauty / We sing our song to thee. / High above Kahlotus waters / Lake of lively grace / Rocky rims in regal hauteur / Mirrored their face / So shall stand our Alma Mater / Her our heart shall bless / Loved by every son and daughter / Dear old KHS." Of course I had to see that lively, graceful lake. But the road was just a dusty track, the signs all gone—and so was the lake! Just a boundless sea of crops and pigweed. So this is how the West, and the world, is drying up, one lively little lake at a time.

In Washtucna, the Progressive Club in 1936 grandly signposted the town's Bassett Park as a "desert oasis," frequented by many species of birds in migration. A narrow freshet still flowed beneath tall cottonwoods. An errant sprinkler got me. The maintenance man, a buff, tanned, and goateed fellow in his thirties who was listening to Nirvana, came to adjust them. "Getche?" he asked.

"Feels good," I said, then laughed. It was in the nineties. House sparrows, goldfinches, mourning doves, and robins bathed in the shade, humans in the swimming pool. An oasis it may be, but it didn't do much for butterflies—I saw only cabbage whites on watercress and mud. Washtucna's main street was about as dead as the

one in Kahlotus, but the school was well kept. I bet there are some
pretty good scraps between the Kahlotus Koyotes and the Tucna
Tigers.

I couldn't seem to find the streamside habitat where Thea and I
once saw the white-skippers numerous near here. I dropped over
to Hooper, next to the Palouse River, where viceroys glided through
the willows and a covey of chukars erupted from clematis. At a wide
spot with a reed canarygrass island, between flat basalt shoals and
shores, a natty Oregon swallowtail glided past. In 1936, the same
year the Washtucna Progressives touted their oasis, Laurence Ilsley
Hewes wrote of this species in *National Geographic*: "Here is game
for the skeptical. . . . Imagine a gorge with the west wall a sand
chute covered with black rock float. The temperature in the shade
of a willow in the bottom may be above 100°. Quietly you move
along among the blistering rocks with the white sand skyline six
hundred feet above. . . . *Oregonia* is a crisp, sharply marked denizen of the arid wind. He is utterly devoid of leisure; his flight is
bold and rapid. The canyon thistles invite him. Far down the steep
slope, near the thread of the drying streamlet, grow these scattered
blooms that are his undoing. . . . Around and across he flashes his
quick reconnaissance, then for a few seconds he hovers, nervously
pulsating splendid wings over the cloying sweet. . . . If your movement is swift and careful, he is in your net!"

When my mother first brought me to Washington on the train
in 1964, filled with Hewes's breathless prose, I insisted on a visit to
the gorge. In just such a place as he described, I found a larva on the
butterfly's host, dragon wormwood. All the way back I fed it parsley
cadged from the porters on the train. The following spring, the day
the pupa finally cracked to give forth my prize, my cat ate it. I sure
as hell didn't laugh at the time, but I chuckled to remember it now.
The official Oregon state butterfly is now seen as a subspecies of the
Old World swallowtail, with which I dallied Solstice eve in Alaska.

Attractive little Hooper had the look and feel of a company
town. The imposing old brick mercantile bore a glass sign reading "MacGregor's—1915." It last pumped gas at $1.00/gallon. At
the new, 1998 Hooper bridge (dedicated to Sherman MacGregor's
memory) thousands of water striders rendered the surface a sil-

ver lamé of sparkles. Down on the black rocks green with algae, an eastern kingbird made a pass at a white thing I earnestly hoped was a *Heliopetes ericetorum,* but it was, of course, a cabbage white. My late picnic of cheese, road onion, Triscuits, and lots of water, with mourning doves singing "No hope, no hope," was interrupted by a man who stopped to check on me. He worked for MacGregor Land & Livestock, which owned everything around—Hooper was indeed a company town. All the fences sported red "M"s. He said it was okay for me to pause in that peaceful pull-off into the alfalfa. As the farmer-lepidopterist Ed Gage once told me about the northern white-skipper, "I found it most common in alfalfa fields of the Columbia Basin. Very nice to watch as you're mowing hay (helps pass the time.)" Not now, in this field.

Dusty, WA. Colfax, WA. The sun rose and set about six times as I rode the chocolate and vanilla waves of the Palouse Hills. I dowsed coffee and gas out of rolled-up Pullman/Moscow, then took Idaho back roads over the 9 percent Kendrick Grade into an orange gibbous moonset. An even smaller county road cut south through Southwick, the big MacGregor "M" posted even here. Then a long, snaky descent to Orofino, where I finally hit the Clearwater River past 2:00 A.M. and turned left, toward Montana.

I woke to and washed in the bright Clearwater River. Evicting grasshoppers and green moths from Powdermilk, I had my granola and flossed—my dental trials over for now, I had to take care of my new David-built goldies. Then rolling smoothly on Powdermilk's new Dave-installed struts, I headed up U.S. 12—called the Lochsa Road, after the Nez Perce name for the river that flows out of the Bitterroot Mountains into the Clearwater.

Every time we drive Lochsa Road, Thea and I stop at a colorful perennial garden at the edge of Kamiah (locally pronounced Kám-ee-eye) to admire the flowers and butterflies, and sometimes buy a plant or two on the honor system. This time the owner-gardener of Bloom-a-gyn Garden, Janet Cruz, was watering when I stopped. With no rain since June, there were no butterflies. But Janet took me back to her vegetable garden and orchard, gave me mulberries and loganberries, and there we watched a lovely Leto silverspot. Floating in dappled sunlight beneath the mulberries, she faked me out for a mourning cloak at first, then perched on dried-up *Viola odorata* by fallen crab apples. On my way out of town, I was given my second "That's okay" cup o' joe in a row. So I didn't mind spending $2.25 for three nice, ripe local peaches from a small stand, especially when the vendor gave me a free bonus peach after I addressed him in Spanish (*"Cuanto cuesta, por favor?"*). I passed through Syringa, that small spot with the pretty name of the state flower, long gone over. There wasn't a lick o' nectar along the road except knapweed, buzz-bombed by the inevitable woodland skippers. The Clearwater was broad and clear and languid and beautiful, its canyon dry, hazy from fires, autumnal.

Lorquin's admirals crossed the road, but not as many as when Thea and I visited David James Duncan a few years earlier in Lolo, farther up Lochsa Road. In *My Story as Told by Water*, he wrote: "Bob . . . had his eyes glued to the air in front of his car, trying with all his might to avoid collisions with the abundance of butterflies . . . an equivalent day for me would involve driving a car sixty miles an hour *underwater* up, say, the Big Hole River, splattering trout after innocent trout all over my windshield and grille."

Near Ashpile Creek, a meadow with a spring reeled me in. Where there be water, there be butterflies. Angles and tortoises, whites and frits and skips all enlivened the muddy green clearing. Another Leto nourished her considerable bulk on tiny yellow tubes, then rose and sailed around the clearing, ascending thirty or forty feet on updrafts with barely flicking wings—between her flashing silver spangles, her backlit beauty, and flying directly into the sun with my binos on her, she threatened my very vision. At the spring, a strikingly different-looking male Leto hung about with northern crescents, both flaming orange.

As the day ran down, past the Bernard DeVoto Memorial Grove of western red cedars, I walked a wetland trail before Lolo Pass. I'd risen a mile from the Columbia to the eastern extent of its watershed. In the hot, wet sedge meadows, Mormon fritillaries again gathered to roost, as in Colorado—but this time on public land, where no one assailed me for enjoying them. Then at Lolo Pass, where I crossed into Montana, the day instantly aged an hour. A logging road lined with pearly everlasting proved fat with frits—

hundreds of Mormons and Hydaspes clambering all over the pearls in the late, hot sun.

"The top of Lolo Pass," Kim Stafford wrote in *Lochsa Road*, "is a place where everything changes." Big gray bread-loaf boulders, a "moose crossing" sign, and waves of purple knapweed—I was in Montana, all right. Since I was shooting Lolo at 8:00 P.M., there was no time to visit Davey J. Duncan, or to become "satisfyingly subtracted" with him again over red wine, as he had described us in his essay: "Just two half-snockered nature dweebs, enjoying a perfect Montana evening."

In Missoula, I tried to call the main Montana lepidopterist, Steve Kohler, but he was off in the field. I'd have to carry on without his advice and trust to my instincts on my next objective, Christina's sulphur. I needed to start picking up some species. In spite of a rich and enjoyable journey so far, I'd seen nothing new in three whole days out.

Sign at a Dairy Queen: "Chill Out with a Artic Rush." That sounded good, but I couldn't countenance the decay of the language. Anyway, I needed coffee, and got my third cup in succession for free—my open-topped steel cup seemed to inspire that gesture. Arriving at my campsite a few minutes before midnight, better than last night's 3:00 A.M., I bedded down near Garrison Junction, where the Flint Creek Range meets the Garnet Range. And I, like Kim Stafford on the Lochsa Road, "in my steel cradle slept."

2. CHRISTINA

U.S. 12 roughly parallels the Mullan Road, where camels were tried for carrying flour to the miners over the mountains. All the other livestock stampeded at the sight of them, so they were used only from 1865 to 1867. The camels are gone, but you can still see beaver slides in the Valley of a Thousand Haystacks. Invented by Dade Stephens and H. Armitage in the Big Hole Valley around 1910, these wooden hay jacks made of lodgepole pine poles look like giant travois or lean-tos. They allowed hay to be piled higher than men with pitchforks could manage, and with less labor.

One of the most popular grasses for haymaking in Montana, as everywhere, is timothy, so perhaps the next thing I saw shouldn't have been the surprise that it was. At noon I turned up the Little Blackfoot Road along Telegraph Creek, about five thousand feet high, just past Elliston. Right away I saw that the air was filled with golden flickers, as if small locusts were swarming. They were European skipperlings—literally thousands of *Thymelicus*, all over the knapweed, in the air, on the road, and everywhere else. As I drove up the creek, I saw *T. lineola* all along. There must be uncounted millions in Montana, I thought. Remarkable to think that when Thea found the first ones at Big Sky (where I was heading), they were so rare that hers comprised the state record.

And to think of the trouble I took to sweep that one individual from the power line right of way in Washington a couple of weeks before! But maybe the biggest wonderment of all was that all along Telegraph Creek, with its jillions of skippers, I saw only a single woodland skipper, when they'd been the abundant one until now. I have wondered whether competitive exclusion of our common native grass skippers might occur when this exotic really gets going.

341

Here, it seemed, that might be happening. Another thing numerous here were painful biting flies, so I cleared out. But before I did, while still upcreek, I caught a female pelidne sulphur—the first new species of this trip.

The top of MacDonald Pass, at 6,320 feet, wasn't what I expected—completely open and very dry, not at all like the Rockies Front habitat due north near Choteau, where Thea and I had enjoyed a wonderful time with Christina's sulphurs two summers ago.

Below the pass, I investigated Cromwell Dixon campground, a more plausible habitat in the trees. I found nobody home except cows. The Forest Service had closed the campground two weeks before on the pretext that bark beetle die-off of the pines had created "hazard trees." But the steers had free run and showed it with copious splats; the loos must have been closed too. Weren't the cattle subject to hazard trees?

The narrow dirt road along the east side, lined with small, healthy pines, thistles, and sheaves of goldenrod, was absolutely loaded with butterflies: hundreds of dark wood-nymphs, callippe fritillaries, sylvan hairstreaks, four kinds of coppers, and many others. Essex skippers occupied almost every flower.

I was about to head to Butte and take one last crack at Christina on Elk Park Pass, but first I nosed into the group camp area east of Cromwell Dixon. Late in the afternoon, it looked all dark and shaded, unpromising. But a glimmer of green on a slender lens of light through the dark firs bespoke a little lushness, and the flicker of yellow wings that might have been a tanager, or imagined, invited me in for a quick look. A meadowlet indeed lay among the forest clearings, moister than anything else around. A bright sulphur rose up, and I caught it—a male Alexandra's. A bigger clearing by the Continental Divide National Scenic Trail offered up a female, also *alexandra*. Then more yellows flew out, all coming to bull thistles. Two uncertain females. And then a male that was the real deal, the unmistakable thing: discrete patches of brilliant orange and yellow, like OJ spilled on country eggs, sunny-side up—*Colias christina*! Sulphurs are all comely creatures, but Thea and I agree that this must be the most beautiful of all. Now I could skip Butte and ease on down to Big Sky with *two* new *Colias*es under my belt: *pelidne* and *christina*.

On the way to Big Sky, a cop stopped me for speed. I was doing forty in a sixty—why was I driving so slowly? he wondered. Then along the winding canyon road, I saw at least twenty-three white crosses for people in a big hurry. That's why. Once at Big Sky, I bedded down in a dark spot as the moon set behind Lone Mountain.

Morning confirmed my impression of the night before: the development at Big Sky Resort was tenfold over when I taught here ten years earlier. It was a dreadful place then, I thought, or rather, a wonderful place with dreadful things done to it, à la Squaw Valley or Sun Valley or Crested Butte. And so much more so now.

I carried on just the same. I found a European skipperling, near its point of discovery by Thea, the long-gone stable. But the area around the gumbo of the resort was depressing. I had to get uphill or get out. I drove up to the base of the ski run road and tried to sneak past the maintenance building, but a young blond woman came out. "Can I help you?" I gave her my pitch and my card. Ask and receive. "Well, feel free to drive up the road," she said. "I'll radio ahead that you'll be on the mountain." She asked how long I'd be, and I said twenty minutes or so, but of course I was wildly off.

The steep, stony track got me to better, moister, more flowery habitats than the nuked base where I used to hold classes. I drove to where it became impassable for Powdermilk, soon gated anyway. The subalpine basin had things on the wing, but the morning was cool and cloudy. High above I saw the rockslide where Paul Opler had found pale crescents, a species not usually seen at high altitude. I climbed the ski run to reach it. The sun came back, and as soon as I got to the toe of the rockslide, there it was—*Phyciodes pallida*. I hadn't seen this largest of crescents for years and had given up on it for this year. Many of these black-spotted oranges shadowed the rocks, the pearl-studded females quite grand. It felt fine to be on the rockslide, one of my best-beloved habitats, if a little lonely without Magdalena. Pikas and nuthatches tooted their respective beeps.

The butterfly I most hoped to find at Big Sky was the relict fritillary, part of a guild of northern Rockies endemics including Gillett's checkerspot. Plenty of *Boloria* flew up and down the ski run, but every one I netted was *B. chariclea*, the arctic fritillary. I thought I *saw* one *B. kriemhild* perched, but it evaded me on the treacherous slope. These very similar species differ in one having inward-pointing chevrons on the margin, the other outward; you must look closely to be sure of the relict's outies versus the arctic's innies. Some thirty species rose out of the rocks and veg, including a chryxus arctic, one big white female Christina, and more pretty pelidnes. But the big deal came along as I picked my careful way down the steep and rocky run, checking out the small fritillaries, when a pale brown waif apparated on my left by the edge of the forest. It was Hayden's ringlet, a butterfly I'd never before seen at Big Sky. That it was very worn did not dilute my delight. This took much of the pressure off the afternoon to come.

No one came to fetch me after my 20 minutes become 120. Finally down, I walked up the stream at the bottom, above the bloated so-called village. My classes often found *Boloria kriemhild* there. These lush riparian meadows presented a whole new faunal element, with northwestern frits and northern checkers and an arctic skipper that took me back to Bonanza Creek in Alaska. But the only *Boloria* was an innie—at least until a smolder in the damp grass ignited into a silver-bordered fritillary: *Boloria selene,* the moon goddess, my only sighting other than the one Jim had caught in an Illinois marsh. Further redeeming this paradise lost, a resplendent, black-and-white monster of a Weidemeyer's admiral sucked on some sort of gall secretion on a currant.

With Kriemhild apparently past, my work here was done. But there was no way I was not going to Targhee Pass. I dropped down the mountain, down the road, down to West Yellowstone, and west on the 20 to Targhee. John Lane, in sharing tips for the year, had written me a poem about this place and its historical associations. Now I had a chance to put it into practice.

OLD FRIENDS' REUNION AT YELLOWSTONE

Up highway twenty from the Snake River plain
as you travel to Old Faithful's domain
there is a mountain pass, Targhee by name
'tween two historical gents of fame,
with Gallatin ahead and Fremont behind,
friends Gillett and Hayden you may find.

At Howard Spring you can rest your truck,
stop for a picnic, and try your luck.
Access is easy, without shilly or shally;
with some luck (and some sun) they'll add to your tally.

It was July 16 I found to be fittin'
when at yellow flowers they were a-flittin'.

An old California friend.

As soon as I arrived at the pass, I saw how lucky I was to have seen *E. gillettii* at Gothic and *C. haydenii* at Big Sky already, for they wouldn't be flying here now. The season was just too far gone, those yellow flowers all bloomed out. Hayden's ringlet, like Gillett's checker and the relict fritillary, is another of the guild of Northern Rockies endemics. Its cocoa-powder brown wings, eyed with orange rings, pupiled with blue, all inside a shimmering silver rim, may be the best example I know of the subtle and the spectacular mingled in the same package. And we already know the red-banded Gillett's checker. I'd harbored visions all year long of meeting them here together, "with Gallatin ahead and Fremont behind." And so I did, for I had them fresh in my mind's eye, and their images evoked anew here on Targhee by Johnnie's verse. Before leaving, I walked down a two-rut road winding between astered banks and declaimed the lines to the hoary, patient aspens. With my steel water bottles full of Howard Spring's Continental Divide water, I set out down the broad, flat Henrys Fork of the Snake.

The radio said big storms were coming, with highs in the forties in central Wyoming and possible *snow* in Sheridan. The sun bobbed on the Buffalo River, and a shade off a full moon rose over the Yellowstone. I cruised the backside of the Grand Tetons by moonlight, contemplating the last rose of summer as I ate my bonus peach.

3. NOKOMIS

Two days behind schedule, I had to cut bait. I'd planned to double back north and east from Jackson Hole and cross Togwotee Pass, where the theano alpine abounds in the short-turfed alpine bogs. It was the last *Erebia* I'd missed and still had a chance to see. But with August halfway spent, I might have been too late for *Erebia pawloskii* already. And with that weather forecast, Togwotee might well be snowing. So I turned right at Jackson and scurried south on 191 to Vernal for tomorrow's big hope: the Nokomis fritillary.

After a windy night with cold clouds rising, the 7:00 A.M. wind felt like October. Sneaking around unlovely Rock Springs, I remembered the briefcase full of manuscripts stolen from me in 1970, outside a hotel telephone booth in the old part of town. Months later it was recovered in a robber's cache in the mountains—too late for most of my magazine assignments, but at least I got my journals and cheap binoculars back.

The way led down through sage and juniper toward Flaming Gorge, wild country of huge vistas across deep cut-rock valleys and open range. Four dark mustangs and a colt crested a rocky knoll in a western cliché, and four stymied pronghorns paced the length of a snow fence, sprawled across the grassland like a superlong beaver slide. Signs pointing each way said I was situated between Mustang Draw and Antelope Flat. "Beware of Deer" depicted Donner mounting the air in "The Night Before Christmas." All these ungulates apart, the road was mine.

The sun came out and the air warmed as I entered Utah and the Hilliard-Baxter-Mancos Formation before nine. At a viewpoint for Flaming Gorge Reservoir, two pinyon jays flew into piñon pines, as was only right. The coal-bearing Frontier Formation folded into the Cretaceous, fluvial Dakota, then Early Triassic fossil sand dunes of the Navajo. Burned skeletons of juniper poked from pink rock before Dutch John, the takeoff point for Little Hole and Dripping Springs. Across Flaming Gorge Dam I entered the Browns Flat Precambrian volcanic ash. Up into lodgepoles the mauve Lodore Formation kicked in, then in Uintah County, the also-purplish Madison Formation from the Mississippian.

Another Red Cloud Mountain rolled by, with none of the high, moist verdure of the one Scott and I had climbed a short month ago, before an 8 percent grade crawled nine miles down into the Great Basin. A yellow hairpin curve sign announced "9 more." The Pennsylvanian Weber Formation "produces oil." My highway monopoly dissipated behind a pod of road whales called "Wilderness" and "Pioneer," using that oil at a clip. We traded the Ashley National Forest for big mines. At the last hairpin, the Park City Formation gave up its phosphate to a giant mine and its oceanic holding pond. After the Triassic Moenkopi and Chinle formations, the Mississippian and Navajo reappeared, and then the Jurassic Carmel—produces dinosaurs! I was getting close to the *T. rex* of western frits.

Now the Jurassic Morrison Formation, familiar to me from its type locality at Morrison, southwest of Denver, famous for Dinosaur Ridge and the nearby Red Rocks amphitheater. That favorite venue of the Beatles, where we sneaked in to any number of Peter, Paul, and Mary concerts, is actually of the Fountain Formation. Then there is the Lyons Formation—"produces Dale's Pale Ale"—whose pink flagstones face much of the University of Colorado in Boulder, my immediate destination. The Morrison Formation bands them all together. Finally, the Mancos popped up again. The whole mess, Mancos to Mancos, was a cross section of the Uinta Anticline.

At last I rolled into Vernal, Utah, and stopped for some of that good ol' Weber Formation oil at the Sinclair station. Main Street was Valhalla for hawkmoths, a paradise of petunias erupting from prolific planters and hanging baskets from one end of town to the other. Up the road then into Dinosaur National Monument, where I got to use my Federal Lands pass, and where every southwest flourish may be seen, from classic red rock canyonland to white rock cliffs and hoodoos, painted hills, slick rock, and desert varnish.

Wind and water scooped triple dips of Neapolitan ice cream from the stone. Pronghorns cut through the sage above a loop of the Green River and loopy rows of cut alfalfa on the bottomland ranches. At the end of the road, I came to Josie Bassett Morris's homestead and fritillary farm right at noon, sunny and warm despite the Pleistocene forecast.

Winy clusters of berries thrust from the sumac. As soon as I pulled up beside the first patch of giant reed and stopped to look for its habitué, the Yuma skipper, a bright fresh male *Ochlodes yuma* snapped out of the blades and spread his wings on a woody root at the base. No nets allowed here, but I watched it well: big (for a skipper) gold wings, narrow stigmata, pale fringes, fine black borders. Yuma, all right; a bonus here.

In the shade beside the spring, Great Basin wood-nymphs flip-flopped about the gravel parking lot. I put out my banana bait, good and rotten by now. On my first look out onto the meadow, I saw big orange—but it was a monarch, not Nokomis, on a tall, bright pink milkweed. Cabbages and painted ladies piped nectar from the water mints. Venturing into the moist fields near Josie's old stock pen brought me among tall yellow composites, two kinds of milkweed, and short joe-pye weed, which I'd never seen before growing wild in the West. Monarchs nectared on all of these, Yuma on the joe-pye.

And then *the* bright being appeared—a male *Speyeria nokomis apacheana*. It flew and disappeared behind the joe-pye, but I saw it! Would there be any more? Apparently not like Yuma, of which scores or hundreds dashed all around. Extensive reed beds of *Phragmites australis* grew nearby, so no wonder there were so many. The massive grass with its waving, fleecy heads is very close to the thatching reeds of Europe, which are introduced and problematic along the East Coast and now spreading along western waterways. But *this* great reed is indigenous, with its native skipper coeval. A perfect green-backed female Yuma landed right in front of my face. Massive for a grass skipper and nugget gold on top, she was champagne pale below. The males, a little yellower, looked the color of straw (or dried reeds) at rest.

The dozens of monarchs, very fresh to very worn, gave many

false alarms for *nokomis*, but they flew much more languidly. An enormous, superannuated doubletail drifted over. The stream cut a red-dirt canyon lined with blue willow and goldenrod. Down by the water grew Canada thistle among knapweed under tamarisk and box elder—scarcely an indigenous scene, thanks to its agricultural history, but nectarish for all that. Nokomis appeared stage left and almost dropped down to the thistles, but a monarch rose to engage it, darn its exoskeleton, and the frit flew the coop into reeds and water brush. Yet as he rose, I saw his wings flash quicksilver against green-olive when closed, intense Apache orange when opened again—the unmistakable combo of Nokomis.

In the middle of the main stand of joe-pye and daisy, near where I saw the first *apacheana*, bedding deer or a williwaw had made a place where the reeds lay flat. Yumas were all over it in a flurry, like woodlands in our backyard in Indian summer. Then back toward the old stock pens, a huge male Nokomis sprang up and swooped back down three or four times. He lit, but since a cloud came over, he spread his wings to the sun, being a horizontal basker. I still hadn't beheld the glorious ventrum except in flight. Yet I couldn't complain at this vision of fresh, generous vanes as red as Oriental poppies. Nokomis, a denizen of desert seeps, flies in late summer and the earlier males were just coming out.

Back at the cabin, I thought of Josie Bassett Morris and her life here. Child of eastern sophisticates who homesteaded nearby at Browns Park, she set up her own homestead on Cub Creek in 1913. Here she lived in her wigwam—log cabin, anyway—farming the meadows and divorcing four husbands over the next sixty years. I lifted a lunchtime beer to Josie and her grit; to Nokomis, Daughter of the Moon by Longfellow's lights (the female might not fly for another fortnight); to Gitche Gumee, Yuma, and Paul Opler and Evi Buckner, since this spot was another of their hot tips. My old faithful locality, a compromised Colorado seep in uranium country, no longer supported Nokomis. "By the shining Big-Sea-Water" it is not, around here; desiccation is the greatest risk for this species.

Josie used two box canyons as natural corrals. Their contorted, eroded rock walls grab the eyes with mesmerizing patterns. In Hog Canyon, the smaller box, Yuma nectared on knapweed and purple

Cleome. A lush meadow held a pair of monarchs *in copula,* hanging from goldenrod in a lovely cleft delta. I tried not to put them up but did, and they flew into a tree—more usual anyway for the postnuptial flight. Oddly for NPS land, grazing is allowed—a grandfathered, public relations thing, according to one ranger I asked. The cows used an overhang as a loafing place and latrine. Their desiccated flakes, stacked up against a shaded wall, offered ready fuel for any clandestine campers.

I stood on the culvert and scanned the mint stream once more before leaving. Blue darners and blue-black wasps traded places over the algal pool with monarchs and Yumas. I mistook an Indian paintbrush for a Nokomis—they are *that bright.* And the same ancient, beat-up, bird-struck, faded-out two-tailed tiger swallowtail— I'm sure of it—drifted in and nectared on a milkweed. She was just about frayed out but doing fine. Butterflies are not as fragile as people think.

Crossing into Colorado, unable to stay awake on the long run of the 40, I sneaked an hour's sleep in the shade of big cottonwoods in Maybell. Then on to Hayden and past the handsome brick ranch house of my great-great-uncle John Whetstone. He, his brothers, and their father, my great-great-grandfather Elias Whetstone, had several ranches all through Routt County and the Blue River country, sadly lost to the family long before my time. Of course the town shares its name with Hayden's ringlet, both taken from Ferdinand Vandeveer Hayden, leader of the enormously influential Hayden Surveys of the West.

Anne E. Dickinson met the Hayden party in Colorado in 1873 and wrote: "I looked at him, and all the little party with ardent curiosity and admiration, braving rain, snow, sleet, hail, hunger, thirst, exposure, bitter nights, snowy climbs, dangers of death for the sake not of a so-called great cause, nor in hot blood, but with patience and unwearied energy for an abstract science." While any comparison with my own venture might seem absurdly presumptuous, it was about to come true at least in the particular of snow and sleet.

From Steamboat Springs to Oakville, past more Whetstone places, I had to brake for five raccoonlets in the road and for a tiny fawn, straddling the line. Once on the I-70, I had moonlight to Eagle, then heavy rain, becoming *snow* after Vail. At the freeway's highest elevation—10,600 feet—heavy snow fell through wild lightning. So much for my foolish hopes of a little more alpine collecting up here! Exhaustion and snow blindness drove me to nap on top of Vail Pass. I awakened to even heavier sleet, lightning, and thunder. Then came mile after downhill mile through several inches of snow, hail, and ice on the pavement. I could barely stay straight at ten miles an hour; most of the trucks had long since left the road, so I was almost alone out there. Where was Nokomis now?

When I pulled off for gas and coffee at Dillon, the odometer read 377,377.0 miles and the clock insisted it was 5:00 A.M. I felt like roadkill and my eyes like lizard skin. After one more paralytic nap in Clear Creek Canyon, I pulled into Boulder at 7:00 and collapsed in the safe shelter of Jan and Amy's House of Chu. August 16 in the Front Range would be cold and rainy all day long. Not that it made any difference to the inert form in the guest room, who didn't arise until friends Larry and Jean came for potluck, bearing brownies and Dale's Pale Ale direct from the Lyons Formation.

4. DOWN EAST FOR COPPERS

Just twenty hours after I'd arrived in Boulder, very early on August 17, Jan took me to the bus for Denver International. By 11:00 P.M. I was driving a new, azure blue Subaru Forester through a warm Maine night, instead of a venerable ivory Honda Civic through a Rocky Mountain snowstorm.

I almost didn't get there. My Delta flight went from Denver to Atlanta, then supposedly on to Bangor, but at 4 P.M. it was still in Atlanta. The plane was pulled for mechanical problems, and not replaced—the flight was just cancelled. They gave me two bad options: spend the night there, or in Boston. I happened to overhear someone mention a flight to Portland (Maine!), rebooked, and ran for the gate. I got the last seat on the plane, just as the door was about to close.

Black swallowtails dallied in a meadow behind the state wildlife office when I met my hosts the next morning in Bangor. Beth Swartz and Jonathan Mays worked for the Maine Department of Inland Fisheries and Wildlife, in the Reptile, Amphibian, and Invertebrate Group. We motored north in their state truck, toward the Dwinal Pond Flowage Wildlife Management Area, near Winn in Penobscot County. Beth is a fit and field-tanned woman who far prefers outdoors to office. We found much in common in terms of technology (aversion to) and natural history (passion for). Jonathan is that rare and wonderful combination of great general naturalist and youth, the sort of person who gives me hope that the discipline will not perish from the earth along with so much of its focus. I was immediately comfortable with both of them and felt we might have been together for days, not hours, by the time we reached the habitat and set out on foot.

In warm sunshine, Beth, Jonathan, and I walked a woodsy road and slough edge to Mattakeunk Stream. The type subspecies of the boreal Atlantis fritillary, dark chocolaty around its silver spots and about half the size of Nokomis, scissored through sunbeams in the clearings. Jonathan also netted a female great spangled frit, very different from both the *cybele cybele* farther south and the *cybele leto* I'd been traveling with in Idaho. L. Paul Grey, the late silverspot wizard whose son I'd met by chance in the Magdalena Mountains of New Mexico, had lived not far from here. No doubt he had fun with these northeastern species and their variation, but he had to travel to see the full chaotic bloom of *Speyeria* in their evolutionary cauldron, the intermountain West.

Stepping out onto the boggy wetland, we entered a dwarf savanna of shrubby cinquefoil (*Potentilla fruticosa*). This yellow-flowered bush, a rose, hosts the butterfly we'd come for. It didn't take a minute for Beth to spot a tiny male Clayton's copper, and then we all started seeing them, some still fresh. The state-endangered *Lycaena dorcas claytoni*, far removed from most of the range of the dorcas copper, occurs no nearer than the Gaspé Peninsula. Vigorous surveys have been conducted for it, and management studies are under way here, one of the best colonies. The new males shone like shiny brown pennies.

As we penetrated deeper into the fen, we found the coppers' headquarters in thick cinquefoil shrubbery, backed by cedars and intertwined with bog laurel and spirea, pink fringed orchids blooming about their feet. Here flew many coppers, more of the dark brown-and-orange females than males this late in the flight, brighter and fresher overall. They looked much like the high-elevation purplish coppers I'd found at Big Sky just a few days earlier. Otherwise they struck me as smaller and slower, more deliberate in flight, than the common and wide-ranging *L. helloides* in general. When I observed as much, Beth said, "Right—to me, they fly like a puppet on a string." Being a birder, she picked out that flight pattern first. The Clayton's were basking on *Myrica* and nectaring on *Potentilla*, males flashing their dull purple subtly in the sun. In the biggest cinquefoil patch, several coppers might be seen at once, if you knew what you were looking for.

Our expedition for rare Maine coppers, soggy underfoot but undemanding, turned out such a delight that I truly didn't want to leave. The day grew hot and remained clear, with a pleasant breeze and few mosquitoes. But dorcas was not our only objective. My original hope for this trip was to find all three coppers I hadn't yet seen this year. Besides Clayton's dorcas, that meant the maritime copper and the bog copper. The Québecois maritime, along with the maritime swallowtail, had fallen victim to the exigencies of time, distance, expense, and borders. But I could still see the bog copper, our smallest, distributed from the Great Lakes to Labrador and south through the Mid-Atlantic states. Since Dwinal Flowage was really a fen, more alkaline than acid, the bog copper didn't occur here. We had the rest of the afternoon to hunt it elsewhere, and some good bogs in mind, but it was late in the season for it, with no guarantee it would still be on the wing.

Walking out, we saw a Compton tortoiseshell on a cedar stub, a viceroy basking on a maple, and a northern crescent in charge of a sunny glade—all old friends from my recent travels. But when Beth spotted a white admiral on a birch, that was something new. A good look in a classic setting, it was the first real *Limenitis arthemis* of the year. Yet it did not count as new, since it is widely considered to belong to the same species as the very different red-spotted purple, with which it hybridizes across a broad geographic band. It was not as big as the Weidemeyer's admiral I'd just drooled over at Big Sky in Montana but just as striking in full black tie, especially against the copasetic birch bark.

Beth, Jonathan, and I had driven south to Caribou Bog by Mud Pond, part of the Hirundo Wildlife Refuge, a trust of the University of Maine. The caribou were long gone, but we hoped to look for bog coppers on a habitat known as the "moss lawn" by their colleague, Philip deMaynadier. But it was a very wet go, and we failed to find a way into the dense shrubs and saturated sphagnum. So we skittered on to Orono Bog, near the University of Maine, where there was plenty of cranberry for bog copper larvae but no nectar, and no coppers. I looked for eggs a little while from the boardwalk, but we were just too late, in the year, in the day. So this turned out to be a one-species detour. The carbon cost of that wee brown copper doesn't bear thinking about, but such a honey it was.

As another white admiral glided through the late sun, I hated to break up that sweet team. But I was joining another, my Santa Barbara supporters, in their migratory summer habitat here in Maine. I drove the blue Forester to Blue Hill and met Debra Piot at Westcott Forge for a bite. We walked over to the park, where hundreds of people had gathered to hear John and some thirty other musicians in an outdoor concert of the popular Jamaican steel band Flash in the Pan. It was almost all steel drums, with a back section of other percussion called the Engine Room. As the energetic music got going, the dancing began. I hadn't seen such lively action since Solstice in Fairbanks—long summer nights do that in northern places. Coveys of pretty girls bopped away, attended by aloof and goofy guys. The happy nubility took me back to my own sixteenth summer, when I'd spent similar August eves on the Maine shore (albeit with rock 'n' roll instead of calypso) with fellow science students in Bar Harbor, just around the convoluted shore from here. Debra danced with me as John flailed away on his drum, everyone happy as gnats in the summer's night.

5. DUKES UP!

In St. Louis, one warm evening later on August 19, I claimed my pretty copper Mitsubishi Eclipse. I named it Bronze Copper, and we set out for the Subtropics. I snatched a plate of good, solid food at a Waffle House, downed to the banter of Nancy, the cheery blond waitress, and a short round cook with tiny pigtails all over his head. Ray cherished and channeled Ray Charles. The jukebox featured a load of songs written especially for Waffle House by artists who are fans of the chain. I plunked in twenty-five cents and selected "Waffle House Doo Wop" by Eddie Middleton. Ray and Nancy were rockin' along with the patrons. Thus fueled and jumped up for the run down the Mississippi, I boogied south through Festus as Roy Orbison and gray tree frogs dinned in close harmony.

The next morning, at the Mississippi River overlook at Thebes, bagworms on bald cypress told me that I wasn't in Maine anymore.

Before we parted last time, Jim Wiker had invited me back to southern Illinois in August for the late-season cane butterflies. He'd been such a great host last time that I decided to take him up on it. But now, when I got to our rendezvous at Horseshoe Lake, I had no idea where to find Jim and Sally. I looked around as turkeys ran alongside and cicadas thrummed in the rising humidity and heat. Tall marshmallow ringed the lake, mostly white with purple centers, some pink. It was native, but the big emergent water lily with high flowers was exotic lotus, nothing to do with the little leguminous *Lotus* on which so many of the rare western lycaenids feed.

"Seen anyone with a butterfly net?" I asked the campground host. He knew just who I meant. I found Jim and Sally at their trailer. Turned out they'd put up the standard paper plates with arrows and butterflies and "Bob," but I'd somehow overlooked them.

Munching Sally's quesadillas under their camper canopy, we caught up and made plans, in case the rain ever quit. When it showed no signs of letting up, we hopped in the Bronze Copper and drove to the Cache River Wetlands Center. The Cache splits the Shawnee and Ozark hills, the upland land bridge between the Ozark Highlands with the Appalachians, the Central Lowlands, and the Eastern Gulf Coastal Plain. We walked the paths in light rain. The meadows provided plenty of partridge pea for cloudless sulphurs. Pickerelweed, a famous skipper magnet, bloomed beside the water; but the only one braving the drizzle was the least of all with the greatest name, *Ancyloxypha numitor*. Why is it that the daintiest butterflies are the ones that so often brave the rain, like these least skippers, pearl crescents, and tailed-blues that dodged the drops across the path?

Driving back, Sally called "Stop!" for a "Free Squash—Stop & Pick" patch by the road. Jim and Sally plucked zucchini and various other cucurbits between the corn and soy fields as I recovered road-killed swallowtails. Later, Sally would prepare an excellent meal of pork and those free squashes, prepared in several toothsome ways.

But first, in the early eve, from six to seven, Jim and I visited Ray McCrite's farm. We shot the breeze as a necessary precursor to traipsing on his land, and for the pleasure of it: crops, weather, whatnot, and by the way, butterflies. Ray's buzzcut son joined the conversation and amazed us both by announcing out of the blue (had there been any blue) that he was going to vote for Obama. This was a long way south of Chicago, in old Klan country. "I just think he'll do better than the other fella," the son said, "and I'm sick of Bush, and that war in *I*-raq." Jim asked him how he thought his friends would vote. "Well, they wouldn't tell you so to your face," he said, "but when they get to that ballot box, I think a lot of 'em'll vote for Barack." Jim had just been telling me that he thought it would work the other way around.

After the formalities, we drove up to the old cemetery. From there we walked up the ridge into a canebrake, much like bamboo. Between the heat, humidity, and tall, tangled jungle, this Illinois farm felt just like Papua New Guinea. Then, out of the green gloom, brown forms materialized. I could see they were pearly-eyes . . .

but to my astonishment, they proved to be *all three* species of *Enodia*—*anthedon, portlandia,* and *creola*—the northern, southern, *and* creole pearly-eyes, all together. In fact, all three sucked sap on the same tree trunk at the same time! Jim, who'd seen this phenomenon before, said "*Damn,* I'm glad you're seeing this! Nobody believed me."

You have to look closely to be sure of the IDs, and they were tetchy in low light. I netted them all to be dead certain. Among the subtle differences, northern has black-based antennal clubs, while the southern's apiculi are all yellow. The creole's forewings draw out into curved, blunt points, making them easier to tell. All three, all right. Six or eight or more pearly-eyes mothed about a big white oak, swirling, tussling, coming back to the sap in the damp dimity. Two of them were new for the year, one a lifer. The only other *Enodia* I'd logged was the *portlandia* that Andy and I had found at the end of Easter, just before getting busted by the farmer with whom we had failed to shoot the breeze in advance. The soft, cool browns of the pearly-eyes were only enhanced by the dusk. Their opalescent eyespots and violet eye shadow detracted from their charm no more than the company of the gemmed satyrs in attendance.

We heard a gun boom, then came upon a squirrel hunter, who was darned surprised to see us up on that ridge. "Hope we didn't spoil your hunt," I said.

He said, "You probably haven't helped it any . . . but that's the way it is," and smiled. He asked what we were hunting, and when we told him, he didn't seem to think it any odder than his own pursuit. He had a couple of big plumes sticking out of his pocket, and we heard the gun twice later, so he did okay. Jim, who used to hunt squirrels, reckoned he was after the larger foxes, not grays. Rounding the toe of the ridge through the steamy air, we saw a last pearly-eye flitting about the dark path at 7:45 P.M. It might be the closest thing to a nocturnal butterfly in the United States.

Regal moth wings lay around by guilty-looking American toads under the lights in Olive Branch when we stopped for a bottle of wine to complement our squash dinner back in the park. Afterward, my bed folded out where the dining table had been. Before sleep we shared remarkable coincidences—like the time they came here, as planned, instead of attending a dear friend's funeral, and Jim found his first *Erynnis funeralis* in Illinois. Or how yesterday, as I was opening my mouth to tell them of our canopy crane adventure, Sally asked, "Are there any butterflies that feed on mistletoe?" No sooner did our reciprocal Dumpster stories reach their happy endings than we all dropped off.

Sitting on the dock of Horseshoe Lake in the morning, I watched the great flared boles of bald cypresses sit into their own reflections in this old oxbow of the Ohio River. Whirligig beetles swirled the surface of the green-brown water, mullet jumped, and *hundreds* of purple martins hawked the surface, midlake. More martins gathered on bare boughs of old cypress candelabra in the lake, chitter-chattering and warbling, or forayed overland. I had never seen a fraction as many purple martins in my life, all put together. There was otter spraint on the dock; twice we'd disturbed an otter from the roadside the night before, sending it slithering into the ditch. Insects shrilled like fishing reels.

Those reflections meant clearing skies, and a zebra was chasing its long tails around the trailer. We returned to McCrite's farm to work the old pasture and hay fields below the ridge. Again, *Lethe portlandia, anthedon,* and *creola* all showed in quick succession, in interspecific clusters. The Carolina satyr with them was a surprise, as very few had been seen in Illinois. A skippery hillside produced Hayhurst's scallopwing and, at last, a much-deferred Peck's skipper. We had a couple of glimpses of likely yehl skippers, another cane butterfly, but not for sure; Jim checked a number of cane leaf nodes for their larvae, without luck. And then in the streambed—*at last!*—a lacewing skipper! I'd been looking for this natty number in every patch of cane since April. The fancy female sat semispread on a cane spear—number 350, as near as I could tell.

Our copious sweat drew a hackberry butterfly to land on each of us in turn. A little later, a 'fly kept landing on my triceps as I had my binoculars up. I almost swatted it but looked first, and saw it was a harvester! The beautiful mite was taking my salt—just like the first one I ever saw, which dropped out of the sky onto my sweaty wrist in an Ohio wood.

Uniquely among American butterflies, *Feneseca tarquinius* consumes animal flesh. I don't mean that the one on my arm was about to take a bite out of me but that its larva grew up on a diet of woolly aphids. The uncommon adults, ignoring nectar, hang around the aphids' alder hosts and visit moisture, mud, and sunny spots—and sweaty people.

Plus poop. Soon after my visitor departed, I came across six harvesters and six pearly-eyes together on a fresh cow pat in the stony streambed. The oblivious harvesters, unlike any other butterflies in looks, displayed their deep russet, pale misty plum, and pumpkin unders, orange-and-black jack-o'-lantern uppers, plus their furry, checkered sox. Then there were the pearly-eyes, with their namesake mother-of-pearl, lilac, fawn, and taupe. What a stunning array, all on a single meadow muffin. I just watched and watched.

At a pond near the bottom, a mass of whirligig beetles in a silver-black beach ball broke into Brownian motion when a train of white-tailed skimmers disturbed them. I could easily see how butterfly watchers become seduced by the odes, as dragonfly enthusiasts abbreviate their beloved odonates. Small frogs squirted into the water with plops, and green tree frogs took their rest on sunflower leaves. A great spangled fritillary female was twice the size and pallor of the one in Maine. Big blue clouds on a female tiger, green on a spicebush, both burrowed deep into purple ironweed: were they the apotheosis of this swallowtail summer?

At the trailer, clouds back in their accustomed place over the park, we counted up and watched rough-winged swallows and dragonflies hawk a prodigious hatch over the lawn. But it seemed we weren't finished for the day. Sun spots teased, so we headed out to scan some woodland sedge patches along an old railroad right of way east of the lake, where Jim studied moths. Here we were looking for a different race of Appalachian browns than we'd found up north, and especially for Dukes's skipper. From the road, we descended into the sedge marsh. We soon spotted the brown, which alighted on a leaf right in front of my face. *Lethe appalachia appalachia* really did seem quite different from *L. a. looewi*, though I wouldn't want to have to describe their traits on an essay test.

Squelching around in the green shade, we looked and looked and scratched and sweated and looked some more. It was late, after seven o'clock, and raining off and on. However reluctantly, we were ready to give up. We gathered up Jim's light traps and started out, when he said, "Bob! Look here! It is . . . it's a *dukesi!*" And it was. The husky dark dart flew around the glade a couple of times, then perched, and we each got a good look—Jim at both surfaces, I at the dorsum. There was the rounded, black and gold hindwing and diagnostic black forewing. Jim deferred to me to net it, but I took a top stroke instead of a sweep, and it waggled out the side and away. We didn't see it again. When Jim returned the next day, I later learned, he found and netted the Dukes's in the very same place. But I was happy with a definitive look, pulled out at the last minute.

That's not all I pulled out of that sedge marsh, those fields, and the canebrake. Back at the trailer, I scraped and scratched at legions of chigger bites. I rubbed on hydrocortisone cream, but I still had a terrible time trying to sleep with all the tiny mites. They numbered over a hundred, all over my feet, ankles, legs, thighs, scrotum, buttocks, and waist. I'd forgotten to tuck in my field pants in the canebrake. Besides, as Jim pointed out, they came from all sides and above, as well as below. In misery, I scratched and scratched, making it worse and worse. I made it through the night only with the cortisone, an ocean of Benadryl lotion, and a stiff hairbrush to rake my soft, sore skin into nervous exhaustion.

I thought I heard a good deal of scratching from Jim and Sally's compartment too.

6. OH, OH, DIANA

After thunderstorms all night, the rain was bucketing down as I approached Cairo, Illinois, where the Ohio and Mississippi meet. GrandPop brought Tom and me here in 1956, and I never forgot how to say it properly: "KAY-roh." Soybeans grew inside the levee, ironweed purpled the verge along 127. In Future City, empty billboards succumbed to kudzu. The Old Custom House swaggered next to the Dollar General, Sherwell's BBQ, and the Mighty Rivers Worship Center. The KKK has a history here; Sally told me it was a place to watch myself and maybe not spend a night. To me it just looked battered, like Port Arthur minus the hurricanes. Cairo is a place with which time and the two rivers have had their way.

Alexander County is shaped like a molar with roots. At the bottom of the right root, I crossed the Ohio into Kentucky with its many barges at bay, close to the confluence. I stopped at Wicliffe Mounds to change into shorts and apply hydrocortisone. A bright orange thing dancing around the Bronze Copper was a tawny emperor. As I claimed my Kentucky road map, Karen at the visitor center allowed as how she knew of Pyles over in Carlisle County, whence my people sprang. She also knew the lepidopterist Bill Black over in Paducah (Tom and I had cracked up calling it "Poddycuh" on that '56 trip) and gave me his phone number. When I called Bill for tips, he confirmed what Jim had told me, that Kingdom Come State Park was the place for the Diana fritillary. He also mentioned Black Mountain (no relation), where the early hairstreak (*Erora laeta*) used to be found.

In Bardwell, I bought a copy of *The Carlisle County News*, to which GrandPop subscribed all his life. It had the same blurry town council pictures as our *Wahkiakum County Eagle*. I passed the little white clapboard house where the *News*, founded in 1894, when GrandPop was six, is published. On into Fancy Farm, "Home of the World's Largest Picnic & BBQ, 1st Sat of August." Miss Polly Harper, the longtime grand dame of the Democratic Party and the picnic, must have been gone by now. When I saw her on a previous visit, I learned she had suffered a girlhood crush on my father. Now I didn't even recognize the old Pyle farm. As GrandPop would say, "It's all changed up around here." Specifically, there was not a lick o' tobacco to be seen anymore—it was all corn and soy—and the graceful old tobacco barns were about gone too. I once took a hickory stick from a barn on the old home place, used to drape tobacco leaves to cure from the rafters. It now resides in a cluster of walking sticks that includes Marsha between field seasons.

I crossed Kentucky Lake on the Tennessee River to the Land Between the Lakes. The roadside near Golden Pond scintillated with blues and swallowtails around ironweed and boneset. A plain person in a horse-drawn buggy crossed the dual carriageway into his farm, in the setting sun. Passing through Bowling Green, I swear I saw Burnham & Sons, Mortuary & Crematorium. On the Cumberland Parkway, a red moon rose.

Highway 27 was a mess on the way out of Somerset. But after the exit for a natural arch in Dan'l Boone National Forest, the Cumberlands got wild in a hurry. Atop the limestone eye of the arch, like an eyebrow, red maples and sassafras were already turning to reds and oranges, but most of the picture was tired green. Finding myself in the Great Gulf Scenic Area and the Eastern Time Zone, I wended along any old road. It was nice down there in the hollow. But feeling that I should be getting on east toward Diana, I turned around on a limestone bench. Across the road I saw a flutter on a joe-pye—and it was Diana! A male, chipped but bright. I watched it, caught it, examined it, released it onto a flower, watched it again at length, touched it, and it rose up, outtasight. Exactly. That rich tan on the inner hindwing below, like doeskin gloves or a well-groomed buckskin horse, is like no other butterfly I know except maybe *Vindula* in New Guinea. His silver is reduced to slender crescent moons. A bird bite allowed me to see a chunk of the orange-skin upperside; and then he spread, for some time. One-third orange, two-thirds black, the male Diana would be perfect for Halloween, along with the little harvester as its trick-or-treat sidekick. And such black! One of the broadest expanses in butterflies, save certain swallow-tails, even more than Magdalena, with a tinge of inky blue, hinting at the female's indigo shimmer. I wondered if I would see her in Kingdom Come.

As it happened, I didn't have to wait. East of Whitley City, I crawled along a county road with hedges of ironweed, joe-pye, and tall yellow daisies, beside clovery hay fields. There I spied a big female Diana nectaring spread-winged on joe-pye. Her underside was brown on black; above, black on the inner half where the male is, then those clear, bright blue ovals where he is orange. I wondered if they had similar UV reflectance patterns, like the yellow and black females of the eastern tiger swallowtail, both reflecting the same pattern to the males. She too was huge, more than three and a half inches. I replaced her on the joe-pye weed, and she went back to it.

Two of her comimics were here too, a black female eastern tiger with massive bright blue patches and a black swallowtail, ditto, on clover. All three mimic the pipevine swallowtail, which carries un-palatable compounds from its *Aristolochia* vine hosts. Advertising its toxicity with its brilliant blue shimmer, *Battus philenor* gains protection from birds that have had an educational nip of one. As with monarchs and viceroys, so powerful is the evolutionary drive toward mimicry that a suite of swallowtails has come to resemble pipevines to fool the birds. And not just several swallowtails but also red-spotted purples and female Dianas. This mimicry ring has given us several of our most beautiful butterflies, including the wildly aberrant fritillary before me in this hedge.

I ascended the Cumberlands, joe-pye lining the road as canteen for battalions of great spangled frits and eastern tigers. Williamsburg came with a plastic clot on I-75—Wal-Mart, Wendy's, Burger King, and the rest—though behind the mercantile thrombosis, white steeples peered above the trees. A sign said, "Feels like home," but it was no place that Crockett (to the north) or Boone (the national forest) would recognize as home.

Sally Gap Missionary Church, Mossy Gap Baptist Church. "Can't sleep? Don't count sheep, talk 2 the Master." "Jesus Saves—Turn or Burn." Poplar Missionary, East Jellico and Pine Flat Baptist. Julip, Honeybee, Marrowbone; Lick Fork, Big Bottom. Finally to the last two folds in the long Kentucky map, Cumberland Gap to the south and Redbird Mission to the north, and onto the Kingdom Come Parkway. Kudzu was a frilly drop cloth over the forest wall, a telephone pole and guy wire completely upholstered. A sign pointed to Flat Lick, and there was flat-picking on the radio, but the topography was anything but flat. I came to Cumberland, then turned uphill to Benham, a little company town in a deep hollow, where I took a room in the old Benham Schoolhouse Inn. Run by Kentucky State Parks, the pink-bricked, white-towered confection was far more commodious than my usual arrangements.

As I drove up the hollow on Sunday morning, a radio preacher went on breathlessly: "Praise God! Read it! If the Bible says it, take it!" I saw a big "Barack" sign across the street from the red-brick, boarded-up Lynch Colored High School, which later became West Main High School. Coal from thirteen hundred feet underground first shipped out of Portal 31 in Lynch on November 2, 1917; 1,243,000 tons went out in 1919. But to me it looked more like a silver mine, as a butterfly bush near Portal 31 was thronged with silver-spotted skippers and great spangled fritillaries. On the radio, the preacher reamed his small congregation for a considerable time, then said, "Ah'm gonna have mercy on ye, just like Jesus did; Ah'm gonna hush!"

At its crest, a sunny clearing with crown vetch and yellow daisies, the road crossed into Virginia. Black Mountain, the highest point in Kentucky, stretched off to my right. At 11:00 A.M., I drove up to the radar tower and FAA facility and beyond to a junction of dirt roads running off in several directions. It was Frit City and Goddessville combined, sextets of Cybeles and Aphrodites and a single Diana on milkweed, all enormous, plus a silver-spotted skipper attending these faerie queens like a page.

The traffic up there was mostly quads, their drivers tending toward friendly. One heavyset four-wheeler said, "Hey, friend," as he passed, and put out his hand for some drive-by skin. Another asked if I was catching snakes. I said no, butterflies, and he said,

"Ah'd rather ketch buhttaflahs than *snakes*." Snake hate runs deep in Kentucky, as I knew from my father's attitude, him having grown up in Carlisle County. With several poisonous kinds, you can see why. Three good ol' boys in a pickup (two of them young) with sticks in back (for snakes?) told me the ginseng's all gone, too many people pulling young plants.

I wasn't after ginseng, but sweet little mountain blackberries, black raspberries, and tall blueberries crowning the top were all ripe. In Diana's colors, the black 'n' blue berry day threatened to overshadow the butterfly day if I didn't stop picking fruit and get on with it. A two-toned wood-nymph flew over, reclaiming my attention. I'd grown up with illustrations of these vast, eastern *Cercyonis pegala* in Holland and Klots, but I'd never seen them in real life. In an open, weedy field, I caught one—a monstrous female, the size of the big frits, with vast cream patches enclosing bright eyespots that recalled her old name, blue-eyed grayling. Nearby, her relative, a northern very-pearly-eye, had just escaped his chrysalis, his brown wings still soft as silk. His abdomen squirmed and squirted a dollop of red meconium as he crawled up a clover to finish drying.

A clunker leaking fumes of alcohol and tabaccy, and a rendezvous of noisy quads, threatened to mar the afternoon. I escaped down a steep side track, where I spotted an amazon of a Diana, her blue like a morpho's in the right light. Another one nectared with a Cybele on joe-pye, their wings rubbing together as they shifted about, floret to floret, sharing the pot. Diana had dramatic, symmetrical pecks out of all four wings by some uneducated bird. The flower grew crowded as a second great spangled jumped aboard. Diana flitted to the next one up, where her companion promptly joined her. Too near, I inadvertently broke up the tea party. Diana circled, flew into Akito's mouth, out again, down to a red-capped canister of wasp and hornet killer, and onto a bank of traveler's joy.

Watching Diana evoked a pair of wildly anachronistic memories. First, W. J. Holland (in his classic *Butterfly Book*) telling how, as a shy boy in Salem, North Carolina, during the Civil War, he saw his first Diana and gave chase. To his utter mortification, she flew right in front of a girls' school. "I would rather have faced a cannonade in those days than a bevy of boarding-school misses," he wrote, "but there was no alternative." With "the dreaded females at the windows," he rushed past as "the rascally porter bawled out after me: 'Oh it's no use; you can't catch it! It's frightened; you're so ugly!' " He "made an upward leap, and by a fortunate sweep of the net succeeded in capturing my prize." Second, as background music for Holland's adolescent ordeal, I heard Neil Sedaka's plaintive lyrics from a century later: "Oh, oh, wait for me, Di-a-na!"

But I was inconstant to Diana, only one of my desires on Black Mountain. The other was the early hairstreak, which I'd all but given up on when Mt. Greylock in Massachusetts proved inaccessible back in May. Charlie Covell had told me, and Bill Black confirmed, that the rare second brood of *Erora laeta* used to be found up here. Charlie worried that it had been collected out. That seemed unlikely to me, with such a creature of the canopy, but I could see how ecological changes might have affected it. By now, I'd had several possible sightings. One lycaenid was a certain summer azure and another a worn gray hairstreak. But one small gossamer in a hazel might have been *E. laeta,* and a little bluish flicker in an apple tree over pokeberry looked like it, as did one more rapid streaker in the hedge. I had walked miles of dappled road, since *E. laeta* often sits on dirt roadbeds, with no joy.

Near day's end, I staked out the summit site of the former ski chalet, the classic locality. Muffled country music emanated from a cinder-block hut on top, the station one of the towers was broadcasting. I found the benchmark on a big rock—elev. 4,139.247 feet AMSL—and stood on top of Kentucky. Little hairstreaks flew around maples, oaks, and sometimes down onto the copper fern and claret shrub heath of the old ski slope, now an ocean of *Clematis.*

Just then, a tiny, pale butterfly alighted on brush in front of me, just out of reach. I hesitated, unsure whether to look or leap with the net; decided to look, and as I raised my binos, it flew—all in a second—so I got neither a bird in the hand nor a bird in the binos. It perched thirty feet up, where distance, angle, and light deprived me of a perfect image. The shade and size matched a worn *laeta,* and I saw some red marks, but neither the blue-green background nor the distinct pattern of brick-red dashes showed clearly. It wasn't the close look at a fresh individual that I'd enjoyed with its sister species in New Mexico. Finally it flew away, high over the oak.

This was a tough call—maybe the toughest of the year. The butterfly's appearance, behavior, habitat, and locale all argued for *Erora laeta,* and no other plausible candidates offered themselves up. It lacked the red and white stripes of a red-banded hairstreak, which doesn't fly *up* in any case, and bore the field marks of no other species I could think of. I believed I saw *Erora laeta* up there, and when I described it to Rick Cech, author of *Butterflies of the East Coast,* he felt there could be no doubt. But would the committee accept it?

I would chew on this one all the way back across Kentucky, and a lot longer. If only I'd swung, if only it had perched a second longer or a little lower, if only . . . but what is, is. Someday, maybe in New England, maybe back here, I will see it as well as I'd seen its sister species in New Mexico. But for now, at least I knew that the early hairstreak still survived on Black Mountain.

There was no longer any need to go to Kingdom Come State Park. I'd already had high times with Diana, and I would just have to pay for the privilege of not swinging my net if I drove up there. No, when I left Black Mountain, it would be down the back side—plunging into Virginia, my feet and tires firmly on solid ground. I guess I just wasn't ready for Kingdom Come.

Did I say "on firm ground"? Then what was I doing hanging over this creek, one wheel spinning in midair, Bronze Copper's shiny frame hung up on the side of a bridge, in danger of plunging deeper into this coal-country canyon?

On the "Virginia Welcomes You" sign, someone had buckshot the redbird. Winding, down hairpin after hairpin, I dropped right into a pit and got my first look at mountaintop removal coal mining. The first Virginia town, actually named Appalachia, was just one ridge removed. Largely prefab, it looked temporary, existing at the mine's pleasure. The older part had the usual shut-down downtown, but schools and churches looked intact, and there was even a working drive-in movie at the edge of town. When James Fisher arrived from England to join Roger Peterson on their 1953 *Wild America* jaunt, he recognized his first cloverleaf, baseball diamond, and Boston's only skyscraper. But, wrote RTP, "he failed at a drive-in motion picture theater, which had to be carefully explained to him."

I passed WAXM, whose music I'd heard by default atop Black Mountain. Buckeye trees lined the road, their handlike leaves already turning coppery red. I tossed one on Bronze Copper's dashboard. Around ten in the evening, I stopped for coffee at the old Riverside Market, produce and roses outside, hardwood floors within. "Been in my family since 1942," said Vic, who ran it with three of his six brothers. I was too late for coffee, so I got chocolate milk, and he gave me a South Carolina peach, twice the size of the ones I had picked from Debra's tree in Maine, now all gone. "Is it still all coal around here?" I asked.

"Coal, methane, and some natural gas down deep," he said. "It's coming back, since coal and gas are so high now—everyone's digging a hole. Even Halliburton's in here, tearing up the woods before strip mining. Now the river runs muddier quicker and rises faster." It wasn't hard to see in what Vic described, as I'd already witnessed at the missing mountaintop by Appalachia, why coal is seen as a threat to Diana, several endemic salamanders, and many other Appalachian organisms, as well as to climate.

W. H. Edwards, the great nineteenth-century lepidopterist who first recognized that the radically different male and female Dianas were the same species, lived in Coalsburg, West Virginia. In his time, the coal came from underground and the habitat remained largely intact upstairs. But now the companies use the vicious and unforgiving practice of mountaintop removal to exploit near-surface, low-sulphur deposits, such as the Coalsburg Seam. As Rick Cech described it in his magisterial *Butterflies of the East Coast*, MTR involves forests being cleared, mountain peaks blasted away, and leftover rock and mining byproducts dumped into adjoining valleys and pits, "leaving a flattened topography, lingering pollution, and buried headwater streams." The companies' pretensions of restoration, writes Cech, "verge on ludicrous."

Vic took an interest in my unspecified rambling. "One of my brothers did it by truck," he said, "then again by motorcycle, another hitchhiking." With a faraway look, Vic said it'd been a long time since he'd traveled like that, but he certainly understood pulling over and just putting your head back, wherever you find yourself.

Where I found myself was in coal town after coal town. A little after midnight, somewhere on a one-lane ridge road between Virginia and West Virginia, I came to the junction of Panther Road and Butterfly Road. Panther Road dissipated into dirt roads too iffy for me, sending me back to Dividing Ridge Road, past Mary Lou Old Regular Baptist Church and Dry Tripe Road. Hurley High, Home of the Rebels, had a big Confederate flag across its doors. I took another wrong turn, into uphill dirt after a few miles. I found my way back into Kentucky on a tiny one-lane about 2:00 A.M., low on gas. My maps were no more useful than the signs, or their absence. Once more in Hurley, I found gas. The station wasn't really open all night but opened at 2:30 A.M. to get breakfast ready for the morning-shift miners and coal truck drivers. Several white-shirted lads loitering on the porch of the Baptist church (why, for heaven's sake, at that hour?) gave me varying directions to the road I wanted. But first I pulled over and just put my head back.

I awoke in Verner Blankenship Park, where Japanese knotweed lined a stream whose water quality I would not want to find out directly. A pair of kingfishers was either encouraging or depressing, for their sake, I wasn't sure which. They wouldn't even give you tap water in the otherwise decent diner where I had breakfast. On the counter sat a collection jar for Baby Brittany—eye out of place, no hard palate—something in the water? I continued up the savaged stream, crossed by dubious bridges to houses and coal piles; under big conveyors that were all lights last night; past Pawpaw Grocery, past tidy homes and beat shacks and trailers, past Raspberry Road; and found the unposted turn by the broken concrete steps to the church that the boys had told me about. I needed to take another critical turn past the second church house, then cross the ridge, in order to reach my objective—Stopover, Kentucky, the easternmost town in the long state.

I'd done an end-to-end of my old Kentucky home, genetically speaking. I noticed that Knox Creek, the second road I gave up on last night, came here after all. Stopover Mini-Mart, Stopover Church of God—"Revival Aug. 7–20 various speakers." This was a butchered landscape, much like our own in southwest Washington, except mining instead of logging, older and more densely popu-lated, where people make adequate life as best they can just the same.

I did not stop long in Stopover but forged on to Majestic. Who could pass that up? Dodging coal trucks in my lane, I found my way there. Bonfires in the creek bed, shacks on stilts, the boarded-up People's Market by the wooden trestle, brown stripe of sprayed knotweed all along the edge. . . . Majestic it wasn't, named no doubt for the colliery. Folks were sitting out on their porches, whether tidy bungalow or junkyard. Trash, when contained, went into el-evated wood-and-link bins or old freezers—because of bears?

Driving up a road signed "Majestic Park," I saw kudzu in grapey and pale purple blossom. Seven feet high in a joe-pye, a great pray-ing mantis polished off a black female tiger, grasping then dropping one hindwing, which I recovered. The road followed the Tug River, filthy with silt, tires, plastic, and a dead dog still poised in its last throes. Heron tracks and striders suggested that the river wasn't quite dead yet.

Across a bridge, litter claimed what could have been a beauty spot: a metaphor for the whole region. Broken-dashes and silver-spotted skippers cared only for the ironweed. A basking comma showed purple rims but no black highwings—the wintering form already. And in a muddy, rutted glade, beneath the hot overcast, a summer azure and another small lycaenid that might have been *Erora laeta* flickered but never lit.

It wasn't even one of the supernarrow, rickety bridges but a nice, wide, concrete one with low curbs. Majestic Park, as it happened, wasn't upriver after all but right back at the turn. I pulled into it but, finding it nothing much, turned out again. Distracted by another kingfisher, amazed to see it on this smutty stream, I took my eyes off the bridge, turned too soon, and put a wheel right over the edge, with a terrible clunk. Shit!

I'd just been thinking about the hazards of all those narrow bridges, but when I came to cross one, I paid too little attention. Now I was in a right fix, and for all I knew, at risk of slipping into the deep-cut gully if I made a wrong move. The Bronze Copper was hung up, and I was stranded. Folks stopped to see if they could help, or just to gander at the stupid Yankee. One couple left their kid in the car in the narrow road, without blinkers, to take a good look. Fortunately, only three or four coal trucks came along, and none of the near-collisions were *that* near. Four fellas stopped, shook their heads, tsked, swore, spat, and looked at the situation from every angle. They allowed as how they could maybe lift us off. But the car was way too heavy, and I could just see one of them getting hurt, or the car sliding on down into the slimy creek. I persuaded them not to try.

"Have ye called a wrecker?" asked one.

"Someone said they did for me," I replied. "Greg Fields. But no sign of him."

"'N' there ain't lahkly to be," he said, exchanging looks with the others.

"But hey," piped another, "don't Paul Cote have a wrecker?"

"Sure do," said a third, "and he lives raght there," he went on, pointing to the nearest house, on the hill across from the park. "You go up 'n' ask 'im, 'n' he'll surely help ye."

I said I was afraid to leave the car there, one fender in the road with the coal trucks zooming by, so they went to fetch Paul for me, and he followed them down.

Paul Cote looked the situation over as if it were an everyday thing and I was no dumber than the next guy. He decided that he could not safely jack her, or pull her, as the chain would wreck the curved and painted bumper. "And she's too pretty to tear up," he said. So he simply hooked on to the rear axel, held fast, and told me to back up the same way I'd gone in. I was afraid we'd plunge deeper into the abyss, smash the front end on the sharp concrete corner, or rake the undercarriage. But his plan worked beautifully, and he soon had us off.

I was damn lucky. There was no obvious damage, and I hoped none underneath, where the chassis had struck the curb. Poor Bronze Copper—it *sounded* awful! Paul gladly accepted twenty-three dollars, all the cash I had. I thanked him roundly, and we were away, in high spirits, back into West Virginia. A spigot's-worth of beer joints lurked just over the near-dry Kentucky border. As much as I'd've liked one, I passed.

Matewan was the setting of the infamous Matewan Massacre of 1920, a labor battle in which mining company goons starved out striking families and then shot both miners and the steadfast sheriff. It was also home to the feuding Hatfields and McCoys. I met Cathy McCoy in the storefront visitor center. When I asked her if all is forgiven, she said, "Yeah, people more or less get along these days," then told me how one Hatfield shot down six McCoys. Just like the Campbells and MacDonalds at Glencoe, I guess; it'll never *really* be over, just kudzu instead of heather.

Speaking of kudzu, I saw a feud of a different stripe in Matewan. On a path above the Tug Fork, which was the state line, *Buddleia* duked it out with kudzu over the riprapped slope above the river. Between them, these notorious, adventitious weeds created butterfly nirvana. Twenty-one species thronged the butterfly bush, including a hoary edge and a wild indigo duskywing, plus a bumble-bee hawkmoth and a great many bees, wasps, and flies. Why so many silver-spotted skippers? I wondered. Then I remembered that their larvae happily consume kudzu.

Among the hundreds of swallowtails present, a male tiger chased a black female tiger from West Virginia into Kentucky, and a randy male pipevine hit on all the black 'n' blue species. One robust *Papilio polyxenes* was every bit as orange below as any *P. brevicauda* shows. It became my make-believe maritime swallowtail, like my pretend-parnassian back at Boloria Junction. Wondrous, how it fluttered its forewings constantly, nectaring without ever quite settling. Surely this was one of the richest, most numerous, and most memorable displays of the year. If only *Buddleia* and kudzu would stay put in places like this ruined riverbank, where nothing else would grow. But kudzu is one of the most expansive exotic plants in the South, and butterfly bush is spreading into native habitats in the West.

It remained only to see Lovely, Kentucky, and nearby Beauty. Lovely lay just over the river from Kermit. I'd like to say it was just that, and I suppose it was neither more nor less than most of these little coal towns. At least the hardwood hills around were lovely, especially in a couple of months; the early brown leaves were already falling. By a little cemetery on the edge of town, below the coal trestle, the radio played sweet mountain music and the cicadas thrummed in the sycamores above a muddy brook. Lovely, for all that.

Up the line in Beauty, the first home hung a banner that read, "Frog Parking Only—All Others Will Be TOAD." The steep wooden gables of the most beautiful house peeked out from behind trees on the hill, abandoned. Beauty did seem cared for, though, with lots of crepe myrtle in bloom. "Let's make Beauty a Place of Beauty" urged "Your Catholic Neighbors." Buck Creek Old Regular Baptist had a seductive garden, but in view of my morning's performance, I declined to hazard the narrow, curbless bridge over Buck Creek. One Appalachian fall was enough.

8. WAKE UP, LITTLE SUSIE

As the Democratic Convention began on the radio, Barack Obama's ascension was under way in Denver—something my Kentucky-Colorado family would never have believed. When my great-grand-mother—we called her Gi'mah—came to live with us in Aurora, I was fascinated if repelled by her habit of chewing snuff and spitting into a coffee can. Here in Kentucky, I found that people chew a lot of what they call "moist snuff." There were stains and plugs all over, like the red betel nut blotches on the ground in Papua New Guinea that I first took for blood, assuming it a violent place indeed. Any Kentucky convenience store offers twenty varieties or more of snuff.

I had come into one such shop to ask the whereabouts of the Everly Brothers monument in Central City. After a sign at the exit from the interstate, there were no further clues. Tucked away on a brick sidewalk near City Hall, it was a handsome stone with a photo of the lads on black granite, declaiming: "From Brownie, to Iowa, to Knoxville, to Nashville, to Hollywood and England and around the world. . . . Don and Phil have taken the music of Kentucky, as taught by their parents, and now they are bringing it back home to Central City. August 25, 1988." That was twenty years ago yesterday.

Seeing me admiring the stone, Sheila came out from the Chamber of Commerce Tourism Commission to say hello. She told me they have a community college thanks to the brothers. For fourteen years they did benefit concerts here to bankroll the scholarship fund. Now the Chamber hopes to start a museum. Sheila and Sharon were putting together a giant card to the boys, a collage of Xeroxed single and album covers with notes from visitors, and asked me to write one. I picked "Wake Up, Little Susie," as it was one I could really relate to. "They were actually from Brownie, a little town nearby," said Sheila. "But this is coal country, and Brownie isn't there anymore." Mr. Peabody's coal train has hauled it away, just as in John Prine's song about Paradise, Kentucky. This *was* in Muhlenberg County, by the way. As I wished them good day and took off, a cloudless sulphur flew past the monument.

West of Madisonville, I saw smallish, dark butterflies crossing the parkway. Then at Kuttawa, on the northern edge of Land Between the Lakes, Little Poplar Creek Boat Ramp had buckeyes all over the boneset—they were what I'd been seeing. A mass movement was under way, as happens with buckeyes sometimes. I crossed Barkley Dam, which creates the lakes that the Land Between is between; and then the Kentucky Dam on the Tennessee River, as another chunk of Muhlenberg County shipped out in a long Union Pacific coal train. Kentucky Dam City looked as motley as a used Band-Aid, all the verges buzzcut. Sumac was turning reds and oranges—well, it was almost September—when I passed Mayfield again, after a huge oval through my forebears' native state. At about three, I arrived at Little Bayou du Chien.

Charlie Covell, when I visited him in Gainesville, had given me directions. I'd heard alluring tales of the place, especially from field trips of Kentucky Lepidopterists, of which Charlie is sachem. Little Bayou du Chien was supposed to be almost subtropical, and rich in butterflies, including a couple of skippers I was still after. Twelve-foot ragweed, next to a woody slough opposite sorghum fields, gave it a jungle feel from the start. As I entered the swamp, the hot, wet day on the bayou certainly felt tropical. A red-spotted purple coursed by, here where Charlie has found hybrids with viceroys. A motion-triggered camera strapped to a tree caught me as I caught an Appalachian satyr. I don't know what they were after, but they were surely in for a disappointment.

I came to a bridge—single planks on stringers, with limbs nailed up for rails—over the dark weed and uncertain depth of the bayou. Hunters must have built it. It looked a little sketchy, especially after my recent history with bridges. I stepped across gingerly. It took me to a trail into the woods, another to the sedge marsh. Corn-patty scat looked like a small bear's offering; a white-tailed fawn hopped across a halfhearted soy field, her flag about as big as she was. At the far end of the marsh cum field, I saw something I didn't understand, with purple wings and a propeller. It was a model mallard with rotating wings, once wired to spin, but whether a decoy or a scareduck, I couldn't say.

There were skippers, all right—cloudeds, Zabulons, fieries, duns—but the rare biggies never appeared. I did, however, find something wonderful. What led up to it was a gigantic and gorgeous golden orb weaver on her zigzag web. Happy not to have found it with my face, I bent to sniff a honeysuckle and almost put my face in another one. Many more webs, with their great silver anchor cables, glittered in the sun along the bayou, some spun in planes so close they looked communal. Gazing up at their tracery, I noticed a troupe of butterflies flying in crazy chains about a sweet gum. Looking into it I saw commas, a viceroy, a red admirable, a question mark . . . what was the deal here?

Then I found the big attraction: a swamp maple, oozing sap from mass sapsucker drillings. The sap was actually *foaming* out, like a maple syrup float but fermented! I could smell its wine on the air. I took a fingerful and licked it—delicious and vinous. There must have been fifteen or twenty butterflies in all, no sooner honing in on the sap than engaging in high-speed aerial conga lines. A red admirable and a skimmer alighted on Akito's new bag, side by side, and a ruby-throated hummingbird came in to the tasting. None of them stuck their tongues right in the foam, as I did, but they played and dabbled all about the tree. I watched the sap foam bubble out and ate some more. It would be great on pancakes, better than anything they had at the Waffle House. At last an admirable escaped and followed my example, but only briefly, before diving back into the mob. Soon a comma settled to sip, and then a viceroy, less flappable. As always, it was hard for me to leave the party.

I rubbed down and changed into less sweaty, less chiggery, looser clothes, and left Little Bayou du Chien, headed for one last stop with the Bronze Copper. Westerly into the darkling pink of the Mississippi bottomlands, there were still fireflies, even over soybeans. At Hickman, where the ferry from Kentucky to Missouri was closed for low water, most of the fine old brick, stone, and wooden buildings were boarded up. A boy on a bike respectfully told me that all the jobs had gone to Union City, Tennessee. So I headed in that direction myself, through Sassafras Ridge, past a tent meeting, and on into Tennessee, where I crossed the Mississippi on the bridge I'd reasoned must be there somewhere.

The next day came bright and clear in eastern Missouri. The unsprayed country road to French Village was pixilated with flowers and flickering wings. Now on the edge of the Ozarks, I kept an eye out for the endemic Joan's swallowtail, almost identical to the black; but all the dark swallowtails I saw were black tigers, spicebushes, and pipevines.

I paused by a meadow that ran down to a clear stream full of fish, with silvery checkers and pearl crescents on stream bank flowers—I was not in coal country anymore but limestone. Parting the head-high boneset and goldenrod, I finally found long-sought crossline skippers, in a foursome. The last one sat on the same flower head as its close look-alike, the tawny-edged, in a perfect field-guide pairing. Then, on wet algae on a stone in the middle of the stream, a snout butterfly, only my second of the year—just wait. A very small, very fast inkling danced now-you-see-me, now-you-don't circuits round and round a tiny island. If it was Linda's roadside-skipper, another Ozark specialty, I would never know for sure.

By the time I reached St. François State Park, it was already half past three. On a tip from Jim, I was here to find swamp thistle and, around it, the swamp metalmark—endangered in the North and only in Missouri still robust. Going on vague directions, I cast about for appropriate habitat. On the dappled path down to the river perched a gray comma and a tatty old question mark, and a comma circled and landed on my sweaty shoulder, where I could see only its shadow: a three-anglewing spot. On the pebble beach, a perfect blue-green spicebush swallowtail sat beside a blue-green shotgun shell.

Running Deer Trail led to a sandy, willowy, and sunny beach where Philenors quaffed boneset nectar. Their larvae, horned like black and red jester's caps, gobbled Dutchman's pipe twining up the boneset to the blossom, a full-service store. Great patchy sycamores, some five feet across the trunk, depended over the river, purling into the end of the day.

On the way out of the park, I checked the butterfly garden, but everyone had gone to bed. Then, along a dirt road that felt right, black-eyed Susan swayed on limestone pavements—and swamp thistle! I pored over it for roosting metalmarks or eggs, then left, hangdog.

But it was much better than what came next. Somewhere past Lee Pyle Road, I entered the Great Wen of St. Louis. Over the next few hours, I negotiated traffic into the city; found Amtrak; was told to scat by a highly exercised policeman because of a guy with a gun; took the wrong exit in construction mess and crossed into Illinois against my will; unloaded the contents of the Bronze Copper into a room at a Days Inn; got the car back to Budget 1.5 hours late and talked my way out of a late fee; found a bite o' grub; walked a couple of miles back to the motel; and repacked my sweaty, muddy, buggy clothes while listening to a recap of Bill Clinton's and Joe Biden's speeches at the DNC. As I was about to board one of its trains in a few hours, I was delighted to hear Joe mention Amtrak as a priority. Finally, a shower and a real bed, for four or five hours. Yes, even without Linda's skipper and the swamp metalmark, the stream and the meadow had all this beat by a country mile.

Obama and Biden were nominated: mirabile dictu! Too few hours later, the shuttle driver to the MetroLink, Michael of Kenya, was beaming. I made the Kansas City Mule and relaxed into the long ride across Missouri. Rolling along the Missouri River breaks, crossing the Osage River, highballing past great masses of thistles that swept by too fast, I logged seventeen species of butterflies out the train window. In Kansas City, the butterfliers Sara Scheil and Linda Williams took me to Kauffman Garden for sixteen more. Then we sat out a major thunder-and-hailstorm in Raytown with Sara's parents, our dear friends George and Alice Scheil, eighty-four and eighty-eight. Linda and I found a monarch larva on George's milkweed, to his delight, as he'd seen none this year.

After rightly venerated KC barbecue, it was time to return to the station. I'd charged my rarely seen mobile phone at the Scheils' house. Now, on a bench outside the grand Union Station in cooled-off, rain-fragrant air under yellow clouds, I checked my messages. I had just one, from Wiker. He'd obtained coordinates for the precise spot where the metalmarks had abounded a year ago yesterday, in St. François State Park. It lay just yards away from where I'd begun my search—but in the opposite direction.

9. A PINK SPHINX

Crossing Kansas on Train Number 3, the Southwest Chief, I chewed on the bitter fat of maybes, the crummy cud of what-ifs, with respect to missed dates and bricked skippers. French toast and coffee in the diner helped as we rolled across Baca National Wildlife Refuge. A foam of white pelicans broke off a prairie marsh, and troops of turkeys preened in the morning sun among multiple mounds of prairie dogs. Morning's light argued that what I really *should* do was skip the should'ves and be grateful for what *was*. And what was, was big brother Tommy meeting me in La Junta. Driving north to Rocky Ford in his tan Ford Econoline, latest in a long dynasty of second-hand vans, Tom stopped in Comanche National Grassland for me. There I barely missed a small presence in the stiff wind that was probably Oslar's roadside-skipper—oh, boy, another one to rue! But help was on the way.

Tom said, "I feel a donut attack coming on!" So in Rocky Ford we bought gas, coffee, and donuts, why none of the famous cantaloupes I can't imagine, and turned toward Colorado Springs. Some ways west of Punkin Center, I spotted a dense stand of spreading buckwheat (*Eriogonum effusum*) and prevailed upon Tom to stop again. Hopping out, I saw blues, and also discovered one of my sandals missing.

"How much do you love me?" I asked Tom. I well remembered that expression of exasperation with his dumb kid brother, but also the indulgent smile. Tom drove the twenty-three miles back to our last stop to fetch the errant Birkie. By the time he returned, I had found two species, a Texas lupine blue and three Rita blues. Coming through Maybell on my way east, I'd missed a tip-off for *Euphilotes rita*, a beauty with wings the color of flax petals and a broad orange ribbon. So here at last was one for the plus column, just when I needed it. I was so pleased with my find that Tom did not spoil it by telling me the sandal was lying right there on the pavement when he got back from the three-gallon roundtrip, having fallen under the van when I got out. It would be almost a year before he told me the silly truth. Now, back here in Colorado, where our father's family had come after Kentucky, I hoped my picked-up luck would continue.

Next day, after visiting with my musician-medic nephew, Michael, I left Tom and Mary's home on Nokomis Circle with them, bound for the Pike National Forest. Soon we were wending Muir Woods Trail and Olympic Way, all the streets in Wildwood Recreational Village named for national parks and evoking stops along my way. At Filing Number 2, Lot 271, we found the weekend trailer of my niece Heather and her husband, Pete Doolittle. After the homeowners' association potluck, my grandnephews Grant and Jerrod showed me their wonderful fort of deep clefts in big pink granite boulders and lodgepoles. It was much grander than the brown-dirt, cottonwood-root forts their granddad Tom and I made do with out on the plains east of Aurora. We searched the rabbitbrush for butterflies, but it was late at this elevation, cool and cloudy besides, and we saw just one errant pierid.

From there, Tom and Mary drove me to Jefferson in South Park, where they handed me off to Jan and Amy Chu at the fudge shop. We three proceeded to Glen Isle on the Platte in Bailey, where we overnighted. The old, bark-slabbed, orange-and-green shingled lodge looked just as I remembered it. So did the round great room, with its wagon wheel ceiling around a broad log spoke in the center. Proprietor Barbara Tripp greeted us in the lobby. I surprised her by saying that we had met in 1964, when my mother and brother Bud had stayed there, and again in 1966, when JoAnne and I began our honeymoon at Glen Isle. There in the dog-eared registration books was the evidence:

8/22/64—Helen L. Lemmon, Robt. & Howard Pyle—
774 Revere St., Aurora, Colo. Chevrolet 1954 PN4084 Room B.

7/30/66—Mr. & Mrs. Robert and JoAnne Pyle—845 Detroit St., Denver, Colo. Chev II 1962 Tarryall Cabin.

Up the pine staircase in Room B, I remembered the brass beds, the watercolor of alpine sunflowers, and the little secretary where I wrote butterfly notes. A needlepoint sampler said, "Pleasant Hours Fly Fast"—certainly true for Barbara Tripp. In her nineties, she still adds to her amazing collections of Indian dolls, baskets, and bygones that jam the round room. She worries about the future of the place, but she and Glen Isle have many admirers who love this oasis of the old time and hope to preserve it.

On August's last dawning, a crystal blue Sunday at Glen Isle, a little girl was spinning on a wood-and-steel merry-go-round from the fifties, powered by her dad. Weidemeyer's admirals and red admirables visited hummingbird feeders in front of Gardenside Cabin, beside the tumbling Platte where we had stayed. After breakfast in Bailey at the Cutthroat Cafe, we went in search of Mead's wood-nymph, just as Mom and I had forty-five years before.

When Theodore Mead undertook his stagecoach travels in Colorado in 1871, collecting for his future father-in-law, W. H. Edwards, he too stayed in Bailey. One of the butterflies he discovered here was a distinctive new wood-nymph with its ocelli set in rusty patches. Edwards named it for him, with Bailey as the type locality. Mom, Bud, and I found *Cercyonis meadii* along the road behind Glen Isle, where Jan and I now walked. Among pine whites and other early autumn butterflies, ochraceous Colorado branded skippers hugged yellow and purple asters. We tried up into the Lost Creek Wilderness area, where many black, white, red, and tussocky tiger moth larvae devoured milkweed. But there was no sign at all of *Cercyonis meadii*, a mystery.

On our way back to Boulder, we followed Buffalo Creek down to the North Fork of the South Platte. Goldenrod bound up in wild hops hosted a colorful assembly: *Adejeania vexatrix*, a big, hairy red tachinid fly; *Lycomorpha grotei*, an equally bright, wine red lichen moth; and several *Lycaena arota*, Jan and Amy's first-ever tailed coppers. It was only when we got back to the House of Chu, completing my great big circle from Boulder to Bangor and back and reuniting with Powdermilk, that I thought: Why the heck didn't I search those hops for the larvae of hops azures?

We initiated the last third of the year with an expedition for an endangered skipper, one with a complicated nomenclatural history.

Formerly considered a mountain race of *Hesperia pawnee,* it was dubbed the Pawnee montane skipper for conservation purposes. Since then, both *pawnee* and *montana* have been assigned as separate subspecies of the prairie-dwelling Leonard's skipper. So now it is known as *Hesperia leonardus montana,* but thanks to the Federal Register, the common name "Pawnee" stuck.

Almost retracing yesterday's route in reverse, Amy, Jan, her field pal Larry, and I motored along the Front Range back to the Platte, and on down to Deckers. While we awaited our rendezvous, Jan and Amy spotted a satyr behind the shops, and Larry and I caught it: a small male *Cercyonis meadii,* after all. Then Boyce Drummond arrived. Having come all the way from his home in Fort Collins, he met us at the biker-crowded Deckers store at eleven. A good friend and a world-class tropical lepidopterist, Boyce had worked on courtship and mating in parnassians and run the Pikes Peak Research Station at Florissant since moving to the Rockies. For years he had served as primary consultant on the Pawnee montane skipper for the Forest Service—and today, for us.

Boyce led us up to the Trumbull demonstration project, a prefire treatment area. Between the 1996 Buffalo Creek and 2000 High Meadows fires and the 2002 Hayman and other fires, some 40 percent of the skipper's critical habitat was lost, according to Boyce. The Trumbull unit underwent fuel reduction to prevent such a cooking conflagration. *Liatris,* the love object of skippers from Kissimmee to Ketchum and beyond, purpled the pineland between mountain barrel cactus and bunch grass. We walked among it for a long time, looking for skippers. Edwards's fritillaries and Mead's wood-nymphs, an apt pair, followed their different flight paths among the trunks of the ponderosas.

Several skippers pounced on the gayfeather, but they were mostly Colorados. Boyce reckoned he saw some montanes fleetingly; having monitored them for years, he knew one when he saw it. When one finally settled down, he raised a hue to call us over. The fresh male repeatedly visited a good swale stand of gayfeather. I got a long, satisfying look from all sides as it perched on a flower head: clear daffodil spots against a tawny ground, with white margins and sharp black stigmata—handsome!

Successful in our search, we repaired to the Bucksnort Tavern in Sphinx Park. This hamlet barely thickens a sandy track between towering granite onion domes, one of them said to resemble a pink sphinx. In the cool cave of the knotty-pine and slab-sided watering hole, we tipped Bucksnort Ale to the skipper's future, doing our best to ignore that the ale was made by nearby Coors.

I'd been here once many years before and had begun to think Sphinx Park was like Brigadoon—either it came and went at mysterious intervals or I'd dreamt it in the first place. In fact it came too damn close to disappearing for good—pub, canyon, and all. Had the infamous Two Forks Dam been built, that darling of Denver Water would have inundated not only Sphinx Park but also Sprucewood tavern upstream, where Tom and I washed down cheeseburgers with regular Coors after tubing the way-too-dangerous Chutes on my thirtieth birthday; the Chutes themselves; Platte Canyon, the most popular hike-bike trail near Denver; and other riparian wonders. "So, did the skipper stop the dam?" asked Amy.

"Near enough," said Boyce. Maybe it wasn't entirely the Pawnee montane skipper that stopped the dam, when the Denver doctor and lepidopterist Ray Stanford discovered it in the canyon, but it certainly didn't hurt the cause, either. "Here's to Ray, too, then," I said, and we ruined another Bucksnort in honor of our old friend and skipper mentor.

The next place Boyce and I dirtied a piece of glassware was in his own study. After I reunited with Powdermilk at the House of Chu, she and I rolled smoothly north through Lyons, pausing only to admire its Lyons Formation flagstones and to take delivery of a discount case of Dale's Pale at the brewery for the return trip. I found Boyce in his Dakota Ridge home, where Sophie the Mastiff crunched her *T. rex* head into my crotch for a memorable greeting upon arrival. When I was again able, I collected Akito, somehow left in Boyce's car at the Bucksnort. I was also presented with a beautiful Certificate of Observation of the Pawnee montane skipper, cleverly made for me by the butterfly's keeper. After red wine and chicken stew with his family, we talked books and butterflies till late in Boyce's magnificent library, and I ended up staying over. I had a three-cat night, partly to protect me from Sophie.

On the third of September, Boyce and I called Thea and badly sang "Happy Birthday." She was feeling well, recovered from the surgery, and the chemo not holding her back from enjoying summer. An hour later I was swishing the flowered, grassy swales of Virginia Dale, near the Wyoming border on beautiful U.S. 287, looking for swale satyrs. Not finding any, I called Boyce to ask if I was in the right place, and lo—he was in Virginia Dale too, about half a mile away! He'd passed me in Fort Collins while I was getting coffee, and then, Powdermilk feeling frisky, I'd passed him on the road without noticing. Boyce had followed me in order to restore my left-behind Dopp kit to my possession. We plunked about a bit together, and then he had to get back.

Boyce directed me to the Benedictine Abbey of St. Walburga. Right away, near the entrance, I observed *Neominois ridingsii wyomingo*, cryptic against the grass and granite. It is a near-relative of the Ridings's satyr I had found with Scott near Lake City. The Pelham *Catalogue* considers them conspecific, but some feel they are separate. *N. r. wyomingo* was discerned and named by James Scott of Lakewood. We had grown up on opposite sides of Denver as avid teen lepists, exchanging letters in appalling handwriting. Much later, we both wrote books on North American butterflies. Jim found the two satyrs indistinguishable, except that they flew at different seasons and *ridingsii* preferred uplands while *wyomingo* kept largely to the grassy swales. Such was not my experience here, with all of them on open, gravelly upland rather than in the swales. Still, I was happy as a grasshopper to see them. Their subtle clay and straw with cream bands and black lightning streaks appeal to me. Very mothy, and in flight grasshopperish, swale satyrs are hard to follow. When netted, they try to crawl out from under the rim.

The low-domed stucco abbey sat among pink granite boulders, hills, and narrow canyons. Born in England in 710, St. Walburga became a Benedictine missionary to Germany and abbess of a double monastery. She died in 779. From her relics flows healing oil still used by the sick who seek intercession. Her handsome bronze statue here held an oil jar in her left hand, a shepherd's crook in her right. From under her veil, she looked down at fritillaries and swallowtails visiting monarda and phlox at her feet. Women in brown robes and veils like hers worked the gardens, one of them driving a tractor. She had a blue ball cap on her white coif, sunglasses, and a pretty smile for me. Little did these women know what special creatures exist under their benign care.

Life was not as pleasant, I would guess, for Virginia of Virginia Dale. This famous stage station of the Overland Route to California, from 1862 to 1867, was established by Jack Slade and named for his wife. Located on the old Cherokee Trail of 1849, it became a favorite campground for emigrants. Jack Slade committed his first murder at thirteen in Illinois, later allegedly killed a drinking buddy in Wyoming, and docked a man's ears before shooting him in Colorado. He ran an efficient stage stop but was fired for stealing sixty thousand dollars from one of his own stages, went to Montana, and was lynched by vigilantes in 1864. What became of Virginia was not revealed by the state's signs.

Some notes from those times echoed a gentler timbre, such as this from Edward Bliss, an Overland Stage passenger in 1862: "At midnight we drew up at Virginia Dale Station. . . . Nature, with her artistic pencil, has here been most extravagant with her limnings. Even in the dim starlight, its beauties were most striking and apparent. The dark evergreens dotted the hillsides, and occasionally a giant pine towered upward far above its dwarfish companions, like a sentinel on the outposts of a sleeping encampment." Near the Wyoming state line, I wrapped myself around one fine pine somewhere between dwarfish and towering. I was surprised at how warm its bole felt against my belly and thighs. I could see why the oyamel fir trunks are so beloved of the winter monarchs in Mexico, for what Lincoln Brower has called "the hot-water bottle effect." It still felt like summer now, but nights were not far off when I would welcome a hot-water bottle, not to mention some two-way hugs. Pines are fine, but they can't hug back.

10. THE GHOST OF KB

In Laramie, over a Rosebud Strong Ale and a rare buffalo burger, I debated routes home. I'd planned to head north and a little east, nudging into Nebraska and Dakota, maybe finding the true Pawnee skipper, and visiting Devils Tower. A westerly route, on the other hand, past Rawlins, Muddy Gap, and Lander, would mean a small last chance of finding a theano alpine at Togwotee Pass. Wondering which way to go, I thought of my friend KB.

One more kid lepist in Colorado, Karölis Bagdonas was born of Lithuanian parents. His dad, PeeWee, was a Boulder County coal miner. KB studied at Fort Collins and taught back east, bringing students out west to study butterflies each summer. He came to the University of Wyoming and enlisted the Flying Circus, a merry band of students auditioned with a butterfly net. The BFC careened around the Rockies doing butterfly counts and sampling little-known habitats, subsisting on Hamm's and trout that PeeWee caught every day. Karölis maintained a research house in Dubois, Wyoming, from which he and his students ventured into the high Absaroka and Wind River ranges, gathering clues to climate change and grizzly bear predation on miller moths. Eventually KB became professor of biology in Huntsville, Texas, where he died too damn young, just months before.

I was sitting there sipping and feeling blue at the prospect of passing through Dubois without him when up to my table strode a pale presence. My mouth dropped—it was the very ghost of the young KB! Davin Bagdonas was dining at the pub with three Nordic sylphs—sister Helena, bride Marla, and mother Sylvia. I followed him back to their table, where we talked about their dad, and their lives now. I recalled Davin and Helena as flaxen-haired sprites with nets in a meadow at Union Pass, where we'd sought Hayden's ring-lets and Gillett's checkers, their dad a benevolent tomte spirit in the background. In recent years, KB on wheels, they'd been there to help him at the lep meetings. Now here they were, handsome blond graduates embarked on lives that will always be colored by butterflies and wildlands. Dav would soon be measuring glaciers in climate-warming studies. When I left, I was still shaking my head.

I took the western route after all, where it's not just glaciers that are retreating. Ice Slough, where I camped west of Rawlins, used to be where travelers dug ice, five or six inches thick about two feet down. William Clayton's 1848 "Latter-Day Saints Emigrants' Guide" called this little flowage into the Sweetwater the "ice spring." "Today," said the sign, "due to a number of factors, the slough has nearly dried up and little ice forms." And wasn't that just the story, around the West? I thought of Kahlotus's missing lake, and the dried-up Nokomis seeps of the Great Basin, and now Davin's shrink-ing glaciers. Beyond the Sweetwater, beyond the Little Popo Agie and its great sump known as The Sinks, black cows stood beside the sign to Bison Basin. The Wind River Range, with fresh snow, rose on the left. Fort Washakie, where I bought tiny Shoshone beaded earrings for Thea's birthday, then Crowheart, with a cold, lowering sky and rain on sage: the drifters' perfume. Into the Red Desert, which inspired Paul Ehrlich's experimental introduction of Gillett's checkerspot to Gothic. Then the snowy Absaroka looming over it all: KB's Happy Hunting Grounds.

From the start, I could see that Togwotee Pass was a bad bet for butterflies. Fresh snow clung here and there on high and north-fac-ing places. I hiked over the meadows and bogs anyway, and the sun came out. A crispy salad of asters, lupines, and sedges lined clear, cold trickles. Red-tailed hawks wheeled with young. I could happily have stayed, but it froze at night, and I saw only two or three live insects. As I pulled away from Togwotee, light snow began to fall on the spent fireweed. But if I was way late for alpines, it was to be quite a night for mammals.

Not far into Grand Teton National Park, a poor ranger was trying to manage a bear jam: "Come on, people," she pled, "get *back*—it's a *grizzly*, for God's sake!" The sleek young male was eating native berries and foliage, not garbage or handouts, and its pelage was a beautiful champagne. By waiting, I was able to watch him without the crowd, and without crowding him. He made me think of KB again, and his groundbreaking discoveries about grizzly bears: how they depend upon migratory noctuid moths for summer energy in the high country meadows and rockslides.

Later in Yellowstone, after dark, between Lake Village and Canyon Village, I came upon a bison walking along the verge. I passed it, nice and slow, with significant eye contact. But a quarter mile on, a flurry of red and blue lights flashed. An SUV had hit a bison at speed, despite the yellow-lighted "Bison on road—Drive Slowly!" signs we'd both seen. The front of the SUV was totally stove in—think what it would have done to Powdermilk! That pathetic, great lump of lost life and fur was being loaded onto a truck with difficulty. The driver sustained some leg injury, but the bison was stone dead. I informed the ranger that another buffalo was walking this way. "That's good information to have," he said, thanking me for the heads-up. I drove on, shaking my head. Dumb fuck, poor buff.

After a snowy pass, the next close call was a pair of eight-point bucks—twins, standing side by side in the headlights—eyes huge, tails small and white with black tips. Next, near Mammoth, a massive cow elk stood smack in the road before me. And finally, just outside the north entrance, a very big buck pronghorn occupied the centerline. Driving slowly, I was okay each time; but all four of these encounters would have been curtains at fifty or sixty.

I camped at Yankee Jim on the Yellowstone River between Gardiner and Livingston, beneath Leo the Lion, smack-dab in Milky Way National Park.

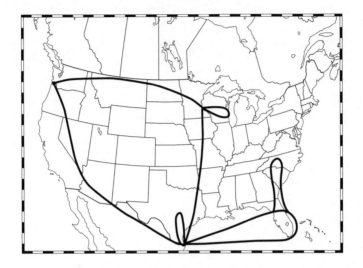

East of the Pecos

The small world of the car
Plunges through the deep fields of the night.

—Robert Bly, "Driving Toward Lac Qui Parle River"

1. GREAT WHITE

When I thought I'd finally be able to resume the hunt, I found that the many thousands of miles under my butt had worn out Powdermilk's second driver's seat. I would have to replace it with the removed passenger's seat. I am as mechanically inclined as a good pig, it didn't quite fit, and I lacked the proper tools; it took me a whole day, but I got it in. When I finally kissed Thea and headed out on September 18, I knew that all this time off the road was costing me species in Arizona. But the ten days at home filled my tank, gave me a retread, and fixed my own struts for three more hard-travelin' months to come.

At Sherwood Campground, the moon glowed red from the same smoke that burned my throat. In the morning, fire helicopters tried to drown out the chickadees and the river. Once under way, as I rounded a bend, Mt. Hood pounced out, enormous and as snowless as I'd ever seen it. Only the weight-watching glaciers and the odd ridge or cirque still held any dirty laundry. Pulling off just before Blue Box Pass to change from cool-morn sweats to hot-day shorts, I put up several Cal torts and a *Polygonia* that was dark enough to be the missing species *oreas*—but everyone was frantic, nobody perching. Lorquin's admiral crossed the road as I crossed the 45th parallel— are we in the South yet?

When I crossed over the shoulder of Mt. Hood and dropped into the ponderosa pines and bitterbrush, the very first blooming rabbitbrush had a juba skipper on it, just as it should. Patches of it along a damp road through burned and cutover woods attracted zerene frits and scads of black and white moths. But there would be masses of rabbitbrush from now on, way too much to check with any care. All I could do was to keep my eyes out for white bits that could be the stubborn northern white-skippers, which I have long known by their older name, great white-skipper. The first candidate turned out to be a Becker's white, a double-brooded species with a robust autumn flight. The next, along a leaky pipe on the road down to Lake Simtustus, where purplish coppers patronized the knotweed, was a melanic female cabbage white that looked like a gray marble in flight.

Plunging into the deep, deep canyon that embraces Warm Springs Village on the reservation, I thought, How did the Indians manage to hang on to such a good spot? When I later asked a Warm Springs friend, he said, "Because they gave up most of northern Oregon." Beside the broad Deschutes River, I gathered tiny, rock-hard pears. I took a bite but found them bitter and gritty; hard to believe a ripe Comice belongs to the same species. As I came out of the Rainbow Market, an older Indian man with a long mustache, who looked Tlingit, said "Semper Fi." A younger man was admiring my rig. He liked the rack, the mileage, the whole deal. He offered me "thousands" for it, plus tropical weed and whiskey on the side. If he could just use it for a minute to get to the bank . . .

When I told Richard thanks anyway, he asked me for a dollar for beer. "Look me up if you want to sell it," he said. Then, nodding at the old Marine, "We're Navy, a different breed from him. We've got cash."

East to Brothers and Burns through solid sage, the rain on it almost too fragrant to bear. Coming out of lightning down south, a storm caught up to me and moved off to the north, leaving silver raindrops and tumbleweeds in the headlights, and sage voles skittering over the road. In Malheur National Wildlife Refuge, fog blew off the marshes on a stiff wind. A barn owl ghosted past, as the kangaroo mouse it was looking for fought the wind across the pavement. Then hard rain, and after the squall, pale moths clogged the headlights. I arrived at Frenchglen at midnight. Just north of the fine old Frenchglen Hotel, I slept well under yellowing cottonwoods and awakened to roosters and woodpeckers. A phone booth stood beside a field across the road, so I called Thea to wish her good morning. As we were talking, a familiar form passed by across the road.

"Is that Ruth?" I called.

"No, can't be!" said Thea. Then I saw Rick's familiar russet shirt and beard. Ha! It was our longtime writing and birding friends, Rick Brown and Ruth Robbins, along with the Xerces Society's treasurer, Linda Craig, and their friend Nancy Peterson. If I was surprised, you should have seen their eyes when they spotted me. Rick and Ruth each had a word with the equally amused Thea. Well, if you were going to run into naturalist friends anywhere, this might well be the spot. They had camped nearby and were about to head up Steens Mountain birding.

"Are you hunting butterflies up on Steens today?" asked Linda. I'd've loved to go up the long, high, isolated mass of Steens Mountain with them. So set apart is this alpine rampart between the Alvord Desert and the Malheur Basin that several endemic subspecies of butterflies have arisen there, including distinct races of the zerene, callippe, and Mormon fritillaries. But it was too late for any of them. I waved the others, well met, on their way.

Pulling up the grade, saying, "This feels like a day to see the great white-skipper," I saw a rabbitbrush covered with them! Or so it appeared. Actually, it was bindweed's white blossoms twining over the bush. Laughing at the decoy, I thought I saw a female, but it was just a big checkered-skipper. A dust-pale ringlet gave a third false alarm.

Beneath the Catlow Rim, alongside Roaring Springs Ranch, a golden-mantled ground squirrel nibbled on a road-flat Pacific rattlesnake. A pair of harriers worked a dry valley, the Long Hollow, up to Catlow Valley Road. As most of it would be from here on out, this was big, lonely country. An imposing juniper sign announced the "Steens Mountain Cooperative Management & Protection Area—Private + Public Lands": the final form of the agreement to conserve this long-contested landform. Skirting the Pueblo Mountains, I cut off the bottom of the Alvord Desert, which has its own endemic checkerspot in season. The OR-NV state line was a cattle guard in dusty Denio.

Through the Quinn River Valley, a long stretch of deep yellow rabbitbrush buzzed with a million moths and flies. The long, straight road over the alkali playa was dressed in shadscale and white dust.

It came to an end as narrow 140 ran into U.S. 95. The best endless roads always end too soon. But beyond Winnemucca, past Battle Mountain, Copper Canyon, Buffalo Valley, Antelope Valley, Jackrabbit, and Ravenswood, a sign called U.S. 50 "the Loneliest Road in America."

The Loneliest Road in America was chock-a-block with big trucks. I turned south toward Tonapah on Hwy. 376, also billed as the Loneliest Road in America. An arroyo about ten miles on produced a surprising fresh female of Queen Alexandra's sulphur. As I was about to go on, a *Noctua pronuba* emerged from under the dash and flew to the window and out. This chunky orange underwing moth belongs to Europe but has spread widely in the Northwest in recent years. Did it come from home? If so, I'd just introduced it to Nevada!

The pointy Toiyabe Range rose on my right, the Toquima Range on my left, with Wildcat Peak jutting across a white playa like a mini–Black Rock Desert. The terraced tailing piles from Smoky Valley Gold Mine looked like the bases of enormous Mexican pyramids.

About fifty miles north of Tonopah, I stopped for a white patch on rabbitbrush and found it a male checkered white. And then, just a mile or two on, I spied a small white flutter in my peripheral. Hopping out, I watched a shadow become the first monarch of this particular trip. Following it, I came to a smaller white thing. It basked, I got a good look, and *yes!* A great white-skipper at last. I saw a few more and caught one—wings nacreous, black border pattern pen-and-ink crisp, thorax shiny teal blue from body hair refraction. They were all bright, fresh males. Weirdly, for the season, that monarch was struggling against the wind, heading due north. But it led me right to the skipper.

So at 2:30 P.M., September 21, I was finally back on the books, with *Heliopetes ericetorum*, its very name a jazz riff. I'd hoped to find it on the way home from Montana at a reliable location called Pelham's Boneyard, two weeks ago. That made a *fortnight* without a new butterfly! I'd have to do better than that. But I was plumb happy for it now. Across the vast flats, the Kingdom of Chenopods rolled on. Came the junction with U.S. 6, extension of Sixth Avenue, the south boundary of my childhood neighborhood of Hoffman Heights. Tonapah was a place of casinos, cheap motels, and false fronts. The Mizpah Hotel, the glans-domed courthouse, and some other limestone solids were all built on mine tailings and alkali flats gullied like claw marks on chalk. Southward toward Alkali and Silverpeak, the first Joshua trees appeared. Now I really felt south.

At the Lida turnoff, the former Cottontail Brothel was for sale, along with the rest of the Lida Ranch: "40 to 3,300 acres." Then Scotty's Junction, almost back to Death Valley—no time for his castle, any more than I'd had for Hearst's, across many mountains to the west, last January. There was a defunct brothel for sale here too, with a pink van by a pink and yellow trailer out back. Then I passed one that was in business: Shady Lady Ranch @ Petticoat Junction. A small tarantula crossed the road. Amazingly, it passed safely between my wheels, the eighteen that passed me just then, and four big ones oncoming. Better odds, anyway, than I'd give it at Petticoat Junction.

Down in a moist, green valley lay a hot springs, with horses grazing in marshy bits that looked like Nokomis country. Then on the outskirts of Beatty, a pink sign for Angel Ladies: "free all night truck parking, pull through for truck trailers, free showers, coffee, phone." Leonard Cohen said of his "Sisters of Mercy," "I hope you run into them, you who've been traveling so long." It's not hard in Nevada. But my painted ladies were free, except for the gas. Besides, I had a date the next day with Carole, or at least Carole's fritillary, up in the Spring Mountains.

2. CAROLE, HOW COULD YOU?

The autumnal equinox began glove and wool-cap cool. Up toward the Mt. Charleston ski area, the aspens' gold matched the rabbit-brush. Western bluebirds flashed like sparks around my campsite, and all up the road too. My first assignation was with pretty Vanessa, as a bright little West Coast lady nectared on rabbitbrush by the Upper Bristlecone Trailhead. We had this cul-de-sac at the edge of the Mt. Charleston Wilderness, a few miles from the horrors of Lost Vegas, to ourselves. But my main date, I hoped, would be with Carole's fritillary, a hometown girl here at her type locality.

The geographic and individual variation of fritillaries in the genus *Speyeria* (or *Argynnis*) across the West is so great, their propensity for converging in looks so puzzling, and their presence so widespread, that scores of species were described. It took the careful studies of L. Paul Grey (whose son I'd met in the Magdalenas) and his colleagues, over many years, to sort out the mess, in papers such as Grey's "*Argynnis gunderi:* A Many-splendored Snafu." In their canonical revision of 1947, Grey and Cyril F. dosPassos reduced the number of recognized American *Speyeria* from fifty-four species to just thirteen, with numerous subspecies. Only three of these have been reelevated to species status since: the northwestern fritillary, the rare unsilvered fritillary of California, and Carole's fritillary (*Speyeria carolae*), known primarily here in the Spring Mountains.

Carole Lombard was a much-loved American actress, the most highly paid Hollywood star of the 1930s, and happily married to Clark Gable. On her way home from a midwestern benefit on behalf of War Bonds, at age thirty-three, she perished in the crash of TWA Flight 3 on January 16, 1942. Owing to a navigation error, the DC-3 plowed into Double Gap Peak near Mt. Potosi, thirty-two

398

miles southwest of Las Vegas. When, later the same year, dosPassos and Grey described what they then considered a new subspecies of *Speyeria coronis* from a little way north of there, they named it for Carole Lombard. It was her butterfly avatar I was hoping to meet today.

I walked a ways on the Mt. Charleston trail to admire the bristlecone pines, some of the oldest organisms anywhere. The hillside was fenced and interpreted for the Mt. Charleston blue (*Plebejus shasta charlestonensis*) and its host plant, Torrey's milkvetch. Stakes showed suspected larval diapause sites. Maybe I could have found one, but I didn't want to disturb the butterfly, the plant, or the research. Shouldn't I get half a point for being in the presence of diapausing endangerees, like this, the Palos Verdes blue, and the Cloudcroft checkerspot? Including the Charleston blue, there were twenty-seven endemics recorded there, including Charleston pussytoes, Clokey catchfly, Clokey mountain sage, hidden ivesia, and Charleston tansy.

Down to Deer Canyon, then, in search of Carole's frit. A triangle of other russets bellied up to a full-bore rabbitbrush inside the closed portico of the ski area: a flaming zephyr anglewing, a big pale California tortoiseshell, and a red-bummed bumblebee. A Clark's nutcracker screamed from a long-needle pine. At Deer Creek Road, with its far views over the desert eastward and its seabed dolomite cliffs, I saw a possible fritillary, and a small, fresh, but truncated mourning cloak nectaring on *Chrysothamnus*. As its wings opened and closed, the blue spots went orchid at just the right angle to the sun. Importune as I might, no further frits appeared.

The Hilltop campground had showers, my first in five days. So at midday I stood hugely refreshed, listening to white-breasted nuthatches wittering and nickering all over the ponderosa pines of the deserted campground. I was glad to be there on Monday, as weekends can be a zoo when Vegas refugees pour in for a little cool and real green. At 8,500 feet, it *was* cool, while 88°F down in Las Vegas. By a creeklet, a threesome of the Vanessa sisters—little Annabella, big Cynthia (*cardui*), and showing her red garters, Atalanta—tippling on rabbitbrush, of course.

George Austin was my guide here, through his "Definitive Destinations" piece on the Spring Mountains. He'd found Kyle Creek, lower and flowerier, to have a lot more butterflies than Lee Canyon, where I'd come from. In the campground, I found a new beauty, the Arizona sister, sipping at sand. Charlotte, the camp host, lived modestly in a small camper. She had noticed the sisters but not really looked at them or come to know them by name. I showed her a stunner. At the top of the canyon, 9,600 feet, I found a lodge, cabins, a couple of Indians selling jewelry, and an unseemly number of casino gangsters' manses plunked among the white crags for a national recreation area. The Spring Mountains had offered up Vanessas, Antiopa, and sisters, but no Carole! *She* stood me up.

I coasted down to the 95, all the way to the city limits of the dreaded Las Vegas. I managed to skirt it on the dark and deserted 215 western belt road, with high views over the lurid, leering Strip. Red Rock Canyon road led to surprising Blue Diamond, with no casino, no subdivision, and dark skies. How they must fuss and fight to keep it that way.

Near the summit of the pass at Mountain Springs, on the south side of the Spring range, I camped rough in a bulldozed no-man's-land. Across a hedge, a fancy gated community had its sprinklers on, of all times and places in the water history of the West. For a weary while, I'd woven among the deep dust of worn dirt roads around the edges of this strange, formless settlement, but those places seemed sinister. I was afraid of getting stuck, or found by someone I didn't want to find me. This unlovely spot seemed safe, at least, right near the gate of the rich, who might call the sheriff but would not be inclined to bother me themselves. Still, as the British writer Roger Deakin put it in *Wildwood*, "I roosted in that instinctive blend of weariness and vigilance familiar to the unofficial camper."

After a shaggy sleep, I left my spot at 7:00 A.M. to try to find the places George Austin wrote about for Mojave giant-skippers. I set out right away, without breakfast, to try to catch them cold and torpid. But it was I who was cold and torpid, as I walked out among the abundant yuccas on the flat over the top of the pass, on the north side of the highway. It wasn't until I reached the first band of rock that I saw the small, curve-leaved, sharp-pronged agave that is *Agathymus alliae*'s host plant.

Utah agave, with leaves a few inches to a foot tall, were easy to spot by their six- or ten-foot spent stalks. Few on the lower rocks, they increased along successively higher layers, and the Mojave giant-skippers were supposed to perch on rock walls. So I climbed, more than I'd expected when I left the car with my black sweatshirt on. I was afraid I'd heat up pretty fast with the exertion and the advancing sun, but a breeze kept me cool until I dropped over the summit of the mountain to the lee. I walked around the top for a couple of hours, taking false alarms from grasshoppers and tarantula hawks. Coloro black swallowtails performed aerobatics with checkered whites. I finally caught a tiny male *Papilio polyxenes coloro*—maybe the smallest swallowtail I've ever netted—on a left-handed wing shot with Marsha. Described by Wright in 1909 as a distinct species and thought by Comstock to be a subspecies of the anise swallowtail, this mostly yellow butterfly is now understood to be a southwestern race of the eastern black swallowtail.

The first orange I saw, also hilltopping, was too small and slow for a giant-skipper. Mercifully it perched, and I got a good look. It was an Arachne checkerspot, a Colorado favorite of mine that I'd all but given up on finding. Arachne, of course, was the peasant girl turned into Spider by Minerva, who resented her weaving skills. This very place is the type locality of *Poladryas arachne expedita,* an endemic subspecies described by George Austin. I managed to net a fairly fresh, pale male. The pattern of dots and dashes on this butterfly's wings suggested a spider web to W. H. Edwards, who named the species in 1869.

But no sign of the Mojave skippers! I saw both a loggerhead shrike on an agave wand and a flycatcher in a juniper and wished them both more luck finding the nice big bite of an *Agathymus* than I'd had; if only I could watch and glean the leftovers. But there were none, and I finally had to go. Working my way down, I angled over to the largest rock face on the northeast edge of the mountain. Nada. By this time I was very thirsty, and I had brought no water. Overripe fruits hung from the cacti. I gathered half a dozen prickly pears, and, being careful not to get the glochids in my mouth, I inverted them, squeezed the mushy flesh, and sucked the juice—very tasty and surprisingly refreshing. The purple juice ran down and stained my T-shirt, jeans, hands, and beard, as well as my net and binos. The stains stayed with me for the rest of the trip. Of course, I had some spine tips here and there to remind me too, for the next several days.

I followed a small juniper wash back to Powdermilk. After gobbling a little granola and draining a water bottle, I crossed the highway to check out the arroyo, in case any giant-skippers had come off the hill to moisture on the earth and limestone walls. No go, but a brilliancy at rabbitbrush turned out to be the big fall *autumnalis* type of a Mormon metalmark. A pygmy-blue in the same wash was the smallest I'd ever seen, perhaps the tiniest butterfly of all.

I was alarmed to find a big wet spot under the car's rear end. Dropping to my belly on the hot gravel, I saw that gasoline was leaking out of the pipe from the filling hole to the tank. What was *that*? I repressed an image, right out of Dante, of a Honda shop in Vegas. When I opened the cap, gasoline gushed all over. After it stopped, the drip stopped too. I guess, having been filled up down at Blue Diamond last night, then sitting in the sun at the summit, the gas line had expanded with the elevation and rising warmth; and the pressure caused the leak and the surge. It seemed okay now, to my immense relief.

I drove the mile up to Mountain Springs, an odd place whose roads are mostly gravel and end at gates. A buckeye drank beside an algae-slimed waterhead. Agave stuck up from the hillside, and more buckeyes of the nice, violetish fall form coursed the dry creek bed. Around the bend, actual moisture seeped up in the sand, supporting big beds of blooming mint. At a patch of mud, a dozen or more northern white-skippers puddled along with some of their smaller checkered-skipper cousins. Cream and brown undersides blended like foam on a latte. I angled up the agave hill to a high rock wall for one more giant-skipper check. The difficult scramble down rewarded me with a skipper all right—an orange skipperling, its wingspan briefer than a giant's antenna.

By then I was beat and thirsty, so I dropped into the Mountain Springs Saloon for one Bass and a second, third, and fourth tankard of ice water, out on the patio. Harley bikers were at their beer, as white-skippers and ceraunus blues chugged their own poison at a wet spot by the parking lot. From there I proceeded to Red Rock Canyon National Conservation Area and drove its scenic loop past the strawberry shortcake of the Calico Hills. The road hummed with after-work bicyclists, impatient with my speed.

Down the 215 to the 515, I evaded Las Vegas to the south. If missing *carolae* and *alliae* stung, managing to miss both Pahrump and Vegas was sweet success. Now, where to spend the night? I tried Boulder City, where I had paused in late winter after coming off snowy heights that today were dripping warm. But the so-called rest area there said "no overnight." So down to Needles I drove, across the Colorado into Arizona, and on to the real rest area at Yucca. Yucca: scene of last April's broken date with the Pima orangetips, another heartbreak. Oh, these inconstant butterflies.

3. HAVASU-GILA

London Bridge Road went on forever through the arid outskirts of Lake Havasu City, but not actually to the bridge. A roadrunner crossed too close in front of me into Havasu National Wildlife Refuge, doubtless a better place for it, and potential home of Wright's metalmark and MacNeill's sootywing.

I tried to get down to the Colorado River at Cattail Cove, but state parks wanted ten dollars just to access the shore. The canyon was unspeakably hot and dry with zero nectar. Bill Williams River National Wildlife Refuge seemed a better bet. The manager, Dick Gilbert, gave me the butterfly list, including thirteen species no longer found elsewhere on the Lower Colorado, compiled by Peter Brussard of the University of Nevada at Reno. Pete has studied butterflies and global warming, which was already here at Bill Williams, at 100°F. The headquarters trails, planted with natives and drip-irrigated, gave up only a couple of pygmy-blues on a shred of a tough yellow daisy; but I was taken aback at still more butterfly interpretation, after an utter absence of such information on the public lands just a few years ago.

The steep, dirt Bill Williams River Road bid me up-canyon. Mosquito Flats, even in this torrid, dry regime, lived up to its name. All reeds at its mouth, the river watered impressive galleries of white-trunked Fremont cottonwoods farther up. I walked back into the bosque, where there were no mosquitoes, or butterflies, it seemed—just the generous cottonwoods, real willows, creek willows (*Baccharis*), and lots of tamarisk.

As I stepped into a sunny slant of light, a tiny brown mote flew up through it, butterflylike. It was a metalmark! Perched and spread, it revealed itself not as the rare Wright's but as a fatal metalmark (*Calephelis nemesis*), whose host plant is none other than the *Baccharis*. Half a dozen of the thumbnail-size males lekked in a sunny glade. They rose, engaged, circled the sun shafts up into the cottonwoods; then descended, parted, and perched, only to do it all over again. Metallic marks glinting, they made a spectacle quite out of proportion to their size, as a western brush lizard watched from a cottonwood trunk, leaped to the ground, and clattered off through the crispy leaves.

Coming down the Colorado, I found myself among rough and tumbled country where the Mojave and Sonoran deserts meet among red and black spikes and horns, mesas and walls, saguaros, chollas, and ocotillos. Now I really was south. Trailer towns and resorts lined the riverside all along. I took a nice room at a motel in Parker, for my first night's sleep in a bed since I'd left home. Ruberto's hole in the wall furnished a perfect plateful of taquitos, fish, carne asada, and lengua, for five dollars.

Bailowitz and Brodkin's guide to butterfly hot spots in Arizona led me to the Indian Agency of the Colorado River Reservation. The "fogfruit fields" mentioned in the book had been mowed, but water spouted from a valve in a concrete block, and the flooded grass soothed my poor goathead-punctured feet. No weed seeds are more vicious on tender skin than goatheads (*Tribulus terrestris*), unless they be sandburs (*Cenchrus*), which graced the recommended alfalfa fields near the river. But there were butterflies on the lucerne, and a bino scan revealed a black checker splashed with orange soda. I had found the California patch, one of the Lower Colorado specialties; and as it was number 365, I'd hit the one-a-day mark for the whole year.

I stepped out on a footbridge over a gushing concrete aqueduct. Inviting but lethal, this torrent was Colorado River water sucked out for arid land enormities such as Phoenix, Las Vegas, and Los Angeles. In the agency, where I asked for and was given cold water, the secretary told me that the saturated lawns were just overflow, the pressure so great in the pipes from the aqueduct. Water around there is feast or thirst. A Manitou-sent breeze over the rez blew hot but welcome breath.

Before leaving the river, I checked the Bill Williams once more. I found a strip of blooming *Bebbia*, foodplant for Wright's metalmark, under a cliff. Both the shrubs and the butterflies took advantage of the shade. Three more California patches sucked at the sweet bush, along with an Arizona powdered-skipper. The mothy *Systasea zampa* perched with its pinked wings flat-out, just as metalmarks do. It wasn't Wright's, but it wasn't wrong: a fine new species. It would have been nice if the frassy units lining *Bebbia* stems were larval feeding chambers of *C. wrighti,* but they belonged to someone else.

The sun was still fierce at 5:00. The thermometer boiled up to 108°F. At 7:30, passing into a pocket of cool air that smelled of peppermint, with ice water, an apple from Pelham's Boneyard, and the Navajo station on the radio, I was a happy man. I loved listening to powwow music and the news in Navajo. The next Depression was being averted by the Big Bailout, Sarah Palin was making a spectacle, McCain and Obama were to debate tomorrow if McCain showed up, and I couldn't understand a blessed word in Navajo. The butterflies didn't give a frass pellet about any of it.

The calendar moved inexorably on. I wanted to detour north to Prescott, *fide* Bailowitz and Brodkin, to look for Apache skippers among high, cool pines. But I decided instead to highball it through Phoenix, Beast of the Desert, by night; then on to Superior, to be in place for Boyce Thompson Arboretum on Friday instead of Saturday, which was bound to be crowded. Before crossing the Harquahala Plains, I stopped for coffee, two Fig Newtons, and two big ice waters, sixty-nine cents, sold by the third woman I'd seen styling her hair after Sarah P. Masses of snazzy grasshoppers, crickets, and beetles flocked the store's entrance, their orientation disturbed by the lights. Sixty miles out, crossing the Hassayampa River, I lost Indian radio.

Phoenix was steeped in 93°F at 10:30, and Mesa had fifteen exits, after an hour of conurbation already. At last I escaped the freeway and the battalions of trucks, many more westbound than going my way. I reached Superior by midnight. In the mini-mart, the clerk was munching sunflower seeds. Aida admired my butterfly T-shirt. "I *love* butterflies," she said. "I want to get a swallowtail tattoo." I told her she could see bunches of them, just up the road at the arboretum, where she'd never been.

In a little rest area near the edge of town, a scrappy Chihuahua skittered lopsided along the sidewalk, pooped, scratched earth, barked, and skittered back again. Then a large darkling beetle came along, its speed and gait much the same as the dog's. The night was marginal, between trucks and the Chihuahua trying to drive a boxer away; the boxer just stood and looked at it. The beetle did not get involved.

On the ever-present rabbitbrush next to the park, a bordered patch greeted the next day, making two new patches in two days. At Boyce Thompson Arboretum, I spoke with Director of Education Chris Kline, a student of migrating monarchs in the Southwest. We went through the butterfly checklist and he suggested spots, but he couldn't go out with me, as he had a busy day ahead. Equipped with water, sunscreen, and fruit, I headed out into the swirl of butterflies, especially sulphurs of various kinds. What seemed to be a small pale dogface was my first Mexican yellow. Empress Leilia, athwart a beavertail pad, checked in as the next novelty, one of hundreds I'd see along with a few hackberry emperors around the many *Celtis* trees.

Now here was a butterfly garden worth the name: what a change, after recent weeks, to be immersed among hundreds of butterflies, many of them cloudless sulphurs. The demonstration garden shimmered with scores of Philenors in the lantana, so many I could hear them fluttering like monarchs in Mexico, and mirrored if not mimicked by phainopeplas making their Lash La Rue sounds. Three small gemstones shared a single three-petaled yellow flower with a snout—pygmy-blue, Palmer's metalmark, and elada checkerspot—*Texola elada*, brand-new. A big autumn Mormon metalmark sat there too, in the same field of view as Palmer's, inches apart, both distinctly bigger and different from the same kinds in spring: this was *Apodemia* 101, right there in the garden. Here was a northern white-skipper, but wait . . . what was that one? Why, it was *Heliopyrgus domicella*, Erichson's white-skipper, in the same bed of *Bidens*. Another Arizona powdered-skipper spread its wings on a Rocky Point ice plant.

Blue-tailed stripy skinks, spiny lizards, and lots of little brown ones skittered everywhere. The day reached 100°F, but there was shade. One monarch—for all the hundreds of queens—spread on a mesquite. I came to a stone hut built into the cliff, the Hobbity, vine-hung Clevenger House. A family of five lived in it from about 1900 to the 1920s, working a truck farm in the valley. Thompson bought their holding and used their abode as a playhouse for his kids. Now the staff dried and displayed herbs there and used it as a cool refuge, which it was for me too—with a water fountain, even. What fun the Clevenger and Thompson children must have had playing here!

As the trail ascended the canyon, many-armed saguaros reached up against the creviced pink cliffs. A wooden suspension bridge crossed the dry wash of Queen Creek to the Cliffs of Xami. And there, right along the High Trail under the cliff, beyond the rock pool (in spring) where Chris said I should look, the first Xami hairstreak flashed by. The colors of both golden and Sandia hairstreaks, it was smaller and fancier than either. I was able to watch it nectaring on a tiny white fleabane. The underside showed the gold and the green along with lavender, russet, and blue, with a double-peaked white stripe and elaborate tails. Another perched on the tip of a short shrub with birchy leaves, as Chris said it would, and sawed its hindwings. It had been bird-struck on the left side. I had a fine time with at least four of the highly restricted, seldom seen Xamis, from my perch on the butt-molded, concrete bench set into the cliff by the imaginative Thompson.

His own winter home, PicketPost House, was built on the rock top across the canyon. Gracious but not extravagant, it was confected of stucco and tile with bowed windows. Thompson, a mining promoter, financial magnate, and Red Cross officer, owned the Magma Copper Mine near here. A trip to Russia in 1917; concern over damage from mining, logging, and overgrazing; and a keen interest in botany all inspired his belief that wise plant use could help solve global food problems. He determined to establish "the most beautiful and useful garden of its kind in the world"—and a darned good butterfly spot, as it happened. I stayed until I figured out that a pair of indulgent young rangers on a golf cart were waiting for me to leave so they could go home themselves.

I adjourned to a bar in the largely boarded-up, beat-up Superior, which throve during the heyday of Boyce Thompson's Magma Copper Mine. I attempted to "hear" the presidential debate between loud CDs and semiprogressive lectures from the barkeep, who liked 1955, minus the racism. I asked the black barmaid to lower the volume on the music so we could hear the debate, but she seemed less than riveted by it. Most of the clientele was oblivious, never mind McCain was their senator, out in the beer garden. Cooled off, I drove up into the Tonto National Forest and camped at Oak Flat, off Magma Copper Mine Road.

I slept hard and secure in the cool mountain air. At eight Saturday, I rose to warming sun and a scene of sunflowers, buckwheats, and jimsonweed, with pygmy-blues and Philenors out my door. An Arizona sister circled about its Arizona white oak as if guarding the campsite. I ranged about after breakfast, but all the butterflies were old friends, and it was already close to 100°F by the time I broke camp.

In Miami, I ditched my aluminum. The recycler Reville Evancs ("Call me Rev!") told me about cars, scrap, cans, and his grandma's turquoise, some of which he wore, big nineteenth-century lumps worth thousands. A fella wanted one that his grandma didn't find, worth around $12,500. Rev said he'd take a big truck with certain specs for it. Tailings lay all about. "The big days of mining are dead here," he said, "but scrapping is strong." Turquoise too, apparently. "Copper & Cattle, Where the West Began," read a billboard for People for the West. I thanked Rev, took my thirty-five cents, and ran.

On the road to the Pinal Recreation Area, northeast of Globe, butterflies came to flowers of dodder draping the mesquite like orange electrical wire. Atop the Pinals, I did not get into pines as I had hoped, for Apache skippers; but the crossing was worth it for spectacular saguaros down the other side. Winkelman Flats Park on the Gila River crawled with pygmy-blues and Palmer's metalmarks. The only water for miles, the Gila ran under mesquite and cactus. A big family picnic was under way on the riverside, people diving and swimming to the sounds of horseshoes clinking and loud, happy Mexican music.

I went into the Gila myself, more than sweet after the swelter, in a sprinkle of rain from a gold and purple sky. When I emerged, in the breeze, I was actually cool. A fishing mom got a good trout, and a boy dove from a rope swing over and over. A pink rainbow—other bands understated, the pink broad and bright—arced over the Gila River.

In Tucson I'd hoped to see Jim Brock, coauthor with Kenn Kaufman of my field bible. I called, but his daughter was marrying that very night! A great caterpillar man, JimBob told me to come back if I could and he'd show me *Lerodea arabus* larvae in his backyard. So I slipped down through the city and on toward the Santa Ritas.

In the Canada Ranch rest area, thousands of longhorn beetles scrambled all over my table, my food, and myself, stuck on with their sharp tarsi and hard to pull off. The lights attracted an amazing array and density of insects. Any real entomologist could do very well here, but would get no sleep. One trooper and one Border Patrol agent swung through slowly during the night. A lady slept in her well-packed van with the door open and her feet out, so I guessed I was safe too. I drifted off with high hopes for lots of species in these legendary Arizona canyons, now that I was finally down here.

4. HAVE SOME MADERA, MINERVA?

The snouts were moving in Madera Canyon, and puce wild petunias lined the roadside. Azures flew about in Whitehouse Picnic Area. Sure they should be a new tally, I was disappointed by the Pelham *Catalogue*'s dictum that *cinerea* is a subspecies of our backyard *Celastrina echo*. The *Catalogue* giveth, the *Catalogue* taketh away. Some future edition, when the azures of the West are better understood, will giveth this one back. But then the annum's initial tailed orange appeared on a yellow, brown, and green cottonwood leaf, elegant in both crypsis and harmony of colors. *Eurema proterpia* is distinctive for its pert little tails and for the luminous depth and intensity of its orange.

On the trail down to the creek, a black scrap fluttered out of the meadow and into Marsha's bag. It was an elf! I'd never seen this species outside Mexico. Wildly atypical for a checkerspot, *Microtia elva* has longish jet wings banded with orange, like larger longwing mimics. Called a "rare stray" in the field guide, it is a great find anytime, one I never expected to see. Just after that, an Arizona metalmark spread on a trailside daisy. So I didn't feel too bad when the first roadside-skipper, orange and speckly like a Toltec, alighted by the creek for about a nanosecond, affording neither a good look nor a net shot. Of course, at that time I still thought that I would be seeing plenty of roadsides.

Among the many yellows, a couple that looked like the uncommon Boisduval's flew by, but they never stopped for me to make sure. Antiopa basked flat on a tripod of long grass caryopses hanging over the water, holding on where they came together. Then, all of a sudden, it was raining! The well-known Arizona "monsoons" were largely past, but remnants could, and often did, come up any afternoon. But by the time I reached the turnaround at the top of the canyon, the sun was back, and with it a striking black butterfly sunning in the creek bed. This was the dark type of the tropical buckeye, *Junonia evarete*, with the clearly descriptive subspecific name *nigrosuffusa*. Up a side road to Bog Spring Campground, I picnicked between two couples doing the same. They made me wish Thea were there with me; how she would enjoy it! And how much more I would as well.

Poking my nose into the woods, I observed a brown-backed woodpecker low in an oak. A new acquaintance for me, it had a breast that was spotty like a thrush's. Then down in a wash of sycamore and alligator juniper, I heard growly cries as a bobcat sauntered sideways out of my view, prey in its mouth, almost as near as the one in Carmel Canyon. Down the road to Green Valley, a party of Empress Leilias danced around a sprawling prickly pear under mesquite. No hackberry trees nearby, they were visiting purple fruit, basking on pads, and roosting communally on grass heads. Recalling the sweetness of the prickly pears, and their all but indelible stains, I was not surprised that Leilia liked them too. Madera Canyon was good to me, with thirty-three species, seven new, and great natural history to boot.

Nogales, on the other hand, could only be called bleak. The downtown was practically Mexico but with no obvious street life. Ineluctably sucked into the border crossing line, I barely ducked out before the black hole. I was looking for food when I clunked up against the border wall, down a dead end. Two Border Patrol agents appeared immediately. They didn't eat around there but recommended Exit 4: "You'll find Taco Bell, anyway." And that's all there was, along with other fast-food joints. Damned if I was going to do that, I blundered onto another dark road, back toward the border. Turning around, I saw a strobe light and heard loud music—could it be? Across the tracks, in a dirt truck yard, stood the wagon and canopy of "Adrian's Tacos."

DJs played Mexican music and manned the strobe, while old Sr. Adrian roamed the picnic tables as maitre d', taking orders. Between his hearing aid, the music, and my bastard Spanish, I had some trouble communicating my order. But eventually I ended up with three taquitos, a Coke, and half a glass of a rice and cinnamon drink, horchata, from a big jug that he gave me to try, since I was curious about it. I was happy as the bats mothing overhead. As I pulled out, the DJs were playing a song about *cerveza,* of which Sr. Adrian had none.

I had come to Nogales to look for a fabulous butterfly only recently described and never yet found north of the border. Andy Warren and George Austin discerned the new species of palm-feeding owl butterfly among Mexican museum specimens. Inventively, they auctioned the naming rights, raising a significant sum for butterfly research. The winning bidders chose to honor their aunt, Minnie Minerva, and her surname became the specific epithet: *Opsiphanes blythekitzmillerae.* Fair enough. But they missed a fine opportunity to use her simpler middle name, since the goddess Minerva's familiar and symbol was an owl. I, anyway, perhaps alone, shall call it Minerva's owl.

Andy told me the species occurred within fifty miles of the border and should be sought around palms, where it might come to bait. My plan was thus to set out rotting bananas around palm groves in hopes of attracting the fruit-loving insect. It would be a spectacular find, this orange, eye-spotted enchantress the size of a swallowtail, the first owl butterfly ever seen in the United States outside a butterfly house. Well, it was a lovely idea. But there were no palms in Nogales as far as I could see, other than a few towering coconuts, certainly not the nice, thick grove I'd pictured beside the border crossing, which was all concrete, steel, and asphalt. So much for Minerva's owl.

I drove up to Peña Blanca Lake, a reservoir in the Atascosa Range, where some folks had enjoyed a fifty-species day earlier in the year. I camped for two-fifty in the simple Lower White Rock campground under one of the best star skies in history. Almost as many desert checkered-skippers seemed to be rotating around the camp's grassy patches in the morning. Before the heat grew heavy, both an Arizona purple and its model, a pipevine swallowtail, tapped wild red four-o'clocks and wild blue morning glories—almost too much blue on blue, that. As for spectacle, a puddle club in Peña Blanca creek bed took the cake: eighty tailed oranges with guest dogfaces, Mexican yellows, dainty sulphurs, and lupine blues. When a newcomer bungled in, disturbing them into an explosion of flight, the result was psychedelic—like a rainbow shattering in the air before my face. Three new species reported for duty, one by one: first, a trio of *Dymasia dymas,* the tiny checkerspot—shaped like an elf, marked like Arachne; second, a bright Mexican fritillary, like the variegated but bigger and clearer orange; and third, the violet-clouded skipper, whose larvae Jim Brock had promised to show me in his backyard.

The camper in the red truck next door hailed me as I walked back to my campsite. I'd heard him snoring in the night, unfazed by falling acorns drumming on the roof of his camper shell. George from Pittsburgh wore a white hankie knotted in the corners over his head, à la Nabokov. Between jobs, he'd come camping with a lady he met playing euchre at the AMVETS in Rio Rico. Noting George's binoculars, I asked if he was a birder. "A what?" he asked. "I don't understand all that western lingo."

Well, as Kenn Kaufman liked to say of the wilder times during his Big Year, "This is the West." George told me where to go to find the stream still running, where there were "lots of butterflies." He'd walked up there the day before with his lady friend, and they'd bathed in the pools. So on this nonbirder's advice, I headed up the wash from the bridge.

Two funereal duskywings perched under an ash in formal attire, a pair of undertakers awaiting the cortege. Then a roadside-skipper, darker this time like a dotted, zipped over a dry runnel, touched down, and vanished, giving me no chance to net or ogle it. I'd anticipated roadsides all over the place, but they were all but absent, even when they appeared! George was right about the water, though—pooling, purling, delightful. When I came to a round, deepish mere silvered by the ripples of water bugs, I stripped and joined them, and they glittered past my face.

Soft laughter in the brush behind me offered the only evidence of the people whose presence was hinted at by the detritus in the streambed and a passing BP agent. After dressing, I went to Peña Blanca Lake itself for a quick look. I watched one last Philenor go to roost in an oak, and a mass of little black melitiine larvae on a sunflower, one or two hundred on a single leaf, the adjacent leaf completely skeletonized. When later I spoke with Jim Brock, he agreed that the caterpillars were probably those of bordered patches.

Now that I'd seen *Lerodea arabus*, there was no need to revisit Tucson, except to see Jim and Joan, and I couldn't count them. Seriously, I couldn't bear the thought of the steaming city. So I headed for Patagonia—a shrine-mecca for birders and butterfliers where I'd never been, though Thea had gone there on a field trip I missed in favor of a council meeting. When I got there, plumb beat, I camped in the town park. I situated myself well away from the "No Overnight Parking" sign to provide plausible deniability. In the morning, I found I'd parked right beside the town butterfly garden. The fellow watering glared at me but never spoke. I filled my water bottles at the café where I recovered my hat, left there the night before. I felt better to read that Peterson and Fisher often lost things too—a wallet here, binoculars there—but I'm pretty sure I was beating their record.

I'd also been reading Edwin Way Teale's American Seasons books along the way. In his chapter "On Idle Days in Patagonia" in *Wandering Through Winter,* Teale spoke of "the white wooden building that housed the Post Office." It's gone for a brick one now, and the route I wanted, leaving from the "S side of the Post Office," was torn up with construction. But I found my way at last to Hershaw Creek, and up it to the Draw of the Roadside-Skippers—as many as eight species, according to Bailowitz and Brodkin.

Now I saw the cost of those extra days at home: *Amblyscirtes* skippers were done. I'd missed most of that whole genus. Since I was there anyway, and the draw had moisture, I shod myself, creamed up, and went to see what I could find. It wasn't bad. A stretched-out cotillion of Arizona sisters was simply spectacular. Little calliche-gray and warty canyon tree frogs hopped all over the muddy streambed. Then a butterfly alighted beside me on the mud that I took for one of the ubiquitous snouts until I looked closely and yipped, "Jeez, that's no snout—it's an ag!" And it was—a perfect *Agathymus aryxna,* Arizona giant-skipper. An even bigger one, a female with more banding beneath, landed next. Lumbering and cryptic parked against the rocks, then fast and flashy when she went into overdrive, like a '59 Caddy with a 486, tail fins spread wide.

So the draw did me well, roadsides or no. And the giant wasn't all: working my way up the canyon, I also found the sheep skipper in the bed and the white-barred skipper in a grassy flat, both robust dusted skippers of the genus *Atrytonopsis*. Since the former used to be called *A. ovina* and it lives where desert bighorns range, I gave it the common name "sheep skipper" in my Audubon field guide as a mnemonical pun. Though reassigned to *A. edwardsii*, sheep skipper it remained. By whatever name, the three big new bugs nicely assuaged the absence of all those little ones.

Back in the Patagonia Butterfly Garden, a white crab spider on a white zinnia relaxed its grasp on a fiery skipper as a cabbage white sought just the right spot to settle down. All the birders in town were after the Sinaloa wren. "Seen that wren yet?" another gray-beard asked me as I left town through the Sonoita Creek Preserve.

"Not yet," I said, and I didn't even try to explain everything I'd seen instead.

5. TERLOOT AND GERONIMO

Across the Canelo Hills, through the gap between the Whetstones and the Huachucas, I crossed to the valley of the San Pedro. Skimming Sierra Vista, I arrived at the Carr Canyon home of Hank and Priscilla Brodkin just in time for their salmon, squash, and spud dinner.

Wednesday, October 1, was the day for our big Garden Canyon expedition. The much-admired naturalist and photographer Bob Behrstock, next-canyon neighbor of the Brodkins, would join us. Jim Brock was planning to come along too, but sadly, a pet emergency at home prevented him from making it. Garden Canyon in Fort Huachuca is one of those mythic names among butterfly folk for the abundance and diversity of its leps, but you have to negotiate the Army's rules and closures to visit. I'd been there during Lep Soc field trips and the yearly Invertebrates in Captivity conference, simplified by Gary Nabhan as "Bugs in Bondage."

We encountered no resistance from the United States Army, sailing through the checkpoint; I wasn't even asked to show my permit. We were detained, however, by great purple hairstreaks at a puddle and tailed oranges at scarlet *Zauschneria*. Sisterhoods of *Adelpha eulalia* crowded wet tire tracks at each successive ford. At the upper picnic ground, nearly a mile high, several giant-skippers shouldered up at mud. They were more Arizonas, which feed on Palmer's agave; it grows mostly in the grassland, but the habitats meet up here. Another lunker dawdled on Popsicle-pink New Mexico thistle. Called the dull firetip, *Apyrrothrix araxes* is "dull" only in relation to other firetip skippers in the Neotropics.

The place really was gardenlike, with marshy meadows and stream running full. Relicts of cooler times and northerly associations, these isolated Arizona summits are commonly referred to as "sky islands." A thorny mimosa called "wait-a-minute bush" caught my net and held me back as I lunged at the first big red-bordered satyr that flopped into the meadow, with a bird-struck margin. A stunning female followed, quite erebioid. These big browns took me right back to the North Slope of Alaska and the Colorado alpine. Not that *Gyrocheilus patrobas* really does have boreal or Arctic affinities. It is actually our sole United States representative of the pronophiline satyrs, a group that reaches its evolutionary apogee in the Andes—Southern Hemisphere butterflies that have evolved convergently with *Erebia*, the brown-and-rust ringlets of northern alpine regions.

At the top of the canyon for cars, we explored around the landmark cabin. Here we found the other *Agathymus*, the endemic Huachuca giant-skipper, also mudding. The massive gray-furred body, the long orange-banded, brown wings—what a beast! Priscilla photographed a giantess on the host agave, sipping shiny drops of some sweet exudate—tequila juice? I tasted it, of course poking my hand on the *really* sharp spines of the muscular blue leaves. The larvae bore into the stems and rootstocks of *Agave parryi huachucensis,* also endemic to the oak forest on this particular sky island. *Agathymus evansi* was named in honor of Brigadier W. H. Evans, a great student of skippers. I dubbed it "The Brigadier," both for him and for its golden epaulets, but that vernacular did not stick.

The last great Garden Canyon find, spied by sharp-eyed Priscilla, was Terloot's white. A male, it looked almost like the pine white I'd seen with David Branch, but the forewing cell was all black. The female is a horse of a completely different color. Brick red to burnt orange, black-veined like the males, she resembles nothing so much as a small monarch—very odd indeed for a white! I am convinced of the truth of an old idea, that female Terloot's mimic monarchs. I've found the two butterflies together, and the first time I saw a female Terloot's, I thought it was a viceroy—a mimic mimicking a mimic!

As the alternative name Chiricahua white implies, it reaches the Chiricahuas and some other sky islands such as here in the Huachucas, and south to Michoacán in Mexico. As for the other

common name, Terloot's white, I do not know much about Baron
Popelaire de Terloot. But when Herman Behr named the species in
his honor, in 1869, he misspelled the worthy noble's name, doom-
ing this marvelous butterfly to bear in perpetuity a scientific epithet
both silly and erroneous: *Neophasia terlooii*.

It was hard to leave the garden, but Hank had an appointment,
so we headed down for a butterfliers' lunch at a German bakery in
Sierra Vista. Then Bob Behrstock took me to Miller Canyon to visit
Bentley's Hummingbird Garden. We chatted with the prickly but
well-liked hummer attractor and apple farmer, Tom Bentley, and
bought some apples. I kept my net out of sight; Tom made it clear
that he doesn't care for "wolf-huggers," but he also has no love for
collectors. The white-eared hummer was the big deal here now, but
we were looking for the uncommon black checkerspot. Hank had
recently found it nearby, and so did we: two fresh ones in the roadside ditch, displaying their crisp underside pattern of black chains
on buff and ocher.

South of Carr Canyon, I strolled with Bob B. and his partner,
Karen LeMay, around their splendid garden. We sipped lemonade as tailed oranges sipped tithonia nectar and red admirables
and mourning cloaks went for ripe fig drippings. Bob picked figs
for me, and Karen gave me orange cosmos and tithonia seeds for
Thea. They pack their seeds in bags labeled with Bob's photos of
rare butterflies visiting the very plants. He introduced the cast of
grasshoppers around the yard, handling them gently, showing me
the red and blue tibiae of one kind, the red wings of giant black
and green lubbers. When I commented on the herringbone pattern
on one species' blue femurs, he said, "Well, the one with the *real*
herringbone"—he looked around for just a moment, reached, and
grabbed like a mantis—"is this one, *Melanoplus differentialis*." Bob
loves them all. "But," he said, "they're eating everything; and the
crab spiders probably got twenty-five tailed oranges yesterday."

Taking leave of all these like-minded souls, I dropped south to
Coronado National Memorial. Up-canyon, bordered patches varied
greatly, banded orange like a California patch, black like a black
checkerspot, or black and white striped like a mini admiral. The
view from Coronado Pass took in the San Rafael Valley from beyond

Baboquivari in the north to the Sierra Madre Oriental in the south, the border slicing in between. On the east, San Pedro River Valley ran under San Jose Peak, described by a marker as "the Mexican monolith that stands as a silent sentinel over [Coronado's] route." Coronado National Memorial commemorates the Spanish explorer's historic march in 1540, to symbolize "both the importance of the Hispanic-Mexican background in southwestern history and culture, and the close relationship existing between the Republic of Mexico and the United States"—a closeness now exemplified by the steel wall under construction on the plain to the east. I could see it marching across the San Pedro Valley, sections coming to meet each other, like some modern version of the Transcontinental Railroad. Except that while that project's last spike brought people together, the last rivet in this one is meant to keep people apart. The butterflies will ignore the wall, but what about El Jaguar?

On top of Coronado Peak, I sat in the Ramada where Thea and Mark Garland had discovered the second United States record ever for the dusky emperor. I had to leave a day early from a butterfly-watching trip we'd been leading in southern Arizona. When Mark and Thea brought the group here, she noted several butterflies flying around the top that she had never seen before—the Mexican hackberry feeder *Asterocampa idyja.* They photographed it for proof, setting off a flurry of visiting butterfly watchers eager to share in the treasure. I had no such luck today, but I did spot mournful dusky-wings alighting on spent sunflower heads, and my first green skipper, *Hesperia viridis,* hilltopped in the slanting sun.

Down in the valley, the Palominas Assembly of God's big sandy garden was alive with orange butterflies on orange cosmos. The BLM's river access at San Pedro Riparian National Conservation Area was alive too, but with mosquitoes and five Gambel's quail running down the rutted road before me, unwilling to deviate, one with a double topknot.

Along the highway north of Douglas the next morning, desert broom was just starting to bloom. It was every bit the magnet I remembered from the monarch chase, plastered with a dozen kinds of butterflies and a huge array of wasps, bees, flies, and other pollinators. One blooming broom had both the largest and the smallest hairstreaks I'd ever seen, just inches apart. The teeny ones were Leda ministreaks, which I'd been seeking for days, smaller than a dime. The big one was a *huge* great purple hairstreak that would have overlapped a silver dollar. Viewed end-on, the maxi-streak's fancy tail apparatus flared out and wiggled on the wind. If a bird hadn't already discovered the butterfly's bad taste, surely it would strike those tails. Nectaring right next to it was an iridescent black-and-blue wasp with a bright orange abdomen just like the hairstreak's: a two-member Muellerian mimicry ring, right there—either one a nasty surprise for a naïve verdin or phainopepla.

The Geronimo Monument at Apache said that the surrender of Geronimo to General Miles on September 6, 1886, in Skeleton Canyon, "forever ended Indian warfare in the U.S." In 1934, when the monument was erected, they didn't yet know about Pine Ridge. The monument is a handsome stone-built column of twenty feet or so. Geodes were set into several concave stones, but they have mostly been chipped away. One of the holes still had its black widow (or her progeny) that I'd found there twelve years before. I couldn't see her, but her egg baskets were right there in the web. Once Thea had found dung beetles rolling their loads all around this tower.

And so to Portal, and the other sky island I meant to visit, the Chiricahuas. I made camp in the only open campground and drank hot green tea, my candle lantern and headlamp full of moths and crane flies, mantids and walking sticks. A broad-beamed hooded skunk waddled away from me in its snowy greatcoat, and the next thing I knew was the cackled chorus of Mexican jays and acorn woodpeckers in the blinding A.M.

Sun fell hard on the amazing, honeycombed orange rocks of Cave Creek, where Geronimo hid out for years before General Miles brought him in. Nabokov's satyr came and landed on my picnic table. There could be few more suitable visitors, since Vladimir Nabokov himself came to Portal in 1954, collecting on sunny days and working hard on *Lolita* during the more frequent rainy ones. I set out my bait trap with overripe banana and Behrstock-LeMay figs, to see what it might draw. Right away another satyr, bird-struck on one precious-gemstone hindwing patch, came to the sweets, plus two darkling beetles. It wasn't long before the Nabokov's satyr was joined by more, and by the canyonland satyr as well. These two western relatives of the gemmed satyr are very similar, so especially good to see side by side like this.

Before I even left camp, I checked off my first Florida white, a female with long charcoal-tipped forewings. Then a moose of a crescent, the *arizonensis* subspecies of *mylitta*—new to me, if not a full species for the list. The campground water was off, so I made my ablutions in Cave Creek, and then I drove up to the "South Fork Zoological Botanical Area—closed to use of recording equipment," but not to butterfly nets as far as I could see. At South Fork Forest Camp, which has no camping, I met a birder or two looking for trogons. Right off, a distinctive Ares metalmark flew up the road and landed on a sycamore leaf. What's a mere elegant trogon to an orange-flared Ares metalmark? The long isosceles triangles of the wings made it a male; soon a larger, rounder female turned up on yellow daisies.

In the Chiricahua Wilderness area, alligator juniper berries were serried so thick on the ground that they resembled pale blue hailstones. An Arizona sycamore had fallen across the stream, a covered bridge painted in flaky swirls of olive, buff, brown, and lime, carved in sensuous curves, curls, bumps, and swellings. Looking down from it, I saw a giant-skipper beside the stream. It was very big, and I wondered if it could be the Bear. That's another of my familiar names that didn't make the cut for the NABA committee's list, though it is surely a far better name for our largest skipper, *Megathymus ursus,* than their "ursine giant-skipper." But it was merely an Arizona, after all.

I hadn't seen everything I could have in Arizona by a long shot. Ten months later, Bob Behrstock would write me of the broad-banded swallowtail, drusius cloudywing, and many-spotted skippers in their backyard, none of which I'd found. Clearly, had I come earlier, the list would be longer by several roadsides and others; but it wouldn't have Terloot's white or the red-bordered satyr on it. Short of a Learjet, I'm not sure how anyone would ever see them all. But there was no jet for me, and the road went on forever.

6. THE RED SATYR

The tiniest bunny in the world stood there in the middle of the road. I thought I'd missed it, but there lay the little lump. Its unmarred body was hot in my hand, which it did not cover. I showed the Border Patrol fella who came to see why I'd turned around, and he petted it. "Cute," he said, and it was, but dead. He looked sad too. I laid it in soft vegetation such as it would have liked to nibble. The next little cottontail got across okay.

Then it was a black-tailed rattlesnake—gorgeous, with seven or eight rattles—rich mustard, yellow-gold, and black. This snake was alive and coiled when I went back. Marsha made a good snake stick, as she always has, to shoo it back into the grass. Another BP officer watched this and followed me for miles. After the next snake, he stopped me and I explained my business. He said, "Ten four, sir," then asked if I was a herpetologist, like his dad. "Every time I see a snake out here, he wants to know all about it," he said.

The snakes multiplied, and almost every time I stopped, a Border Patrol agent pulled out of the brush and checked me out. One said he just wanted to make sure I was okay, and that he was enjoying the conversation. "But I've got guys in the back," he said, and had to go. By Columbus the sad tally was ten blacktails hit, three not. There was also a flattened, marbled Great Plains toad, and a speckled garter snake that twined on my hand, though its head was crushed. The black wraith on the verge, however, was alive, a possible jaguarundi. Leaving New Mexico, I burrowed through El Paso, across from the bloody streets and bright lights of Ciudad Juárez, into Texas again for the back end of the night.

The Davis Mountains, painted purple with mistflower, must have had rain. I slowed for two sets of turkey vultures on black wild hogs, and a lubber noshing on a tarantula patty in the road. Then a live tarantula crossed the pavement, avoiding the spider-killer wasp I'd just seen. It had a cute chocolate duck bill on its butt, and a fetching golden thorax. I admired its fastidious, high-stepping gait. A sad, splay-winged, short-eared owl hadn't made it. But remarkably, it had two vesta crescents visiting its carcass—the first time I'd ever seen butterflies come to bird carrion.

Stopping along a stream to stretch my legs, I saw rusty-patched browns on the wing and thought they were the red satyrs I was after. But they turned out to be Mead's wood-nymphs, easily twice the size of the ones we'd seen in Colorado. It was hard to believe they were the same species. The real red satyr, I guessed, was a lost cause. I'd had high hopes for it in Arizona, but they remained unfulfilled, as the butterfly failed to show at site after site.

Up at the McDonald Observatory, there was no sign of Apache skippers as I lunched on my last bit of cheese and an Arizona apple from Miller Canyon—only godbeams in the west, thunder in the north, and then rain. A short butterfly day, with nothing new save the gargantuan Mead's wood-nymphs and crescents at a dead owl, just as quarter-pounder grasshoppers came to half-pounder tarantulas and vultures to a half-ton hog. Why would anyone not want to join this great carousel of life and death when the day comes? The Davis Mountains were rainy ridge after misty ledge, ten levels deep; and a rainbow arced over Mt. Fowlkes, ending at the observatory's silver dome.

Fort Davis featured the "Rattlers and Reptiles" museum, "the largest live rattlesnake exhibit on the planet." Maybe I'd had enough rattlers last night—"the largest dead rattlesnake exhibit on the planet." In Alpine I foraged a Coney Island at a Sonic and, miles on, slept to the songs of the night insects in a tree-shaded picnic area, sheltered beneath Emory oaks by a stream.

At Elephant Mountain Wildlife Management Area, most of the wildlife was red-winged grasshoppers. I rolled on past Kokernot Mesa and Santiago Peak. Seas of low yellow daisies and waves of fuzzy gray-and-purple flowers colored the Chihuahuan Desert. Past Agua Fria Mountain, Packsaddle Mountain, Hen Egg Mountain with its little bump, Ten Bits Ranch.

Rising off the plain into Big Bend National Park, I pulled into Sotol Vista. A small thing flew up to meet two hilltopping black swallowtails. Settling on a silverleaf, it gave itself away as a Chinati checkerspot, its wings like a pattern of potsherds. Half a dozen of these endemics, currently listed as a subspecies of the theona checker, chased each other and a smaller, darker fulvia checkerspot. In between the Leanira I'd missed in Oregon and the black checker from Miller Canyon in hue with a chain-link pattern below, fulvia was an unexpected treat. I examined these uncommon regional specialties up close and at length: numbers 399 and 400.

At the west end, Cottonwood Camp had been flooded out by the rampaging Rio Grande, as was the road from Castellon to the Santa Elena Canyon view. A woman awaiting her son from a raft trip couldn't reach the usual take-out through knee-deep mud. She hoped he'd come on down; if he didn't, he could end up in a whole other wilderness canyon. She said the Mexicans hoarded water in a reservoir and, when it got dangerously high, let it out too fast. Now all the habitat, like the campground, was under fresh mud. Golden-fronted woodpeckers and summer tanagers held out in battered cottonwoods.

I took campsite number 3 at Basin Campground, the only one open in the park, thanks to the floods. Beneath wondrous rocks all around, folks were trooping back from a ranger talk on herps. How well I remembered being on the giving end of ranger campfires in Sequoia National Park. After their lanterns went out and the night blackened, Jupiter hung suspended from the quarter moon as the Pleiades rode the southern sky.

High winds moved in during the night. Despite blue skies, sun, and warmth in the lee, the basin was too windy for butterflies on October 7. It really was that—a deep scoop out of a wall of the Chisos Mountains. Red and brown volcanic and metamorphic horns, humps, lumps, and ladders soared all around. At Basin Store, a roadrunner worked the grilles of automobiles in the parking lot. Skulking from car to car, it ran out and nabbed something attractive off a grille, then ducked behind the next car. I'd seen house sparrows foraging this niche, but roadrunners? Well, why not? Roads and cars do rather go together.

A clerk in the store told me about "some special butterfly" she thought had been seen down the Window Trail. It was a long way down there in the heat and wind. I walked the sewage lagoon road to a deserted gulch instead. Nice and lonely in the dappled shade, a bright saffron female of a tropical leafwing spread on a branch above the dry bed. The road brought me out past the grown-in sewage ponds with a meaningful sign: "Open Tanks—No Trespassing." On the safe side, I found a colony of shiny brown Rawson's metalmarks. One kindly alighted right next to a fatal metalmark, so that I could compare their differences.

Back at the store, I picked up one Shiner Bock and one Lone Star for the presidential debate later on. Then as I was leaving the basin, at Cave Creek Junction, a giant-skipper flew by my window—but which one? It was likely too late for the Bear. Both century plant and lecheguilla grew on the hills around, so it could have been either the Chisos orange or Mary's giant, but there was no telling which one for sure.

At Dugout Wells, a Big Bend patch-nosed snake lay alive and unhit. What a pretty pink snake, with peachy stripes and belly and an unusual curvature of the nose. Across the hills, I reached the river overview where a sign on the Mexican side of the Rio Grande read "Blizzards-Enchiladas-Cold Drinks." The Chisos loomed purple against sky the color of that snake's belly. I looked for saltbush sootywings; out of one saltbush I tapped came three genuinely sleepy oranges. Five black vultures soared over the border and back at Boquillas, flipping about twenty fingers each at all immigration agents everywhere. White ponies and white-bellied donkeys foraged the bosque on the Mexican side.

Back in radio reception near Panther Junction, I holed up to hear those who would be prez "debate" on a great radio station out of Marfa, Texas. Repeat their lines ad nauseam, more like; but at least Barack answered one audience-generated question straight, that health care was a right, not a privilege. His opponent sounded desperate and mean. I rolled on down to Marathon and past Longfellow, entering the last leg easterly, sad to lose good Radio Marfa. Instead of the vicious AM tower of babble after the debate, I opted for George Noory on Nostradamus.

The morning sky blended the colors of the breasts of the Say's phoebes hanging about their old nest in the picnic shelter, with the rose wing linings of pyrrhuloxias, and the petals of mallows blooming out in the acacia scrub. The sounds were the many sweet songs of the mockingbird and the harsh "whack" of the cactus wren. Wings of sleepy oranges and variegated fritillaries littered the pavement.

Everywhere was the capital of something. Alamo Village was "the Movie Capital of Texas." Sanderson, "the Cactus Capital of Texas," was about three-quarters shuttered. Of four cafés, only Mi Tierra Mexicana was open. Jaime Rodriguez made excellent *migas,* and Dolores served me extra *miel* for my tortillas. As I paid my small bill and left, a *Eurema mexicana* flew out from behind Mi Tierra Mexicana.

Bordered patches swarmed around sunflowers on a Sanderson back street. I remembered their larvae en masse at Peña Blanca Lake, hundreds of them leaving delicate traceries instead of leaves. Sanderson seemed to be the Horny Cat Capital of Texas, judging from their caterwauling. I set the dogs to howling and barking on three sides too, when I waved my net by the stadium at crescents, checkers, and metals. A strong smell of purple crossflower filled the air, or since that adventitious weed blends the scents of cheap perfume with essence of cat pee, maybe it was just the randy cats I was smelling.

Good ol' U.S. 285—I knew it well in Colorado—took off north toward Fort Stockton as the Texas Pecos Trail. I took a whim to try it, just a little, before I left red satyr range for good. Many butterflies crossed the road. By a culvert I got a net full of sandburs, all for a snout, plus one on my rear, and then sat on it in the car. I passed into Pecos County and turned up the 2400 road. Before it crossed back into Terrell County, I stopped to goggle a flowery green roadside with lots of lovely natives in ones and twos.

Butterflies were the expected ones: vesta crescents, tiny checkers, all the sulphurs. Then a dark butterfly materialized on a boneset. Could it be? Surely not on a flower—they're not supposed to nectar. I'd probably miss it and never know for sure. But I caught it, and it *was*—a red satyr, *Megisto rubricata!* Life butterfly, grail, and the reason for this wild-card detour. I was thrilled, never mind that I'd stepped on a long acacia thorn in my Crocs. Worn but no less beautiful for that, with its bright russet patches and yellow-rimmed, silver-shadowed eyespots, this male was much smaller and more delicate than the red-rimmed satyr of the sky islands or the Davis Mountains red-eyed wood-nymphs. What a delight and relief. Now I could turn back toward the Rio Grande without regret.

Besides Powdermilk, only white pickups seemed to ply this Farm Road, an actual category of the Texas Department of Transportation. I saw a big patch of purple verbena and boneset across a fence with an easily climbed gate. The flashing blue Mylar of a superb Philenor, caught in a crab spider's chelicerae, seduced me across that fence. Several skippers met me on the other side. As well as sachems, I bricked a sootywing and saw, missed, and finally caught a fine new branded skipper, the pahaska. And then I got busted.

"Mornin', sir," said the Texas state trooper as he pulled up and climbed out of his cruiser. Tall and handsome, slim-waisted and broad-shouldered in his crisp tan and blue uniform with smart red piping, he was anything but a prisoner of the donut shop. "I believe you're on the wrong side of that fence." As cordial as could be, he made it clear that I should probably come back over to his side, and that everything around there was private, posted or not (which this land was not). "You see," he said, "we've got no public BLM land around here, like you've got out west." He went on: "The problem is, the ranchers around here'd as soon shoot as ask. They'd do it."

I said, "Thank you, sir," complimented his uniform, and climbed back over the mesh gate. But first, I deprived the big fat crab of her spicy pipevine swallowtail.

Back across, I was busted again by the landowner, who'd driven past, seen me in there, and come back. He was pleasant too, clean-cut, and also handsomely turned out in western shirt and hat. His pretty wife sat beside him, their baby between them, much like the couple in the middle of the night in Hope, New Mexico, last spring. "You're welcome to all the butterflies you want," he told me with a congenial smile. "We'd just appreciate your doing it off our private land." Fair enough. Wouldn't have shot me, I'll bet.

A little farther on, checking clumps of tiny daisies on the limestone verge, I saw my first *Mestra amymone* drift off into the mesquite. I grew up with the pretty common name "amymone" for it, as used in Brown's *Colorado Butterflies*. It requires a bit of syllabic gymnastics, though no more so than "anemone." I find it infinitely preferable to NABA's name, "common mestra," which sounds like a mess. Such a dainty of orange peel and oyster shell both deserves and requires a euphonious name, like amymone.

Speaking of names, the signs on most of the many white pickups going by read "Halliburton." What mischief (and money) were *they* making, up there on the Stockton Plateau? At a dry wash just into Terrell County, a flotilla of checkered-skippers perched on a mini mountain of mud. Both white and desert, they sorted out by species, reminding me of matching catboats marooned at low tide.

In the happy aftermath of the red satyr, I drove and drove without incident to just north of Laredo, where I stabled my trusty mount and less than trusty brain at a palatial rest area around four in the morning. I didn't pull out again until noon that day. How could I leave, with thirty-four species nectaring on mauve asters in the irrigated lawn? Three of them were new: Julia's skipper, the Texan crescent, and the oversize red-and-black crimson patch. Also the typical theona crescent, which, for the time being, included Big Bend's Chinati crescent as a race. If this was what the highway oases had to offer, what would the parks and reserves be like in the Lower Rio Grande Valley?

The first one I tried, Falcon Dam spillway, familiar to me from butterfly festivals, was closed—ever since 9-11. A million migrating dragonflies ignored the order, as did scissortails all along the fences, taking advantage of all the odes. I drove out the dam until I saw guys with rifles and a Mexican flag, and that was the border; I had to go through Customs and Immigration coming back, but the nice young agent with braces had noted my mistake and waved me through. I braved the blighted drive through the 83 corridor to Mission, McAllen, and on up to Edinburg, where I took a room at the Echo Hotel. Straightaway prone, I slept through my wake-up call, if it ever came.

7. FLOYD, JUNE, AND BEN

Burger King was a bust. The reason I'd come directly to Edinburg was to visit a particular franchise, famous among butterfliers for the huge colony of red-bordered pixies on the massive guamuchil tree behind it. These exquisite metalmarks are catch as catch can for the most part, to be counted on only around a good pixie tree, and this is one of the best in the valley. But there was no sign of pixies, the setup seemed wrong, and the tree gone, though the car wash was next to it as remembered. I was perplexed.

So I drove down-valley to Weslaco, where I met Floyd and June Preston in Estero Llano Grande State Park. After months of conspiracy over where and when we could intersect this year, I was only an hour late. It was mighty good to see these friends of almost half a century. I met them in 1961, at my first meeting of the Lepidopterists' Society, held at Rocky Mountain Biological Lab. My family had already gone home from their cabin at Crested Butte, so it was unclear how I would to get from Aurora to Gothic and back, a six-hundred-mile trip. As it turned out, a trio of veteran lepists drove me over the mountains for the meeting, and Floyd and June volunteered to return me to Aurora. In the event, I had no idea of how to reach my home, and they drove me around greater Denver for hours before we found it.

I met them now in a linear descendent of the camper they'd driven that summer, the latest incarnation of Preston's Portable Pad and Lepidopterology Lab. For many years, Floyd and June have traveled around the country, mostly the West, collecting target butterflies for the Florida Museum of Natural History. Now eighty-five years old, they are still going out each year, thousands of miles per summer. Few lepidopterists have contributed more to our understanding of the nation's butterfly fauna and its conservation needs than June and Floyd. Now we had a fine reunion, as they scrutinized my list with relish and gave me tips for where to seek particular species. They had also helped me to obtain permits for several parks and reserves. Over lunch of apples, oranges, and granola bars, Floyd showed me their field books and his amazing file of cards—old punch cards, unpunched, of "target bugs"—which they used for advance research on potential sites.

Floyd and I walked the redbrick park walks, my first of many times, while June napped. From the get-go, new species appeared, such as the pale-banded crescent, the laviana white-skipper, the brown longtail, and the wavy black sickle-winged skipper. Later, on my own, I walked the Green Jay Trail, almost oblivious to the tiny skeeters devouring my calves as half a dozen fabulous Mexican bluewings flapped around me. They alighted on a trunk or a leaf, briefly spread their big, black-and-blue banded wings, then closed to show their ashen black, gray, and brown undersides—like a cloak's or an admirable's, beautiful but ignored by most viewers in favor of the flashy upperside. Down in the understory, small black mazans scallopwings played hopscotch with sunbeams.

Back at the camper, Benton Basham had arrived from his nearby trailer. Thea and I had met and liked Benton when we'd been here for the Mission Butterfly Festival. A retired anesthesiologist, Ben has a farm in Tennessee but winters each year in Weslaco. Very well known in bird circles, with one of the highest life lists of all in the ABA (American Birding Association) area, he's a great example of what we call Birders Gone Bad: bird watchers who shift their attention largely or partly to butterflies. More to the point, in 1983 Benton undertook a United States and Canada big year for birds, the first to tally more than 700 species: 711, to be exact. He'd been a mentor to Kenn Kaufman and many others, and now he'd become a respected butterfly watcher and photographer.

That evening the Prestons hosted Ben and me to dinner at Milano's, a fine old country Italian restaurant, for June's favorites: baked eggplant parmigiana and tiramisu. She said, "At our age, you go from living to eat to eating to live," but their gusto and obvious delectation gave that assertion the big fat lie. As I recalled from many visits over the years, they knew how to have fun—completing each other's sentences and stories, laughing at old lovers' japes, Floyd meeting June's stylized complaints with sheepish and loving grins—that hadn't changed at all. "What'd you do, swipe my fork?" June would accuse, and he'd call her "The Government." The years and frailties have brought their frustrations and limitations, yet they carry on, and on, with humor and loving kindness.

The next day, Saturday, October 11, I returned to Edinburg with the Prestons. They showed me the Pixie Tree, and no wonder it hadn't looked right—it was at a *different* BK, which also had a car wash next to it! Mine was on *business* 281, while the real one is just off the 281 expressway. There was the big tree by the take-out window, just as Thea and I saw it when pixies were dripping from it in every life stage. According to Floyd, the owner loves the attention and protects the tree. But, to our sharp surprise, there were still no pixies: the bright things were nowhere to be seen. Maybe a little later?

Floyd found the cheapest gas at Flying J, so he drove the big camper (tiny by motor home standards but heavy on its pickup bed) out of the way to get it. They kindly filled my tank as well, and bought me lunch. Then we drove east on the Kika de la Garza Highway past Edcouch, past sugar cane, past the smoky W. R. Cowley Sugar House of Rio Grande Sugar Growers, and north at Santa Rosa toward Sebastian. Rain came, smelling fresh after hot valley streets. Standing water would be good for butterflies, if the sun came back. Our destination was the Longoria Unit of Las Palomas Wildlife Management Area, one of their frequent study sites. Going afield with Floyd and June during one of their amazing peregrinations was one of my dearest ambitions, and they thought this might be their last year on the road. (It wasn't—they went out in '09.) Floyd and I walked west, while June went east, net in one hand, cane in the other. Every fifteen minutes, they checked in on walkie-talkies: "What's up, doc?" "How you doing, kiddo?"

Red-bordered and lost metalmarks were both abundant on frost flowers. Just two days later, both would be far fewer and the numerous queens joined by bright, fresh tropic queens, also called soldiers. Giant swallowtails and zebras sipped on lantana in a fine juxtaposition of color and form. A citrus-stained Julia longwing sailed over mating queens, and sicklewings parked like so many Batmobiles all over eupatoria, balloon vine, and everywhere else. A Turk's-cap white-skipper was new, named for its host mallow, which looks like an unopened scarlet hollyhock. Amymones, snouts, and emperors visited clusters of anacua trees' ripe golden berries, perhaps accounting for their lack of interest in my bait trap.

We met up with June at the gazebo in the east unit. They held hands as Floyd helped her along, calling her "June-Bug." June's hair was trussed up in a disposable blue surgical cap, but her famous still-blond waves would come out for dinner.

Later, in the park, I helped Floyd back the truck into the tight space allotted for it and get it up on blocks. If my competence at sixty-five is a tenth of Floyd's at eighty-five, I'll be happy. I found a burger and a Lone Star at Fat Daddy's BBQ and talked with two dove hunters. I told them I once killed a band-tailed pigeon with the side of my house as it fled the Cooper's hawk, then plucked it and baked it in wine; and that I'd been hunting Las Palomas (the Doves) that very afternoon. "How was it?" one asked. When I said "Not bad, for butterflies," I ruined what little cred I'd gained as a pigeon hunter.

I camped in Powdermilk beside the P-Pad in the close, humid night, stewing in my sweat and swatting mozzies. I knew I should have made screens for the windows. Soon after that I accepted Ben's invitation to move into a spare bedroom in his trailer, and I ended up living there for weeks, off and on. Most of the dwellers of the trailer park at Estero were forced out to make way for the new World Birding Center, their concrete pads jackhammered with just a few grandfathered in. Ben said that he got to stay on for now since he is "the number one birder," and because he volunteers his expertise to the park.

Ben's little community was thinly populated by an odd cast known variously to him as the Naked Lady, the Crazy Man, and so on. His trailer was handy to the Prestons' campsite, to the visitor center, with its friendly, cordial corps of mostly women rangers, and to the ever-productive brick butterfly walk. Fresh things showed up in Estero's gardens almost every time I looked, such as a silver-banded hairstreak, enameled in a deep blend of blue-green, with flourishes of bright white and violet; or the histrionic white-striped longtail, whose display of both named features was way over the top.

I was eager to get to Santa Ana National Wildlife Refuge, one of the last good slices of old valley flora. The refuge loop road was open to drive on weekends just a little longer before the winter tram would take over. Right away, I saw a malachite on coyote scat—the first of forty or more of the legendary, lime green and mother-of-pearl giants I would see that day. An edge of frost flower and scorpion's-tail heliotrope offered up a common mellana, three very rare Rosita patches, and dozens of white peacocks and amymones with similar color schemes of pearly gray and peachy pink. One red-banded peacock stuck out among all the white peacocks. A pair of potrillo skippers haunted the borage, and mimosa skippers were closely followed by a mimosa yellow, much like the little yellow but for the absence of one tiny black spot. After light rain, the road was gridlocked with hundreds of sicklewings, every ringtail turd a parking lot for Batmobiles.

The Jaguarundi Trail down to the Rio Grande broke up in a cloud of phosphate green and blue bayou in the last few yards as a dozen each of malachites and bluewings arose, plus one black-and-white-and-red-all-over Fatima—what a show! The banks were strewn with abandoned clothing. I'd made it halfway through the refuge by closing time. I headed out, stopping here and there beneath the Spanish moss for more treats, until a young wildlife officer chased me out. She was nice about it but probably not amused.

Ben and I adopted a pattern for our butterflying around the valley. He drove his van, and I picked up the gas and our morning's fresh-made breakfast tacos: huevos y chorizo por ninety-nine cents, at the local Stripes. The Aerostar took off early for our Upper Valley Big Day. Heading west, Ben explained that 90 percent of the original habitat in the LRGV had been destroyed. Going out every day, he knows all the best remaining bits. The garden of the Seedeater B & B in Zapata furnished an astonishing display: thousands of butterflies of forty-four species. Two malachites together were the biggest I'd ever seen, like fancy saucers. Queens and giant sulphurs swarmed an expanse of *Eupatorium odoratum*. Spectacular big skippers such as the coyote cloudywing, the zilpa longtail, and the purple-washed panoquin enlisted on the roster here, standing out in the general flurry.

In San Ygnacio, a Texas tortoise crossed the road. Many of the stone, wood, and stucco casitas in this very attractive, ungentrified village looked unoccupied; I couldn't imagine why they hadn't all been snapped up by birders and butterfliers, as windsurfers have done with the cabins and bungalows of Hood River, Oregon. The center was a real Mexican village *zócalo*, with one difference: it was deserted. In Mexico, which was only a couple of soccer fields away, it would be thronged with folks, day and night.

Pink coral vine draped many of the walls and wires, bearing beaucoup butterflies, including a tawny beauty of a female curve-winged metalmark. To reach a high, deep-seated hairstreak, we appropriated a pallet from a stack in an empty lot, with which I laddered up to the top of the van to sweep the 'streak with Akito at greatest extension: it was a mallow scrub-hairstreak instead of some fabulous Mexican novelty, but what fun!

In Falcon, we visited Pastor Barry's Butterfly Garden at Falcon Heights Baptist Church. Right away, on purple duranta, a Texas powdered-skipper appeared to go with the last week's Arizona powdered; and a Celia's roadside-skipper—atlastaroadside! Next to them, a couple of big Marius hairstreaks, male and female, sucked the sweet nectar. They resembled big gray hairstreaks, but blue and slow. What Ben and I both first took for a purplewing at fruit bait, with lots of hackberries and tropical leafwings, turned out to be a very worn bluewing. At Salineno, Ben's usual river access points were flooded, but a coral vine west of Roma had my first dusky-blue groundstreak. Chachalacas and the Border Patrol played tag down along the Rio Grande.

At our last stop, the Cemeterio de Roma, kids in masks were taking Halloween pictures among the old graves. The Mexican olives, where Ben often saw green-backed ruby-eyes, were visited by only pipevine swallowtails. At Wendy's in Weslaco, Ben's preferred eatery, we counted up the day's spoils. Then back at the Prestonmobile, we rendered up our report: eighty species, nine of them new. Then to Benton's to pack and catch two hours of sleep before heading to the McAllen Airport, with accommodating Ben, for a quick flight to Florida. My first dip into the valley had been rich, and there was much more to come.

8. BY-CATCH

What was this strange skipper? At Jackie Miller's behest, I'd returned to Florida to take part in the McGuire Center's Butterfly Fest. Jaret Daniel and I were coleading a butterfly walk at Morningside Nature Center, assisted by swallowtail friends palamedes, tiger, and zebra. The biggish skipper, its margins broadly blacked and rounded, alit and spread on sumac. We concurred that it was clearly *Problema byssus*, the byssus skipper: a lifer for me.

That afternoon, the UF grad student Brett Boyd took me to a pristine, piney sandhill splotched lavender with *Carphephorus* and *Liatris*, and populated by the objects of our desire—the uncommon, elusive, and local Meske's and dotted skippers. In a clearing bright with backlit frits and sulphurs, we watched at least a pair of each. The golden Meske's and grayer dotted dart between the purple crowns while dodging Akito and an enormous *Argiope* web that spanned the flower glade.

After Butterfly Fest, Jackie Miller, Alana Edwards, and Cathy Malone took me out for gulf grouper at Bonefish. By rights I should have treated them, for this trio of Florida butterfly wise women had done as much for the Big Year as anyone. When my work in Gainesville was finished, Alana drove me south to Haines City. At Buck and Linda Cooper's mobile court, Lake Regent Village, we devastated a chicken with raspberries and several kinds of potatoes and pears. The Rays beating the Sox in game seven for their first Series berth was just more Florida natural history to me but a matter of consequence to some present.

Monday, October 20, came the promised return to Kissimmee, for "seas of *Liatris* and skippers." As we drove the old north road through lake, hill, and retirement country, Buck pointed out the

436

changes. He and Linda are some of the only born locals they know around there. Central Florida used to be all cattle on open range. Kissimmee City, fancy now, was a cow town in Buck's youth. All the growth was because of Disney, seeping out from Orlando, which Peterson and Fisher described in 1953 as a "charming inland town." Back then Kissimmee Prairie was "an endless sea of grass stretching from horizon to horizon . . . only an occasional clump of palmettos in the distance betrayed that we were in Florida."

Instead of Kissimmee Prairie proper, we traveled through Holopaw to Bull Creek Wildlife Management Area, where we rendezvoused with Jack Shaw and Kay Eoff, experienced butterfliers from Gainesville. Unlike with birders, running into the other butterfly watchers is a recent phenomenon. But these days one does, and that's how Lucy Bruce also joined our party. The day was sunny, the breeze cool, and not much yet flew. Lopsided Indiangrass, host for the Florida dusted skipper and others we sought, made a beautiful scrim on all sides, and rose rush nodded in the breeze. The tide had largely gone out already on the sea of *Liatris,* but more bloomed close to the pines, where hooded pitcher plants yawned and blue jays wheedled. A spring peeper clung to rabbit-tobacco beneath a runner oak that cupped a pinelands tree frog. Bachman's sparrows skulked in the palmettos, and big, slow mosquitoes cruised for blood—"galley nippers" in Cracker, according to Kay.

A palmetto skipper apparated onto purple *Carphephorus.* Next a nice Delaware showed up, and then a male Meske's. Things were beginning to pop when Jack spotted a Florida dusted skipper (*Atrytonopsis loammi*), the heart of today's quest, on gay feather. Its clear white spots made more of a skull face than the happy face Alana sees in them. A very fresh one was asymmetrical in pattern, as all of us saw. It had sharp, small skull spots on the right hindwing with lots of frosty dusting, and none on the dull brown left side. But the very next one was symmetrical, and I saw Alana's happy face after all. Still another *loammi* was cursed with a lopsided Dick Cheney smile, poor thing. Over the next couple of hours we all found *loammi,* at least ten in total, along with an array of other grass skippers: a rich brown and compliant monk, its cabbage palms growing nearby; the only arogos since Boulder County; tawny-edged and broken-dash, fiery and whirlabout, ocola and twin-spot; and finally, beside a roundel of scrub oaks, our sole dotted skipper of the day.

After Linda's elegant lunch, we tarried in Rainville Cemetery, where Confederate graves rose under Spanish moss hanging from turkey oaks. Buck recited the final stanza of "Thanatopsis" in honor of the long dead, two of whose identities were revealed on carved-wood nameplates: Haughty and Denkem Cubbedge. Wonderful names, worthy of Florida's open pine flatwoods before the rise of slash pine plantations and Disney World.

Back in Boca, Alana's atalas had eaten themselves out of house and home, but a *Eumaeus* reunion was still in the cards. Jackie had arranged for Akers Pence to escort me to the Everglades and points south. As director of the statewide Butterfly Community Inventory, Akers knew many of the best localities. A "mature" graduate student and lepidopterist, tall and lanky with long silver hair, Akers had a look of constant delight with the natural world, a wry and ready laugh, and a distinctive, fastidious manner all his own: overall, a likably strange guy. I knew from the start we'd have a good time.

At Deering Estate, the naturalist Alice Warren led us down a rockland trail where I could not believe we were in Miami. Native *Lantana involucrata* overhung the path with its small white flowers and purple berries. Atalas nectared all over it, in a superb display that I wished Thea could have seen. I loved playing with atala up close in Alana's yard, but to see a prolific population in more or less native habitat completed the experience. Not altogether native—a foot-long Cuban night anole, yellow slash on its shoulder, slouched on a pine limb overhead. Alice drove us down to Deering mansion's coastal lawn in her truck. By the North Palm Grove, a great dag-gerwing nectared at *Bidens,* close and fresh. Beyond the hammock, in a meadow on an archaeological dig site, dina yellows and Florida whites both appeared for only their second sightings of the year.

The senior reptile keeper, Adam Stern, also served as butterfly monitor at Miami Metrozoo. In the windy afternoon, we followed the young, goateed Miami native on his pine rockland transect, looking for Bartram's hairstreak. A female gulf fritillary searched for passion vine as a male searched for her, but Bartram's remained in its secure, undisclosed location. Back at the zoo, when I inquired whether they had a Komodo dragon, Adam reached into his pocket and gave me a tooth from the huge lizard. And when I learned that their new $60 million facility would include giant otters, and drooled, he took us behind the scenes to visit the wonderful *Pteronura* pair: five feet plus, with blunt heads and flattened tails. The dog otter charged when I got too close to the nipply, basking female, nuzzled the chain-link, and let out a long, squeaky hum.

We called on tiny Mary Krome Park in Florida City by dusk, as Jupiter rose behind a constellation of *Nephilas*—hundreds of huge spiders arrayed against the sky, fortunately strung high above face level. Several big hammock skippers played tag around the top of an orchid tree, their crepuscular display somehow avoiding all of those webs.

The next day began in disappointment: Robert Is Here was closed till November, so no Key lime milk shake; and at Navy Wells, there was no sign of Mr. Bartram around his crotons, just a golden-shafted flicker with red Y on its nape. In the national park, Long Pine was also closed, for a prescribed burn, so we opted for equivalent pine rockland near Gumbo Limbo and walked the ride in a cool breeze. Warty toadlets hopped over mouse pineapples lying lumpy by the path. Something flickered, *red*-shafted this time—no bird but a Florida leafwing—for which we'd barely dared hope. The only full species limited to southern Florida, *Anaea floridalis* seemed to be nearly extinct. It flew out of the pine clearing in a fast flap, much like the tropical leafwings I'd just been watching in Texas. Akers said, "That's even better than Bartram's," and I had to agree.

Driving out, we spoke of exotics. Akers said pythons were a huge problem in the park, and he'd gladly drive over them. I concur with their control, but after all the roadkill, that seemed hard, especially as the pythons might be only injured. Just then a fat snake appeared on the road before us. Akers veered but braked when we saw it was no python. We got out. The four-foot serpent, darkly banded, thick in the middle with skinny black tail and broad brown head, slithered toward me. It humped up, reared, and flopped like a lowrider before slipping into the ditch. Cottonmouth, I thought.

At Castellow, a.k.a. Hammer's Hammock, we walked the trails, which Akers knew well. The butterfly trip ended as it had begun, with a ruddy daggerwing, its long tails outlined against a pearly sky. "Look up there, hon," said Akers, "the Florida tree snails are gorgeous," and indeed the *Liguus fasciatus* were numerous and fine up in the sunburn trees. Sorry to wrap up the field trip and break up the act, we blasted off from Miami to Jupiter and reached Florida Atlantic University in time for my lecture that night.

Afterward, with Alana and her colleagues Emilija Stanic and Taylor Hagood, I helped clean up several platters of "hog snapper." A Florida fish that feeds on crustaceans and hangs about lobster traps, it is "almost by-catch," according to the restaurateur. It was tasty and fine. Later, as I was falling asleep next to the one-eyed Skipper at Alana's house, the term came back into my head: "by-catch"—that which ends up in your net without your direct intent. It seemed an apt category for much of my experience during this whole big, weird year.

9. CAROLINA IN THE DINER

A couple of days later, on October 16, I was swinging a golf club instead of a butterfly net. It had long been my plan to swap a day on the links for a day of leps with my oldest friend, Jack Jeffers. It was supposed to happen last spring, then in summer; but one thing and another kept putting it off. If this was going to take place at all, it had to be now. There were even a couple of potential butterflies I could pick up on the way. Probably not with a golf club, though Charlie Covell *had* once caught a meadow fritillary with his driver.

The Silver Star departed Delray Beach on schedule. My seatmate, Tamra from Tampa, asked me questions about the loo, doors, and so on. "I've never . . ." she started. "Ridden a train?" "Right." I'm a sucker for dinner in the diner, especially in Carolina, so I had crab cakes and Cabernet opposite a retired microbiologist from Hunter College in the Bronx. We talked about Obama and McCain, now anointed. "May the best man win," she said, but it was pretty clear who she thought that might be.

The three women working there—Server Michelle, Steward Kashika, and Chef Fatima—stopped me on my way out of the dining car. "Excuse us," said Kashika, "but we were wondering, what do you do? You look so . . . *wise.*"

I said yes, I was indeed a professional wise man, following stars and looking for babies in mangers. Fortunately, they all laughed. I could have stopped there but went on and told them what I was really following. "Not so wise," I said. "But I do keep good company." At least they hadn't called me Santa, or taken me for you-know-who.

Jack collected me at the train in Raleigh and took me home to his pleasant cul-de-sac, all in early autumn foliage of sweet gum, maple, and other eastern deciduous trees. There was an undeveloped lot next door, but Jack and Lorée's son, Jake, wasn't much drawn to play in it, or build forts. Jack and I would have positively lived out there. He made me cayenne shrimp for lunch, and we reconnected across fifty-five years.

In 1953 the Jefferses moved in across the street from us in Hoffman Heights, on the edge of Aurora, Colorado. Jack and I attended school together from first grade through twelfth, often in the same room, and we grew up close friends. When I went nuts over butterflies in fifth grade, Jack joined me, and for years we built and swung nets together, mostly along the High Line Canal. Jack also loved golf. When not chasing butterflies, we often played a makeshift neighborhood course, tree to tree, with golf balls and croquet mallets.

Jack became a varsity golfer in both high school and university, and now he had retired to an area where he could golf as often as he wanted, on a great array of courses. At a class reunion, Jack joined me on a butterfly walk I'd been drafted to lead, and I walked the golf tournament with him, playing three holes when the course steward wasn't looking. We agreed to reciprocate again during the Big Year, doing a bit of each.

Saturday, October 25, was golf day. First, Ping-Pong with Jake, a game Jack and I used to play endlessly on my back porch; next, Jake's church-league basketball game. And then on to golf! We had planned to play my virgin whole game but didn't, given Jack's cold. Instead, we each drove a bucket at the driving range. Jake was great for his height, and Lorée impressive with her featherweight pink driver. I drove a couple of 150 yarders, to Jack's smacks of 250-plus, and duffed only one, with his good instruction. Jack said he wouldn't have been embarrassed to be on the course with me. Next we went to the putt-putt course, where again I did not completely disgrace myself, nearly pegging a hole in one. We also watched butterflies, as a bit of sun came out: a buckeye basking, a female cabbage white, fiery skippers on white *Buddleia,* and a couple of very sleepy oranges the same color as the pumpkins we bought for a carving party that evening. I won no prizes for my jack-o'-lantern, but I did ace the day's final competition, winning the 847 peanut

M&M's in the "guess how many M&M's in the big jar" contest. I shared a few of them.

Sunday was butterfly payback, as Jack and I visited Sandhills Game Land down on the coastal plain. We stopped first at Weymouth Woods Nature Reserve, outside of Southern Pines. The funny ranger directed us down her favorite path to some splendid blue-spotted gentians. We met a couple hunting pterodactyls with their small son. None of those turned up, but clouded skippers clung to lavender asters along the Bog Trail, a variegated fritillary flew over matching cinnamon ferns in open pinewoods, and buckeyes and tailed-blues flitted alongside. At nearby Indian Camp Park, on a little lake, eufala skippers called on white asters, and several kinds of sulphurs improved upon the day.

For the rest of the afternoon we explored one sandy road after another, searching for patches of promising autumn nectar. At one stop, Jack chased down and netted a pesky little sulphur. Despite different strokes for different lives, he hadn't lost his touch with a net any more than with a Ping-Pong paddle or a putter. As we navigated the Sandhills, we kept seeing the same red car. The fifth time or so we met this sporty model, the driver stopped. He was a herpetologist from Raleigh. Funny that the only other person we met out there all day, aside from a few kids messing about, was a naturalist. From my drawing and notes he confirmed that the Everglades snake was a cottonmouth.

At last, along Old Laurel Hill Road, we came upon a good stand of gayfeather blooming in burned-over woods, and a few skippers to show for it—least, dun, clouded. My big hope for Carolina was the hunky yehl skipper. In a forest with quite a bit of cane, its host plant, I was faked out momentarily by a large, dark female fiery. I told Jack we had yehl. We got all giddy like the kids we'd been, chasing March tortoiseshells and autumn goatweeds, until I looked more closely in the bag. In the end, *Poanes yehl* proved as elusive as those pterodactyls. But the links and leps caper had panned out, at least enough to let us know that we're still here, still willing, and still able, after all these years.

10. ON A MISSION

When Benton met my plane, we went to see Floyd and June to sign permits and render my report. We found their camper at the Split Rail trailer park—they called it the "Broken Stick"—where they had moved. The Prestons were wearing their evening caps, as it was much cooler than when I'd left. Even in the valley, autumn was moving in.

The next morning, I awoke to the soft voices of birders. The magpie-jay was right outside Ben's trailer. As number one birder, of course he welcomed all comers. This fabulous Mexican bird, with its fancy crest and extra-long azure tail feathers, was almost certainly introduced and had not been accepted as a U.S. record; but everyone was coming to see it just in case, and because it was so spectacular. I rose and got my own look. A newcomer on the park's brick walk was no less phenomenal: a glorious guava skipper, with its orange juice face, sapphire stripes, and ruby spots. Almost as grand, several Brazilian skippers tapped yellow trumpets of a spreading esperanza on the Crazy Man's place near Ben's.

For the next couple of days, Ben and I motored around the various valley gardens and reserves. At the Frontera Audubon Society Preserve in Weslaco, an aster patch offered up an exquisitely formal tailed aguna, cream stripes on chestnut, long black tails. A real fish patch of mistflower floated my first brown-banded skipper, and we both viewed a very rare malicious skipper: I saw the ventral striations and wing shape sharply, and Ben saw the distinctive dark marks of the forewing. "I showed Jeff Glassberg his life malicious skipper too," said Ben, referring to the founder of NABA. Formerly assigned to *Synapte malitiosa*, the Texas species is really *S. pecta*, yet no common name has supplanted "malicious."

444

We sent Floyd and June off to their further rambles with one more shared dinner. Dessert featured Key lime pie, helping make up for my missed milk shake in Florida City. As we compared checklists and shared stories, Floyd quoted his mom's saying about fat versus lean times: "Chicken today, feathers tomorrow!" I think they offered the quip almost as grace for each fortunate meal. I reciprocated with GrandPop's Kentucky version: "That was mighty fine what there was of it, and plenty of it, such as it was."

From there, Benton drove us west to the town of Mission, which styles itself the Butterfly Capital of the Valley. Thea and I have participated in several Texas Butterfly Festivals in Mission. We enjoyed them, but I had to lead so many field trips and give so many talks that we had little time to explore for ourselves. One year's festival saw the discovery of a certain *Duranta* hedge at Mission West RV Park. So attractive was its bloom that it proved more fruitful than any of the reserves or field-trip sites, and everyone flocked to "the Hedge." But Thea and I didn't get to see it until our last day, and then only briefly.

So I definitely wanted to see the Hedge on this visit, and that's where we went next. We found the bloom largely past and the number of butterflies modest. But Ben said there were always olive-clouded skippers along the bottom on the western edge, outside the park. I netted a swirling pair, of which one was eufala and the other olive-clouded, just as he said. Ben is not only keenly observant but also richly associative: he remembers what's where, and how to find it. I could see how he got to be the number one birder. Though he'd become an excellent butterflier, he didn't trouble himself over taxonomic niceties, such as the fact that the olive-clouded had been subsumed under the violet-clouded skipper in the Pelham *Catalogue*. Even so, I was just as happy to see it.

Later we explored several sites in the Mission area along with the experienced lepidopterist and folksinger Mike Riccard, running into various of the valley butterfly cognoscenti as we went. At the Old Pump House, thank goodness, red-bordered pixies appeared at last: two *Melanis pixe* on the mistflower, not very fresh but unmistakable. There is simply nothing like them, with their coal black, yellow-tipped, longish wings, crimson-spotted at the base of each and around the trailing edges of the hindwings. It's a good thing these turned up, given Burger King's poor performance. Right nearby, a fresh, two-tone clytie ministreak let me catch it with tweezers for a good close look.

A little way upriver, or up-wall as it now is, lies the NABA Butterfly Park, which was Jeff Glassberg's great vision. We were welcomed by a gold-spotted aguna, a silver emperor (a.k.a. Laure), and a gorgeous yellow-tipped flasher. Hundreds of butterflies adorned a single clump of South Padre eupatorium, including a giant of a crimson patch, all the royal danaiines, and my first white-patched skipper of the year. Jan Dauphin, a sweet-natured butterfly maven in her hat of many pins, was there with her photography partner and husband, David. The Dauphins' website is the definitive state-of-the-valley butterfly resource. She showed me a plummy glazed pellicia, all the colors of a swollen shiner, and tried hard to find me a cracker, without success.

The bait stations had mostly old dried oranges on them, with only tawny emperors visiting. A volunteer told me that the black bear would sit around under them, waiting for fresh fruit to be put out. A broad, brew-daubed log, crossing the creek, hosted an assemblage of hackberries, malachites, and bluewings, as well as my first two red rims: favorites of mine, with their rose-bordered wings of jet. We worked bed after bed of nectar plants, where farmed-out fields once stood.

One butterfly I'd especially hoped to see at NABA was a tiny bit of a thing called the cyna blue. It had recently been seen in a patch of frogfruit near the HQ. Formerly confused with *Zizula gaika*, an African species, it was thought to have come in with camels that Jefferson Davis brought to the southwestern deserts. Now it is known to be an indigenous species, *Z. cyna*. When I finally saw my first, one year later in Mexico, I knew it instantly. No other blue is so dainty, so daintily marked, and so easily missed.

As I searched for cyna, a thirty-person border break took place right next to the wall in progress. I heard *"Andale, andale"*; there was a lot of dust. The Border Patrol gave chase, and somewhere in the background, someone was playing "Scotland the Brave" on the bagpipes. Welcome to the NABA Butterfly Park!

In the afternoon, Benton and I drove to Bentsen State Park. This is another one of the so-called World Birding Centers and, in fact, the headquarters of this nine-headed hydra. How you can have nine "centers" of something, I don't know; maybe "South Texas birding ganglion" would be more accurate. As at most of the centers and other reserves, the big attraction for butterflies was the managed gardens. And as in most of them, the chief plantings were eupatoria, white plumbago, lantanas, Turk's-cap, and a few others. Bentsen also had some nice big Mexican olives, which large skippers like. A mass of yellow-and-black flower scarabs covered grapes on the bait station, packed in with many emperors and one gargantuan malachite.

Benton told me in harsh terms what he thought about policy changes that led to the closing of Bentsen's campgrounds and drive-through privileges for the public. Now, to get into the park proper across the canal, one must walk or bicycle. Since he suffered a stroke a few years ago, and then many months of therapy and recovery, Ben is not able to walk the distances necessary to explore the park without driving in. Same with Santa Ana Refuge. So he is limited to the gardens, which he walked in a very methodical and stylized manner, pointing with his stick to share each new delight.

Next Ben took me to the over-the-top "campground" outside Bentsen, an upscale RV park whose users commonly stable $100,000 Volvo tractor-trucks to pull their immense fifth-wheelers and split-level motor homes. Many of them sport Jesus fish, making me wonder how these gargantiomobiles will fit through the needle's eye. Some of the units even have palatial carports and cottages to augment the aluminum wombs, apparently inadequate in their own extravagance. All of this display replaced humble, actual camping in Bentsen Park, to Ben's disgust. I take his point; there is no longer anywhere to pitch a cheap tent (or park a Powdermilk) at these World Birding Centers. But Ben gets his own back by using the RV park's gardens. He likes the place in spite of himself, because the owners love butterflies and plant a lot for them, with a small butterfly garden at almost every site. They don't spray, and they don't lock or police the gates. Watchers are welcome. Plus, I was able to take Marsha into the RV palace, unlike any of the other gardens we'd been to all day.

Along the well-flowered adobe border of the place, known locally as "the Wall" (or "the *other* Wall"), we found Marius, clytie, and lantana scrub-hairstreaks, the last one a harbinger of Hawaii. Palace or no, we vastly preferred this most welcoming wall over the grim and lifeless one of steel and concrete, rising so near to the south even as we watched.

These were just the first of several pilgrimages to Mission. But now I had another quest that needed to be made, quixotic as it might be.

11. THE BEE CAVES

Heading north in Powdermilk, who had been stabled these many days, felt darned good, just to be getting out on my own again. This trip went against Ben's considered judgment, based on "Strategy, strategy." No doubt he was right, strictly in terms of the number of new species I could find, versus the continual train of novelties in the valley. But I really wanted to make one last try for the Apache skipper.

At the McGuire Center, with Jackie Miller's help, I had studied specimens and literature in preparation for the coming hunt. Bill McGuire, patron of the institution, had himself researched the Apache skipper. I studied his pin labels and manuscript for clues. Now I was driving toward Austin, in hopes of seeing the isolated population that McGuire planned to describe as a new subspecies of *Hesperia woodgatei*.

A quick look at Estero that morning produced thirty-three species, and a brief stop into the Longoria Unit revealed thirty-nine. None of them were new, except once more I thought I saw Boisduval's yellow, but couldn't catch it. Under a lens, little *Caria ino* revealed a train of rubies around its emerald eyes and topaz-studded sable robes. Spent chrysalides of emperors and snout shells hung all over the hackberry boughs. Great green lynx spiders sucked on tamenund juice while guarding prodigious brown silk egg sacs. Sicklewings, whose name was changed from *Achlyodes thraso* to *Eantis tamenund*, glided everywhere on their peculiar, bent wings. Longoria too could be renamed: the National Tamenund and Amymone Preserve.

I crossed the King Ranch toward Sarita, Kingville, and Kleberg County. Beside me lay a guide to butterflying in Texas, written by our friend Ro Wauer, the former park naturalist at Big Bend. On

Ro's suggestion, I pulled into Dick Kleberg Park, where he had found rare definite patches roosting in long grass. Walking, sweeping, and searching the tall vegetation before, during, and after sunset, I found no sign of *Chlosyne definita.*

However, I discovered eight different kinds of butterflies roosting for the night: a bordered patch, a ceraunus blue, and three species each of checkered and grass skippers. The tropical, white, and desert checkered-skippers all perched together on grass, as did the fiery, eufala, and Julia's skippers. The eufala turned up in the net when I swept the vegetation, along with an amazing volume and diversity of hoppers, crickets, singers, odes, lacewings, beetles, long walking sticks, spiders, and many others. My flashlight revealed the pale wedges of more checkered-skippers all through the dry sward.

As I looked down by the river, a couple of park employees called out to me. "Watch out for the crocodile!" they said. "We saw one." They meant alligator, of course. But having very nearly fallen from an upset canoe onto the back of a twelve-footer in the Trinity Bayou one time, I do not treat Texas gators as a joking matter, and I watched my step. Northward through the night, past Swinney Switch, I found a convenient rest area. I'd slept in too many actual beds lately.

Halloween morning found me at Lake McQueeney, east of New Braunfels, where Mike Riccard had given me directions to an old broad-winged skipper site. *Poanes viator* was the one I'd missed on my last marsh slog with Jim Wiker, and this was likely my final crack at it. The lake was hard to reach, with no public access; subdivisions had taken almost the whole shore.

At length, I found some unfenced, remnant wild rice, *P. viator's* host plant, around a boat-trailer storage lot. The broadwings remained at bay, or more likely extinct, but I enjoyed munching wild rice kernels as I looked. Delicious, stripped from the heads with my fingers, they made a nice follow-up to the pumpkin donut I'd had for breakfast.

In New Braunfels, the Wurst Fest was under way. I drove up past the Wurst Hall to Comal Springs, whose impressive flow rushed out of the canyon bottom in a fast, fresh runnel and spread into broad pools in the park. I bent down to the spring and washed the heat, sweat, and dust of two days from my feet, hands, and face. Then I walked Panther Canyon, a good place for hermit skippers, according to Ro. No hermits haunted Panther, but a Texas powdered-skipper did, and a bright new brood of gemmed satyrs danced through the juniper woods. I still had an acacia spine in my Crocs from Red Satyr Day, so I sat on a rock and dug it out as a red admirable basked full-out in a sun spot on the streambed's white limestone. I was thinking of Jack, and the epiphany of our first red admirable in a barnyard by the High Line Canal, when a man taking his iPod for a walk shouted, "Out here butterfly catchin'?"

"Just seein' what's here," I said.

"I haven't seen that many around," he said as he strode right through a flutter of *gemma*, right past wide-spread Atalanta. She ignored him too.

At the top, I'd noticed kids from the nearby high school conducting brief assignations in the woods. They looked more like deals than trysts. A lad came down the trail without earbuds, transported in his reverie, whether by the woods or his score, I couldn't say. I favored the former and wondered if that admirable might catch his eye, heart, life, as that other one had taken mine. A wasp caught a snout, and quite a tussle ensued in the leaves and dust until the butterfly was subdued. Then the wasp neatly clipped away the wings and flew off with the streamlined package: a *Vespa* Wurst Fest!

The River Road followed the shallow green Guadalupe in late sun through lemony sycamores and cinnamon cypresses. It was a picture, away from the many tour and inner-tube rental signs. Most spelled it "toobs." The many camp, picnic, and launch sites were all private. River Road had no traffic but a toob shuttle or two, and two cops who stopped to see if everything was jake with me, parked in the middle of a bridge to see the stream. When they saw I was indeed okay, they said, "Good deal!" and headed on.

The next police I saw were organizing traffic in Sattler. The entire town was one big Halloween party at six o'clock, well before dark, or even dusk. Everyone of all ages wore costumes as they marched the kids around town, where all the businesses had treats for them. At a country café out of town, I picked up my own treat, a piece of homemade pumpkin pie and hot coffee for dinner, and drove on.

In Dripping Springs, I poked my nose into a little country bar for directions to Bee Cave. An old cowboy directed me to "the Bee Caves," as he called it. Bill McGuire's specimen labels in the McGuire Center indicated habitat for the disjunct local Apache skippers along Bee Cave Road, and my conversation with the lepidopterist Chris Durden of Austin confirmed that the colony had still been there in recent years. But Bee Cave was not what I'd expected it to be. The city hall was in one of the biggest, most pretentious shopping malls I'd ever seen. I actually entered an ignoble book barn to consult the Texas DeLorme atlas and gazetteer, too big and expensive to buy, and I wouldn't buy it there in any case. I located the habitat, found a place to camp nearby, and called Thea to say boo.

Then I drove into Austin, in hopes of finding one of my favorite beers at the Lovejoy Tavern. What a fond ambition. Halloween in Austin might as well have been a pope's mass or an Obama rally, except for the outlandish dress. Tens of thousands of costumed young welled and flowed through the Sixth Street precinct. Every face you could find in all of the dusted skippers' dots was here in masque. Many of the women were scantily clad, and horned Bush-devils abounded. Traffic moved like grapes in green Jell-O. It took me an hour just to escape. Back at my quiet campsite, I settled in with a bottle of pumpkin ale. It wasn't Dennis Hopper IPA, but I had it all to myself. Trick or treat!

November announced itself on the soft voices of people arriving for a Saturday church breakfast. "Welcome All Who Enter Here" read the little wooden sign for the Church of Conscious Harmony. I'd taken them at their word. So did the eight-point buck that walked through the parking lot where I'd slept. I thanked a well-groomed couple—gray-streaked, swept-back black hair, pepper-and-salt goatee—for their hospitality. "Any time," said the gent.

"You know," said his wife with a sly smile, "we have a chapel too."

The Apache skipper site was just down the road, and the sun was peeking over the limestone ridge at nine o'clock. Traffic roared on Bee Hill Road, all the angry engines, everyone thinking he was a NASCAR driver, but many bicycles hummed by as well. When the first skipper slipped down a flowery 'dozer track opposite Grace

Lane, I thought for a moment I had Apache—but it was a crisply spotted female sachem, which people often mistake for branded skippers. I walked down along a power line cut through oak-juniper savanna. There'd been a lot of juniper cutting and shredding for fuel reduction, and tall yellow composites filled the clearings. They attracted many butterflies but no *Hesperia*.

At noon I found Chris Durden's Cuernavaca–Old Bee Cave Road site. On the Old Bee Cave roadbed, a small-flowered gayfeather was out. This is supposed to be the main nectar source, as it is for skippers everywhere it grows. The hilltop was torn to bits, 'dozed and scooped for a new communications tower, but the roadsides teemed with butterflies of twenty different kinds, including scores of American painted ladies and ocola skippers. After the tower swarm, the dirt road entered a good wire-grass, oak, and juniper habitat with lots of *Liatris*, then narrowed to a pleasant woodsy trail. You could fool yourself that you were in Texas wilds but for the snarl of traffic on Bee Cave Road and views of the palaces of the plutocrats between the trees. It was very hot where the road ended at another, higher tower. I was ready for shade, water, apple, and nuts. Nuts is right—no Apaches, though the habitat and season should have been just right.

Finally I tried Cypress Arm on Lake Travis, where the Prestons' punch cards said they had found *Hesperia woodgatei* on skeleton-leaf goldeneye. The flowers were there but not the Apaches. The lake level was way down, the setting dry and fallish. When I later spoke with Chris, he said the six-year drought was likely the cause; he only hoped the skipper survived at all. This is how climate events deplete the overall picture: common, generalist species persist, while specialized, more particular animals drop out.

As the first day of November closed out on me, I had to let the Apache go. Only one of my goals for this trip could still be achieved. So I headed back downtown, only to find Sixth Street again blocked off, this time by skeletons and skulls in the Día de los Muertos parade. But after the Day of the Dead died down, I found a parking spot, walked, and located Lovejoy's. It looked closed—for good, but a small light shone over a black sign for "Tap Room and Brewery." It was as basic as I remembered, shabby and comfy, nothing for show, full of hirsute regulars on barstools and at dark tables. On the chalk-board: "The Order of the Fez—Lovejoy's World Beer College—start today! $2.50—full pour!" So far, so good. But where was Dennis Hopper on the long list of draft beers?

I approached the bar. Comely, tattooed Catherine asked my fancy. Girding for disappointment, I said, "It's been years . . . do you still have Dennis Hopper Ale?"

Catherine look quizzical, then sad; and then she brightened. "You're in luck!" she said. "We have it on tap for the first time in eight months!"

I was delighted. And, despite a new brewmaster a year ago, the recipe was as toothsome and hoppy as I remembered—pure humu-lus oil!—and splendid. I burrowed into my pint like a *Papaipema* larva in a hop-vine stem. *One* species, at least, came through for me on this trip.

Standard Time came back as I dropped from Austin through San Antonio and on back down to the valley. The Burger King plot thickened. I checked the right franchise, and there were still no pixies to be seen in the pixie tree. But in using Ro Wauer's Texas butterflying guide, I'd noticed that he gave still a third location for the pixie-tree BK, on Raul Longoria Road! Due diligence required me to check that site too. But there was no hamburger shop at Raul Longoria and Sprague, just a Family Dollar on the north and a Dollar General on the south. Ro, like me, had confused the address. But now that I was there, thanks to Ro, I found myself next to the Edinburg Wetlands World Birding Center, with its "six acres of butterfly garden," and I thought I'd better give it a look-see while here.

As I entered the sea of mistflowers, a Fatima appeared against red lobelia and Turk's-cap, flying up at everything going by; then alighted by a crimson patch—what a lot of red in one spot. And it went from there. Several Hispanic families came through the butterfly garden on their way to the wetland to see the fabulous heronries. As one little girl said, "There's a lo-o-ot of butterflies!" I detected nothing new, but when I left at 1:00 P.M., much later than I'd intended, I'd seen forty-seven species, almost all on *Eupatorium betonicifolium* (Padre Island mistflower). A lot of butterflies indeed. Back to Ben's too late for the field, we went to Wendy's.

Monday came clear for our Big Day downriver, and it went by in a blur. First we met Ben's friend Martha Blanton at her home place, Los Ebanos Preserve. She and her husband, Taylor, are trying to maintain this wonderful estate, supporting it mostly by weddings. They'd lost a great deal to Hurricane Dolly, including a sabal palm four feet in diameter. Martha and Ben discussed the merits of different eups and lantanas—"desert lantana will not die"—as we walked about the paths. Though there was plenty a-wing, none of it was new.

Next came the Inn at Chachalaca Bend, where the innkeepers, Curt and Rosemary Breedlove, greeted us genially on a golf cart and escorted us into the preserve. We walked to a grove where Julia's and dun skippers guarded their posts. The great find came when I swept a grassy field, a skipper flew, and I netted it: a good female of the rare hecebolus panoquin. When worn, this species is easily confused with ocola and purple-washed panoquins.

At Palo Alto Battlefield National Historical Park, like everywhere else, there was a mistflower-based butterfly garden occupied by the usual suspects. The best bit was a silver argiope's stitchwork. The spider had spun a great X, which would make a fine logo for the Xerces Society. Henceforth to Resaca de la Palma State Park and World Birding Center, Brownsville. Looking around the obligatory butterfly garden, we right off the bat encountered a lifer and a grail: the blue metalmark (*Lasaia sula*).

I'd wanted to see this incomparably clear, cool, shimmering blue insect for years, and here it was: half a dozen males, in fact, and all the looking we could want, except for the rolling clock. I'd always found the very idea of a *blue* metalmark outrageous, and the silver-banded hairstreak among them didn't harm that impression. Then still another wish fulfilled: a purplish skipper with as striking a dot as any dog called Spot, and with one of the best names: *Nyctelius nyctelius nyctelius*, the violet-banded skipper.

A friendly and charming young ranger who knew her butterflies, Katherine Miller, drove us in her state truck into a wildwood remnant on a generally closed road. She had seen band-celled sisters in this palmy resaca in the past, and they did not flake out for us. A bright male flew out from the trees like any feisty admiral, with another tailing it. Until they sorted out their territorial rights and one took off, we enjoyed fine watching of both—fresh males—perching, spreading, and jetting all around us. Even with the heat and mosquitoes, how I wanted to walk in there for hours and hours!

Instead, we took off for El Jardin des Colores in Brownsville. This private school for little ones and its adjacent garden are run by one of courtly Ben's many doting lady friends. Perhaps they were drawn by his Tennessee charm and gnomish smile, since it couldn't have been his summer Santa beard, much like my own. Marilyn and her gardener, Jose, welcomed us into the little backyard Eden. Two blue metalmarks posed, both females this time, the fresher one's lavender just matching the blooms of the mistflower that supped her. An immense, intensely hued guava skipper tanked up on some long-styled white blossoms, a perfect accouterment to the Jardin des Colores.

Sabal Palm Audubon Sanctuary is the reserve most debated when it comes to the border wall. It was also the only one of the day's destinations, so far, where I had been before, several times, for tours and festivals. I remembered it as hot, buggy, and semiproductive. All that applied today, except it was almost nonproductive. Ben said the garden used to be much better but wasn't much now at all. We walked about a mile's loop, a real push for Ben with his semiparalyzed left side, but he gutted it through well.

Bizarrely few butterflies appeared on the wild *Eupatorium crucita* patches in the sun at Sabal Palm: one red admirable, one pipevine swallowtail, a female mazans scallopwing, and a southern broken-dash, not common here and very rich russet below. Odonates were more numerous by far—giant and eastern pondhawks among them. And I finally saw green jays well, those improbable, tricolor paint chips of the border forests and feeders. The time spent at Sabal Palm could certainly have been better invested at the day's final destination, but you never know: there could also have been something fabulous. The days for discovery here may be limited. Thanks to the planned border wall, Audubon later announced that the sanctuary would close for the summer of 2009. With the wall built on the levee, the entire preserve would be cut off in the no-man's-land behind the wall, virtually ceded to Mexico. Its future hangs on a pending lawsuit with the government, provision of a gate or not, and border politics.

We'd hit our southernmost point, in fact the southernmost point of the year not counting Florida, at Brownsville. From there we turned northeast up the Gulf, across the Rio Grande's ignoble outlet. Demonstrating his oft-repeated "strategy, strategy!" at every turn, Ben dashed across the bridge to Port Isabel on South Padre Island. Or tried to dash—the five o'clock traffic was thick as Texas crude in winter. The island is largely a high-rise mess, even more so since the hurricane tossed things about. There is the big, long, wild reserve and beach up north, but we had no time for that. We picked our way through the vacationing crowds to yet another World Birding "Center"—that polynucleate pretense—and found its grounds largely barren, the day late and breezy. And yet . . . Ben's strategy paid off again. There on a Padre Island mistflower, beside a too-mowed lawn, sat a teensy *Panoquina panoquinoides*, which Andy and I had missed on Easter in Florida. I spotted a candidate, then a eufala, and then *it* for sure!

Ben came through. The obscure skipper was exactly that for which we had come to this extreme. Its breeding habitat was down in the hard-to-navigate salt marsh; the adults came up to the lawn in search of sweets. It was warmly colored, really shaped like a miniature salt-marsh panoquin, if not quite as drawn out. I saw the three crucial spots very well, twice or three times, before it flew. Among all the mess and junk, I thought, that one fine little skipper sits. That's practically haiku, and it works for me.

Finally, Laguna Atascosa National Wildlife Refuge. The road out there was long and terribly potholed. I harbored fond memories of being there with Thea and Mark Garland and our tour, when we encountered Jeff Glassberg and his tour. Jeff was flustered that we were picnicking in the ramada where he'd intended to stop with his optics-only, no-net group. Jane Ruffin suggested that we actually *could* lunch together, and so we did, Jeff scrupling to break bread with us netters after all. That time was rainy but midday. I remember another, sunnier visit when the hot shore was teeming with pygmy-blues on the glasswort. Now it was almost night. A communal roost of queens fluttered in the last, low-angled sun in an acacia. Another roost held twenty or more tropic queens, including two pairs *in copula*. A nessus hawkmoth hover-sipped in the coming dusk. We were too late for Laguna.

But it had been a memorable day, with fifty-six species, four of them new. Ben enjoyed showing off his places and people and having the butterflies where they were meant to be, and I was happy to see them. When Ben asked me which of today's butterflies made the greatest impression on me, I responded that the beauty of the blue metalmarks was unforgettable, the band-celled sisters were elegant and fine, the lilac-banded skipper a total delight, and the hecebolus panoquin awfully exciting to confirm in hand; but I had to say that my favorite of all was that little obscure skipper. "I *thought* that's what you'd say," said Ben. "Wonderful, wonderful."

Ben showed me the spot where he once watched an ocelot. He had also seen jaguarundi in this refuge. We stood vigil for some time, but cats did not come padding. An armadillo rooted in the verge, three deer crossed the road at the crest, and heading out, we spotted a big hog across the marshland. A pauraque called down dark on the day.

13. BOG HOPPER

"Cheese Next Exit." I guess I was in Wisconsin. Wisconsin, in November, on a butterfly hunt? As I rolled past Holsteins and stone-bottomed barns, brown oak-leaf drumlins, corn stubble, and winter weeds, I had to remind myself why I was here, and why I wasn't completely bats.

Election Day, Tuesday, November 4, Ben had taken me to the Harlingen airport. As I was about to board the Sun Country (amazingly) nonstop flight to Minneapolis (of all places), a butterfly flashed past the terminal window—I believe it was a painted lady— my last sight of a Texas butterfly of this trip. Or of any butterfly for many days to come.

The year's original plan had me teaching a writing workshop on the train from Winnipeg to Churchill, Manitoba. We were going to visit the polar bears, and I would look for immature butterflies on the frozen Arctic tundra. I accepted the offer because it would make a change, and it would pay some bills back home. But the whole thing was axed for lack of sign-ups. So when I received an invitation to take part in a Children & Nature Network meeting in Minnesota, I again accepted. I was an adviser to this initiative, which was inspired by Richard Louv's book *Last Child in the Woods*. It seemed that a butterfly Big Year ought to include a northern component in winter, and it would get me to some states I'd otherwise have missed.

I wrote several upper midwest lepidopterists to ask their advice on seeking immature blues, coppers, checkers, skippers, and others in winter. Their comments ranged from "That RMP is one ambitious guy" to "basically a fool's errand." No one gave me much cause for hope. But I thought I'd have a go, anyway.

That night, Barack Obama was elected president of the United States. I joined a jubilant election party in C&NN President Cheryl Charles's hotel room. Next day I walked around the Minnesota Landscape Arboretum in a balmy twenty degrees, looking in a lightning-split hollow tree for cloaks in the crannies, then for spring azure pupae among the osier dogwoods. After the gathering, I left Chanhassen in a rented Mazda called the Tailed Maroon, after a satyr of that description I once knew in Hong Kong. Snow spattered the windshield.

At a rest area, there was interpretation for sphagnum, the barrens, and the Karner blue butterfly, in whose pursuit I had come. Before dark, I reached the Baraboo home of Ann and Scott Swengel, the blue's chief devouts in those parts. Scott's spud and scallop soup led into nature chat that could have outlasted their remarkable, long-term regime of butterfly study and monitoring. Scott was a former employee of the Crane Foundation here, and Ann had been longtime keeper of the national Fourth of July Butterfly Count data. I slept in their "spare" room, full of books, journals, papers, artifacts, and now me.

Up at 7:00 A.M., we set out north, soon passing Bosshard Bogs —cranberries, just like home. Dike 17 Wildlife Area in the Black River State Forest had been assembled in the 1930s from government buyouts of poor farms, then developed by the CCC for duck habitat. Today it includes white pine barrens, wetlands, and grassland habitats for Blanding's turtles, timber wolves, and Karner blues. For an hour we knelt, lay, and squatted on the snow-patched ground, reticulated with red British soldier lichens and a mosaic of winter leaves and grasses, examining dead lupines for Karner blue eggs. Sand grains, snow drops, fungi, and lichens all yielded false alarms. Our knees went wet, our toes cold.

The indefatigable butterfly team of the Swengels made a sweet sight, knelt over their work together. Stretching out our chilled limbs, we climbed the high, windy observation tower, from which we watched skeins of tundra swans. Timber wolf tracks as broad as my hand pressed into the sandy trail leading back to the field car. "Food for the dudes," said Scott, and lunch appeared.

Our next attempt was a bog trot in search of bog copper eggs.

Beyond North Settlement Road, we walked into the bog in Jackson County Forest from Highway 54. The going was difficult in the tussocks, vines, birches, snow, and water. I tripped on a vine and fell flat, frigid water filling my borrowed rubber boots, soaking my jeans. Dense stands of dwarf cranberry crowded tussocks in breaks in the tamarack woods, but searching them meant sprawling on knees and gloves until we got too damn cold. No copper eggs turned up, but I munched a bunch of good, crisp, tangy cranberries, so big for their tiny leaves. Then there was the beauty of the bog, its reds, greens, browns.

After warming up, we resumed the Karner blue hunt at Bauer-Brockway Barrens, a state natural area in Jackson County Forest. Right off, Scott found an egg cemented to an herbaceous stem next to a lupine. With our hand lenses, we clearly saw the flattened, dimpled, and ornamented white donut. Then Ann and I found one each laid on lupine pods, conspicuous on the dark, hairy beans. She and Scott had not attempted this before; it was fun to see something new for them, with them, in their own intimate territory.

This was a big deal for me. The Karner blue, now a cause célèbre across the Upper Midwest, was one of the Xerces Society's first conservation projects, in the mid-seventies. The butterfly had been distinguished as its own taxon and named by Vladimir Nabokov while he was curator of butterflies at Harvard, and it later cameoed in his novel *Pnin*. Decades later, the society director Robert Dirig obtained a letter from Nabokov in support of Xerces' efforts to protect the Albany Pine Bush population in New York. I'd been much involved with this animal for years, but I'd never seen it, and an egg was much better than nothing. Though it was at that time listed as a subspecies of the Melissa blue, Nabokov and Dirig both considered the Karner blue distinct, and most authorities agreed it would eventually be elevated as such. As this book goes to press, that prediction has just come true, in the first revision of Pelham's *Catalogue*.

We finished our bog crawl over a meal of local cranberry brats and New Glarus Bog Ale at the Bog Restaurant, warmly glowing in its piney walls and furniture. Proprietor Charles said this was the Bog's last night, thanks to a bankrupt lodge and a failed Flintstone theme park. I wondered if the timber wolves and Karner blues might inherit this boggy landscape after all, and so they may; but happily, the Swengels later informed me the restaurant has since reopened.

Back on Birch Street, we talked butterflies, fire, people, and other mutual passions and plaints into the night. The Swengels have done a great deal of rigorous research on the impact of intentional burning on butterfly populations. Their findings have been received with a "kill the messenger" attitude by The Nature Conservancy and others. Bluntly voicing their often iconoclastic and inconvenient beliefs, based on sound science in service to conservation, Ann and Scott inspire strong feelings. Their work is beginning to affect policy and practice. I like them a lot and hugely admire their dedication to natural history, which shames most of us, or should.

Two days later I was again on my knees, this time at the Riveredge Nature Center just west of Lake Michigan, north of Milwaukee. I'd led butterfly walks there during the warm days of summer, but this was different. Su Borkin, lepidopterist at the Milwaukee Public Museum for thirty-some years, met me for a long-planned hunt for the swamp metalmark—the species I'd so narrowly missed in Missouri. A covey of young Riveredge naturalists joined us. Out in the very field where I'd netted meadow fritillaries, Su pointed out *Cirsium muticum*, host plants of *Calephelis muticum*. She gently poked about the bases of the swamp thistles, and on the second or third one, unearthed two caterpillars plus their woolly cast skins and eggshells. One reacted to the warmth of her hand by rearing its head; the other turned its posterior up and shot poop.

This site occupied just half an acre. In her extensive site assessments for the Fish and Wildlife Service, Su found very few appropriate habitats in the state. One lies in the kettle moraine country, another along a power line right of way, then there is this site. There are maybe twelve historic colonies, but just the three active populations known in Wisconsin. So Riveredge really is a significant habitat for this state-listed species.

"Given how small the sites are," Su told us, "you have to have some optimism that there are some more sites lurking. But from what I've seen, it seems unlikely." If not for the more robust Missouri colonies(!), *Calephelis muticum* would likely be listed already. Intolerant of fire, the species may have suffered from burns, but succession is responsible for most local extinctions, with larch, birch, dogwood, and ninebark taking over marshes. So to manage for it, you need to reduce the biomass without crisping the critters. I was thrilled to see those larvae. It was especially, wickedly sweet to have a second chance, having come so close in Missouri. Now it remains, as for the Karner blue, to see them fly one day.

Su and I drove out Blue Goose Road to Cedarburg Bog preserve. We walked a trail over a piney drumlin she calls her Mourning Cloak Wood, then out onto cedar and tamarack bog. Ice cracked beneath bridges and scarlet pitcher plants, gin Popsicles in their mouths, poked up through rose-red sphagnum. We sprawled on the boardwalk, my plan ever since Orono Bog, and searched dwarf cranberry leaves for bog copper eggs.

We took our candidates (for there were some) back to the University of Wisconsin, Milwaukee, Field Station, where Su once based her research, to examine them. The director, Gretchen Meyer, had been a student of Remington and Francie Chew at Yale and gladly provided lab space and microscopes. Our "eggs" all turned out to be white fungal disks, but we had enjoyed the search. We debriefed over my life cheese curds at the DQ in Saukville. "Not the *best* cheese curds," said Su. But they were cheese curds, it was Wisconsin, and it was warm.

The next day, I left the home of my Riveredge friends Barb and Don Gilmore. They'd flown to Seattle for their twenty-fifth anniversary, so I walked Spaniel Sheila at seven. Sniffing the crisp white selvage, she got excited when a duck hunter's shotgun boomed. Sheila loves nothing like hunting with Don. I was sorry to disappoint her as we walked back, leaving our footprints on the frosty grass, but I had my own hunt to resume, and a dog wouldn't help.

Wisconsin is easy on the eye. Dusty sumac crowded against the fencerows. On my way to Oshkosh, near Horicon Marsh, I passed Brownsville—a million miles in every way from Brownsville, Texas, where I could be right now surrounded by butterflies, inflating my stalled total. Here, the cold, clear sky was full of geese. Into Winnebago County and then, b'gosh, I was in Oshkosh, a life garment-brand location. I would have loved to have seen the yellow and purple tapestry of goldenrod and New England asters all over these fields just a month ago. The "World's Longest String Cheese" could be seen at Weyauwega, near the Waupaca County fairgrounds.

Somewhere between Highway 10 and Rustic Road 54W, barns and silos replaced adult superstores and billboards. After Appleton, Almond, and Amherst, beyond Wild Rose, past Plover and south of Vesper, I found Ron Arnold's inviting home on the back forty of his family farm. We visited in the warm inside, then took off for the field. In our respective rigs, we drove deep into sandy bogland of Jacob Searles Cranberry Company holdings, in the township of Cranmoor. Snow fell in small pellets, and the temperature dropped. A young white-tailed buck flashed his big white flag for Armistice Day. Snow blew along the ice in the bogside ditch. This was not Texas anymore.

In summertime, Ron had seen fifty to sixty Harris's checkerspots at once here, an uncommon beauty I'd encountered only once ever, in Vermont. Having come now to look for its diapausing larvae, we were surprised by a flying lep—a November moth, winging its way through the falling snow. We entered the marsh and poked through flat-topped asters, Harris's host plant, as our fingers froze. I found feeding damage and egg mass remnants, and Ron retrieved a mote of silk. I was hoping the larvae might still be present in communal nests in winter; my research and queries had yielded conflicting results on this point, but I'd located no one who professed to actually finding any.

A big flock of black-capped chickadees descended onto poison sumac's white berries. We went until our toes and fingers froze, and then went some more, maybe two hours in all. As we left, sleety snow had collected in wide, loopy stripes on the ditch ice. Heading out, I saw a lot more aster. So when we got to the blacktop and said our goodbyes, I turned around and went back, stopping to watch hundreds of sandhill cranes glide over low, getting out before the really heavy weather closed in. I suspected their example should be heeded. But after my toes warmed up, I went out again into a deeper, reedier marsh. There I collected aster stems with leaves on until nearly dead dark.

As I tucked my big, unruly bouquet into the trunk, a withy cutter drove by, his willow switches piled in the back of his pickup. We nodded at each other, a nod without questions, winter harvesters with our different harvests. The sandy road was white and slick with snow beside the ditch. I eased on out with care, holding no desire at all to slip into that ditch, through that ice, especially after that bridge in Majestic, Kentucky.

In my room at the Antlers Motel in Eau Claire, I ransacked my bale of aster herbage, making a mess of pappi and dried leaves like roll-your-own tobacco all over the carpet. I selected and bottled up a bunch of rolled leaves to check with a dissecting scope back home. In the event, I would actually find one live larva—not Harris's checkerspot but a casebearer, a microlepidopteran of the family Coleophoridae. These minute moths, as larvae, make houses rather like those of caddis flies from silk and bits of leaf and other materials. The end of this one suggested a three-cornered hat. From these shelters, they stick out feet first and feed.

The following spring, having hibernated in its tiny case, the caterpillar was still alive. I gave it fresh new Douglas aster (*Aster subspicatus*) leaves, our native, from our own dooryard. It fed at first, then went torpid for several weeks, but then began roving and apparently feeding again. At that point I wrote to Jean-François Landry, a Canadian scientist and expert on the colephorids, for his advice. He suggested misting it to mimic dew, and being patient, but also warned me that parasitism is a frequent bane.

Indeed, on the nineteenth of August, I found an even tinier wasp in the rearing chamber. A colleague of Jean-François's in Ottawa identified it as a member of the chalcidoid genus *Perilampus*. From its case and host, the parasitized micromoth larva matched *Coleophora bidens*—but that species is known to feed only on the seeds of asters and goldenrods, not the leaves, whereas our creature made minute mines in the leaves, rolling up bits of the epidermis like tiny green cigars. This struck Jean-François as very strange. It could be a new species, as might the wasp, but he could not make a positive ID from the case alone.

I may one day have to go back and look for more. Meanwhile, my bog trot yielded a third trip lepidopteran, and two specimens for the Canadian National Collection. The remarkable thing is that, if not a Harris's checkerspot, some mote of actual life came out of that cold dusk thrash through snowy weeds in a Wisconsin marsh. Imagine that.

The following morning, driving toward the Twin Cities, I placed my pillow fight's–worth of winter asters in a suitable same-species spot. Then I drove to St. Paul and dropped into Garrison Keillor's Common Good Books, a great little basement bookshop with an unusually broad wall of poetry. I bought the proprietor's own com-pendium, *Good Poems,* for the long train trip home. At my friend's house in Minneapolis, I sat back and read Robert Bly. When Robert Johnson returned from giving a reflexology session, he showed me his latest fine book-making project, for a collection of Bly's poems. He prints the texts and builds the elegant bindings, and his ex-traordinary books reside in the rare book collections at Harvard and Yale universities. Robert asked, "Can I go to the bog with you tomorrow?"

Cedar Creek Ecosystem Science Reserve was recommended by several lepists, even those who thought I was nuts. Robert and I searched cranberry leaves on the floating bog from narrow, two-plank boardwalks. Luann and Mary from the field station visited us, and Mary, in her nice work clothes, hunted with us for an hour. Robert looked all around a deer bone that he took for an omen.

Amazed, I gazed back at them, this professional woman and this noted book artist, out here combing the winter bog for invisible bits of life, on my behalf. I wanted Robert to find eggs almost as bad as I'd wanted anything all year. He attended to one place better than I, who shifted from spot to spot as I got stiff and cold. He also bent, reached, and squatted better, though he is taller and about the same weight. When he had to leave, I was sad to see him go without any eggs in his basket.

I had one more hour, lying on the boardwalk or in soft and yield-ing sphagnum. I checked many a tiny leaflet and saw bits of fluff, skeletonized and nipped spots, and the tiny domes that bear the spores of Ascomycete fungi. Then, rooting one last time through my original hummock, I noticed an off-white oval mote on my fin-ger. I got it safely back to the lab, where Mary and Luann, excited, rounded up a scope. The tiny unit proved indeed to be an egg—but not of the bog copper. It was a little eccentric, too elongated, and lacked the ornamented pillbox look of any lycaenid ovum. So the last United States copper missing from my list would remain that way.

But that was no disgrace. Later, David Wright, the only person I know who has actually found them (and one of the very few who has looked) wrote me this: "It is amazingly difficult to find *epixanthe* eggs." Maybe I got all these people—Ann, Scott, Su, Ron, Robert, and Mary—out on a wild-goose chase, crawling through winter bogs in the frozen North in search of mythic motes, for nothing. But we had fun. We found the eggs of Karner blues, the wild worms of marsh metalmarks, and a cool casebearer. And we got *out*: that never needs an apology.

And if one could look forward as one looks back, there would have been even more to celebrate. The following July, Ann Swengel wrote to me that "the bog copper eggs we failed to find as adults are abounding as adults. On July 4th . . . we found swarms." Scott added, "The first two Karner blues we saw this year in Bauer-Brockway Barrens were, respectively, flying circles around the lupine plant where you found an egg, and less than a meter from where Ann found an egg. The place was loaded with Karners this year." And over at Riveredge, Su Borkin found the swamp metalmarks in good shape too, and may have seen the very ones we petted as woolly first instar larvae.

Robert made me a great grilled cheese, massaged my feet, and put me on the Empire Builder, pulling out of St. Paul at midnight. Two mornings later, chatty passengers wakened me in time to see the Columbia River, all pink in the sunrise. I washed my face and, in a stroke of magic, came out to the vestibule just in time to look right into the Fish Patch, its burdock and wintervege as red as its summer monarchs in the dawning. I took Robert's buttered raisin bread, a banana, a little Amtrak granola, milk, and coffee into the dome car. Mt. Hood emerged around a bend, and with the moon still high, the sun erupted out of the cold magma walls, casting a yellow sun glade all down the Great River of the West. At Hood River, my two-month giant circuit was complete, for this was where I'd left the river to head south toward Texas.

And then there was Thea, meeting me in Kelso with a huge hug. We drove home through the Columbia White-tailed Deer Refuge, listening to *A Prairie Home Companion*. When Garrison Keillor and Andra Suchy sang "The Bramble and the Rose," our wedding song, we stopped, got out, and danced our way right down the middle of the refuge road.

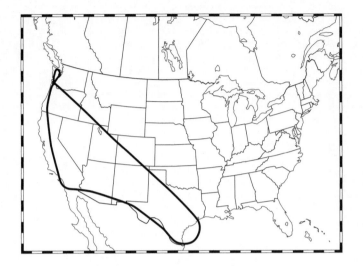

Back and Forth

What is the blue road anyway but an opportunity to poke

at the unseen and hoping the unseen will poke back?

—William Least Heat-Moon, *Blue Highways*

1. TEJAS THANKSGIVING

The Naked Lady died the night before Thanksgiving. Maybe she was thankful to go, as she was in misery according to her neighbor, Benton Basham, which is why she didn't wear any clothes. I'd slept poorly with new chigger bites acquired since I'd come back to Texas, always itching from 2:00 to 4:00 A.M. when the histamines were at their peak. Maybe it was chiggers that made the Naked Lady miserable in the first place.

Just before boarding my plane in Portland, I'd seen the weather map in *USA Today*: it called for a high temp in Brownsville of 64°F— yikes! I hoped I wasn't returning to a cold week in south Texas. On the long flight, I added up the species still possible to see in the LRGV, and it came to about 120. Of course, many of those very rarely turn up on the United States side of the border. But if I could see one-quarter of them, I'd be in reach of my goal.

As Ben and I began my final week in the valley, Mission shivered under a cool overcast. A few things were flying, but the air had been warmer in Washington when I'd left home. Our first great find was the Kellys from Kokomo—Phil and Joanne, intense and brainy naturalists as committed to having fun as to seeing butterflies. Eager to help the cause, they had already set up a cell phone chain among the people butterflying the valley that week, all searching on my behalf. I was touched.

We all headed over to the NABA Butterfly Park. Among the slim pickings, a Mexican silverspot materialized from the chilly air. Shocking pink at the base of its ventral forewings like a Virginia lady, with a pouch of Mexican silver coins spilled all across its hindwings, it seemed unreasonably brilliant, considering the weather. "I love it, I love it," enthused Benton. "To me, that's a fabulous bonus insect for your list. They usually start later, and in light of the last few days, especially." As the day warmed by degrees, a gray hairstreak with reddish bars skipped onto a patch of eups. It remained while Ben set the telephone relay in motion. It was truly a wonder how quickly everyone assembled—suddenly there were more butterfliers than butterflies! We all got good views, including flickers of the russet upperside that made it a male ruddy hairstreak.

Then someone said, "Father Tom is coming—stay on the bug!" When the well-liked priest arrived, all the way from Harlingen, I examined crimson patch caterpillars on flame acanthus with him. Another who answered the call was Dave Hanson, a very experienced observer. A purple-washed panoquin had been mistaken for a hecebolus, and it was Dave who spotted the error, an easy one to make. As we watched together, Dave referred to a female *Phoebis philea* as "a flying tangerine," and I warned him that I would probably steal that description. Then he gave me a field lesson in telling *Eurema nise* from *E. lisa* on the wing. Ben had his own method. I saw their points, but the mimosa yellow is so similar to the little that I prefer to make that call at rest or in hand.

Ben said, "Let's beat path," and I heard "Rosita patch," setting off a false alarm. A great big Evans's panoquin, one of my heavy wants, was spotted; but sadly the hue failed to go up for that one. Jan Dauphin tried and tried to find it for me, to no avail.

The next day came brighter, partly thanks to my first two-barred flasher. *Astraptes fulgerator* is the stunner called "flashing astraptes" in my 1982 field guide. First on white plumbago, it shifted to shrimp plant for a good long look: turquoise blue inside white bars on black, with long blue, furry scales coarsely combed like a big boa. A rare "white-tailed longtail" proved to be a brown longtail with a bird dropping on it. The Kokomo butterfliers, coming down the walk at Estero, spotted a giant white. Big as a baseball, this was one of my long-standing desires. It landed right above Ben's head and he got a photo. Then a beautiful guava skipper showed up on the plumbago. It was always hard to get out of that place.

Every morning we picked up a large Dr Pepper for Ben, a coffee for me, and two packets of peanuts each. Ben plunked his peanuts right into his Dr Pepper, apparently a common practice in the

South but a new one on me. First stop, Frontera Audubon, right there in Weslaco. We thought we were watching a clytie ministreak, but neither of us was really happy with it. Fortunately Ben got a good photo, which Andy Warren later determined to be a rare red-spotted hairstreak (*Strymon rufofusca*).

On our way to Mission, we got a hot call from Dave Hanson that a white angled-sulphur had turned up at the NABA park. When we got there, Dave had the giant sulphur staked out under a potato plant leaf, against which it was extraordinarily cryptic. A tear in the wing showed a glimpse of the top, like a slit skirt revealing a bit of shapely leg. Then over at the Bentsen RV palace, where monarchs fanned the flame vines all along the fence, a West Coast lady was flying and perching along a dirt track. An uncommon insect here, though a backyard butterfly for me, Annabella had Ben much more excited than the flasher. He called the Indianans, and they came pronto, for a lifer all around. Ben gushed, "Wonderful wonderful. I love it I love it." Things Ben liked were "fabulous" or "incredible," and he often doubled up on the superlatives, just to make sure.

So that's how it went, garden to garden, butterfly to butterfly, across the valley. Ben felt that strategy argued for my keeping vigil "where it's happening," in the valley, in the gardens, in reach of the cell phone alerts; and no doubt he was right. He said I should spend the rest of the year there and forget about Hawaii, with its few species, and I asked him if he wanted to handle the ensuing divorce.

I hankered to experience the *inside* of the border reserves, not just the tended edges, and therefore decided to hike deep into Santa Ana National Wildlife Reserve the next day. That would leave Ben out, but as his main objective was to help me in my Big Year, he gave me pointers for Santa Ana, adding that I probably wouldn't see much new in there.

"The rain and hail have really knocked things back," said the English volunteer at the refuge desk in the morning. Indeed, the numbers were vastly fewer than on my previous visit. The eups and scorpion's-tail so productive before were all dried up. It almost started well, as I walked a crossroad and a smallish green butterfly flew a circle around me and disappeared into the forest. It was almost certainly a blue-eyed greenwing, or sailor as NABA likes to call it; but a four-spotted greenwing, a very rare stray from across the river, had been recorded here this year too, so I couldn't be sure. Then came the bloody tram stinking up the air, its *loud* interpretive bullhorn frightening off the wildlife. What a racket one woman with a microphone can make; I heard her for a mile over the birdsong. Cars had been banned during tram season to reduce human impact, and that's defensible, but the tram itself seemed plenty intrusive to me.

At the old cemetery, I finally found some nectar. Yellow composites and lantana bloomed in the untended butterfly garden. As I had my lunch of nuts, banana, and water, no curds, no whey, on the butterfly gardener Glenda Blankenship's memorial mossy tuffet, a potrillo skipper came and sat down beside me. Then I laid out my rotten bananas on rotted old palings and posts, and on the big, flat tomb of D. Christoval Leal Fallacio, died 5 August 1876, forty-three years old. Wouldn't you know that the tram would come again just as I put out my bait, and that the guide would bring her group into the graveyard? I mumbled something about permits, taking part in a long-term butterfly survey, and the interpretive opportunity of the malachite and amymone already on my bait, and left by the back way.

Santa Ana did have its rewards that day. On the Vireo Trail, much longer than the advertised .9 mile, I unsheathed my collapsable hand net for a nonlethal self-tutorial on petite fawn-spotted and chunkier clouded skippers. I concluded that many of the calls I'd watched folks make for fawn-spotteds had really just been small cloudeds. Then, back at the cemetery, all I found at my bait were the very same malachite and amymone, plus ants and wasps. But along the nearby Owl Trail, a pair of splendid red rims flew up between a bluewing and a malachite—now that's fancy!

Heading out Resaca Trail to the road, I watched the spectral flutter of twenty or more zebras, barely moving their wings before my face, surely the lowest gear to keep a butterfly aloft. As James Fisher described it in *Wild America*, "It does not beat so much as quiver its wings, and with a shivering delicacy picks its way very slickly through the undertangle of the most jungly complication." Here they were going to their communal roost in Spanish moss, as coyotes set up a sunset howl to the west. No garden had that to offer.

At Jaguarundi Crossing, I turned one more time down to the Rio Grande. The moment I hit the bank, a Border Patrol speedboat shoomed up below me with two agents aboard. Impressive! Had they tracked me with infrared or motion sensors? After exchanging niceties, they wished me a pleasant evening and good birding and shoomed back downstream again. And evening it was. Way past closing, I hoofed it out on the Jaguarundi, Oriole, and Bobcat trails, and finally the road, because I hated to break all the spider webs across the narrow paths. Pauraques perched on the road in front of me in the deep dusk, and as I approached, they hopped like grass-hoppers, came down a few feet away, then flew up and around, flashing their big white wing bars and calling their high "ca-quat ca-ca-quat-quat-quat-Wewooo!" These chunky goatsuckers are related to the nighthawks I watched swarming in the Methow Valley back in August, but their voices are entirely different. As I came out on the dike, a few fireflies still stoked their cool fires beneath Saturn and Jupiter. So I had a fine time in Santa Ana. But Ben was right—I saw nothing new. Except, everything.

At midnight, heavy rain fell on the tin roof and awnings of the trailer. In the foggy morning, on our way to the Pumphouse, Ben rubbed it in a bit, telling me about the 106-species day he and his son Jeff had logged while I was up in the barren North. We stopped for a roadkilled barn owl. Ben loves owls; on his Big Year, through strategy, he made sure he had all nineteen species by June 30. He doubted I could reach five hundred species at this point. The de-tested, spectacularly ugly border wall was going up right beside the Pumphouse gardens, cutting off part of the trail. Christmas lights were up too, all in butterfly shapes. In the cool morning, those were about the only butterflies to be seen. But soon we spotted, and Ben photographed, a real butterfly to celebrate. The teleus longtail is a good find, which people often think they see but almost never really do.

We were heading to Bentsen when Phil called with an alert for a yojoa scrub-hairstreak and a green-backed ruby-eye, the latter a special desire I'd looked and looked for. We all met at the appointed La Coma (or saffron plum), a bush with small yellow flowers on which Thea had once photographed a great purple hairstreak in the Hill Country. There was indeed a great purple on it, as well as a mallow scrub-hairstreak and a dusky-blue groundstreak. But the yojoa and the ruby-eye had flown the coop. Except for that teleus longtail, the day was something of a downer.

The "jam" that Ben took me to at Siesta Village that evening—a sort of trailer park hootenanny with eighteen guitarists and assorted other oldsters and their instruments playing mostly Merle Haggard—improved upon it only by degrees. Some 107 such jams took place in the valley every week among the Winter Texans, and I think Ben attended about half of them. Benton is a scholar of country music, and when I didn't know a certain Tennessee songbird, he was genuinely appalled. For me, the best bits were the brownies at the break; the old gents swooning over the flirty lady with the nimbus of silver hair and the fringed satin-and-chambray shirt, when she sang "Blanket on the Ground"; and the ninety-something fella with a happy smile and a beautiful square squeezebox labeled "Stradivarius," whooping up a snappy polka.

Wednesday came with sun, and Ben's helper and friend Maggie bringing us pancakes and a big bag of oranges and grapefruit she'd picked. As the rangers proudly showed us, water had been let back into the Resaca Llano Grande, and it was full of white pelicans. I hoped they didn't get drift from the crop-duster that had been grunting back and forth all morning. I hoped we got no drift, either, it was that close. Upvalley at the Bentsen RV palace, happily, no spray is allowed. The day before, a resident described a butterfly to me, and I responded that it was probably a crimson patch. Today, she asked us to look at her caterpillars—they were hundreds of crimson patch pups! A giant white flew past. "We big-time rarely get cabbage butterflies in the valley," said Ben, confirming the diagnosis of *Ganyra josephina*.

Then an emergency call came from across the street: young Troy from Ohio had rounded up another yojoa. This one stayed put for us. Eight sets of eyes confirmed it: a lot of butterfly experience, gathered in one spot. Then Chris Durden, noted expert on fossil butterflies and father of a good Seattle friend of ours, showed up from Austin. I was glad to thank him in person for his cordial help with the phantom Apache skipper, though I wished I could have told him I'd actually found it.

The party shifted to the RV park. At the entrance, on orange lantana, I spied a very scarce Isabella longwing. We assembled the cadres in minutes, and everyone got to see and photograph it. A member of one of the great Neotropical mimicry complexes, Isabella flashed its own particular version of the oft-copied tiger-stripe pattern of orange, black, and yellow. Its antennae were almost chartreuse! The next day I would find a second Isabella in the park's lantana beds, then a Julia, then a zebra—three species of longwings in about as many minutes. I thought, Now, how about a *Heliconius erato*, for four? An erato actually appeared, but not until I was long gone, a couple of days later.

A shout went up: there was a greenstreak outside the Wall. We all watched it well, and several good photos supported our joint conclusion that it was the rarer Clench's greenstreak, *Cyanophrys miserabilis*: brilliant green with maroon spots along the edge below. Only the Kokomonians missed it, having explored upriver that day. I enjoyed almost as much as the greenstreak watching four ardent butterfliers, all with cameras "on the bug," Jan's pins glittering on her hat in the slanted sun.

Ben and I finished the day at the Hedge, where I saw the best purple ever on a purple-washed skipper. A huge (inch-plus) jumping spider with fancy banded leggings held her own on a prickly pear pod, eating a honeybee. She turned her eight eyes toward me and clutched her prey tighter when I peered, as if I wanted it for myself.

What I really wanted next was something other than Wendy's. Ben found us the Sunrise Cafe in old Weslaco for garlic fish and enchiladas. Relaxing with a Negro Modelo for me and a nonalcoholic piña colada for him, Ben told me about his erstwhile anesthesiology practice, and the good livelihood he made and lost twice, first to divorce, then to his stroke. He described his beloved Tennessee farm and how his neighbors sometimes drove him wild. "I've been to university and had to relearn a lot of things," Ben said. "These people, they've never gone anywhere but the bathroom."

Thanksgiving came, my last day in the valley. The Naked Lady's demise caused a stir in the park. Even so, we got away early, thanks to a call from Phil about another green-backed ruby-eye at Bentsen.

On our way, he called again—there was a tropical greenstreak at the RV palace! We made the twenty miles in a hurry and picked up the double play. *Cyanophrys herodotus* sat still on eups in the RV park, just eighteen hours and a couple of hundred feet away from yesterday's *C. miserabilis,* and crisply field-marked to show the difference. Then we hastened over to the Bentsen lantana. The rubyeye, probably the same one we missed two mornings ago, was still there. Two minutes later, the massive skipper buzzed off. I saw the mottling, the bright spots, those improbable ruby globes; I missed the green back but know it was there. The powerful, intelligent insect no doubt habitually roosted in this nectar garden, near its beloved Mexican olive blossoms.

I wanted to penetrate the backways of Bentsen as well as Santa Ana. The park volunteer and excellent butterflier Rick Snider offered to be my guide. There were big native La Comas, where we might find some novel hairstreaks. The beginning was a bummer: as I came out of the gents', Rick said there'd been an Evans's panoquin— the biggest and brightest of these jet-winged skippers—on a bush right there by the door, and it had just flown off. Foiled again.

Across the canal, we walked roads to old campgrounds. Whitecollared peccaries snuffled oranges at a bait station with green jays and altamira orioles. Rick showed me a tree hole with a screech-owl in it. The ear tufts looked like broken wood, increasing the owl's impressive crypsis. I could smell the sweet scent of the biggest saffron plum from many yards away. Along with crowds of snouts and queens, it did have 'streaks and skippers, including a striking whitepatched skipper. There was nothing new or unusual, but at least I'd had a look beyond the gardens.

NABA was closed for the holiday, but someone had the combination. By the gods, that white angled-sulphur was still there under the same leaf, five days later! Was it estivating? It hadn't moved a millimeter. At the bait sat a red rim and Empress Laura but not her consort, Pavon. Then, as I was spreading Ben's special brew on the big log over the wash, a general call went up: "Pavon!" I ran, and there was *Doxocopa pavon* all right, on a fruit basket. I asked if anyone wanted to see the upperside, and everyone did, so I caught it with forceps, gently spread it, showed the gorgeous purple male all around, and released it unharmed. If I am banned for life for the offense, it would be worth the looks on those faces as everyone got to see the rarely displayed dorsum up close. Beautiful Pavon, Thea's favorite butterfly from Mexico, has a Day-Glo chartreuse tongue that almost steals the show from its amethyst flash.

The last hunt of the day was a mission to find a bottle of wine in Mission. It wasn't easy, but I wanted to take a bottle to Thanksgiving and we succeeded. Phil and Jo from Kokomo, with their friends Jim and Sue, had invited us to their rented cottage in the RV palace for Thanksgiving dinner. After a heavy day in the field, these good folks did turkey and the rest for all the local and visiting leperati. Jan and David were there, and Mike and Sherry, and Dave and his woolly pup with its amazing rescue story, and Troy, and Ben and I, and others. It was a good time to recall all the great spottings and tell stories on ourselves, as we got suitably stuffed. "Makes a break from Wendy's," I said. "Listen at you!" said Ben.

Full of turkey, mashed potatoes, and warm confederation, Ben was mellow even without the wine that has never passed his lips. Pass my lips it did, as I raised my glass several times to this odd but mostly merry band of butterfly nuts. For a Real Good Time, dial 1-800-LEP-LRGV, and when someone answers, say, "Stay on the bug!"

2. LAGUNA IN WINTER

After In-Ko-Pah, Jacumba, and the Tecate Divide, I got to sleep for almost four hours before meeting Koji Shiraiwa. But before I dropped off, the run from Weslaco west replayed before my eyes in bits and snatches.

Leaving Ben's, I got a good news–bad news joke. The good news: I actually found the only English-speaking radio station in the valley, and it was broadcasting the blues. The bad news: the pledge drive was on.

A last look at the pixie tree by the BK *still* produced no pixies. A last look at Edinburg Wetlands yielded an orange skipperling sitting side by side with a southern skipperling—two flecks of gold that between them wouldn't cover an old English ha'penny.

Taking back roads through the valley, I saw thirty pounds of *tripas* offered for $13.90 and nearby taquerias advertising *menudo*. One man was selling various sizes of doghouses; just beyond him, another offered Doberman pups. Farmers sold corn from pickup beds, signified by stalks erect in the corners. Fixflats Mecanico: it was like leaving Mexico.

At the San Agustin Park Reserve, number 70 on the valley birding and butterflying map, hermes satyrs worked the dry grass beneath the whole cast of Texas sulphurs. There was no park, just wild, rutty roads, up and down through chigger-ridden thorn scrub and *Opuntia*, with none of the cross-border Mexican swallowtails I'd hoped for as goodbye gifts.

Beyond Falcon, an Audubon's caracara sat on roadkill, a great horned owl occupied a telephone pole against pink cloud, a bat flew between them, and moths came out.

Walking out into the streets of Laredo, I saw no young men in cowboy outfits, almost no one at all. On the way out of town, I saw one old man in a cowboy hat hobbling along with a cane. I wanted to say "I see by your outfit . . ." but I reckoned I'd scare him half to death. Then he was gone into the dark streets of Laredo, which rang with train whistles.

In the deep, steep Pecos River Canyon at Eagle Nest, the bridge soared over pink and gray outcrops sculpted like ravens' beaks, and honeybee combs the size of big-screen TVs interleaved beneath an overhang.

It was November 29, and deep autumn was here. Cottonwoods were big golden globes, the grass was stiff yellow straw. I thought butterflies were all over, from here on north. But then the sun warmed the rims of the canyon, a yellow tarweed opened out, and fourteen species of butterflies came to it, including a southing monarch and the biggest female dwarf yellow I've ever seen. So much for butterflies being done.

At Langtry, the home of Judge Roy Bean and now his museum, a sleepy orange had found a white bachelor button, the sole flower in the garden. The Jersey Lilly Creamery offered ice cream and postcards.

Near the Continental Divide north of Antelope Wells lay a kit fox, just hit. With its silver guard hairs, soft russet behind the ears and legs, petite muzzle, big feline ears, not much larger than our cat, it is surely one of the most beautiful American mammals—how much more so in life.

Awakening cold, somewhere between Six Shooter Draw and Van Horn, I said in the cow store, "It's a little chilly"; and the old cowboy replied, "Hell, it's break-ass cold!"

A tow-truck driver called over, "Hey, man, you getting away from the cold weather?" I wasn't sure if it was my tags or the Santa Claus gag. I told him if he was very good, I'd see him in about a month. "I love ya, baby," he called in his gravelly voice. "God bless ya!" And in Gila Bend, a drunken, potbellied man addressed me in front of a store. I thought he was fixing to panhandle, but instead he said, "God bless you, brother," several times. One should never take blessings for granted, or lightly.

As I passed a brightly lit Border Patrol check station, maybe my last of the year, one of the agents called "Merry Christmas." At the Ag checkpoint, I handed the official the peels of my last Texas tangerine. I did not mention Maggie's oranges and grapefruits squirreled in the back: high crime, but I was determined to get them home to Thea.

East of Ocotillo, I hit Pacific sea level and found the great oldies station out of Calexico that I'd had last January. There was no pledge drive on.

I awoke again after seven to a lightening sky, sunrise, and a rowdy wind, in California. I'd driven 1,524 miles from Ben's house and had some 1,150 to go. I was mistaken, there was one more Border Patrol roadblock. Since I was waiting in a line, I called to wish Thea good morning and happy December. The Border Patrol agent told me that California Highway Patrol was there too, so be careful with the cell phone, illegal while driving. That was very nice of him. I was going to miss those guys.

I met Koji a little past nine at Descanso Park and Ride, and we headed up Noble Canyon via Pine Valley again, as we had back in June. I had written him with a proposition. I recalled an article in the *Journal of the Lepidopterists' Society* from many years ago about Japanese lepidopterists who made sport of hunting hairstreak eggs on their host plants in winter, sometimes tucked deep in the crevices of bark. I asked him how he felt about going out to hunt mountain mahogany hairstreak eggs when I came back through, and he readily agreed. He'd never done it, but he was willing to try.

Likely ladies and whites crossed the road before us as we rose into the Laguna Mountains, which we had to ourselves. At the top, a grand viewpoint and Koji's favorite *Satyrium tetra* site, we began searching among the mountain mahogany leaves, as I had proposed we do. It was wonderful to be able to push through the chaparral without fear of ticks or chiggers. Back in July, below Fandango Pass in the Warner Mountains, I'd sought and failed to find this hairstreak among old-growth mountain mahogany. The shrub is evergreen here, so it made sense that the eggs might be on leaves instead of bark.

It didn't take long—there they were! Within five minutes, Koji found five eggs clustered on the underside of a small, fresh leaf.

Each egg, the size of an insect pinhead, was pearly gray-white, flat-tened like a fat disk, pitted in a fine honeycomb, and furred with minute bristles. A broad white ring surrounded the central depres-sion, or micropyle. They reminded me of fancy-siped little tires.

Seeing quite a bit of feeding damage, we looked farther. Upright in bright sun at 71°F, I found this more pleasant than looking for bog copper eggs prone in the snowy sphagnum with wet, cold feet, though that had its points too. Koji found another cluster of four, then I found one of five on a chewed-up leaf. He came up with a bunch of thirteen, lined up in the interveins of the lower surface in rows of four, four, three, and two; and then four more on the same branch. We found thirty-one eggs in all cemented to the densely hairy leaves. The two trees with eggs grew very near the buckwheats on which the *tetra* love to nectar. Koji said *S. tetra* differs from other *Satyrium* in its robust thorax and strong flight, like a skipper in the net. A good start to the day, the month!

Next, we drove east on I-8 to Kitchen Creek, where Koji had found a new Sonoran blue colony that spring. Sonora was one of my saddest misses, and I'd have loved to take a pupa home and watch it hatch in the early spring. We both looked for the pupae among healthy little *Dudleyas* growing out of moist granite grum. I thought I found one right off, but it was a .22 bullet! The leaves here were small, new growth; the old leaves were dried and gone, so leaf mines would not be helpful. The larvae prefer the flowers in any case. We had no luck there—we just didn't know the proper substrate for pupation.

We continued east on I-8, all the way back to In-Ko-Pah, to look for the larvae of the California giant-skipper (*Agathymus stephensi*) on *Agave deserti*. The agaves grew all over this landscape of moun-tain, boulder, and pointy plants, where speedy skippers drop eggs randomly. Young larvae bore into the fleshy leaves near the tips, where they winter before going down into the stems in spring. Koji showed me the beautiful trapdoor from which an adult had exited, at the base of a thick blue leaf, and then a trapdoor with its round manhole cover in place. There were lots of larval nests but, so far, only old ones. Then Koji called, "Bob! Eighty percent confidence this is a skipper!" He let me look for myself, and I spotted it too.

The caterpillar was *out* on the surface of the leaf. Its head was dug in, but its black cap, the black ring behind the head that makes it a skipper, and the speckled, pearly body all showed well when Koji split the leaf and it backed out.

"I'm sorry," he said. "He's upset with me." It secreted a liquid from the head when he touched it. Squat and roly-poly, it expelled a bright green frass pellet as we watched. Koji decided not to try to keep it through the winter; it would burrow back in just fine. He took close-up photos before it did. The flesh of the cut agave leaf had a delicious scent. To Koji it smelled of soap, and indeed, it was growing next to jojoba.

"So, it's December, and he's still active," Koji said. "I guess they come in and out, in and out." The leaves were freckled with the caterpillars' holes and beauty-spotted with their mines beneath the cuticles. When full-grown, an inch plus, it would be the type of "worm" supposed to be found in a good bottle of Mezcal tequila; though Mexican distillers usually plunk in a beetle grub these days. I replaced the larva at the base of a nearby leaf, with thanks. That made four identified giant-skippers. I would have been happy with one.

With two out of three of our day's objects in the figurative bag, we made a second try for the third. Tall dead flowering stalks of agave lay across junipers. Yuccas, chollas, other cacti, and great bubbles of boulders lounged all around, as we drove all the way east and north into Anza-Borrego State Park. "I came out this way almost a year ago, at night," I told Koji. "I'd no idea I'd be coming back here and seeing it by day." At 2:00 P.M., it was 80°F outside.

We drove to the end of Plum Canyon Road, a famous *Philotes sonorensis* locale, then hiked. It took us a while to find the *Dudleya*. One ceraunus blue came out, giving me a momentary thrill—had a Sonoran blue jumped its season? The sun dropped below the canyon walls. For an hour we climbed the rocks, searching cranny and duff, overhang and crevice, turning many a stone and leaf. The problem was, we didn't really know what the larvae do or where they go: how far is the walkabout? Do they attach with a girdle before they pupate, or just lie there? In a side canyon we looked all over a rock of white quartz with leaves of black mica and one *Dudleya*, where Koji always finds eggs. We did not find pupae. I ought to have looked for ova or larvae in April.

The long freeway drive to the pleasant seaside oasis of Rancho Pines was worth it for the tuna salad and shrimp pasta prepared by Rumiko and shared with sons Yuji and Hiroki. Over Sapporo beer, Koji showed me the little pupal pellets he'd reared from brown elf-ins, arrowhead blues, and—Sonorans! Speckled and rounded, they weren't far off the looks of the wood rat turds that kept fooling us. Couldn't we have found just *one*? But two out of three wasn't bad, and it was soothing to finish the long day in Koji's happy and soft-spoken household. Then real sleep in a real bed before the long haul home.

In the morning, mist clearing, I entered I-5 for the next thousand miles. Over the veiled and voluptuous landfill that is L.A., the smear cleared to blue at Santa Clarita. The curvy hill called The Grape-vine, closed for snow last spring, was summerish now. The Sonoran was just one of three endemic California blues I had missed. But I was half a year late for the other two, the San Emigdio and veined blues. In the afternoon I turned off at Smokey Bear Road to Koji's locality for San Emigdio blues and walked sandy paths up-canyon, but in the big, yellow, crispy mounds of the saltbush foodplant, I might as well have been seeking leprechauns as larvae. The only blues about were scrub jays and lazuli buntings among dried-out rabbitbrush and buckwheat. A black fleck over the Sespe *might* have been a condor, but it was so far, so small, it could have been a turkey vulture, or even a plane.

Down the steep mountain, fog came thick enough to rate the term pea souper. I'm not sure that's why I stopped in Santa Nella for another bowl of Andresen's pea soup. The biggest user of peas for split pea soup in the country, they serve over 2 million bowls per annum. I'd done my bit, having supped one one-millionth of their year's output. Except for coffee and almonds to go with Rumiko's tangerines, there would be no more searches until Oregon. I was lucky that the weather hadn't driven me to the coast. "Watch for Snow," said the sign, but the only snow in sight lay high on Mt. Shasta. Night and the next day somehow went by.

Seven minutes past the Oregon line, I was on the Mt. Ashland

Road in late sun, watching for *Polygonia* and paintbrush. Neither hibernal Oreas anglewings nor the winter larvae of Leanira checkerspots decided to join me. But on a golden chinquapin, I ferreted out a golden hairstreak's pupal shell. Poring over several more bushes well after sunset, fingers wicked cold even in two pairs of woolen gloves, I finally found one live egg. It wasn't a new species, as we'd found the adults on the day of the mistletoe and the canopy crane. But at least it was not a day without a butterfly, and maybe the last butterfly of the year at that, in the North.

But not the last lepidopteran. A couple of days after I got home, Thea and I drove to Port Townsend for Fayette and JoAnne's annual Swedish Christmas party. The Sunday after, walking off the good ale, potato sausage and pickled herring, custard and krumkake, I hiked up to the prewar concrete batteries of Fort Worden State Park. Looking for overwintering nymphalines, especially *Polygonia oreas,* I penetrated deep into the tunnels of Alanson Randol Battery. Rounding a curve, I looked into a galaxy of golden eyes gleaming back at me! My flashlight beam had struck the eyeshine of moths—thousands of *Triphosa haesitata,* vine maple inchworm moths—hibernating there. The handsome and extremely variable moths—chestnut, banded black-and-blond, or olive, an inch and a half across with delicate striations and pinked edges—clung to the rusty, limy old walls, shingled over each other in one of the greatest lepidopteran spectacles I've ever beheld.

I stepped out into the luminous dusk, astonished.

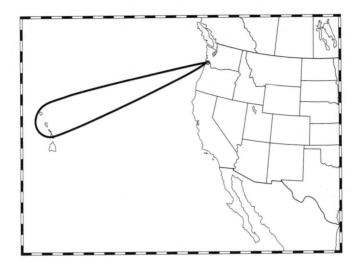

❧ RAY THIRTEEN ❧

Kauai Blues

Two observers . . . cannot adequately survey the avifauna
of an often mountainous and overgrown island of some
550 square miles. . . . Observation is made difficult by
the dense forest and by frequent rains.

—Frank Richardson and John Bowles, *A Survey of the
Birds of Kauai, Hawaii*

1. KAHILI

On the long, easy flight over cloud and ocean in a 757, I read Frank Richardson's *Birds of Kauai*. My old professor had devoted a sabbatical year to the subject, exploring the island's remaining native wilds in the process. He gave me the book in 1969, and this was my first chance to use it. At Honolulu airport, David Branch's big sister, Jeanne Branch Johnston, greeted us with leis. Kindly hosting both ends of our excursion, Jeanne took us home to Kailua on the H3, over the pass, through green even deeper than home. Hundreds of high waterfalls plunged past high, ragged peaks, like the Columbia Gorge squared. The reason for all the waterfalls was hard and constant rain. It was beautiful. But it didn't look good.

Hawaii had been kissed by Pacific storms, licked by the rain, slobbered by squalls for weeks. Many of the roads were flooded and beaches were closed thanks to silted waters and sewage overflow. Like the fiftieth state, the forty-ninth is a place you can go and never see the sun. Fortunately, the butterfly season is a little longer in Hawaii, like a year, as opposed to six weeks or so in Alaska. But you can miss it just the same, unless you have a few weeks to hang around, waiting for the sun. We had just ten days.

Jeanne and David had survived the horrific 1946 Hilo tsunami as children. She has since become a major authority and consultant on tsunamis. A cofounder of the great tsunami museum in Hilo, she was now finishing a worldwide compendium on the topic. After hearing about it, I slept with strange stormy butterfly dreams, awaking now and then to the sound of the rain. But Sunday on Oahu came with sun after all. Beside Jeanne's pool and down her flowery block under an overhanging mountain of acacia scrub, I saw our first Hawaiian butterflies of the trip: gulf fritillaries nectaring on yellow hibiscus and bougainvillea. All these organisms were introduced, of course, like most of the lowland fauna and flora in these islands that so many consider "paradise." Edenic, perhaps, but hardly endemic. Hawaii is far past the Fall, biologically speaking.

On the way back to Honolulu, almost all of the waterfalls were already gone! We'd been extremely fortunate to make the passage just at their peak. At the airport, Thea and I took a walk around the "grounds"—a dead loss but for one female gulf, one moth, lace-necked and zebra doves, Chinese mynas and pink-headed Java sparrows (a lovey pair under a concrete freeway abutment), and a beautiful golden-plover, worming like a robin beneath the bright colors of the lei stands. In the Chinese Garden Court, Japanese white-eyes chipped about the foliage, and a European couple from Connecticut asked me if they were hummingbirds. A red-vented bulbul, with its pert black crest, silver scaling, and scarlet underbutt, perched behind our bench, giving out soft whistles.

We flew to Kauai, and a short flight it was. We collected our Ford Focus, a white version of the Red-disked Alpine, at Lihue Airport. Looking for a grocery store, Thea spotted two large butterflies flying down a weedy lane in the late light, likely monarchs. Then she said, "Is that a butterfly? It looks like a hairstreak roosting." She had spotted a long-tailed blue, a.k.a. bean butterfly (*Lampides boeticus*), gone to roost six feet up in tall grass. White-banded and tailed, it does suggest a hairstreak. Like all of Hawaii's eighteen species of butterflies but for the two endemics and maybe the migrants, it was introduced from elsewhere; in its case, Asia. But it was new for the year, and thus a start.

After snagging an ono fillet at the Market Diner down Nawiliwili Road at the head of the bay, we drove west on Highway 50. A dirt road with a bullfrog in the middle led up into Kahili Mountain Park, where a Christmas party was under way in the school gym. By successive approximation we found our way in the dark, over a muddy lip and across a barely tracked sward, to Cabin 26 with its outdoor shower. Thea had tracked down this somewhat remote and affordable Seventh-day Adventist camp and convinced them that our search fit their criteria for nonmembers to stay—basically, Good Works. She selected the midrange lodging, and it seemed just right—neither spartan nor elaborate. A stream was rushing outside after all the rain, and a good moon was on the rise.

Heavy rain fell again on the middle day of December. After coffee on the covered porch facing the stream, we showered exposed to the rain, a pleasant sensation. As we paid our tariff in the office, Charlotte wished us a blessed day. How could it miss? In Koloa, we poked our noses into a ukulele shop with its symphony of beautiful woods, koa ukes for thousands, but even the cheaper versions seductive. A sugar mill museum displayed old photos of how it once was around here, when people made a living without tourists.

We had a problem. When Dory had delivered us to the Portland airport at dawn, I'd left Akito's aluminum pole in the back of her Element. All we had were Akito and Mini-Marsha's hoops and bags, with no handle for either. I figured a length of bamboo would do just fine, and how hard could it be to find a bamboo pole in Hawaii? First, we stopped at a nursery on the way into Lihue. They had no bamboo, but they did have hypnotically fragrant, deep purple orchids, an extremely affectionate gray kitten named Silver Bells, and our first island cabbage white, disappearing over a white-flowered tree. Now where?

Our mission ended at Ace hardware, where the only bamboo poles came in the form of cheap tiki torches. I tested several and found one torch that fit just right, its sharp, punji-stick end sliding right into either net's aluminum receptacle. I bought it for $2.99 and laid out another $2.99 for duct tape, which proved extraneous, the fit was so snug.

We found our way to the beach through the grounds of the Marriott Hotel, required to provide public access but not to signpost it. Graded after the storm, the red-dirt beach was not especially attractive. Facing the seawall and Matson docks, it fronted a resort such as we've never visited and never want to. Between showers, redemption came in our first sure Kauai monarch, up by the faux Hellenic golf course and viewpoint.

It was time for the farmers' market at Kukui Grove Center on Nawiliwili Road. The market was held in the lower-level parking lot behind the Kmart. We were allowed to walk around and select a pineapple, but transactions couldn't be settled until 3:00 P.M. Since it was only about 2:00, and the day was hot and humid though cloudy, we decided to seek a cold drink up in the mall.

As we climbed the ramp to the main level, past a grassy slope, Thea said, "I think I saw pygmy-blue." Based on a quick glimpse, I agreed with her guess. Then we noticed more vegetation across the lot, beyond Kmart's Dumpster pen. Several of the blues flitted over the far slope, too big and too blue to be pygmies. I realized then that they must be lesser grass blues (*Zizina otis*), a recent introduction to Oahu. Jim Snyder's discovery, only last March, was reported on the cover of the *News* of the Lepidopterists' Society—the butterfly equivalent of appearing on the cover of *Rolling Stone*. I'd hoped to find it on Oahu when we got back there, but now here it was on Kauai!

A new species for the island, and doubtless the first county record ever collected with a tiki torch, this was also our second big find in a mall. A few years back, Thea had business in an office building by the Vancouver, Washington, Mall. While I waited for her outside the building, I noticed a larger skipper nectaring among the woodland skippers in a garden. It was the first sachem ever recorded in Washington State.

The habitat here was close-mown lawn, a little longer on the steepest slope. Sensitive plant (*Mimosa pudica*), a powder-puff legume and a common pan-tropical lawn weed, dotted the grass with pink. *M. pudica* also happens to be the preferred host plant of *Zizina otis*. The minuscule blues came tumbling down the hill in ones and twos, pausing to sip nectar from small yellow and white composites. Contra Dustin Hoffman in *Rain Man*, Kmart did not suck; but the blues did, at Kmart. The brightest males shone brilliantly blue, the females less so. While Thea went back to claim our pineapple, I collected several pairs to document the new island record without denting the local population. (Of course, Hawaiian biologists would prefer that I had wiped it out.) These would furnish the basis for DNA studies to determine whether Oahu and Kauai lesser grass blues came from the same source. The tiki torch worked fine, by the way—under heavy cloud yet. Later, a tropical thunderstorm broke as we had our deferred guava nectar and lychee green tea in a little Asian bakery in the old town.

That night we reached Jim Snyder by telephone in Honolulu, and he confirmed that our *Zizina* were the first record for Kauai. A new introduction to the island is nothing to celebrate, but we marked the occasion with tuna steak, stir-fry from the farmers' market, and wine. For dessert, 85 percent cocoa chocolate and, of course, macadamia nuts.

The next day glowed pearl, and the breeze came cool and pleasant. After heavy rain through most of the night, the stream rushed high behind our cabin. A ring-necked pheasant strutted the lawn among golden-plovers and chickens. We were surprised to find chickens all along the roads, on the lawns, and just about everywhere else on this island. Feral brown and black hens and handsome, blue-green plumed roosters acted like they owned the place. None looked too big, so perhaps they were prey for people and cats, and in fact we did see some pretty banged-up cats. A white-eye was taking apart the yellow acacia flowers in the wall of exotic tropical vegetation across the stream.

On the way up the east coast of the island, we saw a few cabbage whites and monarchs. Then beside Kilauea School, our first Asian swallowtail (*Papilio xuthus*), the only swallowtail in the islands, flew over the car. I asked two Hawaiian policemen shooting a speed gun near the school how to get to Kilauea Point: "Go to the big pine tree, turn right, and go on down to the end." We did just that. Sunshine came in dribs and drabs. At the end of the road, on a bank of Bay Biscayne creeping-oxeye, fiery skippers nectared among a bunch of small grays that resolved into *Strymon bazochii*. In Texas, this is called the lantana scrub-hairstreak, and Ben and I had seen it next to the RV Wall. Here in Hawaii it is known as the smaller lantana butterfly, as it is one of two species introduced long ago (vainly) to combat the spread of adventitious lantana.

My Federal Lands Pass, still good for two more weeks, got us in. We walked up to the point and the lighthouse. Across the south gut, hundreds of red-footed boobies flew to and from their boobery on the steep green cliffs. On the opposite slopes, Laysan albatrosses lay up beneath casuarinas. Several were being released from cages, having been brought back from a golf course they visited every day. Overhead, great frigatebirds and white-tailed tropicbirds soared against the clouds. Around patches of lantana, as was only right, flitted smaller lantana butterflies. One coy painted lady, either

American or regular, one swallowtail, and one gulf fritillary shot across our bows on the stiff breeze. Thea found the gulf's red larva on a passionflower vine beside the dramatic lighthouse.

After that, in the land called Hanalei, we surveyed the maintained taro beds of Hanalei National Wildlife Refuge, where Hawaiian ducks and gallinules plied the ancient Polynesian waterways. Beyond Wet and Dry coves, at the beaches below the wild Na Pali Coast Trail, the high, brown water roiled with storm debris. It was no picture from a travel poster, but I walked to the water and waded at least. Then it was all the way back around the island, in the always early-falling tropic dusk. It wouldn't be long until we'd be at the other end, up above those Na Pali wilds. That was what we'd come for, the native part, the part Frank Richardson wrote about in *The Birds of Kauai.*

2. KOKE‘E

Our last morning at Kahili, Thea and I walked up toward a dense mountainside stand of Norfolk pines. On the way, we passed a banana grove and had a look-in. A leaf with several cut-out tents flopped in the rain. I worked my way to the tree, pulled the tents gently apart, and found six banana skipper larvae, probably third in-star, snug in their chalky white flocking. Then Thea called, "There it is!" An adult *Erionota thrax* appeared above us, ricocheted back and forth a few times, and went to rest on a banana flower. The fabulous insect applied its long scarlet proboscis to the maroon *Musa* bracts, apparently for some sweet stuff on the surface. Native to Indonesia, it is as big as the green-backed ruby-eye of Texas. We both saw its gold spots and that crazy red tongue, and Thea made out its own ruby eyes. When I'd corresponded with Dan Rubinoff at the Bishop Museum about Hawaiian butterflies, he'd told us that this species is seldom seen, especially since biocontrol in the banana planta-tions with a braconid wasp parasitoid. Jim Snyder confirmed that impression.

After checking out of our cabin, we drove into Lihue to meet the *Golden Princess* cruise ship in the harbor. Our friend Beth Ros-sow and her traveling companion, Bob Seaman, had come in on that floating, vertical city. Both of them work wilderness detail in Olympic National Park, and they enjoy the utter contrast that a sea cruise provides. Close habitation with 2,600 other passengers, under luxurious conditions (which they had obtained at a bargain price), must be about as far as you can get from the solitude of remote trails in the national park. We'd agreed to meet Beth and Bob and give them a little shore leave.

We drove up to Wailua Falls, a turbid chocolate malt of immense volume after all the recent rains. We'd hoped for a hike there, but the trails were all muddy and slick. Coming down, at a pullout thick with purple porterweed and orange dodder, we caught one of the many gulf fritillaries and placed it on Beth's nose. But we also found several lesser grass blues in the verge, a substantial range extension already; so it wasn't restricted to the mall after all. We took Beth and Bob to our other great find, the Market Diner, then back to their ship. It was time for us to head northward along Kaumualii Highway, toward Koke'e.

In the driveway of an old estate beyond Salt Pond Beach, large orange sulphurs swept among towering magenta bougainvillea. We'd seen the orange giants, a recent addition to the Hawaiian list, on our trip to the Big Island a few years before. After Waimea, the Russian Fort Elizabeth interpretive site abounded with bean blues on weedy, white-flowered beans along a rock wall. A garden of yellow and purple lantana, on a street corner off Waimea Canyon Road, might as well have been a Texas butterfly garden with its impressive flush of gulf fritillaries, fiery skippers, smaller lantana butterflies, large orange sulphurs, monarchs, and a northern cardinal. But once we left civilization and struck uphill, the fabled Waimea Canyon was fog-filled, rim-to-rim.

In the heights of Koke'e, a dispersed forest community, we found Laura Arnold's house. As soon as we met, she took us into her garden to gather greens. Then she made us a burgeoning salad and a delectable soup of carrots, sweet potatoes, spinach leaves, kale, basil, and various other local ingredients. Swaddled by the dense Koke'e fog, we spent a cozy evening with Laura and her tortoise-shell kitten, Ketzela, getting to know each other.

The previous year, I had taken part in the filming of a monarch movie with a German public television company. During our travels with monarchs from Michigan to Michoacán, the cameraman Klaus Miebach and I had made friends. He told me about his friend Laura on Kauai and recommended we contact her if we ever went there. So we had, and she'd kindly invited us to stay.

Laura had lived in this capacious two-level "cabin" in this damp green location a few miles above Waimea Canyon lookout for about ten years. An astute freelance naturalist, she takes part in rare bird surveys and carries out botanical inventory, among other jobs, including massage. Over ginger tea, we discussed butterfly strategies up in Kauai's wilder, wetter highlands. When it was time to turn in, she gave us her big, comfy bed in the front room, which came with the cat. And when we awoke and climbed out from under the blankets, we were still just as swaddled, in cold thick fog instead of warm goose down.

Rain made for less than the most welcoming conditions for hunting butterflies, birds, and host plants in the mesic forest of Koke'e State Park. But the ceiling raised just a bit, with a thin hint of sun, and I thought I saw a small butterfly in Laura's koa-rich backyard. It was very likely, but not certainly, a Blackburn's bluet—our foremost quarry here.

Before we set out, Laura wrapped her well-used climbing shoes with duct tape. I was delighted to see that I was not the only one. My battered field shoes, more than ready to shed their soles and heels, had been held together with duct tape for months. As difficult as I am to shoe, when I get a pair that fits, I don't give them up till they utterly disintegrate.

In her truck, Laura drove us on four-wheel-drive roads into the deep woods. We walked a slippery trail among koa and fog, down to Koke'e Creek and back up Halemanu Road. A side trip took us up to the Cliff Trail, with its white-tailed tropicbirds and fabulous views into the interior. I made a pratfall on the slick, red-dirt muck and learned why predyed, red-dirt T-shirts are both a joke and a hot item on the island.

Laura is a superb plantswoman, as is Thea, with different floras at their disposal. She showed us the red-berried hahakua (*Cyanea leptostegia*); the *Lobelia* named hame; a brilliant red fungus called the starfish stinkhorn (*Aseroe rubra*), its hue echoed above by singing apapanes; and many others. Laura knew not only the names of the plants but also their lore, traditional uses, and personalities. An amakihi honeycreeper flew through the fog. Up Pu'u o Kila Lookout, there was not a bit to be seen. Thea photographed me from behind on this futile hunt, a Goretexed gorilla in the darkening mist. Walking back down, we examined koa buds for *Udara* eggs, but we could barely see our hands before our faces. We were ready for the cozy cabin, the cat, and the couscous.

On Friday, there was no need for an early start, given the rain, fog, and pancakes. Thea elected to stay behind, rest, and read. Laura and I drove up a road to a mamaki patch. Mamaki (*Pipturus alba*), a member of the nettle family, is the host plant of the other endemic butterfly we were seeking. We found mamaki but had no luck seeking court with King Kamehameha. I nosed up the opposite gully, under a great-grandmother koa, into perfect glades for *Vanessa tameamea*; but no mamaki grew there.

Laura and I descended a long, slick dirt track in search of more mamaki. We pushed her truck perhaps farther than we should have and then hiked, with blue rags of sky showing. Across Kauaikinana Stream, actual sun came out. We raced it to the curves, then up each next slope to beat its fall behind the ridges, as I'd done at Alum Rock Park in February when hunting Sonoran blues. Scrambling up a tributary, Laura found one mamaki, but by then it was in the shade. I rounded a corner into sun. Then, on an ohia tree, I saw movement. Were they small butterflies? Blackburn's bluets? They were—three or four of them. I called out to Laura. She came, and got to see one fly, then perch on an ohia blossom in the last of the beams. Then the mist returned.

It was difficult to leave that ledge. Beyond the ohia, the canyon stretched away to a succession of humps, horns, and pyramids of steep eroded rock, completely upholstered in green. Most of this dense, tropical vegetation—ohia, tree ferns, many species Laura would know but I didn't begin to recognize—was actually native, a fine place to see a native Hawaiian butterfly. *Udara blackburni*, known by many as the Hawaiian blue or the koa butterfly, was named for the Reverend Thomas Blackburn, the first resident naturalist to attend to insects in a serious way. Many of the species he found in the lowlands between 1877 to 1883 have never been seen again, as their habitats changed under agriculture, development, and exotic biota. Almost unique in its appearance, *Udara blackburni* is deep blue above, leaf green below. It evolved in Hawaii from some ancient ancestor that arrived by winds or rafting. The bluet's nearest relatives today, known as hedge blues, occur from New Guinea and Australia to Japan and Sri Lanka.

We walked still farther uphill to Alakai picnic area, a lawn somehow arrived on top of these wild ridges. The spot afforded fine views of Waialeale, the highest, rainiest point of the island. The roof of Kauai loomed under tumbled clouds just east of us—no wonder it's the rainiest place. Between here and there stretched the great Alakai Swamp, only parts of which are swampy. So, we'd come to the Alakai, where Frank Richardson made some of his most memorable and prescient observations on the native birds—at least the Alakai picnic area, on the edge of the edge of the big wild middle.

There might have been great hilltopping up here a little earlier. While I imagined what I might have seen in the midday sun, Laura sang beautiful, unselfconscious thank-you chants of her own device. In her lovely voice, she sang to the eastern sky, the plants, the birds, and the golden-plovers on the lawn. She knew all the trees and shrubs and often giggled in recognition or made soft sounds of delight to them. Yet she was not at all woo-woo, rather, a darned good botanist who actually cared about the individual plants themselves.

Roosters crowed in the distance, a sound never far away on this island. But elepaio, that feathered gnome of Hawaiian forests, spoke too in the fading light. Laura turned her truck around and four-wheeled her up the slick rock runnel with ease. Thea had the gate open and the lights on. Soon we had hot soup and cold pineapple from the farmers' market of the new blues and, for me, a good, hoppy Big Swell IPA from Maui. Stars were out for the first time.

The sun followed suit. Back in the mamaki grove, Laura plunged down the slope while Thea and I looked above. We saw no Kamehamehas, but the giant Hawaiian darner (*Anax strenuus*) came out on top of Pu'u o Kila Lookout, six or seven inches across its glassy Jurassic wings. The clearing mist unveiled the fluted cliffs and knife-blade ridges of Pali, running down to crescent beaches, and Kalalau Valley, the most diverse plant community on Kauai with its mesic cliffs. *Myrica* was the only exotic shrub in view, and plenty of robust ohia trees with their scarlet bottlebrush flowers (ohia lehua) succored the apapane honeycreepers.

Up on Kalalau Lookout, the highest, the new sun drew Blackburn's bluets right out of the a'ali'i and the ohia. We had lush looks at the teal ventrum of one, the apple green of another, and their blue-black tops when they spread to the morning warmth. One bluet basked on naupaka (sea evola), then nectared on ohia lehua. Such green and red together—what a Christmas card they would make! And only five shopping days left.

Kolea the plover settled into a sunny spot on the lawn, wiggling its bottom down into a dimple like a broody hen. A little girl, reaching for her dad's binoculars and pretty darn cute herself, asked, "How cute of a blover is *that*?"

3. KAILUA

Waimea Canyon opened out of the mist on our way downhill from Koke'e. Otherworldly eruptions of greenswords—the Kauai version of Haleakala's celebrated silverswords—fronted the seeming infinity of the canyon's red levels. Laura rode down to Lihue with us, and we parted with promises of future adventures. I got my tiki torch past several levels of TSA checkpoints and onto the airplane. I'd removed the screw-on cap and wick for the fuel canister, which was obviously dry. I'd also left the folded-up net on the pole, covering the end cut sharp as a spear. That may be the only tiki torch ever taken aboard a Boeing 717 as a carry-on—certainly the only one with a butterfly net attached. Security was tight too, Barack Obama and retinue having just flown in for Christmas, shutting the Honolulu airport and delaying our flight.

Back on Oahu, the first day of winter came sunny but voggy. Jeanne pointed out that the high mountains were not as clear as they should be. "That haze has blown over from the Big Island," she told us. "The vog from the new eruption near Kilauea has been really bad over there." The volcanic smog was one reason I hadn't planned a visit to the island of Hawaii this time. I was beginning to wonder if that had been a mistake. I thought we'd see a Kamehameha butterfly on Kauai, and now I was worried about it.

Jeanne drove us into Honolulu via the Kalanianaole Highway, past Sandy Beach and Makapu'u, where David, her brother, our buddy, had done a lot of bodysurfing as a youth. Ditto for Barack Obama, who was said to be doing so this very day. We met Jim and Denise Snyder at a bookstore. Jim, who works for a cement firm, uses his days off and business trips well, having photographed more than seven hundred species of butterflies. They took us to Mauu-mae Trail, where the greater lantana butterfly and mamaki have been seen. But that was out toward Kainawaʻau Nui and Lanipo summits, three to four miles up and down the steep and treacher-ous trail, now badly eroded from the floods. I'd have liked to try, but it wasn't in the cards. We went only the first quarter mile or so, to where Blackburn's bluets glittered all over koas with small-leaved, yellow-puff flowers, very different from those on Kauai. We watched them at length and leisure, as gulf fritillaries and Asian swallowtails passed over.

I wanted to see where *Zizina otis* had officially joined the Hawaiian, thus the American, fauna. Jim was delighted to show it to us. He had discovered the lesser grass blue next to the Waikiki-Kapahulu Public Library, next to Ala Wai Golf Course. Sensitive plant spattered the library lawns with pink. There were hundreds—thousands, probably—of the tiny blues, including mated pairs, all over the park: a confetti of blue. Large orange sulphurs, the latest addition to the Hawaiian list save *Zizina*, flapped about. I think we saw one cloudless giant sulphur too. I predict this will be Jim's next state record.

Adult and immature Hawaiian night-herons hung out behind the library. Two species of *Salicornia* grew on the brackish shore of the Ala Wai Canal, and on them lived western pygmy-blues. Thea watched one oviposit and found the practically microscopic egg, which we all examined with a hand lens. This was a morning of small delights. Just a couple of blocks away, the hordes of Waikiki Beach–goers knew nothing of all this.

We lunched at an Egyptian buffet, the Pyramids, perched on the Mid-Pacific Ridge. Afterward, now that the sun was back and the president gone, Sandy Beach was crowded. Usually brown Koko Crater was green after the rain. Up in the botanical gardens, cabbage whites were big-time common, in Benton's lingo. And in the very same place where Jim and Denise had seen it yesterday, a dwarfish gulf fritillary came out to play for the Winter Solstice. It was about half the size of a normal one, an inch and a half in wingspread.

Swinging by Hamakua Marsh for the endemic Hawaiian coots, moorhens, and stilts, Jim and Denise delivered us home to Jeanne's in Kailua and came in for a cool drink. Over a beer (someone to share one with at last!) I said, "I'm getting a bit frantic, Jim. Isn't there any place we can go on Oahu for *Vanessa tameamea* and *Tmolus echion?*"

Jim thought hard about it. "Most of the places I know—and there aren't many—have been cut off by the floods. But you might try the Lyon Arboretum above Manoa. It's about the only place I can think of that wouldn't involve a long drive and a heck of a hike on those muddy trails, with no guarantee once you got there—*if* you could get there."

So the next day, Thea and I picked up a car at Enterprise and drove to Manoa via the Pali lookout. We got lost on East Manoa, which dissipated to nothing somewhere between mauka and makai. Then when we finally got to Lyon Arboretum, the Mazda's car alarm went off for no discernible reason, ripping open the peaceful scene like an electric can opener in church. Every time we got it silenced and tried to open or close the doors, it began again. We had to drive away until we got it well and truly shut off. The only way to halt the racket with the remote, we finally figured out, was to click the "open trunk" button—intuitive! By then distinctly unpopular with the arboretum's longhaired gardeners and the few visitors, we slunk off into the tropical verdure and hid.

Lyon Arboretum protects the head of a drainage and its native flora, along with many exotic plantings. Clouds sat right on the mountain crest, directly above us. In hot sun and light rain together, we got our first sustained look at *Papilio xuthus*, floating slowly around, searching for citrus. Its pale yellow, black-striped pattern distinguishes it from all of our native tiger and black swallowtails. We set out up the trail. In section 2E, Native Hawaiian Plants, another banana skipper scatted about. A hummingbird hawk, or maile pilau hornworm, nectared on ohia lehua. Clouds came up with the mosquitoes. The path ran upstream, past the Economic Garden and an old weather station ("currently haunted," according to the interpretive guide), toward Little Falls. This was the stretch in which a large bush lantana, the species favored by the larger lantana butterfly, was supposed to be growing, according to Jim. Known in Texas as the red-spotted hairstreak, *Tmolus echion* was introduced from Mexico in 1902 along with the smaller lantana butterfly. Both bombed out at controlling weedy lowland lantanas. The greater became an occasional crop pest but is nonetheless not all that easy to find.

We missed the bush, but the sun came out at a nice ferny clearing with *Heliconia* plants and fruits. Just then a big lycaenid fell out of the sky and alighted on a fern. It was a larger lantana butterfly, all right—bluish above when it dropped through the sunbeam, a pale gray triangle with darker dashes when it settled. We could have continued watching from about thirty feet away, but I wanted to get closer. Wrong move. Barging up the rough trail, I first blocked Thea, who was having a perfectly nice watch. Then I lost its position, got too close, and put it up, high away from the fern, and from us. It never came back, not while we were there. I was sure of the ID, and glad we saw it; but it could have been a more satisfying encounter, had I been less clumsy and impatient.

I'd have liked to stick around and wait for it. I walked up to the high green slot of Little Falls and let the spray cool my heated brow. But the sun was iffy, the day short, and we wanted to climb Diamond Head. So we hoofed on down to the bottom and drove to town. We saw just enough of Waikiki to evoke Thea's memories, from a high school girlfriends' trip, of someplace very different indeed. We made it into Diamond Head just before closing time, paid our six dollars, and walked up the stiff trail as most folks were coming down. It too was much greener than usual, but open, utterly different from the Lyon jungle. Long series of steps and tunnels evoked Fort Worden, but there were no hibernating vine maple moths. Spiral stairs emerged beneath the brow of a battery, where we had to duck and cross a cistern of stagnant water on an old plank—an insurer's nightmare. Amazing they didn't fix it, given the thousands of visitors per day, many of them jumbo-size.

From the lookout atop the tiara, jumbo Honolulu sprawled below. Two painted ladies hilltopped and basked about the summit. We had to lean way over and dash back and forth from porch to tiptop, bemusing the other tourists, to see one alighted well and ascertain it was *Vanessa cardui*. The second, paler lady alighted below a lip of rock; I dropped pieces of dried orange peel to bring it out and saw that it was *cardui* too. Gulf fritillaries and swallowtails also circled the summit, and then the ladies, 'tails, and silver-flashing longwings all chased and twirled around the crown together.

So, how should I regard a xuthus swallowtail on Diamond Head? A pale yellow-and-black banded insect indigenous to Asia, it was first recorded in Hawaii in 1971. Of course it counted on my list, but ought one to enjoy it? I know great, principled biologists in Hawaii who are utterly incapable of taking pleasure in any of the islands' introduced species, be they butterfly, bird, toad, or posy. Many of the exotics are injurious to the indigenous elements, often already endangered, so such an attitude is entirely understandable. Yet while I share their bitter remorse over a degraded biota, and take much keener delight in seeing natives, I've always been able to admire individual organisms out of geographic context: a common waxbill with its pink breast that looks berry-stained from the livid beak; a broad swallowtail soaring high above the human medium below. This ability may be a flaw in a conservationist. But it makes life in the world as we get it more various, more interesting; more lively. After all, it's not the animals' fault where they find themselves; they simply adapt. It is our own biological legacy we live with.

No, the swallowtails, ladies, and fritillaries crowning Diamond Head were no more native than we were. But they made a dramatic spectacle, if one that only we seemed able to behold, as if we were wearing magic glasses. Perhaps we were. Every other eyeball on Diamond Head was seduced by the spectacle of the over-bloated city.

On our way down the trail, Thea discerned a tiny blue on a head of *Emelia,* a rosy composite weed known as Cupid's shaving brush. It was a roosting *Zizina*—the first one ever recorded on Oahu away from Waikiki. The butterfly will spread all over the archipelago before we know it, one more element in the stew of animals from elsewhere, exploiting the tossed salad of Hawaii's feral flora. As if to underscore the point, a striking pair of red-crested cardinals with two orange-capped young mewled from an acacia branch just before the guard gave us the bum's rush out of there.

Before returning to Kailua, we called in at the Foster Botanical Garden, where there was said to be a butterfly garden. We were too late for it, but we rested on an inviting bench before facing the traffic out of the city. I'd been feeling a little off kilter. Frustrated first by the car alarm, then by my gracelessness in the hairstreak glade, I was also anxious about choices made and not made. Should we have driven instead to the north side of the island (where Jim would find dozens of greater lantana butterflies beside disused pineapple fields a week later)? Should we have scheduled in a quick trip to the Big Island for insurance against the unexpected absence of Kamehamehas? Or attempted those high, eroded trails, as I'd been eager to do.

I never imagined that we would miss the Amazon of the Vanessas. Both times I'd been to Kipuka Puaulu in Volcanoes National Park on the Big Island of Hawaii, I'd found it without difficulty. The first time, when I was working for The Nature Conservancy in 1978, dozens of the big brilliant ladies were sucking sap at rat-damaged, endangered *Hibiscadelphus* trees. When Thea and I went five years ago, the trees had been saved, the rampant nasturtiums and crocosmias extirpated, and the Kamehamehas were still there. We saw new lava issuing forth that night, and it was the same color as the neon salmon bands across the butterfly's great black wings: Pele and Kamehameha, dancing across the a'a. This time I'd assumed we could find it on Kauai or Oahu, but I'd guessed wrong.

There was no time for any major effort the next day. On the way to her local beach with her grandsons, Jeanne showed us the Kailua estate where the Obama family was staying. Two Secret Service agents, clad in Hawaiian shirts and shorts, were on their feet when we got within a hundred yards and saw us off with a friendly wave. After a dip, Jeanne took us all for sushi, then to another botanic garden, where a bit of mamaki grew, and we spotted just as many Kamehamehas as we'd had Barack sightings. Then it was time to cross the mountains one last time for our flight home.

Flying east over the Pacific, I quite naturally dwelled on Kamehameha. This missed grail, after all, was right up there with Eversmann's parnassian and the Sonoran blue. Yet the high Pacific airs on Diamond Head, the swirling swallowtails, the shimmering Blackburn's bluets, and those great (if exotic) little grass blues all talked back to me. After all, we'd found fifteen of the eighteen Hawaiian butterflies, and all the new ones we could, except for the King, Kamehameha. We'd had a good shot at Hawaii, a fine time together after all the months apart, and, most important, with Thea well to enjoy it.

And that's when I remembered the words inscribed on that bench at Foster Garden, penned by Esther Virginia Woolpert:

> Ever you seek beauty
> Ever you find beauty.

Right on, Esther.

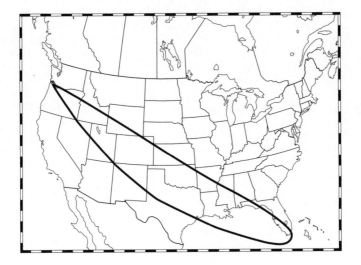

Keys to the Highway

We made a trip into the Gulf; sometimes we dignified it

by calling it an expedition. . . .

We were curious . . . we wanted to see everything our

eyes would accommodate.

—John Steinbeck, *The Log from the Sea of Cortez*

(with E. F. Ricketts)

1. MORE PURPLE

Getting the tiki torch on the Airbus to Portland was an even longer shot, but I did. We flew out in a sweet vapor of plumeria and ginger flower, since Jeanne bestowed leis upon us for our departure as well as our arrival. It wasn't long until those leis, one red, one white, settled around the stout neck of a snowman at daughter Dory's house in Portland. The city found itself in the twenties, traffic barely moving through the thick snow and rutted ice. We arrived on Christmas Eve, in time for me to read "The Night Before Christmas" to our grandson Francis. There was only a little identity confusion between Santa and me.

Christmas morning came way early with the kid and the dogs Lucy and Timo. But Francis loved his colorful Hawaiian chameleon from Kailua. Sweating while shoveling snow from around the car made a change from Hawaiian sweat. Jeb cooked us a splendid prime rib, salt-and-horseradish-encrusted, with a snowlike mound of mashed potatoes and roasted roots, and his unassailable crème brûlée; it is good to have a chef in the family. And in the end, my dawn flight was canceled because of icy runways, so I could relax a little longer before the final journey.

I had struggled over a destination for the last week of the year. Returning to the gardens of south Texas would have been the best strategy for species numbers, as Ben reminded me, but I had been there, and I had done that. The only frequent flier flight I could get *anywhere* south went to Austin, so I toyed with flying there, taking the train to Brownsville, and working the reserves to the east that I'd barely seen before, such as Laguna Atascosa and Boca Chica. But Amtrak nixed that with blackout dates for their Guest Rewards program. I strongly considered the most distal point in the southeastern United States, Dry Tortugas National Park. But NPS reticence, time, difficulty, expense, and especially the likely lack of leps all conspired to scratch that plan. So when Lana and Alana Edwards floated a scheme for the Florida Keys, missed on both prior trips, I jumped to accept their kind and generous invitation. Would anyone else be butterflying both Kauai and Key West this month? I wondered. Would anyone else even *be* in both Kauai and Key West this month?

But when the time came, my nice southerly flight plan through Las Vegas and Charlotte to Fort Lauderdale was canceled. My heart sank when I heard "O'Hare," and with good reason. I got to Chicago a little after 5:00 A.M. on the twenty-seventh, and by 9:00, O'Hare was Canceled Flight Holiday Hell. By the time I got to Fort Lauderdale, a day and a half of fieldwork had been lost, along with the Cuban crescent.

Sun came over the distant Chesapeake and the white plume of Three Mile Island. Then came a blinding sun glade on the channeled water glades and Miami, thick as my airplane sinuses with northern refugees. Then I was back in Florida, in time for Xmas leftovers with the Edwardses. The runway workers with their orange signals wore shorts, instead of Portland's furry parkas.

December 28 was a beautiful morning in Boca Raton. After a head butt from the incredible one-eyed Skipper, Alana and I set out for Homestead. Rick and her boss had indulgently loaned her to me until New Year's. To start, we tried Larry and Penny Thompson Park, a pine rockland remnant. *Richardia* by the roadside, introduced by DNR as a soil holder, breakfasted *Agraulis vanillae*—my last butterfly in Hawaii, first in Florida. Ceraunus blues dotted the Cupid's shaving brush, instead of the grass blues of Waikiki.

At Castellow Hammock dozens of the tiny larvae of Polydamas swallowtails clustered on *Aristolochia*, and adults nectared on purple porterweed. In our pockets, Alana and I carried amethyst crystals, which she had found in North Carolina, to conjure amethyst hairstreaks and purplewings. She had seen them both here before. No luck with the purples on the first visit, but we'd be back.

From there we went to Navy Wells pine flatwood preserve for my third time. Local spotters Linda Evans and Becky Smith joined us, to bring more eyes to the hunt. The pink *Bella* rattlebox moths were still there, and the faithful beauties with their poison-red, blue-backed larvae on devil's potato. As we walked down the same path that I had checked with both Thea and Akers for Bartram's hairstreak, there it was—at last!

Alana spotted it first; then it lit on a bright green coontie. Very fresh, its broad white bands and bright orange wedge were more intense than on Martial hairstreak, as it sawed its ultraprominent false heads energetically: glorious! We all had fine views, and those with cameras got excellent photos. I love the symmetry of these fine 'streaks named for great naturalists—*muiri, thornei, hesseli, bartrami. Strymon acis bartrami* honors the great father and son botanists John and William Bartram, who tramped the whole Southeast in the eighteenth century and wrote about it in their *Diary* and *Travels*, respectively. Walking back, we found another *bartrami* nectaring on false buttonwood in the path, imperturbable. I was able to view it at length on my belly through reversed binos, with no fire ants around. It had the red eyebrows of a male.

Waiting in line to enter the Everglades, I hopped out and checked the verge. On a *Bidens* sat a Martial hairstreak. Its orange looked like frozen concentrate, compared to the fresh-squeezed of Bartram's. Just inside the park sprawled a pair of green iguanas, three feet plus: a lean, alert female; the male stocky, lethargic, missing part of his tail. I was wide-eyed, but this was just the beginning for iguanas. The Florida leafwing did not reappear at Gate 2, but a nice male Florida duskywing flew like a bat and basked on bracken for us. I sampled saw palmetto fruit and found it slightly sweet and tasty, contra the columnist Jonathan Dickinson, who thought it tasted like "rotten cheese steeped in tobacco juice."

That made me long for a Key lime milk shake. Robert Is Here was open again, but huge lines of thirsty tourists defeated us. We settled for fresh strawberry shakes from another, less famous venue. Sucking on the straws like greedy butterflies, we drove back to Castellow. The dingy purplewings were still no-shows, but the shake was great.

We chased our shakes with a dry Belgian ale that Roger Hammer had discovered, for, as Alana explained, an after-the-field beer at the House of the Blue Cichlids is a must for local lepists. In their remarkable garden just before dusk, Roger and Michelle told us they planned to marry. That called for a celebratory meal. But at El Toro Loco, because of the owner's old felony conviction, you have to bring your own drink. Fortunately, Alana had brought some Florida beers for me, so we had some to share and toast the couple with. Popping one, Roger asked, "So how are you coming on your goal?"

"It is still mathematically possible to reach five hundred species," I told him, "if I see almost everything I could down here. But your famous purplewings aren't cooperating."

"Come back to the preserve tomorrow, and have another look."

"Thanks," I said, "but no can do. We've got to get south. This show's almost up, and Castellow has had three strikes already."

"Well, maybe in the Keys, then," he said. "Maybe in the Keys."

We overnighted with Linda and awoke at dawn to the scent of fresh-baked sticky buns. By Key Largo, the day was already going hot. Ospreys peered from pole nests over Tea Table Key Channel. Indian Key Channel gave my first view of Lignumvitae Key, a low green mole on the skin of a bay that got too much sun.

We parked on Lower Matecumbe Key—I knew these names from early Xerces work on Schaus's swallowtail. Melba Nezbed, the manager of Lignumvitae, Windley, and San Pedro Key parks, welcomed us. On the dock, little gnats tickled and nipped, but we were told that the famous mosquitoes were few: good for us, but that could augur poorly for butterflies too. We'd just have to see. The ever-thoughtful Alana had arranged for us to visit Lignumvitae on the state parks service boat.

On the slow scow ride out the channel lined with red mangrove, I knew I'd made the right choice for the week, goal or no. At the wheel was the young Ranger Dustin Clark ("All the good-looking rangers around here look alike," he said). The others aboard were Lance, Bill, and volunteer Mike, who'd put in seven thousand–plus hours over thirty of his ninety years. He had a little yellow-white ponytail, and a McCain-Palin bumper sticker on his car back in the lot. Ashore, Dustin walked us to the house and filled us in on the history of the place.

William Mattheson bought the key for ten dollars in 1909 and built the coral house in 1919 but never stayed there. A noted chemist, he invented the analine dye process for blue coloring but also contributed to mustard gas. He conserved a lot of land for plants and animals yet introduced many species here, including peacocks, white-tailed deer, and Galápagos tortoises, one of which is still alive in Miami Metrozoo. Dustin gave us the tour. Mattheson used *Pinus elliottii densa* (Dade County pine); a slab of it felt like ironwood. The house withstood the fierce 1935 hurricane, which put cormorants right through trees, and coconuts, like cannonballs, through houses. The terra-cotta roof went, but the rest remained, and foundation-to-roof steel rods were later added. There was a fine display of lignum vitae, its purple-red wood, handsome flowers, and seeds, for which the island was named. The largest native short-leaved fig stood beside the house with a small lignum vitae, a Lower Matecumbe lignum vitae snail sliding along its smooth bark.

A rusty '35 Dodge pickup at rest by the edge of the hammock had built all the trails. After the state got the island, nothing could be changed, including the truck. We took one of those trails now and entered the woods, a very rare example of West Indian hardwood hammock. "This is one of the few places where desert intersects with tropical rainforest," Dustin said. We walked a lengthy circuit of trails, seeing no butterflies at all for a long time. Dustin talked about art versus utility. An art major and artisan ranger, he was also an Amish MBA who strongly believed in function to justify art. It was a bee in his Smokey bonnet. I urged him to consider emotional response to "pure" art as a useful "function." But I don't really like to talk much on the trail, so I dropped back.

Then, on a north-side trail, I saw a butterfly alight in full sun on a poisonwood trunk. I could see the ventrum pretty well, and as it flitted onto a leaf, backlit, the wing shape and spots showed that it was *Eunica tatila*—a Florida purplewing, just what we came here for. The slightly hooked forewing and the bright white spots both indicated it wasn't a dingy purplewing, though I hadn't yet seen the purple side. But three minutes later, I had. I heard Alana call and ran to her, and they were watching a fairly fresh male, left hindwing bird-struck, spread-winged on a pigeon-plum leaf in the sun. It really was *amethyst*! The intense hue shifted from violet through deep purple with the angle of the sun. Alana and I smiled and flashed our amethyst amulets, whose grapiness ran just as deep. The nymph started, and then it vanished into the forest. Farther down the trail, two or three more purplewings shone through the violet dapple.

A dead and rusty tractor, used chiefly for its come-along to operate a dredge, displayed the old Caterpillar logo on its radiator. It was the word itself, written loopy, like a crawling larva—surely one of the best corporate symbols ever. When did the company abandon it, and why? A rare white-crowned pigeon flapped noisily over the forest, as big as a passenger pigeon. Its snowy crown glistened in the sun like the old volunteer Mike's hair. We came upon him on the way out, he having just dug out a large stump. His heart had stopped two months ago, and Dustin helped to revive him. "He died on us," the ranger told us, "but we brought him back."

Fiddler crabs plinked across the sandy path to the shore, and Dustin hauled up a horseshoe crab. We walked past, under, and through many trail-spanning webs of red-and-black, crablike thorny orb weavers. Alana's sharp eyes spied mangrove skipper pupae and larvae on mangroves, and those of hammock skippers on Jamaica dogwood, the "fish-poison tree" of Florida Indians who used its rotenone-bearing sap for fishing. Once back across the bight, we shot south, through Marathon. I found that I had left my steel Kleen Kanteen on the dock. Weeks later I got it back, through the efforts of Alana and the good offices of the diligent young Ranger Clark, Steward of the Florida Purplewings.

2. MIAMI BLUE

At the south end of the Seven Mile Bridge, the masses of people on Ohio Key seemed insensible to the masses of butterflies. A stunning display of mangrove skippers and polka-dot wasp moths excited no interest but ours. Bahia Honda State Park was so full that it was closed to any more comers, but seeing our permit and my Xerces Big Year card, in one of its last uses, Assistant Manager Mike welcomed us in. Lycaenids skittered hither and thither above the eastern shore — Cassius blues, almost as tiger-striped below as marine blues.

We'd come to Bahia Honda on the off chance of seeing the Miami blue. This Caribbean species once occurred across much of South Florida, even recorded on Sanibel in the seventies. It contracted, then seemed to disappear, and was considered extinct for years. Then in the fall of 1999, Jane Ruffin rediscovered the Miami blue here on Bahia Honda. There followed years of energetic, concerted conservation efforts; except not so concerted, with different factions and personalities getting in the way of protection as much as bringing it about. Now that a scientific approach was being coordinated out of the McGuire Center, the butterfly had contracted again. Emily Saarinen was conducting her research in the Marquesas, beyond the Keys; no one had reported them from the Keys proper in many months.

So it was pretty darned exciting when Alana called, "Miami blue!" And there it was, for real — one good, clear Miami blue. The butterfly, whose formal name (*Cyclargus thomasi bethune-bakeri*) is much bigger than itself, nectared back and forth between scorpion's-tail heliotrope and miniature wild *Poinsettia* with half-red, half-green bracts. Its chalk submargin, quartet of ink spots at the base, and thin orange crescent were unmistakable.

On the opposite slope, iguanas lolled like a scene out of *Jurassic Park*. A yard-long, orange-spiked male clambered and ate its way through the vegetation. A sunburned boy on a bike, vacationing here from Washington for two weeks, told me that the slope had had twice as much vegetation a week ago. It was disturbing to see the iguanas chowing down on nickerbean, right above where Jane rediscovered the Miami blue.

Along with balloon vine, nickerbean is an alternate host plant for the Miami blue but also the chief host for the ammon blue (also called nickerbean blue), which itself hadn't been seen in Florida for many months. Having witnessed the damage the iguanas were wreaking, I would be relieved to hear six months later that Alana and Paula Cannon had rediscovered nickerbean blues here. For now, it was enough that Alana had conjured for us a Miami blue: one of the rarest, most enigmatic of American butterflies.

Down at Bahia Honda's beach, great southern whites mobbed beach radish, or cakile, as cabbage whites do along the northwest coast. Like everywhere these days, the park had a butterfly garden. A Brazilian skipper joined a bunch of Martial hairstreaks on the yellow flowers of bay cedar. The hefty Brazilian gave us a rare dorsal view of its purple, green, and blue iridescence and clear, pearl spots. Even larger, even pearlier and purpler, a hammock skipper came to this excellent shrub as well. Leading me through round red sea grape leaves on the Silver Palm Trail, Alana stopped abruptly. "I think it's an obscure," she said. Indeed, she'd picked out a *Panoquina panoquinoides* on a porterweed. The demure skipper—the species I had found with Ben on South Padre Island—was only my second one ever.

The traffic was now so slow, we thought there must be an accident. We finally reached Big Pine Key and hopped over to No Name Key, where we were met by my first Key deer, its legs mere chopsticks, a lump of coal for its nose. At No Name Pub, we met the butterflier Bob Kennington for grouper sandwiches under a ceiling of dollar bills, thumbtacked up and marked with signatures and mottoes. Once as anonymous as its name suggests, the No Name, like the Bucksnort in Sphinx Park, has become the victim of its own obscurity, swimming in folks pleased with themselves for being in on the secret.

We gobbled our grouper, signed a dollar, made butterflies on it, and struggled to find a place to pin it up. Then Bob led us back to his comfortably disheveled, two-level house on Little Torch Key. Alana crocheted while Bob checked Key West sites on his computer and I jotted down field notes. When I slept, it was dreamy of Floridian life forms in purples and blues, some seen, some still to be seen, and some to be seen only in dreams.

Up early for the penultimate day of the year, Alana, Bob, and I crossed over to Big Pine Key and found Paula Cannon in her coral garden. I'd corresponded with Paula, the doyenne of Key butterfly students, about what I might see here. She showed us her endangered old man palm from Cuba, her red-flowered *Jatropha,* and a coral grotto with koi and bald cypress shadows. Sulphurs, monarchs, blues, and monks fanned the humid air. Many tortoises scuttled about, including several box turtles scorched in "controlled" burns on the island. Paula had rescued these, including a sad one with its feet burned off.

An attractive woman in her forties with long cashew-colored hair, Paula smiles and laughs a lot, but her eyes carry constant concern. Embattled over fire, mosquito spraying, and lack of appropriate management for many species following hurricanes, she sees the biological condition of the Keys on an inexorable downward slide, as much from wildlife authorities as from any other factor. Insidious mosquito "fogging" is perpetually destructive: she has followed spray trucks down the street to photograph and collect dying butterflies in their wake, and been sprayed doing it. Paula has a few allies and many foes. She is outdoors all the time with her eyes open, while her adversaries seldom go out, "except to burn." Few others are willing to spend time to save what's being lost.

But rather than just jawbone about it, we got out to see the places she was talking about. First, to the National Key Deer Refuge. This interested me since I live near another refuge for a federally listed subspecies of whitetail, the Columbian white-tailed deer of the Julia Butler Hansen Refuge. The Key deer seemed to be doing rather better than the Columbians, perhaps a little too well. As Paula told us, they have become overnumerous (like whitetails in many places), are getting bigger and fawning all year. This makes things tough on native vegetation, thus on specialized butterflies. Common, weedy species like white peacocks do fine along the heavily grazed fire-breaks, but not all the rarities.

In one recent but desultory burn site, we saw two Bartram's and one gray hairstreak on the same spared bush. A teneral female Bartram's wore ice cream sundae colors; she would not be fire toler-ant. If fires are patchy enough, much can survive, but if they are too efficient, local extinctions surely follow: the same story I heard in Illinois and Wisconsin with threatened skippers and blues. Nearby, Alana thought she saw a rare disguised scrub-hairstreak (*Strymon limenia*), very similar to the mallow scrub-hairstreak, but we couldn't find it again.

Then I thought I might have seen a Cuban crescent flying among native sweet acacias, but it was more likely a winter form phaon crescent. The Cuban crescent was one we'd planned to go for if my flight had been on time. Paula gave me three hog plums to eat. "It's a terribly thorny plant," she said, "but the fruits are *so* good." And they were, a thin sweet and sour pulp over a big seed. We also tried the amber, strange but tasty berry of *Brysonima*, or locustberry, host of the Florida duskywing. Palmettos swept the coral to a clean, flat floor beneath their hems. Next to the refuge, the 43.5-acre Cactus Hammock Addition stretched back from the beach. Paula was ap-palled, if unsurprised, when she later learned of a state land ex-change that put this vital parcel, rich in rare cacti, at risk.

Long Beach, at the north end of the Key, was chock-full o' folks; but back from the beach, full o' flowers: fields of *Jaquemontia*, also called sky blue clustervine. Paula was excited to see a tropic queen on it, since it's mostly regular queens here. Four more of the so-called soldiers had captured a clump of sea heliotrope by the shore, their spots much whiter than on Texas *Danaus eresimus*. This habi-tat has had much more nectar *since* Hurricane Wilma, according to Paula, as the white-flowered sea heliotrope has prospered on the battered shore.

We lingered at one sumptuous, fragrant patch of sea heliotrope where a flurry of fieries, Martial, great southerns, and a double hand-ful of fabulous hammock and mangrove skippers made a spectacle of themselves. One amazing porterweed patch supported three au-bergine hammocks, two ink blue mangroves, and a flibbertigibbet of a giant swallowtail female, by Alana's terminology. Meanwhile, up on the bridge, thousands of cars poured by like cold syrup, staggering toward Gehenna. The hot and bothered occupants had no idea of what they were missing down here. Ditto for hundreds of human lobster pots in the RV park. A lone kayaker plied the quiet blue bay.

Dawdling over beach finds, I lost the others when they went back into the woods. Cool big sponges lay about the beach like so many mossy beer barrels. I picked one up and found that it snugly fit the crown of my hat. Unsure which way my companions had gone, I asked an oncoming couple if they'd seen two women and a man. They looked at me oddly and said no, they hadn't. So after they passed I went the same way, stopping for this and that. When I found the others, they cracked up. "Ah," said Alana, "I *see!*"

It seems they too had inquired of the couple, who said the only person they'd seen was "a ranger with a sponge on his hat." Bob's photograph of us shows a grizzled Bacchus with a gnarly growth on his head, planted between two wood-nymphs. It took me twenty minutes to twig to that which was immediately obvious to the other three. So SpongeBob I was, S. B. Field Pants, said pants having admitted just two or three new chiggers that day.

Heading back, we ogled a pair of iguanas perched high in a dead tree, the huge horny male up at the top, the smaller female below, clinging to the bare trunk. Truly an Archeozoic scene, and spectacular dragons they were—if only they belonged there! Skirting traffic on side roads, we made it back to the Cannons'. Their boat bobbed out back on the canal. Paula's husband, Gary, is a much-in-demand marine mechanic. She cleaned, prepared, and cooked some excellent fish that they'd caught in local waters: thin, silver, the size of bread plates, they go by the delightful name of lookdown fish.

Over the delicious meal, I brought up a growing concern of mine. At Long Beach, when we saw the traffic totally backed up, I realized that yesterday's slowdown had the same cause: no accident, just masses of people trying to get to Key West for the New Year's revels. I couldn't imagine subjecting Alana to that ordeal for hours and hours, just to get me there. An alternative plan was bubbling up in my mind: omitting Key West altogether. Perhaps I could spend the day here on Big Pine Key, wandering some of the north-end habitats; or maybe just get to Boca Chica Key. When I had considered a south Texas finish, I'd had in mind putting the year to bed at Boca Chica, a reserve near the mouth of the Rio Grande. Why not this Boca Chica instead?

"Because it's a naval reserve," said Alana. "Besides, it's almost to Key West."

I was still struggling. When I'd thought of going to Key West, I'd pictured myself wandering back alleys, neighborhoods, the fort, and so on, in hopes that something unusual would pop up at that far end of the earth or, at least, the country. But it was a long shot, maybe not worth the hassle. "What I'm really going there for," I said, "is . . ."

"Titties?" laughed Paula.

Well, that convulsed the table. Apparently New Year's in Key West is known for nudity. When we recovered, they all convinced me that I should go to Key West after all. Alana figured there would be less traffic if we went early enough. Thus resolved, we spent a convivial evening looking over Paula's fine drawings and photographs, talking butterflies and birds and conservation ad infinitum. Gary tolerates all this as long as it keeps his Paula happy. And Paula has a huge capacity for happiness, if only the keepers of the Keys would give her a chance to indulge it.

For my part, I had one last day to go.

3. THE LAST BUTTERFLY

So what was that butterfly? It had to be one of the best of all, if I only knew what. As I relaxed into the cooling night at Bogart's, I went over it again and again in my mind's eye, every detail, as I have a thousand times since.

Alana had been right about the traffic. There wasn't much when we left Big Pine at six with Paula's great breakfast burrito. Through mangrove islands, across Boca Chica Key, we came on a cool blue morning to this extremity called Key West at last. Then she was off, back to Boca and her own life. My kind pal and butterfly guide gone, I was back on my own for the conclusion, as it had to be; and in a place I had never seen before.

I heard cock-a-doodle-doos and looked down the parking lot between coconut palms for the rooster. There he was, and a hen, and then more. This, then, was the real connection between Key West and Kauai: chickens! And then three hieroglyphic white ibises paced by, a few feet away. A drop of water hung, then flicked from one long, curved bill as a milky dollop plopped from the other end. It wasn't Hawaii, after all.

A gulf fritillary, just a little nearer the Straits of Florida than the Gulf of Mexico, basked in front of Key West Wildlife Center. A signboard gave tips for removing hooks from birds and announced: "We're very sorry but we do not take iguanas." Tracy, a five-foot-three, redheaded wildlife worker, told me of a red iguana back by the turtle pond longer than she was. They did take chickens, which would be relocated "to wonderful homes off the Keys." A "Missing!!!" poster offered a hundred-dollar reward for Sketch ("she knows her name"), a small brown hen with blue legs and a bumpy comb, missing since October 24. Amber wrote, "I really miss her and can't stand not knowing where she is." How many beach bums brought in a chicken, hoping for the C-spot? I'd sooner seek a bog copper egg blindfolded all across Minnesota than try to track down one special brown hen here.

In Sonny McCoy Indigenous Park, a vast and perfect female giant swallowtail spread wide on a citrus. Her bright red and blue bits, deepest black with yellow bands in a big, toothy smile with mustache, all somehow blended in against the shiny green leaves. Two males tussled over her. In the gumbo-limbo grove, purplewings or not, neon purple morning glories popped out through mauve mistflower. A man, neat and patrician, peered at me with some alarm as I unwound from a smooth and sinuous gumbo-limbo trunk.

I introduced myself to Carl Goodrich, a resident birder and photographer carrying a massive camera. We had friends in common, including Ben Basham. At the marsh observation deck, he pointed out an anhinga, "rather rare in the Keys," near a sleeping great blue heron. We watched Polydamas swallowtails, orange-barred and large orange sulphurs, all of which he knew, and a northern parula. Then he got on a small yellow warbler, and I didn't dare take the time. Carl told me about a good habitat along Government Road, and I set off to try to find it.

North along the waterfront, a seductive, woodsy path marked "City of Key West Nature Reserve" led down to the beach. Just then, from who knows what, maybe yesterday's unfamiliar fruit, I was taken with a most urgent fit of peristalsis. Thank those same gods for a hidden track into deep brush, without fire ants, people, or poisonwood, for the adjacent ocean for a soothing swim, and for no encore. I thought it would be dandy to discover nickerbean blues here, but the chorus lines of blues dancing over the abundant nickerbean were all Cassius, almost as white as the egret eyeing me from the blinding strand.

I turned inland, triangulating toward the habitat tip-off. At a busy corner on Bertha Street, between passing cars and scooters, across the street from where I stood waiting for the light, an orange nymphalid alighted on a clump of *Bidens*. *Vanessa*-size but no lady, it was nothing I recognized. For some reason I thought of *Araschnia lavana*, the European map butterfly, but this was larger, not really very much like it.

The butterfly rose and sailed around a big red bougainvillea. Finally the traffic stopped and I rushed across the street, hoping to find it nectaring there. As I hit the sidewalk, extending Akito's handle and oblivious to the many stares, the nymph came around the bush again and dabbled at the *Bidens* but didn't quite light, just flirted. "Mapwing" entered my mind again—and then I saw why: there were strong striations, not light-on-dark as in *A. levana*, but dark-on-light. I saw pointed, maybe slightly tailed, angular hindwings, and a dark pattern on the bright orange dorsum. Intent on netting it, I didn't try to use the binos.

Closing from fifteen feet, I saw that neither the wing shape nor the markings, more barred than spotted, matched any of the three buckeyes that could be there, and the color was wrong for any lady, frit, or leafwing. I approached, willing the butterfly to settle, begging it to give me either a swipe or a definitive look. But the traffic light changed again, and a big white truck put the butterfly up in its slipstream. Damn!

The mystery butterfly rose high and fast, then sailed off across the street, over a tall hedge of trees. Not waiting for the light this time, I dodged the cars and shot after it, hoping it might have gone down over there. But behind the hedge there were no flowers, just a paved lot without a bush or a butterfly to be seen, and the high, barren backs of condos.

That butterfly was gone, solid gone. But what the hell was it? I walked back east to the beach, in case it had gone there. But all I saw at the south end of Smathers Beach, ignoring all the traffic turning past them, were a dozen stolid turnstones on the rocks. Giant brown pelicans on a concrete pier projected sublime indifference that I did not share.

I abandoned the search, and the big road, for small lanes. Government Road ran east-west just north of the airport, past the Key West Salt Ponds and a remnant hammock that John James Audubon prowled when he came here in 1832. It is now Little Hamaca Park. Yellowtop, lining the road, was alive with common butterflies. Fields of the little native poinsettia projected the holiday season, if nothing else did. Apart from occasional planes landing beside me on the right and a few other walkers, traffic was nil. The large salt pans here had been vital for local use and trade in the early days of

Key West settlement. Today only mangrove buckeyes tapped the salt flat: saffron-banded, buckskin wind vanes surrounding big blue eyes—a fine sight that Audubon himself would have beheld, right here. The salty mud was herringboned by shore bird tracks and spattered with mahogany mangrove leaves.

An old fella and his wife pulled up in a battered pickup. He said, "Fifty years ago, you woulda really seen a lot of bugs in here."

"Oh, yeah?"

"That's right. There was papaya, guava, all kinds of fruit in here—and thousands of butterflies, all kinds."

"Wish I would've seen that. At least there's this strip."

"You wouldn't believe it, but before that, it was all watah. The Army had it. Then they drained it with a six-inch pipe, and people started planting seeds. All kinda birds 'n' bugs back then." We exchanged Happy New Years.

Little Hamaca Park offered the best shred of Key hammock-mangrove-transition woodland. A mangrove skipper at orchid morning glory: like sapphire set in rose quartz. A nature trail led to the Riviera Canal, full of little blue fish. I watched ornate jellies with pinwheel tops, about the size of Vienna sausage tins, pump through schools of fish that crowded around their purplish, pleated caps and fancy parts. As pretty as butterflies, they flowed through on the tide as if in procession, each with a classroom of blue fish in attendance—nipping, cleaning, or what? Two old German shepherds and a green iguana doing pushups watched me from a yard on the opposite bank.

As the last day entered old age, I retraced my path back to the south. Overhead, as if throwing a wrap-up party for me, giant monarchs, swallowtails, and sulphurs played around the platters of wine red sea grape leaves. The final butterflies of the day, of the year, were a fiery skipper, a mangrove buckeye, a cloudless sulphur, and— now that I was on the Gulf side of the Key—a gulf fritillary, all going to roost.

I made it out to Flagler Avenue and speed-walked its many bustling blocks for much of the length of the key. I was determined to catch the last sunset over the Caribbean. Stealing glances at my creased map, I tried to judge the path of the setting and figure where I could intersect it. I ran the last two blocks to South Beach. It reminded me of jogging to make the ferry on Catalina, only this time, just as sweat-soaked, I made it.

I put my feet in the sea and my rear on an algal-covered coral tump that the tide had not long ago left, and watched the last few minutes of the sun's descent into a hazy west. A funnel-like, diagonal contrail ran right up through it, like a sea spout. Ships sailed beneath, pelicans soared over. I did my best to ignore the din of a party on the hotel deck above me, and I thanked the really old testament god Pan that the homing battalion of rented Jet Skis didn't rip the pink gap between the sun and me until after the sun had set. Then they all hit the riprap and exploded in a brief but spectacular burst. At least that's what the sky looked like. A gold-chained man at the wedding party looked down, tipped his champagne flute, and said, "We'll never see another one like that."

I lacked my Kleen Kanteen to tip back at him, and I wasn't sure if he meant the sunset or the year. Either way, I looked back up at the gold-chain guy, smiled, and said, "You're right, sir. Never one like that."

Well, my work was done, and I could quit right there. But there was more. I had the night to face—New Year's Eve in Key West—before I could go home. Pointing toward the belly of the beast, I passed Hemingway House and hit Duval Street, just starting to liven up. I stepped into Bogart's Irish pub, whose corbeled brick whitewashed front and green awnings really looked the part. The interior was cool, open, and pleasant. Very, very thirsty, I ordered one pint of Smithwick's Irish Ale and two pints of ice water and bellied up to a plank between two pillars facing the street.

My thoughts returned to that butterfly, the one that wasn't in the field guide. Suddenly I knew why the European map butterfly had come to mind—there *is* a North American map butterfly—the orange mapwing! I'd forgotten all about it. Now I searched my dusty convolutions for whatever they could tell me. *Hypanartia lethe*, a Mexican species, made no sense here. Its appearance in Pelham's *Catalogue* owed to one dubious old Texan record. Yet the image of the orange mapwing that came together from books I'd studied over the years really did resemble that fleeting butterfly—the color,

size, pointy hindwing, and especially those maplike, varicose striations—it had them all.

Of course, there was no counting it. I'd neither caught it nor
photographed it, or even seen it well. I was far from sure. And even
if I were, what would it mean? That it was an escape or release (that
plague of serious students of butterfly distribution); or else that it
had somehow crossed the Gulf of Mexico. Of course, birds do that
after storms from the west; some butterflies probably do too. Andy
Warren would later say that my sighting was almost certainly not *H.
lethe,* that another, Cuban species of *Hypanartia* was slightly more
likely; but it too would be a new United States record. When I con-
sulted a Cuban butterflies website, I knew that the darker, tailed,
unstriated *H. paullus* was not my beast.

Later still, Jon Pelham would urge me not even to mention that I
might have seen *H. lethe* in the Keys, lest I cast doubt upon all of my
observations. Then too, such a remarkable find on the very last day
of the quest would seem pretty darned hokey. And yet, and yet . . .
if not here, then where? I'd left the Keys for last precisely because
they *might* turn up something outlandish, as they have before. After
all, Key West is just 400 miles from Yucatan. Besides, as that noted
Florida lepidopterist Dave Barry is wont to say, "I am not making
this up." It happened, and I hereby report it, for what it's worth. Not
much, perhaps. I suppose it probably wasn't *Hypanartia lethe.* But it
was *something*—something I've never seen before.

But most of that analysis lay in the future. Right here and now,
in Bogart's, I discovered that I'd drained the beer and both waters.
And when I looked up, I found myself quietly bawling my eyes out.
It wasn't for the empty pints, or for the butterfly I lost and will never
see again. I guess it was just because the whole thing was all over.

I walked down Duval Street, as one is meant to do here on New
Year's. It was all mobs of tourists and peacocks, block on block.
Paula was right about the titties, to the extent of one pair of barely
clad cuties escorting a Methuselah of a roué, and a trio of naked,
not nekked, body-painted women in trompe l'oeil, who are said to
proliferate here during Fantasy Fest. I had to admit that the sight
of a sleek tuxedo sprouting breasts was arresting. But the nakedest
person was a sinuous, high-stepping fellow with a silver half-thong

curling around one skinny cheek, and a tiny silver fig leaf cupping his junk.

Most of the young women wore low-cut party gowns or cocktail dresses and high heels; the promenade looked more like the prom than Carnival. Some wore butterfly bodices, but they weren't in the field guide, either. I'd thought I might see body-painted butterfly wings for a final species, but no cigar. Well, that's the wrong idiom—many of the millers were smoking cigars from Cuban cigar vendors lining the route along with extortionate rum and beer stands. Young roosters strutted with a ten-dollar cocktail in one hand and a phallic stinker in the other, crowing, the air thick with their exhaust.

The epicenter was a human thrombosis where frenzied throngs awaited midnight, when instead of an orange ball, Sushi the six-foot drag queen would drop in a giant red pump. I watched Sushi go up and must admit that s/he was very good—deep-voiced, campy, almost sexy, utterly unfazed by the madness. But I felt like a beetle under a shag rug in a hothouse, crammed against people by more people, unable to breathe. I considered unfurling Akito to clear my immediate perimeter, but I could barely move as it was.

Once I escaped that fissile nucleus, I wasn't about to fight my way back in at the midnight hour to see Sushi's descent. I withstood more than celebrated Auld Lang Syne several blocks away, where the kissy crowd thinned out. From a dirty public phone, I called Thea at Ann and Alan's New Year's party. They were playing Boggle by the fireside. I'd much rather have been there, doing that. I sneaked around the back streets, back to Bogart's.

Cigar smoke invaded the pub's open windows on shouts and squeals. Someone had puked, and the reggae was too loud. But the corner sofa where I nursed another Smithwick's beat the hot crowd by a mile. I guess I just preferred the company of hammock and mangrove skippers, buckeyes, sulphurs, and lep dweebs to these merry hordes milling in a miasma of beer and boredom. But that's harsh. Many looked happy, walking or rolling by in pedicabs. It was their party, not mine. At least, if I wasn't into it, I was in costume. Inside of just one block, I got "Mr. Survivor Man, I love you!" "Dr. Livingstone, I presume?" and "It's Ernest Hemingway! Wow, you're alive!" I was surprised that *that* one took so long down here, but I'll take it over Kenny Rogers any day.

Maybe it's just hard to take such a crowd after so much solitude. As I maundered away the hours over my bottomless Smithwick's and several more pints of ice water, the Irish bartender kept asking me if I was happy. I told him yes, quite happy, but I was actually pretty blue. And completely spent. I just wanted the night to be over.

And then came Amanda. Sweet, young, mildly drunken Amanda, who suddenly flitted into my life. Pretty and blond, in a nice black and white dress, she'd been at the bar for some time. I was half asleep over the dregs of my beer when she approached and asked me for a light. When I told her I didn't have one, she asked, "Well, can I sit with you?" Then, without warning, she popped down onto my lap.

"What's up with the hat?" she asked, "and that net, backpack—the whole deal?"

I said, "I study butterflies." Amanda told me she'd been to Indonesia, and loved seashells, birds, and butterflies. I said, "You must have seen a lot of them in Indonesia."

"Birds, or butterflies?" she asked. Amanda was Amish, from Delaware. I wondered if she knew young Ranger Clark, another fallen Amish, but I didn't ask. "I'm not going back," she said. "I work at Teasers now." She might have been twenty.

Amanda's friend Marlys tugged at her, trying to get her to come join their pals for a bite to eat. "We're starved," she whined, pulling Amanda's arm. Ditch the geezer, I knew she was thinking. Amanda stayed for a few more moments. Then, as she got up to follow Marlys, she asked, "Where can I find you?"

I just shrugged. I didn't even give her my Xerces card with my story on the back—good enough for Louisiana cops, the Border Patrol, and everyone else, I guess, except a beautiful young Amish dancer in Key West.

Amanda gave me a little hug, kissed my cheek, wished me luck with the butterflies (too late!), and disappeared into the finally dwindling crowd. I, feeling in equal parts avuncular, ancient, and amazed, sank back into my dirty couch and smiled. The barkeep called, "You still happy down there, mate?"

In his foreword to my first book, *Watching Washington Butter-flies*, Roger Tory Peterson wrote this: "It has been suggested that butterflies may symbolize a boy's adolescent dreams of the fair sex, gossamer and floss creatures to be pursued, and—just possibly—possessed." RTP wasn't being sexist: in those days, almost all lepidopterists were men, and all the young collectors I knew were, regrettably, boys.

Not to be pursued, and certainly not possessed, this particular creature of gossamer and floss was a godsend from all the rustic deities with whom I'd been spending my time—the dryads and nymphs, satyrs and fauns, Aphrodite, Astarte, Diana, Selene, maybe even Sushi—a single, shimmering grace note on an otherwise grim night. Ephemeral, lovely, and welcome, she merely fluttered through the tattered end of my used-up year, and then she was away, to somewhere else.

"Yes, thank you," I replied, "quite happy." Then I turned to the window. "There," I said, to no one at all, "goes the last butterfly."

4. HOME

The barman nicely kicked me out of Bogart's at four. I heard a rooster crow, and pedicab bells tinkling, but the crowds had evaporated. I walked south and found the entrance to Fort Zachary Taylor State Park, surrounded by the Navy's Truman Annex. The entrance station was closed until 8:00 A.M., so I walked in half a mile or so until I came to a fenced gate across the winding road. I chose a tree for a bedstead, slung my pack into a V of roots for a pillow, lay down on the ground, and slept maybe a solid hour or two. Dawn came cloudy, not that it really mattered anymore.

I saw someone go up the road, open the gate, and return, so I rose and walked on into the fort. I was reading the historical interpretation when a skinny whitebeard known as Bicycle Charlie pedaled up on a tricycle and told me I was not supposed to be there—"It's only seven-thirty"—and that I'd have to walk all the way out and pay my buck fifty after it opened at eight. I told him that it was unseemly for two Santas to be arguing on New Year's and that I'd gladly pay my twelve bits on the way out, but I wasn't walking back now. He pedaled off. A little later, Ranger Kip appeared in a golf cart and said, "What're we going to do about this?" He accepted my dollar fifty and wished me Happy New Year. Later I saw Charlie, a volunteer, yanking out exotic weeds; perhaps he'd regarded me in much the same way.

Gulf fritillaries woke the year up as they had put the last one to bed. The weedy fields on old bay fill outside the fort's moat had loads of butterflies on gaillardia and yellowtop but, almost to my relief, nothing I hadn't already seen. Beyond the severe castle I came to the last bit of beach before the Navy's angle cut it off, across the bay from the downtown waterfront. At the isolated end, from a small algae-slick concrete pier, I stripped off naked (it *was* Key West) and swam in the warm aquamarine sea. It felt better than good on my months of scratches, stickers, bites, and weary muscles and bones. I was amazed and grateful to find this wild Caribbean dip, all alone between the jammed beach back in the park and the thousands of overhung celebrants in town.

Not that I was really alone: schools of tiny silver fish surrounded me, flickering this way and that like sandpipers in flight. Then I noticed the pipefish. From the dock, I could see them well with my binos, their slender bodies, pert tails, pipe cleaner mouths. Mostly they milled in one small area protected by rocks. But when they saw something they wanted, they bent their bodies once and then, pow! Off like arrows! Their tails and beaks, about a foot apart, were turquoise, like the water out there, like the tips of a great southern white's antennae. As I watched them, a great southern white flew off the Navy's bare chunk of coral, past me, and out, out, into the blue-green ocean, Cuba-bound. So that, I said to the pipefish, must be where they go to dip their clubs.

Back by the fort, I heard another ranger telling a fellow that there was a palm warbler in the acacias where I had seen it in the morning. She approached me, and I thought, What have I done now? But she said, "You look like someone who could teach me something." Lu Dodson used to be a barmaid at the original Margaritaville, which was one level of last night's Hades. She and her husband have been volunteering in parks for ten years. It transpired that she'd read *Chasing Monarchs* and *Where Bigfoot Walks*, and the column that I wrote in *Orion* for many years until this trip put an end to it. I told her about my earlier contretemps with Bicycle Charlie. Lu laughed and said that he'd peddled 35,000 miles on his tricycle—farther than I drove Powdermilk in all of 2008. Then she took me back to Volunteer Village to meet her neighbor who worked on the butterfly garden and gave me wraps from last night's ranger party for lunch.

Master Gardener Bonnie led us to see orange dogs—giant swallowtail larvae—and their pupae, some liquescent, some good. She'd moved them to wild limes when too many had defoliated one citrus tree. There'd been a nice piece of habitat for native brush rabbits and cotton rats next door, until the Navy cleared it after 9-11. Now they mow it, Lu said, but at least the broad-winged hawk likes hunting there. She kindly offered to drive me to the Greyhound station at the airport, saving me the Key-length walk I'd been resigned to—an unexpected outcome after the morning's imbroglio.

Over a Yuengling and the local paper in the airport lounge, I saw Sushi on the front page. She was huge, having just arrived at her apogee. There, in the farthest back of the crowd below, up against a wall, barely visible, a tiny mote with a beard and a butterfly net, was I.

On the long ride up the whole of the archipelago on the big grey dog, I updated my checklists and dozed. The keys were shadowy, green-black smudges, sinking into an aqua sea. I changed buses in Miami, rode on to Fort Lauderdale, and boarded my flight to Portland, first class again through a fluke of holiday ticketing. Things you hate to hear while passing the cockpit might include, Captain to Copilot, looking over the flight plan, "That one looks like a nine, what you think that one is?" But I guess they figured it out. I took my vitamins with the first screwdriver I'd drunk in years.

As we crossed the Cascade Crest, the Oregon forest was all flocked, Hood River's orchards a ream of manuscript pages, white with black lines, laid out to dry. Houseboats glittered on the snow-melt-swollen Columbia as we banked to land. Thea would be waiting to meet me on the other side of Security, eager to tell me about the elk she'd hit on the way in, how they both came out okay, but her car, not so much. I saw it was already greening down there, and it wasn't going to be very long until spring. I wondered when the first echo azures would be out.

The End

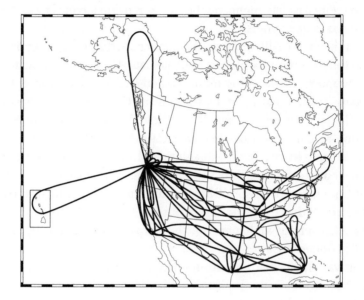

❧ AFTERWORD ❦

COULDA DONE BETTER, BUT I DON'T MIND

After any big undertaking, one inevitably asks oneself, So how'd I
do? How do I feel about it? How might I have done better? What
would I do differently? And what would I recommend for anyone coming after? Then too, one naturally asks, What did I learn?
How am I changed? And of much greater importance, in this case,
how have the butterflies changed? The land itself? And their survival dance together?

How'd I do? is easy to answer, at least in terms of sheer numbers.
I had set an arbitrary goal of 500 of the Pelhamian ideal total of 800

species. Some of my friends and colleagues avowed that they'd be surprised and delighted if I got half, or 400. My stalwart old friend and optimist Ray Stanford said he thought I could get 600. To me, 500 seemed a challenging but not unreasonable target. That turned out to be a good guess.

In the end, I tallied 478 species, as certified by my distinguished and tough committee: Jonathan P. Pelham, Curatorial Associate of Lepidoptera, Burke Museum of Natural History and Culture, University of Washington, and author of the *Catalogue of Butterflies of the United States and Canada;* Dr. Andrew W. Warren, the *Catalogue*'s editor, Senior Collections Manager at the McGuire Center for Lepidoptera and Biodiversity of the Florida Museum of Natural History, University of Florida, and author of *Butterflies of Oregon;* and Dr. Paul A. Opler, Professor of Bioagricultural Sciences and Associate Director of the C. P. Gillette Museum of Natural History, Colorado State University, and author of the eastern and western Peterson Field Guides to Butterflies.

It was Opler's hard question—How will people be able to trust your determinations of species?—that led to the certification committee in the first place. This is a large and perennial concern with Big Years. In his marvelous book *Birdscapes,* Jeremy Mynott wrote about birders engaged in "extreme pursuits" such as Big Years. Considering the rules they are always making for themselves, he wrote: "God doesn't care and won't settle it. Nor will Nature." True enough. So I sought the next best authority, appointing Pelham, Warren, and Opler to vet my results. The committee scrutinized not only my list, but also my notes and voucher specimens.

I wanted to be held to a high and rigorous standard, and I got it; the list would be several species longer if we had gone with a criterion of high probability, parsimony, or circumstantial likelihood rather than demonstrable certainty. For example, the committee threw out the early hairstreak from Black Mountain. They corroborated the great majority of my determinations, and corrected a few erroneous IDs.

In the end, I guess you could say that, while I didn't quite reach my goal, I did all right at 96 percent. Of course, there is nothing else with which to compare my results. I was like the person who wins Best of Show at the fair as the sole entry.

Another concrete objective of the project was the Xerces Society Butterfly-A-Thon. By soliciting monetary pledges for each species seen, we hoped to raise a significant sum for butterfly habitat conservation. In aid of this objective, and to raise and satisfy interest in the project overall, I agreed to write and post two weblogs about it. I am not the most electronically adept or sympathetic soul going. In the end, I constructed my entries by handwriting the dispatches on various objects picked up along the way—postcards, leaves, birch bark, beer mats—and sending them in by U.S. mail to the Xerces and Orion societies, where adept young staffers scanned and posted them online. The two artifact-based antiblogs, separate and complementary in their contents, appeared throughout the year. See them at http://www.xerces.org/butterflyathon/ and http://www .orionmagazine.org/index.php/butterfly/.

In addition to my spontaneous dispatches, the antiblogs include many splendid photographs of the species, places, and people I encountered, taken and donated by kind companions in the field, since I did not take pictures. Whether they helped elicit support or not I cannot say for sure. But I was shocked and delighted to learn that pledges to the Butterfly-A-Thon amounted to some $45,000, all of which will be spent directly on Xerces Society butterfly habitat conservation projects.

What would I (or should I) have done differently, in retrospect? A thousand little things, I'm sure: push farther on a given day, get going earlier, give up sooner and move on. Drop the net over a particular butterfly instead of swishing for it, or the reverse. Arrange for a stiffer rim for Akito (but then I couldn't have folded it up). Don't chat so much (though I was pretty antisocial on the whole). Don't drive off that bridge.

My strategy could have been sharpened, as Ben Basham constantly reminded me, by skipping some of the single-species quests, such as the Apache skipper, in favor of more time in the proven productive areas, especially the Lower Rio Grande Valley. In fact, if I'd wanted to ensure five hundred species or more, I would have begun and finished in the valley and spent months, not weeks, there in between. But would I have had as much fun? I do regret missing out on most of New England, the Great Lakes, and the Upper Midwest in summer, with its Dakota and Poweshiek skippers, not to mention

Canada. I'd have loved to visit the Great Dismal or the Carolina coast with the pickerelweed in full bloom. But as for that, talk to the gods of weather, the masters of time.

I know I lost time, and therefore species, to the preparation of materials for the antiblogs; to visiting, as little as I did; to my curiosity about the land and the culture through which I moved; to exigencies such as sink stoppers down valve covers; and to the little sleep and forage I managed to snag between rolling up the miles. But sleep and eating, on some level, are necessary; and all the other distractions served to enhance the richness of the overall experience, and I hope the telling of it too.

Speaking of means, how did my idea of "grails" pan out? Of the forty or so designated grail species, I found thirty. It was wonderful to commune at last with Gillett's and Baltimore checkerspots, Sandia and Avalon hairstreaks, Behr's sulphur, atala, Ross's alpine, and the Georgia satyr, to name just a few. It was fine to have better encounters than my prior ones with Nokomis and Idalia, Diana and Christina, among others. And how about those giant-skippers? Going for the grails in faith that the commoner species would show up along the way worked out pretty darned well. So did the daisy-petal model for the individual trips or rays, though the "flower" (page 537) would look a little more like one if I lived in, say, Topeka.

Of course, I missed some too. My main disappointments may be listed as Eversmann's parnassian and the Mt. McKinley alpine in Alaska, the Sonoran and veined blues of California, the short-tailed swallowtail of the Maritimes, and the Kamehameha in Hawaii. While I did very well on certain genera, such as *Polites* and *Euphyes* skippers, sulphurs, coppers, and fritillaries, I did poorly on road-side-skippers and crackers. There were some inexplicable absences, such as the Hobomok skipper (see "Silly Misses" under "Statistics"), and others—like the cyna blue and the Cuban crescent—that simply eluded me again and again.

And yet, as far as luck goes, how can I be said to have had anything but extraordinarily good luck, when all of seventy-two species—any one of them easily missed—appeared to me as singletons? And for every miss or disappointment, there was what I have consistently called a *grace note*: for what else to call the white wedge of the Olympia marble poking up in the Texas cemetery I came upon by accident; the brown smudge of the red satyr just where I had hoped to find it, at the last possible instance; or the Florida leafwing's momentary dash at the end of an Everglades day?

From a Morrison's silver-spike on an opening bear grass blossom in the New Mexico spring to a Karner blue's egg in the depth of the Wisconsin winter, from the sea otters of Moss Landing to the swallow-tailed kites of Marys River, even to the Daphne in a hospital garden or a mass of moths in a gunnery tunnel, I saw something wonderful every single day of the year. Good fortune stands out overwhelmingly in my memory. Misfortunes, aside from the weather, were almost incredibly few. People behaved considerately toward me, or at least civilly, with very few exceptions. Authorities seldom forgot their manners, and often helped me out. I had no dangerous encounters at all, that I was aware of. Extraordinary kindness found me, again and again.

Most of my trials were minor, some funny, and always survivable. You could say I lucked out, gleaning the benisons of happenstance that sometimes come to those who are open to them, when the world is closely watched and hunches are indulged. Plus, I picked my partners well; remarkable Powdermilk, never a breakdown or even a flat tire in almost 33,000 gas-sipping miles. Miraculous Marsha, broken and arisen these many times, and her sidekicks, Mini-Marsha, Akito, and the tiki torch. Most of all, though with me only rarely, Thea—with her infinite indulgence and encouragement, keen perception, and insistence on getting well and keeping me on the road.

Now that I have broken the ice on the copper's bog, as it were, I suppose others will inexorably try their own hand at this gambit. They are welcome to it, and they will very likely shatter my "record": it will be like the year I held the discus-throw record at South Junior High School, because we were the first class to attend and compete. So what tips can I offer those who follow? (1) Have better weather: don't pick a La Niña year. (2) Avoid family health crises; but if you must have one, make sure it involves a supporter as robust and heroic as Thea was for me. (3) Make better use of electronic aids than I did. Of course, almost anyone who would undertake such an ordeal would do this as a matter of course, because most serious field folks I know—butterfly, Bigfoot, or otherwise—

are both gearheads and web adepts. If you have the stomach for endless e-mails, charging batteries, and, may the gods help us, list-serves, you may well find more butterflies than I, who do not, managed to spot. (4) Take a field companion more often, preferably a devoted photographer and a good netsman/woman, but only if s/he doesn't talk too much in the field, drinks beer after hours, and is willing to share the driving (before the beer). Having to do most of the driving was one of my toughest challenges. If you can afford it, hire Jim Wiker, Koji Shiraiwa, Alana Edwards, or Ben Basham for the whole year. (5) Study up on the immatures; you could find even more in winter than I did. (6) Most aspirants will have some sort of van, SUV, or RV. Fine; you'll be more comfortable. But be sure it is as reliable as Powdermilk, and you'd better pick a year with cheaper gas than 2008. (7) Have more money. (8) Finally, never mind the numbers. If you need to beat me, have at it, and more power. Get it out of the way. Then slow down, and let the butterflies lead. You'll see just as many as you see; and much more besides.

Every day I looked into the lives of creatures doing what they do to survive, doing the best they can in the face of a cold spring, a warming world, wildfire, and everything else that we exact from the land. But the land, the habitat, and the butterflies are not what Peterson and Fisher found on their *Wild America* trek in 1953, nor Kenn Kaufman as the hobo of *Kingbird Highway* in the early 1970s. The human population has doubled in each interval, and with it, the wildness has more than halved. I anticipated that the Big Year would become a stitchwork transect of the condition of butterfly well-being, and so it did. Butterfly habitats and populations have vastly diminished for many species, and they are going down yet.

But not all of them: I also observed rarities that have recovered, or are increasing, in some beloved and well cared for places. And certain species that proliferate in anthropogenic settings are probably more abundant than ever. Butterfly gardens and greenbelts help to keep common species common, as I saw from Fort Myers to Matewan, Brownsville to Boulder. Wilderness areas, national and state parks and forests, and preserves of various kinds protect good populations of many species. Yet I witnessed more examples of butterflies depleted from inappropriate management of "conserved" land than from any other factors besides outright development or intensive agriculture. Fire, especially—both wildfire and intentional, "controlled" burns conducted too large, too often, and too hot —endangers our aridland endemics and grassland specialities. Will Ottoe and Hermes survive the flames, intentional and otherwise?

Even though I saw monarchs on more days than any other species, their numbers in the West were way, way down and everywhere else, only middling. This condition owes at least in part to drought. In the winter of 2009–2010, monarchs in Mexico were at their lowest recorded ebb. Will they recover once again, or continue on down? Meanwhile, the Uncompahgre fritillary perches precariously on alpine heights too little snowed upon.

The great drying and warming are under way and, with them, the dying and shrinking away of some butterflies, the expansion of others. The Avalon hairstreak seems safe on its island heights, Diana in its Appalachian redoubts, the Magdalena alpine on its high, rocky ridges and cirques. But each has its threats, in the forms of fire, mountaintop removal, and the warming that is even now expelling Magdalena's pal, the pika. I wish I could say the Butterfly Big Year left me sanguine about the state of our butterflies, but that would be asking a lot after forty years' involvement in their conservation. Yes, it is undeniably good to see the resurrection of the Palos Verdes blue and all the attention paid to the Karner blue. Good work is being done, with good results. But nothing I saw convinced me that the Xerces Society will be anything but busier in the coming years.

And yet: there remains, and will continue to remain, still more delight and diversity than any one of us could possibly apprehend in a year or a lifetime. If you are willing to look between the enormities and the erosion, you will find it. Whether for a year across the continent or for an afternoon in a vacant lot, the butterflies and all the rest carry on as best as we allow them to do. But only by getting *out there* among them, between the best of what's left and the ruts of what's lost, will we care enough to save the remnants and to restore the land in the aftermath of our kind's excesses.

The checklist will surely change in years to come, as will the range maps. But butterflies will still be here, whether anyone is around to enjoy them or not.

APPENDIX:

STATISTICS AND SPECIES TALLY

SPECIES

Goal: 500 spp.

Total, Certified 09/09/09: 477 (+1 species elevated) = 478

   +Species pending elevation: 5 (potential total of 483)

   +Eliminated likelies: 4

   +Bricked likelies: 8

   +Narrow misses: 13

   +Silly misses: 3

   +Surprising misses: 5

   +Easily could'ves: 34+

   72 + 478 = 550+, a plausible total for a similar effort

— RMP Life Butterflies: 158 (one third of total)

— "Grails" seen vs. sought: 30 of about 40, or 75 percent

— Average species seen per day: 10.1

— Most species seen in a day: 80 (October 20, Lower Rio Grande Valley)

— Days with zero species seen: 86

— Species seen just one day: 140

— Actual singletons (just one individual seen): 72

— Top fifteen species by number of days seen: little (Lisa) yellow, 36 days; giant swallowtail and sleepy orange, 39; pipevine swallowtail, 41; gray hairstreak, 42; queen, 46; buckeye, 49; red admirable, 54; fiery skipper, 56; cabbage white, 61; orange sulphur, 63; gulf fritillary, 68; cloudless sulphur, 74; painted lady, 78; and Number One, monarch, seen 92 days of the year.

544

— New county records: 134 (per BAMONA state coordinators)
— Other species of animals seen and identified (or can likely be identified from my notes).

Except for birds, numbers are approximate, and include roadkills and sign. With a little more time and energy than I had left over, these poor numbers could vastly be increased for most of these and several other groups, the moths alone by hundreds. I observed many additional organisms with no effort at ID. The point of this exercise is to barely hint at the vast diversity that welcomes any attentive observer on the road and in the field (and this is only animals—though I greeted many old and new floristic friends with pleasure, I attempted no tally of the plethora of plants that graced the journey!).

mammals (73)
birds (344)
reptiles (50)
amphibians (20)
fish (10)
moths (40)
caddis flies (2)
flies (8)
hymenopterans (14)
beetles (12)
heteropterans (8)
orthopterans (13)
odonates (23)
arachnids+ (20)
earthworms (1)
millipedes (1)
mollusks (30)
crustaceans (5)
echinoderms (2)
jellies (1)

= 677 species + 478 butterflies = 1,155 TOTAL SPECIES

TRAVEL

— Miles Powdermilk driven: 32,544
(of 387,034 total on the odometer at conclusion of the journey)
— Powdermilk mileage: 42 miles per gallon average, best tank 49 mpg
— Flat tires: 0
— Breakdowns: 0
— Miles driven in rental and other cars: 7,989
— Total miles driven: 40,533
— Miles by air: 37,616
— Miles by rail: 4,135
— Miles by boat: 122
— Miles by bus: 435
— Rough total distance traveled in 2008: 87,739
— Miles driven per species: 95
— Total miles traveled per species: 183
— Carbon cost per species: don't ask.
— Carbon mitigation: see first two items.

BUTTERFLY-A-THON

— Donors: ~600
— Average pledge per donor: $77.00
— Average pledge per species: $.80
— Total amount raised for Xerces Society habitat action: ~$46,000

EXPENSES AND ESSENTIALS

— Overall expenditure: $16,132
gas: $2,687; lowest $1.58 per gallon, highest $5.50, average $3.47;
auto upkeep: $1,117; auto rental: $1,351; air and Amtrak: 0; food
and drink: $5,481; supplies, $410; lodging: $1,901 for 33 nights;
camping: $79 for 13 nights; specs and dental, $455
— Cost per species: $33.82
— Days ill: 0
— Plastic water bottles bought: 0
— Steel water bottles used: 5, refilled n^x
— Peanuts consumed: incalculable

SPECIES CERTIFIED

Scientific names used for space. Common names easily found in Jim
P. Brock and Kenn Kaufman, *Kaufman Field Guide to Butterflies of North
America* (Houghton Mifflin Harcourt, 2003). Order of species and all
spellings according to Jonathan P. Pelham, *A Catalog of the Butterflies of
the United States and Canada* (*Journal of the Research on the Lepidoptera*
40: 2008).

HESPERIIDAE
001. *Phocides pigmalion*
002. *P. polybius*
003. *Epargyreus clarus*
004. *Polygonus leo*
005. *Chioides albofasciatus*
006. *C. zilpa*
007. *Aguna asander*
008. *A. metophis*
009. *Urbanus proteus*
010. *U. dorantes*
011. *U. teleus*
012. *U. procne*
013. *Astraptes fulgerator*
014. *A. anaphus*
015. *Achalarus lyciades*
016. *A. toxeus*
017. *Thorybes bathyllus*
018. *T. pylades*
019. *T. confusis*
020. *T. mexicana*
021. *Cabares potrillo*
022. *Cogia calchas*
023. *Apyrrothrix araxes*
024. *Pellicia arina*
025. *Staphylus mazans*
026. *S. hayhurstii*
027. *Pholisora catullus*

028. *Hesperopsis libya*
029. *Timochares ruptifasciata*
030. *Chiomara georgina*
031. *Ephyriades brunnea*
032. *Erynnis icelus*
033. *E. brizo*
034. *E. juvenalis*
035. *E. telemachus*
036. *E. propertius*
037. *E. meridianus*
038. *E. horatius*
039. *E. tristis*
040. *E. zarucco*
041. *E. funeralis*
042. *E. baptisiae*
043. *E. afranius*
044. *E. persius*
045. *Eantis tamenund*
046. *Systasea pulverulenta*
047. *S. zampa*
048. *Pyrgus centaureae*
049. *P. ruralis*
050. *P. communis*
051. *P. albescens*
052. *P. philetas*
053. *P. oileus*
054. *Heliopyrgus domicella*
055. *Heliopetes ericetorum*

056. *H. macaira*
057. *H. laviana*
058. *Cartercephalus palaemon*
059. *Piruna pirus*
060. *Agathymus evansi*
061. *A. aryxna*
062. *A. stephensi*
063. *Megathymus yuccae*
064. *M. cofaqui*
065. *Erionota thrax*
066. *Perichares adela*
067. *Ancyloxypha numitor*
068. *Oarisma garita*
069. *Copaeodes aurantiaca*
070. *C. minima*
071. *Thymelicus lineola*
072. *Calpodes ethlius*
073. *Panoquina panoquin*
074. *P. panoquinoides*
075. *P. errans*
076. *P. ocola*
077. *P. lucas*
078. *P. hecebola*
079. *Synapte pecta*
080. *Amblyscirtes vialis*
081. *A. aesculapius*
082. *A. alternata*
083. *A. celia*
084. *A. belli*
085. *Nastra lherminier*
086. *N. julia*
087. *Cymaenes tripunctus*
088. *C. trebius*
089. *Lerodea eufala*
090. *L. arabus*
091. *Lerema accius*
092. *Oligoria maculata*

093. *Hylephila phyleus*
094. *Hesperia uncas*
095. *H. juba*
096. *H. colorado*
097. *H. ottoe*
098. *H. leonardus*
099. *H. pahaska*
100. *H. metea*
101. *H. viridis*
102. *H. attalus*
103. *H. meskei*
104. *H. lindseyi*
105. *Polites peckius*
106. *P. sabuleti*
107. *P. draco*
108. *P. mardon*
109. *P. themistocles*
110. *P. baracoa*
111. *P. origenes*
112. *P. mystic*
113. *P. sonora*
114. *P. vibex*
115. *Wallengrenia otho*
116. *W. egeremet*
117. *Pompeius verna*
118. *Atalopedes campestris*
119. *Atrytone arogos*
120. *Problema byssus*
121. *Poanes zabulon*
122. *P. taxiles*
123. *P. massasoit*
124. *P. aaroni*
125. *P. melane*
126. *Stinga morrisoni*
127. *Ochlodes sylvanoides*
128. *O. agricola*
129. *O. yuma*

130. *Paratrytone snowi*

131. *Anatrytone logan*

132. *Quasimellana eulogius*

133. *Euphyes pilatka*

134. *E. conspicua*

135. *E. berryi*

136. *E. dion*

137. *E. dukesi*

138. *E. bimacula*

139. *E. arpa*

140. *E. vestris*

141. *Asbolis capucinus*

142. *Atrytonopsis hianna*

143. *A. loammi*

144. *A. pittacus*

145. *A. edwardsii*

146. *Nyctelius nyctelius*

PAPILIONIDAE

147. *Parnassius clodius*

148. *P. smintheus*

149. *Battus philenor*

150. *B. polydamas*

151. *Eurytides marcellus*

152. *Papilio machaon*

153. *P. polyxenes*

154. *P. zelicaon*

155. *P. indra*

156. *P. xuthus*

157. *P. cresphontes*

158. *P. canadensis*

159. *P. glaucus*

160. *P. rutulus*

161. *P. eurymedon*

162. *P. multicaudata*

163. *P. troilus*

164. *P. palamedes*

PIERIDAE

165. *Kricogonia lyside*

166. *Nathalis iole*

167. *Eurema daira*

168. *E. mexicana*

169. *Abaeis nicippe*

170. *Pyrisitia proterpia*

171. *P. lisa*

172. *P. nise*

173. *P. dina*

174. *Colias philodice*

175. *C. eurytheme*

176. *C. occidentalis*

177. *C. christina*

178. *C. alexandra*

179. *C. harfordii*

180. *C. meadii*

181. *C. canadensis*

182. *C. tyche*

183. *C. scudderi*

184. *C. gigantea*

185. *C. pelidne*

186. *C. interior*

187. *C. palaeno*

188. *C. behrii*

189. *Zerene cesonia*

190. *Z. eurydice*

191. *Anteos clorinde*

192. *Phoebis sennae*

193. *P. agarithe*

194. *P. philea*

195. *Aphrissa statira*

196. *Anthocharis sara*

197. *A. midea*

198. *A. lanceolata*

199. *Euchloe ausonides*

200. *E. olympia*

201. *E. creusa creusa*
202. *Glutophrissa drusilla*
203. *Neophasia menapia*
204. *N. terlooii*
205. *Pieris angelika*
206. *P. marginalis*
207. *P. virginiensis*
208. *P. rapae*
209. *Pontia beckerii*
210. *P. protodice*
211. *P. occidentalis*
212. *P. sisymbrii*
213. *Ascia monuste*
214. *Ganyra josephina*

LYCAENIDAE
215. *Feniseca tarquinius*
216. *Lycaena phlaeas*
217. *L. cupreus*
218. *L. arota*
219. *L. hermes*
220. *L. dione*
221. *L. editha*
222. *L. xanthoides*
223. *L. gorgon*
224. *L. rubidus*
225. *L. heteronea*
226. *L. hyllus*
227. *L. dorcas*
228. *L. helloides*
229. *L. nivalis*
230. *L. mariposa*
231. *Hypaurotis crysalus*
232. *Habrodais grunus*
233. *Eumaeus atala*
234. *Atlides halesus*
235. *Rekoa marius*

236. *Satyrium fuliginosa*
237. *S. semiluna*
238. *S. behrii*
239. *S. californica*
240. *S. sylvinus*
241. *S. titus*
242. *S. edwardsii*
243. *S. calanus*
244. *S. liparops*
245. *S. auretorum*
246. *S. tetra*
247. *S. saepium*
248. *S. favonius*
249. *Chlorostrymon simaethis*
250. *Cyanophrys herodotus*
251. *C. miserabilis*
252. *Callophrys affinis*
253. *C. dumetorum*
254. *C. sheridanii*
255. *C. perplexa*
256. *C. gryneus*
257. *C. muiri*
258. *C. thornei*
259. *C. hesseli*
260. *C. xami*
261. *C. mcfarlandi*
262. *C. johnsoni*
263. *C. augustinus*
264. *C. mossii*
265. *C. polios*
266. *C. irus*
267. *C. henrici*
268. *C. niphon*
269. *C. eryphon*
270. *Electrostrymon hugon*
271. *E. angelia*
272. *Calycopis cecrops*

273. *C. isobeon*
274. *Strymon melinus*
275. *S. avalona*
276. *S. bebrycia*
277. *S. yojoa*
278. *S. martialis*
279. *S. acis*
280. *S. bazochii*
281. *S. istapa*
282. *Tmolus echion*
283. *Ministrymon leda*
284. *M. clytie*
285. *Erora quaderna*
286. *Lampides boeticus*
287. *Leptotes cassius*
288. *L. marina*
289. *Brephidium exilis*
290. *B. pseudofea*
291. *Zizina otis*
292. *Cupido comyntas*
293. *C. amyntula*
294. *Celastrina lucia*
295. *C. echo*
296. *C. neglecta*
297. *Udara blackburni*
298. *Hemiargus ceraunus*
299. *Philotiella speciosa*
300. *P. leona*
301. *Euphilotes battoides*
302. *E. glaucon*
303. *E. bernardino*
304. *E. enoptes*
305. *E. columbiae*
306. *E. rita*
307. *Glaucopsyche piasus*
308. *G. lygdamus*
309. *Cyclargus thomasi*

310. *Echinargus isola*
311. *Plebejus idas*
312. *P. anna*
313. *P. melissa*
314. *P. saepiolus*
315. *P. icarioides*
316. *P. shasta*
317. *P. acmon*
318. *P. lupini*
319. *P. glandon*
320. *P. podarce*
321. *Calephelis muticum*
322. *C. virginiensis*
323. *C. nemesis*
324. *C. perditalis*
325. *C. rawsoni*
326. *C. arizonensis*
327. *Caria ino*
328. *Lasaia sula*
329. *Melanis pixe*
330. *Emesis ares*
331. *E. emesia*
332. *Apodemia mormo*
333. *A. virgulti*
334. *A. palmeri*

NYMPHALIDAE

335. *Libytheana carinenta*
336. *Danaus plexippus*
337. *D. gilippus*
338. *D. eresimus*
339. *Limenitis arthemis*
340. *L. weidemeyerii*
341. *L. lorquini*
342. *L. archippus*
343. *Adelpha fessonia*
344. *A. eulalia*

345. *A. californica*
346. *Dione moneta*
347. *Agraulis vanillae*
348. *Dryas iulia*
349. *Eueides isabella*
350. *Heliconius charithonia*
351. *Euptoieta claudia*
352. *E. hegesia*
353. *Boloria eunomia*
354. *B. selene*
355. *B. bellona*
356. *B. frigga*
357. *B. improba*
358. *B. epithore*
359. *B. astarte*
360. *B. freija*
361. *B. chariclea*
362. *Speyeria diana*
363. *S. cybele*
364. *S. aphrodite*
365. *S. idalia*
366. *S. nokomis*
367. *S. edwardsii*
368. *S. coronis*
369. *S. zerene*
370. *S. callippe*
371. *S. egleis*
372. *S. atlantis*
373. *S. hesperis*
374. *S. hydaspe*
375. *S. mormonia*
376. *Asterocampa celtis*
377. *A. leilia*
378. *A. clyton*
379. *Doxocopa pavon*
380. *D. laure*
381. *Biblis hyperia*

382. *Mestra amymone*
383. *Eunica tatila*
384. *Myscelia ethusa*
385. *Marpesia petreus*
386. *Vanessa virginiensis*
387. *V. cardui*
388. *V. annabella*
389. *V. atalanta*
390. *Aglais milberti*
391. *Nymphalis vaualbum*
392. *N. californica*
393. *N. antiopa*
394. *Polygonia interrogationis*
395. *P. comma*
396. *P. satyrus*
397. *P. progne*
398. *P. gracilis*
399. *P. faunus*
400. *Anartia jatrophae*
401. *A. fatima*
402. *Siproeta stelenes*
403. *Junonia coenia*
404. *J. evarete*
405. *J. genoveva*
406. *Euphydryas gillettii*
407. *E. editha*
408. *E. chalcedona*
409. *E. colon*
410. *E. anicia*
411. *E. phaeton*
412. *Poladryas arachne*
413. *Chlosyne janais*
414. *C. rosita*
415. *C. theona*
416. *C. cyneas*
417. *C. fulvia*
418. *C. nycteis*

419. *C. gorgone*
420. *C. californica*
421. *C. lacinia*
422. *C. hoffmanni*
423. *C. acastus*
424. *C. gabbii*
425. *C. palla*
426. *C. damoetas*
427. *Microtia elva*
428. *Dymasia dymas*
429. *Texola elada*
430. *Anthanassa tulcis*
431. *A. texana*
432. *Phyciodes graphica*
433. *P. picta*
434. *P. orseis*
435. *P. pallida*
436. *P. mylitta*
437. *P. phaon*
438. *P. tharos*
439. *P. cocyta*
440. *P. pulchella*
441. *Anaea troglodyta*
442. *A. aidea*
443. *A. andria*
444. *Lethe portlandia*
445. *L. anthedon*
446. *L. creola*
447. *L. eurydice*
448. *L. appalachia*
449. *Coenonympha haydenii*
450. *C. tullia*

451. *Cyllopsis pyracmon*
452. *C. pertepida*
453. *C. gemma*
454. *Hermeuptychia sosybius*
455. *H. hermes*
456. *Neonympha areolata*
457. *Megisto cymela*
458. *M. rubricata*
459. *Cercyonis pegala*
460. *C. meadii*
461. *C. sthenele*
462. *C. oetus*
463. *Gyrocheilus patrobas*
464. *Erebia vidleri*
465. *E. rossii*
466. *E. disa*
467. *E. magdalena*
468. *E. fasciata*
469. *E. epipsodea*
470. *E. discoidalis*
471. *E. callias*
472. *Neominois ridingsii*
473. *Oeneis melissa*
474. *O. bore*
475. *O. chryxus*
476. *O. nevadensis*
477. *O. uhleri*
478. *P. samuelis* (elevated to species status in revision to Pelham *Catalogue*, 2010; belongs between 313 *P. melissa* and 314 *P. saepiolus* above)

CLOSE CALLS: SHOULDA'S, COULDA'S, AND WOULDA'S

SUBSPECIES LIKELY TO BE DESCRIBED SOON OR ELEVATED TO SPECIES STATUS

Erynnis juvenalis clitus
Anthocharis sara thoosa
Euphilotes "on heracleoides"
Plebejus lupini texanus
Chlosyne theona chinatiensis

These would raise the actual total to 483.

SPECIES LIKELY SEEN BUT NOT IDENTIFIED WITH CERTAINTY

Nastra neamathla
Eurema boisduvaliana
Erora laeta
Dynamine dyonis

INDIVIDUALS SEEN BUT MISSED, SO UNIDENTIFIED

Amblyscirtes 1 (eos?)
Amblyscirtes 2 (tolteca?)
Amblyscirtes 3 (oslari?)
Amblyscirtes 4 (linda?)
Hesperia sassacus?
Agathymus mariae/
    chisosensis?
Neonympha helicta?
Key West "mystery
    butterfly"?

All of these would have brought the total to 495.

NARROW MISSES IN TIME OR SPACE

Poanes viator
Panoquina fusina
Agathymus alliae
Parnassius eversmannii
Lycaena epixanthe
Strymon acadica
Philotes sonorensis
Boloria kriemhild
Speyeria carolae
Thessalia leanira
Erebia pawloskii
E. mackinleyensis
E. occulta

SILLY MISSES

Poanes hobomok
Pieris oleracea
Celastrina ladon

SURPRISING MISSES

Erynnis martialis
Poanes yehl
Anthocharis cethura
Euchloe lotta
Mitoura spinetorum
Parrhasius m-album

All of these would have brought the total to 517.

SPECIES I READILY COULD HAVE SEEN WHERE I WENT OR NOT SO FAR AWAY

Hesperopsis alphaeus
Amblyscirtes texanae
A. simius
A. hegon
A. exoteria
A. nysa
Astraptes gilberti
Autochton cellus
Hesperia woodgatei
Parnassius behrii
Papilio ornythion and
    other Mexican swallowtails
Colias nastes
Celastrina humulus
Polygonia oreas
Apodemia nais
Strymon alea
Plebejus emigdionis
P. neurona
Zizula cyna
Eunica monima
Chlosyne harrisii
Phyciodes batesii
P. frisia
Erebia youngi
E. lafontainei
Oeneis alpina
O. polyxenes
O. jutta
+ many others in the Lower Rio Grande Valley

These show how the total could easily reach 550+.

ACKNOWLEDGMENTS

A proper thank-you for such a dependent enterprise as this could easily exceed the checklist of butterflies itself. I hope everyone will accept that this shorthand version, minus the usual modifiers and endearments, implies no less than uttermost appreciation.

But first, certain ones whose service rendered exceeded any measure of normalcy: Mía Monroe and Steve Meyer; Barbara and Barry Deutsch; Debra and John Piot; Lana, David, and Alana Edwards and Rick Nevulis and Skipper; Buck and Linda Cooper; Lee and Jackie Miller; Pat and Clay Sutton; Fayette Krause and JoAnne Heron; Charlie Covell and family; Kojiro Shiraiwa and family; Kenelm and Betty Anne Philip; Jim Wiker and Sally Agnew; Jan and Amy Chu; Boyce Drummond; David Branch; Dave McCorkle; Floyd and June Preston; Benton Basham; Akers Pence; Ann and Scott Swengel; Su Borkin; and Laura Arnold.

The Xerces Society (especially Sarina Jensen, Sean Tenney, and Scott Black), and all the donors to its Butterfly-A-Thon; the Orion Society (especially Jennifer Sahn, Hal Clifford, Scott Walker, and Katie Yale); the Washington, Eugene-Springfield, North Central Florida, and Atala chapters of NABA, and its Texas Butterfly Park; our national forests in toto, especially the U.S. Forest Service Wind River Canopy Crane on the Gifford Pinchot NF; all the U.S. Border Patrol agents who watched over me and livened my nights with cordial conversation; and all the farmers, ranchers, rangers, and officers of the law who forgave me my trespasses.

Kenn Kaufman for the inspiration of *Kingbird Highway*, for cheerleading, and with Jim Brock for their invaluable field guide; Jon Pelham for his essential *Catalogue*, and with Paul Opler and Andy Warren for their certification duties and so much more; and the authors of all the other field guides, papers, and other resources I depended upon.

The shared enthusiasm of my kind and astute agent, Laura Blake Peterson of Curtis Brown, Ltd., and Lisa White at Houghton Mifflin

Harcourt for the idea of this book made it happen. Lisa's edit was superb, tolerant, and good-natured, Susan Brown's copy edit essential, and their colleagues at HMH—Tim Mudie, Teresa Elsey, Beth Burleigh Fuller, Martha Kennedy, Paul Lobue, and George Restrepo—helped make it the handsome book it is, with the invaluable aid of the designer, Lisa Diercks. Taryn Roeder and Katrina Kruse eased its way into the world.

And so many more, surely not all named here, who helped in one way or a dozen: Doug Aguillard; Keith and Katrina Andrews; Richard Arnold; Ron Arnold; Sue Arnold; Zach Arsineaux; George Austin; the Bagdonas family; Rick Bailowitz; Greta Ball; Bob Behrstock and Karen LeMay; Rob Bellinger; Ira Beltz; Richard Benning; Chris Benshoof; Haven Best; Mavynee Betsch (always); Ken Bible; Bill Black; Martha Blanton; Carol Boggs and Ward Watt; Brett Boyd; Patrick Boyle; Curt and Rosemary Breedlove; Hank and Priscilla Brodkin; Rachel and Bob Brophy; Lincoln Brower; Bill and Alexis Brown; John Brown; Rick Brown and Ruth Robbins; Lucy Bruce; Pete Brussard; Evi Buckner; Shayna Butler; Ed and Judy Butterfield; John Calhoun; David Campbell; Paula and Gary Cannon; Jennifer Carillo; Carrie of Santa Catalina; Steve Cary; Kurt Caswell; Dave Chagnon, Paul, Che, and their coworkers at Stirling Honda; Cheryl Charles; Francie Chew; Bonnie Ciegler; Dustin Clark; Chris Cline; Howard Close; Jimmy Coleman; Jack and Jesse Connor; Catarino Contreras; Barry Cook; Paul Cote; Linda Craig; Robert Cramer; Mark Creighton; Larry Crowley; Janet Cruz; Robert Dana; Jaret Daniel; Jan and David Dauphin; Ray Davis; Todd Davis; John Dayton; Philip deMaynadier; Dan Derrick; Lu Dodson; Heather and Pete Doolittle; Phillip Drivens; David Droppers; Chris Durden; Judy Durrah; Catherine Edison; David Edwards; Granger Ellington; Susan Elliott; Deirdre Elmansoumi; Tom and John Emmel; Kay Eoff; Linda Evans; Maya and George Exum and Carol Carver; Jerry and Louise Fall and BioQuip; Sarah Fetterly; Firkin; Joel and Noreen Fitts; Five M's; Joe Fontaine; Larry Gall; Deborah Galloway; Christina Garcia; Martha Garcia; Mark Garland and Paige Cunningham; Dick Gilbert; Tommy and Edie Giles; Barb and Don Gilmore; Walt and Natalie Glass; Jeff Glassberg and Jane Scott; Carl Goodrich; Prescott and Robin Grey; Gerald Griggs; Patty Groth; Louise Hallberg; Roger Hammer; Paul Hammond; Dave Hanson; Jim and Bea Harrison; George Hart; Taylor Haygood; Fred Heath; Dave Heft; Tom, Iliana, David, and Cristina Hellyer; Alice and Bob Henry; Joey Hernandez; Carry Hiestand; Tod Hisaichi; Travis Hoover; Walter Houle; David Inouye; Rodney James; Jack, Lorée, and Jake Jeffers; Stephanie Jijon;

Betsy and Dan Johnson, Glenn Johnson; Jeanne Branch Johnson; Paul Johnson; Robert Johnson; Susan and Ted Kafer; Akito Kawahara; Jay Kelly; Phil and JoAnne Kelly; Bob Kennington; Will Kerling; Ketzela; Kenneth Key; Mike Klein; Chris Kline; Sunny Knutson; Steve Kohler; Brad Kolhoff; Carolyn Kremers; Art Kruckeberg; Jean-Francois Landry; John Lane; Robert Langston; Tom and Sue Leskiw; Jack Levy; Bob LiaBraaten; Terri Lollio; Jim Louvier; Ellen Mahoney; Robin Mallow; Kathy Malone; Steve Marck; Susan Maresco; Thomas Maring; Luann Marrote; Kathy Martinez; Debbie Matthews; Cathy Maxwell; Jonathan Mays; Joanna McCaffrey; Dorcas and Cope McClintock; Mary McCollum; Ret McCoy; Ray McCrite; William McGuire; Joe Meeker; Pete Melendez; Gretchen Meyer; Caterina Meyers; Microbrewers all; Klaus Miebach; Don Miller; Katherine Miller; Mitch Miller; John Mimosa; Mark Minno; Monterey Bay Poetry Consortium; Jean Morgan; Laurie Ness; Melba Nezbed; Martha Nitzberg and Mark Conover; George Noory; Krist Novoselic and Darbury Stenderu; Dave and Jo Nunnallee; Liam O'Brien; Maryanne and John Ogden; Tom O'Hagan; Larry Orsak; Richard Owen; Jennifer Owen-White; Nancy Peterson; Ann Potter and Dave Hays; Jerry Powell; Jim Price; Howard W. Pyle; Tom, Mary, and Mike Pyle; Alan Rembos and Sue and Marcy; Mike Renda; Albert Rendon; Mike Riccard; Harold Rice; Jim Riley; Mary Ritch; Jo Roberts; Beth Rossow; Dan Rubinoff; Jane Ruffin; Brian Russart; Paul and Sandy Russell; Emily Saarinen; Alfred Sanchez; Scott and Ruth Sanders; Sarah's granola and Heidi's tamales; Paul Saris; Vic Scheffer; George, Alice, and Sarah Scheil and Betsy and Tom; Erin Schramer; Matt Schroeder; James A. Scott; Bob Seaman; Janet and Richard Selzer; Dee Serage-Century; David Shaw; Jack Shaw; Katha Sheehan; Everett Skinner; Rick Snider; Jim and Denise Snyder; Mary Spivey; Toby Sprunt; Ray and Kit Stanford; Emilija Stanic; Adam Stern; Don Stillwaugh; Beth Swartz; Rod Swensen and SCAA; David and Kory Taylor; Elaine Terrell; John and Pat Thomas; Barbara Tripp; Terry Truman; Bill Tydeman; Mike and Kathy Uhtoff family; Idie Ulsch; Dory, Jeb, and Francis VanBockel; Al Wagar; Eric Wagner; Diane Warner; Alice Warren; Samuel Watson; Ro Wauer; Dan Wetzel; Marc White; Eddie Williams; Jerry and Cyndi Williams; Linda Williams; David Wright; Kevin Wright; Mike Yavlick; Adrian Yirka; and John Yochum. And of course, Kenny Rogers.

The Rain, for flowers, foliage, freshness, rest, tension, drama, and perversity. Every single butterfly along the way.

And is it any wonder that my final, biggest, and perpetual thanks are for Thea?